Opera in
Seventeenth-Century
Venice

The publisher gratefully
acknowledges the generous
contribution provided by
the Director's Circle of the Associates
of the University of California Press,
whose members are

Edmund Corvelli, Jr.
Leslie and Herbert Fingarette
Diane and Charles L. Frankel
Susan and August Frugé
Florence and Leo Helzel
Sandra and Charles Hobson
Valerie and Joel Katz
Ruth and David Mellinkoff
Joan Palevsky

Opera in
Seventeenth-Century Venice

The Creation of a Genre

ELLEN ROSAND

University of California Press
Berkeley • Los Angeles • Oxford

Publication of this book was made possible by generous
grants from the National Endowment for the
Humanities, The Gladys Krieble Delmas Foundation,
the American Musicological Society,
and Gordon P. and Ann G. Getty.

University of California Press
Berkeley and Los Angeles, California

University of California Press, Ltd.
Oxford, England

Library of Congress Cataloging-in-Publication Data

Rosand, Ellen.
    Opera in seventeenth-century Venice : the creation of
a genre / Ellen Rosand.
        p.   cm.
    Includes bibliographical references and index.
    ISBN 0–520–06808–4 (alk. paper)
        1. Opera—Italy—Venice—17th century.   I. Title.
ML1733.8.V4R67   1991
782.1'0945'3109032—dc20   90-40399
                                                          CIP
                                                          MN

Printed in the United States of America

1 2 3 4 5 6 7 8 9

The paper used in this publication meets the minimum
requirements of American National Standard for
Information Sciences—Permanence of Paper for
Printed Library Materials, ANSI Z39.48-1984. ⊗

For my parents,
Gertrude Fineman and Lester Fineman

Contents

◆   ◆   ◆

Illustrations

◆   ◆   ◆

Unless otherwise indicated, all illustrations are from the Biblioteca Nazionale Marciana, Venice.

Musical Examples

◆　　◆　　◆

Acknowledgments

◆   ◆   ◆

This book represents the culmination of research carried out over the past two decades. At every stage of its elephantine gestation, I have benefitted from the encouragement and criticism of friends and colleagues. Nino Pirrotta inspired my earliest attempts to understand opera in Venice and has remained a guiding spirit, a model of passionate and humane scholarship for my work ever since. Over the course of innumerable miles in Riverside Park, and then by post and phone, my erstwhile jogging companion Piero Weiss listened to ideas, read and reread drafts, translated, edited, and bore with me. Joseph Kerman was the first to recognize the book implicit in my disparate studies and ideas on Venetian and operatic topics, and he was also the first to read through the completed manuscript (no footnotes), which he subjected to the full treatment of his characteristic critical, but always responsive, pencil.

As readers for the University of California Press, Lorenzo Bianconi examined the text with a fine-tooth comb, sparing me the embarrassment of countless minor errors and several major ones; Howard Brown, with humor and sympathy, found his share of lacunae and redundancies; and Philip Brett, going well beyond the call of duty, made many excellent stylistic suggestions. I am indebted to Gary Tomlinson for the challenge of his ideas and stimulating queries over the years and for his specific suggestions more recently; to Andrew Porter, who long ago promised me a *New Yorker* editorial job on the manuscript and kept his word; and to Maria Teresa Muraro, whose friendship, hospitality, encouragement, and access to the Venetian libraries at the other end of an international telephone line were invaluable assets in the completion of my work.

I am grateful, too, to my former student Beth Glixon for making fair copies of the musical examples, to Christian Moevs for a large number of translations, and to my editors at the University of California Press, above all, to Doris Kretschmer for her sustained enthusiasm, to Peter Dreyer for his gentle editorial touch, and to Jane-Ellen Long, who calmly shepherded the manuscript through the final gauntlet of publication.

It is with pleasure that I acknowledge the National Endowment for the Humanities, the American Council of Learned Societies, the American Philosophical Society, the Gladys Krieble Delmas Foundation, and the Rutgers University Research Council for their support of a succession of research trips to Venice, each of which was intended to be the last.

This book could not have been completed without the sustenance, forbearance, and considerable intervention of my family: my sons Jonathan and Eric, who grew up tolerantly—and too fast—in the company of a sibling more demanding than any sister or brother, and their father, my husband David Rosand, whose passion for and knowledge of things Venetian nourished mine, and whose professional skill as a writer, editor, artist, and critic and intuition as an opera lover have had their impact on every page of this volume. Finally, I wish to express publicly my immense private gratitude to my parents for having waited patiently and supportively through many difficult years for me to finish this book, and to whom I lovingly, and thankfully, dedicate it.

Editorial Procedure

◆   ◆   ◆

Editorial intervention has been kept to a minimum. Clefs have been modernized for voice parts only; the original clefs are indicated at the outset of each piece, along with the original key signature and meter, if any. For ease of reading, key signatures have usually been added when they are implied by the sources. Original note values have been maintained. An attempt has been made to regularize the barring. Thus, while pieces are generally barred according to the source, where additional bar-lines are required these are dotted. Changes of meter are provided where maintaining the same meter would produce measures of irregular, inconsistent length. Editorial accidentals as well as notes missing in the sources are enclosed in brackets. All expression and tempo markings are original and are indicated in italics. Figures are generally those in the sources. Occasionally a figure is added in brackets where the harmony might otherwise be ambiguous.

Poetic texts in the musical examples follow those of the manuscript sources; they have not been altered to conform to the texts quoted from the librettos. Punctuation has been clarified, however, and abbreviations have been expanded. In addition, the beginning of each poetic line has been marked by capitalizing its initial letter. In quoting from librettos and manuscript documents, I have chosen to retain the original capitalization and punctuation as well as spelling. Occasionally, however, punctuation and accents have been added to clarify the meaning.

Abbreviations

◆   ◆   ◆

AcM	*Acta musicologica*
AMw	*Archiv für Musikwissenschaft*
CM	*Current Musicology*
DBI	*Dizionario biografico degli italiani*
JAMS	*Journal of the American Musicological Society*
JM	*Journal of Musicology*
Mf	*Die Musikforschung*
ML	*Music and Letters*
MQ	*The Musical Quarterly*
MR	*Music Review*
MT	*The Musical Times*
NRMI	*Nuova rivista musicale italiana*
RIM	*Rivista italiana di musicologia*
RMI	*Rivista musicale italiana*
StOpIt	*Storia dell'opera italiana*

Library sigla are those used in *RISM* (*Répertoire international des sources musicales*) and listed in *The New Grove Dictionary of Music and Musicians* (London, 1980).

Introduction

◆   ◆   ◆

Opera in Seventeenth-Century Venice rather than "Venetian Opera in the Seventeenth Century": the difference is significant. My concern is with the development of a particular art form in a very particular place. Opera did not originate in Venice, but, as with so many inventions that flourished on the lagoon (printing, for example), what was conceived and born elsewhere found a most nurturing environment in the Most Serene Republic. With the political stability of its oligarchic structure and the economic democracy that sustained it, Venice offered a unique situation for the elaboration of others' inventions. The opening of the Teatro S. Cassiano in 1637 marked the beginning of an important new phase in the history of the young art. What happened to opera in Venice during the seventeenth century was fundamental to the art itself: there and then, opera as we know it assumed its definitive identity—as a mixed theatrical spectacle available to a socially diversified, and paying, audience; a public art.

Born in Florence, and further developed in Rome, opera essentially defined itself as a genre in Venice. There, and only there, three conditions existed that proved crucial for its permanent establishment: regular demand, dependable financial backing, and a broad and predictable audience.

Regularity of demand was guaranteed by the Venetian calendar. Carnival season had been a major tourist attraction in Venice for at least a century. Traditionally hospitable to extravagant entertainments of all kinds, it readily accommodated the latest fashion, music-drama, to display before an audience that was already prepared by the carnival atmosphere to enjoy it.

Dependable financial backing derived from the Venetian sociopolitical structure: competition among patrician families, essentially a self-ennobled merchant class, encouraged investment in theaters as a means of increasing wealth and status. A few powerful families sustained the major expenses of constructing new theaters or adapting old ones for operatic productions. But a broader aristocratic base supported these theaters as annual leaseholders of boxes. Indeed, a list of such subscribers from any season in any theater offered a who's-who of Venetian society.

The audience for opera, drawn from the carnival crowds that annually swelled the population of the city, was unusually large; it was also unusually diverse. Carnival was a time of masks, social license, the blurring of class distinctions. When foreign tourists took their places in the theaters, they were surrounded by the full spectrum of Venetians, from the patricians in the boxes to the *volgo* in the stalls. The significance of this varied audience cannot be overestimated. It was responsible for the breadth of opera in Venice and the range of its appeal. It also provided the basis for the celebration of the myth of Venice that formed such a significant aspect of the public message of opera in the Serenissima: the spectacle of opera mirrored the spectacle of miraculous Venice herself.

Nourished by these particular conditions, opera took quick and healthy root on the lagoon: the first historic spectacle at S. Cassiano in 1637, *Andromeda*, spawned another in 1638, three more in 1639 (in two theaters), five in 1640 and 1641 (in three and four theaters respectively), and as many as seven in 1642.[1] Success begat success. The more they saw of this spectacular new art form, the more audiences wanted, and what they wanted had to be (or seem) new. The need to supply such a steadily expanding and increasingly demanding market placed great pressure on the muses of librettists and composers. They sought to develop procedures that would speed up the creative process, maximizing the appearance of novelty, of brilliant invention, while allowing them, as efficient craftsmen, to draw on their own—and others'—previous works. Their efforts soon resulted in the establishment of a conventional poetic and musical language and a conventional structural core for plots, one that could support a variety of superficial modifications—a change of setting, an extra complication, or some new topical allusions.

This conventional core not only sustained infinite variation in Venice; it was portable elsewhere. Indeed, just this portability was one of its essential features. For even as it offered hospitality to the new art, a permanent home, Venice sent it out again to the rest of Italy and, eventually, Europe. The troupes responsible for the first Venetian performances of opera were traveling companies ema-

1. The chronology of the first five years is as follows: *1637: Andromeda* (S. Cassiano). *1638: La maga fulminata* (S. Cassiano). *1639: Le nozze di Teti e di Peleo* (S. Cassiano); *Delia* (SS. Giovanni e Paolo); *Armida* (SS. Giovanni e Paolo). *1640: Gli amori d'Apollo e di Dafne* (S. Cassiano); *Adone* (SS. Giovanni e Paolo); *Il ritorno d'Ulisse in patria* (SS. Giovanni e Paolo); *Arianna* (S. Moisè); *Il pastor regio* (S. Moisè). *1641: Didone* (S. Cassiano); *Il ritorno d'Ulisse in patria* (S. Cassiano or SS. Giovanni e Paolo); *Le nozze d'Enea e Lavinia* (SS. Giovanni e Paolo); *La ninfa avara* (S. Moisè); *La finta pazza* (Novissimo). *1642: La virtù de' strali d'Amore* (S. Cassiano); *Narciso ed Ecco immortalati* (SS. Giovanni e Paolo); *Gli amori di Giasone e d'Isifile* (SS. Giovanni e Paolo); *Sidonio e Dorisbe* (S. Moisè); *Amore innamorato* (S. Moisè); *Alcate* (Novissimo); *Bellerofonte* (Novissimo).

nating from Rome—Venice was initially only a stop on their tour. They found a stable base of operation in Venice, but only during Carnival; off season they still earned their livelihood elsewhere, carrying with them the products of the Venetian stage. Elsewhere, however, the product had to be modified to appeal to different audiences and to suit different performing conditions: topical and local Venetian allusions, for example, would hardly be effective in, say, Bologna or Milan, and temporary theaters in such cities often lacked the possibility of sophisticated stage effects available in Venice. The conventional core, however, which comprised the basic features of the genre, could be adapted accordingly.

The chronological coverage of this book is less than the full seventeenth century promised by its title. Rather, it deals with the forty-year span between the opening of the first and last opera houses of the century: S. Cassiano in 1637 and S. Giovanni Grisostomo in 1678. This limitation is not arbitrary. By 1650 all of the important elements of opera had been laid out, and the next two decades were a period of consolidation. The opening of S. Giovanni Grisostomo, however, marked a change in attitude toward the art, the end of what we can now see as the first of the cycles (all of them of about forty years) that were to shape and reshape opera during the course of its subsequent history: an arc moving between the extremes of aesthetic principle and extravagant overripeness. The 1680s heralded the beginning of a new cycle: the development of the so-called reform movement that culminated in the enthronement of Metastasio. The opening of S. Giovanni Grisostomo also coincided with a general increase in operatic activity outside Venice, much of it in public theaters, and, consequently, of the definitive establishment of opera as a pan-Italian—indeed, fully European—phenomenon. The developments of the final decades of the seventeenth century thus belong to a new chapter in opera history.

Between 1637 and 1678, in nine different theaters, Venetian audiences saw more than 150 operas. These were the work of some twenty composers and nearly twice that many librettists. Several individuals stand out among them, for different reasons: the composers Claudio Monteverdi and Francesco Cavalli and the librettist Giovanni Faustini, to name the most prominent. Each of them had a shaping influence on the developing genre. But that influence is not always easy to measure. Monteverdi, for instance, was fully recognized as the greatest composer of his time, and his reputation lent enormous aesthetic prestige to the new genre in Venice. He was also an experienced opera composer, and his lessons to his various librettists in the writing of operatic poetry had important consequences for the future. The influence of his musical style, in particular his approach to text-setting, can be traced in the operas of Cavalli as well as those of other composers, such as Giovanni Antonio Boretti and Antonio Sartorio. But the impact of his operas themselves is less evident. *Il ritorno d'Ulisse* and *L'incoronazione di Poppea* are masterpieces of the genre—the latter is the only opera of the period to enjoy any real place in the twentieth-century repertory—but they were not typical of their time. They represent the culmination of Monteverdi's own development as a madrigalist and interpreter of dramatic poetry, but they did not serve as models for the future: no subsequent opera in Venice quite matches the rich musical elaborations of *Ritorno* or the mimetic and ethical force of *Poppea*.

Closer to providing such models were the works produced almost yearly by the collaboration of Cavalli and Faustini over the course of the decade 1640–50. It was essentially through them that opera in Venice assumed its characteristic physiognomy. But these works made their impact more through repetition than as individual aesthetic objects, demonstrating and reinforcing their successful formulas season after season. High as the quality of some of these operas may have been, it was the regular rhythm of their production that was most significant historically—and their replicability.

For the formula assured its own continuation, at once instigating and permitting its adoption and expansion by other librettists and other composers, who devoted their energies to supplying the market. However powerful, the impact of all individuals—Monteverdi, even Cavalli and Faustini—was relative. Their particular contributions were absorbed, swept up by a general tide of accumulating convention. The product that emerged, opera, was in this respect a group effort.

The complexity of the sources of the developing genre is reflected in the shifting focus of this book, which approaches the material from a variety of critical perspectives: from focus on a single individual (Monteverdi in chapters 1 and 9, Giovanni Faustini in chapter 6, and particularly Cavalli in the chapters devoted to the developing conventions), an intellectual movement (the Accademia degli Incogniti in chapter 2), or a theater (the Teatro Novissimo in chapter 3, S. Giovanni Grisostomo in chapter 13) to particular works that embody different stages of the development. *La finta pazza* (1641) at the beginning, the first operatic hit, exemplifies the confluence of the local and traveling companies (in chapters 3 and 4); *Giasone* (1649), in the middle, represents a moment of equilibrium in the cycle, a perfectly adjusted meeting of music and drama, the model of the genre to future generations (in chapters 9 and 11); *Orfeo* (1673), in its highly attractive, explicit way, displays the symptoms of decadence that had been gradually infecting the genre since midcentury (in chapter 13).

Other topics involve broader, more general issues that are critical to the history I am writing: the aesthetic soul-searching involved in trying to define a bastard genre seeking to combine music and drama (in chapter 2), the emergence of the professional librettist (in chapter 6), the rise of the prima donna (in chapter 8). Most significant of all, and the subject of four full chapters, is the emergence of conventions within the works themselves, the enabling structural units that unified all the individual efforts of composers and librettists. Those conventions are of various kinds and sizes, affecting the several aspects of the works, from the relationship between text and music (in chapter 9) and formal structures for arias (in chapter 10) to dramatic situations suggesting particular musical settings (in chapters 11–12).

The shifting focus of this approach has resulted in a book whose structure might best be described as bipartite (perhaps "rounded binary" would be more accurate). The first eight chapters constitute an A section that is primarily concerned with extramusical issues: the aesthetic definition of opera, the chronology of theater openings and productions, the publication and contents of librettos, the iconography of Venice, and the changing roles of librettist, composer, and singer. The B section (chapters 9–12), attending more precisely to the works themselves, analyzes the development of musical, musico-textual, and musico-dramatic conventions in some detail. And the concluding chapter returns once more to the level of cultural and historical generalization, a final *sententia* on ripeness and decadence—with implications of eventual renewal.

Although the contributions of most of its individual members were anonymous, and difficult to distinguish from one another, the group responsible for the creation of opera in seventeenth-century Venice left a large body of commentary on what they were doing and why. Their letters, contracts, and libretto prefaces not only provide the documentary basis for our reconstruction of the past, they lend a personal, individual dimension to institutional history. To suggest the vitality of the ambience in which opera developed, I have quoted abundantly from this wealth of contemporary commentary, particularly in the A section of this study. The B section is embedded in a documentary context of another kind: a large number of musical examples, mostly complete pieces, drawn from the full range of works produced during this period. Here, for the first time, composers like Ziani, Boretti, and Sartorio take their place alongside Monteverdi, Cavalli, and Cesti as full participants in the development and confirmation of operatic conventions.

Venetian opera was established as a field for study relatively early in the history of musicology, with important steps taken before the end of the nineteenth century. Chief among the pioneers, most appropriately, was a Venetian, Taddeo Wiel, whose primary research facilitated the early efforts—by several German scholars (Hermann Kretzschmar and Hugo Goldschmidt, then Egon

Wellesz), and a Frenchman (Henry Prunières) — to place the music of Cavalli and Cesti in historical perspective.[2] That perspective was broadened in 1937 by Helmut Christian Wolff's dissertation on the later seventeenth century, which focused on Venetian works by composers other than Cavalli and Cesti. A new era of Venetian studies was initiated in the 1950s, when the burgeoning literature on Monteverdi yielded a significant monograph on the composer's Venetian operas by Anna Amalie Abert. And in that same year, 1954, Simon Towneley Worsthorne published the first substantial monograph on Venetian opera, in which he considered the librettos and staging of the operas as well as their music. The 1950s also saw publication of the first of Nino Pirrotta's and Wolfgang Osthoff's many contributions to the field, which approached the material from a variety of special angles, all of them with profound implications for our understanding of the larger phenomenon of opera in Venice. Both Pirrotta and Osthoff expanded the study of Venetian opera to include its social context, which, they demonstrated, offered significant insight into aspects of the creation, function, and meaning of the art.

The literature continued to grow in the course of the following decades with the publication of documentary studies that focused on the history of the theaters, by Remo Giazotto and Nicola Mangini, and a number of monographic dissertations, articles, and books on various figures and topics: William Holmes and Carl Schmidt on Cesti, Thomas Walker (a dissertation unfinished but nonetheless valuable), Martha Clinkscale, Edward Rutschman, and myself on aspects of Cavalli, and Jane Glover on Cavalli and on the Teatro S. Apollinare and the 1650s. More recent dissertations have continued to expand the field of study: Peter Jeffery on the manuscripts in the Contarini Collection, Beth Glixon on recitative, and Harris Saunders on the Teatro S. Giovanni Grisostomo. These recent contributions have clarified our understanding of the role of individual figures and institutions in the history of opera in Venice. At the same time there have been important advances in the definition of the repertory itself. Claudio Sartori's libretto census, in particular, has finally made it possible to clarify the chronology of operatic activity in Venice, and to measure it against that of other centers.

In the past decade or so, however, the most important work in the field has been in the realm of social history. In a series of major publications Lorenzo Bianconi, Giovanni Morelli, and Thomas Walker have enriched and refined our view of these operas by uncovering the social and political matrices in which they were formed, the external forces that helped to shape the works of art; and their interpretations have been based upon the richest foundation of primary

---

2. For the specific publications of these scholars, and those mentioned in the following paragraphs, see Bibliography.

documentation. My debt to these scholars—and to their students in Italy—can be read in the frequency with which they are cited in the footnotes to the following pages.

Opera in Seventeenth-Century Venice builds on this previous scholarship. Although it aims to survey the entire field, from a variety of perspectives, its particular agenda is signaled by its subtitle: *The Creation of a Genre*. Its thesis, as already suggested, is that opera received its most lasting theoretical, as well as practical, definition in the public theaters of seicento Venice. I have used the words of the librettists themselves, and the message they convey through their often jocular, ironic, and defensive tone, as indications of contemporary attitudes toward the phenomenon of opera. And I consider their words a critical framework for discussion of the repertory. This has been done for the Arcadians who followed, and for the Florentines who preceded, but never for the seventeenth-century Venetians, precisely because their voices were never taken seriously. What they offer, in fact, is nothing less than an aesthetics of opera, as relevant today as it was then.

Just as their theoretical discussions can be applied to opera in general, so the practical realization of their ideas, the conventions they developed, continued to shape the operas with which we are most familiar. Modern opera-goers will recognize in those conventions the roots of favorite scenes: Cherubino's song, Tatiana's letter, Lucia's mad scene, Ulrica's invocation, even Tristan and Iseult's love duet, all trace their lineage back to seventeenth-century Venice. There, too, is the beginning of another phenomenon that modern opera-goers will recognize: the hedonistic contract between audience and singers, and its first concrete manifestation, in the da capo aria.

One reason that modern audiences may initially fail to appreciate the relationship of these conventions to their own experience is that they were created with disarmingly simple materials. Although the techniques of baroque scenographic spectacle were far from simple—in fact they have hardly been equaled since—the musical means of seventeenth-century opera were comparatively limited; the orchestra was small, the chorus virtually nonexistent. Voices were for the most part accompanied by continuo instruments; arias were short, ensembles few and far between. The forces, in other words, were not overwhelming. But the creators of these operas exploited their resources fully and subtly. Contrast, though on a comparatively small scale, was of the utmost importance: between speech and song, vocal and instrumental sound, string and continuo accompaniment, high and low voices, and between serious and comic moments. A couple of chords on the harpsichord might thus have been sufficient to create the impression of a fierce battle (*Il ritorno d'Ulisse*), three soloists singing together the effect of a chorus of followers (*L'incoronazione di*

Poppea), and a single juxtaposition of two unrelated tonal realms a fundamental conflict of personalities (Seneca and Nerone in *Poppea*).

Given a chance to speak for themselves, to instruct us in their ways, seventeenth-century operas appear less archaic, less distant than, until recently, we have been led to believe. Not only were they made of the conventional units that have continued to shape opera to our own time, but they appealed to audiences in ways that remain essential to operatic experience. Their plots, however apparently exotic and gratuitously intricate, confronted fundamental realities, universal human passions—love, jealousy, ambition. They dealt with social issues and moral dilemmas—honor, fidelity, deception. Self-conscious from the beginning, the art that combined drama and music continued to make the most of its inherent implausibility by testing it constantly against a standard of verisimilitude. Even as it created depths of mimetic chiaroscuro, drawing an audience into the reality of its fictional pathos, it inevitably found moments in which to reinvoke disbelief: the singer directly addressing the audience, the text directly addressing the art, the topical allusion to life outside the theater. Perhaps the most obvious legacy of Venetian opera to modern practice is the phenomenon of the prima donna, the star singer who comes to outshine all else, who makes of the composer's art a vehicle for herself. But that perversion of original values, too, was part of the very vitality of the art, part of its dynamic rapport with its audience.

In witnessing the development of opera on the Venetian stage, we recognize an art we already know. Opera in seventeenth-century Venice is the art of opera itself.

1

• • •

Far recitare un'opera a Venezia: Origins and Sources

This night, having . . . taken our places before, we went to the Opera where comedies and other plays are represented in recitative music by the most excellent musicians vocal and instrumental, with a variety of scenes painted and contrived with no less art of perspective, and machines for flying in the aire, and other wonderful motions; taken together it is one of the most magnificent and expensive diversions the wit of men can invent. . . . This held us by the eyes and ears till two in the morning.

John Evelyn, *Diary*

The experience that so delighted the English visitor to Venice in 1645—and for which he purchased tickets in advance—was a type of entertainment that had been established in that city for only eight seasons, since 1637: public commercial opera.[1] The history of its origins in Venice is the story of the beginning of the art as we still know it.

Opera is a mixed theatrical genre, a combination of drama, music, and scenic spectacle, and the balance of those constituent elements has always been a source of its vitality. That same balance is also the source of its problems as an art, raising aesthetic dilemmas that have challenged every generation since its creation. Nevertheless, whatever its uneasy sense of itself as a genre, opera has survived because it is essentially a popular art, because it has managed for nearly four centuries to pack houses, to marshal all its contributing forces to entertain audiences from a broad range of society. With all its expensive magnificence, its fantastic illusion of sound and sight, its glitter of talent and temperament, opera is public spectacle.

Opera has been spectacular from its beginning—but it has not always been public. The birthdate of opera is traditionally set at about 1600, its birthplace Florence. But the art that was created in Florence at the turn of the seventeenth century is in many ways unlike the sung drama we have come to recognize as

1. *Memoires of John Evelyn*, ed. W. Bray (London, 1819), 1: 191. The opera was *Ercole in Lidia* (Bisaccioni / Rovetta), performed in 1645; according to Evelyn, the performance took place during Ascension week. But see ch. 3, n. 101 below.

opera. Indeed, in many respects the earliest operas—from Mantua and Rome as well as Florence—were more closely linked to the past than to the future. They manifest a closer kinship with such theatrical predecessors as humanist plays with music or the intermedi of the sixteenth-century courts than with the subsequent development of the genre. What we regard as opera was fundamentally an urban development, created with the tastes of a large, cosmopolitan, and varied audience in mind.[2]

The first operas, *Dafne*, *Euridice*, *Orfeo*, *Arianna*, like the intermedi before them, were courtly entertainments; the earliest of them, *Dafne*, even shared its subject matter and poet with an intermedio of 1589.[3] They were commissioned and created to celebrate specific political or social occasions, and were performed before an invited patrician audience. Productions enjoyed the relatively unrestricted budget of aristocratic patronage, and the music and poetry were subject only to the patrons' taste and the exigencies and decorum of the occasion.[4] The collaborators in these productions—poets, composers, scene and costume designers—were essentially servants of the court, and their works were conceived as celebration. Verbally and visually, iconographic conceit and allegorical allusion extolled a ruling dynasty—Medici, Gonzaga, or Barberini—besides marking the specific occasion.[5] The splendor and lavishness of the productions reflected further glory on the ruler, brightening his image at home and abroad.

Usually these works were produced only once, though court chroniclers were charged with preserving them for posterity through detailed descriptions that appeared in print. We learn a great deal about Peri's *Euridice* and Caccini's *Il rapimento di Cefalo* from the account by Michelangelo Buonarroti the Younger, a Medici courtier who was a poet and dramatist in his own right as well as the first editor of his famous grand-uncle's poetry.[6] And Monteverdi's *Arianna* is brought to life through the chronicle of the Mantuan court reporter

2.   See Lorenzo Bianconi's eloquent treatment of the distinction between courtly and public opera in *Il seicento* (1982), translated as *Music in the Seventeenth Century* (Cambridge, 1987), 163–66. All citations are to the English edition.

3.   The third of the five intermedi for *La pellegrina* celebrated Apollo's victory over the serpent Python. The text was by Ottavio Rinuccini: librettist not only of *Dafne* but of *Euridice* and *Arianna* as well. The relationship between the two treatments of Apollo's victory is discussed in Barbara Russano Hanning, "Glorious Apollo: Poetic and Political Themes in the First Opera," *Renaissance Quarterly* 32 (1979): 485–513. On these intermedi in general, see Nino Pirrotta and Elena Povoledo, *Li due Orfei* (1969, 1975), translated as *Music and Theatre from Poliziano to Monteverdi*

(Cambridge, 1982), 212–36. All citations are to the English edition.

4.   Although *Orfeo* (Striggio/Monteverdi) was not written for a specific political occasion, but as a carnival performance under the auspices of a Mantuan academy, it shares most of the distinctive features of the other works.

5.   For Medici iconography in the first Florentine operas, see Hanning, "Glorious Apollo."

6.   *Descrizione delle felicissime Nozze della Cristianissima Maesta di Madama Maria Medici Regina di Francia e di Navarra* (Florence: Marescotti, 1600), partly transcribed in Angelo Solerti, *Gli albori del melodramma* (Milan, Palermo, and Naples, 1904), 2: 113. See L. Rossi, "Michelangelo Buonarroti, il Giovane," *DBI* 15 (Rome, 1972): 178–81.

Federico Follino.[7] The early Florentine and Mantuan operas find analogues in Barberini Rome, where for more than a decade operatic entertainments enhanced the image of the papal court. They also find an echo later in the Paris of Louis XIV, where each one of Lully's and Quinault's *tragédies lyriques* began and ended with an encomium to *le roi soleil*.

This kind of opera, "performed in the palaces of great princes and other secular or ecclesiastic lords" ("fatta ne' palazzi de' principi grandi, e d'altri signori secolari o ecclesiastici"), was the first and most praiseworthy of the three categories of musical spectacle distinguished by the Jesuit Giovan Domenico Ottonelli in his moralizing treatise *Della Cristiana moderatione del teatro* (1652).[8] This category he labeled the princely. The second category, the academic, linked to the first and of nearly equal status, was the kind "put on sometimes by certain gentlemen or talented citizens or learned academicians" ("che rappresentano tal volta alcuni gentiluomini o cittadini virtuosi o accademici eruditi").

Opera in Venice, however, was of an entirely different order. Ottonelli called it "mercenaria." Musically and conceptually, of course, this "mercenary" opera was indebted to the earlier models produced at Florence, Mantua, and Rome. The idea of wholly sung drama would have been unthinkable without the first experiments of Rinuccini, Peri, and Caccini. Nevertheless, opera in Venice was more profoundly affected by other factors. Above all, it responded to the unique sociopolitical structure of the Republic and its distinctive urban fabric. Opera as we know it, as an art appealing to a broad audience, had its origins in this special environment. Venice nurtured opera's development in a variety of ways and for a variety of reasons.

Venetian Foundations

The Most Serene Republic of St. Mark had long enjoyed a distinctive reputation as a haven of freedom and stability, a state with its own special position in the world and in history. What modern historians have come to know as the "myth of Venice" played a role not only in preparing the ground for the establishment and subsequent flourishing of opera there, but also in the actual substance and message of what was mounted on stage.

---

7. *Compendio delle sontuose feste fatte l'anno MD-CVIII nella città di Mantova* (Mantua: Osanna, 1608); see Solerti, *Gli albori*, 2: 145–46. *Orfeo*, not being politically inspired, was not accompanied by such a description.

8. The topic is treated in book 4, n. 3 of Ottonelli's treatise: "Delle commedie cantate a nostro tempo, e di quante sorti, e di che qualità si rappresentino." The relevant passages, as cited in Ferdinando Taviani, *La commedia dell'arte e la società barocca: La fascinazione del teatro* (Rome, 1969), 509–13, are given in Appendix II.3 below. See also Lorenzo Bianconi and Thomas Walker, "Dalla 'Finta pazza' alla 'Veramonda': Storie di Febiarmonici," *RIM* 10 (1975): 406–10.

Unique among the Italian states, Venice could not boast a Roman foundation. Rather, it owed its origins, as a haven for those fleeing the invading barbarians, to the fall of the Roman empire. Claiming to have been founded on the day of the Annunciation, 25 March 421 (according to the dominant legend), Venice promulgated itself as the first republic of the new Christian era, and therefore as the only legitimate successor to fallen pagan Rome. The greatness of the Venetian state was to be seen in its longevity and its political continuity; by the seventeenth century it had already lasted longer than ancient Rome. On a more practical level, the famed stability of Venice was said to depend on two special factors: its site and its constitution. The governmental structure of the Republic was celebrated for being a *regimen temperatum*, a perfectly balanced state. Venice, according to its own myth, had realized the classical ideal of mixed government. The Doge represented the monarchical component, the Senate the aristocratic, and the Maggior Consiglio the democratic. As a constitutional oligarchy, Venice concentrated political power in a relatively restricted patriciate; within the nobility, however, that power was distributed in a way that precluded any individual or clan from assuming an undue share. This harmony of power was the prerogative of perhaps 2 percent of the population. That the disenfranchised majority seemed content, that patrician Venice suffered no serious internal dissension, appeared only to confirm its privileged state of grace. And that sanctified state was further manifest in the very image of this splendid city, founded miraculously upon the waters; unwalled, yet unconquered for more than a millennium. The physical city itself stood as proof of its uniqueness.[9]

The Venetian ruling class, although restricted and hereditary, was actually more open than that of other states. It comprised a large number of families of equal rank—equal in theory, that is, if not in practice. What especially distinguished the Venetian nobility was its active and privileged involvement in commerce. The ruling patrician was also a merchant of Venice, and his economic enterprise extended beyond investments in trade and banking to include all the arts—and so, eventually, opera. The Tron, Vendramin, Grimani, Giustiniani, and Contarini were among the leading families of the Venetian patriciate, and they were the most important backers of opera in Venice. Beyond the obvious desire to enhance family prestige, their interest in the art was largely commercial; they invested in opera houses primarily for financial gain, and the

---

9. For literature on the myth of Venice, see Ellen Rosand, "Music in the Myth of Venice," *Renaissance Quarterly* 30 (1977): 511–37, n. 1; and, more recently, David Rosand, " 'Venetia figurata': The Iconography of a Myth," in *Interpretazioni veneziane: Studi di* storia dell'arte in onore di Michelangelo Muraro, ed. David Rosand (Venice, 1984), 177–96, and James S. Grubb, "When Myths Lose Power: Four Decades of Venetian Historiography," *Journal of Modern History* 58 (1986): 43–94.

profit motive could not help but affect the product. Expenditures were carefully limited, imposing strictures on librettists, composers, and scene designers. The spectacle of the courts could hardly be indulged. In Venice, opera was a business.[10]

Venice had its own traditions of elaborate public pageantry, its own expanding calendar of annual politico-religious festivals: the Marriage to the Sea celebrated on Ascension Day, victory at Lepanto on the Feast of Sta. Giustina, and the Feast of St. Mark, to name only a few. It celebrated special occasions as well, its ducal coronations and royal visits. And all of these celebrations involved elaborate entertainments featuring music, spectacle, processions, and theatrical presentations.[11] But opera did not emerge in Venice from such a background of occasional or ceremonial spectacle; it had different progenitors. Its roots were, and remained, in the carnival season, with its established tradition of theatrical performances by troupes of itinerant players, performances for which tickets were sold.[12] These activities became especially intense after the crisis of the Interdict (1605–7), when, with the expulsion of the Jesuits from Venice, the *comici*, who had been excluded by them, returned to the city with impunity.[13]

Crossroads of east and west, Venice was a port city characterized by a lively cosmopolitan and even exotic atmosphere. Its carnival celebrations earned in-

10.   For three contrasting models of opera patronage in the seventeenth century, in Rome, Venice, and Reggio Emilia, see Lorenzo Bianconi and Thomas Walker, "Production, Consumption, and Political Function of Seventeenth-Century Opera," *Early Music History* 4 (1984): 209–96.

11.   Perhaps no series of events could match those mounted by the Serenissima in honor of the visit of Henry III in 1574. For a documentary history of that visit, see Pier de Nolhac and Angelo Solerti, *Il viaggio in Italia di Enrico III re di Francia e le feste a Venezia, Ferrara, Mantova e Torino* (Turin, 1890); also Angelo Solerti, "Le rappresentazioni musicali di Venezia dal 1571 al 1605," *RMI* 9 (1902): 554–58; and Margaret Gilmore, "Monteverdi and Dramatic Music in Venice, 1595–1637" (MS).

12.   A vivid picture of the flourishing theatrical life of fifteenth- and sixteenth-century Venice is provided by Maria Teresa Muraro, "La festa a Venezia e le sue manifestazioni rappresentative: Le compagnie della Calza e le *momarie*," in *Storia della cultura veneta dal primo quattrocento al concilio di Trento*, 3.3 (Vicenza, 1983): 315–42; see also Elena Povoledo, "Scène et mise en scène à Venise: De la décadence des compagnies de la Calza jusqu'à la représentation de *L'Andromeda* au Théâtre de San Cassian (1637)," in *Renaissance, Maniérisme, Baroque*, Actes du XIe Stage

International de Tours (Paris, 1972), 87–99. For a concise discussion of the traditional Venetian carnival activities, see Edward Muir, *Civic Ritual in Renaissance Venice* (Princeton, 1981), 156–81; and, more recently, with emphasis on its sociological implications, Peter Burke, *The Historical Anthropology of Early Modern Italy* (Cambridge, 1987), ch. 13, "The Carnival of Venice."

13.   The return in full force of the comedy troupes in 1607, just after the Interdict, is documented in the diary of Gerolamo Priuli, who reports the presence of three different companies of actors at the same time (quoted in Nicola Mangini, *I teatri di Venezia* [Milan, 1974], 34). See also Mangini's discussion of the relationship of the *comici* and *teatri stabili*, 33–35; and Pompeo Molmenti, "Venezia alla metà del secolo XVII descritta da due contemporanei," in *Curiosità di storia veneziana* (Bologna, 1920), 313, 317. By the late 1620s the actors were performing at the same theaters that would soon host operatic entertainments: S. Cassiano, S. Moisè, S. Salvatore, and SS. Giovanni e Paolo. See Elena Povoledo, "Una rappresentazione accademica a Venezia nel 1634," in *Studi sul teatro veneto fra rinascimento ed età barocca*, ed. Maria Teresa Muraro (Florence, 1971), 119–69; also Mangini, *I teatri di Venezia*, ch. 2, "Il seicento."

ternational renown and made the city, long a necessary stop for travelers, a special attraction for tourists. The population of the city, which hovered around 50,000 during most of the seventeenth century, swelled to nearly twice that number each year for the approximately six to ten weeks of Carnival (from 26 December, the Feast of St. Stephen, to Shrove Tuesday).[14] That season of liberation, of the dropping of social barriers and distinctions, was celebrated by fireworks, ballets, masquerades, bull chases, fights. Much of the excitement was provided by the dramatic entertainments performed throughout the city, indoors and out, by resident groups as well as visitors, bands of *comici dell'arte* who arrived in Venice in time for Carnival and dispersed when it was over. Just such a group, a traveling company of musicians, headed by Benedetto Ferrari and Francesco Manelli, brought opera to the lagoon for the first time. It was during the carnival season of 1637 that opera in Venice began.

Almost exactly the same company had appeared in Padua the previous year. It returned to Venice in subsequent seasons, along with other similarly constituted groups inspired by its success.[15] These groups were responsible for producing operas of Ottonelli's third and least respectable category, for which the Jesuit reserved most of his admonitory passion: "the mercenary and dramatic musical representations, that is, the ones performed by those mercenary musicians who are professional actors, and who, organized in a company, are directed and governed by one of their own, acting as authority and head of the others" (Appendix II.3b).

Such traveling companies soon yielded to more permanent, locally based troupes and a more stable structure as the impact of the new entertainment made itself felt and began to be exploited by Venetian entrepreneurs. Nevertheless, many of the distinctive qualities of the first operas in Venice, those produced by Ferrari's company, survived. Since opera remained confined to carnival season, its potential audience remained essentially the same: a heterogeneous mix of patricians and *cittadini*, tourists and travelers, Venetians and foreigners, all of whom paid for the privilege of being entertained.[16]

14.   On the fluctuating population of Venice, see R. T. Rapp, *Industry and Economic Decline in Seventeenth-Century Venice* (Cambridge, Mass., 1976), 176–77.

15.   Such traveling opera companies, most of them from Rome or trained there, had appeared elsewhere in Italy before 1636. See Nino Pirrotta, "*Commedia dell'Arte* and Opera," in *Music and Culture in Italy from the Middle Ages to the Baroque,* henceforth cited as *Essays* (Cambridge, Mass., 1984), 353–54; and id., "Tre capitoli su Cesti," in *La scuola romana* (Siena,

1953), 28–34; also Bianconi and Walker, "Dalla 'Finta pazza,' " 395–405.

16.   Although diverse social classes were represented in the audience, the proportion of seats reserved for gondoliers and courtesans has probably been exaggerated; see Bianconi, *Seventeenth Century,* 184. Lower-class opera-goers may have been irrelevant for the economic structure of the theater, as Bianconi claims, but, as I argue below, they had an impact on the aesthetic character of the works that were performed.

Commercial success was of primary concern, and that could be achieved only by creating works with broad audience appeal. Opera in Venice was distinguished from that in Florence and other courts of Italy by the nature of its audience and by its socioeconomic base. Public approbation was important not only to the financial backers; it affected composers, librettists, and scenographers as well. These were independent professionals, who were themselves often involved financially as well as artistically in their own productions. The aim was to turn a profit. The success of an opera depended on its appealing to a large and varied audience; it had to play for a season, to keep the house filled night after night.

Although initiatives of the private sector, the opera houses, like every other Venetian institution, were regulated by the government. An enterprise as public as the theater, attracting crowds of *forestieri* as well as Venetians, obviously required responsible scrutiny. Regulation involved various magistracies, including the *Provveditori di comune* and, more gravely, the Council of Ten; it was designed to ensure the well-being of the public as well as of the state as a whole. Theater buildings were regularly inspected for safety hazards and had to be licensed each season before productions could even be advertised. Opening and closing times, and even the price of librettos sold at the door, were established by government decree.[17]

Monteverdi in the Wings

The Venetian experiment of Ferrari and Manelli took immediate root. Their return with a new production the following season affirmed and confirmed the existence of opera in Venice as a seasonal occurrence. Ferrari and Manelli were not, however, the first composers of opera to reach Venice, though they may have been the first to bring opera to the Venetian stage. Claudio Monteverdi, undoubtedly the most celebrated opera composer of his day, had been living in Venice since 1613, when he assumed the position of *maestro di cappella* at San Marco (fig. 1). Monteverdi was the composer of numerous theatrical entertainments in addition to the two famous Mantuan operas *Orfeo* and *Arianna* of 1607–8. Most recently his "favola pastorale," *Proserpina rapita*, had been performed in Venice, in the Palazzo Mocenigo, in 1630. Yet the seventy-year-old composer remained aloof from the new operatic activities. Perhaps it would have been unseemly for the *maestro di cappella* to express overt interest in the public theater;[18] possibly, too, his advanced age discouraged him from under-

---

17. See Cristoforo Ivanovich, *Minerva al tavolino* (Venice: Pezzana, 1681), 405–7 (Appendix II.6s).
18. The same factor probably restrained his San Marco colleague, Giovanni Battista Rovettino, from

participating in opera. For Monteverdi's reluctance, see Nino Pirrotta, "Early Venetian Libretti at Los Angeles," *Essays*, 321–22.

1.   Giovanni Battista Marinoni, *Fiori poetici raccolti nel funerale del molto illustre e molto reverendo Signor Claudio Monteverde* (Venice, 1644), title page.

taking so large-scale a project as an opera. Whatever the cause, his silence is remarkable not only to us. It was noticed by several of his contemporaries. One of them, probably in late 1637 or 1638, commented expectantly that Monteverdi might surprise everyone and produce an opera for Venice after all: "God willing, one of these nights he too will step onto the stage, where everyone else is about to appear, with the production of a musical drama," to which the appreciative response was: "Even if he doesn't actually appear, he'll be there in spirit, since he was so powerfully behind the whole business."[19] Clearly Monteverdi's participation was expected; and it was missed. In 1640 the librettist Giacomo Badoaro claimed to have written the text of *Il ritorno d'Ulisse in patria* for the express purpose of encouraging his friend Monteverdi to enter the operatic arena:

> From the author to the Most Illustrious and Reverend Signor Claudio Monteverdi, Great Master of Music. Not to compete with those inspired minds, which in these very years have published their compositions in the Venetian theaters, but to stimulate the virtue of Your Excellence to make known to this city that in the warmth of the affections there is a great difference between a true sun and a painted one, I dedicated myself, as a matter of principle, to compose *Il ritorno d'Ulisse in patria*. (Appendix I.7a)

It was not until 1640, then, after three seasons of observing the operatic activities of younger musicians from the sidelines, that Monteverdi finally—and, it would seem, still reluctantly—made his move. He first revived an old opera, *Arianna*, which ostensibly required little of his time or energy. Then he produced a new one, *Il ritorno d'Ulisse in patria*, which obviously must have required a great deal of both.[20]

Although *Arianna* was one of Monteverdi's favorite works,[21] reviving it in Venice, thirty years after its creation, would seem to have been an unlikely, even unworkable, enterprise. The conditions of opera production, not to mention the aesthetics of opera and Monteverdi's own style, had changed radically. To be sure, some revisions were made in the work, apparently to suit new, Venetian conditions. These included the cutting of many of the choruses and the alteration of some passages specifically linked to the original performance in Mantua, as well as elimination of the designation *tragedia* from the title

---

19. "Dio voglia non se avanzi anco sopra delle scene dove tutti li altri sono per capitare una di queste sere con una Comica, et musicale rappresentatione." "Se non vi sarà in atto vi potrà essere in potenza perche haverà consigliato forte il tutto" ("Satire, et altre raccolte per l'Academia de gl'Unisoni in casa di Giulio Strozzi," I-Vnm, It. X, 115 [7193], fifth satire, f. 61ᵛ; quoted in Ellen Rosand, "Barbara Strozzi, *virtuosissima cantatrice*: The Composer's Voice," *JAMS* 31 [1978]: 251 n. 34).

20. Two librettos of *Arianna* were printed in Venice, one in 1639, the other in 1640. The earlier, *L'Arianna: Tragedia del Signor Ottavio Rinuccini . . . rappresentata in musica* (Venice: Salvadori, 1639), appeared without the composer's name—and very possibly, therefore, without his approval. It surely

did not correspond to a Venetian performance, but merely reprinted the original text of 1608 verbatim. The 1640 libretto, however, *L'Arianna del Sig. Ottavio Rinuccini, posta in musica dal Sig. Claudio Monteverdi, rappresentata in Venetia l'anno 1640* (Venice: Bariletti, 1640), clearly corresponded to a performance in that year. Monteverdi had already expressed a desire to alter *Arianna* for a performance in Mantua in 1620, which apparently never took place (cf. letters of 17, 21, and 28 March 1620 in *Claudio Monteverdi: Lettere, dediche, e prefazioni*, ed. Domenico de' Paoli [Rome, 1973]).

21. See Gary Tomlinson, "Madrigal, Monody, and Monteverdi's *via naturale alla immitatione*," *JAMS* 34 (1981): 86–96.

page.[22] Despite such adaptive changes, the opera remained very different in tone, structure, and content from any of its contemporaries on the Venetian stage. Clearly, however, Monteverdi's reputation must have been more than sufficient to compensate for the inevitable stylistic incongruities.[23] The dedication of the libretto to one Bortolo Stacio, signed by the printer, gives some sense of the composer's exalted status:

> Now that Arianna, the most praised of dramatic compositions in Italian theaters, returns to the stage in Venice, the work of Signor Claudio Monteverdi, most celebrated Apollo of the century and the highest intelligence of the heaven of harmony, I take the occasion to no longer keep my [respect] hidden from you, but, by offering it in the name of Your Excellency, to manifest [that respect] to the world by means of its new reprinting. (Appendix I.6a)

And this is reinforced by Benedetto Ferrari's oft-mentioned sonnet of homage to the older master, whom he addressed as "l'Oracolo della musica" (Appendix I.6b).

Arianna was a monument to Monteverdi's past glory; *Il ritorno d'Ulisse in patria* boldly affirmed his present powers. Any hesitation on the composer's part must have been dispelled by the success of the new work, which ran for ten performances in Venice and was produced in Bologna as well,[24] for he wrote two more operas before his death in 1643. *Le nozze d'Enea e Lavinia* was produced in the 1640–41 season and *L'incoronazione di Poppea* in 1642–43.[25] Three new operas in four years: an amazing creative spurt for a 75-year-old composer whose operatic career had long seemed finished.

The radical differences between these late works of Monteverdi and his first opera, *Orfeo*, have been noted by every student of the subject.[26] The evolution

---

22. The choruses are placed between *virgolette* (inverted commas), the standard means of indicating textual cuts in performance. The prologue, originally addressed to Carlo Emmanuele of Savoy, was revised and addressed to the Venetian doge. See Nino Pirrotta, "Early Venetian Libretti," *Essays*, 320–21. The differences between the two librettos are briefly mentioned in Domenico de' Paoli, *Claudio Monteverdi* (Milan, 1979), 455–56.

23. Despite its anachronistic appearance, Pirrotta regards *Arianna* as having encouraged a new interest in classicizing themes among Venetian operas ("Monteverdi and the Problems of Opera," *Essays*, 251).

24. Pirrotta (ibid.) claimed that the Bologna performance of *Il ritorno d'Ulisse* was its premiere, another indication of Monteverdi's initial reluctance to participate in Venetian operatic life; but this was convincingly disputed by Wolfgang Osthoff ("Zur Bologneser Aufführung von Monteverdis 'Ritorno di Ulisse' im Jahre 1640," in *Mitteilungen der Kommission*

für Musikforschung [Vienna, 1958], 155–60). Osthoff's source for his dating of the Bologna performance, *Le glorie della musica celebrate dalla sorella poesia, rappresentandosi in Bologna la Delia, e l'Ulisse nel teatro de gl'Illustriss. Guastavillani* (Bologna: Ferroni, 1640), identifies some of the performers: Madalena Manelli played the role of Minerva (and Venere in *Delia*), while Giulia Paolelli was Penelope (and Delia). On the dating of *Ritorno*, see ch. 3, no. 36, below.

25. The title *Le nozze d'Enea in Lavinia* is given in the only printed document for the performance of the work, the *Argomento e scenario* (1640); I have adopted the more conventional form of the title from some of the manuscript librettos.

26. Those differences prompted Nino Pirrotta to propose, for an essay attempting to explain or account for them, the whimsical title "Opera from Monteverdi to Monteverdi" ("Monteverdi and the Problems of Opera," *Essays*, 248).

of Monteverdi's own style would be enough to account for the major differences between the works. But, although *Orfeo* and *Poppea* do indeed exemplify two important points in his development, they also serve to illustrate vividly the distinctions between court and public opera. These distinctions can be brought into relief by a comparison of the surviving sources.

Orfeo and *Poppea*

The score of *Orfeo*, like those of its operatic predecessors in Florence and most of its successors in Rome, was published, although not until two years after the work was performed.[27] Dedicated by the composer to the patron of the Mantuan production, the publication was commemorative, its purpose to preserve the event for posterity.

> The fable of Orpheus, which has already been represented in music under the auspices of your Highness on a small stage at the Accademia degli Invaghiti, now having to appear in the great theater of the universe to show itself to all men, there is no reason that it should allow itself to be associated with any other name than that of Your Glorious and Fortunate Highness. To you therefore I humbly consecrate it, so that you, who as a benign star were propitious at its birth, with the most serene rays of your grace, will deign to favor the progress of its life.[28]

Indeed, the edition, using the past tense, records a number of details of the original performance, particularly regarding specifics of orchestration, not fully indicated in the music itself. For example, a song at the beginning of act 1 "fu concertato al suono de tutti gli stromenti" ("was accompanied by the sound of all the instruments") and a ballet shortly thereafter "fu cantato al suono di cinque Viole da braccio" ("was sung to the sound of five viole da braccio").[29] There are even occasional references to staging, such as this near the beginning of act 2: "Questo ritornello fu sonato di dentro da un Clavicembano [*sic*], duoi Chitaroni, & duoi Violini piccioli alla Francese" ("This ritornello was played from within by a clavicembalo, two chitaroni, and two small French violins").[30] And, at the beginning of act 5: "Duoi Organi di legno, & duoi

27. *L'Orfeo: Favola in Musica da Claudio Monteverdi Rappresentata in Mantova l'Anno 1607. & novamente data in luce. Al Serenissimo Signor D. Francesco Gonzaga, Principe di Mantova, e di Monferrato, . . . In Venetia appresso Ricciardo Amadino. MDCIX* (facsimile published by Adolf Sandberger, Augsburg: Benno Filzer, 1927; henceforth cited as *Orfeo*). Atypically, the score was reprinted in 1615 (facsimile published by Denis Stevens, Westmead, Farnsborough, Hants, England: Gregg International Publishers, 1972).
28. "La favola d'Orfeo, che già nell'Academia de gl'Invaghiti sotto gl'auspitij di V.A. fu sopra angusta

Scena musicalmente rappresentata, dovendo hora comparire nel gran Teatro dell'universo a far mostra di se a tutti gl'huomini, non è ragione che si lasci vedere con altro nome signata, che con quello dell'Altezza V. glorioso, & felice, A lei dunque humilmente la consacro, affinch'ella che a guisa di benigna stella le fu propitia nel suo nascimento, con i Serenissimi raggi della gratia sua, si degni di favorir il progresso della sua vita" (*Orfeo*, composer's preface).
29. *Orfeo*, 8, 10.
30. *Orfeo*, 27.

Chitaroni concertorno questo Canto sonando l'uno nel angolo sinistro de la Sena, l'altro nel destro" ("Two wooden organs and two chitaroni accompanied this song, one of them playing in the left corner of the stage, the other in the right corner").[31] But several directions are given in the present tense, suggesting that the purpose of the print may have been somewhat broader: to serve not only as a historical document but as a practical one as well, a kind of generic score providing the basis for future performances.[32] In fact, the score offers several choices, such as that for the opening toccata "che si suona avanti il levar da la tela tre volte con tutti li stromenti, & si fa un tuono piu alto volendo sonar le trombe con le sordine" ("which is played three times with all the instruments before the curtain rises, and if one wishes to use muted trumpets, this piece should be played a tone higher").[33] Perhaps the most striking, most curious choice is offered for Orfeo's central number, "Possente spirto," where the singer is directed to perform only one of the two lines, the first unadorned, the second a highly elaborated version of the first: "Orfeo al suono del Organo di legno, & un Chitarone, canta una sola de le due parti" ("Orfeo, to the sound of the wood organ and a chitarone, sings only one of the two parts") (fig. 2).[34]

The libretto of *Orfeo* was also printed, two years earlier, presumably shortly before the first performance of the opera.[35] It matches the printed score quite closely, with the single major exception of the ending; the score alters the original myth so that the opera ends happily.[36] Although published by the ducal

31. *Orfeo*, 89.
32. However, we have no reliable records of later performances of *Orfeo*; see Iain Fenlon, "The Mantuan 'Orfeo,' " in *Claudio Monteverdi: Orfeo*, ed. John Whenham (Cambridge, 1986), 18. The revival of scores that were published was somewhat exceptional, but Peri's and Rinuccini's *Euridice* (1600) was apparently performed in Bologna in 1616; Loreto Vittori's *Galatea*, published in 1639, served as the basis for a performance in 1644 (see Bianconi, *Seventeenth Century*, 170); Domenico Mazzocchi's *La catena d'Adone* (1626) was performed in Bologna in 1648 and Piacenza in 1650 (see Bianconi and Walker, "Dalla 'Finta pazza,' " 426 n. 194, 433 n. 219); and Stefano Landi's *Sant'Alessio* (1632) was performed in Reggio Emilia in 1645.
33. On the transposition of the toccata, see Wolfgang Osthoff, "Trombe sordine," *Archiv für Musikwissenschaft* 13 (1956): 77–95.
34. *Orfeo*, 52. A contemporary publication by Bartolomeo Barberini, *Secondo libreto delli motetti* (Venice: Vincenti, 1614), which provides two versions of each of its pieces, may shed some light on this. As Barberini explains in his preface to the reader, the first version, unornamented, is for those singers lacking "dispositione di passeggiare," that is, those

unable to perform the embellishments, and for those with "dispositione," who already know the rules of embellishment and can do it themselves; the second, ornamented, is for those unschooled in the methods of embellishment but technically able to perform them. Pirrotta (*Music and Theatre*, 277), suggests that the unadorned version may have been intended to be sung as written. It is hardly likely, however, that a singer engaged for the title role of an opera would have lacked "dispositione di passeggiare." The most reasonable explanation, suggested to me by Lorenzo Bianconi, combines the function of documenting the past (this is how Francesco Rasi, the original Orfeo, sang the piece in 1607) with concern for the future (here is the skeleton, ornament it as you wish).
35. *La favola d'Orfeo: Rappresentata in musica il carnevale dell'anno M. D. CVII nell'Accademia de gli Invaghiti di Mantova, sotto i felici auspizij del Serenissimo Sig. Duca benignissimo lor protettore, In Mantova, per Francesco Osanna stampator Ducale . . . 1607.* There were probably at least two performances (see Fenlon, "Mantuan 'Orfeo,' " 9–18).
36. There is a full literature on this alteration. Pirrotta was the first to suggest that the apotheosis preserved in the score was part of the original ending, which had to be modified because the performance

2.   Claudio Monteverdi, *L'Orfeo, favola in musica* (Venice, 1615), p. 52.

printer, this libretto was not designed primarily as a commemorative document. Thus it fails to mention either the composer or—and this is more unusual—the poet. It was used by the audience as an aid to following the action.[37]

---

site was too small ("Theater, Sets, and Music in Monteverdi's Operas," *Essays*, 258–59, and "Monteverdi's Poetic Choices," *Essays*, 291 n. 44) and was then restored for a second performance. Fenlon ("Mantuan 'Orfeo,'" 16), although agreeing with Pirrotta that the apotheosis did not take place at the first performance, holds to the more traditional view that the bacchic finale was the original one.

37.   See *Orfeo*, ed. Whenham, appendix 1, letter 9: "The play has been printed so that everyone in the audience can have a copy to follow while the performance is in progress."

In contrast to the score of *Orfeo*, that of *Poppea* was never printed. It survives in two manuscript copies, neither of which can be linked with its initial performance. Documentation for that first performance is slim indeed, resting solely on a scenario—a scene-by-scene synopsis of the action that was printed not for commemorative reasons but, once again, for the practical purpose of helping the audience in the theater to follow the performance.[38] The scenario mentions neither the composer nor the poet. In fact, there is no printed documentation whatsoever for Monteverdi's authorship of the music. Two librettos eventually appeared in print, but not until 1651 and 1656. The latter, published along with his other librettos by the poet himself, Gian Francesco Busenello, mentions the original date of performance on its title page but fails to include the composer's name.[39] As for the 1651 libretto, published in conjunction with a Neapolitan revival, it lacks the names of both the composer and the poet, as well as the original date.[40]

The two manuscript scores of *Poppea* might best be described as performance scores.[41] They memorialize expedients adopted for one or several specific performances after the premiere (figs. 3a, 3b). Transpositions, cuts, rearrangements, not all of them fully worked out or reconciled with one another, are indicated in various strata throughout both manuscripts. Preserved, it would seem, by chance, these scores owe their survival to the fact that the opera was revived; both are probably connected with the revival that took place in Naples in 1651.[42] Evidently, despite Monteverdi's enormous reputation, there was no interest in preserving the music of the first performance of *Poppea*.[43] That music per se had no practical value except as a basis for subsequent

38.   *Scenario dell'opera reggia intitolata La Coronatione di Poppea. Che si rappresenta in Musica nel Theatro dell'Illustr. Sig. Giovanni Grimani, In Venetia, 1643, presso Gio: Pietro Pinelli*; the scenario is available in a modern edition in Claudio Gallico, *Monteverdi* (Turin, 1979), 92–96. For a full discussion of scenarios, see ch. 2 below; also Ellen Rosand, "The Opera Scenario, 1638–1655: A Preliminary Survey," in *In cantu et in sermone: For Nino Pirrotta on His 80th Birthday*, ed. Fabrizio della Seta and Franco Piperno (Florence, 1989), 335–46.

39.   See *Delle hore ociose di Gio: Francesco Busenello. Parte prima. All'Eminentissimo Principe Il Sig. Cardinal Ottoboni* (Venice: Giuliani, 1656).

40.   *Il Nerone overo L'incoronatione di Poppea, Drama musicale dedicato all'Illustriss. & Eccellentiss. Sig. D. Inigo De Guevara, et Tassis* (Naples: Molli, 1651).

41.   I-Vnm, It. IV, 439 (9963), facsimile ed. by Giacomo Benvenuti (Milan: Bocca, 1938), and Forni reprint (Bologna, n.d.); and I-Nc, Rari 6.4.1.

42.   Wolfgang Osthoff was the author of two classic articles on the sources of *Poppea*: "Die venezianische und neapolitanische Fassung von Monteverdis 'Incoronazione di Poppea,' " *AcM* 26 (1954): 88–113, and "Neue Beobachtungen zu Quellen und Geschichte von Monteverdis 'Incoronazione di Poppea,' " *Mf* 11 (1958): 129–38. More recently, the origin and provenance of these scores have been discussed and extensively reevaluated by Alessandra Chiarelli, " 'L'incoronazione di Poppea' o 'Il Nerone': Problemi di filologia testuale," *RIM* 9 (1974): 117–51; see also Peter Jeffery, "The Autograph Manuscripts of Francesco Cavalli" (Ph.D. diss., Princeton University, 1980). The most recent reexamination of the sources, by Alan Curtis ("La Poppea impasticciata, or Who Wrote the Music to *L'incoronazione* [1643]?" *JAMS* 42 [1989]: 22–54; and preface to Claudio Monteverdi, *L'incoronazione di Poppea*, ed. Alan Curtis [London, 1989]), suggests the possibility that some of the surviving music may be by one or more younger composers.

43.   Busenello, to be sure, intended to immortalize his original text by printing it in his 1656 collection.

3. a,b.   Claudio Monteverdi, *L'incoronazione di Poppea*, I-Vnm, It. IV, 439
(=9963), fols. 65v–66.

performance. The differences between the scores and other sources confirm the fact of multiple performances, and the kinds of alterations in each document indicate the liberties taken with the original opera—transposed here, cut there—in response to changing conditions of performance.

One major difference between the scores of the two operas that is only partly explained by their different functions concerns orchestration. The score of *Orfeo* is not only much more specific in its instrumental requirements (listing them, however incompletely, in its front matter), but it calls for a much larger, more varied instrumental group, essentially the late Renaissance orchestra that was customarily used for court entertainments; and this is deployed alone, in a large number of purely instrumental movements, especially dances, as well as in combination with voices, with particular expressive functions. In its successive strophes, for instance, "Possente spirto" displays first violins, then cornetti, then double harp, and finally violins again, the variety enhancing the moving power of Orfeo's prayer.[44]

The *Poppea* scores, on the other hand, contain considerably fewer instrumental movements, and the voice is invariably accompanied only by a bass line. Furthermore, they contain no instrumental specifications. This notational reticence is more than a matter of expediency. It reflects an actual difference in instrumental practice between the Mantua of 1607 and the Venice of 1642. The chief components of the typical Venetian opera orchestra, as attested by a few widely scattered documents, were a large continuo group (several harpsichords and several theorbos), which was evidently deployed in various combinations to accompany the voice. The two treble parts written out in most ritornelli and sinfonie were taken by two violins.[45]

The different orchestral requirements of *Orfeo* and *Poppea* underline the distinctions I have been making between court and urban opera. The instrumental display of *Orfeo* formed part of the court spectacle in Mantua. The reduced band of *Poppea* satisfied the economic conditions of a commercial en-

---

44.   On the typical intermedio orchestra, see Robert Lamar Weaver, "Sixteenth-Century Instrumentation," *MQ* 47 (1961): 363–78; id., "The Orchestra in Early Italian Opera," *JAMS* 17 (1964): 83–89; and Howard M. Brown, *Sixteenth-Century Instrumentation: The Music for the Florentine Intermedi*, Musicological Studies and Documents 30 ([Rome], 1973).

45.   The two violins were sometimes joined by alto and tenor instruments, the viola da braccio and the violetta. The chief documentary evidence for the makeup of the Venetian opera orchestra is found in two different sets of pay records, which date from 1658–59 (in the account book for *Antioco*, I-Vas, Scuola grande di San Marco, *busta* 194: unnumbered)

and 1665 (for a revival of *Ciro*, b. 194, c. 268): that is, considerably later than *Poppea*. Nevertheless, it seems unlikely that the orchestra changed much until late in the seventeenth century, when trumpets were introduced. For a discussion of these documents, see Denis Arnold, "Performing Practice," in *The New Monteverdi Companion*, ed. Denis Arnold and Nigel Fortune (London, 1985), 319–33, esp. 329–31; also Jane Glover, *Cavalli* (London, 1978), 106–12; and Edward Tarr and Thomas Walker, " 'Bellici carmi, festivo fragor': Die Verwendung der Trompete in der italienischen Oper des 17. Jahrhunderts," *Hamburger Jahrbuch für Musikwissenschaft* 3 (1978): 143–203.

terprise. It allowed theaters to function without large stable orchestras. It also tended to focus greater attention on the singers.

A Mantuan opera of 1607 could be fixed, commemorated in print as a rare, even unique, object, a jewel in the crown of a ruling prince. Not so a Venetian opera of 1643. It was but one of a succession of similar events that would be remembered only as long as the season lasted, and then discarded—unless subsequently revived. Whereas we owe our knowledge of the music of Monteverdi's *Orfeo* to the desire to preserve a moment of dynastic celebration, our knowledge of *Poppea* depends upon a more professionally utilitarian motive, the appropriation of a past event for the purposes of the present. Only because *Poppea* was revived, given renewed life on the stage, do we know anything of its music. *Orfeo*, although immortalized by the act of publication, embodied a tradition of court entertainment that was essentially over. The very survival of *Poppea*, imperfect as it is, testifies to its continuing vitality, to its function within a living tradition of public opera.

The Documents of a History

As the case of *Poppea* attests, the distinctive and cohesive character of the Venetian operatic tradition is exemplified by the nature of its surviving documents. These fall into two general categories: manuscript and printed, categories that themselves implicate a set of further distinctions, between the musical and the textual, the professional and the public. The manuscripts, that is, the scores, representing the professional side of things, are preserved, if at all, largely by accident, by virtue of the fact that they were reused. Relatively few have, in fact, survived. The nature and purpose of the printed sources, the public documents, primarily librettos, were very different. Quite apart from their practical function of serving the audience during performances, librettos were deliberately created for the purpose of documenting the individual work. Published in large enough numbers to have ensured the survival today of several complete sets, they record the chronological development of Venetian opera from year to year. The sheer accumulation of librettos—there were nine after four seasons, thirty-five after ten, and over one hundred by 1667—provides concrete evidence of the momentum of opera mania in seventeenth-century Venice.

In addition to appealing to the collectionist tendencies of a number of *letterati*, such as Apostolo Zeno, whose complete sets have come down to us,[46] the

46. The Biblioteca Marciana in Venice possesses three such sets. The most nearly complete, containing a number of second editions, and possibly from the collection of the eighteenth-century bibliographer Antonio Groppo, is Dramm. 907–1126, which covers the years 1637–1796. The others are Dramm.

librettos inspired another type of historical record: the operatic chronology, for which they supplied the basic source material. The earliest of these publications, neither yet a chronology nor devoted exclusively to operatic or Venetian texts, was explicitly designed to take stock of the rapidly growing genre of the libretto. Leone Allacci's *Drammaturgia*, published in Rome in 1666, declares its purpose in the printer's preface: to preserve an undervalued and therefore highly perishable product:

> It often happens that, after being read, librettos are rejected, and they are no longer valued, because of the silly things that are found in most of them, so that copies are lost, and not only is the memory of those obscured, who with great effort and study made some name for themselves, but also their countries and families. Since, in the opinion of some, [librettos] are in no small part derived from antiquity, and indistinguishable from one another in invention as well as subject matter, there having been no new discoveries [of ancient plays], they have become so tediously similar in subject matter, usually concerning the disappearance of babies or children during the taking or sacking of a city, that readers assume they have already read them, and they intentionally abstain from seeing them, clearly recognizing them, as Burchiello said, to be patchworks of old rags, twisted and pilfered from here and there, without beginning or end, head or tail. (Appendix II.4)[47]

Allacci's volume, which underwent an ambitious revision in the eighteenth century,[48] was soon followed by the first true chronology. This was the work of the Dalmatian Cristoforo Ivanovich, himself the author of several librettos. "Le memorie teatrali di Venezia," published in Venice in 1681 (2d ed. 1688), formed an appendix to Ivanovich's *Minerva al tavolino*, a collection of letters on the subject of the wars against the Turks.[49] By providing a list of the dramas performed in Venice, Ivanovich, like Allacci before him, hoped to rescue them from oblivion: "From the reading of the dramas cited in the catalogue of the present 'Memorie,' posterity, for various reasons, will heap greater praise upon the authors than they received when their works were first performed" (Appendix II.6ff). Ivanovich's catalogue forms the climax of a lengthy essay on the

---

3448–3578 (1637–1750), from Zeno's collection; and Dramm. 1127–1418 (1637–1836), from the Rossi legacy. Another virtually complete series is the Cicogna Collection at the Casa Goldoni. There are several others outside Venice, including I-Rig, I-MOe, US-Wc Schatz, and US-Lau. The most comprehensive listing of librettos, which includes the location of multiple copies, is found in Claudio Sartori, "Primo tentativo di catalogo unico dei libretti italiani a stampa fino all'anno 1800" (MS in the Ufficio Ricerca Fondi Musicali, Milan).

47.   Although he lived in Rome, Allacci maintained close connections with operatic life in Venice. He belonged to the operatically important Venetian Accademia degli Incogniti (see ch. 2 below).

48.   *Drammaturgia di Leone Allacci accresciuta e continuata fino all'anno MDCCLV* (Venice: Giambattista Pasquali, 1755).

49.   On this important publication, see Thomas Walker, "Gli errori di *Minerva al tavolino*: Osservazioni sulla cronologia delle prime opere veneziane," in *Venezia e il melodramma nel seicento*, ed. Maria Teresa Muraro (Florence, 1976), 7–20; see also Miloš Velimirović, "Cristoforo Ivanovich from Budva, the First Historian of the Venetian Opera," *ZVUK* [*Yugoslav Music Review*] 77–78 (1967): 135–45.

origins and contemporary practice of opera in Venice, which draws, in large measure, upon the prefaces of the printed librettos. His discussion of Venetian operatic practice remains by far the most explicit and reliable we have; and his chronology served as the foundation of all subsequent chronologies, notably those of the eighteenth-century writers Giovanni Carlo Bonlini (1730) and Antonio Groppo (1745).[50]

These chronologies, generally trustworthy with respect to titles, authors, theaters, and dates of performances, are less dependable for information not regularly available in printed librettos—most crucially, composers' names. Indeed, Ivanovich, particularly for the years preceding his arrival in Venice in 1657, tended to attribute music rather haphazardly (especially to Cavalli). Many of his attributions, repeated by Bonlini and Groppo, have remained unexamined, unchallenged, and uncorrected until recently.[51]

Another still insufficiently acknowledged shortcoming of all three volumes is their failure to recognize the inconsistent application of dates in the librettos they catalogued. That is, they ignored the whole problem of *more veneto*, dating Venetian style. Because the Venetian year traditionally began on 1 March, Carnival (and the opera season coincident with it), generally over by the end of February, was considered to belong to the previous year. Thus a libretto dated 1640 *m.v.* actually belonged to 1641, modern style (or 1640–41 if it appeared before 1 January). But not all Venetian dates were given *more veneto*. This is made clear in some cases by a discrepancy between title page and dedication date; the libretto of Cavalli's *Giasone*, for example, bears the date 1649 on its

50. [Carlo Bonlini], *Le glorie della poesia e della musica contenute nell'esatta notitia de teatri della città di Venezia* (Venice: Bonarigo, [1730]) both acknowledged his debt to Ivanovich's catalogue and recognized its shortcomings: "Il primo, anzi l'unico, che fino ad ora abbia dato al Pubblico qualche succinta notizia in tal genere [dei' drami], fu il Dott. D. Cristoforo Iwanovich . . . il quale se ben Schiavon di natali, è andato del pari in dottrina, ed eruditione a i più fioriti Ingegni Italiani della sua età. Questo famoso Auttore sul fine del Primo Tomo della sua *Minerva al Tavolino*, pone un breve Trattato, a cui da il nome di *Memorie Teatrali della Città di Venezia*, e quivi dopo aver dato in ristretto qualche contezza de' Teatri noti sino a nostri giorni, va tessendo un Catalogo de' Drami in Musica sino a' suoi giorni parimente in quelli rappresentati, e s'estende nella seconda Edizione delle sue virtuose fatiche sino all'Anno 1687. Ma questo Catalogo in alcuni Drami riesce non poco fallace, ed in altri ancora mancante, cosicchè non è giunto a quella perfezione, che sarebbe desiderabile in una tale materia. E per verità fattone un rigoroso

rincontro con i Libretti ch'abbiamo in stampa, vi si scorgono circa quaranta sbagli di non poco rilevo, particolarmente nella notizia non ben esatta de' veri Maestri di Musica" (preface, 4–5). Antonio Groppo, *Catalogo di tutti i drammi per musica* (Venice: Groppo, 1745), referred to all three of his predecessors, Allacci, Ivanovich, and Bonlini, but without criticizing them (preface, 5–6). A more recent chronology, largely based on the others, is Livio Niso Galvani [Giuseppe Salvioli], *I teatri musicali di Venezia nel secolo XVII, 1637–1700* (Milan, 1879). See also the chronology in Francesco Caffi, "Storia della musica teatrale in Venezia" (MS I-Vnm, It. IV, 747–49 [10462–65]).

51. On Ivanovich's shortcomings, see Walker, "Errori." Walker's corrections resulted in a substantial reduction in the number of works ascribed to Cavalli, from forty-two (nearly a third of them missing) to the much more reasonable number of thirty-three (only five missing); the definitive list is given in Thomas Walker, "Cavalli," *New Grove* 4: 24–34.

title page, but the dedication is dated 30 January 1648. Clearly, then, the date on the title page should be read in modern style, that of the dedication *more veneto*; the work was performed during the 1648–49 season, not that of 1649–50. Other cases are not so clear and can be resolved only through triangulation, using evidence external to the librettos themselves.[52]

In contrast to the librettos, whose preservation is virtually complete, the proportion of surviving scores is small. In particular, very few scores remain from the first—and, arguably, the most decisive—decade of operatic activity in Venice. Of the nearly fifty operas performed there between 1637 and 1650, music has survived for only thirteen, and by only three of the dozen or so composers known to have been involved: Monteverdi, Cavalli, and Sacrati.[53] No music at all survives from the operas of either Ferrari or Manelli, two of the most important composers of the decade, who were largely responsible for creating the musical style that came to be associated with opera in Venice.[54]

Through various circumstances, a number of the surviving scores were dispersed among libraries throughout Europe—including those in Modena, Florence, Naples, Oxford, Paris, and Vienna. Most of them duplicate scores held in the primary repository for this music, the Contarini Collection of the Biblioteca Marciana in Venice.[55] The 113 opera scores in the Contarini Collection (the period covered extends to 1684) owe their preservation to the efforts of two individuals: in the first place to Francesco Cavalli (1601–76), the com-

52. Such confusion has affected the dating of works as important as Monteverdi's late operas. According to Ivanovich, three operas by Monteverdi were performed in 1641: *Il ritorno d'Ulisse in patria* (S. Cassiano), *Le nozze d'Enea e Lavinia* (SS. Giovanni e Paolo), and *Arianna* (S. Moisè); and one in 1643, *L'incoronazione di Poppea*. Bonlini, who tried to take *more veneto* into account by introducing what he called the autumn season (for those operas that began before the first of January but continued to be performed until the end of Carnival), revised Ivanovich's chronology, ascribing *Arianna* to 1640, *Il ritorno* and *Le nozze* to 1641, and *Poppea* to autumn 1642. In fact, however, the coordination of various kinds of evidence permits a still more reasonable chronology, the one assumed on p. 18 above, which allows for the effort involved in readying a production for the stage. *Arianna* and *Ritorno* were performed in 1639–40; *Le nozze* (and *Ritorno* revived) in 1640–41 (the preface to the scenario of *Le nozze* mentions *Il ritorno* as having taken place the previous year); and *Poppea* in 1642–43 (scenario dated 1643). In the present study, all dates are given in modern style unless otherwise indicated.

53. Sacrati joined this elite group only very recently, with the important discovery by Lorenzo Bianconi of a score of *La finta pazza*, which will be published shortly in facsimile in Drammaturgia musicale veneta.

54. We can, of course, extrapolate some knowledge of their style from their non-operatic music, as Alessandro Magini did in his thesis at the University of Bologna, "Indagini stilistiche intorno *L'incoronazione di Poppea*" (1984): esp. ch. 3; see also id., "Le monodie di Benedetto Ferrari e *L'incoronazione di Poppea*: Un rilevamento stilistico comparativo," *RIM* 21 (1987): 266–99; and Curtis, preface to *L'incoronazione di Poppea*.

55. The only two scores from before 1650 not duplicated in the Contarini Collection are *Il ritorno* (A-Wn 18763), which may have been brought to Vienna by Benedetto Ferrari, and *La finta pazza* at the Isola Borromeo (see Lorenzo Bianconi, preface to Giulio Strozzi and Francesco Sacrati, *La finta pazza*, ed. Lorenzo Bianconi and Thomas Walker, Drammaturgia musicale veneta 1 [in press]).

poser best represented in the collection. Near the end of his career, probably about 1670, Cavalli apparently arranged to have his operas recopied with a view to preserving them for posterity.[56] He clearly regarded them as important property, a significant part of his legacy, and made special provision for them in his will.[57] These fair copies, plus some of his autographs (which, we may assume, would also have been copied had he lived longer), eventually found their way into the Contarini Collection.[58]

The other *collezionista* responsible for the preservation of the scores was Marco Contarini himself, patrician and patron of opera, who built two theaters for private operatic performances at his villa at Piazzola, just northwest of Venice. Between 1679 and sometime before his death in 1689—probably in 1684—Contarini gradually and purposefully amassed a collection of scores.[59] Most of the scores in his collection date from earlier than 1679, the year his operatic productions began, and so cannot be connected with his own performances. Indeed, we should regard the entire Contarini Collection, fair copies as well as autographs (figs. 4, 5), as commemorative rather than functional documents, reflecting the desire of both Cavalli and Contarini to preserve a musical heritage.

Imperfect and incomplete as the musical sources may be, they far exceed those for the visual component of these operas. For an idea of what the works

56. His latest scores were apparently copied first; and then the scribe seems to have started at the beginning and worked forward as far as 1650. On the copying of Cavalli's manuscripts, see Glover, *Cavalli*, 65–72. The matter is exhaustively treated in Jeffery, "Autograph Manuscripts," passim.

57. Cavalli's will distinguished between specially bound volumes (the fair copies) and some other scores, which were left to his student Caliari. The document is transcribed in Taddeo Wiel, "Francesco Cavalli (1602–1676) e la sua musica scenica," *Nuovo archivio veneto*, n.s., 28 (1914): 142–50. The details are summarized in Glover, *Cavalli*, 31, and in Jeffery, "Autograph Manuscripts," 81–86. Cavalli's library must also have included the Contarini copy of *Poppea*, which shows evidence of his hand (see Jeffery, "Autograph Manuscripts," 114). Osthoff's suggestion that Cavalli directed the Naples revival of *Poppea* ("Neue Beobachtungen," 137–38) has not been substantiated. The presence of his hand and some of his music in the manuscript merely indicates that he was involved in some way with the version of the opera that was eventually performed in Naples.

58. The Contarini Collection, which included material other than opera scores as well, was acquired

by the Marciana from Contarini's distant heirs in 1839; see Taddeo Wiel, *I codici musicali contariniani del secolo XVII nella R. Biblioteca di San Marco in Venezia* (Venice, 1888; repr. Bologna: Forni, 1969). Some clue to the order in which Contarini acquired the manuscript scores is provided by a handwritten list of operas found on the inside cover of a printed volume of Frescobaldi keyboard toccatas now in the Biblioteca Marciana (I-Vnm Musica 39). According to that list, dated 14 June 1681, which includes none of the Cavalli autographs, most of the scores were acquired in 1681 and 1682, and a few in 1683. (The list also includes a number of works not in the present Contarini Collection.) See Glover, *Cavalli*, 67–68. The most complete discussion of the development of the Contarini Collection, including a list of its contents, is found in Giovanni Morelli and Thomas Walker, "Migliori plettri," preface to Aurelio Aureli and Francesco Lucio, *Medoro*, ed. Giovanni Morelli and Thomas Walker, Drammaturgia musicale veneta 4 (Milan, 1984), CXL–CXLVI.

59. Contarini apparently employed his own copyist for some of them, in particular, those in Hand A (according to Morelli and Walker, "Migliori plettri," CXLV).

4. Francesco Cavalli, *Gli amori d'Apollo e di Dafne*, I-Vnm, It. IV, 404 (=9928), f. 85v (copy).

5. Francesco Cavalli, *Oristeo*, I-Vnm, It. IV, 367 (=9891), f. 41 (autograph).

actually looked like on stage, the historian is forced to rely primarily on de-scriptions in librettos and to extrapolate from the few published engravings of scene designs.[60]

Beyond the primary source materials—the librettos and the scores—other kinds of documents bearing on the history and development of opera in seventeenth-century Venice are preserved in various archives. The most sub-stantial and important are two large *buste* in the Archivio di Stato, Venice, known by students of the period as 188 and 194.[61] Comprising hundreds of folios each, they are the papers of Marco Faustini, who served as an impresario at various theaters from 1651 to 1668, working with every important com-poser, librettist, and singer of the period. His papers, which cover earlier years as well, include a wide variety of documents: from correspondence with agents, singers, and composers (Cesti, Cavalli, and Ziani) to contracts and theater budgets. Collectively, they supply the basis for a richly detailed history of opera during the period of his activity.

Other notable and more recently discovered Venetian archival sources in-clude two *buste* of Cavalli documents from the Archivio S. Lorenzo[62] and one from the Monastero di Sta. Maria dell'Orazion a Malamocco in the Archivio di Stato,[63] and the theater documents in the Archivio Vendramin, now housed at the Casa Goldoni.[64] Still to be fully mined is a cache of documents found in the State Archives in Hannover among the correspondence of Johann Friedrich, duke of Brunswick-Lüneburg. The duke was an important political ally, sup-

60.   The stage designs for Venetian productions of this period were rarely published; but those that were are frequently reproduced. See, for example, Per Bjurström, *Giacomo Torelli and Baroque Stage Design* (Stockholm, 1961); Simon Towneley Worsthorne, *Seventeenth-Century Venetian Opera* (Oxford, 1954, rev. ed. 1968); Ludovico Zorzi, Maria Teresa Mu-raro, Gianfranco Prato, and Elvi Zorzi, eds., *I teatri pubblici di Venezia (secoli XVII-XVIII)*, exhib. cat. (Venice, 1971); Franco Mancini, Maria Teresa Mu-raro, and Elena Povoledo, eds., *Illusione e prattica te-atrale*, exhib. cat. (Venice, 1975); Hélène Leclerc, *Ve-nise et l'avènement de l'opéra public à l'âge baroque* (Paris, 1987).

61.   Scuola Grande di S. Marco, *buste* 188 and 194, henceforth cited as *b.* 188 and *b.* 194. They were first mentioned in 1887 by Bartolomeo Cecchetti, "Carte relative ai teatri di S. Cassiano e dei SS. Giovanni e Paolo," *Archivio veneto* 34 (1887): 246. See also Wiel, "Francesco Cavalli," 135–36 n. 2, and Henry Pru-nières, *Cavalli et l'opéra vénitien au XVIIe siècle* (Paris, 1931), 305–6 n. 3. Hermann Kretzschmar, to whom Wiel sent transcriptions, published an article about

them in 1907: "Beiträge zur Geschichte der vene-tianischen Oper," *Jahrbuch der Musikbibliothek Peters* 14 (1907): 71–81. They were inventoried, somewhat inexactly, by Remo Giazotto, "La guerra dei palchi," *NRMI* 1 (1967): 245–86, 465–508; 3 (1969): 906–33; and quoted extensively in Bruno Brunelli, "L'impre-sario in angustie," *Rivista italiana del dramma* 3 (1941): 311–41; Remo Giazotto, "Nel CCC anno della morte di Antonio Cesti: Ventidue lettere ritrovate nell'Archivio di Stato di Venezia," *NRMI* 3 (1969): 496–512; and Carl Schmidt, "An Episode in the His-tory of Venetian Opera: The *Tito* Commission (1665–66)," *JAMS* 31 (1978): 442–66.

62.   I-Vas, Archivio S. Lorenzo, *buste* 23 and 24. These are discussed in Glover, *Cavalli*, ch. 1, as well as elsewhere.

63.   *Busta* 3; formerly part of the S. Lorenzo ar-chive. These documents contain important informa-tion on Cavalli at S. Cassiano; see Giovanni Morelli and Thomas Walker, "Tre controversie intorno al San Cassiano," in *Venezia e il melodrama nel seicento*, ed. Maria Teresa Muraro (Florence, 1976), 97–120.

64.   I-Vcg, Archivio Vendramin 42 F 1–16.

plier of arms, and frequent visitor to Venice during this period.[65] These papers include letters and reports from the duke's agents in Venice, among them the composer Sartorio and the librettists Pietro Dolfin and Nicolò Beregan, who were entrusted with hiring musicians for him. A particularly rich source of operatic gossip is provided by the letters of the duke's secretary in Venice, Francesco Maria Massi.[66]

Travelers to Venice, who formed an important component of the operatic audience, were occasionally stimulated to comment on the operatic scene in their letters or diaries. Few as they are, these comments shed considerable light on the place of opera in the life of the city.[67] Somewhat more formal are the weekly *avvisi* reporting the news from various cities that circulated around Italy and abroad in manuscript and, eventually, printed form, from the late sixteenth century on. Several series of manuscript *avvisi* from the late seventeenth century have been preserved, in which information about opera is part of the detailed description of everyday Venetian events.[68] A number of issues of the Parisian journal *Le Mercure galant*, from the same period, contain lengthy reports of opera in Venice.[69]

All of these sources, taken together, allow us to assemble a history of opera in Venice. The most fundamental of them, however, are the printed librettos. In regularly supplying dates and names—of patrons, theaters, librettists, sometimes of composers, singers, and stage designers—as well as the actual texts that were sung, they provide the foundation of that history. But they provide much more. Their prefaces and dedications are rich in information. Their form and

65. Niedersächsisches Haupt-Staatsarchiv Hannover, Aktes-Korrespondenzen italienischer Kardinäle und anderer Personen, besonders Italiener an Herzog Johann Friedrich, Cal. Br. vols. 1–6 (624–29). On the importance of the dukes of Brunswick-Lüneburg to Venetian political—and operatic—life, see Bianconi and Walker, "Production," 269–70; also, in passing, Craig Monson, "*Giulio Cesare in Egitto* from Sartorio (1677) to Handel (1724)," *ML* 66 (1985): 313–37.

66. There were similar correspondences with other foreign princes interested in Venetian opera, such as the duke of Modena and Mattias de' Medici (archival material in I-MOs Particolari and I-Fas); also I-Rvat (Archivio Chigi), I-Vmc (correspondence of Polo Michiel), I-R (Archivio Colonna).

67. Such figures include John Evelyn (quoted on p. 9 above), Sir Philip Skippon (*Journey through the Low Countries, Germany, Italy, and France* [London, 1682; repr. 1752], 520–21); and Francesco de' Pannocchieschi; see Molmenti, "Venezia alla metà del sec. XVII," 313, 317. See also Alexandre-Toussaint de Limojon, Sier de Saint-Disdier, *La Ville et la République de Venise* (Paris: Barbin, 1680).

68. A number of series are preserved in Venice at the Biblioteca Marciana and the Archivio di Stato. For a summary of these, see Eleanor Selfridge-Field, *Pallade veneta: Writings on Music in Venetian Society, 1650–1750* (Venice, 1985), chs. 1 and 2.

69. Written anonymously by Chassebras de Cremailles during the 1680s, they were collected and republished by Pierre d'Ortigue de Vaumorière in *Lettres sur toutes sortes de sujets* (Paris: J. Guignard, 1690). These descriptions are quoted extensively in Harris Sheridan Saunders, Jr., "The Repertoire of a Venetian Opera House (1678–1714): The Teatro Grimani di San Giovanni Grisostomo," Ph.D. diss. (Harvard University, 1985), ch. 1. The earliest surviving sources of this kind reporting on opera in Venice date from the early 1660s; they appeared in *Il rimino*, a newssheet published in Rimini that was a compilation of *avvisi* from various cities. See Nevio Matteini, *Il "Rimino," una delle prime "gazette" d'Italia: Saggio storico sui primordi della stampa* (Bologna, 1967).

content change with the developing genre. Carefully read (on and between the lines) and considered in their entirety—from their actual poetic content (form, subject matter, and organization) to the layout of their title pages, from the publishers' and authors' prefaces to the dramatis personae and last-minute addenda—they offer a precise record of public opera at the most important period of its development, just as it was taking shape. It is against the facts and running commentary provided by the librettos that all the other sources, including the music, yield their full historical meaning.

2

• • •

Dramma per musica:
The Question of Genre

"Drama for music": this was the term by which opera librettos were generally known in the seventeenth century. The subtitle under which they were usually published, *Dramma per musica*, expresses quite effectively, even eloquently, the ambiguous nature of the libretto as a genre. Alone, these little books were but shadows, texts needing music (and staging) to endow them with life. Never intended to stand on their own, they were admittedly, glaringly, and self-consciously incomplete. Evaluation of their quality could not rest on their merits as literature or drama—the elegance of their poetry, the tautness of their plot structure, the verisimilitude of their action. Librettos had to be judged by the efficacy of the musical setting they inspired, the dramatic conviction of the combination: libretto plus music, a combination that, ideally, would exceed by far the simple sum of its parts.

Although every writer of librettos was aware of the extent to which the definition of his work depended on another artist's efforts, that awareness was not always shared by literary critics. Lacking appropriate instruments for evaluation, they often tried to judge librettos by purely literary standards, without considering them in the proper context, that of the opera house.[1] From the beginning of their history, librettos suffered abuse from critics for their failure to measure up as literature. The issue was most urgent for the earliest and most sensitive of these critics, those who had the most to lose—or gain: the librettists themselves, the inventors or creators of the genre. Critical abuse began as critical self-abuse.

---

1. Some writers, such as Ludovico Antonio Muratori, displayed an acute ambivalence in their attitude toward opera: as literary critics they condemned it, but as members of the audience they applauded it enthusiastically. See Sergio Durante, "Vizi privati e virtù pubbliche del polemista teatrale da Muratori a Marcello," in *Benedetto Marcello: La sua opera e il suo tempo*, ed. Claudio Madricardo and Franco Rossi (Florence, 1988), 415–24. These critics lacked appropriate categories for judging theatrical works. See also Lorenzo Bianconi, "Il cinquecento e il seicento," in *Teatro, musica, tradizione dei classici*, Letteratura italiana 6 (Turin, 1986), 356–63.

It is worth noting that *dramma per musica* did not suggest itself immediately as a designation for operatic texts. It emerged only after librettists had wrestled for some time with the question of defining just what it was they were producing; and it developed not in the occasional operas produced during the first decades of the century in Florence and Rome, but later, in Venice, where the operatic experience was constant and intense. Ottavio Rinuccini's first two operatic texts, the mythical dramas *Dafne* and *Euridice*, bear no generic subtitle at all, while his third libretto, *Arianna*, is labeled a *tragedia*; Striggio's *Orfeo* is called a *favola in musica*; and in Rome librettos were variously referred to as *dramma musicale*, *commedia musicale*, *opera musicale*, or *attione in musica*.[2] The first Venetian librettos, too, exhibited a striking variety of generic designations, some of them borrowed from the past, others obviously invented ad hoc: *favola*, *opera scenica*, *festa teatrale*, *dramma*, *opera drammatica*, *favola regia*, *opera regia*, *tragedia musicale*, *opera tragicomica musicale*, *dramma musicale*, and others. One notable feature of this list is that only a few of the terms allude to the absent, yet central, ingredient, the music; the others imply self-sufficiency and could have been—and were—applied to any kind of dramatic work. The familiar and curiously neutral term *opera* appears in several of these subtitles. Originally applied to every category of written or improvised play, it became associated with a particular kind that was neither tragic nor comic but mixed features of both. Plays set in exotic lands, featuring royal or princely protagonists and eventful plots with happy endings, were called *opere regie* or *opere reali*. Busenello's *L'incoronazione di Poppea*, for example, was termed an *opera regia*. Although *opera* occasionally appeared unmodified in conjunction with some early librettos, it did not assume its modern significance until much later.[3]

It was not until the middle of the seventeenth century, then, after more than a decade of vigorous operatic activity—more than thirty operas by some twenty librettists and ten composers, in five theaters—that Venetian librettists began to designate their works *dramma per musica* with any consistency, thus signifying

2. Nino Pirrotta has emphasized the significance of generic distinctions in early opera. He attaches considerable importance to the designation *tragedia* for *Arianna*, regarding that opera as the first real attempt to recreate tragedy in music. Its two predecessors, the *favole Dafne* and *Euridice*, represented, in contrast, "the brief pastoral phase of opera" ("Monteverdi and the Problems of Opera," *Essays*, 245–46). Barbara Russano Hanning, however, prefers to regard all three of Rinuccini's librettos as manifestations of the same impulse toward tragedy. See her "Apologia pro Ottavio Rinuccini," JAMS 26 (1973): 252; also id. *Of Poetry and Music's Power* (Ann Arbor, 1980), ch. 1, esp. 18.

The generic subtitles for the early Roman operas occur in the *argomenti*, which were usually printed. The librettos, which were not printed as a rule, merely use the term *dramma*. For a list of Roman subtitles, see Margaret Murata, *Operas for the Papal Court, 1631–1668* (Ann Arbor, 1981), appendix 2.

3. On the use of the term *opera regia* in *commedia dell'arte*, where it seems to have referred to works exhibiting Spanish influence, see Cesare Molinari, *La commedia dell'arte* (Milan, 1985), 49. Pirrotta, "Commedia dell'arte and Opera," *Essays*, 355 and nn. 33–34, regards this designation as the source for the term *opera*. An early use of *opera*, unmodified, appears in the scenario of *Le nozze di Teti e di Peleo* by Orazio Persiani (1639) in a descriptive passage.

recognition and acceptance of the imperfect state of their creations. Although it may seem like a matter of mere semantics, the terminological consensus thus reflected on the title pages of printed librettos actually represented a significant step in the history of the art. It was one of many indications that opera had aesthetically come of age, that it had achieved the status of a genre in its own right.

Lack of agreement on the question of categorizing subtitles was only one symptom of the malaise that appears to have afflicted most early Venetian librettists. The librettos offer many other indications of their authors' uneasiness with opera as a genre, of their concern with the propriety of mixing music and drama. Early prefaces and notes to the reader are filled with librettists' explanations and excuses, with justifications and defenses of their work. These writings enable us to witness, through their parental eyes, the birth pangs of *dramma per musica*.

The self-defense erected by the librettists to express their existential discomfort was two-pronged and paradoxical. On the one hand, they energetically justified the new genre; on the other, they repeatedly denied the seriousness of their commitment to it. Neither moral qualms nor aristocratic nonchalance, however, kept them from swelling the torrent of activity. Preoccupied with finding forebears to legitimize their bastard art, librettists turned up ancestors in every period, from classical antiquity to the day before yesterday. Among ancient authors called for the defense, the most frequently cited was, of course, Aristotle, bolstered by various others — including Homer, Virgil, Aristarchus, Lucan, Horace, Plutarch, Diodorus, Cicero, Strabo, Lucretius, Terence, and Seneca. Librettists also evoked the Tuscan classics Dante and Petrarch; masters of the modern Italian tradition such as Ariosto, Tasso, Chiabrera, Guarini, Marino, and Salvadori; and the Spanish dramatists.[4] In most cases, librettists' actual need for such authority — and their use of it — was quite superficial. Often they simply cited authorities rhetorically, as a preemptive strategy, in order to emphasize their purposeful departure from them. But they also invoked precedents from the past to justify various aspects of their works. In their search for precedents and their reinterpretation of the past for their own purposes, our librettists differed little from sixteenth-century authors.[5]

4. One of the few Spanish dramatists actually cited was Lope de Vega; the significance of Spanish models, however, is often mentioned. On the influence of Spanish drama on members of the intellectual community of seventeenth-century Venice, see Benedetto Croce, "Appunti sui costumi e letteratura spagnuola in Italia," in *Nuovi saggi sulla letteratura italiana del seicento* (Bari, 1949), 235–39, and Antonio Belloni, *Storia letteraria d'Italia: Il seicento* (Milan, 1943), 354–61.

5. For extensive discussion of and quotations from the full range of sixteenth-century critical commentaries on the ancient authors, see Bernard Weinberg, *A History of Literary Criticism in the Italian Renaissance* (Chicago, 1961).

The Accademia degli Incogniti

Their shared approach to libretto-writing, in particular their attitude toward authority as a source of justifying precedent, can be traced to a common background. Almost without exception, the librettists of the 1640s traveled in the same intellectual and social circles. They were Venetian aristocrats, and they belonged to the Accademia degli Incogniti, the successor, in a sense, to the large number of Venetian academies that had sponsored theatrical entertainments since the middle of the sixteenth century.[6] Founded in 1630 by the patrician Giovanni Francesco Loredano, the Accademia degli Incogniti included among its members nearly every Venetian intellectual of any importance, many of them future senators or councilors, and also a number of prominent non-Venetians.[7] Indeed, for several decades the academy functioned as an unofficial seat of political power in Venice. Aside from personal contacts, the group wielded its influence through the publications of its members, most of them prodigious writers—of novels, moral essays, and religious tracts, as well as opera librettos. In fact, as we shall see in the next chapters, the Incogniti were much involved in the whole phenomenon of opera in Venice, not only as authors but as founders and managers of the most successful opera theater of the 1640s, the Novissimo, which flourished from 1641 to 1645. The commanding role of these literary patricians guaranteed the close connection between politics and early opera in Venice, a connection fundamental to the establishment and success of the genre on the lagoon.

The basic philosophy of the academy derived from the teachings of the Peripatetic Cesare Cremonini, professor of philosophy at the University of Padua, with whom many of the members had studied. Cremonini was notorious for his strict interpretations of Aristotle and his heterodox religious views—he was brought before the Inquisition several times. He inculcated in his students the necessity of questioning accepted dogma, and he forcefully promoted Aristotelian arguments against belief in God as creator and provider. Skeptical of the immortality of the soul, he preached the importance of the here

6. The standard sources of information on Venetian academies include Michele Battagia, *Delle accademie veneziane* (Venice, 1826) and Michele Maylander, *Storia delle accademie d'Italia* (Bologna, 1926–30); but see also I-Vmc, MSS Cicogna 3010–13, used extensively in Gilmore, "Monteverdi and Dramatic Music in Venice."

7. The "forestieri" included such well-known literary figures as Gabriele Chiabrera savonese, G. B. Basile napolitano, Leone Allacci da Sciò; also from outside Venice were Maiolino Bisaccioni da Iesi, Pietro Paolo Bissari vicentino, and Scipione Herrico

messinese. These names are given in *Le glorie degli Incogniti overo gli huomini illustri dell'Accademia de' Signori Incogniti* (Venice: Valvasense, 1647), which contains articles on 106 members of the academy, each of them including a bibliography as well as a portrait. The group was obviously much larger, but Giovanni Battista Fusconi, the secretary of the academy, who signed the dedication of the volume, explained that to include all of the members would be "un voler restringere la grandezza dell'oceano in un sol fiume."

and now, and the value of physical pleasure above Christian morality. Such teaching set the intellectual and moral tone for our librettists, who had the opportunity of discussing the implications of their studies with Cremonini as well as many other matters at the meetings of their academy.[8]

Those meetings were usually organized as debates. The topics ranged from philosophical exchanges on such profound issues as the relationship (or not) between body and soul to the (perhaps) somewhat less serious question of the relative power of tears and song in promoting love.[9] Regardless of the significance of the question, all these debates required the same forensic skills, the ability to argue either side of a question with equal conviction. The Incogniti defended, on principle, the validity of multiple points of view, multiple interpretations. Equivocation and ambivalence were fundamental to their stand on all matters; they were taught to question every proposition, to see the other side of every issue.

The motto of the academy symbolized these aims: *Ignoto Deo*.[10] The political influence of the Incogniti, in keeping with their name, was usually covert and indirect, operating behind the scenes; and they often wrote in a secret, but obviously highly allusive, language. Their operatic involvements were not always overt either. While some of them affixed their own names to their librettos, others hid behind academic aliases or anonymity. Giacomo Badoaro, for example, left unsigned the letter to Monteverdi that prefaces *Il ritorno d'Ulisse*, and his authorship of the libretto itself is only revealed four years later in the preface to another libretto, *Ulisse errante*—or half revealed by his academic title "Assicurato Academico Incognito." In another case, the actual author of the libretto *Amore innamorato* (1642), which is signed by Giovanni Battista Fusconi, seems to have been intentionally obscured.[11]

These attitudes—the heavy emphasis on Aristotle, the training in debate, and the appreciation of equivocation promoted by the academy—strongly conditioned the impact of the Incogniti writers on the development of opera. The

8.   On the Incogniti, see Giorgio Spini, *Ricerca dei libertini: La teoria dell'impostura delle religioni nel seicento italiano* (Rome, 1950), 2d ed. (Florence, 1983), 147–99; also Rosand, "Barbara Strozzi," 245–49; id., "Seneca and the Interpretation of *L'incoronazione di Poppea*," *JAMS* 38 (1985): 36–47; Bianconi and Walker, "Dalla 'Finta pazza,' " 410–24. For Cremonini's actual participation in the theatrical life of Venice, see ch. 5 below.

9.   The Incogniti debates appear in several publications, among them *Discorsi academici de' Signori Incogniti havuti in Venetia nell'academia dell'Illustrissimo Signor G. F. Loredano* (Venice: Sarzina, 1635); and Giovanni Francesco Loredano, *Bizzarrie academiche* (Venice: Sarzina, 1638).

10.   It referred to the unknown god worshiped by the Athenians, as reported by St. Paul. For further on the motto, see Lionello Puppi, "Ignoto Deo," *Arte veneta* 23 (1969): 169–80. This motto was depicted iconographically (in one of the Incognito publications) as a globe on which a river representing the Nile is shown with its source veiled because it was unknown; see Rosand, "Barbara Strozzi," 248 and n. 27.

11.   The real authors were the Incogniti Pietro Michele and Loredan himself; see Rosand, "Barbara Strozzi," n. 22, and Bianconi and Walker, "Dalla 'Finta pazza,' " 421 n. 175.

very ambiguity of sung drama appealed to them. It gave them the opportunity to exercise their forensic skills, as illustrated by the variety of defenses and definitions they erected: classical precedent, the inconsistencies inherent in the ancient rules, their limited applicability to the present—all of these were marshaled in defense of their efforts. They wrote librettos that claimed to be tragedies in order to flaunt both their classical education, their knowledge of "the rules," and their iconoclastic tendencies, their commitment to the moment, their respect for modern taste.

The issue most crucial to them, to which they directed most of their defensive energies, involved the propriety of sung drama. This, of course, had been central to the Florentine theorists of opera half a century earlier, who had sought to defuse it in two somewhat contradictory ways: by the adoption of a musical style that was uninflected enough to pass for speech and by a choice of plots in which musical speech was appropriate. This double strategy is clearly articulated by the anonymous author of a Florentine treatise on opera from about 1630, *Il corago*:

> To begin with characters or interlocutors that musical setting seems to suit best, for secular plots the ancient deities such as Apollo, Thetis, Neptune and other respected gods seem very appropriate, as do demigods and ancient heroes, among whom one might especially list rivers and lakes, and especially those most famous among the Muses, such as Peneus, the Tiber, and the Trasimenus, and above all those personages whom we consider to have been perfect musicians, such as Orpheus, Amphion, and the like. The reason for all this is that since each listener knows all too well that at least in the more familiar parts of the earth ordinary men do not speak in music, but plainly, speaking in music is more consonant with one's conception of superhuman characters than with the notion and experience one has of ordinary men; because, given that musical discourse is more elevated, more authoritative, sweeter, and more noble than ordinary speech, one attributes it to characters who, through a certain innate feeling, have more of a sublime or divine quality. (Appendix II.1b)

The Florentine solutions, however, did not satisfy the requirements of Venetian librettists. They evidently did not regard the Florentine operas—assuming they even knew them—as sufficiently authoritative to justify their own activities. In any case, it was the Venetians' need to establish a pedigree for sung drama that provoked their interest in ancient theatrical practices. It was an interest that was to be shared by most subsequent theoreticians or critics of opera, including Metastasio.

Their ad hoc investigative procedure involved several steps: first, to establish that music had functioned in various ways in classical drama; then, to demonstrate the relationship of their works to classical drama, by pointing out either similarities or differences. Similarities naturally justified themselves, but differences required further differentiation of the source material. They could be explained as deriving from inconsistencies or ambiguities in the classical authors themselves or else as reflecting the librettist's desire—condoned by those very same ancient authors—to satisfy modern taste, even if that meant going against tradition.[12]

Music and Drama

In considering the function of music in ancient drama, the Incogniti librettists, very much in the tradition of sixteenth-century literary critics, rehearsed all the possibilities: that ancient drama was sung throughout, that only the choruses were sung, that none of it was sung.[13] In the end, however, it hardly mattered what evidence they adduced. Their conclusion was always the same: regardless of ancient practice, the requirements of modern taste alone were sufficient to justify *dramma per musica*.

Few librettists were as confident and succinct—and as circuitous—on the matter as Vincenzo Nolfi in the preface to his *Bellerofonte* (1642). He readily accepted the classical precedent of sung drama as the least controversial feature of his activity, declaring axiomatically that his was "a kind of poem that has returned to the original nature of drama as far as singing is concerned." But he rejected historical precedents for every other aspect of his libretto, proclaiming it to be entirely modern, geared to a culture "that no longer acknowledges Epicharmus as father, nor Sicily as homeland, nor Aristotle as law-giver" (Appendix I.19d). But then, in another twist, he went on to defend the idea of novelty and change of taste on the very basis of the precedent he had previously

---

12. A rather nice example of their characteristic reasoning is provided by Busenello in connection with his libretto *La prosperità infelice di Giulio Cesare dittatore* (1646). He cites Seneca the dramatist to justify his rejection of modern taste embodied in his choice of five acts rather than three: "If the acts are five and not three, remember that all ancient dramas, and particularly the tragedies of Seneca, are divided into five acts" (Appendix I.12a). But Seneca the man justifies the opposite attitude toward modern taste—acceptance: "It is necessary to satisfy modern taste to some extent, always keeping in mind the praise that Tacitus bestowed on Seneca, that is, that he had an imagination made to order for the taste of his times" (Appendix I.12c). See Rosand, "Seneca," 40–41.

13. All of the interpretations were based on a rather ambiguous passage from Aristotle's *Poetics*, ch. 1 (1447b): "There are, lastly, certain other arts, which combine all the means enumerated, rhythm, melody, and verse, e.g. dithyrambic and nomic poetry, tragedy and comedy; with this difference, however,

that the three kinds of means are in some of them all employed together and in others brought in separately, one after the other" (*The Complete Works of Aristotle*, Revised Oxford Translation, ed. Jonathan Barnes [Princeton, 1984], 2: 2317). See, for example, Benedetto Varchi, *Lezzioni della poetica* (1553–54); Giraldi Cintio, *Discorso intorno al comporre delle comedie e delle tragedie* (1543/54), quoted in Weinberg, *Literary Criticism*, 433–44; Lodovico Castelvetro, *Poetica d'Aristotile vulgarizzata e sposta* (Vienna, 1570), 33, 146; and Francesco Patrizi, *Della poetica, La deca istoriale* (Ferrara, 1586). See also Giorgio Bartoli's letter to Lorenzo Giacomini, summarized in Claude Palisca, "The Alterati of Florence: Pioneers in the Theory of Dramatic Music," in *New Looks at Italian Opera: Essays in Honor of Donald J. Grout*, ed. William W. Austin (Ithaca, N.Y., 1968), 31–34. The entire issue is discussed most recently and fully in Claude Palisca, *Humanism in Italian Renaissance Musical Thought* (New Haven, 1985), ch. 14, "Theory of Dramatic Music."

rejected, dropping the names of various authorities in his wake: "All customs change, and even the most depraved novelties can please, as Scaliger said in regard to the Amphytrion of Plautus. If the various Cratinuses, Aristophanes, and Terences were alive today, they too might change their ideas" (Appendix I.19e).

Pietro Paolo Bissari, more specific in his classical citations and more expansive and circumstantial in his discussion (as well as more consistent), prefaced his *Torilda* (1648) with a lengthy disquisition on classical drama. His aim was to show that every aspect of his libretto—machines, gods, dances, frequent changes of scene, infusion of comic elements, and even the placement of the orchestra in the theater—was based on classical precedent. Musical setting was second on his list, following frequent scene changes: "Nor would it be at variance with that practice for drama to be staged with music, since it is known that Phrynicus was elected Captain for this reason, that he had his tragedies sung with melodies and musical art that were modes appropriate for battle" (Appendix I.25b). Bissari, who was more anxious than most of his colleagues to establish the continuity between ancient drama and his own work, concluded his essay on an unusually positive note by suggesting that "in all of these works the ancient institutions seem revived rather than interrupted" (Appendix I.25e).[14]

Most writers, however, took a more tentative and circumspect stance, clothing their defenses in more theoretical garb. The anonymous (=Incognito) author of *Le nozze d'Enea* (1640 [1641]), for example, evidently believed that only the choruses of ancient drama were sung; but that hardly prevented him from justifying his own theatrical efforts, though it complicated his argument. He opened his defense by distinguishing between two types of tragedy, "di lieto fine" and "d'esito lugubre" ("called *tragichissima* by Aristotle"), and then offered the usual explanation, modern taste, for having chosen the former type for his libretto:

> In order to accommodate myself to current taste, I have chosen a tragedy with a happy ending, rather than otherwise. Considering in addition that since it is to be sung, and not simply recited, such a tragedy seemed more appropriate: although not because I am certain that in ancient times melancholy tragedies were not also sung, or at least the choral part; but it is certain that such a practice was gradually abandoned, to the point where, even in "happy" tragedies, music had become an external, merely ornamental feature. (Appendix I.9c)[15]

14. *Torilda* was one of the few librettos that explicitly offered spoken performance as an option. Another was Giulio Strozzi's *La finta savia* (1643).
15. The author of this libretto derives his two kinds of tragedy from Renaissance commentaries on Aristotle. *Le nozze d'Enea* was long assumed to be the work of Giacomo Badoaro, an assumption questioned and tentatively dismissed in Walker, "Errori," 11–12, and Anna Sweykowska, "Le due poetiche venete e le ultime opere di Claudio Monteverdi," *Quadrivium* 18 (1977): 149.

Somewhat later in the letter, the author returned, again obliquely, to the issue of the function of music in ancient drama. He explained his substitution of ballets for "classical" choruses between the acts of his work on the grounds that sung choruses only had an effect when the rest of the drama was not sung (i.e., he assumed that in ancient drama only the choruses were sung): "Given that the entire tragedy is sung, to sing the choruses as well would become too tiresome; therefore, in order to please the spectators more with variety, ballets have been introduced" (Appendix I.9i).

Even those librettists who were unwilling to admit that music had played any part at all in early classical drama found a way to link their works with the past. Giacomo Badoaro, for example, to judge from his preface to *Ulisse errante* (1644), considered the complete musical performance of a drama to be very far from ancient practice. But he exploited the lack of consistency among ancient playwrights on other issues, such as the appropriate number of characters in a drama or the necessity of a prologue, to justify a wide variety of modern practices.

The author who perhaps more clearly than any other articulated the Incognito librettists' attitude toward classical sources, and the one who certainly presented them most cynically, was Gian Francesco Busenello, Monteverdi's collaborator in *L'incoronazione di Poppea*. In a letter to his friend Giovanni Grimani, proprietor/impresario of the Teatro SS. Giovanni e Paolo, written upon the presentation of his drama *Statira* (1655), Busenello aired the entire controversy about the correct performance of ancient tragedy, systematically undermining the relevance of each of the issues in the debate. In general he discouraged the use of ancient precedent as a standard for measuring modern efforts. Since his poetry was designed to be sung, he argued, ancient poetic models should not be applied to it, the assumption being that ancient poetry was not sung (Appendix I.13b). But, he continued, like the skilled polemicist he was, "even if we allow that the poems of the ancient Greeks were sung, as some maintain, and that Homer himself was both the poet and composer of his own songs, that music was different from ours" (Appendix I.13c). Finally he deflated the significance of the whole investigation of ancient practice, refusing "to be the judge of whether it was the ancients or the moderns who brought musical plays into the theater" (Appendix I.13d). His attitude regarding the futility of such investigation is perhaps best captured by the final sentence of the preface to another of his librettos, *La prosperità infelice di Giulio Cesare dittatore*: "And may those who enjoy enslaving themselves to the ancient rules find their fulfillment in baying at the full moon" (Appendix I.12b).[16]

---

16. See also a similar remark in the text of another of Busenello's librettos, *Didone* (1641), in Gian Francesco Busenello, *Delle hore ociose* (Venice: Giuliani, 1656), 53: "Non possono i Poeti a questi dì / Rappresentar le favole a lor modo, / Chi ha fisso questo chiodo, / Del vero studio il bel sentier smarì."

These early Venetian librettists' preoccupation with the genre of their works was not unambivalent. For at the same time as they defended their combination of music and drama either on the grounds of classical precedent or as a response to the demands of modern taste, they also blamed a variety of defects in their librettos, such as lapses in decorum, form, or style, on the special exigencies of music. These shortcomings, they claimed, were the inevitable result of combining two incompatible artistic media. The question of how music and drama must modify each other when they are combined is, of course, the central aesthetic issue of opera, and it is to these librettists that we owe the first and most articulate airing of the issue. Their need to justify opera, because it was new, prompted them to expose and attempt to resolve the inconsistencies, imperfections, and compromises inherent in it. Concern with this issue abated after some years of operatic experience, but it never completely disappeared.

Music served as scapegoat for a variety of literary offenses: for inelegant language, mixed meters, varied characters, and so on. One author, Niccolò Enea Bartolini, the librettist of *Venere gelosa* (1643), proceeded from the defensive premise that because his work was created to be sung, it should nonetheless not fear comparison with those that are merely intended to be recited. The implication, of course, was that it might otherwise be considered thoroughly inferior: "And if its poetry is not filled with aphorisms and witticisms, it cannot on that account be called either cold or lacking in spirit. I have maintained a high style, and with diversity of meters and propriety of language have sought to stimulate the imagination of the composer" (Appendix I.21).

The anonymous author of *Le nozze d'Enea* also cited music as a blanket excuse for all sorts of lapses in his poetry, in particular his use of varied meters to distinguish between high and low characters:

> And so to adapt to the characters, and to the emotions that they are to express, I have made use of a number of different meters; that is to say, I have given *versi sdruccioli* to people of low condition, and *versi brevi* and *tronchi* to choleric types, though knowing well that the better Tuscan tragedians used only lines of seven, eleven, and occasionally five syllables. Nevertheless, given that the ancient Greeks and Romans, in addition to the iamb, also used trimeter, tetrameter, and other meters in their tragedies, I do not see why [such variety] is prohibited to us, at least in the case of six- and eight-syllable lines. And besides, musical tragedies are entitled to a freedom not enjoyed by those that are merely spoken. (Appendix I.9f)

The same justification served for his mixture of characters—in particular, his introduction of comic characters within a serious plot:

> I have made use of this fellow [Numano, called "the Strong" by Virgil] as a comic character, since I could not find in the author anyone more suitable [for such a role], and because I knew the disposition of many theatergoers, who prefer jokes like this to serious things as we see that Iro of our friend was a marvelous success. But re-

ally I would not have introduced this sort of character in a different kind of [i.e., non-musical] tragedy. (Appendix I.9e)

For Busenello, writing for music required the abandonment of poetic elegance and classical poetic forms. In the preface to *Statira*, he acknowledged the low style of his poetry; more ambitious literary embellishment, he implied, was not suitable for musical drama:

> I would have been more eloquent in writing this play, and would have concentrated my faculties to elevate the style somewhat, if the brevity and conventions required by the [musical] stage had allowed it. It is one thing to compose an ode or a sonnet, in which enthusiasm is permitted to thought, and ecstasy to the imagination in exciting the ears with sweet stimuli and the heart with a sensual sparkle, by contriving a soothing and ingenious conclusion; it is another thing to compose a play, in which the characters are under constraints, and use common speech, and if the tone becomes too elevated it loses its seemliness and decorum. (Appendix I.13a)

And in the letter on *Statira* already mentioned, he explained that he had tried to follow the style of the best Italian authors instead of ancient writers in his "elocutions." Since he was writing poetry for music, with its "measures and numbers, irregularities and alliterations geared to music, Greek forms, such as strophes and antistrophes, hymns, idylls, and odes, are all irrelevant" (Appendix I.13b).

But the impact of music on drama went far beyond mere inelegance and infelicities imposed on its poetry; it thoroughly undermined its verisimilitude. It was difficult for any audience to believe that singing was speech. What sparked all of these librettists' preoccupation with the genre, their attempts to justify the combination of music and drama, either through classical precedent or modern taste, was their discomfort with the question of verisimilitude. This issue underlies all their defenses, although it is actually mentioned only rarely. One of the few authors to do so was Giacomo Badoaro, in the preface to *Ulisse errante* (1644). After having characteristically blamed his own specific failure to observe the ancient rules of drama on the special demands made by music, he addressed the question of verisimilitude: "It is normal today for the purpose of pleasing the spectators . . . to introduce improbable situations so long as they do not disturb the main action." Having introduced music into our dramas, he continues,

> we cannot avoid the implausible, namely, that men should carry on their most important transactions while singing. Moreover, in order to enjoy variety in the theater, we are used to music for two, three, and more voices, which causes another unlikelihood: that several people conversing together should suddenly find themselves saying the same thing simultaneously. (Appendix I.8j)

The joining of music and drama could simply not be achieved without the loss of verisimilitude. No matter what precedents might be adduced, song could not pass for speech. As all these librettists recognized, and as Badoaro acknowledged, the impact of *dramma per musica* depended on an audience believing either that the singers were in fact really speaking, or else that they meant to be singing. The complete acceptance of the genre required the acceptance of unverisimilar action—and clearly, this never happened.

Verisimilitude, the eternal operatic embarrassment, continued to cast a shadow over opera well after 1650, but the focus narrowed somewhat from general skepticism of the whole enterprise to specific concern with the nature of the musical language itself. Badoaro's distinction between speech and song was rendered more precise in the by now classic formulation of this dilemma in a libretto of 1651 by Francesco Sbarra, *Alessandro vincitor di se stesso*:

> I know that the *ariette* sung by Alexander and Aristotle will be judged as contrary to the decorum of such great personages; but I also know that musical recitation is improper altogether, since it does not imitate natural discourse and removes the soul from dramatic compositions, which should be nothing but imitations of human actions, and yet this defect is not only tolerated by the current century but received with applause. This kind of poetry today has no purpose other than to give delight; thus we should adjust to the practice of the times. (Appendix I.29e)

By 1651, through use, musical "speech," that is, recitative, had become thoroughly acceptable. But "song," that is, the arias, still posed a problem. Sbarra's statement is corroborated by the continued reluctance of librettists to introduce arias into their dramas, and their attempts to construct and invent evasions and pretexts for them. The development and persistence well beyond the middle of the century of conventional situations in which singing was either natural or purposely unnatural—songs within the drama, for instance, or scenes of madness and sleep—bear witness to the unresolvable contradiction posed by the mixing of music and drama.

Dramatic Structure: The Unities

In addition to defending their general involvement in opera by such shows of erudition, these early Venetian librettists also cited precedents from the past to justify certain specific features of their works. Their individual decisions regarding observance of the unities, division into acts, and the use of chorus were carefully examined in the light of classical authority. One of the most hotly debated topics concerned the appropriateness of adhering to the so-called Aristotelian unities of time, place, and action. Originally conceived by sixteenth-century literary theorists and commentators on Aristotle as merely one aspect of the larger issue of genre—in particular the distinctions between tragedy, comedy, and the epic—the unities had become an increasingly specific focus of discussion.[17] The subject continued to concern seventeenth-century writers.

The crux of the problem for the sixteenth century was the disagreement as to whether Aristotle had addressed the unities at all in his *Poetics*. In fact, Aristotle set some store on unity of action in tragedy—as opposed to the epic, which by definition encompassed many actions.[18] And he alluded to the unity of time when he observed that tragedy limited itself to what can occur during a single revolution of the sun—whereas the epic, again by definition, knows no such limits.[19] The third unity, that of place, did not figure at all in the *Poetics*. A number of the sixteenth-century elaborations and interpretations of the *Poetics*, however, did concern themselves specifically with the unities. One of these, Castelvetro's *Poetica d'Aristotele vulgarizzata et sposta* (1570), seems to have been the first to articulate unity of place as a rule and to formulate the concept of the three unities as they were subsequently understood—in France as well as Italy.[20]

The "rules" were originally interpreted as being genre-specific, applicable to tragedy only, and not to comedy or the epic; but a number of commentators, including Castelvetro, tried to adapt them to other genres as well. It was this attempt during the sixteenth century to broaden their application that stimulated librettists' concern with the unities. The question was most pressing—and most relevant—in those early Venetian librettos that aspired to the status of tragedy. The anonymous author of *Le nozze d'Enea*, for example, whose preface I have already quoted, made a special effort to define his work as a *tragedia* (though *di lieto fine*) and considered the problem of the unities at great length.[21] Significantly, librettists' concern with the unities diminished in proportion to their growing acceptance of the generic legitimacy of *dramma per musica*.

As for the literary theorists of the sixteenth century, so, too, for their seventeenth-century heirs the unities represented only part of the larger ques-

---

17. See the summary in Joel E. Spingarn, *A History of Literary Criticism in the Renaissance*, 2d ed. (New York, 1908), 56–63, 84–96; also Weinberg, *Literary Criticism*, passim.
18. The relevant passage in the *Poetics*, ch. 5 (1451a) reads: "Just as in the other imitative arts one imitation is always of one thing, so in poetry the story, as an imitation of action, must represent one action, a complete whole, with its several incidents so closely connected that the transposition or withdrawal of any one of them will disjoin and dislocate the whole" (*Complete Works of Aristotle*, ed. Barnes, 2: 2322).
19. *Poetics* (1449b): "[Epic poetry] differs from it [tragedy], however, in that it is in one kind of verse

and in narrative form; and also by its length—which is due to its action having no fixed limit of time, whereas tragedy endeavours to keep as far as possible within a single circuit of the sun, or something near that" (*Complete Works of Aristotle*, ed. Barnes, 2: 2320).
20. See Weinberg, *Literary Criticism*, 502–17 for Castelvetro; chs. 9–13 treat the various Renaissance interpretations of the *Poetics* in great detail. See also Piero Weiss, "Neoclassical Criticism and Opera," *Studies in the History of Music* 2 (1987): 1–30.
21. Only a few other authors explicitly considered their works to be tragedies. Paolo Vendramin, for example, called his *Adone* (1640) a *tragedia musicale*,

tion of genre. But the topic nevertheless received special emphasis in the apologies of the librettists, perhaps because it came into direct conflict with one of the most essential requirements of the new operatic genre: variety. It was difficult for librettists to reconcile these two principles, the one theoretical, the other practical, but they spilled considerable ink in the attempt. As usual, their explanations took one of two forms: either they demonstrated how their works were unified—interpreting that concept with considerable freedom—or else they justified the fact that they were not.

Some authors minimized the distinctions between their works and classical drama. Fusconi, for example, in his preface to *Amore innamorato* (1642), states that the work "follows all the good rules taught by the masters: it ends within the span of one day, or little more; it has one plot line, with no extraneous events; and it does not stray at all from established custom" (Appendix I.27a). But no sooner has he affirmed his observation of the unities of time and action than he deftly—and predictably—undermines the significance of that affirmation by invoking modern taste:

> But I do not think it makes sense to go to the trouble of defending something even the authors themselves were careless about. Especially given that our present age is made up of private opinions and interests and thus does not believe in any rules except those of whim and of passion. (Appendix I.27b)[22]

Giulio Strozzi, in the preface to his *Delia* (1639), adopts a similarly casual tone in minimizing the extent of his departure from the unity of time, implying quite effectively that a slight abuse of that unity is his only transgression. After defending his plot and characters by citing classical precedents, he confesses: "I have taken the liberty of a couple of hours: I don't know if Aristotle or Aristarchus will grant them to me" (Appendix I.15g).

But other librettists seem especially bent on preserving the unity of time above the other two. The author of *Le nozze d'Enea* found it necessary to stretch the boundaries of place, choosing a large geographical region rather than the corner of a city for his action, but he accepted the unity of time without question:

> As for the physical setting, whereas for myself I would have chosen a city, or a part of one, as good tragedians, our friends both ancient and modern, do, nevertheless, in order to give the audience pleasure through variety, I have taken a little piece of the small portion of Italy that is Latium, so that the action can be now in court, now in the woods, and elsewhere, as the occasion requires. But as for time, I did

---

and Badoaro's *Il ritorno d'Ulisse in patria* is labeled a *tragedia con lieto fine* in one of its manuscript copies (I-Vmc, MS Cicogna 192, no. 3330).

22. It is perhaps noteworthy here that the libretto in question treats a mythological subject, in which the unities are more easily followed.

not want to diverge from the rule so often laid down by the master of true knowledge, which stipulates for tragedy the span of one day or a little more. (Appendix I.9d)

Unity of time was particularly significant in this instance: it seems to have served an important function with respect to dramatic verisimilitude. In explaining, later in the same essay, why he has chosen to divide his drama into five acts rather than the more modern three, the anonymous author alludes to the relationship between dramatic and real time:

> And although the modern practice is to divide even spoken plays into three acts, I have preferred to divide mine into five, so that with more pauses the audience might rest from the mental effort of following a series of depicted events, and to this end I have settled on such a division. And also to adapt, at least in appearance, the timespan of the imitation to the duration of what it imitates. Given therefore that the action of the play covers one day, it would seem indeed that that is how long the play should last; but since this would be too inconvenient and tedious for the audience, the same continuous plot is divided into acts, so that one imagines that between one act and another more time elapses than actually does, and in this way, all told, one attains the span of one day. (Appendix I.9j)

Since the play could not possibly last as long as the time represented on stage, four intermissions—rather than two—made the illusion that much more suggestive.[23] Unity of time as a concept is addressed more explicitly by another librettist we have already heard from, Bissari, in his preface to *Torilda* (1648): "These operas do not fail those rules of quantity in that they generally represent the events of a single day in the prescribed limit of four hours" (Appendix I.25d).

One of the fullest discussions of the unities, as well as of other aspects of "classical" theory, to be found in these early librettos is Badoaro's preface to *Ulisse errante* (1644), his "Lettera dell'Assicurato Academico Incognito." Badoaro's generous airing of various possible interpretations of the "rules" was intended to assure the reader that his own decision to treat them in the freest possible manner was an educated, conscious one: "This opera necessarily required some transgression of the rules. I do not consider this a fault, and if others insist that it is, it will be a conscious, and not inadvertent, error" (Appendix I.8e). According to Badoaro, none of the three unities, no matter which interpretation is followed, accords with modern taste. Here is his scholastic defense of his position on the unity of time:

---

23.   It was important for the author to preserve the illusion that the time represented on stage was equivalent to that actually spent by the audience in the theater. For an analogous interpretation of the function of intermedi to enhance the dramatic verisimilitude of a play by framing it in unreality, see Pirrotta, *Music and Theatre*, "Temporal Perspective and Music," esp. 127–29.

As for the span of time covered by the plot, some wanted to allow a limit of eight hours, and no more, others one revolution of the sun, some two days, others three; and even these uncertain rules were not always observed by Aeschylus, by Euripides, or by Sophocles, in some of whose plots months go by, and even years. Others said that it was more than sufficient if the story could be grasped without effort in one act of memory, and I myself could accept this opinion. The precepts of poetics after all are not permanent, because the mutations of centuries give rise to diversity in composition. (Appendix I.8g)

Badoaro's apologia here, his justification for the stretching of time to its useful—if not logical—limits, recalls the sixteenth-century literary defenders or modernizers of Aristotle.[24] That justification was to supply the theoretical basis for exploitation on the part of later Venetian librettists to an extent Badoaro himself could hardly have imagined.[25]

As far as unity of place was concerned, the same argument applied. Ancient tragedy was different from modern drama, a difference Badoaro documents by a quick summary of its development adapted from Horace:

In its earliest days, Tragedy was recited by the poet alone, his face tinted with the dregs of crushed grapes. Later characters were introduced, and masks; and then choruses were added, and music, and sound effects, and scene-changes, and dances replaced the choruses; and perhaps in the future, as times change, our descendants will witness the introduction of still other forms. (Appendix I.8h)[26]

Since ancient tragedy was so different from modern drama, it followed that its rules could no longer be strictly applied. But free application of the rules resulted in a breach of verisimilitude—the very sin these rules were created to mitigate:

At one time changes of place were abhorred in these plays, but at present, in order to please the eyes, what was once prohibited seems to be prescribed, so that every day greater numbers of scene-changes are devised; now, in order to increase the delight of the audience, one thinks nothing of introducing some improbabilities, as long as they do not disfigure the plot. (Appendix I.8i–j)

24. The argument is particularly reminiscent of Francesco Buonamici, *Discorsi poetici nella Accademia fiorentina in difesa d'Aristotile* (Florence, 1597); see Weinberg, *Literary Criticism*, 689, 696–97.
25. The stretching of time to cover many days, even years, was not uncommon in some librettos (see, for example, *Didone*). Most relevant for the production of *Ulisse errante* itself, the temporal elasticity provided the opportunity for a great number of scene changes to accommodate the scenography of Giacomo Torelli, newly moved to the Teatro SS.

Giovanni e Paolo from the Teatro Novissimo. See Worsthorne, *Venetian Opera*, 41.
26. Badoaro's account of the evolution of classical drama seems to derive from a conflation of Aristotle's *Poetics* and Horace's *Ars poetica*—along with Aristotle's text the most important focus for translation and commentary during the sixteenth century. The two works were often conflated or jointly interpreted. See Marvin T. Herrick, *The Fusion of Horatian and Aristotelian Literary Criticism, 1531–1555* (Urbana, Ill., 1946), 406.

Badoaro does claim unity of action for his drama, but he does so by vastly stretching the definition of unity through elaborate verbal sophistry:

> The plot . . . aims to be *una unius* [one in unity]. Unified, then, is my plot, because the subject unity is Ulysses; the formal unity is his errancy; nor do many errors constitute many plots, but only many parts of a plot, which constitute a single and great action, such as Aristotle advocates. (Appendix I.8c)

He argues from both sides of the question, proving unity of action at the same time as he defends its absence:

> If someone objects that this subject is not appropriate for the stage, I will say that it is, hoping that as soon as he has heard the work, he will change his mind. If he says that it contains multiple plots, I will say that I was the first to point it out, and that can easily be seen from the subdivisions of the action that I send him, here enclosed, for this purpose. As for the adventures that befall Ulysses while traveling, it is true that they are multiple actions, but in respect to the intention of the traveler, which is to get back to his country, they are but a single action. (Appendix I.8b)

And he adds:

> If these arguments are convincing, let them be accepted; if not, let it be said that I have wished to depict the greatest misfortunes experienced by Ulysses on his voyage home. Those who create their subjects out of their own imaginations do very well to proceed in strict accordance with the rules; given that the choice is theirs, they are wise to follow common practice; but he who commits himself to the hero of a known tale cannot take him on without the details of the events that necessarily go with the story. (Appendix I.8d)

Badoaro's emphasis on the incompatibility of the unities and modern practice was also expounded by several other spokesmen for the new genre. Busenello touches on the question of the unities in almost all of his writings. Revealing his acute awareness of the distinctions between ancient drama and his own librettos, he draws upon a wide variety of defenses to support his departures from classical precedent; his final defense, however, is always the same: modern taste. In *Didone* (1641) he excuses his breach of the unity of time by citing the precedent of Spanish drama: "This opera is influenced by modern opinions. It is not constructed according to the ancient rules but, according to Spanish usage, it represents years and not hours" (Appendix I.11a).[27] In *Giulio Cesare* (1646), however, he simply confesses to abusing the unities of both time and place without presenting a formal defense, citing as justification only his

---

27.   Busenello was presumably referring here to the dramas of Lope de Vega, whose views on the unities were specifically articulated in a letter to the Florentine playwright Jacopo Cicognini, in which he urged

desire to please the public. Here the poet makes Tempo, one of the allegorical characters featured in the prologue, his mouthpiece:

> Here you will see years / Epitomized in hours. / . . . Who could ever object / If one melodious night reveals to you / The happenings and deeds of a thousand days? / . . . And I, in order to delight you, / Disciples, or rather teachers, of Alcydes / With flattering art, / Have enclosed more than a year in an evening: / Without using either couriers or ships, / Without changing your seats, you will discover / Thessaly, Lesbos, the Lighthouse, Egypt, and Rome. (Appendix I.12d)

As far as unity of action is concerned, Busenello calls upon Guarini as a witness for his defense in the preface to *Gli amori d'Apollo e di Dafne* (1640):

> The other things in the present play [aside from the Apollo-Daphne plot] are episodes interwoven in the manner that you will see; and if perchance someone should judge that the unity of the plot is broken by the multiplicity of love stories (that is, of Apollo and Daphne, of Tithonus and Aurora, of Cephalus and Procris), let him be reassured by remembering that these interweavings do not destroy the unity, but rather embellish it; and let him remember that the Cavalier Guarino, in his Pastor Fido, did not intend a multiplicity of loves (that is, between Myrtillus and Amaryllis, and between Sylvius and Dorinda), but rather used the love story of Dorinda and Sylvius to adorn his tale. (Appendix I.10)[28]

Busenello sounds suspiciously like Badoaro when he demonstrates, by means of historical exegesis, the incompatibility of ancient rules and modern taste: neither Greek tragedy (originally performed on a cart with mud on the actors' faces), Homer (whose characters spoke three, four, or even five cantos in a row), nor Seneca (whose acts consist of but a single scene with chorus) would appeal to a modern audience; by extension, neither can the rules that governed them serve modern drama.[29]

It is worth noting the dates of Busenello's statements. Although, with the exception of *Statira* (1655), his librettos were among the earliest performed on the Venetian stage, neither they nor his prefaces appeared in print before 1656— that is, well after the establishment of *dramma per musica* in Venice. If he seems somewhat more radical in his pronouncements than his fellow librettists, more responsive to modern taste, it may be because he is observing the scene in retrospect, having been bolstered by their success as well as his own.

---

him to compose in the new style and not to follow the old rules for the unities; see Belloni, *Il seicento*, 354.

28.   Busenello also invoked Guarini in the letter he wrote to Giovanni Grimani in connection with his libretto of *Statira* (1655), when he compared *Il pastor fido* favorably with Tasso's *Aminta*; the letter is excerpted in Arthur Livingston, *La vita veneziana nelle opere di Gian Francesco Busenello* (Venice, 1913), 369–79. See below, Appendix I.13b–d.

29.   He made these three points in the *Statira* letter; see Livingston, *Vita veneziana*.

Division into Acts

The division of their dramas into acts seems to have been a much simpler proposition for the librettists than adherence to the unities. To begin with, they had only two choices: three acts or five. Classical precedent as articulated by Horace was unambiguous: five-act division was the accepted norm for ancient drama.[30] But strong competition was readily available from the living tradition of the *commedia dell'arte* as well as from Spanish drama, with their three-act structures.[31] By its very simplicity, in fact, the choice between five or three acts focused the librettists' dilemma with particular clarity. It demanded a commitment, one that could not be hedged. Whatever the decision, it was an immediate confession that classical precedent either was or was not being followed. Given librettists' alleged discomfort with the necessity of abusing the unities, it is surprising how few of them chose the five-act format.

We have considered the defense by the librettist of *Le nozze d'Enea* of his five-act format on the basis of verisimilitude: five acts offer twice as many intermissions as three, hence twice as many opportunities for the audience to imagine the passage of time. It is interesting that this author does not even attempt to cite classical authority for his choice, but somewhat sheepishly acknowledges the modern preference for three acts. Busenello, on the other hand, justifies the five acts of his *Giulio Cesare* (1646) with a perfunctory bow to classical precedent: "If the acts are five and not three, remember that all ancient dramas, and especially the tragedies of Seneca, are divided into five acts" (Appendix I.12a). But *Giulio Cesare* happens to be Busenello's only five-act libretto.[32] And, as we have seen, he shows no compunction in dismissing classical precedent in the prefaces to his other librettos—and even in the preface to

---

30. Horace, *Ars poetica* (*The Complete Works of Horace*, ed. Casper J. Kraemer, Jr. [New York, 1936]), 403: "A play which is to be in demand and, after production, to be revived, should consist of five acts—no more, no less."

31. All of the scenarios in Flaminio Scala's *Teatro delle favole rappresentative* (Venice, 1611), for example, are in three acts. Significantly, however, most of the literary dramas by the same and other authors, which were designed to be read rather than staged, are in five acts. See, for example, Flaminio Scala, *Il finto marito* (1618) in *Commedie dei comici dell'arte*, ed. Laura Falavolti (Turin, 1982), 215–365. A number of early Roman librettos, themselves rather strongly influenced by the Spanish tradition, were also in three acts. These include *La rappresentatione di Anima e di Corpo* (1600) and *Eumelio* (1606), as well as Giulio

Rospigliosi's *Erminia sul Giordano* (1633) and Stefano Landi's *Sant'Alessio* (1634). The "rules" of Spanish drama in the seventeenth century are articulated in Lope de Vega, *Arte nuevo de hacer comedias en este tiempo* (Madrid, 1609). Lope himself abandoned the "rules" of tragedy, including five act division and the "unities," in his plays. In the letter to Cicognini mentioned in n. 27 above, for example, he recommended the ordering of "actions . . . to cover the space not just of a day, but of many months, even years."

32. And despite contrary evidence in the libretto itself (allusions in the preface and prologue), it may also be the only one never set to music. It was certainly not performed in 1646, the season for which it was intended, since all of the Venetian opera houses were closed in that year. See Walker, "Errori," 16.

Giulio Cesare with respect to other issues. Busenello reveals his true nature here, and the true functioning of his education. For him and his fellow academicians, the entire arsenal of precedent existed to be used or discarded as needed. And the needs changed frequently. What passed for legitimate one day failed the next. In any case, five-act librettos were exceedingly rare in Venice, even in the early years of generic insecurity.[33]

Three acts may have been the accepted norm for modern opera librettos (as they were for Spanish drama and *commedia dell'arte*), but at least one of our early authors was moved to justify his choice. In the preface to his first libretto, *Delia* (1639), Giulio Strozzi claims three-act division as natural: "I have divided the work quite deliberately into three acts, a division common to all things: beginning, middle, and end"; and he defends it against the silent proponents of the "classical" five acts by distinguishing between ancient drama and his own work: "The ancients made five in theirs, because they interspersed them with singing [i.e., choruses]. This work, being wholly sung, has no need of so many pauses" (Appendix I.15e).[34]

After the early 1640s, the three-act division, a clear bow to modern taste, became completely conventional for *dramma per musica*; five acts, however, remained the norm for spoken dramas.[35] The issue did not arise again until the end of the century, when a few of the most radical neoclassicizing librettists, especially Frigimelica Roberti, but also Zeno, used five-act division as an emblem of their orthodoxy.[36]

---

33.   Among the few were Paolo Vendramin's *Adone* (1640), the anonymous *Le nozze d'Enea* (1641), and Badoaro's *Il ritorno d'Ulisse in patria* (1640) and *L'Ulisse errante* (1644)—but the score of *Ritorno* is in three acts and the other operas may also have been altered; we cannot know since their scores are lost. For a brief discussion of the differences between the manuscript librettos of *Il ritorno d'Ulisse* and the single extant score, see Wolfgang Osthoff, "Zu den Quellen von Monteverdis *Ritorno di Ulisse in patria*," *Studien zur Musikwissenschaft* 23 (1956): 67–78.

34.   In defending his division into acts, Strozzi implicitly and incidentally acknowledged his belief that ancient drama was only partly sung, and therefore not a model for him. His choice of the term *azzione* rather than the more common *atto*, however, smacks of self-conscious classicism that is undermined by the tripartite division. Such classicizing or pseudo-classicizing word choices were typical of Strozzi. In a similarly oblique acknowledgment of classical precedent, he ostentatiously gave the three acts of his next two librettos, *La finta pazza* (1641) and *La finta*

savia (1643), Greek labels: "Protasi," "Epitasi," and "Catastrofe," thereby implying an awareness of ancient practice that would be belied by the three-act division itself. (These terms appear in Donatus's fourth-century commentary on Terence, i, 22, 27; see W. Beare, *The Roman Stage* [London, 1964], 217 and ch. 25, "The Roman Origin of the Law of Five Acts.") In another instance, Strozzi dignified the un-unified place of his *Proserpina rapita* with a Greek term, *anatopismo*, defined in the libretto as "un error di luoghi havendo qui per vaghezza il Poeta congiunto insieme il Lago di Pergusa, il monte d'Etna, il promontorio Pachino, etc."

35.   All of the plays written by Giacomo Castoreo for the Teatro ai Saloni were in five acts (with musical intermedi). Castoreo's librettos, however, were in three acts.

36.   Most of Frigimelica Roberti's librettos have five acts. They and other five-act librettos by such poets as Zeno and Pariati were a specialty of the Teatro S. Giovanni Grisostomo; see ch. 13 below.

Chorus

Another apparently clear-cut choice for early librettists involved the use of a chorus. Its presence in ancient tragedy was axiomatic; both Aristotle and Horace were clear about its importance, ascribing to it several different roles within the action.[37] The pastoral, too, made use of choral passages, which, however, were usually more tangential to the plot than those of tragedy. Opera, insofar as it was considered a revival of Greek tragedy, was thus bound to include choruses. And yet modern taste dictated otherwise, at least in Venice. Indeed, one of the conventional distinctions between Venetian opera and its predecessors hinges on the importance of choral episodes. Florentine, Mantuan, and Roman operas of the first half of the century employed them extensively, both within and between acts, where they served musical and dramatic purposes. In some of the earliest of these operas, choral passages provided the primary articulations within an otherwise nearly continuous flow of recitative, and thus contributed importantly to the shape of the works.[38] Venetian operas, on the other hand, are notable for their lack—or paucity—of choruses. They concentrate instead on soloists, using a variety of vocal styles to project the drama.[39]

An illustration of the contrast in the use of chorus between early opera and the Venetian *dramma per musica* is provided by a comparison of Monteverdi's early and late operas, a comparison already made with respect to their orchestral usage. In the tradition of the pastoral, and following the Florentine precedent, *Orfeo* contains multiple choruses—of nymphs and shepherds, of infernal spirits—that frame and comment on much of the action. In *L'incoronazione di Poppea*, however, there are only two choruses: Seneca's followers reacting to his decision to die, which requires only three singers for its performance (it is essentially a chorus of soloists), and Nerone's courtiers celebrating Poppea's coronation. A still more striking contrast is offered by the two versions of

37. See Weinberg, *Literary Criticism*, 914–16. Aristotle, *Poetics*, ch. 18 (1456a): "The Chorus too should be regarded as one of the actors; it should be an integral part of the whole, and take a share in the action" (*Complete Works of Aristotle*, ed. Barnes, 2: 2330). Horace, *Ars poetica*, ed. Kraemer, 403–4: "The Chorus should discharge the part and duty of an actor with vigor, and chant nothing between the acts that does not forward the action and fit into the plot naturally. The Chorus must back the good and give sage counsel; must control the passionate and cherish those that fear to do evil; it must praise the thrifty meal, the blessings of justice, the laws, and Peace with her unbarred gates. It will respect confidences and implore heaven that prosperity may revisit the miserable and quit the proud." Extensive description of the chorus is absent in Horace's discussion of comedy (p. 406).

38. In Peri's *Euridice* and Cavalieri's *La rappresentazione di Anima e di Corpo*, for instance. The chorus certainly played an important role in later Roman operas based on the model of tragedy. See Margaret Murata, "Classical Tragedy in the History of Early Opera in Rome," *Early Music History* 4 (1984): 101–34.

39. The absence of choruses is analogous to the reduced importance of the instrumental movements in Venetian, as opposed to early court, opera. See Donald J. Grout, "The Chorus in Early Opera," in *Festschrift Friedrich Blume*, ed. Anna Amalie Abert and Wilhelm Pfannkuch (Basel, 1963), 151–61.

Rinuccini's *Arianna*, the original one for Mantua in 1608 and the revision for Venice in 1640. The libretto printed in 1640, as already observed, differs significantly—though subtly—from the original one. In addition to lacking the generic subtitle *tragedia*, it places many of the original choruses between *virgolette*. It would seem, then, that the designation *tragedia* was associated with extensive choruses. The changes in the 1640 version brought *Arianna* more closely into line with the increasingly conventionalized Venetian *dramma per musica*—though it was still far from typical.

Not even the most classicizing of the early Venetian librettists included many choruses in their dramas, and those they did include occurred within, rather than at the ends of, acts. As usual, they felt self-conscious enough to call attention to their lapse. The author of *Le nozze d'Enea* gives a characteristically thorough, and learned, defense:

> The chorus was an integral part of ancient tragedies, entering not only as a charac-
> ter, but singing, mainly between the acts, accompanied by gestures and dancing,
> and with those characteristic lamentations and outbursts. But in modern plays it is
> less important, and in some it does little more than separate the acts. Since I have
> introduced even several choruses within each act, I have not used them at the ends;
> because given that the entire tragedy is sung, singing the choruses as well would
> become too monotonous; and thus to give the audience greater satisfaction with va-
> riety, ballets have been introduced, derived in some way from the plot, just as the
> ancient choruses danced to sung tetrameter, a meter very well suited to the move-
> ments of the body. (Appendix I.9h–i)

Here the complete musical setting of the drama served as a double excuse, both for not writing choruses between the acts and for including ballets instead, which, in addition to providing that essential commodity, variety, could, by stretching classical theory a little, actually be justified as an extension of the ancient practice of choral dancing.

Bissari, too, in the preface to *Torilda*, defends his substitution of ballets for choruses between acts with a similar excuse: the choruses danced.

> In the divertissements [*scherzi*] and dances that are woven into modern perfor-
> mances, ancient practices are revived . . . which made their tragedies less
> monotonous. . . . Because the new stagings are embellished with these things, it
> cannot be said that they lack the customary choruses, especially since the choruses
> appeared mainly in dances: and those dances, to which song will be added, will not
> be dissimilar to that hyporchema of which Atheneus writes, which was distin-
> guished by being sung and played. (Appendix I.25c)[40]

40. Most operas of the 1640s contained ballets at the ends of their first and second acts. True to classical precedent, these were usually linked in some way, however loosely, to the dramatic events of the operas. For a summary of the changing function of these ballets in seventeenth-century opera, see Katherine Kuzmick Hansell, "Il ballo teatrale e l'opera italiana," in *StOpIt*, 5 (Turin, 1988): 177–92.

Modern Taste and Ethics

Behind all of these specific decisions—about the use of chorus, division into acts, and even adherence to the unities—lay a central conflict between traditional rules and modern taste. That conflict touches on an even more fundamental issue, to which these librettists were especially sensitive, one at the very basis of their whole enterprise: the purpose of their works.

The overt commercial values that had shaped opera in Venice from its earliest days gave a new focus to the question, but in addressing it, librettists were following an old tradition, that of the sixteenth-century writers who attempted to understand and communicate the aims of drama in the light of ancient poetic theory.[41] They acknowledged Aristotle's emphasis on emotional catharsis, but generally followed Horace in regarding their purpose as involving both delectation (*il diletto*) and edification (*l'utile*). The exact definition of these terms, as well as the proportion of the two ingredients in any single work, however, were matters that required considerable discussion. Following Horace, most previous theorists had allowed a mixture of the two aims, the one being a necessary means to the other. So, too, with our librettists, although their generic insecurity led them, at least during the 1640s, defensively to emphasize *l'utile* above *il diletto*.

An effort to demonstrate ethical content evidently inspired such elaborate interpretations as the one offered by Giulio Strozzi in the prefatory "Allegoria" of his libretto *Delia*:

> But since . . . I did not work at random in structuring this plot, I shall tell you its allegorical meaning. The sons of the Sun . . . are wretched mortals, subjected to punishment by him for their pride and audacity. The Cyclopes represent the evil vapors. . . . The Sun shoots the Cyclopes, that is, those pernicious fumes, with arrows . . . and overcomes evil. [The Sun pretends to be] the shepherd of Admetus, that is, of the wise prince, who contributes by appropriate means to our salvation. . . . Like the sacred poems, this entire composition can be spiritually applied to the human soul, which seeks to unite with God, by whom it is received in glory. (Appendix I.15b)[42]

Strozzi claims a high moral significance, indeed, for a text that might seem a rather unlikely vehicle.

Moral scruples appear to have been operating once again in the preface to his next libretto, *La finta pazza*, in which he defends the apparently low tone of the work: "Do not laugh at the humbleness of the name ['The Feigned Madwoman'], nor at the [low] nature of the subject, because I wished to keep

41. See Spingarn, *History*, 47; also Weinberg, *Literary Criticism*, 505–8, on Castelvetro.
42. Such an allegorical gloss continues the kind of moralizing impulse that had made pagan texts like Ovid safe for centuries of Christian readers.

my claims modest, and my invitation narrow, so that, without high-sounding titles, I could much more easily live up to the low expectations of the work" (Appendix I.16b). Not only is the apparent modesty of the libretto intentional, but so is the seemingly indecorous behavior of one of the principal characters, Deidamia, who feigns madness. Her action, however, offers a moral lesson: as Strozzi reminds his readers, "many great men, through feigned madness, have put into effect their wisest counsel, to the great benefit of the nation" ("molti huomini grandi con simulata pazzia hanno effettuato i lor prudentissimi consigli in gran benefitio della patria").

Didactic value of a more specific kind is ascribed to Deidamia's madness by Bisaccioni. In his commentary on Strozzi's work, he interprets it as a practical lesson in child-rearing, illustrating "how wary fathers should be, in raising their children, to provide for them and foresee the dangers they face" ("quanto debbano i padri star oculati nel provedere e prevedere i pericoli dei figli nell'allevarli"). And this lesson in turn proves that, unlikely as it may seem, "stage works should be heard and considered more for edification than for pleasure" ("l'opere sceniche dovrebbono per utile, più che per diletto udirsi, e considerare"). The message certainly transcends the medium.[43]

Some librettists, however, made a point of denying moral purpose to their works. The oft-quoted anonymous author of *Le nozze d'Enea* asserts that although the Horatian *l'utile* is in fact the "fin principale" of poetry, his aim is "diletto maggiore" as well as the Aristotelian excitation of the passions:

> But although it is true that tragedies with tragic endings are superior to the other kind [i.e., his tragedy "di lieto fine"], even this kind is capable of exciting the passions; and besides it produces greater pleasure, which, even if it is not the principal aim of poetry, as edification is, still must be much sought after by the poet, especially since it is demanded by the temper of the times, to which poets have always adapted themselves in large measure. (Appendix I.9b)

And the librettist of *Bellerofonte* no longer even felt the pull of *l'utile* as he boldly rejected Horatian authority and proclaimed *il diletto* as poetry's chief purpose: "Of the two aims of poetry that Horace taught, only pleasure remains. In this age men have no need to learn the way of the world from the writings of others" (Appendix I.19f).

Denial no less than affirmation of ethical aims calls attention to an issue that obviously concerned these librettists. Such aims might be difficult to discern without the authors' hints, but they were inherent in many of these texts, even the most unlikely of them, those that seem especially hedonistic and amoral. One early librettist, Paolo Vendramin, offers a key to the interpretation of such

---

43. *Il cannocchiale per la Finta pazza, dilineato da M[aiolino] B[isaccioni] C[onte] di G[enova]* (Venice: Surian, 1641).

texts in ethical terms. In the prologue to his *Adone*, he comments on the tragic death of the hero, pointing out the moral of the story: "Se stupor, se pietà sia, che v'ingombre / Spettatori a tal fin; fattevi accorti, / Ch'i diletti de l'huom tutti son corti / E le gioie d'Amor tutte son'ombre" ("Spectators, whether it be shock or pity that weighs you down / At such an ending; be aware / That all the pleasures of man are brief / And all the joys of love are shadows").

Vendramin's moral lesson could be applied even under the opposite conditions; a happy ending could be as instructive as a tragic one. This point is crucial to the interpretation of one of the most problematic librettos of the period, Busenello's *L'incoronazione di Poppea*—and undoubtedly to that of others as well. Poppea's illicit rise to power, which culminates in her coronation as Nerone's empress, is built on lust and the death and exile of apparently innocent, moral individuals. In the end, however, despite the overwhelming victory of Poppea, the work is less a celebration of the vices of murder and lust than a cautionary tale. The audience, undoubtedly familiar with their Seneca, knew that Poppea's triumph was only momentary and that she would soon be violently killed by her husband. The lesson of her story, then, although only implicit, can be considered no less moral than that of Vendramin's *Adone*.[44]

After the middle of the century, when their number had increased markedly, most librettists abandoned the theoretical defense of their works; they could now accept as axiomatic the premises argued by their more academically inclined predecessors. Some, however, still felt compelled to account for the gap between the ethical aims of ancient drama and the more hedonistic purposes of their own works. As late as 1667 Nicolò Minato asserted the ethical intentions of his *La caduta di Elio Seiano* quite explicitly in his preface:

> And if you come across some who say [the actions] are not to their liking, look closely and you will see that they are people of low condition who are unable to comprehend the elevated sentiments of a heroic soul. Remember that the performance of these dramas was invented by the ancients to teach perfection in morals, and thus the actions that are represented in them must be modeled after the idea of what should be, if not after what actually is. (Appendix I.43)[45]

And the publisher's preface to the anonymous *Achille in Sciro* (1664) still concerns itself with the aims of drama: "If this play does not proceed according to the strict rules of Aristotle, [at least] it follows the pleasant custom of the age, being a new kind of composition, which, unlike the ancient ones, has as its aim more to delight than to instruct" (Appendix I.54).[46]

---

44. This interpretation is amplified in Rosand, "Seneca," 34–52; see also Pirrotta, "Monteverdi's Poetic Choices," *Essays*, 316.
45. On *La caduta di Elio Seiano* and its twin, *La prosperità di Elio Seiano*, see Craig Monson, "A Seventeenth-Century Opera Cycle: The Rise and Fall of Aelius Sejanus" (manuscript).
46. According to Bonlini, *Le glorie della poesia e della musica*, 66, the author of *Achille in Sciro* was Ippolito Bentivoglio.

The issue became especially pressing in the case of some of the more lascivious librettos of this later period, although not all librettists attempted to excuse their salaciousness with the same circuitous and pathetic justification as Giacomo Castoreo in the preface to his *Pericle effeminato* (1653):

> If I have not maintained either decorum in the characters or verisimilitude in the incidents, do not find fault with me, since I am following the misguided custom, introduced by many and practiced by all. Those metaphors that go by the name of playful, though they stray rather far from moral propriety, listen to them if you wish, but know that my intention was never to introduce obscenity into them; rather it was to induce you to mourn with me the depraved corruption of the century, in which poetic talent, which in other times was used to intimidate tyrants with civility of conduct, can find no means to delight you except through the effrontery of indecent jokes. (Appendix I.40b)

Much later, in the preface to his *Alcibiade* (1680), a thin pro forma reference to morality was all that Aurelio Aureli could muster to excuse his thoroughly licentious libretto: "You will enjoy a few lascivious though restrained actions, composed by me with the sole aim that you learn to shun them, and not to imitate them." ("Goderai di qualche scherzo lascivo ma pero moderato, composto da me a solo fine, che tu impari a sfuggirlo, e non ad imitarlo.")[47]

For the first generation of librettists—the Incogniti Busenello, Badoaro, Bartolini, Bisaccioni, and Strozzi, who were truly academic in their education and interests—the authority of the ancients was part of their cultural heritage. It loomed in the background, waiting to be applied whenever and however it was needed. The main purpose of all of their citations, as Badoaro neatly put it, was to show that they knew the rules: "In every age the road of invention has been shown to be open, and we have no other obligation in regard to the precepts of the ancients than to know them" (Appendix I.8k). What they did with them after that was a matter of individual choice.

Subject Matter

One area in which the impact of ancient precedent remained evident, at least on the surface, was in the choice of subject matter. The stories were old. A number of the earliest Venetian operas, like those in Florence and Rome, had mythological subjects. Most of them were based on Ovidian tales (probably filtered through modern translation and adaptation, especially that of Anguillara): *Andromeda, Adone, Apollo e Dafne, Arianna.*[48] Others treated mythological char

---

47. Further on the question of moral decadence in Venetian librettos, see Bianconi and Walker, "Production," 267.
48. *Le metamorfosi di Ovidio ridotte da Gio. Andrea dell'Anguillara in ottava rima* (1554). The importance

of Anguillara as a source for Ovidian transformations in seventeenth-century opera plots is discussed in Bianconi, *Seventeenth Century*, 218–19; see also Ellen Rosand, "L'Ovidio trasformato," preface to Aurelio Aureli and Antonio Sartorio, *Orfeo*, ed.

acters more freely: *Amore innamorato*, *Venere gelosa*, *Delia*. Still others, borrowing their plots from Homer and Virgil, recounted the exploits of Greek and
Trojan heroes: *Le nozze di Teti e di Peleo*, *Il ritorno d'Ulisse*, *Didone*, *Le nozze
d'Enea*. Another important category of libretto was the romance derived from
more recent Italian literature, from Ariosto or Tasso: *Bradamante*, *Armida*. In
most cases, the librettist relied on an earlier literary or dramatic model; newly
invented plots were uncommon during the first decade of opera in Venice. Yet
the nature of the source determined the librettist's attitude toward it, the extent
to which he followed or elaborated upon it. Mythology, dealing with the exploits of the Olympian deities, allowed relatively free rein to the librettist's
imagination. The various events of divine careers were self-sufficient, lending
themselves to isolation as well as to combination and permutation. They could
also be combined with those of other gods with whom they intersected, linked
by their common Olympian citizenship. A divine cast could be expanded or
contracted at will, characters could be added for their particular attributes—
their comic potential, for example, like Momus or Mercury. Their characterization left more room for invention or imagination, for expansion. Most important, mythology not only permitted the suspension of disbelief, it actually
encouraged it. Gods and goddesses were automatically exempted from the rules
of human behavior.[49]

History, on the other hand, whatever its mythological dimensions, made
greater claims on verisimilitude. The Trojan War had causes and results; it had
a beginning and an end. Ulysses and Aeneas, though legendary, were human
beings with well-known histories and destinies; their adventures were replete
with historical implications and consequences. It is no wonder, therefore, that
early librettists felt more strictly bound by human history than by divine myth,
and that they felt compelled to justify any liberties they took as far as plot
development was concerned.

One of the most notorious revisionists in this sense was, predictably,
Busenello. His treatment of the Virgilian episode of Dido and Aeneas bows so
deeply to "modern taste" that it verges on the absurd: he supplied that quintessentially tragic story with a happy ending. And yet he found full academic
justification for his departure.

> And because according to good doctrine it is permissible for poets not only to alter
> [fictional] stories but even history, Dido takes Iarbas for her husband. And if it was

---

Ellen Rosand, Drammaturgia musicale veneta 6
(1983), X–XI.
49. Cf. *Il corago o vero alcune osservazioni per metter
bene in scena le composizioni drammatiche*, ed. Paolo
Fabbri and Angelo Pompilio (Florence, 1983) (Appendix II. 1b). The willingness of audiences to accept
gods' and goddesses' singing had important implications for the development of occasions for arias in
early opera.

a famous anachronism in Virgil that Dido lost her life not for Sychaeus, her husband, but for Aeneas, great minds should be able to tolerate that here there occurs a marriage that is different both from the stories and the histories. He who writes satisfies his own fancy, and it is in order to avoid the tragic ending of Dido's death that the aforementioned marriage to Iarbas has been introduced. It is not necessary here to remind men of understanding how the best poets represented things in their own way; books are open, and learning is not a stranger in this world. (Appendix I.11b)

The convention of the happy ending in tragedy, of course, was hardly new with opera. Aristotle himself had confronted the issue. Judging the happy ending more proper to comedy, he recognized its use in tragedy as a form of pandering to audience taste.[50] Renaissance authors deliberately exploited the option. Giraldi Cintio, for example, all of whose tragedies end happily, acknowledges their generic impurity by calling them *tragedie miste*. He, too, admits that his motive was "exclusively to serve the needs of the spectators, and to make them [the tragedies] more pleasing on the stage, and to conform better to the usage of our times."[51] The issue remained problematic into the seventeenth century, and the rationale for the happy ending the same, its appeal to popular taste—as Giulio Strozzi reminds us in defending his tragedy *Erotilla*, written in honor of the marriage of the prince of Sulmona.

> But what have tragedies to do with weddings? In truth the incongruity would be great if mine were not one of those tragedies that are allowed to have a happy ending and to leave a sweet taste in the mouths of the spectators. . . . It is true that, according to the rules of Aristotle, such tragedies seem less perfect, but in accordance with the taste of the day, which is the rule of all rules, they are received with greater enthusiasm, and listened to with greater patience. (Appendix I.14a,c)[52]

Within this same passage, Strozzi makes a further distinction, one also emphasized by Renaissance writers, between tragedy with a happy ending and tragicomedy:

> Nor do I want anyone to baptize it a tragicomedy, because it would show that they do not understand the significance of that term, nor know in what sense the ancients used it. For they called tragicomedies only those comedies in which some more noble and tragic characters were inserted, such as heroes or gods; but they never used that term for tragedies to which they gave happy endings. (Appendix I.14b)

---

50.   Aristotle, *Poetics*, ch. 13 (1453a).
51.   Quoted from Weinberg, *Literary Criticism*, 1: 442.
52.   *L'Erotilla: Tragedia di Giulio Strozzi*, saggio primo, terza impressione, in *I saggi poetici di Giulio*

Strozzi (Venice: Alberti, 1621). This is the same distinction made by the author of *Le nozze d'Enea*, between *tragedie lugubri* and *di lieto fine* (Appendix I.9b–c).

That distinction, as we shall see, proved to be of particular relevance in the subsequent development of the Venetian libretto.[53]

In any case, whether in tragedy or tragicomedy, the happy ending already boasted a lengthy operatic pedigree, having been introduced in the first surviving opera from Florence, Peri's *Euridice*, and used on many subsequent occasions. Busenello nevertheless felt compelled to justify the practice in his *Didone*, perhaps because the tragic outcome of the story was so well known. Whatever the reason, he seems to have been the first librettist to cite ancient authority—though he is rather vague on exactly which authority he is referring to—to justify the practice in opera.

Other librettists, however, stuck more closely to their sources, at least in the early period. In *Il ritorno d'Ulisse*, for example, Badoaro follows the *Odyssey* quite faithfully. But when he treated the same subject in another libretto, *Ulisse errante* (1644), he took many more liberties with his source. The contrast, as pointed out by Badoaro himself in the preface, was intentional, a response to critics of his earlier work who had apparently judged it lacking in invention.

> Many years ago [i.e., four] I produced *Il ritorno d'Ulisse in patria*, a drama wholly derived from Homer and deemed excellent by Aristotle in his *Poetics*, and even then I heard dogs barking, but I was not slow to respond with stones in my hands. Now I present *Ulisse errante*, which consists, in substance, of twelve books of Homer's *Odyssey*. I have partly reduced the episodes, partly built up the subject with inventions as I deemed necessary, without departing from the essence of the story. (Appendix I.8a)

Although *Il ritorno d'Ulisse* is indeed close to the *Odyssey*, it does not follow it exactly. Badoaro's play with dialogue is naturally much shorter and more focused than the Homeric epic, in which the action is described rather than enacted. The generic distinction is one to which Badoaro, predictably, was extremely sensitive. He nimbly explains the difference, though with reference not to *Il ritorno d'Ulisse* itself but to *Ulisse errante*:

---

53. Originally the term *tragicomedy*, as coined by Plautus, referred to a play that combined elements of both tragedy and comedy in mixing kings, gods, and servants. The happy ending does not seem to have figured significantly in Plautus's original definition, though Renaissance writers such as Giraldi Cintio used the term for tragedies with happy endings. See Weinberg, *Literary Criticism*, 210. The most complete discussion of tragicomedy in the Renaissance is by Battista Guarini, *Il Verrato* (Ferrara: Galdura, 1588), discussed in Weinberg, 658–68. See also his *Compendio della poesia tragicomica* (Venice: Ciotti, 1601). Guarini defined tragicomedy as a combination of tragedy and comedy that "takes from the one the great personages, but not the action; the verisimilar plot, but which is not true; the passions moved, but blunted; pleasure, not sadness; danger, but not death. From the other, controlled laughter, modest jests, the contrived knot, the happy reversal, and above all the comic order" (*Il Verrato*, f. 19v, quoted and translated by Weinberg, 659–60). On tragicomedy, see the *Princeton Encyclopedia of Poetry and Poetics*, ed. Alex Preminger (Princeton, 1965), 865–68.

If some wit should assert . . . that it is a subject more suitable for an epic than a tragedy, I will say that whoever wishes to read it in an epic will go to Homer's *Odyssey*, and whoever wishes to hear it as a tragedy will come to the theater of the Most Illustrious Signor Giovanni Grimani, where, in a short time, and with less effort, he may behold it in greater splendor upon the stage. (Appendix I.8f)

The characterizations in *Il ritorno d'Ulisse* are generally based on Homer, but they are developed in various ways. The secondary figures left greater latitude for expansion than the protagonists: less is known about them, their histories are less important. One in particular, the beggar Irus, gains much fuller characterization at Badoaro's hands. Labeled a "parasito" by Badoaro (and in Monteverdi's score, "parte ridicola"), he has a much more prominent role in the opera than in the epic, providing the opportunity for a full range of comic imitations—blustering, stuttering, crying. His effect is hardly comic, however, when, having been roundly beaten by Ulisse, he is not propped passively against the courtyard wall to scare away stray animals, as in the *Odyssey*, but actively determines to commit suicide.[54]

The abuse of decorum perpetrated on this "tragedia" by the presence of a comic character such as Iro was noted by the anonymous author of *Le nozze d'Enea*, who modeled an indecorous comic character of his own on him.[55] Once again, the desire to satisfy modern taste inspired breaking the "rules"—in this case, those of genre. But a precise precedent for doing so was easy to find; the anonymous author had a number of models besides Iro to choose from, and even earlier ones. He could have looked to Ermafrodito in Strozzi's *Delia* of 1639, to whom Strozzi had called particular attention in his preface: "I have introduced here the hilarode of the Greeks in the person of the playful Ermafrodito, a novel character, who, between the severity of the tragic and the facetiousness of the comic, sits very nicely upon our stage" (Appendix I.15f). Strozzi himself had modeled his character on a still earlier one, who had appeared on stage the year before: Scarabea, from Ferrari's *La maga fulminata*.[56] And he acknowledged his debt explicitly in Ermafrodito's first speech:

Con lusinghe ladre	With deceitful sighs
Mercurio mio padre	Mercury my father
Venere assaggio:	Tasted Venus.
Nacqui di bella Dea;	I was born of a beautiful goddess
E la nudrice mia fù Scarabea.	And my nurse was Scarabea.

54. See Ellen Rosand, "Iro and the Interpretation of *Il ritorno d'Ulisse in patria*," *JM* 7 (1989): 141–64.
55. The relevant passage is quoted on pp. 43–44 above. See also Appendix I.9e.
56. The modeling of Ermafrodito on Scarabea was evidently one of the many revisions to the libretto, which Strozzi claimed to have sketched for a different purpose, some ten years earlier (Appendix I.15h); see also Bianconi and Walker, "Dalla 'Finta pazza,' " 411 and n. 137.

L'han gia molti udita	Many have already heard her,
Vecchia rimbambita	The old woman grown childish,
D'amore cantar,	Sing of love.
Ma non è maraviglia	But it's no wonder,
D'una Tiorba, e d'un Poeta è figlia.	Since she's the daughter of a theorbo and a poet.

Latte Scarabeo	Scarabean milk
Mi fece un Orfeo	Made me an Orpheus
Si lungo, e sottil:	So long and thin.
Son di Venere figlio,	I am Venus's child,
Ma nel restate à Scarabea simiglio.	But in all else I resemble Scarabea.

In all these cases, the comic character provides relief from the serious drama, and in so doing represents a breach of the rules of tragedy. Although the perpetrators were self-conscious about it, at least they felt they were not alone. They could rely, with comforting tautology, on one another's example for justification.

This solidarity, supplying one another with support or precedent, marks an important turning point in the development of Venetian opera. The practice actually began as soon as it could, with the second opera performed in Venice referring to the first, and it grew up alongside and quite soon replaced the function of invoking classical models. Librettists cited one another's works, as they had done and continued to do with all sources, quite intentionally, with full awareness of their twin needs: for specific precedents and for a general history of their own, both of which would support the legitimacy of their activity. Such cross-references were a crucial component of opera's increasingly secure establishment in Venice, at once creating and recording its own history.

The growing number of such cross-references produced a decisive shift in the equilibrium between ancient authority and modern taste. By concretizing the concept of modern taste, these specific examples gave it greater weight, and certainly greater relevance for contemporary efforts. The borrowing of material from one libretto in another over an extended period of time eventually resulted in the establishment of a set of conventions that defined Venetian opera as a genre.

Badoaro's elaboration on Homer in *Ulisse errante*, like Busenello's alteration of Virgil in *Didone*, reveals another important trend in the development of the genre—one that, although established in the early 1640s, gained momentum rapidly in the course of the decade. This was the tendency toward increasing freedom in the adaptation of sources, toward increasing *inventione*. But in this same early period, not all librettists felt obliged to apologize for taking liberties with sources. Giovanni Faustini did just the opposite. In the preface to his second libretto, *Egisto* (1643), he admits not to excessive *inventione* but to a borrowing: "I confess to you that I have taken the episode with Cupid from Ausonius, with the same license that the Latin poets used to take the ideas of the Greeks in order to adorn their own stories and epic compositions" (Appendix I.31b). The essential difference between Faustini's libretto and those we have been discussing, implied here but not stated, is that the remainder of his text is not taken from any obvious source, but is freely invented, suggesting a different model: tragicomedy rather than tragedy.[57]

This contrast between librettists who defended invention and one who defended borrowing stands for a basic dichotomy in the early history of opera in Venice. Badoaro and Busenello, the Incogniti apologists, represented one side; Faustini and others, to be discussed in the following chapters, represented the other. The academic theoreticians and the practical men of the theater: these two currents, epitomizing the struggle between theory and practice, were the main tributaries of the new genre, *dramma per musica*. From the beginning of its history, opera in Venice was shaped by this dialectic. The professional theater men, like Ferrari and Manelli, brought opera to Venice; the academics, the writers whose views on the nature of tragedy and its relation to their own theatrical efforts we have been considering, helped to provide it with intellectual and historical substance.[58] Although they themselves did not use the term, choosing *tragedia* or *dramma* instead, their efforts bear major responsibility for defining *dramma per musica* for the future. In airing and then dismissing the "rules" as inconsistent or irrelevant, the Incogniti librettists disposed of the issues that troubled them as intellectuals well versed in the classics, helping to clear the ground and set opera on a firm footing for their less intellectual, more pragmatic successors. Their theoretical defenses lent a patina of legitimacy to the bastard genre.

57. Faustini's librettos, which were the models for most librettos written in the second half of the century, almost seem created to fulfill Guarini's criteria for tragicomedy (see n. 53 above).

58. For evidence of tension between the two groups, see Ferrari's pointed anti-academic comments in the preface to the Bologna edition of his *Pastor regio* (1641) (Appendix I.5a). One figure seems to have bridged both worlds: Giacinto Andrea Cicognini, a professional theater man, was reported also to have participated in the "erudita conversatione" with members of the Incogniti, Loredan, Pietro Michele, Herrico, and Strozzi. See Angelo Bontempi, *Historia musica* (Perugia, 1695), 188; quoted in Bianconi and Walker, "Production," 213 n. 11.

3

• • •

Da rappresentare in musica:
The Rise of Commercial Opera

The agreement among librettists on the designation *dramma per musica* conferred a certain aesthetic legitimacy on their art, affording it a definite place in the taxonomy of genres. But this consensus was not the only sign that opera had achieved some legitimacy by the mid seventeenth century. We can follow its establishment as an independent art form in the primary documentary sources, especially the librettos. They testify to the thickly competitive atmosphere of the theatrical world of Venice and to the rapidly developing self-consciousness of that world.

The relationship of printed libretto to performed opera changed radically during the first decade. The change is revealed most succinctly on the title pages, epitomized in the forms of a single verb, *rappresentare*. Its appearance in the past tense, *rappresentato*, suggests that the work has already been performed. In the infinitive, *da rappresentare* or *da rappresentarsi*, it indicates that the opera is yet to be performed. If the verb does not appear at all, the libretto was probably not associated with a performance but published for some other reason.[1] Judging, then, from their title pages, librettos of the late 1630s and early 1640s were routinely published, if at all, after a work had been performed (*rappresentato*), whereas later ones were usually published beforehand (*da rappresentarsi*).

As with most generalizations, this one requires qualification. The change from *rappresentato* to *da rappresentare* was neither linear nor consistent. *Da rappresentare* on a title page does not guarantee that the work was ever actually performed, while *rappresentato* could refer to an event of ten or more years earlier; each libretto needs to be evaluated individually. But the exceptions, rather than undermining the generalization, give it greater weight, since their departure from convention was usually explicit and intentional.

The considerations that determined whether a libretto was published before or after a performance are embedded in the complex early history of opera in

---

1. Pirrotta was the first to point out the importance of careful scrutiny of title pages ("Early Venetian Libretti," *Essays*, 317–24). The absence of any verb at all on a libretto title page often signified a purely literary print or reprint; on literary prints, see Robert S. Freeman, *Opera without Drama: Currents of Change in Italian Opera, 1675 to 1725* (Ann Arbor, 1981), 24.

Venice. A libretto printed before a performance served a very different purpose from one printed afterwards. The latter could only have a commemorative value; it could recall the aura and even some of the details of a past success, reminding those who had seen the work what it was like and suggesting for those who had not just what they had missed. On the other hand, a libretto printed ahead of time could function as advertising for a forthcoming performance, to attract an audience; in addition, of course, it could serve the audience in the theater, as an aid to following the action on stage. The increasing incidence of publication beforehand confirms opera's changing status: its growing stability during the 1640s, both as a regular part of the carnival season and as a genre. Some of the forces that eventually prompted the shift from after to before are revealed by an examination of the librettos published during the first four seasons of operatic activity in Venice.

The arrival of the first opera company headed by the poet-musician Benedetto Ferrari to produce *Andromeda* at the Teatro S. Cassiano during Carnival of 1637 has been described many times. The earliest and fullest description—and a chief source for all the others—is contained in the libretto itself, which appeared in print some two months after the opera was performed (fig. 6). Another early account, only in part derived from the libretto, is that of Ivanovich in *Minerva al tavolino*, an account allegedly based on a report given to him in 1664 (i.e., nearly thirty years after the event) by Marchese Pio Enea degli Obizzi, whom he claims to quote directly. According to Pio Enea, the first step toward *Andromeda* had been taken the previous year in Padua, when a special kind of tournament, entitled *Ermiona*, was produced, probably on 11 April:

> In the year 1636 the generous desire was born in some friends and companions of mine in Padua to arrange a tournament; so I, in order to further dignify it, took up the story of Cadmus, and composed an introduction for it, which was then set to music in the form in which it appeared in print for all to see. For this purpose a spacious place, adjoining Pra della Valle, was enclosed, and with horse-drawn machines, as are seen in these drawings, a magnificent spectacle was effected. The concourse of Venetian nobility, *cavalieri* from the mainland, and students from the university was great, even though the performance took place in the month of October, which is normally devoted to vacation.[2] Whether because of the good fortune of the *cavalieri* who composed it, or the merits of those who performed in it, it was universally applauded. . . . From this it followed that the next year, under the sponsorship of a number of noblemen, various excellent professional musicians got together, through whose efforts there appeared, in 1637 at the S. Cassiano theater, *Andromeda* by Benedetto Ferrari, poet, composer, and excellent theorbo player. (Appendix II.6k)

2. Although Ivanovich gave October as the month of the performance, the libretto of *Ermiona* gives the possibly more plausible, because more specific, date of 11 April, which is confirmed by letters of Pio Enea to the duke of Mantua from 10 March and 14 April; see Bianconi and Walker, "Dalla 'Finta pazza,'" 410 n. 132.

L'ANDROMEDA

Del Signor
· BENEDETTO FERRARI.

Rappresentata in Musica
In Venetia l'Anno 1637.

Dedicata
ALL'ILLVSTRISSIMO
SIG. MARCO ANTONIO
PISANI.

Con Licenza de' Superiori, e Priuilegi.

IN VENETIA, MDCxxxvII.

Preſſo Antonio Bariletti.

6. Benedetto Ferrari, *Andromeda* (Venice, 1637), libretto title page.

Pio Enea's account of the influence of *Ermiona* on *Andromeda* is substantiated by a comparison of the librettos of the two works.[3] It was probably no mere coincidence, then, that just a month after the Paduan spectacle, in May 1636, the brothers Francesco and Ettore Tron, members of a prominent noble family and proprietors of the Teatro S. Cassiano, were granted permission by the Council of Ten to reopen their old theater as a "theatro de musica qual se prattica in più parte per lo diletto de l'insigni pubblici."[4] Originally constructed for the purpose of presenting plays, the theater had been closed since a fire had damaged it in 1629.[5] The Tron brothers were not the only ones seeking to capitalize on the success of *Ermiona*. As we learn from the commemorative libretto of the work published in 1638, *Ermiona* was performed by a traveling company made up of many of the same musicians who were to perform in *Andromeda*.[6] The company, too, was apparently hoping to repeat a previous triumph.

The shared cast is indicative of more profound similarities that link *Ermiona* and *Andromeda*, from the organization of the spectacle to the nature of the audience that witnessed it. Indeed, *Ermiona* introduced two important new elements that became crucial to Venetian opera. As distinct from a typical court opera, it was not commissioned to celebrate a special occasion;[7] and the audience was a relatively mixed one—*nobiltà veneta, cavalieri della terraferma*, and *scolari dello studio*.[8] Furthermore, the theater in which *Ermiona* was performed, with its multiple tiers of boxes built to accommodate that diverse audience, may well have served as the model for Venetian opera houses, with their various rows and categories of boxes. The Paduan arrangement is described in the libretto as follows:

3. See Pierluigi Petrobelli, " 'L'Ermiona' di Pio Enea degli Obizzi ed i primi spettacoli d'opera veneziani," *Quaderni della Rassegna musicale* 3 (1965): 125–41.

4. Mangini, *I teatri di Venezia*, 37. In December 1628 the Council of Ten had assumed control of "le maschere, commedie et li musicali interventi." See ibid., 31, and Giazotto, "La guerra dei palchi," 252.

5. According to Ivanovich, who sketches a history of each of the theaters (see Appendix II.6p).

6. *L'ERMIONA del S. Marchese Pio Enea Obizzi Per introduzione d'un Torneo à piedi & a cavalli E d'un Balletto rappresentato in Musica nella Città di Padova l'Anno M.DC.XXXVI dedicata Al Sereniss. Principe di Venetia FRANCESCO ERIZO descritta dal S. Nicolo Enea Bartolini Gentilhuomo, & Academico° Senese* (Padua: Paolo Frambotto, 1638). This libretto may have been published as an afterthought, inspired by the publication of *Andromeda*. It may, therefore, rep-

resent an attempt at corrective history, an effort to emphasize the connection between *Ermiona* and the blossoming Venetian opera. The *Ermiona* company, listed in the libretto, included Girolamo Medici, Madalena Manelli, Anselmo Marconi, Antonio Grimani, Felicita Uga, Giovanni Felice Sances, composer of the music, and Francesco Monteverdi, first three of whom appeared in *Andromeda* as well.

7. Like a typical court opera, however, it received only a single performance; see Petrobelli, " 'L'Ermiona,' " 127. For a recent attempt to emphasize the differences rather than the similarities between the two works, see Silvano Benedetti, "Il teatro musicale a Venezia nel '600: Aspetti organizzativi," *Studi veneziani* 8 (1984): 185–220.

8. The makeup of the audience is also mentioned in the preface to the libretto; see Mangini, *I teatri di Venezia*, 38.

Five rows of galleries circled all around, one above the other, with parapets of mar-
ble balusters; the spaces, large enough to accommodate sixteen spectators each, were
separated by partitions, which were finished on their exterior ends like columns,
from which supports of silvered wood held the candlesticks that illuminated the theater. The two highest and most distant rows were filled with common citizens; in
the third sat the students and foreign nobility; the second, as the more worthy place,
was for the rectors and the Venetian noblemen; and in the first there were the gen-
tlewomen and the principal gentlemen of the city. (Appendix I.1)[9]

As for *Andromeda*, its libretto was published not by the author, Ferrari, as
we might expect, but by the printer Antonio Bariletti, who signed the dedication to the Venetian nobleman Marco Antonio Pisano, dating it 6 May 1637
and referring to the performance as having occurred two months earlier ("già
son due mesi"), or during the previous Carnival.[10] Bariletti's dedication, cast in
the characteristically ornate and effusive language of such addresses, offers as his
purpose in publishing the libretto the desire to provide the heroine Andromeda
with a living protector, thus assuring her a permanent sense of security, or, we
might say, immortality.

After the dedication, Bariletti addresses a lengthy note to the reader, which
begins with a bow to the company responsible for the production: "To the
glory of the musicians, who in the number of six (in addition to the author)
staged *Andromeda* with great splendor and refinement, at their own expense,
with a little extra help, and no less for the pleasure of those who have not seen
it, I have deemed it fitting to give a brief account of it in this form" (Appendix
I.2a). Ivanovich's—or Pio Enea's—version of this episode adds one crucial detail: "con la protezione di più Nobili." Ferrari's troupe may have footed most
of the bill (according to Bariletti), but the company enjoyed patrician patronage
in some way—"qualche consideratione," in Bariletti's words. This is an important point: it raises the question of the financial underpinnings of the new
genre. Presumably "la protezione di più Nobili" of Ferrari's troupe was a reference to the Tron family and, possibly, the noble families who rented boxes.

Bariletti's note to the reader is followed by a detailed description of the
production, with special emphasis on the visual effects and on the amazed
response of the audience to the magic of the stage transformations: "The curtain
having disappeared, the stage was seen to be entirely sea, with such an artful
horizon of waters and rocks that its naturalness (although feigned) inspired
doubt in the audience as to whether they were really in a theater or on an actual

---

9. On the influence of the tournament theater, see
Bjurström, *Torelli*, 38–39.
10. Since Carnival that year ended on 24 February,
the performance probably took place shortly before
that.

seashore" (Appendix I.2b).[11] The description also identifies the cast by name and provides some incidental details about the music.[12]

Madalena Manelli romana (Francesco's wife), who played the part of Andromeda "mirabilmente," also sang the prologue "divinamente."[13] This was followed by "una soavissima Sinfonia" played by "più forbiti sonatori," among whom was the "author" (i.e., poet) of the opera "con la sua miracolosa Tiorba." The part of Giunone was sung by Francesco Angeletti of Assisi; that of Mercurio exquisitely by Don Annibale Graselli from Città di Castello, who also sang Ascalà Cavalier "con mille gratie di Paradiso," and Perseo. Francesco Manelli of Tivoli, "autore della musica dell'opera," portrayed Nettuno "egregiamente," as well as Astarco Mago. (This is the only mention of the composer.) Protheo was played "gentilissimamente" by Giovanni Battista Bisucci bolognese, who also sang Giove "celestemente." At the end of the first act there was sung "first, from within, a madrigal for several voices concerted with various instruments; and then three beautiful young men, dressed as Cupids, came out to perform a most gracious ballet for intermezzo. . . . To the accompaniment of a mellifluous instrumental melody Astrea appeared in the sky and Venere in the sea." Astrea was played "gratiosamente" by Girolamo Medici romano, and Venere "soavissimamente" by Anselmo Marconi romano.

These, then, were the singers who participated in *Andromeda*—seven rather than the six cited by Bariletti earlier in the preface. Four were from Rome (Madalena Manelli, Girolamo Medici, and Anselmo Marconi, plus Francesco Manelli from nearby Tivoli); one each from Assisi (Francesco Angeletti), Città di Castello (Don Annibale Graselli), and Bologna (Giovanni Battista Bisucci). The only Venetian involved in the production was Giovanni Battista Balbi, "inventore del balletto" and "ballarino celebre."[14] More interesting perhaps than their place of origin is the fact that, with the exception of the two Manelli, all these singers were currently employed in Venice, at San Marco, suggesting that their presence on the lagoon was neither casual nor temporary. While we do not have similar information about every early opera cast, this one and some others suggest that the San Marco musicians took no small part in early operatic activity in Venice.[15]

11. The scenographer, though not mentioned, was probably Giuseppe Alabardi, or "Schioppi veneziano"; see n. 17 below.

12. The full description is printed in Worsthorne, *Venetian Opera*, appendix III, 168–69.

13. No prologue is recorded in the libretto, however.

14. Balbi had a long career, first as a choreographer, later as a scenographer and impresario. He produced operas for Naples in the early 1650s and was responsible for the scenography for the Venetian production of *Alessandro vincitor di se stesso* in 1651. For his subsequent career, see Bianconi and Walker, "Dalla 'Finta pazza,' " 406 n. 125, and nn. 33 and 76 below.

15. See Mangini, *I teatri di Venezia*, 39; and Francesco Caffi, *Storia della musica sacra nella già cappella ducale di San Marco in Venezia (dal 1318 al 1797)* (Venice, 1853; rev. ed., ed. Elvidio Surian, Venice, 1987), 398: "tutti, non uno eccettuati, tutti coloro che

Although the foreigners in Ferrari's band were perhaps fewer than Bariletti's description implies, the mixture of travelers and local musicians that performed in both *Ermiona* and *Andromeda* matches Ottonelli's description of the typical operatic troupe of "mercenarii musici." These groups were generally self-sufficient, but they were occasionally forced to draw upon local talent to supplement their number.

> They strive to assemble enough accomplished companions so that the company alone, composed of paid professional actors, is sufficient to carry out the undertaking, without having to call upon the assistance of other singers or players. Sometimes they succeed in this intent, and sometimes not. And when they do not succeed, they do not give up, but go with the company, which is at least partly formed, to a major city; . . . and they take steps to find out, if they do not know already, what singers and players are available in the city, either secular, ecclesiastical, or monastic, who could be invited—for pay, or else exhorted with affection, and also sometimes almost forced, with the aid of important intercessors—to accept one or more parts as assistant musician in a public theater, in order to reach a sufficient number to have the drama or musical play heard, seen, and enjoyed by the listeners and spectators. (Appendix II.3c)

Bariletti's extended description of the action is followed by three sonnets (one of them by Busenello) dedicated to Benedetto Ferrari, "l'Autore, Poeta, Musico, e Sonator di Tiorba Eccellentissimo," the dramatis personae, and, finally, the actual text of the drama. The volume concludes with more poetry: six sonnets by Ferrari "In lode de Signori Musici più celebri, ch'intervennero nell'Andromeda," and three more by other authors in his honor.

With this elaborate volume Bariletti expressly sought to give permanence to an otherwise ephemeral event. Publication of the libretto would assure *Andromeda* a fixed place in history. For this purpose, the actual text of the drama—a rather disconnected series of episodes—was probably the least important part of the publication.[16] Rather, it was the wealth of information about the performance, the evocation of the event itself, that had the greatest impact on subsequent operatic developments in Venice. The sonnets contributed by a number of important Venetian citizens served to lend an air of respectability to the

---

quel dramma [*Andromeda*] cantarono furono distintissimi cantori della Capella ducale." Manelli was appointed to San Marco on 3 October 1638—that is, after *Andromeda* (I-Vas, Proc. de Supra, Chiesa actorum 144, f. 28ᵛ, 3 Ott. 1638: "che iij codotto per cantor Basso in Chiesa di S. Marco Francesco Manelli con salario di ducati sessanta all'anno"); see also Pierluigi Petrobelli, "Francesco Manelli: Documenti e osservazioni," *Chigiana* 24 (1967): 53. But Caffi's list contains too many names. It includes Guidantonio Boretti, whose first operatic appearance

occurred the season after *Andromeda*, in *La maga fulminata*, and Francesco Antegnati, who sang in neither *Andromeda* nor *La maga fulminata*. One San Marco singer who performed in *Ermiona*, but in neither *Andromeda* nor *La maga fulminata*, was Francesco Monteverdi, the composer's son. He did appear in *Le nozze di Teti e di Peleo* in the following year, however.

16. See Petrobelli, "'L'Ermiona,'" 129–30, on similar lack of coherence in *Ermiona*.

publication. Bariletti's enthusiasm for his project was obviously inspired by its novelty. Subsequent librettos, though often highly informative, rarely supply comparable detail, particularly about the music.

As if to confirm the effectiveness of Bariletti's publicity, the following year witnessed the second Venetian opera production, *La maga fulminata*, performed at the same theater by essentially the same troupe. Ferrari again wrote the text and Manelli the music; the scenographer was Giuseppe Alabardi, called "Schioppi veneziano," who had possibly served in the same capacity for *Andromeda*, although his name was not mentioned.[17] Four of the original singers took part—Angeletti, Bisucci, and the two Manelli—and there were three new ones: Felicita Uga romana, who had sung in *Ermiona*, Antonio Panni reggiano, and Guido Antonio Boretti from Gubbio.[18] Like the libretto of *Andromeda*, that of *La maga fulminata* was published after the first performance, but sooner, possibly before the end of the run. The dedication is dated 6 February, which was still well within the carnival season and probably quite close to the actual date of the premiere. It is likely, in fact, that the libretto was already in press when the first performance took place (fig. 7).

In this case the librettist himself must have played a significant role in the publication, since he signed the dedication, to Viscount Basilio Feilding (*sic*), the English ambassador to the Serenissima.[19] And in that dedication he offered a rather charming—and informative—justification for the print:

> It was enjoyed and applauded by you in the theater; may it not displease you in your study. A beautiful woman entices in public, and delights in private. I have already presented to Your Excellency musical tokens of my respectful service [i.e., *Musiche varie*]; now I offer you poetic ones, because I want my homage to you to compete in permanence with the years; and (if it were granted me), I would like it to last for eternity. (Appendix I.3a)

Again, the aim was permanence and signaled an implicit recognition of the fleeting, ephemeral quality of performance.

The note to the reader that follows can be interpreted in the same light. Like that in *Andromeda*, it is signed by the printer, Bariletti, and it offers a similarly

17. The sets were probably the same for both operas; see Bjurström, *Torelli*, 43. Alabardi, a painter, was responsible for the scenography of several pre-operatic spectacles as well. They included *Rosilda*, a tragedy by Tobia de' Ferrari, performed by the Accademia dei Sollevati in 1625, and *Proserpina rapita*, a text by Giulio Strozzi set to music by Monteverdi and performed in Palazzo Mocenigo in 1630. See Povoledo, "Una rappresentazione accademica," 144–47 and fig. 84, which reproduces Alabardi's single scene for *Rosilda*. See also id., "Lo Schioppi viniziano pittor di teatro," *Prospettive* 16 (1958): 45–50.

18. Felicita Uga had been in Venice since 1634; see Povoledo, "Una rappresentazione accademica," 136–37, 152. Boretti is not to be confused with the future composer Giovanni Antonio; see Ellen Rosand, "Boretti," *New Grove*, 3: 48.

19. Feilding was the dedicatee of Ferrari's *Musiche varie a voce sola Libro secondo* (Venice: Magni, 1637) as well as of Manelli's *Musiche* of 1636, published by Madalena Manelli "ad istanza d'alcuni Cavalieri" (possibly an attempt to secure a Venetian position for Manelli).

7. Benedetto Ferrari, *La maga fulminata* (Venice, 1638), libretto title page.

detailed description of the performance and a rave review. With regard to the opera company itself, it is actually more informative. Bariletti repeats and expands upon the information provided in the *Andromeda* preface, including some previously unknown facts about the composer, as well as details concerning economic matters. His observations reveal considerable sensitivity to the novelty as well as the larger importance of Ferrari's whole enterprise:

> If the *Andromeda* of Benedetto Ferrari, represented in music last year, was pleasing to the utmost degree, this year his *Maga fulminata* fulminated all minds with wonder. Not content with having sweetened the waters of the Adriatic with the unique sound of his ever-so-sweet theorbo, with the most refined concerts of two volumes of music published by him,[20] he has wished also to gild this clime with the dark characters of his pen. It fell to me to publish his *Andromeda*; and I have been honored as well with his *Maga*, which was impressed on hearts before it was impressed on paper. Welcome it, readers, as the most noble offspring of an illustrious author, who from his own resources, and those of only five fellow musicians,[21] and with the expenditure of no more than two thousand scudi, has been able to steal the souls of the listeners with the royal representation [*reale rappresentatione*][22] of that play; similar undertakings cost princes infinite amounts of money.[23] In addition, where can you find in our time a private virtuoso who has been granted the courage to put hand to such tasks and to discharge them with honor, as he has done, whose glory, and that of his companions, is applauded by the universal acclamation of the Most Serene City of Venice? Meanwhile, welcome no less my intention, which is to be of use to you and please you by offering to you, by means of my presses, the illustrious labors of such a noble virtuoso, and by describing to you the musical performance of the work, which went as follows. (Appendix I.3b)

This then is followed by a scene-by-scene description that, although quite elaborate, is somewhat less rich in musical references than that of *Andromeda*.

As in the *Andromeda* print, the description of the action of *La maga fulminata* is succeeded by a clutch of sonnets in praise of Ferrari by various Venetian literary figures, and the text of the drama is followed by three more poems, one of them by Ferrari himself.[24] Again, these contributions seem intended to lend a kind of literary legitimacy to the publication. One novelty in the libretto is the portrait of Ferrari, aged thirty-four, which is inserted in most copies just before the text of the drama (fig. 8).

20. These were *Musiche varie a voce sola del Sig.r Benedetto Ferrari da Reggio* (Venice: Magni, 1633) and the previously mentioned *Musiche varie a voce sola del Sig. Benedetto Ferrari* (note the absence of Reggio), libro secondo (1637).

21. Bariletti here slightly underestimated the number of musicians. There were, as we counted, seven names listed in the libretto.

22. On the cost of the production, see ch. 5 below; *reale rappresentatione* is equivalent to *opera regia*, for which term see ch. 2, n. 3, above.

23. The reference to the expenses of princely productions reveals Bariletti's appreciation of "Venetian" opera. Cf. Ivanovich's similar acknowledgment of the difference between "princely" and "mercenary" opera (Appendix II.6g). It is a difference acknowledged by other authors as well; cf. the expression *affatto reale* in the preface to *Bellerofonte* (1642) (Appendix I.20a).

24. The authors included at least one future librettist, Francesco Sbarra.

8. Portrait of Benedetto Ferrari, from the libretto of *La maga fulminata* (Venice, 1638).

The Beginning of Competition

The publicity created around *Andromeda* and expanded in connection with *La maga fulminata* paid immediate and lasting dividends. Interest was such that the libretto of *La maga fulminata* quickly sold out and was reprinted in the same year.[25] More significant, by the next year a second opera company had been formed and a second theater converted for use as an opera house: the Teatro SS. Giovanni e Paolo.[26]

Owned by the Grimani family, the original Teatro SS. Giovanni e Paolo was probably built sometime between 1635 and 1637. According to Giustiniano Martinioni's revision of Francesco Sansovino's standard guide to Venice, the wooden theater was soon moved from its original site on the Fondamenta Nuove to a location nearby (in Calle della Testa at Sta. Marina) and rebuilt, part in stone, part in wood.[27] The move and reconstruction, which probably occurred sometime in 1638, were arguably stimulated by the Grimani family's desire to exploit the political potential of the new genre, to compete with those families who had already invested in it. This motivation is clearly acknowledged in Bonlini's account: "In the year 1639, following the example of the theater of S. Cassiano, the first *Opera in Musica* was recited . . . in that of SS. Giovanni e Paolo, built a short time after the two already mentioned [i.e., the two S. Cassiano theaters], not only for the purpose of emulating them, but also to overshadow their fame."[28] The Grimani theater certainly exceeded that of S. Cassiano in size as well as magnificence, for in 1645, even after several other theaters had opened, it was referred to as the most comfortable and beautiful in the city: "il teatro, stimato più commodo, e bello di questa città."[29] This reputation it maintained for close to forty years, until the construction of a new Teatro Grimani, the S. Giovanni Grisostomo, in 1678.[30]

25. With a few minor changes: copies in I-Vmc and US-Lau.

26. Mangini, *I teatri di Venezia*, 56, considers SS. Giovanni e Paolo to be the fourth opera theater, after S. Cassiano, S. Moisè, and S. Salvatore. But only S. Cassiano had as yet been used for opera. Ivanovich, *Minerva*, 399, lists it as third, after S. Cassiano and S. Salvatore; Bonlini, *Le glorie della poesia*, 20, as third after two S. Cassiano theaters, one of them our opera house, the other a theater built in the preceding century, where spoken dramas had been performed.

27. Francesco Sansovino, *Venetia città nobilissima et singolare . . . con aggiunta di tutte le cose notabili . . . da D. Giustiniano Martinioni* (Venice: Curti, 1663), 397. For Ivanovich, see Appendix II.6p; see also Mangini, *I teatri di Venezia*, 56.

28. "L'anno 1639. ad esempio del Teatro di S. Cassiano fu recitata la prima Opera in Musica . . . in quello di SS. Gio e Paolo, già eretto poco tempo doppo li due accennati ad emularne non solo, ma ad offuscarne la Gloria ancora" (Bonlini, *Le glorie della poesia*, 20). For the two S. Cassiano theaters, see Mangini, *I teatri di Venezia*, 19–26.

29. In a letter from the Florentine ambassador in Venice to Matthias de' Medici cited by Bianconi and Walker, "Dalla 'Finta pazza,' " 435 n. 229.

30. It is difficult to estimate the exact sizes of the individual theaters during this period. Some certainly had a greater number of boxes than others, and some, such as S. Moisè and S. Apollinare, had the reputation for being particularly small. Comparative figures are available for a later period, from the reports of Chassebras de Cramailles published in the *Mercure galant* of March and April 1683 and from notes made on a trip to Venice in 1688 by the Swedish architect Nicolas Tessin; see Per Bjurström,

Ferrari's troupe, reconstituted to include, among others, two experienced theater men, the scenic designer of *Ermiona*, Alfonso Chenda "detto il Rivarola," and the librettist Giulio Strozzi, moved to the new theater in time for the 1639 season, when they produced not one but two operas.[31] Both season and theater were inaugurated with a setting of Strozzi's *Delia* by Ferrari's usual collaborator, Manelli. Ferrari's own authorial efforts were reserved for the second production, *Armida*, for which he wrote not only the text but the music as well.

In the meantime, a new company, an "Accademia per recitar l'Opera," had taken charge of Ferrari's former theater at S. Cassiano.[32] It, too, consisted of a composer, a poet, a ballet master, and singers, including several veterans from Ferrari's troupe.[33] Unlike Ferrari's, however, it was not in any sense a traveling company. Its composer and leader was Francesco Cavalli, a Venetian who had already made something of a name for himself in the realm of sacred music at San Marco and was soon to dominate the operatic field. His chief associates — the librettist Orazio Persiani and the ballet master (scenographer) Balbi — were also local residents, and most of the singers belonged to the San Marco chapel.[34] The new company began its activity with a collaboration between two of its founders. Cavalli's setting of *Le nozze di Teti e di Peleo*, a libretto by Persiani, was performed in 1639, during the same season as *Delia* and *Armida* at SS. Giovanni e Paolo.

In the space of three seasons Venice had seen five new operas, by three librettists and three composers, at two theaters. These numbers were to increase dramatically the very next year, 1640, when a third theater, the Teatro S.

"Unveröffentlichtes von Nicodemus Tessin d. J.: Reisenotizen über Barock-Theater in Venedig und Piazzola," *Kleine Schriften der Gesellschaft für Theatergeschichte* 21 (1966): 14–41. These descriptions and figures are all cited and discussed in the appropriate chapters of Mangini, *I teatri di Venezia*.

31. Chenda was an architect as well as a scenographer of vast experience. In addition to building the theater in Padua where *Ermiona* took place, he had been responsible, earlier, for constructing a theater in his native Ferrara. He worked at SS. Giovanni e Paolo until his death in 1640 and was followed there by other illustrious scenographers: Giovanni Burnacini, responsible for *La finta savia* in 1643 and possibly, before that, *Le nozze d'Enea*, *Narciso ed Ecco immortalati*, *Gli amori di Giasone e d' Isifile*, and *L'incoronazione di Poppea*, was succeeded, though only briefly, by Giacomo Torelli; see p. 102 below. For more on Chenda and Burnacini, see Bjurström, *Torelli*, 44–45; also Mancini, Muraro, and Povoledo, eds., *Illu-

sione e pratica teatrale, 54–62. Strozzi had been writing dramatic texts for Monteverdi since the late 1620s.

32. See Morelli and Walker, "Tre controversie," 98–101. The company was founded on 14 April 1638, that is, some nine months before its first production. It dissolved in 1644.

33. Bisucci, from *Andromeda* and *Maga*; Felicita Uga, from *Ermiona* and *Maga*, whose presence in Venice, since 1634, anticipated Ferrari's by some years (see n. 17 above); and Balbi, who had participated in all three previous productions. Though a choreographer, Balbi may have acted as scenographer in this company.

34. See Morelli and Walker, "Tre controversie," 98, 102. Mangini, *I teatri di Venezia*, 40, claims that after Ferrari's departure, the Tron brothers took over the running of their theater themselves. But this seems to have happened after Cavalli's first few seasons.

Moisè, owned by the Zane family, opened its doors to opera.[35] Its two productions raised the number of new operas in a single season to at least four (most likely five): *Arianna* (Rinuccini/Monteverdi) and *Il pastor regio* (Ferrari/Ferrari) at S. Moisè; *Adone* (Vendramin/Manelli) and probably *Il ritorno d'Ulisse* (Badoaro/Monteverdi) at SS. Giovanni e Paolo;[36] and *Gli amori d'Apollo e di Dafne* (Busenello/Cavalli) at S. Cassiano. In this year, the names of two new librettists (Vendramin, Busenello) and one new composer (Monteverdi) were added to the fast-expanding roll of opera makers.[37] Approximately five productions per season remained the norm until 1645, when theatrical entertainments and all other carnival activities were suspended by government decree because of the war with the Turks that had begun early that year.[38]

The economic arrangements supporting the individual undertakings at S. Cassiano, SS. Giovanni e Paolo, and S. Moisè differed in detail, but they shared the special tripartite, cooperative organization that characterized opera production in Venice well into the eighteenth century. Indeed, although the system developed gradually over a period of years, its origins and structure are evident in the first S. Cassiano venture. There were essentially three agents responsible for the operation: theater owners, impresarios, and artists. Theater owners, like the Tron, Zane, or Grimani, belonged to the great patrician families of Venice;

35. According to Ivanovich, *Minerva*, 399, the Teatro S. Moisè was the fourth theater to be opened in Venice, after S. Cassiano, SS. Giovanni e Paolo, and S. Salvatore; but no operas were produced at S. Salvatore until 1661. Bonlini, *Le glorie della poesia*, 21, also lists it fourth, but after the two at S. Cassiano and SS. Giovanni e Paolo.

36. Although *Ritorno* was traditionally ascribed to the 1641 season, Osthoff ("Zur Bologneser Aufführung") has argued that the 1641 Venetian performance was a revival and that the opera actually had its premiere in Venice the year before, just prior to the Bologna performance of 1640, a performance documented by *Le glorie della musica* (cited in ch. 1 above). That *Ritorno* had been performed in Venice by 1640 is documented by a reference to the opera in a book by the Incognito author Federico Malipiero published in 1640, *La peripezia d'Ulisse overo la casta Penelope* (Venice: Surian, 1640) (Lettore: "Ella fù una fatica motivatami . . . da una Musa, e da un Cigno, ch'entrambi abitando l'arene dell'Adria, ne formano appunto un richissimo Parnaso di meraviglia. M'apportò'l caso ne' Veneti Teatri a vedere l'Ulisse in Patria descritto poeticamente, e rappresentato Musicalmente con quello splendore, ch'è per renderlo memorabile in'ogni secolo. M'allettò cosi l'epico della Poesia, com'il delicato della Musica, ch'io non seppi rattenerne la penna, che non lasciassi correrla dietro'l genio. Viddi d'Omero le prodigiose fatiche rapportate dalla Grecia nella Latina Lingua. L'udij recitativamente rappresentate. L'ammirai poeticamente nella Toscana ispiegate. Parvemi, che lo portarle nella prosa fosse appunto fatica adeguata, a cui pretende co'l fuggir l'ozio d'involarsi alla carriera de' vizij"); and by the preface to the *Argomento et scenario delle nozze d'Enea* (Venice, 1640) (Appendix I.9a).

37. Curiously, Ferrari's company (at least the Manelli part) seems to have been simultaneously active at S. Moisè and SS. Giovanni e Paolo in 1640. And Cavalli seems to have begun an association with S. Moisè in 1642, while he was still involved at S. Cassiano (Nino Pirrotta, "The Lame Horse and the Coachman: News of the Operatic Parnassus in 1642," *Essays*, 333–34). Contracts were apparently not as exclusive as they became later. It is worth noting that many of the composers and librettists, and probably the singers as well, moved back and forth between theaters with some frequency. Ferrari, for example, moved from S. Cassiano (1637, 1638), to SS. Giovanni e Paolo (1639), to S. Moisè (1640, 1641). Manelli moved from S. Cassiano (1637, 38) to SS. Giovanni e Paolo (1639–40). Monteverdi worked at S. Moisè (1640) and SS. Giovanni e Paolo (1640, 1641, 1643). Busenello moved from S. Cassiano (1640, 1641) to SS. Giovanni e Paolo (1643).

38. See Bianconi and Walker, "Dalla 'Finta pazza,' " 416 n. 154.

they invested in the buildings themselves, but generally delegated responsibility for what went on in them to an impresario—or a society (like Cavalli's) or troupe (like Ferrari's)—with whom they contracted seasonally. That party either supplied itself or hired at its own expense singers, players, and workers of various kinds. Besides paying the rent, the impresario or society covered operating costs for such necessities as scenery and illumination. The expenses were offset and profits made by receipts from the rental of boxes and by ticket sales.

The capital derived from box rentals depended on the number of boxes as well as the prices charged for them—which, at least in some theaters, depended on the position of the box. In both these matters individual theaters differed considerably. Figures for the earliest period are lacking, but by 1666 S. Cassiano had ninety-eight boxes (twenty-nine in each of the first two tiers), which rented for twenty-five ducats each.[39] SS. Giovanni e Paolo, although the "most magnificent" of the theaters, seems to have had fewer, only seventy-seven, which were arranged in four rows.[40] The number of boxes in S. Moisè during this period is unknown, but the theater had the reputation of being uncomfortably small, so presumably there were fewer, if any.[41]

Most boxes were rented in perpetuity, but paid for on a seasonal basis by members of the aristocracy, Venetian and foreign. Individual tickets, purchased nightly, were of two kinds: the *bollettini* were required for everyone entering the theater, including box-holders; *scagni*, purchased for an additional sum, entitled

39.   According to *b*. 194: 18. See Giazotto, "La guerra dei palchi," 260; Bianconi and Walker, "Production," 223. The importance of the income derived from box rental is emphasized in Ivanovich, *Minerva*, 401–4, 410.

40.   *B*. 194: 135. But the original number may have been higher, since in 1645 Giovanni Grimani indicated that two boxes (per row?) needed to be eliminated because the people in the end boxes could not hear the singers well, presumably because they were too far over the stage; see n. 86 below. The plan of the theater, drawn by Tommaso Bezzi, which dates from late in the century (after 1678), shows boxes extending over the stage to the sides (illustration in Mangini, *I teatri di Venezia*, no. 15). The number of boxes, in any case, was increased to 5 rows of 29 each, or 145, by 1683 (as reported by Cramailles in *Le Mercure galant*); see n. 30 above.

41.   Pirrotta ("Theater, Sets, and Music," *Essays*, 262) interpreted two pieces of information provided in the prologue to *Sidonio e Dorisbe*, performed at S. Moisè in 1642, as indicating that the theater had no boxes (in fact, he suggests [263–64] that other theaters may not have had boxes either until later). The first is a description of the theater as a "narrow and poorly decorated room." The second is a stage di-

rection indicating that Tempo, one of the characters speaking in the prologue, is to take a place near some ladies, whose gambling he has interrupted. Pirrotta cited 1688 as the date when boxes (two tiers) were added, but this may have occurred earlier, in 1668, when, according to Taddeo Wiel (*I teatri musicali veneziani nel settecento: Catalogo delle opere in musica rappresentate nel secolo XVIII in Venezia [1701–1800]* [Venice, 1897], XLIII), the theater was entirely rebuilt. It must have had boxes by 1673, since a letter from 4 February of that year to Duke Johann Friedrich of Brunswick-Lüneburg from his agent in Venice, Francesco Massi, discusses the rental of boxes in S. Moisè as well as in S. Cassiano, SS. Giovanni e Paolo, and S. Samuele (Appendix IIIB.19). Another theater famous for its small size, S. Apollinare, had only forty-eight boxes, in three tiers, which rented for twenty ducats per season (*b*. 194: 92–102). Mangini (*I teatri di Venezia*, 63 n. 4) claims that the Teatro Novissimo did not have any boxes at all, but this is belied by the documents reporting their construction, quoted in Benedetti, "Il teatro musicale," 200–201; see also Bjurström, *Torelli*, 36. For a glimpse of the politics involved in box rental, see Appendix IIIB.20.

the holders to seats in the parterre.[42] The artists, who originally participated in the running of the theater (such as Ferrari's troupe or Cavalli's), eventually became employees of the impresario. Among them, the librettist became financially independent of the others, deriving his income exclusively from libretto sales and the largesse of his dedicatees.

Despite the proliferation of theaters and new works, opera remained confined to the carnival season.[43] Even allowing for a reasonable rehearsal period, opera companies were essentially unemployed for at least half the year. This hardly presented a problem for Cavalli and his troupe, since they were employed elsewhere in Venice. But several members of Ferrari's company, including Ferrari himself, did not yet have fixed posts. For several off-seasons they continued the itinerant ways that had brought them to Padua and Venice in the first place, producing four of their Venetian operas in Bologna in 1640 and 1641, and two in Milan several years later.[44]

The Scenario and the Libretto

Several of the operas of 1639 and 1640, like *Andromeda* and *La maga fulminata*, were memorialized by librettos issued after the performances. Two of them, however, also received advance publicity. *Delia* and *Le nozze di Teti e di Peleo* were both announced by a new kind of publication, one that was to become quite common during the next decade or so: the scenario. The *Argomento e scenario della Delia* and the *Breve espositione della festa di Teti e Peleo*, slim pamphlets of thirty-three and twenty-three pages respectively, were printed before their operas were performed (*da rappresentarsi*). The former bears the date 5 November 1638, whereas the libretto is dated more than three months later, 20 January 1639. The latter, undated, probably appeared closer to the date of the libretto, 24 January 1639, with which it is usually bound, though it was clearly a separate publication with its own title page and pagination. The dedications of both scenarios were signed by the librettists (figs. 9, 10).

42. See Bianconi, *Seventeenth Century*, 182–89, and Morelli and Walker, "Tre controversie," 103–4; also Ivanovich, *Minerva*, 401–4, 410.

43. On the unusual reopening of the Teatro Novissimo after Easter, see n. 73 below.

44. The works performed in Bologna were *Delia* and *Il ritorno d'Ulisse* in 1640, and *La maga fulminata* and *Il pastor regio* in 1641; those performed in Milan were *Il pastor regio* and *Delia* in 1646–47 (when the Venetian theaters were closed); they had been given in Genoa in 1645 (along with Cavalli's *Egisto*); *Il pastor regio* was performed again in Piacenza in 1646; see Bianconi and Walker, "Dalla 'Finta pazza,'" passim, and Armando Fabio Ivaldi, "Gli Adorno e l'hostaria-

teatro del Falcone di Genova (1600–1680)," *RIM* 15 (1981): 136, 143, 144, 147–51. Ferrari's was the first of a number of traveling opera companies that were responsible for bringing Venetian opera to the provinces and making it a national (later international) phenomenon; see Bianconi and Walker, "Dalla 'Finta pazza,'" 397–405. The name "Febiarmonici," which came to be used generically for such groups, originally referred to a specific one associated with productions of a particular opera, *La finta pazza*. Ferrari's company was referred to more descriptively as the "annuale comitiva dei più leggiadri Musici dell'Italia" (in Manelli's dedication of the Bologna edition of *La maga fulminata* [1641]).

These scenarios essentially fulfill the promise of their titles. They contain a synopsis and a running description of the action, material that had been incorporated, along with the actual text of the drama, within the more ambitious librettos of *Andromeda* and *La maga fulminata*. In addition, the scenario for *Delia* includes a lengthy preface by the author clearly aimed at arousing public interest in the forthcoming production. It also calls attention to the unprecedented event of a second new production within the same season, Ferrari's *Armida*. This was all part of a public relations effort on behalf of the new theater. Strozzi did try, however, to disguise the rather blatant propagandistic purpose of the scenario by suggesting that it had the practical function of providing basic information about the action for the benefit of the scene designer: "Because the sublime intellects of Your Lordship [the dedicatee, Ercole Danesi] and of Signor Alfonso Rivarola [the scene designer] cannot philosophize about the stage-machinery if I do not reveal to you what I have been doing day to day with my pen, I am sending you this summary of my Delia" (Appendix I.15a).[45] Accordingly, the dedication is followed by a scene-by-scene plot description and an explanation of its significance. Then the publicity campaign begins in full force:

> Signor Giovanni Grimani . . . has chosen Delia to be the first opera to appear in that most noble theater, which he, with such generosity of spirit, has caused to be born, so to speak, in the space of a few days in this city of Venice, and which is destined to last many years for the sole benefit of music. And indeed it seemed to me that the stones joined together by themselves, as if induced by the harmony of new Amphions, so little was the effort with which this ample and solid theater rose from the foundations; in which I hear that a production of Signor Benedetto Ferrari is also scheduled to be performed this year, a noteworthy effort, because without using either words or ideas from Tasso, he has simultaneously composed and embellished with music a new Armida, which will be, as the other two of these past years, the marvel of the stage, since it is currently being ennobled by the machines of Your Lordship and Signor Alfonso, and honored (as will be the Delia that precedes it) by the voices of some of the most melodious swans of our Italy. I send you, in conclusion, the number of characters that make up my Delia. (Appendix I.15c)

The scenario concludes with a wonderfully informal and informative postscript, redolent of Strozzi's characteristic advertising tone:

> I was forgetting to tell you that Signor Francesco Manelli romano, who, as you know, to great applause clothed Andromeda and La maga fulminata of Signor Benedetto Ferrari with music, has demonstrated this time an excess of his affection and the summit of his talent in honoring my Delia. I know what I am saying: Venice will be astonished to hear what heights are reached by the effort Signor Manelli has made in this work. He has an admirable way of portraying the words [*un'imitatione*

45. Atypically, the dedicatee collaborated on the scene designs and staging. Strozzi's remark calls spe-cial attention to the scenography, obviously an at-traction of this—any—production.

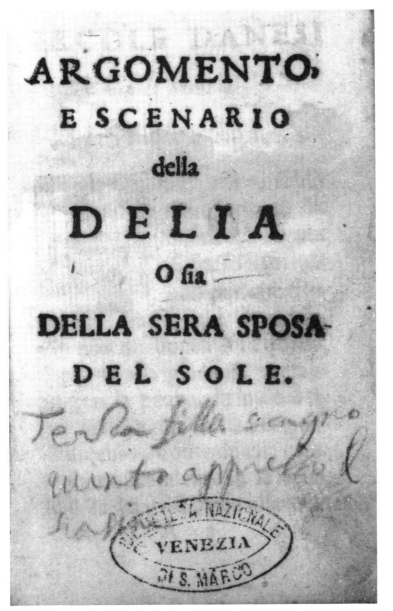

ARGOMENTO,

E SCENARIO

della

DELIA

O fia

DELLA SERA SPOSA-

DEL SOLE.

9. Giulio Strozzi, *Delia* (Venice, 1639), scenario title page.

BREVE
ESPOSITIONE
Della festa Teatrale

Del Signor
ORATIO PERSIANI,

Posta in Musica dal Sig.
FRANCESCO CAVALLI

Da Recitarsi nel Teatro
DI S. CASCIANO.

L' Opera è intitolata
LE NOZZE DI TETI,
e di Peleo.

10. Orazio Persiani, *Le nozze di Teti e di Peleo* (Venice, 1639), scenario title page.

di parole mirabile], a distinctive, varied, and delightful harmonic style [*un'armonia apropria, varia, e dilettevole*]; in short, when this effort comes off the press it will be known whether I have spoken out of self-interest or rather, instead, have cheated the truth. (Appendix I.15d)

Beyond the utilitarian function of identifying the composer, this particular passage serves also to justify Strozzi's own efforts. By invoking its two predecessors, Strozzi places his work in the context of an already established, if recent, operatic tradition, thereby claiming a legitimacy based on successful precedent. *Andromeda* and *La maga fulminata* buttress not only his *Delia* but the whole enterprise at SS. Giovanni e Paolo.

The *Peleo* scenario does not share the self-advertising tone of *Delia*, but it does provide a few important bits of practical information about the performance not given in the libretto—information clearly intended to attract a local audience: the place of the performance, the name of the composer, and the general provenance of the singers, who were both foreigners and local (some "conceduti all'auttore da diversi potentati," others "stipendiati nella Cappella della Serenissima Republica Veneta").[46]

These little volumes, the *Delia* scenario in particular, were evidently responding to a new force in the marketplace: theatrical rivalry. With two theaters now in operation, competition had begun. The function of scenarios, however, was not limited to advertising; once they had attracted an audience, the synopsis and scene-by-scene descriptions helped it to follow the complicated action on the stage. As publications, scenarios had many practical advantages over librettos. They were much shorter, most subsequent examples comprising fewer than twenty-four pages, or a single duodecimo fascicle, in contrast to several times that number in most librettos, and so they were cheaper to print. They could also be produced far more quickly. And, since they did not contain any actual dialogue, they could easily be published in advance of a performance, going to press as soon as the librettist had outlined the action, before he had completed the versification.

A melancholy witness to the largely practical function of scenarios is their poor rate of survival. Lacking even the meager literary merits of a libretto, and having no permanent value outside the particular performance they described, they were likely to have been disposed of immediately after the performance, like our present-day playbills: theatrical ephemera, pale historical records of a single past event, and not especially worth saving.[47]

46. This confirms Ottonelli's point about borrowing locals; see p. 72 above.
47. Because of their poor rate of survival, the general dearth of scenarios after the 1640s is not absolute proof that they never existed. I have been able to locate only nineteen, covering the period from 1638 to 1655, a few in unique copies. These are listed in Rosand, "Opera Scenario," appendix.

In most cases, scenarios were soon followed by librettos. For at least two early operas, however, *Il ritorno d'Ulisse* (1640) and *Le nozze d'Enea* (1641), commemorative librettos seem never to have been published,[48] and for several other operas, including *Didone* and *L'incoronazione di Poppea*, librettos were published so long after the scenarios that they can hardly be considered documents of the same occasion.[49] Significantly, and unusually, however, there are contemporary manuscripts of all four of these librettos, some of them in multiple copies.[50] These rather anomalous examples involve the works of only three men: Badoaro, Busenello, and the anonymous author of *Le nozze d'Enea*—the three most academic of the early librettists. Clearly their failure or reluctance to publish their librettos—or even, in two cases, to admit authorship—was no coincidence. It is likely that these aristocratic authors hesitated to identify themselves with the commercial aspect of publication. Their elaborate defenses of the genre itself suggest that their reluctance to publish may have been compounded by some sense of discomfort, which made them unwilling to pass off their products as literature.[51]

Similar discomfort probably accounts for the publication of a number of early librettos under pseudonyms, or else by someone other than the author, such as the printer or stage designer. Whatever the reason for dissembling or obscuring authorship, by the mid 1640s any reluctance, modesty, or squeamishness on the part of librettists, no matter how aristocratic, had been overcome by a desire to participate in the action.

Scenarios filled the twin needs of publicity and practical assistance for about a decade, from 1638 to shortly after the middle of the century—that is, during the period in which *dramma per musica* was assuming its identity. By 1650, however, they had virtually disappeared; their demise coincided with the increasing trend toward publication of librettos before rather than after performances. These librettos incorporated the functions of the scenario within their more ambitious purpose. Some of them even specifically claimed for themselves one of those functions, that of helping the audience to follow the plot:

48. A scenario survives for *Le nozze d'Enea* but not for *Il ritorno d'Ulisse*, although one may well have been published and lost.

49. But no scenario survives for *Apollo e Dafne*, whose libretto was also published well after the performance.

50. Those for *Poppea* have been studied by Chiarelli (" 'L'incoronazione di Poppea' "); those of *Il ritorno* by Osthoff ("Zu den Quellen"); those of *Le nozze* have not yet been studied, but would reward comparative analysis. Other manuscript librettos that would bear further study are those of *Apollo e Dafne* in I-Pu, I-RVI, I-TVco; and *Didone* in I-Fn I-Vmc. For a complete list of these manuscripts, see Rosand, "Opera Scenario," 340 n. 8.

51. Badoaro's name is nowhere evident in the libretto of *Ulisse errante*; only his academic alias identifies him. But he gives himself away by referring to his *Il ritorno d'Ulisse*, which he had already (though not publicly) admitted having written in the letter to Monteverdi that prefaces one of the manuscript copies of the libretto (Appendix I.7).

The desire was born in me to have [this text] printed in order to satisfy those who enjoy such things [as operas] more when they are accompanied by reading. (Appendix I.8n)

I composed the present work to be recited at the Teatro Novissimo, which, since it was to be published for the greater convenience of the spectators, I wished to bring into the world adorned with the name of Your Illustrious Lordship. (Appendix I.23b)

It is obvious from their front matter that librettos, unlike scenarios, represented the author's investment.[52] His name was featured prominently on the title page, to the exclusion of that of any of the other collaborators, and he signed the dedication. Other information about him, irrelevant to the specific performance but flattering to his image, was often included, such as a list of his works or encomiastic sonnets by other authors in his honor. Not only did librettos frequently fail even in prefatory material to provide the names of composer and scene designer, but a number of them conspicuously lack significant information relating to the specific performance, such as the name of the theater.[53] Indeed, some point distinctly away from the particular performance to a loftier end, revealing their aspirations to the permanence of literature. Scenarios, in contrast, tended to emphasize practical information, and they were as likely to mention the composer, singers, and stage designer as the librettist.

The financial involvement of the librettist in the printing of his text is confirmed by Ivanovich, who devoted an entire chapter of his "Memorie" to the subject, "Qual fu prima, e qual'è al presente l'utile dell'Autore del Drama." Looking back on the first Venetian operas, Ivanovich saw them from the jaded perspective of a witness to dozens of subsequent works. To him they represented a golden age: "In the beginning, when *dramma per musica* first appeared in Venetian theaters, the authors were satisfied with the glory that came from applause" (Appendix II.6z). But as time went on, he continues, the number of theaters increased and there were not enough dramatists to supply them; it was then that financial rewards began to be offered to poets in order to attract them to music drama. "Because of this the custom was introduced (still current today) of leaving to the author of the drama, as a reward for his efforts, everything that is realized from the sale of the librettos printed at his expense, and from the dedication that he makes, according to his own choice, and this profit depends on the success of the opera" (Appendix II.6aa). Ivanovich's golden age,

---

52. Occasionally, under special circumstances, the investment was made by another party, such as the printer, stage designer, or theater impresario, but never the composer. See ch. 6 below.

53. Rather than naming the specific theater in which a performance took place, the libretto of *Torilda* (1648), for example, provides the generic information that it is intended "per i Veneti teatri."

if it ever existed, was shorter than his account implies. If he judged motivation by publication, perhaps he had in mind those aristocratic academics who never or only retrospectively involved themselves in the publication of their works. They were soon followed and outnumbered by authors avidly interested in publishing for profit.

A demand had to exist before a librettist would risk such an investment. During the first five years that demand was created by the success of each individual production: librettos published afterwards capitalized on it. On the other hand, printing a libretto ahead of the performance, before its success was proven, was risky; besides, it put a great deal of pressure on librettist, composer, and even on the singers. So much was done at the last moment—the musical setting, the casting, the rehearsals—that it was difficult to establish a text that accurately reflected the finished work. Within a few years, however, the cumulative success of the genre as a whole was evidently sufficient to justify advance publication of librettos despite all the pressures. Sporadically after 1642, consistently after 1650, they appeared ahead of the performance. The rare occasions later in the century when librettos were not printed until afterwards seem always to have been the result of special circumstances. Rather than trying to establish correct texts sooner, which was an impossibility given the mechanics of operatic production, librettists developed various methods of minimizing the inevitable discrepancies between the printed librettos and the words finally sung.

The Teatro Novissimo

The first Venetian librettos, then, with a few notable exceptions, were printed after the fact, when the operas had already been produced, *rappresentato*—presumably with success. The exceptions prove the rule. Virtually all of those printed ahead of time were for operas performed at the Teatro Novissimo, a theater with its own special story and influence.[54] The fourth theater to present opera in Venice, the Novissimo differed from both its predecessors and successors in several important respects. Although it had a shorter life span than any of its competitors—only five seasons of activity can be documented—and although it produced fewer operas—only six—the Novissimo had a greater impact than any other single theater on the establishment of opera in Venice.

Unlike its predecessors, it was not a preexisting theater converted or reconstructed for use as an opera house. It was a brand-new building—hence,

---

54.   These include *La finta pazza* (1641), *Bellerofonte* (1642), and *Venere gelosa* (1643). Another, *Amore innamorato* (1642), not for the Novissimo but for S. Moisè, was also printed ahead of time, possibly to steal the thunder from a very similar opera, *La virtù* *de'strali d'Amore*, which was scheduled to compete with it at S. Cassiano; see Pirrotta, "The Lame Horse and the Coachman," *Essays*, 328. Atypically, the text of *Amore innamorato* is preceded by a complete scenario of the kind normally published separately.

undoubtedly, its name—constructed specifically to house "opere eroiche, so-lamente in musica, e non commedie" ("only heroic operas in music, not plays").[55] From its inception, the project represented a concerted effort on the part of a group of Venetian noblemen rather than a single family. Its manage-ment by committee rather than by an individual proprietor was one of its unique features.

On 30 May 1640, "diversi cavalieri," together with the patrician Luigi Michiel, had signed a contract with the Dominican monks of SS. Giovanni e Paolo agreeing to oversee construction of and to manage a theater on a property adjacent to the monastery. These "cavalieri" were members of the Accademia degli Incogniti, whose involvement with the enterprise determined the entire course of the Novissimo's brilliant though brief career.[56] We have already con-sidered the Incogniti from the point of view of their theoretical writings, which had a fundamental influence on the definition of opera as a genre; their impact on its social, practical, and economic structure, specifically through their ac-tivities at the Novissimo, was equally profound. They were largely responsible for the creation of the model spectacle that defined Venetian opera for the rest of the century. Primarily through their influence, that model combined aspects of Ottonelli's second and third categories of opera, the academic and the mer-cenary: "those presented sometimes by various gentlemen or talented citizens or learned academicians for one good reason or another" and those "presented by those mercenary musicians, actors by profession, who, organized in a com-pany, are directed and governed by one of their own, as the chief authority and head of the others" (Appendix II.3a,b). For the Incogniti hired a group of traveling musicians from Rome to carry out their program.

Individual members of the Academy like Pio Enea, Strozzi, Badoaro, and Busenello had participated in opera from the outset and were active in various theaters, but it was only at the Novissimo that the Incogniti acted as a group. Their influence permeated all aspects of the endeavor, which served as the perfect focus for their abundant energy and multiple talents. The broad base of financial support they commanded with the help of their patrician associates permitted, at least initially, a certain extravagance that could not be taken for

---

55. Its name distinguished it from the "Teatro Nuovo" in the same parish, that is, SS. Giovanni e Paolo; the pertinent documents are quoted in Mangini, *I teatri di Venezia*, 62. See also Bianconi and Walker, "Dalla 'Finta pazza,' " 415–17, and Bene-detti, "Il teatro musicale," 200–209. On the Novis-simo in general, see Guglielmina Verardo Tieri, "Il teatro Novissimo: Storia di 'mutationi, macchine, e musiche,' " *NRMI* 10 (1976): 555–95.

56. The story is somewhat more complicated. On 2 October, 1640, three noblemen, Girolamo Lando, Giacomo Marcello, and Giacomo da Mosto, urged

that the monks lease the theater for 200 ducats to one Geronimo Lappoli, "forestiero," on the condition that only operas be performed ("non intendendo, che per nisun modo si rappresentino comedie buffone-sche o di altra natura, ma solo delle sopradette ero-iche opere in canto"). In the summer of 1642, when the friars agreed to widen the theater by twelve feet, the contract was renegotiated at 300 ducats. Lappoli renewed it for two more years in March of 1643, but the rent for the second year—1645—was never paid. See Bianconi and Walker, "Dalla 'Finta pazza,' " 415; also Benedetti, "Il teatro musicale," 203–4.

granted in other commercial theatrical efforts.[57] Moreover, the fame and reputation of the group lent enormous prestige to the undertaking. Most important, the Academy possessed a built-in mechanism for publicity, a pool of writers with well-lubricated pens who could supply a full range of verbal resources, everything from libretto texts to advertising copy. The internally generated publicity surrounding the inaugural production at the Novissimo, *La finta pazza*, was sufficient to assure opera an indelible spot on the cultural map of Europe.

The most striking aspect of Incognito publicity, however, and their most fundamental aim, was political. In keeping with their close association with the ruling Venetian patriciate, these writers repeatedly asserted a connection between the magnificence of Venetian operatic spectacles and the splendor of the Serenissima herself. Their involvement in these spectacles was a projection of their patriotism, a way of polishing the image of Venice. A connection between splendor on the stage and the image of the city had been implicit in the patrician involvement in earlier theatrical ventures as well, particularly in the three other opera houses, but it was made explicit for the first time in connection with the Novissimo. The Incogniti not only participated in the phenomenon, they defined it. It was the Incogniti who laid the groundwork for the political interpretation of the development of Venetian opera advanced some thirty years later by Ivanovich. As we shall see, much of the verbiage surrounding the individual productions at the theater was devoted to embroidering an elaborate defense of the traditional myth of Venice.

When the Novissimo opened its doors during Carnival of 1641, Venice's fifth consecutive opera season, it faced stiff competition from the three older theaters. S. Cassiano, still being served by Cavalli's troupe, was planning to mount a production of *Didone* (Busenello/Cavalli); SS. Giovanni e Paolo had two Monteverdi operas scheduled, *Le nozze d'Enea* and a revival of *Il ritorno d'Ulisse*, probably performed by Ferrari's and Manelli's troupe;[58] and S. Moisè was preparing a production of Ferrari's *La ninfa avara*.[59]

La finta pazza, with which the Novissimo vociferously initiated its activity in early January, became the first and possibly the greatest operatic "hit" of the century. It set the standard for measuring operatic success. The production

---

57. An indication of the kind of indirect patrician support that sustained the Novissimo venture is the fact that Giacomo Badoaro was one of Lappoli's creditors when he defaulted on rental payments in 1645. See Bianconi and Walker, "Dalla 'Finta pazza,'" 415, and Benedetti, "Il teatro musicale," 205.
58. The assumption is based on the fact that they had taken *Ritorno* to Bologna the previous season.

59. The total of four operas at theaters other than the Novissimo confirms the information in a letter from Prince Matthias de' Medici, who reported in 1641 that he had heard "tutte queste Comedie cantate, che sono al numero di Cinque"; see Bianconi, *Seventeenth Century*, 193; also Bianconi and Walker, "Dalla 'Finta pazza,'" 402 n. 105.

combined the theatrical know-how of arguably the most experienced and able librettist in the business, Giulio Strozzi (fig. 11),[60] possibly the moving force behind the whole Novissimo venture, and the formidable talents of three newcomers to the Rialto. These were the scene designer Giacomo Torelli, "engineer to the doge," who, after several spectacular productions at the Novissimo, was called to France in the service of the queen;[61] the Parmesan composer and impresario Francesco Sacrati, who subsequently collaborated on four more operas in Venice and was compared flatteringly with Monteverdi; and his protégée, the soprano Anna Renzi, who became the first "prima donna" in operatic history.[62]

The success of *La finta pazza* was choreographed carefully from the start. In accord with recently established custom, a scenario was printed before the premiere, its dedication signed 4 January 1641. Strozzi was by now an old hand at writing publicity for the inauguration of theaters, having performed this function for SS. Giovanni e Paolo two years before. But the title page of the scenario for *La finta pazza* is especially—and uniquely—explicit in its claim for attention:

> ARGOMENTO E SCENARIO DELLA FINTA PAZZA. *Drama di Giulio Strozzi.*
> Da rappresentarsi con solenne apparato di Musiche, Macchine, e Scene, il presente Carnovale, dell'Anno Mille e seicento quarantuno, nel Theatro Novissimo della Città di Venetia. (fig. 12)[63]

Atypically, however, and for the first time in Venice, Strozzi also published a full libretto before the premiere, which also contained a considerable measure of propaganda.

---

60. Strozzi, the author most recently of *Delia*, had been writing dramatic texts for years. He had undoubtedly improved his skills with the help of Monteverdi, his collaborator on the abortive *La finta pazza Licori* (1627) (see Gary Tomlinson, "Twice Bitten, Thrice Shy: Monteverdi's 'finta' *Finta pazza*," *JAMS* 36 [1983]: 303–11); *I cinque fratelli* (1628), a non-theatrical work; and *Proserpina rapita* (1630) (see Paolo Fabbri, *Monteverdi* [Turin, 1985], 280–83).

61. On Torelli in Paris, see Bjurström, *Torelli*, 122–95; also Cesare Molinari, *Le nozze degli dei: Un saggio sul grande spettacolo italiano nel seicento* (Rome,

1968), 163–70; and Raimondo Guarino, *La tragedia e le macchine: "Andromède" di Corneille e Torelli* (Rome, 1982).

62. On Sacrati, see Claudio Sartori, "Un fantomatico compositore per un'opera che forse non era un'opera," *NRMI* 5 (1971): 788–98. The comparison to Monteverdi occurs in the preface to Badoaro's *Ulisse errante* (1644). On Anna Renzi, see Claudio Sartori, "La prima diva della lirica italiana: Anna Renzi," *NRMI* 2 (1968): 430–52, and ch. 8 below.

63. It is the only scenario with so much information on the title page; normally the title of the work sufficed. See Rosand, "Opera Scenario," appendix.

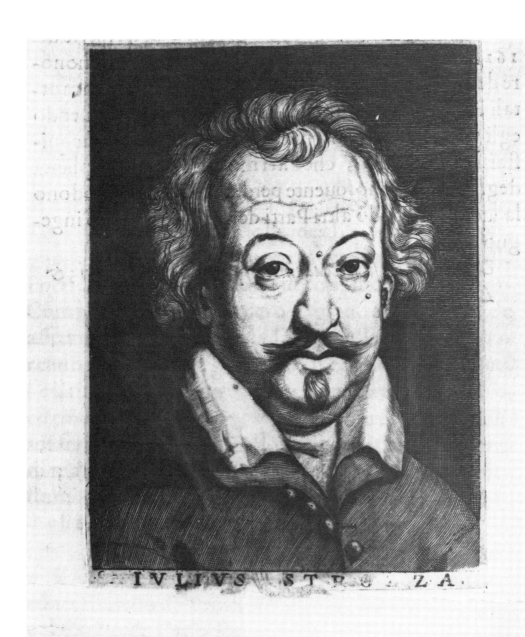

IVLIVS STROZZA

Carmine struct a tuo tremulis dum stabit in vndis
Urbs immota, tuus, Strozze, manabit honos.

11. Portrait of Giulio Strozzi, from *Le glorie degli Incogniti* (Venice, 1647).

ARGOMENTO,

E SCENARIO

DELLA

FINTA PAZZA.

Drama di Giulio Strozzi.

Da rappresentarsi con solenne apparato di Musiche, Macchine, e Scene, il presente Carnouale dell' Anno Mille e seicento quarantuno, nel Theatro Nouissimo della Città di Venetia.

Con Licenza de' Superiori.

IN VENETIA,
M DC XXXXI.

─────────────

Per Gio: Battista Surian

12. Giulio Strozzi, *La finta pazza* (Venice, 1641), scenario title page.

In his preface to this libretto, Strozzi provides extensive information about the production. He begins with a little self-promotion, linking the work to his previous successes and complimenting himself for his management of the plot: "This is the eighth theatrical effort that I find myself having made; five of them have already trod the boards more than once,[64] and in this one I have succeeded quite well in untying more than one knot without magic, and without resorting to supernatural and divine assistance" (Appendix I. 16a).[65] In addition, he praises in elaborate if obviously rhetorical terms the contribution of Sacrati and his band of singers, above all Anna Renzi:

> The poverty of my ideas is made up for by the treasure of the music of Sig. Francesco Sacrati from Parma, who has known how to adorn my verses marvelously with his harmonies, and just as miraculously he has also been able to assemble an excellent chorus of so many most exquisite swans of Italy; and all the way from the Tiber, in the most extreme cold of a horrid season he has brought to the Adriatic a most gentle Siren, who sweetly steals the heart and charms the eyes and ears of the listeners. The city of Venice must be grateful to the diligence of Sig. Sacrati for the favor of the most skillful Signora Anna. (Appendix I. 16c)[66]

Although neither libretto nor scenario mentions Torelli by name, the scenario refers frequently to the magical effects of the stage designs (which, as we have already seen, were atypically mentioned on its title page). Torelli's contribution received its due in another volume, the *Cannocchiale* (telescope) *per la finta pazza* by one "M. B. di G." This elaborate publication, of fifty-five pages, vividly describes the visual effects of the opera. Probably published after Easter, certainly after the opera season had closed, it was evidently intended to augment the effect of the publicity campaign for the opera and the theater by prolonging the memory of its success.

---

64. Besides *Delia* (1639) and *Proserpina rapita* (1630), he may have meant *Erotilla tragedia* (1621), *Il natal d'Amore, Anachronismo* (1621), and possibly *La finta pazza Licori* in dialogue form, as it was apparently performed in Palazzo Mocenigo in 1627 (see Monteverdi's letter of 5 June 1627 in *Lettere*, ed. de' Paoli, 253; English trans. in *The Letters of Claudio Monteverdi*, ed. Denis Stevens [Cambridge, 1980], no. 96, p. 323). *Erotilla* and *Il natal d'Amore* were spoken dramas, but the text of part of the latter (3.1), revised, was set to music by Giovanni Rovetta in 1629. Strozzi's bibliography, including works that were never published, is given in *Le glorie degli Incogniti*, 281–83.

65. This may be a competitive reference to the plots of earlier Venetian operas, nearly all of which involved magical or supernatural solutions. *La finta pazza* does include divine characters, but they do not resolve the plot. For a libretto and facsimile of the score, see *La finta pazza*, ed. Bianconi and Walker.

66. Sacrati's role as head of the troupe of performers was evidently similar to Ferrari's, but he was probably not financially responsible to the theater owners, as both Ferrari and Cavalli had been. His function as impresario at the Novissimo—and the preeminence of that theater—is documented by an interesting letter from him to Matthias de' Medici dated Venice, 19 November 1641, or slightly more than a month before the opening of the new season: "Qui è già calato mezzo Roma, fra cantatrici, e musici, ma sin'hora poco v'è di buono, ed io posso gloriarmi che non è venuto, ne verrà alcun personaggio quest'anno, che prima a me non siimi offerto." And he continues by reporting that Matthias's singer, Michele Grasseschi, had offered himself and been accepted, as had been the "castratino" of Archduke Leopold (letter in Sartori, "Un fantomatico compositore," 798).

This becomes clear in the volume itself. The cryptic author's initials are those of Maiolino Bisaccioni, count of Genoa, Incognito, and eventually the author of several librettos in his own right.[67] Bisaccioni begins by justifying the publication of this unusual volume, the very title of which declares its purpose of bringing the spectacle closer to the reader. The scenario as well as the libretto, he says, have both been published in order to serve those members of the audience too far away to appreciate the production, either because of absence—never having made it to the theater at all—or because of distance—having attended the performance, but being seated too far from the stage (thus implying that the theater was uncommonly large). But these publications did not do justice to the machines, the costumes, or the crowds, a shortcoming that the *Cannocchiale* would attempt to rectify. Bisaccioni hoped that even the remotest of readers would be able to imagine what was seen by the front-row audience in the theater.[68]

Although obviously intended to serve as propaganda for the Teatro Novissimo, and especially, perhaps, as publicity for the scene designer, Torelli, the *Cannocchiale* supplies, in passing, a number of interesting details about the brief history of opera in Venice up to that point. It gives an idea of the kind of competition that was already rampant, competition that its very publication documents. And it asserts explicitly for the first time the relationship between opera and "the miraculous city of Venice" that was so essential to the development of the genre there, emphasizing the function of the art as a projection of the Venetian self-image: "May the eyes of those even in the most distant and secluded foreign countries enjoy in these pages what eyes and ears have enjoyed in this city, which in its every aspect surpasses the bounds of the marvelous" (Appendix I.17b). The subject of the final phrase is the city of Venice rather than the spectacle itself. This is part of the litany of the myth. The book claims to address a readership extending from Venice to Italy at large and the entire world.

In the past, theaters may have opened in other places as well, and a single one was sufficient to render a people famous and memorable for an entire century. But Venice has rejoiced in no fewer than four at the same time, all

67. These included *Ercole in Lidia* (1645), the last opera to be performed at the Novissimo, *Semiramide in India* (1648), at S. Cassiano, and *Orithia* (1650), at SS. Apostoli. Neither the *Cannocchiale* nor any of his librettos appears in the bibliography of his works in *Le glorie degli Incogniti*. For his bibliography, see V. Castronovo, "Maiolino Bisaccioni," *DBI* 10 (Rome, 1968): 639–43.

68. "I considered these days, that Sig. Giulio Strozzi's composition of the *Finta pazza*, the machines invented by Sig. Iacomo Torelli, and the mu-sic woven for them by Sig. Francesco Sacrati were a sky worthy of being contemplated by everyone, but so far from so many people that it would diminish the value for the many who came to view so noble an undertaking if one did not make it possible for everyone to see and admire it; the scenario was printed, and also the libretto, but the machines and the costumes and the actions remained far from the view of the audience, and thus unappreciated" (Appendix I.17a).

competing with one another in size, scenography, music, staging, and machines (Appendix I.17c). Bisaccioni's rather gradual historical buildup culminates predictably in a bold demonstration of the superiority of the Novissimo to all other theaters, a superiority that relies in part on the perfection of its construction, carried out with the help of Torelli.

> The last of these [theaters], which as it happens was called the Novissimo, surpassed all belief because in the space of six months it was built from the foundations and perfected with the assistance, for its construction as well as for the sets and machines, of Sig. Giacomo Torelli from Fano; who came to exercise his talents in military matters in the service of this August Senate, and, impatient of idleness, has shown what his talent is capable of. (Appendix I.17d)[69]

After these general remarks, the *Cannocchiale* moves to specific description of the opera itself, concentrating primarily on the staging, the marvels of the machinery, the speed and smoothness of the transformations (one of them so simple that "a single fifteen-year-old boy set it in motion"), and the success of the pictorial illusion.[70] It also comments on the singers, adding to the information provided in Strozzi's preface to the libretto. Several remarks on the star of the show, Anna Renzi, amplify what we know of her from other sources: "Signora Anna Renzi from Rome, a young woman as skillful in acting as she is excellent in music, as cheerful in feigning madness as she is wise in knowing how to imitate it, and modest in all her habits" (Appendix I.17e). The part of Acchille was played by a "young castrato from Rome (like all the other musicians brought in from various places) of beautiful appearance, who resembled an Amazon in his mixture of warlike spirit and feminine delicacy" (Appendix I.17j).[71] Bisaccioni also singled out a singer from Pistoia for special praise, reporting that he sang "so delicately that the souls of the listeners, as if drawn through the portals of the ears, raised themselves to heaven to assist in the enjoyment of such sweetness" (Appendix I.17i).

One of the most important contributions of the *Cannocchiale* is the insight it offers into the effect of the work on the audience, most of whom attended two, three, or even four performances (Appendix I.17f). The scenery was so well painted that the audience forgot that they were in Venice, the illusion so overpowering that "the eye did not know where to stop, for that shallow scenic space knew how to feign an immensity of sea and land" (Appendix I.17h). Such

---

69. Torelli's participation as architect of the Novissimo is confirmed in a letter now in the Biblioteca Correr, Venice, quoted in full in Mangini, *I teatri di Venezia*, 63.

70. "[U]n solo Giovanetto di quindici anni le dava il moto" (*Cannocchiale*, 21). These descriptions are quoted at length by Mangini, *I teatri di Venezia*, 64–65, and Bjurström, *Torelli*, 53–58.

71. This may have been the first operatic appearance of the Roman castrato Atto Melani (born 1626); see Bianconi and Walker, "Dalla 'Finta pazza,' " 414 n. 147.

was the art of the scene painter that the eye was deceived into thinking that painting was sculpture, that flatness was depth (Appendix I.17k).

Bisaccioni attempted to recreate the excitement of being in the theater, of actually experiencing the work as it unfolded: "When the theater was filled to its utmost capacity with spectators, who were impatiently awaiting the movement of the curtain, a sinfonia was begun, of instruments played no less expertly than sweetly, after which the curtain rose with incredible rapidity" (Appendix I.17g).[72] His description concludes with a publicist's confirmation of the success of the work that borders on the tautological. The opera's fame has caused unusually large crowds to gather in Venice—an implicit credit to the efficacy of the advance advertising.

> The public's desire to see it again never ended; and thus, however many times it was repeated, the place was crowded with people, and many were led to curse their own laziness when they arrived and had to leave because they could not find any place to sit. Nor did the long period between the end of Carnival and Easter lessen the desire in the city to see such an applauded work again, even though familiarity normally breeds contempt; and thus it was necessary to reopen the theater and perform it a number of times, which further spread the fame of this delightful spectacle to the cities of Italy and beyond, and was the reason that, quite exceptionally, Venice was filled ten days early with the crowds that normally gather for the devotions and ceremonies of Ascension Day. (Appendix I.17l)[73]

For all its *campanilismo* and self-promotion, the *Cannocchiale* can be trusted in its general outlines. Its reporting involves exaggeration rather than invention, for many of its observations can be validated from other sources. In a second printing of the libretto, a note from the publisher to the "frequente compratore" explains that he was forced "by the avidity of the readers of this work to print it twice in one month, such was the approbation received from every tongue by the *Finta pazza* at the Novissimo theater in the city of Venice, where it was performed with regal display twelve times in seventeen days" (Appendix I.16d).[74] The printing of a second edition as well as the information

---

72.   Notice that the curtain was raised, not lowered; both systems were apparently in use; see Pirrotta, "Theater, Sets, and Music," *Essays,* 256 n. 8.

73.   This passage indicates that the Novissimo reopened after Easter, at least in 1641. It seems also to have done so in 1645, when John Evelyn reported having seen a performance there in June. But this was highly unusual; see Bianconi and Walker, "Dalla 'Finta pazza,' " 416 n. 154.

74.   This was not actually the first libretto to have required a second printing—*La maga fulminata* was (see p. 77 above). That the first printing was sold out suggests it had been published before the performance; it may even have been calculated to sell out

by a limited press run. Twelve performances within seventeen days must have been a large number for 1641. (The ten performances of *Il ritorno d'Ulisse* in 1640 [Appendix I.7c] were evidently considered worth mentioning.) Although documentary evidence for number and frequency of operatic performances is scarce, the numbers must have gone up as the century progressed. In 1649 there were eighteen performances of *Giasone* (Morelli and Walker, "Tre controversie," 15), and Robert Bargrave reported sixteen performances of an opera in 1656 (Michael Tilmouth, "Music on the Travels of an English Merchant: Robert Bargrave [1628–61]," *Music and Letters* 53 [1972]: 156). In the 1658–59 season there were

provided in it about the success of the work—the number of performances, the amount of applause—continued the publicity campaign initiated by the scenario, the first libretto, and the *Cannocchiale*.[75]

The Venetian success of *La finta pazza* was enormous. But the work made its fullest impact in subsequent performances outside Venice, where it was brought, variously altered and rearranged, by a succession of traveling opera companies—most famously in Paris under the auspices of Torelli and Balbi, one of the first of a series of Italian operas performed in the French capital.[76] The glow of success enjoyed by *La finta pazza*, fanned as it was by the full deployment of the Incogniti publicity machine, continued to surround the productions of the Novissimo. Strozzi wrote no further librettos for that theater, returning to SS. Giovanni e Paolo, but Sacrati continued to serve as composer-impresario, Torelli as scenographer, and Anna Renzi as prima donna. The season of 1642 saw two new productions. The first, *Alcate*, on a libretto by Marc'Antonio Tirabosco, was set not by Sacrati but by Manelli, and Torelli seems to have had no part in it.[77] The libretto, atypically for this theater, was published after the performance, on 13 February 1642. The real successor of *La finta pazza* was the second production of 1642, *Bellerofonte*, with a libretto by Vincenzo Nolfi, music by Sacrati, machines by Torelli, and starring Anna Renzi.

In fact, *Bellerofonte* seems to have been even more elaborate than its spectacular predecessor. Its libretto and scenario, like those of *La finta pazza*, were both printed before the performance. As we learn from a note to the reader attached to the end of the libretto, the scenario came first: "Various things in the opera were altered and corrected after the scenario was printed; thus if in number of scenes or in some part of what is presented in them you find some

twenty-four performances of *Antioco* from 25 January through 24 February, sometimes seven days per week (see Bianconi and Walker, "Production," 224); and in 1669, there were thirty-five performances of *Argia* (see I-Vcg, Archivio Vendramin 42 F [44], unnumbered folio, illustrated in fig. 24). Audiences apparently were accustomed to seeing the same opera more than once, to judge from Maria Mancini Colonna's remark that in 1666 she had seen *Tito* (Beregan/Cesti) five times in succession (see Alberto Cametti, *Il teatro di Tordinona poi di Apollo* [Tivoli, 1938], 2: 335).

75. Among the additions to the second edition of the libretto are three encomiastic sonnets in praise of Anna Renzi by Francesco Melosio, a librettist whose first work was performed the following season at S. Moisè, and two passages of text "inadvertently omitted" from act 2 (from scene 4 for Venere and Vulcano and from scene 7 for Giunone), but they were also omitted from the first edition, without comment.

76. Balbi, whom we know from *Ermiona*, *Peleo*, and *Delia*, choreographed the ballets for Paris. On this production, see Henry Prunières, *L'Opéra en France avant Lulli* (Paris, 1913), 68–77. The French documents seem to suggest that the work was not sung throughout. This led Sartori ("Un fantomatico compositore") to the conclusion that it was not a real opera; see also id., "Ancora della 'Finta pazza' di Strozzi e Sacrati," *NRMI* 11 (1977): 335–38.

77. There is some problem about *Alcate* with respect to Torelli and the involvement of the Incogniti. Bjurström (*Torelli*, 58) mentions a libretto, F-Bn Yth52325, with the conflated title *Alcate overo il Bellerofonte* (Venice: Surian, 1642). This may be the publisher's mistake (or, more likely, Bjurström's, since the libretto is not listed in Sartori, "Primo tentativo"). Bjurström (*Torelli*, 73–74), claims that Torelli's sets for *La finta pazza* and *Bellerofonte* could easily have been used for *Alcate*.

divergences from the one to the other, do not immediately become critical; take everything with goodwill, because our only aim is to minimize your boredom and maximize your pleasure" (Appendix I.19h).

The scenario was probably prepared by the theater management, since it is unsigned, bears no author's name on its title page, and continues the publicity campaign initiated the previous year by the *Finta pazza* publications. Indeed, it is atypical of scenarios in opening with a preface. Reminding the reader of the extraordinary success of the opera of the previous year, which had rendered the Novissimo "worthy of the favor and applause of the whole city," it praises the forthcoming opera, *Bellerofonte*, "likewise a musical drama," which, it is hoped, will maintain if not improve the reputation of the theater. *Bellerofonte* is "the very recent work of Signor Vincenzo Nolfi, gentleman of Fano." Although the work was a rush job, it is nevertheless a masterpiece, which, in any case, is largely owing to the generosity of the patrons, "questi Signori interessati," who spared no efforts in obtaining however many machines the poet felt necessary (Appendix I.19a).[78]

The preface to the scenario concludes with several paragraphs addressed "to the curious reader" by Torelli, unnamed but identified as "l'inventore delle machine." In a conventionally self-effacing note laced with only a touch of paranoia, he divulges the curious information that his sets are being plagiarized. His swipe at the narrowness of the theater is the only indication we have of any deficiency at the Novissimo:

> If in the scenes and machines I have constructed for you you do not find that perfection and beauty that you deserve and that you have a right to expect in virtuosic emulation of other celebrated and most noble theaters in such a glorious country, forgive me because the desire to delight you won over my awareness of the weakness of my talent. Appreciate the little that I can offer you in relation to the great deal that I wish to offer you; I confess that the imperfections are infinite, nor do I allow myself to be flattered by the speed with which others have adopted, perhaps in order to use them, things first invented, established, and, I might even say, bestowed, by me. Whatever they are, they are certainly the simple fruits of my invention. The site of the Teatro Novissimo cannot give you a full idea of things, as its narrowness would make it impossible even for an extraordinary architect to work perfectly.[79] Let this too convince you to excuse and bear with me. My weaknesses, in any case, will be largely covered up by the brush of Signor Domenico Bruni of Brescia, who with his usual success painted the sets. (Appendix I.19b)

In contrast to that of the scenario, the preface to the libretto of *Bellerofonte*, signed by the author, is less concerned with propaganda than with aesthetic

78. Fano was also Torelli's home town. Torelli's machines must have been expensive if the queen of France was concerned about their cost in *La finta pazza* (see Bianconi and Walker, "Dalla 'Finta pazza,' " 416 n. 152). This passage reminds us once again that because it drew upon the resources of a group of patricians, the Novissimo organization enjoyed a comparatively solid financial situation.

79. In fact, the Dominican friars agreed to correct that deficiency—see n. 56 above.

issues, of more specific relevance to the librettist as poet than as servant of the theater. But Nolfi offers a novel, and revealing, excuse for his literary short-comings: his deference to the wishes of the scene designer: "You are wasting time, O Reader, if with the Poetics of the Stagirite [Aristotle] in hand you go tracking down the errors of this work, because I confess freely that in composing it I did not aim to observe any precepts other than the desires of the scene designer" (Appendix I.19c). And again, slightly later: "The tale that was crumbling because of its antiquity has been restored by my pen in a dramatic form, under the constraint of very little time, in order to be crowned by the beauty of the theatrical machines and sets" (Appendix I.19g). The preface is followed by Torelli's note, reprinted from the scenario, and the front matter of the libretto concludes with poems addressed to the poet, two of the singers (including Renzi), and the composer.

The unusual emphasis on the scenographer in both the scenario and the libretto is capped in a third publication issued shortly after the performance. A deluxe commemorative quarto volume similar in function to the *Cannocchiale per la finta pazza*, this book was published under the aegis of Torelli himself and accordingly emphasizes the visual aspects of the production to an even greater degree. In addition to an elaborate narrative account of the performance, the entire text of the libretto is reproduced, along with ten engravings of scene designs.[80]

From our point of view, the most interesting section is the "Descrittione de gli Apparati" by Giulio del Colle. In its effort to place first the machines and then the Novissimo in their proper context, this report provides a veritable history of opera in Venice up to 1642, isolating many of the elements that were to prove crucial to its development—though much of this was recognized only in retrospect by later historians. Del Colle's description was obviously an important source for Ivanovich, who used it, amplified with information culled from later librettos, as the basis for his history of Venetian opera.[81]

Del Colle opens with a typically chauvinistic encomium to Venice and its unique history, including the usual favorable comparison to Rome, which it surpasses by virtue of its singular and miraculous site and, especially, in the number and magnificence of its theaters. Particularly in recent years, these have produced works that would have caused ancient Rome to blush with shame at being so surpassed (Appendix I.20a). The most magnificent of all, of course, is

80. *Il BELLERO FONTE: Drama Musicale Del Sig*^r *Vicenzo Nolfi da f. RAPPRESENTATO NEL TEA-TRO NOVISSIMO IN VENETIA DA GIA-COMO Torelli Da Fano Inuentore delli Apparati, DEDICATO Al Ser*^{mo}. *ferdinando II Gran Duca di Toscana 1642.*

81. Lengthy excerpts are quoted in translation, and several of the engravings reproduced, in Worsthorne, *Venetian Opera*, appendix V; see also Bjurström, *Torelli*, 58–73, cat. nos. 3–10, and figs. 18, 20, and 21 below.

the Teatro Novissimo, which, "built two years ago, has really caused a sensation and has deserved and won acclaim. This year it presented *Bellerofonte*, a drama by Signor Vincenzo Nolfi from Fano; and since, for many reasons, the things introduced in it are worthy of minute description, I have decided to undertake the task, however imperfectly" (Appendix I.20b).

Del Colle then goes on to describe the action of the drama itself, commenting on the various singers as he sketches the individual characters. He mentions only three by name: Giulia Saus Paolelli from Rome, who had resided and performed in Venice for the previous three years; Michele Grasseschi, a contralto on loan from Prince Matthias de' Medici of Florence; and Anna Renzi romana, "true embodiment of music and unique marvel of the stage, who, during the course of the performance first gave vent to, then hid, then disguised, then revealed, and then lamented her amorous passions." But he gives the city of origin for most of the others and, more important, supplies vocal ranges for all of the roles, which would be otherwise unknown to us, since the music of *Bellerofonte* has not survived. His complete list comprises Innocenza (soprano from Parma), La Giustizia (a castrato from Rome), Nettuno (tenor from Parma), Paristide (tenor from Pistoia), Il Re (bass from Siena), Regina Anthia (Signora Giulia Saus Paolelli romana), Defiride, the nurse (a castrato from Parma), Pallade and Diana (two soprano castratos), Melistea (a castrato from Pistoia), Eolo (a Sienese bass), Bellerofonte (Signor Michele Grasseschi, contralto), and Archimene (Anna Renzi romana) (Appendix I.20c).[82] Most of del Colle's text, however, is devoted to a vivid description of the costumes, sets, and the workings of the machinery, in which he emphasizes the novelty of Torelli's inventions. As in the similar descriptions in the *Cannocchiale* and even in the earlier librettos of *Andromeda* and *La maga fulminata* so long before, a special point is made of the amazed reaction of the public, its inability to penetrate the illusion.[83]

After *Bellerofonte*, activity at the Novissimo began to slacken somewhat. Only one opera was produced during each of its next (and last) three seasons: *Venere gelosa* in 1643, *Deidamia* in 1644, and *Ercole in Lidia* in 1645. Sacrati and

82. Giulia Saus Paolelli, who starred as Penelope and Delia in the Bologna productions of *Il ritorno d'Ulisse* and *Delia* in 1640 (and presumably in the Venetian productions as well), became a very successful stage personality in Venice. She was praised by Fulvio Testi in a letter of 3 December 1633 to the duke of Modena (*Lettere*, ed. M. L. Doglio [Bari, 1967], 1: no. 473), and by Leonardo Quirini (*Vezzi d'Erato* [Venice: Hertz, 1653]).

83. In act 1, scene 3: "Slowly descending, the two clouds bore the goddesses to the ground on either side of the stage, with a movement both unexpected and marvellous, without showing how it was arranged, and straightway scattered through the scene without the means being understood by the amazed audience" (Worsthorne, *Venetian Opera*, 178). And later, "Amore made an entry, flying from the left with great speed to the middle of the scene. He wounded [Anthea]. . . . Then, rising again, he flew to the right, drawing the eyes of the theater which, astonished, tried in vain to penetrate the machinery and discover the artifice" (2.10; Worsthorne, 181). This was truly *l'arte che nasconde l'arte*.

Torelli seem to have been directly involved only in the first of these; in fact, following Strozzi's lead, they both began to work at SS. Giovanni e Paolo. Sacrati collaborated with several other composers there in a joint setting of Strozzi's *La finta savia* already in 1643, and he provided all of the music for Badoaro's *Ulisse errante* in 1644, for which Torelli served as scenographer. Anna Renzi, too, moved over to SS. Giovanni e Paolo after *Bellerofonte* to sing in *L'incoronazione di Poppea* and *La finta savia* in 1643, though she returned to the Novissimo in 1644 and 1645 for *Deidamia* and *Ercole in Lidia*.[84]

In fact, the theater of SS. Giovanni e Paolo and the Novissimo had always been linked, by geographical proximity and outlook as well as personnel. Strozzi, as we know, had written his *Delia* for the Grimani theater in 1639, before the Novissimo was built, and many other members of the Accademia degli Incogniti, including Busenello, Badoaro, and the anonymous author of *Le nozze d'Enea*, were active there rather than at the Novissimo. It was natural, then, for Strozzi to have returned to SS. Giovanni e Paolo and to have brought his Novissimo colleagues with him in 1643. Torelli, for his part, may even have found the older theater more congenial to his scenographic technology. At least one of his inventions, the fine machine for changing all the sets simultaneously by means of a lever or winch moved by a weight, described in the eighteenth century, may have originated there.[85] SS. Giovanni e Paolo was certainly the larger theater. In fact, although in 1645 it was deemed the most comfortable and beautiful theater in Venice, as we have noted, Giovanni Grimani himself thought it was too deep and should be shortened by two boxes because "those facing the stage hear the performers poorly."[86] It is just possible that the general exodus from the Novissimo to SS. Giovanni e Paolo was in some way connected to the signing of a new rental contract at the Novissimo by Gironimo Lappoli in 1643, though the nature of the relationship between the two events is uncertain.[87] The fact that Strozzi's operatic trilogy—which began with *La*

84.   Renzi was joined at SS. Giovanni e Paolo in 1643 by the Roman soprano Anna di Valerio or Anna Valeri; see Wolfgang Osthoff, "Filiberto Laurenzis Musik zu 'La finta savia' im Zusammenhang der frühvenezianischen Oper," in *Venezia e il melodramma nel seicento*, ed. Maria Teresa Muraro (Florence, 1976), 174, and a letter from one of Cardinal Mazarin's agents in Piacenza of 25 March 1643 (F-Pre, Corr. polit., Parme, t. 2, ff. 39–41), quoted in Margaret Murata, "Why the First Opera Given in Paris Wasn't Roman," in *L'opera tra Venezia e Parigi*, ed. Lorenzo Bianconi (in press); see also Curtis, "*La Poppea impasticciata*," 42 n. 28.
85.   "Fù nel Teatro SS. Giovanni & Paolo in Venezia ch'inventò la bella machina di mutar in un tratto tutte le scene per mezzo di leva o di argano mosso da

un peso" (Francesco Milizia, *Memorie degli architetti antichi e moderni* [Parma, 1781], 2: 213). But there was confusion over the names of the two theaters. He could have meant the Novissimo in the parish of SS. Giovanni e Paolo. Moreover, the invention is alluded to in the first of the Novissimo librettos. See ch. 4 below.
86.   "E che sarebbe bene farlo due Colonnate, cioè due Palchi meno di quello è di presente, perchè quelli che sono in faccia alla Scena, sentono poco i Recitanti" (Bianconi and Walker, "Dalla 'Finta pazza,' " 229).
87.   See Mangini, *I teatri di Venezia*, 65 (on Girolamo [=Gironimo] Lappoli). Other SS. Giovanni e Paolo operas with Incognito connections include *Il ritorno d'Ulisse* (1640–41); *Narciso ed Ecco immortalati*

finta pazza and included *La finta savia* and *Romolo e Remo*—was split between the two theaters suggests that SS. Giovanni e Paolo was considered in some sense a natural twin or even heir of the Novissimo.

But in 1643, despite the loss of Strozzi, Sacrati, and Anna Renzi, the energy of the Novissimo was still far from spent. *Venere gelosa*, by all (admittedly prejudiced) accounts, was just as marvelous and successful as any of its predecessors. The text, by a new librettist, Niccolò Enea Bartolini,[88] was published as expected before the premiere and reprinted at least four times in Venice and also in Padua; it contains the characteristic Incognito peroration on the aesthetics of opera, but is not especially informative about the performance. Nor, atypically for the Novissimo, does a scenario seem to have been published for the purpose. Torelli, however, made up for this with another commemorative volume, the last of his efforts in that direction, issued in 1644.

The title of this publication, *Apparati scenici per lo Teatro Novissimo di Venetia nell'anno 1644 d'inventione e cura di Iacomo Torelli da Fano*, is neutral, making no reference to any specific opera. Indeed, even the dedication of the volume seems purposely noncommittal. It simply introduces the designs as having been made for the Teatro Novissimo and shown "this past Carnival to the eyes of Venice in the representation of a musical drama."[89] The description of the opera in question by Bisaccioni, the author of the *Cannocchiale*, makes it clear, however, that it was *Venere gelosa*, performed during the previous season (1643). But the printing of the *Apparati scenici*, whose dedication was signed by Torelli on 24 January 1644, was a year late if it was intended to commemorate only *Venere gelosa*, and in fact only nine of the twelve plates relate to that work. The other three probably illustrate *Deidamia*, the opera then on the boards.[90]

Furthermore, of the eight stage sets listed in the libretto for *Deidamia*, the five not included in the *Apparati* could have been drawn from those of *Venere gelosa*.[91] Thus, while the *Apparati scenici* describes only *Venere gelosa*, it in fact

---

and *Gli amori di Giasone e d'Isifile* (1642); *L'incoronazione di Poppea* and *La finta savia* (1643); *Il principe giardiniero* (the Incognito connection derives from the note to the reader, which is signed by Fusconi) and *Ulisse errante* (1644); *Romolo e Remo* and *Bellerofonte* (1645); *Deidamia* (1647); *Torilda* (1648); and *Argiope* (1649).

88. Bartolini is familiar to us as the author of the narrative description of the Paduan *Ermiona* seven years earlier.

89. "questo Carneval passato all'occhio di Venetia nella rappresentatione d'un drama musicale" (*Apparati scenici*, dedication).

90. Bjurström, *Torelli*, 89–94, cat. nos. 20–22; also

Bianconi and Walker, "Dalla 'Finta pazza,' " 416 n. 153, and figs. 17, 19, 22, and 23 below.

91. And some from *La finta pazza* or *Bellerofonte* as well; see Bjurström, *Torelli*, 91. Presumably this was necessary because Torelli was no longer available to create new sets at the Novissimo, having moved by 1644 to SS. Giovanni e Paolo. Torelli himself may have authorized or suggested the use of some old sets for *Deidamia* because he was pressed for time, especially if he was already contracted to produce *Ulisse errante* for SS. Giovanni e Paolo. His unrealized promise to publish the stage designs of *Ulisse errante* is another indication of the time pressures under which he operated.

illustrates both *Venere gelosa* and *Deidamia*—and not only three of the latter's sets but probably all of them. This is confirmed in a note to the reader appended to the volume.

> These sets were so marvelously and exquisitely presented that they convinced their maker to allow them to be seen this year, 1643 [1644], also. And in truth he judged very wisely, since people have derived inexpressible satisfaction from them, to the extent that many thought they were new, and others that they had been improved; and this because of the addition of other very beautiful sets included here [i.e., the three already mentioned], and because the drama turned out to be marvelously beautiful: whence it was shown that to repeat beautiful things even twice is commendable. (Appendix I.22c)

Like the *Cannocchiale* and the deluxe *Bellerofonte*, the *Apparati scenici* sheds valuable light on the current state of opera in Venice. It begins (like *Bellerofonte*) with a capsule history of the city and its theaters in order to place the Teatro Novissimo and especially the featured production, *Venere gelosa*, in their proper context—on a pedestal, as the culmination of a brief but glorious tradition. In so doing, it makes its own considerable contribution to the blossoming mythology:

> Venice, always and on every occasion extraordinary, and never tired of displaying her greatness, has discovered the remarkable also in virtuoso entertainment, having introduced a few years ago the presentation in music of grand drama with such sets and stage-machines that they surpass all belief; and what the richest treasuries can produce only with difficulty (and only rarely) in royal halls [*Regie Sale*] here we see easily achieved with private resources, not only in one, but in three theaters [*tre orchestre*] at once;[92] and competing with each other for the greatest perfections, they each draw spectators from the most remote parts of Italy. I am not undertaking to write down what was done in *Venere gelosa* because I deem it the most notable of this year's, and this city's, theatrical productions, nor because my choice aims to detract from the others' merits, but rather because I enjoyed this one first, and I have preserved the most vivid memory of it. . . . But not even of this one do I want to write every detail, because it seems to me enough to report the most important things of the drama, as much as is needed to show what its scenic clothes, or shall we say sets, were like. (Appendix I.22a)

The author will tell only as much about the drama as is necessary to illustrate or describe the scenography—by which strategy, of course, he hopes to achieve exactly what he disclaims, to convince the readers of the superiority of *Venere gelosa* to all other operas of the season, especially, we might guess, to the opera at SS. Giovanni e Paolo.

---

92. In 1644 there were actually four theaters (not "orchestras"): S. Cassiano, SS. Giovanni e Paolo, S. Moisè, and the Novissimo.

His description of the effect of the final scene gives a good idea of the audience's reaction and provides a fitting conclusion to the volume:

> At the birth of this scene the whole theater, not just the stage or the buildings, was supposed to rise, and it rose indeed, for with the movement of those great back-drops and the disappearance of the sky, and upon seeing all the parts of that great machine turn and mix in great confusion, not one of the spectators sat still: they stood up and turned around and did not know what they were seeing or what to expect, if not a great novelty; but soon the eye was satisfied, because it saw the scene transformed into a lovely and delightful garden, which was far different from any that have been depicted, either on stage or in print. (Appendix I.22b)

This *Apparati scenici* was the last volume of his stage designs Torelli published in Venice, although he promised a similar one for his next opera, *Ulisse errante*, at SS. Giovanni e Paolo, in a note to the reader in the libretto of that work: "Experience makes me recognize the fact that favors often increase the daring of those who receive them; I received *Ulisse errante* from the hand of the author with the privileged authority to print it in large format with illustrations after the performances, and I undertook this to be able to show to the world the efforts I faced in order to serve these gentlemen well" (Appendix I.8m).[93]

Torelli obviously assumed the responsibility (and profits?) of the librettist in this case. Perhaps permission to publish the libretto as well as engravings of the sets was part of his contract with the theater management, possibly an inducement to leave the Novissimo. Interesting also, given the precedent of the *Cannocchiale* and the deluxe *Bellerofonte*, is the proviso that he should not publish the engravings until after the performance, as if prior publication might diminish their effect. Conversely, the publication of this particular libretto before the premiere (which is implied in Torelli's preface, though not by any verb on the title page) seems explicitly intended to enhance the audience's enjoyment of the performance.

It is evident that by 1644 Torelli's exclusive ties to the Novissimo, like those of a number of his collaborators, had loosened, if not broken altogether. The staging of neither *Deidamia* that year nor *Ercole in Lidia* the next is specifically ascribed to him. And, as we know, 1644 saw the performance of his first, and only, new work for another Venetian theater, *Ulisse errante* at SS. Giovanni e Paolo. This was followed by revivals there of two works that had originally been produced with his sets at the Novissimo: *Bellerofonte* in 1645 and *Deidamia* in 1647. But by then Torelli was gone: in the spring of 1645, after the

93. This passage reveals once more the abstention of a patrician librettist from the publication business. As already observed, Badoaro's name appears nowhere in this libretto; only his academic alias identifies him. It is worth noting that, even without his name, Badoaro would not let this publication out of his hands without the de rigueur aesthetic statement, perhaps one of the longest in any libretto (see Appendix I.8).

opera season, he accepted an invitation from the queen of France and left for Paris, "sacrificing all of his important interests in Venice," thus bringing to a close the Venetian chapter of his career.[94]

Although Torelli was not the only scenographer active in Venice in the early years of public opera (we have noted Alabardi at S. Cassiano, and Chenda and Burnacini at SS. Giovanni e Paolo), he clearly left an indelible mark upon the Venetian stage—and, through the engravings of his designs, upon our knowledge of its visual spectacle.[95] Stage design had traditionally aimed at producing marvelous effects; Torelli's special contribution was to achieve those effects with a mechanical efficiency that enhanced the marvelous. By creating a central mechanism that controlled all the moving parts, he could set the entire stage into simultaneous motion. Light and shadow further contributed to the smooth transition of space, adding the final convincing touches to the illusion of a world in mutation. No longer merely a backdrop or setting, the scenery actively participated in the drama, changing with, and as part of, the action.

Torelli's (and Sacrati's) transfer to SS. Giovanni e Paolo may have represented a significant victory for the management of that theater, but it did not signal the end of the Teatro Novissimo's career as a major opera house or a change in its mission. The Incogniti involvement continued—and with it the propaganda about Venice, about opera, and about the Novissimo initiated with *La finta pazza*—in the two operas that followed Torelli's departure, *Deidamia* and *Ercole in Lidia*, both of them starring Anna Renzi. These marked the librettistic debuts of Scipione Herrico and Bisaccioni, though the latter at least was no stranger to matters operatic. And at least one of the new operas, *Ercole in Lidia*, marked the operatic debut of a composer from the San Marco chapel, Giovanni Rovetta.[96] Both librettists proclaim their indebtedness to anonymous collaborators (probably their fellow Incogniti), Herrico because he was a novice, Bisaccioni because he lacked inspiration (Appendix I.23a, 24a–b).

Herrico's dedication to Alvise da Mosto, "Nobile Veneto," borrows the old Novissimo rhetoric and has the familiar ring of Venetian myth making:

> This great city, as it is in its site, so always it has shown itself, and shows itself, to be admirable and extraordinary in its public and in its private actions. In these times foreigners are astonished to see the ornate theaters in which so many dramatic

94. Prunières, *L'Opéra en France*, 68–77, prints the documentation surrounding Torelli's employment in Paris; the passage quoted comes from a letter of 11 September 1645 (372–73).

95. Another early Venetian scenographer was Gaspare Beccari, active at S. Moisè in the early 1640s; see Bjurström, *Torelli*, 43–46; also Worsthorne, *Venetian Opera*, 37–50 ("The Spectacle"); Lorenzo Bianconi, "Scena, musica e pubblico nell'opera del seicento," in *Illusione e pratica teatrale*, 15–24; and Mercedes Viale Ferrero, "Luogo teatrale e spazio scenico," *StOpIt*, 5 (Turin, 1988): 3–24.

96. The composer of the other opera, *Deidamia*, is unknown. The lost score was traditionally attributed to Cavalli; but see Walker, "Errori."

works are presented in music, and which are so ingeniously composed, and so full
of diverse and marvelous effects. Whence the opportunity is offered for many fine
talents to exercise themselves and receive great praise, whether in poetry, or in music, or in the construction of stage-machines, or in other similarly honored and related labors.

    Now, coming to this noble refuge of every virtue, and admiring such fine rival-
ries, I, too, was stimulated by poetic fervor, and that same reason that persuaded me
not to compete with so many skilled men urged me on with a sweet desire to imitate them. Finally, with the continual requests of my friends added to this internal
inclination of mine, I entered the arena to please them, and they guided my style,
which is by habit very far from this kind of poetizing. I have written this work for
performance in the Teatro Novissimo, and since it was to be printed for the greater
convenience of the audience, I wanted it to appear adorned with the name of Your
Most Illustrious Lordship, who will deign to receive it as much in my name, as a
token of my loyal service, as in the name of those who had a part in it with me, in
the invention and in the ideas. (Appendix I.23a–b)

Although Torelli was probably not directly involved in designing the scenes
for these operas, he may still have had some hand in the productions. At least
no other scenographer is mentioned in connection with them. As we have seen,
Deidamia probably used sets from his other operas, especially *Venere gelosa*; and
the same may also have been true for *Ercole in Lidia*, since none of the sets
mentioned in the scenario or libretto seem to make demands beyond the variety
available from *La finta pazza*, *Bellerofonte*, and *Venere gelosa*.[97] In any case, the
stage designs played no little part in the impression made by *Ercole in Lidia* on
John Evelyn in 1645:

> This night, having with my Lord Bruce taken our places before, we went to the
> Opera where comedies and other plays are represented in recitative music by the
> most excellent musicians vocal and instrumental, with a variety of scenes painted
> and contrived with no less art of perspective, and machines for flying in the aire,
> and other wonderful motions; taken together it is one of the most magnificent and
> expensive diversions the wit of men can invent. The history was Hercules in Lydia,
> the scenes changed thirteen times. The famous voices, Anna Rencia, a Roman, and
> reputed the best treble of women; but there was an eunuch who in my opinion sur-
> passed her; also a Genoeze that sang an incomparable bass. This held us by the eyes
> and ears till two in the morning.[98]

There has always been some question as to when the Novissimo actually
closed its doors for good. Like much of the confusion surrounding the chronology of early Venetian opera, this uncertainty derives in part from Ivanovich,
who gives two conflicting dates, 1646 in his chapter on the history of Venetian
theaters, 1647 in his chronology. This is his version of the demise of the Novissimo: "Musical performances took place there until 1646, when the theater

---

97. Bjurström, *Torelli*, 97.   98. *Memoires of John Evelyn*, 1: 191.

was completely destroyed, and its site was where at present the Riding-School has been set up, behind the Mendicanti, toward the Fondamenta Nuove" (Appendix II.6q). In his chronology, however, Ivanovich assigns Busenello's *Giulio Cesare* and a revival of *Deidamia* to the Novissimo, in 1646 and 1647 respectively; and various chroniclers, following Ivanovich, have chosen one of those two dates for the closing of the theater. But Ivanovich's confusion was itself the result of an ambiguity in the naming of theaters on the title pages of librettos, between "Novissimo" and "Novo," a designation that referred at this time to SS. Giovanni e Paolo. The confusion was compounded by the fact that the Novissimo and SS. Giovanni e Paolo were both located in the same parish. *Giulio Cesare*, for example, was certainly written for the SS. Giovanni e Paolo, though it was probably never performed,[99] and the revival of *Deidamia*, according to the libretto, clearly took place not at the Novissimo but at the "Teatro Novo."[100]

Evelyn's description of *Ercole in Lidia* of 1645, then, is the last document of a performance at the Novissimo. Whether or not the theater was actually destroyed soon after, as Ivanovich implies, the focus of operatic interest and activity had certainly shifted elsewhere, primarily to SS. Giovanni e Paolo. In the meantime, S. Cassiano and S. Moisè continued to compete as well, each averaging two operas per season. Like all of the theaters in Venice, the Novissimo closed in 1645 and remained closed through 1646 and 1647. But unlike the others, it never reopened.[101] Possibly because of the enormous cost of Torelli's scenographic extravaganzas, which may have accumulated, and because it failed to recoup the expenses of *Ercole in Lidia*, which was apparently interrupted during its run, the theater was bankrupt by 1646.[102] The Dominican friars, unlike the patrician proprietors of the other theaters, were understandably not committed enough to the venture to bail it out. And so, when the Novissimo closed in 1645, it closed forever. The strength of the initial enterprise, which lay in the cooperation of a large number of energetic collaborators, may ultimately have become the source of its failure. No family's reputation

---

99. See the dedication of Busenello's *Le hore ociose*.
100. Likewise, Ferrari's *Il principe giardiniero* (1643) and Strozzi's *Romolo e Remo* (1645), though assigned to the "Teatro Novo" on their title pages, were certainly performed at SS. Giovanni e Paolo. But for some reason they were listed properly by Ivanovich. It may have been common practice to use "Nuovo" to distinguish new or reconstructed theaters from older ones in the same parish; such was evidently the case not only for SS. Giovanni e Paolo but for S. Cassiano and S. Moisè as well.
101. Because of the War of Candia, the government decreed a ban on all public performances, be-

ginning in 1645 (see ch. 5 below). There is some evidence, however, that a few operas may have been performed during those years, but outside of the Carnival season: *Ercole in Lidia* in June 1645 at the Novissimo (where it was seen by John Evelyn) and *Deidamia* in May 1647 at SS. Giovanni e Paolo (a libretto published in that year and indicating performance in that theater bears a dedication date of 30 May).
102. For the documentary evidence for the closing of the theaters, which was part of the general suspension of Carnival activities, see Bianconi and Walker, "Dalla 'Finta pazza,'" 416–17.

and position depended on its success. By 1645 the status of the theater was not important enough to any single individual to inspire the heavy economic transfusion that would have ensured its survival.

Although the bright light of the Novissimo was extinguished in 1645, the effect of that theater on the subsequent history of opera in Venice was permanent. Its activities may have been concentrated in a few short seasons, but in that brief time steps fundamental to opera's development were taken and reinforced. By launching the career of the first "prima donna," the Incognito managers set new standards for singers, elevating them to greater prominence and greater influence in the operatic partnership with composers and librettists. By providing an environment—physical as well as financial—for the exercise of Torelli's special creative talents, they raised the level and importance of operatic stage design, transforming it into an independent art. Most important, they traded on the unspoken but fundamental connection between opera and the image of the Republic. In making that connection patent, the Novissimo Incogniti fulfilled their responsibility as patriotic Venetians. And, by the very energy of their publicity campaign on behalf of their theater and their city, they stimulated interest and excitement in the new art. Their success created a market for opera both in Venice and abroad.

4

• • •

La finta pazza:
Mirror of an Audience

The permanent impact of the Teatro Novissimo is embodied in the opera with which it opened in 1641, *La finta pazza*, a text by Giulio Strozzi set to music by Francesco Sacrati, designed and staged by Giacomo Torelli, and starring Anna Renzi in the title role. It was on this inaugural project, more than on any of its successors, that the energies of the Incogniti were focused most intensely. The fanfare of its launching reverberated well beyond the geographical boundaries of Venice and the chronological ones of the season.

As we have seen, *La finta pazza* was carefully prepared in advance by a systematic public relations campaign designed to whet the appetite of the large audience in Venice for Carnival; and interest was effectively maintained during the run and continued after by intensified propaganda that trumpeted its special marvels—above all, its prima donna and scenographer—and recounted the particulars of its success: twelve performances in seventeen days, the same audience attending not one or two but as many as four performances, crowds turned away at the door. And, in a move that was unprecedented in Venetian operatic history, the theater actually reopened after Easter to accommodate the throngs who had come to Venice for the express purpose of seeing the celebrated work.

All this publicity, printed and widely distributed, gave the opera a special reputation abroad. And that reputation was confirmed by live performances. Thanks to the efforts of a variety of traveling companies, *La finta pazza* made the rounds of opera houses throughout Italy and beyond. A performance by the Accademici Febiarmonici in Piacenza in 1644 was followed the next year by one in Florence as well as the one in Paris. Three years later, in 1647, a group known as the Accademici Discordati (a name chosen, perhaps, to contrast with the Febiarmonici) produced it in Bologna.[1] It appeared in Genoa in 1647, Reggio

---

1. Sacrati himself was probably involved in the Bologna production as a member or leader of the Discordati; see Bianconi, *Seventeenth Century*, 194.

Although apparently the name of a specific academy, "Febiarmonici" was also used generically to refer to opera companies in Naples, Milan, Turin, and

Emilia and Turin in 1648, Naples and Milan in 1652, enjoying what might be
considered its final run as late as 1679, or nearly forty years after its premiere.[2]
So soon after that premiere did *La finta pazza* become public property—with
a life of its own, independent of its origins, and subject to alterations—that as
early as 1644 Strozzi felt impelled to publish the "true" *Finta pazza* in a third
edition, in order to assert his paternity as well as the integrity of the original
text:

> I willingly undertook this third printing of the true *Finta pazza* because I saw
> that some wandering musicians [i.e., the Febiarmonici] have had it reprinted else-
> where in various ways, and that they go around performing it as if it were their
> own. The author takes little notice and would be glad to be able to thank God had
> his compositions been improved for him. Hence you will be the judge by reading
> the one and the other, and if you should not discover any improvement, you will
> say, if it was such a success altered, what must it have inspired in its original form,
> when in the mouth of Signora Anna Renzi, with the music of Signor Sacrati, and
> with the machines of Signor Torelli, it stupefied Venice itself. (Appendix I.16e)

Strozzi was evidently referring to the libretto published in Codogno, which
reflected the Piacenza performance; in 1644 it was the only one that had been
published "elsewhere," without any mention of either Strozzi or the Venetian
origin of the work. The kinds of changes he had in mind are spelled out in a later
edition of the libretto (Bologna, 1647), whose text is the same as that of Piacenza but with a different prologue. According to the preface of the Bologna
libretto: "The one who produced it for the first time outside Venice cut some
scenes and added others for his convenience. In that manner it was presented.
If it didn't satisfy your taste, don't blame the original author."[3] More specifically, many of the supernatural scenes, which required elaborate machinery,
were eliminated, as well as those referring too directly to the myth of Venice
and other peculiarly Venetian allusions.[4]

Strozzi's "third edition" can be regarded as yet another piece of propaganda
on behalf of the work—and, implicitly, of the Teatro Novissimo—but the
author was obviously responding to a need. Venetian copyright laws offered
protection only within the domain. Beyond, Strozzi's work was common

---

Genoa; see Bianconi and Walker, "Dalla 'Finta
pazza,' " 387 n. 52 and 403–4 n. 114.

2. This revival, under a new title, *Gli amori sagaci*,
took place in Reggio Emilia. It is unlikely, after four
decades, that it contained much, if any, of Sacrati's
original music. With one exception, all of these performances are documented by librettos (the exception is Reggio, 1648, for which only a scenario survives); the sources are all evaluated in Bianconi,
preface to *La finta pazza*.

3. "Chi la fece rappresentare la prima volta fuori
Venetia levò alcune Scene, altre ve n'aggiunse per sua
commodità. In questa maniera è stata consegnata, se
non satisfacesse al tuo gusto non incolpare il primiero
Auttore." There were two editions of the work published in Bologna in 1647, one dedicated to Cornelio
Malvasia by Curzio Manara (I-Bc), the other without dedication (I-Vgc).

4. See Bianconi and Walker, "Dalla 'Finta pazza,' " 424 nn. 182–84.

property, his text available to every plagiarist. This was only the beginning of a problem that was to become severe during the following decades. As the most widely traveled work of its time, *La finta pazza* became in effect a model of the new Venetian genre to the world at large. The ways in which the Febiarmonici productions differed from the original version indicate just how specifically Venetian that original had been.

The initial success of *La finta pazza* was not only owing to publicity or to extraordinary performers and scenography. It derived as well from qualities intrinsic to the opera itself. Strozzi had brought all his theatrical expertise to bear on the creation of a work that would appeal to its audience on many levels. His intellectual background and his previous activity as a panegyrist of Venice and writer and promoter of operatic entertainments enabled him to strike the appropriate chord. His libretto embodied just the right combination of ingredients to both stimulate and satisfy the public he knew so well.

La finta pazza is permeated by a profound self-consciousness, a thoroughgoing awareness of its own various aspects: as a theatrical entertainment in which music plays a special role and as the inaugural work of a unique new theater in the matchless city of Venice. This self-consciousness informs every dimension of the libretto, from the choice of subject, characters, and situations to the language of the dialogue. Reaching out beyond the stage and commenting upon itself even as it unfolds, the libretto weaves a complex and seductive web of connections with the audience. Such self-awareness, of course, is characteristic of theatrical entertainment in general: many of the techniques and devices in *La finta pazza* are commonplaces of spoken theater as well.[5] But *La finta pazza* complicated this potential by the very fact of its being sung: it was as a paradigmatic opera that it made—and still makes—its mark.

The work tells the familiar tale of Achilles on Skyros. Teti, in order to prevent her son from joining in the Trojan War, in which she knew he would die, conveyed him to the island of Skyros, where he lived disguised as one of King Licomede's daughters, revealing his true identity only to Deidamia, with whom he fell in love and produced a son. When Ulisse and Diomede land on the island in search of the missing hero, Acchille cannot resist the call to arms and betrays his identity. His departure for Troy is delayed by Deidamia, who, feigning madness, persuades him to marry her and take her with him. Whereupon they all depart for the war, an ending that is only temporarily happy, since the historical hero's fate is in any case sealed. Within the context of this rela-

---

5. Some of the text was in fact spoken in the Paris production of 1645; see Sartori, "Un fantomatico compositore," 792–93; id., "Ancora della 'Finta pazza,'" 336–37.

tively straightforward plot, *La finta pazza* touches all of the characteristic themes and concerns of early Venetian opera.

Like all successful theatrical entertainments, *La finta pazza* engages its audience in the most central of theatrical questions: the distinction between illusion and reality. On the simplest level, the illusion comprises everything that takes place on stage, beyond the proscenium; it is defined as fiction by the real audience seated in the theater. But the stage illusion has many layers. The cast participates in overlapping, intercalated dramas. The action involving Deidamia and Acchille, initially kept obscured from most of the other characters through disguise and dissemblance, itself temporarily masks a larger conflict among the gods over the outcome of the Trojan War. This in turn conceals— and then reveals—a more relevant story, for the fall of Troy had important genealogical implications for a Venetian audience, who saw history as descending in the progression Troy-Rome-Venice and regarded themselves as the ultimate heirs of the Trojans. Three different levels of illusion intersect here, the last one approaching reality most closely for the Venetian audiences by reminding them, perhaps only subliminally, of their historical lineage.

Beyond these interleaved dramas, the stage illusion of *La finta pazza* is enriched and complicated by several plays-within-the-play, which the characters sometimes participate in, sometimes observe. As observers, they abandon one illusion to create another, for they then appear to share the point of view of the audience rather than that of their fellow characters. Implicitly they cross the frontier of the proscenium, temporarily renouncing ancient Greek citizenship to become modern Venetians.

As early as act 1, scene 6, Licomede lifts a curtain–behind–the–curtain to reveal his daughters on a small stage.[6] When Ulisse and Diomede react as audience to this play-within-a-play in their honor, they speak on two levels, responding for themselves to the actual scene in Skyros and for us, the audience, to the theatrical illusion created in the Teatro Novissimo. Ulisse exclaims: "This is either an earthly theater made by the gods or else a man-made heaven"; and Diomede responds, "Oh, most beautiful scene . . . ," an exchange that draws special attention to the scenography, one of the Novissimo's—and *La finta pazza*'s—greatest attractions.[7]

The most complex and striking play-within-a-play is, appropriately, an opera (3.2). The libretto describes the scene: "Deidamia . . . having heard that

6. This particular scene exploited one of Torelli's scenographic innovations, whereby a small background scene could be opened up within an otherwise flat backdrop. See Bjurström, *Torelli*, 103.

7. ULISSE: "O formano gli Dei / Questi teatri in terra, / O innalzano i mortali / Questi apparati in Cielo." DIOMEDE: "O bellissima Scena. . . ."

commedie in musica are to be performed in honor of the ambassadors, says she wants to participate, since she is an expert in stage machinery and in singing."[8] The opera, however, is evoked rather than seen; it is a creation of Deidamia's imagination:

> What melodies are these? Tell me, what brand-new theaters [*novissimi teatri*], what numerous scenes are being prepared in Skyros? I, too, would like to be part of the effort, since I possess the art of creating a hundred different scenes by a single whistle [*sol fischio*], of counterfeiting seas, erecting mountains, and making beautiful heavens and stars, and opening up Hell, too, on whose Tartarean shores I can form the Styx and Cocytus.[9]

Here, at the height of her feigned madness, Deidamia plays several roles simultaneously to her two audiences, one on stage, the other in the theater. To her nurse and the Eunuch, who share her theatrical space, she is Deidamia gone mad. To the Venetian public, she is first of all Anna Renzi pretending to be Deidamia, of course, and Deidamia pretending to be mad; but she is also the mad Deidamia pretending to be the scenographer Torelli. And finally, her words themselves suggest that she is at the same time also speaking as a member of the audience in the Novissimo observing the marvels of the actual performance in which she is participating.

Her speech reverberates in many directions. *Novissimi teatri* is obviously a punning allusion to the Teatro Novissimo, and *sol fischio* calls attention to one of Torelli's most famous inventions, the system of winches and pulleys that allowed for the simultaneous changing of all the sets. Deidamia's description of Hades even anticipates a scene between Teti and Caronte (3.4). Her next observation is still more pointedly professional and, with an aesthetic as well as practical, even personal, thrust: "Today, when architecture is raining from the stars to ornament so many new and illustrious works, I, too, would like to create lofty and beautiful machines that can make a hundred Orpheuses break their necks."[10] Her remarks acknowledge the prominence of scenography in opera and at the same time suggest the physical texture of life on stage—the evidently real danger to singers of rapid and numerous scene-changes, with heavy sets dropping from above. If her view of opera is somewhat one-sided

---

8. "Udito che in Sciro si dovevano rappresentar Commedie in Musica per honorar gli Ambasciadori, dice di voler anch'essa far la sua parte, come esperta di Macchine e di Canto."

9. "Che melodie son queste? / Ditemi? che novissimi teatri, / Che numerose scene / S'apparecchiano in Sciro? / Voglio esser ancor'io del faticare a parte; / Ch'a me non manca l'arte, ad un sol fischio / Di cento variar scenici aspetti, / Finger mari, erger monti, e mostre belle / Far di cieli, e di Stelle /

D'aprir l'inferno, e nel tartareo lito / Formar Stige e Cocito."

10. "Hoggi, che dalle stelle, / Per tante opere ornar illustri e nove, / L'Architettura piove, anch'io spiegar vorrei / Macchine eccelse, e belle / Di far romper il collo a cento Orfei." This text points up another of Torelli's striking scenographic innovations, the use of a counterweight system that would enable any number of flats to drop down from their storage place behind the upper proscenium.

in its emphasis on scenic spectacle—she is "mad," after all—the response of her nurse is more balanced, giving equal weight to all three traditional components: poetry and music as well as scenography. Nurses, of course, always tell the truth: "Poetry, machines, and song are apt to render even the wisest Sibyl mad; and when you add a love plot, it's no wonder this one has lost her mind."[11]

One further play-within-the-play is referred to, but not seen. Bearing only the most tangential relationship to the plot, it was undoubtedly inserted for the amusement of a special segment of the audience, namely the Incognito management. In this bizarre scene (2.2), Acchille challenges the Captain to a duel in defense of the principle that a young lover can change his affections and his love object whenever he wishes. The duel, reported to have taken place off stage, at the "teatro del porto,"[12] is evidently intended to parody the verbal duels, or debates, that provided the substance and justification for meetings of the Incognito academy.[13] Furthermore, Acchille's challenge provides the occasion for another little private joke. Ulisse refuses the challenge, asserting that he is constant in love and will die a faithful lover—an allusion, presumably, to his appearance in *Il ritorno d'Ulisse*, an opera of the previous season, which was currently being revived at the Teatro SS. Giovanni e Paolo.[14] The expansive musical setting of Ulisse's text, which will be discussed in chapter 9, seems to underline its allusive significance.

In blurring the boundary between fact and fiction, these plays-within-a-play remind the audience of its status as audience witnessing a marvelous entertainment at the Teatro Novissimo. Indeed, if the audience needed any further reminder of where it was, it received it from Torelli's sets, at least one of which probably portrayed Skyros in the guise of Venice.[15]

The libretto bridges the gap between fictional and real worlds in other ways as well. Actors frequently shift their attention back and forth between stage and theater, playing off their fictional companions against the audience by addressing first one group then the other in asides, or by addressing both together in

11. "Versi, macchine e canto / Son atte a render pazze / Le più saggie Sibille; e se v'aggiungi / Un amoroso affetto, meraviglia non è, se da costei / Partito è l'intelletto."

12. In order to save time, as the librettist explains. "Anderebbe qui una richissima comparsa di Barriera, ma studiosi della brevità, habbiamo finto, ch'ella sia di già seguita al porto" (*La finta pazza* [Venice: Surian, 1641], 2.4–5).

13. A number of these debates were printed in Loredano, *Le bizzarrie academiche*. *La finta pazza* also features a scene involving the distribution of flowers (1.6), which may refer to an actual event in which members of the Incogniti participated—another in-

joke. Such an event is described in *Veglia prima de' Signori academici Unisoni havuta in Venetia in casa del Signor Giulio Strozzi* (Venice: Sarzina, 1638); see Rosand, "Barbara Strozzi," 244, 251.

14. On the dating of *Il ritorno d'Ulisse*, see ch. 1, nn. 24, 52, above.

15. Although engravings of Torelli's sets for the Venice production of *La finta pazza* have not survived, one of those for the Paris production of 1645 shows the city of Paris in the background (see Bjurström, *Torelli*, 137); and Torelli's second production at the Novissimo, *Bellerofonte*, featured a view of Venice in the background of one of the scenes (see fig. 16).

language characterized by double entendre. In act 3, scene 5, for example, the Eunuch, searching high and low for a doctor to cure Deidamia of her feigned madness, turns to the audience for help: "If anyone within earshot knows some secret cure for madness, either from his own experience or from that of any of his relatives, please lend it to Deidamia."[16] Like Ulisse's speech in the duel scene, the weight of this text is underscored by a lyrical setting that distinguishes it clearly from its narrative context.[17] While a number of other passages appeal to the audience as a whole, some are directed to a specific component of that audience, such as those "lovely women" addressed in the prologue by Consiglio Improviso.

> You illustrious fair ladies, to whom I dispense my treasures in loves desired, and in whose minds I would enjoy a worthy throne, well do you know that I revolve among the shining and blessed spheres of your eyes, and invite you all to pleasure at every hour. . . . Come, come, turn your eyes here, let a beautiful Fury be your teacher in learning how to explain to lovers changes of heart, and voice, and appearance. In the meantime, I return to the breast of the most beautiful. And which of you does not want me in your bosom?[18]

Then there are the allusions to the mores of modern society, such as Caronte's description of women in act 3, scene 2: "Though they have angelic and divine faces, beautiful women burn to be more beautiful still. They unhook the sun to gild their hair, they paint their lips, they burnish their skin."[19]

A number of references and word choices are amusingly evocative, laden with Venetian relevance. Caronte is the "gondolier of Cocytus," his boat the "*traghetto* of Hell." Beyond the obvious puns, which were probably not lost on any careful listener—on the name of the composer ("questi orror Sacrati") and the impresario (or leaseholder) of the theater ("E stecchi, e spine, e Lappole")—

---

16. "Ma s'altri che m'ascolta, / In se sperimentato, / O ne' congiunti suoi / Havesse alcun segreto / Di sanar la pazzia / L'impresti a Deidamia."
17. See example 3.
18. "Voi belle donne illustri, / Ben lo sapete, a cui / Ne' mendicati amori / Dispenso i miei tesori, /E d'haver godo un degno / Trono nel vostro ingegno: / Che tra le sfere lucide, e beate / M'aggiro de' vostr'occhi, e invito ogn'ora / Voi tutte al godimento. . . . / Su, su, volgete gli occhi, e un bel Furore / Sia vostro insegnamento / Per saper a gli amanti / Spiegar varie dal core / E le voci, e i sembianti / Rivolo intanto alla più bella in seno; / E chi sarà di voi, / Che non mi voglia in grembo?"
19. "Se ben han volti angelici, e divini, / Braman le belle ancor d'esser più belle. / Staccano il Sol per indorarsi i crini, / Tingonsi il labbro, illustransi la

pelle." The toilette of Venetian women was traditionally an issue of public discussion. Appropriate dress and behavior for women as well as men were legislated by Venetian sumptuary laws, and changing fashions were illustrated in the pictorial arts. The subject is amply treated in Pompeo Molmenti, *La storia di Venezia nella vita privata dalle origini alla caduta della repubblica*, 7th ed. (Bergamo, 1927–29). See especially vol. 2, *Lo splendore*, ch. 9, "Il tipo dell'uomo e della donna: Le vesti e gli abbigliamenti." Three particularly rich sources of illustration of womens' dress in late Renaissance Venice are Cesare Vecellio, *Degli abiti antichi e moderni* (Venice, 1589), Pietro Bertelli, *Diversarum nationum habitus centum et quatuor* (Padua, 1589), and Giacomo Franco, *Habiti delle donne venetiane* (Venice, 1610). All three volumes illustrate Venetian women in the act of bleaching their hair in the sun (see Molmenti, 2: 305).

there are probably numerous others that can no longer be recognized today.[20] The text itself contains a number of pointed "academic" references to various poetic styles and conventions. Caronte sings a passage in *ottava rima* (3.4), and Deidamia, as part of her mad act, parodies conventional invocation scenes by singing in *versi sdruccioli*. And there are numerous other affectations of locution and vocabulary.[21]

One central topic that would have been appreciated by all segments of the audience, though undoubtedly on different levels, was the question of sung drama itself. Like most early Venetian operas, *La finta pazza* reveals a preoccupation with the legitimacy of its own genre. We have already investigated the more overt evidence of that preoccupation in the remarks of the librettists about their works. A large part of their self-defense was directed toward justifying sung drama. Strozzi himself was as concerned as anyone about the problem. But the academic background of the librettists notwithstanding, this was no mere intellectual issue. A theater audience, no matter what its composition, could hardly have failed to notice that the characters on stage, though pretending for the most part to speak, were actually singing. *La finta pazza*, playing out the aesthetic issue, makes music part of the illusion, a further enrichment of the theatrical experience. It questions and at the same time demonstrates the validity of combining music and drama, and it implicates its audience in the affirmation, or at least in the discussion. Distinctions between actors who sing and singers who act, between speech and song, are constantly invoked as issues central to the art's own discourse. And the line between the two modes of expression is repeatedly obscured and redrawn.

Lorenzo Bianconi's recent discovery of a score for *La finta pazza* allows us to evaluate the nature of the musical illusion suggested by the libretto. In fact, the levels of musical discourse are nearly as varied as the textual ones. As in most early operas, three can be distinguished from one another: song (illustrated by formal songs such as those sung by the Nurse and the Eunuch), realistic speech (represented by normal, open-ended recitative in *versi sciolti*), and expressive or musical speech (which is portrayed in recitative heightened by repetition, sequence, or some other musical patterning in response to intensity of feeling, to emphasize the importance of certain words or ideas to the drama). In addition to highlighting individual textual points or dramatic moments, the

20. It is surely no coincidence that many of these allusions occur in passages that were cut in editions of the libretto published outside Venice.

21. These include classical quotations parodied or turned upside down (see Bianconi, preface to *La finta pazza*). Such purposeful allusions are explicitly documented in the preface to a later Novissimo libretto, *Venere gelosa* (1643), 14: "Comparve . . . un buffone del Re chiamato Trulla, del quale si servì l'Autore dell'opera per burlarsi di certi Poetastri, e penne de' nostri tempi, che stimando, trovar translato, e Parole sconcie, e fantastiche, si sconciano in trovarne per parlare da strambi, che però stuzzicato da quelle per prenderne diletto, così verseggiò": (and there follows some dialogue).

shifts between these different modes challenge the audience to define and understand their experience. Are the characters speaking or singing? What is the difference? The multiple levels of musical illusion amplify those in the text.

Among the various scenes, characters, and references that play upon the legitimacy of sung drama is one critical figure, the Eunuch, a singer by profession. His job is to guard and serve the daughters of Licomede, or, more pointedly, to entertain them by singing. In two different scenes the Eunuch offers a pretext for repeated references to music, as well as for several actual songs. During the first (1.6), the play-within-the-play that features Licomede's daughters on their own small stage, he is urged to sing; he refuses, unleashing a bitter diatribe against music, thick with double entendre: "Cursed be the day that I met you, Music, eternal death of him who uses you at court. Why can't my chest explode with my vocal chords? I serve a cruel tyrant who, with the liberty of others in her hands, makes free harmony mercenary."[22] References to *corde* and to the enforced mercenary goal of *libera armonia* may be allusions to features of contemporary operatic practice: castration and commercialization.[23] The Eunuch finally does sing, of course, producing a typically lascivious song of advice that compares the fate of unmarried women to that of the rose, appreciated in the morning, scorned by evening. One of the few closed forms in the score, it is directed to its double audience, on stage and in the theater.[24]

The second "music" scene mixes a similar variety of apposite musical references. Again the Eunuch plays the unwilling singer who, having stopped another song after a single stanza, is accused by the "mad" Deidamia of castrating *canzonette*. He himself alludes in various ways to his own ambiguous sexuality, mixing musical and sexual metaphors: references to chords or ducts (*corde*, as above), to serving as bass in the (sexual) music of the world, and to supporting the counterpoint of others.[25] Castratos, of course, represented a

---

22. "Sia maledetto il dì, ch'io ti conobbi, / Musica, eterna morte, / Di chi t'adopra in Corte. / Come scoppian le corde / Che non mi scoppia il petto? / Servo tiranna ria / Dell'altrui libertà, / Che mercenaria fà / La libera armonia."
23. *Corde* may refer to the sperm ducts, which were cut when boys were castrated. The reference to the mercenary use of "free harmony" recalls the reasons some Incogniti advanced for Apollo's refusal to grant Anna Renzi a place in Parnassus: "lo sdegno, che prendeva Sua Maestà [Apollo] dal vedere la Musica, ch'è un attrovato divino, divenuta stromento d'una poco honorata mercantia; mentre osservava l'avaritia di molti, che si servivano del mezzo d'una voce canora per incantare gli animi, acciochè non badassero alla spesa" (*Bizzarrie academiche del Loredano*, parte seconda [Bologna: G. Longhi, 1676], 180–82; quoted in Bianconi and Walker, "Dalla 'Finta pazza,'" 418 and nn. 163–64); see also John

Rosselli, "From Princely Service to the Open Market: Singers of Italian Opera and Their Patrons," *Cambridge Opera Journal* 1 (1989): 24.
24. "Belle Rose, che regine / Sete pur degli altri fiori, / La Natura fra le spine / Chiuse in van vostri tesori: / Già d'un Maggio ornavi il seno, / Hor di Rose l'Anno è pieno.

"Belle Donne, voi, che nate / Per bear gli uomini sete, / Più racchiuse, più peccate, / Più guardinghe, più cadete. / Foste un tempo un sol secondo, / Hor di Donne è pieno il mondo.

"Sembra Rosa la bellezza: / Quando spunta si gradisce: / Sul mattino ella s'apprezza: / Su la sera si schernisce. / Se Donzella non si sposa, / Presto langue come Rosa."
25. This is a conventional sexual allusion; for example, in *Gli amori di Giasone e d'Isifile* by Orazio Persiani (Venice: Bariletti, 1642), Ermafrodite sings: "M'addoppiasti il diletto / Natura e ti ringrazio /

special class of singer. Though they had long performed as church musicians, their appearance on the operatic stage must have elicited particular curiosity on the part of the audience. Knowing allusions to their sexuality were a sure source of titillation.[26]

The presence of a singer in the dramatis personae and the use of the singing scene was a convention borrowed from spoken comedy, but it found special relevance in opera as a reminder of the underlying aesthetic ambivalence of the genre. These singers are not the heroes, the Apollos and Orpheuses, whose musical exploits provided the subject matter of the very earliest operas; they are dramatically extraneous characters, who seem to exist primarily to point up the fact that the others are actors who happen to be singing. Although *La finta pazza* was not the first opera to feature such an extraneous "singer" (there had been one in Strozzi's *Delia* two years earlier), its popularity may have given special impetus to what was to become a long tradition. The singing scene may have been introduced into opera originally for reasons of verisimilitude or for ironic commentary, but it persisted well beyond the period of necessity as one of the best-loved conventions of Venetian opera throughout the century. Indeed, the "music" or "singing" scene has retained its appeal as an aesthetic conceit in opera even to this day.

In addition to the Eunuch, the dramatis personae of *La finta pazza* include several other characters for whom singing was not unnatural, at least part of the time. The gods, for instance, by virtue of their divinity, were exempt from laws governing normal human discourse. Deidamia, while pretending to be mad, released herself from the bonds of realistic behavior. Her singing in fact was a persuasive part of the act that convinced her fellow characters of her distraught condition, and it was enjoyed by the audience made party to her pretense. Obviously, madness was a particularly suitable justification for irrational behavior, for singing rather than speaking.[27] But Deidamia also sang when her

Passando di Donzella in pargoletto / Mi rinovo il piacer quand'io son satio, / E fo con doppio spasso /In Musica d'Amor soprano, e basso" (p. 5). Strozzi's *Delia* contains some similar language; cf. Wolfgang Osthoff, "Maschera e musica," *NRMI* I (1967): 30. See also the much more graphic text of the anonymous mid-seicento cantata, "Lilla vergognosetta" (I-MOe Mus. G. 258), which provides a lexicon for such references. The cantata is discussed by Margaret Murata, "Singing about Singing, or The Power of Music, Sixty Years After," in *In cantu et in sermone: For Nino Pirrotta on His 80th Birthday*, ed. Fabrizio della Seta and Franco Piperno (Florence, 1989), 363–82.

26. The castrato was a favorite butt of sexual satire throughout the seventeenth century. See, for example, the poem by Francesco Melosio, "Difesa di un musico castrato amante" (*Poesie e prose* [Venice, 1704], 436); and the "Lamento del castrato" by Fabrizio Fontana (with text possibly also by Francesco Melosio) in I-Bc Q14, fols. 134ᵛ–39. For a thorough investigation of the castrato during this period, see John Rosselli, "The Castrati as a Professional Group and a Social Phenomenon, 1550–1850," *AcM* 60 (1988): 143–79. While castratos were certainly important in these operas, they did not receive the attention lavished on the female prima donnas. They had not yet achieved the status they would enjoy in Handel's day.

27. For more on madness as an operatic convention, see ch. 11 below; also Ellen Rosand, "Operatic Madness: A Challenge to Convention," in *Music and Text: Critical Inquiries*, ed. Steven Scher (in press).

emotions got the better of her. Emotional excess, which induced a kind of madness, permitted, sometimes even demanded, extravagant musical expression.[28]

Acchille is another character who claims a certain immunity from decorum, and this by virtue of his disguise. Himself only in private, he must pretend to be someone else at all other times; and the deception frees him from having to behave in a verisimilar manner—in fact it requires just the opposite. However unnaturally he speaks—or sings—while disguised, the audience forgives him; it knows he is pretending. Actually, though, Acchille's singing threatens to give him away, for the historical Achilles was well known as a musician, having received musical instruction from Chiron, legendary educator of heroes. His singing, then, is doubly justified, by his disguise and by his training.

Disguise as a device of plot is of particular importance to this opera. Whether introduced for the specific purpose of legitimizing singing or for the more general purpose of stretching verisimilitude, this most obvious (and most superficial) form of pretense lies at the core of *La finta pazza* and literally generates all of its action. Disguise is intrinsic to the story of Achilles' seclusion on Skyros and was undoubtedly one of its major attractions to Strozzi. The account of Papinius Statius (*Achilleis*) must have seemed ideal material for a libretto. Acchille's sexual transformation is made all the more convincing (and humorous) in the opera by the casting of a castrato in the role. The other castrato in the cast more perfectly fit his part: the Eunuch was a "real" one, both on and off stage, in the drama as well as in life. Acchille, on the other hand, despite being a castrato off stage, needed his virility in the opera—the plot depended on it. His high voice, then, gave ironic credibility to his disguise as a woman.

Acchille's disguise, in addition to legitimizing his singing in general, gives him the excuse to extol the delights afforded by transformations, a theme appropriate to any theatrical representation—particularly from the mouth of a castrato—but especially relevant to a Venetian audience during Carnival: "O sweet change of nature, a woman transforming herself into a man, a man changing himself into a woman, varying name and figure . . . how many of you envy my state, that of being both man and girl?"[29] Like several others we have noted, the significance of this passage is underscored by its poetic structure and

---

28. The distinction between song and speech in Deidamia's role is not made especially clear by the poet. Other librettists were perhaps more careful than Strozzi to justify specific formal texts. In any case, the casts and plots of subsequent Venetian operas confirm the continued importance of justifying singing, even through the 1660s; see Pirrotta, "Early Opera and Aria," *Music and Theatre*, ch. 6, and ch. 9 below.

29. "Dolce cambio di Natura, / Donna in huomo trasformarsi, / Huomo in donna tramutarsi, / Variar nome e figura / . . . Quanti invidiano il mio stato, /Per far l'huomo e la donzella?" (2.2).

musical setting: three symmetrical quatrains set lyrically, as a song. Directed pointedly at the audience, it might have served as a theme song for any number of subsequent Venetian operas.[30]

Only a few of the nine operas that preceded *La finta pazza* in Venice utilize disguise, but it is prominent in many later ones. Indeed, *La finta pazza* probably created the vogue for disguise, just as it did for so many other operatic conventions. It is worth noting, though, that in *La finta pazza* a man pretends to be a woman—in most other operas, before as well as after, the disguise works the other way. Admittedly, few other early librettists found disguise as conveniently built into their sources as Strozzi did, but they did not hesitate to introduce it when absent. The plot of nearly every opera of the 1640s, and many later ones, hinges on the disguise and subsequent uncovering of at least one character.

The device was carried to an extreme in the last opera performed at the Novissimo, *Ercole in Lidia* (1645), in which a single character, Rodopea, is so completely disguised that no one, either in the drama or the audience, learns the character's true identity until the final scene of the opera. During the course of action, however, Rodopea appears to reveal her/himself several times, first as a woman, then as a woman pretending to be a man in disguise, then as a man pretending to be a woman, and so on. The librettist's description of the character hardly does justice to the complex gyrations of the plot: "Rodopea creduta donna vestita da huomo scoperta per Alceo figliuolo d'Ercole." The singing actress who played the role was, of course, none other than Anna Renzi. Like the singing scene, the convention of disguise persisted in opera well beyond the period of its specific usefulness. Its pure and timeless value as a theatrical device kept it alive as an operatic convention to the end of the seventeenth century and beyond.

Although the impact of *La finta pazza* was undoubtedly enhanced by Incognito propaganda, its intrinsic appeal is confirmed by its longevity as an operatic vehicle, and especially by the extent to which subsequent operas availed themselves of its most striking features. I have mentioned two: song and disguise; there are others, such as sleep, which is used as a dramatic expedient— Deidamia feigns sleep in order to encourage Achille to speak his mind. But these devices were such common theatrical property that their adoption or transformation into operatic conventions cannot be automatically ascribed to the influence of any single work. This is not true of one, however, undoubtedly the most conspicuous feature of *La finta pazza*: madness, to which its very title drew immediate attention. The appearance of mad scenes in a number of sub-

---

30. See Osthoff, "Maschera e musica," esp. 29–30.

sequent operas surely reflects the influence of *La finta pazza*; it also strongly suggests that the same opera may indeed have inspired the adoption of the other, more general, theatrical devices.

Heiress to the numerous "pazze" of *commedia dell'arte*, tragicomedy, and the pastoral, and progenitor of as many others in musical guise, Strozzi's Deidamia was actually not the first operatic madwoman. But her predecessor, Strozzi's own Licori, to whom she was intimately related, probably never saw the light of the theater.[31] Her successors were much more forthcoming. They seem to have turned up almost immediately, even while Deidamia herself was still ranting on stage. During Carnival of 1641, when Venetian audiences could have seen five different operas at the four theaters then in operation, both *Didone* (Busenello/Cavalli) at S. Cassiano and *La ninfa avara* (Ferrari) at S. Moisè had characters suffering from temporary—not feigned—madness, probably inspired by *La finta pazza*, which was playing to packed houses at the Teatro Novissimo.

Lack of precise dating usually makes it difficult to ascribe priority to one or another opera of the same season. But whether or not it was actually performed first, immediate borrowing from *La finta pazza* would have been facilitated by the printing of its libretto before the first performance. The indebtedness of *Didone* to an earlier model is particularly striking. The madness of Iarba, Didone's eventual husband (one of Busenello's bows to modern taste), was certainly a late addition, since it was not mentioned in the scenario published to coincide with the first performance. The solo scene in which Iarba's madness first manifests itself (2.12) is actually described in the scenario as act 3, scene 1, but without any reference to madness. "Iarba, noticing the too polite reception accorded Enea by the Queen, and discovering that her pretexts for turning away his love and his proposal of marriage are false, enunciates forcefully some truths about love."[32] And his three subsequent mad scenes (2.13; 3.2, 10) do not occur in the scenario at all. The appearance of these scenes in the score and libretto of *Didone* might easily have postdated the opera's first performances, since the score is a fair copy of the performance material and the libretto was not printed until many years later.[33] In any case, the madness begins at the very

31.   This relationship is fully explored in ch. 11 below.

32.   "Iarba, accortosi delle accoglienze troppo cortesi, fatte dalla Regina ad Enea, e scoprendo falsi i pretesti addotti dalla Regina, per escluder gl'amori, e le pretese nozze con lei, dice per martello qualche verità nelle cose d'Amore" (*Didone*, scenario, 3.1).

33.   In Busenello's collected works, *Delle hore ociose* (Venice: Giuliani, 1656). The later addition of these scenes is actually documented by the score of the work (I-Vnm, It. IV, 355 [9879]), for they alone are written in a hand other than that of the main copyist. See Jeffery, "Autograph Manuscripts," 125; also Glover, *Cavalli*, 72; and especially Rosand, "Opera Scenario," 341–42.

end of act 2, at a joint in the drama where it could have been added without difficulty.

Almost as if to excuse—as well as to underscore—the relationship between his work and Strozzi's, Busenello concludes the first of Iarba's three mad scenes with an aside to the audience, a message from the poet through the mouth of a madman:

Non possono i Poeti a questi dì	The poets of these days
Rappresentar le favole a lor modo,	Can't represent stories in their own way.
Chi ha fisso questo chiodo,	He who adheres to this rule
Del vero studio il bel sentier smarrì.	Has lost the path of true learning.

Iarba's sudden transformation from rejected lover into librettist's spokesman commenting on the action is a sure sign of madness![34] Madness may also have been an afterthought in the other opera of 1641, *La ninfa avara*. The publication of its libretto likewise followed the original production, appearing at least a year later—which left plenty of time to accommodate the last-minute insertion of a mad scene.[35]

The 1642 season seems to have been free of operatic madness, but in the following year a mad episode was ostentatiously grafted onto another opera that was originally constructed without it, Faustini's and Cavalli's *Egisto* at S. Cassiano. In the preface to his libretto, Faustini apologized for introducing a mad scene for the hero "in imitation of an action already seen several times on stage," explaining that he had bowed to pressure from an "important person" (the impresario?) who wished to satisfy the performer of the role (Appendix I.31a).[36] While not *finta*, Egisto's madness was temporary, and like Deidamia's served to achieve the desired end, his reconciliation with his recalcitrant be-

34. Cavalli emphasizes this aside by setting much of it to repeated notes at the top of Iarba's range; the character explains the reasons for his madness with maddening logic. It is a sentiment that echoes, amplifies, and particularizes the message in Busenello's opening note to the reader, where he admitted to having embroidered the Virgilian plot to create a happy ending, which he claims is only as anachronistic as Virgil himself: ancient poets followed their own laws, so why can't modern poets do the same? (Appendix I.11b).

35. Pirrotta, "The Lame Horse and the Coachman," *Essays*, 328 nn. 10–11, has identified the strophic aria "Amor proprio è una rapa" from the same scene as a text borrowed from an earlier Ferrari libretto, *Il pastor regio* (1640), which would suggest that the whole scene might have been added later or

revised after it was written. I have not been able to locate the text in edition of *Il pastor regio*, however.

36. Paolo Fabbri argues ("Alle origini di un 'topos' operistico: La scena di follia," in *L'opera fra Venezia e Parigi*) that the "action already seen several times on stage, transferred from spoken to musical drama," refers primarily to the convention of madness in *commedia dell'arte*; but the performer who wanted a mad scene surely had in mind Deidamia's success in the musical drama two years earlier. On this scene and its relationship to exigent "commedia dell'arte" performers, see ch. 11 below. Interestingly, Faustini's apology is omitted from the prefaces to the librettos printed in conjunction with revivals of *Egisto* in Bologna (1647) and Florence (1667), presumably because operatic madness had become thoroughly conventionalized in the interim.

loved, Climene. Madness, feigned or real, but transitory, persisted for a number of years as an expedient, becoming for a while the conventional fate of rejected lovers. Perhaps the last instance of the direct influence of *La finta pazza*, however, occurred in 1657, in an opera by Aureli and Pietro Andrea Ziani, *Le fortune di Rodope e Damira*. In it, Damira feigns madness to regain her husband who has fallen in love with Rodope. The role featured Anna Renzi, "la finta pazza" herself, in her final Venetian performance.

Incognito propaganda was instrumental in assuring the initial impact of *La finta pazza* on its Venetian audience, and that impact provided the impetus for its circulation around Italy. But publicity alone cannot account for its popularity. There was something inherent in the work itself, like the scenario of a *commedia dell'arte*, a basic structure that lent itself to improvisation and accommodation, that made the opera portable. These intrinsic qualities are set into relief by the librettos printed in subsequent years in connection with performances by traveling opera companies in Piacenza, Florence, Bologna, and elsewhere. The extent to which those performances altered the original, cutting all "Venetian" allusions—for example, to the Trojan succession or to the Teatro Novissimo—confirms the parochial relevance of such passages. It also attests to the viability of the work without them. The *venezianità* of the original *Finta pazza*, reflecting the patriotism of the Incogniti, certainly contributed to its initial success at the Teatro Novissimo—we shall examine this in the next chapter. But it was without the Venetian references that the opera was known outside Venice. The local allusions were sustained by a more generic sense of theater. Because it exploited theatrical experience in the broadest possible way, *La finta pazza* could appeal to a wide and complex public, patrician and common, Venetian and foreign.

The success of some later operas equaled that of *La finta pazza*, but the climate for their success owed much to that first operatic hit. Because of its wide dissemination, *La finta pazza* paved the way; it defined the new genre for an audience of unprecedented size. More effectively than any previous work, it demonstrated what opera was and what it could be; it epitomized the means by which opera exercises its fascination on its audience. By its bold and basic music-theatricality, it provided a mirror in which a broad spectrum of society, not only Venetians, could see itself reflected.

5

·   ·   ·

All'immortalità del nome di Venetia: The Serenissima on Stage

The extraordinary success of *La finta pazza* was in large measure a function of its sheer theatricality, its ability to reach out and engage its audience—by direct address, through topical allusions, by scenographic marvels. One strong component of the bond between the opera and its original public was political, depending upon that special self-awareness of the Venetians. *La finta pazza* played to their *venezianità*, to their shared sense of being citizens of a unique state, uniquely situated in time and place.

In this light, Strozzi's choice of subject is of particular relevance, for it affirms one reading of the mythical foundation of Venice. In act 1, scene 4, Venere consoles herself for her future loss of the Trojan War:

> I know the Fate of Asia requires that I be conquered in the end, but destiny will make amends for the great sorrow of my losses. Venetian and Roman will not from the Greek Achilles spring, but from good Trojan blood: And thus I have good reason to be proud.[1]

Taking comfort in the knowledge that, despite the fall of Troy, the Trojans will emerge as the progenitors of two future civilizations, she gives voice to the myth of the Trojan origins of the city on the lagoon.

Other librettos of the late 1630s and early 1640s also exploited the events and personages surrounding the Trojan War and its consequence, the subsequent founding of Rome, as the basis of their plots: *Didone*, *Le nozze d'Enea e Lavinia*, *Il ritorno d'Ulisse*, *Le nozze di Teti e di Peleo*, to mention only the most conspicuous. While the connections between these works, their common historical background and shared characters, would have enhanced their combined, cumulative impact on any audience, the choice of the Trojan theme had

---

1. "So, ch'il Fato d'Asia vuol, / Ch'io rimanga vinta alfin, / Ma ristora il grande mal / Delle perdite mie anco il destin. / Deve il Veneto, e 'l Roman / Non d'Achille Greco uscir, / Ma dal buon sangue Troian: / Onde ho giusta cagion d'insuperbir" (*La finta pazza* 1.4). This scene is cut in all the non-Venetian editions of the libretto.

special resonance for an audience of Venetians. As Strozzi's Venere declares, the fall of Troy is prelude to the future rise of Venice.

The Myth of Venice

In their misty visions of the origins of their city, Venetian chronicles traced two alternative routes back to Troy. One offered a direct line of descent: just as the Trojan Aeneas had founded Rome, so, in parallel course, Antenor had fled burning Troy for northern Italy, there to found Venice—not, significantly, Padua (which more famously claimed him as progenitor).[2] The second version, less direct, but boasting a more celebrated genealogy, went via Rome. The city established by Aeneas developed into the Roman Republic and matured into the full glory of empire, only to succumb to inevitable decline. Once-mighty Rome fell to the invading barbarian hordes, and from the ruins of one great historical epoch there rose a new, divinely ordained republic founded in Christian liberty. The successor to the pagan state created by Aeneas was the Republic of Saint Mark, which, favored by God, was destined to surpass Rome in power and vastness of dominion, glory and abundance of riches. Either way, then, the myth of Venice was based, ultimately, on the Trojan succession.

Integral to that myth of Venice as the safeguard of liberty and justice and preserver of civilization was the Rome-Venice *paragone*. Evolving as a response to the need for historical self-definition, an exercise in political etiology, the myth proved extraordinarily successful at home as well as abroad in promoting the image of Venice. It shaped the political imagination of the Serenissima and came to permeate every aspect of Venetian culture as well. Broadcast in a remarkable variety of literary efforts—including religious and political tracts and histories, in addition to encomiastic poetry and occasional scripts—it assumed pictorial form in the decorations of the Ducal Palace and other public buildings. The personification of the state as an armed female warrior, Venetia, was explicitly modeled on the goddess Roma.[3]

Although the myth had slowly evolved in the course of the Middle Ages—crudely asserted in the chronicles, more elegantly and influentially articulated by Petrarch—events in more recent history stimulated important elaborations of the basic material. The most serious threat to the survival of Venice, the

---

2. Not only was Venice thus founded by a heroic, free, and noble people—and not by fearful fishermen in flight from invading barbarians, another version of its origins—but it was, according to these same chronicles, established immediately after the fall of Troy, long before Rome. For a review of the early sources, see A. Carile and G. Fedalto, *Le origini di Venezia* (Bologna, 1978), 55–68. On Trojan descent as a sine qua non of imperial ambition, see Frances A. Yates, *Astraea: The Imperial Theme in the Sixteenth Century* (Boston, 1975), 50, 130–33.

3. See David Rosand, " 'Venetia Figurata,' " 177–96. For the decorations of the Ducal Palace, see Wolfgang Wolters, *Der Bilderschmuck des Dogenpalastes: Untersuchungen zur Selbstdarstellung der Republik Venedig im 16. Jahrhundert* (Wiesbaden, 1983).

League of Cambrai (1508) and the accompanying papal interdict (1509), forced significant and resonant modifications. That crisis was successfully resolved with the Peace of Bologna (1529–30), but Venice could no longer rely on her military might. With her imperial momentum thwarted, she now emphasized her diplomatic virtues, her role as champion of peace as well as liberty. A new, Renaissance iconography was developed as part of this self-conscious presentation of a new rhetorical image of Venice, one populated by Olympian deities and pagan heroes. It is most publicly announced in the sculptural program of the Loggetta of San Marco designed by Jacopo Sansovino in 1537: in niches, bronze figures of Minerva, Apollo, Mercury, and Peace declare the special attributes of the state; in the attic above, a relief representing Venice as Justice is flanked by others of Venus (Cyprus) and Jupiter (Crete), suggesting the expanse of Venice's maritime empire.[4]

In the Ducal Palace, the central architectural monument of Venetian political power and wisdom, this imagery was brought to still more spectacular life in the paintings of Veronese and Tintoretto. Personified in those canvases were the same virtues, attributes, and qualities that were celebrated again and again in the encomiastic poetry in praise of Venice. Venetian poets invoked the same allegorical dramatis personae in giving voice to the myth. Thus, for example, a poem by Domenico Venier, written before the middle of the sixteenth century and set to music by Baldassare Donato, sings of "Gloriosa felice alma Vineggia / Di Giustizia, d'amor, di pace albergo." Another, also set by Donato, celebrates the "Quattro Dee che 'l mondo honora et ama," the four political virtues of Victory, Peace, Wisdom, and Fame. And, combining these several arts, theatrical presentations in the Ducal Palace gave further life to their message in the late cinquecento. In a masque such as the *Rappresentatione fatta avanti il Serenissimo Prencipe di Venetia Nicolò da Ponte, il giorno di S. Stefano 1580,* the text of which was duly published, the characters include Peace and Victory as well as Wisdom, by now traditional personifications of Venice's political *virtù.*[5] Venice had quite effectively pressed all the arts into service in presenting

---

4. For the development of this Olympian iconography, see David Rosand, "Venezia e gli dei," in *"Renovatio urbis": Venezia nell'età di Andrea Gritti (1523–1538),* ed. Manfredo Tafuri (Rome, 1984), 201–15, with further bibliography. The particularly musical dimensions of Venice's self-image as a harmonically proportioned state are discussed in Ellen Rosand, "Music in the Myth of Venice." On the historical situation and its consequences, see esp. Felix Gilbert, "Venice in the Crisis of the League of Cambrai," in *Renaissance Venice,* ed. J. R. Hale (London, 1973), 274–92, and id., *The Pope, His Banker, and Venice* (Cambridge, Mass., 1980).

5. Wisdom, addressing the other characters, declaims: "Tra voi non cresca lite, / Ambe giostrate al pari, / Ambe siete sorelle, / Nate ad un parto istesso, / Ecco la cara Madre / VENETIA, ch'apre il grembo / Virginal, fatto sol per voi fecondo, / State mill'anni in quest'aurato tetto, / Consolate di Madre, e di ricetto." See Rosand, "Music in the Myth," 528–29, 537. Donato's madrigals were probably sung at one of those uniquely Venetian religious-civic occasions, the joint celebration of Ascension Day and the Marriage of Venice to the Sea — for which see Muir, *Civic Ritual,* 119–34.

herself to the world, and the Venetians themselves were at once participants in and audience to this spectacle.

In the opening years of the seventeenth century, a crisis once again confronted Venice, an open conflict with Rome that led to yet another papal interdict (1606–7). Seizing the occasion, Venetian apologists—led by Paolo Sarpi—reaffirmed the superiority of their city over (now modern) Rome, celebrating it as a haven of religious liberty.[6] And the War of Candia (Crete), beginning in 1645, offered still further occasion for mounting the literary defense of Venice—now as the civilized Christian bulwark against the pagan barbarians of the east.[7]

Among the most prominent of the writers whose pens were in the active service of the Serenissima and who exploited the Rome-Venice *paragone* toward that end was Giulio Strozzi. His epic poem *Venetia edificata* (1624), a monumental verse narration of the founding of Venice, epitomizes the mythic vision of Venetian history (figs. 13, 14). Continuing the long tradition of genealogical epics, Strozzi's "poema eroico" aspires to be the Venetian *Aeneid*—and, by implication, to crown its poet as a Virgil *redivivus*—although Ariosto is fully acknowledged as a more modern model. The author's ornate dedication of his work to the "immortal" name of Venice establishes its reverential tone and encomiastic intent; filling two pages, it offers an epigraphic summary of the myth of Venice:

ALL'IMMORTALITÀ / DEL NOME / DELLA SERENISSIMA REPVBBLICA / DI VENETIA / HEREDE DELL'ANTICO VALORE, PROPVGNACOLO D'ITALIA / ORNAMENTO D'EVROPA, / MARAVIGLIA DELL'VNIVERSO, / SOSTEGNO DELLA CHRISTIANA RELIGIONE, /PRIMOGENITA DI SANTA CHIESA, / ORACOLO DI TVTTI I PRINCIPI. / SPLENDORE DI TVTTI I SECOLI, / SEMINARIO D'INVITTI EROI, / STANZA DI VERA LIBERTÀ, / GLORIOSISSIMA IN PACE, / FORTISSIMA IN GVERRA, / SEMPRE MAGNANIMA, / SEMPRE FELICE, / SEMPRE GIVSTA, / QVESTO BRIEVE COMPENDIO / DELLE VENETE LODI / RIVERENTEMENTE / PORGE, DONA, E CONSACRA, / GIVLIO STROZZI HVMIL SERVO, / ET AMMIRATORE / DI TANTE VIRTÙ.[8]

---

6. On Sarpi, see Gaetano Cozzi, *Paolo Sarpi tra Venezia e l'Europa* (Turin, 1979); also William J. Bouwsma, *Venice and the Defense of Republican Liberty: Renaissance Values in the Age of the Counter Reformation* (Berkeley and Los Angeles, 1968).

7. For some of the literature published during this period, see Emmanuele A. Cicogna, *Saggio di bibliografia veneziana* (Venice, 1847), 259–60.

8. "To the immortality of the name of the Most Serene Republic of Venice, heir to ancient valor, Bulwark of Italy, Jewel of Europe, Marvel of the universe, Defender of the Christian faith, First-born of the Holy Church, Oracle of all princes, Splendor of all ages, Seminary of unconquered heroes, Home of true liberty, Most glorious in peace, Most powerful in war, Always magnanimous, Always happy, Always just, This brief compendium of Venetian praises is reverently offered, presented, and consecrated, by Giulio Strozzi, the humble servant, and admirer of so many virtues" (*La Venetia edificata, poema eroico di Giulio Strozzi, con gli argomenti del Sig. Francesco Cortesi*, In Venetia, MDCXXIIII, Appresso Antonio Pinelli, Stampator Ducale, 2–2ᵛ). The work has a complicated history of publication. Cicogna, *Saggio di bibliografia*, lists a number of editions beginning with one of the first twelve cantos in 1621. The first complete edition of 1624 was followed by others in 1625 and 1626 (see nos. 1825 and 1827).

LA VENETIA EDIFICATA
POEMA EROICO
DI GIVLIO STROZZI.
Con gli Argomenti
DEL SIG: FRANCESCO CORTESI

IN VENETIA *apprefso il Pinelli con licenza, e Priuilegio.*

13. Giulio Strozzi, *La Venetia edificata* (Venice, 1624), title page.

En Juli effigiem Strozzæ vel Apolline dignā. At Venetiam rebus, Veneta quid grandius Vrbe
Grande, sub hac feruet, cum Deus ille canit.   Ista sub hac cecinit Deliŭs effigie.

M. Ant. Romitu Vicet. I.C.

F. Valesio Sculp.

14. Portrait of Giulio Strozzi, from *La Venetia edificata* (Venice, 1624).

In twenty-four cantos *Venetia edificata* recounts the foundation of Venice, combining assumptions of its Trojan origins with a more historical placement of that event in the time of Attila's invasion of Italy. Through the complex narrative—of declining Roman power and virtue, of barbarian destruction and perfidy, of the machinations of an evil sorceress and the prophecies of a good magician (Arthurian Merlin, the essential seer in such historical epics), of love thwarted but eventually rewarded—Venice comes to be founded miraculously on the lagoon for all eternity. Art herself is the agent here. Lamenting the destruction of so many noble cities, she intercedes with God and obtains the divine plans for the new foundation, as well as the holy protection of Saint Mark and the four archangels. Strozzi's verse summary heading canto 11 translates as follows: "Art, in order to mend such great destruction of the works of her illustrious and worthy hand, having ascended into Heaven, strives wisely to express her sorrow to the divine ears: God reveals to his beloved the plan of an eternal city, where in a little cove of the Sea will be enclosed all that Genius, Nature, and Heaven can achieve."[9]

In the front matter of *Venetia edificata* is a prefatory poem in praise of the author by one of Strozzi's future colleagues as Accademico Incognito and librettist, Francesco Busenello. And two of its fourteen stanzas further summarize the basic catechism of the myth:

> Queen of the Sea, Goddess of the waves, metropolis of Faith, nest of Peace, who is only like herself, who lights a perpetual torch in Liberty, who in Heaven sees no glory to which she herself is not heir.
> Sister of Astraea, immortal maiden, who blesses her vassals with sacred laws; she, who is herself both pole and star, nor fears the rage of evil influence: sing of her, praise her, in a thousand ways you will immortalize yourself by praising her.[10]

9. "L'ARTE per riparar tante rouine / Dell'opre di sua mano illustre, e degna / In Cielo ascesa, all'orecchie diuine / Di scoprir'il suo mal saggia s'ingegna: / D'vna Città, che non mai venga a fine, / Iddio l'esempio alla diletta insegna; / Oue si chiuda in picciol sen di Mare / Quant'Ingegno, e Natura, e Ciel può fare" (*Venetia edificata*, 105).

Francesco Cortesi's prose summary of this canto reads: "Dimostra l'undecimo Canto, come l'ARTE veduti gl'incendij di tante, e tante Città, si risolve d'irsene in Cielo a ritrovar il supremo Fattore, e narrategli le sue disgratie, a chiedergli una Città eterna (per cosi dire) dove la libertà, e 'l vero culto non patissero mutatione. Il che fatto, le vien promesso con giuramento dal sommo Monarca, che la Città di Venetia sarà quella, che a tali vicende non verrà in alcun tempo sottoposta. Et data la sudetta Città in cura di San Marco, al quale era stata ultimamente disfatta da gli Hunni la seggia d'Aquilea, e destinati alla guardia di Venetia quattro Angeli, c'hanno la custodia delle nostre vite, entra l'ARTE per gratia fatale da Dio nella Celeste Galleria, ov'in molti quadri svelati vede quanto havea da succedere ne' secoli venturi alla nuova Repubblica: e preso di lassù lo sbozzo, scende in terra a riformarla, secondo' l disegno del Cielo. San Marco havuto da Dio uno squittino, e registro di tutti coloro, a' quali dovrà assistere con particolar protettione, viene alla difesa della nuova Città con gli Angeli sudetti, mentre ella era dalle trame d'Irene [the sorceress on the side of Attila] infelicemente travagliata, essendosi la maggior parte de' Senatori della creduta Oriana [wife of Ezzelino, king of the Dalmatians], & di Degna sua figliuola con gran disturbo della pubblica quiete, e libertà fortemente invaghiti."

10. "La Regina del Mar, la Dea dell'onde, / Metropoli di Fè, nido di Pace, / Che sola se medesma corrisponde, / Ch'accende in libertà perpetua face, / Che nel Ciel sue glorie altro non vede, / Se non se propria di se stessa herede.

Strozzi the dramatist carried the message of his *Venetia edificata* directly into the theater. *La finta pazza* was the first of a trilogy of librettos by him that together span the period from the Trojan War to the founding of Rome. The others were *La finta savia* (1643), dealing with the proto-history of Rome, and *Romolo e Remo* (1645), which concerns its founding. The author himself outlines the structure of the trilogy in an essay at the end of the second work, *La finta savia*:

> These dramas [*La finta pazza* and *La finta savia*] are imperfect poems: the one contains a Greek story, and the other a Latin one; the one leads toward the destruction of Troy, the other refers to the future founding of Rome, which [poems], in the coming years, God willing, we are preparing to complete. . . . The real name of the *finta savia* was Anthusa, which we, for greater elegance, have changed to Aretusa: and the name Anthusa was the third name of the city of Rome. . . . The second name of Rome was Amaryllis, drawn from the loves of Ilia and Mars, which will be expounded by me in the future drama of *Romolo e Remo*. (Appendix I.18c)[11]

And he explained the relationship of his trilogy to the standard Venetian genealogy in the *Argomento e scenario* of *Romolo e Remo*. Here is his description of the prologue: "Aeneas descends on the chariot of his mother, Venus, and seeing Fame drowsy among the clouds, he invites her to broadcast for many centuries the works of his glorious descendants for the future founding of Rome, of whose valor the Most Serene Republic of Venice has remained the eternal heir."[12] The prologue concludes with the following dialogue between Enea and Fama:

"La sorella d'Astrea, l'alma Donzella, / Che in sacre leggi i suoi vassalli bea, / Quella, ch'è di se stessa, e Polo, e Stella, / Ne teme rabbia d'influenza rea; / Canta pur, loda pur, in mille modi / Te stesso eternai nelle sue lodi."

Cesare Cremonini, the intellectual inspiration of the Incogniti, had himself left a model of patriotic poetry, a verse drama on the origins of Venice: *Il nascimento di Venetia* (Venice: Ciotti, 1617). His most explicit declaration of the myth occurs in act 5, scene 14, where Nettuno compares Venice to its predecessors, Athens and Rome: "La dottissima Athene, / Ch'è di già nata, e sorge alta, & illustre / Cadrà, lassa, tantosto / Precipitata da sapor corrotto; / E Roma, c'ha più lungo il nascimento, / Misera oppressa da suo proprio peso / Fia ruina a se stessa. / Vedranno ambe di se mille rivolte, / Soggiaceran ben mille volte, e mille / A tirannico affetto, / Sorgerà questa tua men frettolosa, / Ma vivrà sempre co'l tenor medesimo / Di libertà, di concordia, di pace, / E non cadrà, se non quand'anco cada / Per

non risorger più da l'onde il Sole." In the last scene, the chorus sings a hymn to the Serenissima, using distinctly familiar language: "Così mentre di voglie regolate, / E di chiari intelletti / Nobilissimo numero raccolto / Di libertà sotto l'Auguste Insegne, / Farà di molti senni un senno solo, / E di molti consigli una prudenza. Fortunata Città c'havrete in sorte / Il giusto reggimento / D'una tanto perfetta sapienza, / Composta del saper di molti saggi." For further comment on *Venetia edificata* and Strozzi in the context of Venetian opera, see Osthoff, "Maschera e musica," 33.

11. On this trilogy, see Osthoff, "Maschera e musica," 34–35, and id., "Filiberto Laurenzi," 176–77.

12. "Scende Enea sul carro di Venere sua Madre, e veduta la Fama sonnacchiosa tra le nugole l'invita à portar' intorno per molti secoli l'opre de' suoi gloriosi Nipoti per la futura fondatione di Roma, del cui valore è rimasta eterna herede la Serenissima Republica di Venetia" (*Romolo e Remo*, scenario 8).

ENEA: You, having wreathed her tresses with immortal laurel, divulge that
        today both the walls and the great empire of Rome were founded.

FAMA: Oh happy voyage, oh welcome news.

ENEA: Of whose valor may the Venetian lion remain the eternal heir, planting his
        foot on more blessed shores.[13]

Strozzi reasserted the relationship in his description of the concluding scene of
the opera (3.12), in which Numitore, Flora, Remo, and Ilia "settle their affairs,
pray to Heaven for their prosperity, and invite their peoples, who were of noble
Trojan blood, as the Venetians still are, to applaud their deeds."[14]

    While Strozzi was a particularly vocal patriot, whose commitment to pol-
ishing Venice's image shines through most of his works, he was not the only
librettist to explicate a connection between his themes and the Venetian political
myth. Here, for example, is the author of *Le nozze d'Enea* (1640 [1641]), sound-
ing very much like Strozzi:

> Hymen himself takes the opportunity to touch upon the origin and greatness of
> Rome . . . and then the birth of our Venice, certainly an event, it is safe to say, of
> no less significance, since this most noble city began at the time when Rome fell
> under the yoke of the Barbarians, who, by invading Italy, pushed many of her in-
> habitants, who were not at all ignoble, to take refuge in these lagoons in order to
> escape their fury; and in this way they founded the city . . . which through the
> valor of our fathers attained the greatness for which we admire her now. (Appendix
> I.9k)

In his description of the closing scene, the author takes a final opportunity to
refer to the myth: "Hymen . . . with Venus and Juno . . . unites the happy
couple, foretelling from such a marriage the greatness of Rome, and the birth
and marvel of the city of Venice. Here the opera ends" (Appendix I.9l).[15]

    Perhaps the most explicit statement of the Rome-Venice connection occurs
in the preface to another libretto based on Homeric legend, Nolfi's *Bellerofonte*
(1642), the immediate successor to *La finta pazza* at the Teatro Novissimo.

---

13.   ENEA: "Tu d'alloro immortal conta la chioma / Pubblica hoggi fondate / E le mura, e l'Impero alto di Roma." FAMA: "O felice viaggio, ò nuove grate." ENEA: "Del cui valore il Veneto Leone / Rimanga eterno Erede, / Assicurando il piede / Frà spiagge più beate" (*Romolo e Remo*, prologue).

14.   "vengono à cose stabilite à pregar il Cielo per le loro prosperità & invitano i lor Popoli ch'erano del nobil sangue Troiano, come sono i Veneti ancora, ad applaudire alle lor'Opre" (*Romolo e Remo*, scenario, p. 36).

15.   Not all of the manuscript copies of the libretto have the final scene as described by the author. One that does, however, is I-Vmc Cod. Cicogna 192/2 (3331). The relevant lines replace and continue beyond the tutti for Enea, Lavinia, and the four deities that begins: "Cosa non sia / Nel ciel, nel mondo." The extra lines, spoken by Himeneo, read as follows: "Dall'alte nozze e belle / Qual veggio in girar d'anni / Città sino alle stelle / Erger superba i vanni. / Mà, che del Mondo avrà l'impero augusto / Da sotto il giogo in fin barbaro ingiusto / Caduta fortunata, / Onde qual suol Fenice / Dal rogo in acqua nata / Sorga Città felice. / Vergine, e dove è tutto al fin mortale / Ella sola perpetua, et immortale / Di pura Fè gl'onori."

The special qualities and circumstances of the city of Venice cannot be adequately described, because they exceed any term and epithet with which a worldly thing can be magnified, unless perhaps she be called rival of ancient Rome, or rather, ancient Rome come to life again in our time; in fact, if you consider the majesty of dominion, the dignity of government, the prudence and virtue of the citizens, the magnificence of the public and private buildings, and so many other marks of nobility and excellence, you will find that the expression is well suited to the comparison. In fact, her singular and miraculous site makes Venice superior to Rome, and to every other work of human hands, so that one can only acknowledge her a work of divinity.

Only in entertainments, I still think, and the famous temporary theaters of the Scauti and Curioni, is Venice not equal; but for this it worked in her favor that the Republic of Rome, established at the end of the wars and expansion, and having as a political principle athletic and bloody games, like those to which her citizens were accustomed from their military exploits, and that freed them from certain feelings of pity and tenderness that are almost innate in mankind, engaged herself in these with zeal. But the goals and institutions of this Most Serene Nation are different, and are directed only toward self-preservation, to the public good, and to the security of her subjects, whom she guides and governs with most sacred and truly Christian laws; nor is she, if indeed she takes up the sword of war, in any way ambitious or unjust, but she always either defends her own threatened or besieged states, or else comes to the aid of friends who have been oppressed by the iniquitous appetites of the powerful.

As for scenic spectacles, those instructors of men, which by offering a true model for living set them on the path of virtue, she has in these last years multiplied her power with sets and performances that are indeed regal [*affatto reali*], that would make ancient Latium blush; heavenly harmony, wondrous illusions and stage-machines, most magnificent displays of costumes, and all this in multiple theaters, with almost incredible productions. (Appendix I.20a)

Bellerofonte, especially distinguished by its literal incorporation of Venetian imagery, is the first opera in which the city was actually represented on stage by the scenery. Its prologue concludes with the emergence from the sea, by command of Nettuno, of "a most exquisite and lifelike model of Venice . . . which everyone acclaimed as a tour de force: the eye was deceived by the Piazza, with its public buildings imitated to the life, and it delighted increasingly in the deception, almost forgetting where it actually was, thanks to that fiction"[16] (figs. 15, 16).

After expressing their astonishment at the magical appearance of so beautiful a sight, like an enactment of the paintings celebrating Venice on the ceilings of the Ducal Palace, Innocenza and Astrea, the goddess of Justice, join Nettuno in singing the praises of the Serenissima, concluding the prologue with a (com-

---

16. "D'ordine suo viddesi sorger dal mare in modello la Città di Venetia così esquisita, e vivamente formata, che la confessò ogn'uno un sforzo dell'arte: Ingannava l'occhio la Piazza con le fabriche publiche al naturale immitate, e dell'inganno ogn'hor più godeva scordandosi quasi per quella finta della vera dove realmente si tratteneva" (*Bellerofonte*, p. 9).

15. Giacomo Torelli, stage set for *Bellerofonte* (1642), prologue.
Engraving by Giovanni Giorgi.

petitive) hymn in her honor: "City wise, rich, and noble over any the world admires, Sparta, Athens, and Stagira are but a modest shadow of your greatness. Henceforth the ages to come will see Heaven, swollen with light, rush to your shores as a river to pay you tribute."[17]

17. "Città sopra qualunque il mondo ammira / Saggia ricca e gentile, / Son del le tue grandezze un'ombra vile / Sparta, Atene, e Stagira. / Quindi vedranno i secoli futuri / Correrà i lidi tuoi gonfio di lume / Per tributarti il Ciel converso in fiume" (p. 22). Astraea also appears, along with Neptune, Venus, and Juno, in *Andromeda*; see the preface by Bariletti, in Worsthorne, *Venetian Opera*, appendix 3. For further bibliography on political spectacle, see the items mentioned in n. 4 above; for the late sixteenth century in particular, see Solerti, "Le rappresentazioni musicali di Venezia."

16. Giacomo Torelli, stage set for *Bellerofonte* (1642), prologue.
Engraving by Giovanni Giorgi.

Venice was depicted onstage in another libretto a few years later, Busenello's *La prosperità infelice di Giulio Cesare dittatore*.[18] Like *Bellerofonte*, Busenello's
text gives dramatic life to the traditional myth of Venice's origins, making use
of the standard iconography. In the final scene of the opera (the epilogue)
Libertà and Nettuno play out the myth in detail:

18. This work, as I have already remarked, was
probably written in 1646 for the Teatro Grimani, but
not published until 1656; it does not seem to have
been performed, perhaps because the theaters were
closed during the 1646 season. These passages are
discussed in Livingston, *La vita veneziana*, 206–8.

LIBERTÀ: Ill-treated by Rome, I turn toward the lofty peaks of sublime Olympus, because I foresee my losses clearly, nor do I know when fate will allow me to return to live on earth in safety.

NETTUNO: Stay, Liberty. Your residence will be a glorious and great city, which, virgin and invincible, will have the waves as its foundation and Heaven as its roof. Here you will see divided among a thousand heads the power of authority. Venice will be the name of this supreme and triumphant city, which will make the Adriatic shores famous; epitome of wonders, portrait of the spheres, summary of the world, rich empyrean of the arts, compendium of nature, and abridgement of the great universe. Powerful, and free, and just, in every season three signs will grow bright in the political Zodiac: Virgo, Libra, and the Lion.

LIBERTÀ: And how you console me, Oh, how you increase my dignity, O Neptune; but if only I could see among the models of eternal ideas the lofty cast and immortal image of the city that is more of Heaven than of earth.

NETTUNO: Look there, for Jove, out of his divinity, is showing a small model of happy Venice. And look how, as proof, divine lightning flashes about it, and she, serene in herself, in her radiant circle, renders the sun idle and superfluous.

LIBERTÀ: O blessed dwelling, earthly heaven for togaed demigods, you will reign over the waters, and of your empire nature will be the boundary, and the sun the sentinel.

NETTUNO: Hear, Liberty, listen to what prophetic Neptune foretells: many centuries from now you will sing the praises and I the cheers of immortal VENICE in a joyful style, in the world-famous GRIMANI THEATER.

CORO: Long live VENICE, hurrah, let every pen describe the glories of your name, the histories of your exploits, and may destiny bejewel the crowns of her most generous LION. (Appendix I.12e)[19]

The scene between Libertà and Nettuno is an allegorized reenactment of Saint Mark's holy vision, in which it is foretold that he will come to rest in Venice. Caught in a storm upon the lagoon, Mark finds refuge among its islands; in a dream an angel, or Christ himself, declares: "Pax tibi Marce Evangelista Meus. Hic requiescet corpus tuum."[20] In enumerating the unique qualities of Libertà's new haven, Nettuno charts the three signs of Venice's political

19. The refrain, "Viva Venetia, viva," is standard in the political litany of the Serenissima. Many poems, including one of Venier's set by Donato, end with this rousing affirmation. See Rosand, "Music in the Myth," 527–30. On Donato and Venier, Martha Feldman, "Venice and the Madrigal in the Mid-Sixteenth Century" (Ph.D. diss., University of Pennsylvania, 1987).
20. The "Sogno di San Marco" is, of course, a crucial scene in Venetian versions of the saint's life and as such forms part of the major illustrative cycles in the Church of San Marco and in Tintoretto's canvases from the Scuola Grande di San Marco. For Tintoretto's painting, the execution of which is generally ascribed to his son Domenico, see Rodolfo Pallucchini and Paola Rossi, Tintoretto: Le opere sacre e profane (Milan, 1982), 1: 256; 2: fig. 744. On the legend of St. Mark, see Giuseppe Pavanello, "S. Marco nella leggenda e nella storia," Rivista della città di Venezia 7 (1928): 293–324, and Silvio Tramontin, "San Marco," in Culto dei santi a Venezia (Venice, 1965), 41–73.

zodiac. *Vergine*: founded on the Feast of the Annunciation (25 March), Venice associated herself with the Virgin Mary *ab initio*, as well as with the virgin goddess Astraea, and claimed for her unconquered self the epithet "Venetia sempre vergine";[21] *Libra*: the scales of justice, the chief virtue claimed by the Republic; and *Leone*: the winged lion of her patron, Saint Mark. One of Busenello's aims in his thumbnail sketch of the mythic origins of Venice was obviously to exalt the city's present glories, in particular the Grimani theater. Involving that theater so directly as the stage from which Venice's glories will be proclaimed, he confirmed the political significance of opera, its importance as a means of enhancing the image of the Serenissima.

Busenello's view of opera as one of the jewels of the city was shared by other authors, among them Giovanni Faustini, whose contemporary *Ormindo* (1644) is yet another opera that portrays Venice on stage. The setting of the prologue represents Piazza San Marco, "the most conspicuous part of the city of Venice" ("parte più cospicua della Città di Venetia"), and the protagonist is Armonia, who summarizes the familiar genealogical myth in slightly new—operatic—terms.

> It has been five years already that I have shone on you from gilded stages and illu-minated my glories; your immortal Muses and divine swans adorn my tresses with new garlands. I, who as a child trod the stages of Athens in jeweled buskins, I, who when Greece was conquered and tamed by the victors of Rome saw no splendor or magnificence equal to yours, Most Serene and immortal Virgin.[22]

Harmony, a metaphor for civilization, has passed from Greece to Rome to Venice, whose "pompe e fasti" she deems superior to those of any other place. Here Venice is praised specifically for her hospitality to music, echoing Francesco Sansovino's remark that "music has her own special place in this city." Again, the Rome-Venice *paragone* is invoked in favor of Venice.[23] The illusion of the stage representing Venice itself is reinforced elsewhere in the opera; for example, when Nerillo remarks, touristlike, on the wonders of the city he is seeing for the first time:

21.   See references in the text of *Bellerofonte*, on pp. 134–35 above; also Sansovino, *Venetia città nobilis-sima*, 323. For more on this imagery, see David Rosand, " 'Venetia Figurata.' "

22.   "E' già varcato un lustro / Che sù palchi dorati / In te risplendo, e le mie glorie illustro, / Di novi fregi adornano i miei crini / L'Alme tue muse, e i Cigni tuoi divini. / Io che bambina passeggiai d'Atene / Con gemmati coturni in sù le Scene, / Io, che condotta fui, / Vinta la Grecia, e doma / Da vincitori à Roma, / Non vidi à le tue pompe, à fasti tuoi, / O pompa, ò fasto eguale, / Vergine Serenis-sima, e immortale" (*Ormindo*, prologue, 12).

23.   "Musica ha la sua propria sede in questa città" (Sansovino, *Venetia*, 380). See also Sansovino's description of Apollo, one of the four bronze figures in niches on the Loggetta: "questa natione si diletta per ordinario della musica, & pero Apollo è figurato per la musica. Ma perche dall'unione de i Magistrati che sono congiunti insieme con temperamento indicibile, esce inusitata harmonia, la qual perpetua questo ammirando governo, pero fu fabricato l'Apollo." For further discussion of the place of music in the myth of Venice, see Rosand, "Music in the Myth."

Che città, che città	What a city, what a city,
Che costumi, che gente	What customs, what people
Sfacciata, ed insolente.[24]	Impudent and insolent!

Not all of the librettos based on Trojan or Roman history state the Venetian connection as specifically as *La finta pazza*, *Le nozze d'Enea*, or *Giulio Cesare*. But the mythology was so much a part of the Venetian consciousness that it automatically formed part of the cultural context in which these stories were understood. It most likely underlies operas with Roman plots in which Venice is never even mentioned—such as the best known of Busenello's librettos, *L'incoronazione di Poppea*, notorious for its portrayal of Roman decadence. There is some indication that the work could have been understood by its contemporaries as a moral lesson implying the superiority of Venice over Rome, and suggesting that such immorality was only possible in a decaying society, not in a civilized nation.[25]

This response is offered in a book by a Venetian cleric, Federico Malipiero, who, like Strozzi and Busenello, was a member of the Accademia degli Incogniti. *L'imperatrice ambiziosa* (1642) tells the story of Poppaea and Nero, although it is actually more concerned with Nero's mother Agrippina, the empress of the title. And it is her downfall that inspires Malipiero's philosophical conclusion:

> This was the greatness of a woman, incomparable in every way. Thus did she fall from supreme eminence to the darkest depths, because the higher mortals rise, the more they are subject to uncertainty. Empires are transformed in a flash, like human happiness, which can collapse and be extinguished in a single moment. Often the tombs of one kingdom have become the cradles of another, and from the ruins of a fallen republic has arisen the magnificence of a new one.[26]

24. *Ormindo* 2.6. The confluence of stage and real worlds is a convention of Renaissance theater. A number of comedies by Machiavelli, Ariosto, and others were set in the cities where they were performed. Cf., for example, the opening of Machiavelli's *Mandragola* (1518): "Vedete l'apparato: / Quale o vi si dimostra / Questa è Firenze vostra; / Un'altra volta sarà Roma o Pisa." More pertinent to my point, in Aretino's *Cortigiana* (1534) an entire scene (3.7) is devoted to the praise of Venice on stage. Aretino, for his own good reasons, rehearses the entire litany of the myth of Venice, especially of its liberty and hospitality; see Patricia H. Labalme, "Personality and Politics in Venice: Pietro Aretino," in *Titian: His World and His Legacy*, ed. David Rosand (New York, 1982), 119–32. For further discussion of this convention of spoken theater, see Pirrotta, *Music and Theatre*, 77–78; see also Ludovico Zorzi, *Il teatro e la città: Saggi sulla scena italiana*

(Turin, 1977), esp. ch. 3, "Venezia: La repubblica a teatro."

25. The Venice-Rome *paragone* may be implicit in three later librettos on Roman subjects by Nicolò Minato: *Scipione affricano* (1664), *Mutio Scevola* (1665), and *Pompeo magno* (1666). See Bianconi and Walker, "Production," 257–58, on political pamphlets and their possible relation to two more explicitly political librettos of Minato's, *La prosperità* and *La caduta di Elio Seiano* (1667). See also Monson, "Aelius Sejanus." On the persistence of Roman themes throughout seventeenth-century Venetian opera, including a complete list of titles, see Giovanni Morelli, "Il filo di Poppea: Il soggetto antico-romano nell'opera veneziana del seicento, osservazioni," in *Venezia e la Roma del Papa* (Milan, 1987), 245–74; Morelli considers the political significance of Roman subject matter on 258–62.

26. "Queste dunque descritte fur le grandezze

The implications are clear. Malipiero's invocation of the conventional Rome-Venice *paragone* is only slightly veiled.

Although not always in connection with Rome, Venice as a political or symbolic image figures in one way or another in practically every work produced during the first five or six seasons of operatic activity, whether metaphorically, through choice of plot, or in a more literal way, through direct reference. We have seen her depicted visually. She is personified even earlier in the final scene of Ferrari's *Armida* (1639), where Venetia herself sings her own praises to an audience of Nereids:

> Would I, mother of heroes, support of the glorious Adriatic empire, leave you on a solitary path? Happy is he who rests in this place. My waves are swollen with treasures, and my sands teem with triumphs. When the sea murmurs, it speaks of me, and it says in its language that there is no nation more beautiful outside of Heaven.

And the Nereids respond with the typical encomium to the city (like the conclusion of *Giulio Cesare* and *Bellerofonte*):

> Come, glorious heroes, to celebrate among us, while to the sound of musical harmonies every shore and bank echoes, Long live VENICE![27]

Even *Ermiona*, the lost "proto-Venetian" opera performed in Padua in 1636, contained a number of topical allusions to Venice. In his account of the performance, Bartolini describes Venus stopping to deliver "the praises of the Serene Republic of Venice" ("le lodi della Serenissima Republica di Venezia"), which, he continues, "is the greatest marvel that has ever been in the universe" ("è la maggior meraviglia che mai sia stata nell'universo").[28]

Aside from the Troy-Rome-Venice succession, other thematic relationships to Venetian imagery are established through ancient mythology. *Andromeda*,

---

d'una Donna inarivabile in tutte le cose. Così trabboccò dall'eminenza al profondo, perche quanto più le mortali cose sono ellevate, tanto più sono all'incertezza assoggettate. Gli imperij si mutano a momenti, come la felicità humana traccolla, e fornisce in un punto. Le tombe spesso d'un regno fur le culle d'un altro, e sopra le rovine d'una caduta Republica insorsero le magnificenze d'una novella" (Federico Malipiero, *L'imperatrice ambiziosa* [Venice: Surian, 1642], 184). Malipiero, incidentally, was himself involved with things operatic, and his translations of the *Iliad* and *Odyssey* in the early 1640s may have been responses to the same impetus that led librettists to choose Roman and Trojan subjects. His motive for translating the Homeric epics and writing the histories of great men (such as Solomon, Hannibal, and others) was moral: he hoped to provide *exempla virtutis* for men to follow—an aim he would have

shared with at least some librettists; see Rosand, "Seneca," 47–52.

27. "Io che madre d'heroi, / D'Hadria sostegno il glorioso Impero / Sovra un ermo sentier lascerò voi? . . . / Felice chi riposa in questa sede. / Sono i mici flutti di tesori gonfi, / E le mie arene pullulan trionfi. / Quando mormora il Mar, da me ragiona; / E dice in sua favella, / Patria non è fuori del Ciel più bella." "Venite inclti Heroi / A' festeggiar tra noi. / Mentr'al suono, di musici concenti / Ogni piaggia risuona, & ogni riva / Viva VENETIA viva" (3.6). The *Argomento* describes this scene: "Vengono i due felici Heroi su' l suo [Jupiter's] trono levati dall'Invitta Regina del Mare sempre gloriosa VENETIA, per poi felicemente indirizzargli à i loro Imperi."

28. *Ermiona*, description, 93.

for example, involves a rescue at sea. And even *Arianna* may have been selected for revival in 1640, despite its old-fashioned style, partly for the relevance of its subject matter to Venetian iconography. Ariadne is the subject of one of four paintings by Tintoretto in the Sala Dorata of the Ducal Palace described by Carlo Ridolfi, the seicento biographer of the Venetian painters, as treating "subjects appropriate to the government of that Republic" ("soggetti adeguati al ministerio di quella Republica"). (The others are Vulcan with the Cyclopes, the Three Graces with Mercury, and Mars being chased away by Minerva while Peace and Abundance celebrate together.) According to Ridolfi's reading, the picture portrays the abandoned Ariadne discovered by Bacchus on the beach and crowned by Venus (with a golden crown) declaring her free and welcoming her among the heavenly bodies, "which is meant to signify Venice born on a shore of the sea, and made abundant not only in every earthly good, through Heavenly grace, but crowned with the crown of liberty by the divine hand, whose power is recorded in eternal characters in Heaven."[29]

By the mid 1640s, plots centering around the Trojan War and the founding of Rome had begun to give way to a greater variety of subject matter; connections between these new works and the myth of Venice continued to be maintained, but in different ways. However, the Rome-Venice *paragone* was now firmly ensconced in the history of Venetian opera. This is clear from the first attempt to view that history, Ivanovich's "Memorie teatrali." The connection between Rome and Venice was central to an understanding of the development of Venetian opera, a development Ivanovich viewed in political terms.

His essay opens with an unequivocal statement of the standard tenet of the myth: "Never in the world was there a republic that excelled all other republics as did Rome; nor any other that better imitated Rome than the republic of Venice" (Appendix II.6d).[30] His opening four chapters deal specifically with that relationship. The first tells how "the republic of Venice, imitating the Roman republic, created anew the magnificence of theaters," because both republics understood the secret of successful government: "Through material goods and games, used judiciously, the ruler gains the love of his people, who can never more easily forget their yoke than when sated or diverted by plea-

---

29. "che vuol dinotare, Venetia nata in una spiaggia di mare, resa abbondevole non solo d'ogni bene terreno, mediante la celeste gratia, ma coronata con corona di libertà dalla divina mano, il cui dominio è registrato a caratteri eterni nel Cielo" (Carlo Ridolfi, *Le maraviglie dell'arte* [Venice, 1648], ed. Detlev Freiherrn von Hadeln [Berlin, 1914–24], 2: 43). See Charles de Tolnay, "Tintoretto's Salotto Dorato Cy-

cle in the Doge's Palace," in *Scritti di storia dell'arte in onore di Mario Salmi* (Rome, 1961–63), 3: 117–31. Part of the same scene, featuring Ariadne and Bacchus, is also portrayed in Cremonini's *Il nascimento di Venetia*; see n. 10 above.

30. In a sonnet the Dalmatian poet had characterized his adopted home as "sole heir of Roman glory."

sures" (Appendix II.6d–e). In chapter 4 he compares Venetian theaters to those of Rome, finding many similarities—and incidentally providing important information about the structure of theaters and practice of theatergoing in his own day.

> Present-day theaters can hold a small number of people compared with ancient ones; moreover, instead of stands several ranks of boxes are constructed, most of them for the convenience of the nobility, for the ladies like to stay unmasked there and to feel at liberty. In the middle are benches, rented from night to night with no distinction as to rank, since the use of masks obviates the need for respect that was shown to the Roman senators and matrons, who made a grand appearance; for in this respect too, Venice, born free, wishes to preserve freedom for all. (Appendix II.6h)

Venetian spectacle, Ivanovich admits, cannot match in splendor that of ancient Rome, for the latter, instead of using artifice to portray violence, enacted it literally at whatever human sacrifice (Appendix II.6i). But, whereas the Roman theater, habituating the people to slaughter and horrors, was intended to serve an admonitory function, Venetian theater has a different purpose: "Today, however, musical theater has been introduced, for the lifting of the spirits and as a virtuous diversion, since one can observe the appearance of amusing machines suggested by the drama, which give great delight, along with the spectacle of sets and costumes that satisfy everyone's curiosity to the utmost" (Appendix II.6j).

Although Ivanovich was writing much later, when Venice was clearly at the height of her operatic (though no longer political) power, the importance he ascribes to the Rome-Venice comparison and his emphasis on the political component of opera are, as we have seen, borne out by the earlier sources themselves, from which he clearly derived much of his material.[31] In fact, Ivanovich's patrons, the Grimani family, were quite used to having their theater compared favorably with those of ancient Rome. In the preface to his *Scipione affricano*, performed at the Grimani theater in 1665, Nicolò Minato had invoked the familiar *paragone*: "You will see that the most-famous Grimani theater is capable of rivaling the Marcellus and Pompey theaters, and any other of the most famous ones that glorious antiquity might bring to mind."[32] So, too, had Aurelio Aureli in the dedication of his *Eliogabalo* of 1668 to the brothers Gian Carlo and Vincenzo Grimani, "who no less than the Pompeys and the Trajans

---

31. The similarity between Ivanovich's description of Roman theatrical practices and those from the preface to *Bellerofonte*, quoted above, p. 134, is one of many indications that Ivanovich read the librettos he catalogued.

32. "Lo vedrai nel Famosissimo Teatro Grimano, che sà nell'età nostra emulare i Teatri Marcelli, i Pompeiani, e qualunque altri più illustri sapesse la pomposa antichità nella memoria svegliarti" (*Scipione affricano*, preface, dedication dated 9 February 1664 [1665]).

make themselves known in the world as true Maecenases of the muses by the construction of sumptuous theaters and through the patronage of musicians."[33]

The Reality of Venice

During the late 1640s and 1650s, pressed by the success of opera to search for new sources for their plots, librettists moved away from the Trojan-Roman orbit in an eastward direction, and a number of librettos of this period are set in foreign locales like Susa, Assyria, Media, Tauris. These librettos, however, were no less closely connected to Venetian politics than their predecessors. If less concerned with the legendary origins of Venice, they seem to bear an even more specific relationship to current events. References to and personifications of Venice continue to cultivate or expand upon her image as a stronghold of freedom and haven against the barbarians, but the barbarians are now pointedly Turkish, as if in response to Venice's growing preoccupation with the Ottoman threat to her maritime power.[34] During the 1650s and 1660s, when legendary Roman heroes began to be featured with increasing frequency in opera librettos, their exploits invited comparison with those of Venetian military heroes in the War of Candia (the Rome-Venice equation once again).[35]

Venice's preoccupation with Ottoman power reached its first crisis in 1645 with the outbreak of the war, which drained Venetian manpower and resources for nearly a quarter of a century (1645–69). Its onset inspired an outpouring of patriotic zeal among the Venetian nobility, who were called upon for financial support as well as personal participation.[36] In part because this same nobility was among its chief patrons and enthusiasts, opera could not help but be affected by the crisis. Along with the prohibition of all other public spectacles, opera theaters were closed for the 1646 season, and it was not until several years

33. "che non meno de' Pompei, e de' Traiani coll'erettione di sontuosi Teatri, e con la protettione de' Virtuosi si fanno conoscer nel Mondo per veri Mecenati delle Muse" (Eliogabalo, dedication, 10 January 1667 [1668], p. 2).

34. Two librettos of 1651 featured Alexander the Great, Alessandro vincitor di se stesso by Sbarra and Gli amori d'Alessandro magno e di Rossane by Cicognini, while two operas of 1654 featured Persian subjects, Ciro by Sorrentino and Xerse by Minato. On the significance of these themes, see Wolfgang Osthoff, "Antonio Cestis 'Alessandro vincitor di se stesso,'" Studien zur Musikwissenschaft 24 (1960): 13–43.

35. See Bianconi, Seventeenth Century, 189. The implicit comparison is made explicit by Marco Rosetti in canto 34 of his long poem of 1684–93 commemorating the War of Candia, La sacra lega divisa in

quaranta libri overo canti consacrata al Ser. Prencipe et Ecc. Senato della gloriosissima repubblica (Padua: Seminario, 1696). He praises the Venetian hero Francesco Morosini: "In paragone dell'opere sue sono un nulla quelle degli Scipioni e di Pompeo. . . . Questi pugnarono contro un solo re, e tu con poche forze e molto ingegno di man togliesti a tutta l'Asia un regno" (Antonio Medin, La storia della repubblica di Venezia nella poesia [Milan, 1904], 366).

36. For the patriotic enthusiasm inspired by the War of Candia, and especially its literary expression, see Medin, La storia . . . nella poesia, 315–79. The events surrounding this costly and protracted war are chronicled in S. Romanin, Storia documentata di Venezia (Venice, 1853–61), 7: 343–526; for a modern review, see Roberto Cessi, Storia della repubblica di Venezia (Milan and Messina, 1968), 2: 193–204.

later, when the immediate crisis had passed, that Venice's operatic life returned to full strength—except, as we have seen, for the Teatro Novissimo, which never reopened.[37]

Other critical moments in the War of Candia occurred in 1651, with the Venetian victory at Paros, and again in 1656, with the successful battle of the Dardanelles. Although the outcome for the Venetians was positive—at least in the short run—these military efforts proved costly, drawing heavily upon resources and morale. They also appear to have affected operatic life: several theaters were closed for the 1651 season, and a few remained inoperative for several subsequent years as well.[38] Librettists were among those involved in the events of 1651. A volume commemorating the victory at Paros published in that year contained poetry by Busenello, Aureli, Minato, and Giacomo dall'Angelo, among others.[39]

During this period, references to Venice are usually both more explicit and extrinsic to the actual plots of librettos: they appear either in prefaces or else in prologues (or epilogues), those framing elements marginal to the drama that were traditionally reserved for occasional references to patrons or for other kinds of special communications from poet to audience. Because of their occasional nature, such prologues were rarely repeated when their accompanying operas were performed outside Venice.[40] But for Venetian purposes, practically every libretto prologue of the late 1640s and early 1650s refers to war, to the Turk, and to Venice as the bastion of peace, the most peace-loving nation on earth. In the prologue of *Ersilla* (1648) by Giovanni Faustini, for example, Venere (Ciprigna), goddess of Cyprus,[41] praises the "heroic guests" (presum-

37. SS. Giovanni e Paolo may have opened during the spring of 1647 for a performance of *Deidamia* (see ch. 3, n. 101, above). S. Cassiano and S. Moisè seem to have opened for the 1647–48 season; they were joined by SS. Giovanni e Paolo and SS. Apostoli in 1649–50. The operas listed by Ivanovich for the intervening years—all of them with librettos by Busenello, namely *La prosperità infelice di Giulio Cesare* and *L'incoronazione di Poppea* in 1646 and *Gli amori d'Apollo e di Dafne* in 1647—were not performed then. In his efforts to cover all seasons, Ivanovich may have extrapolated performances from a misreading of the date on Busenello's publication of his collected librettos, *Le hore ociose* of 1656.

38. S. Cassiano was closed from 1651 to 1657; S. Moisè closed from 1650 to 1653; SS. Apostoli closed in 1653.

39. *Le glorie dell'armi venete celebrate nell'accademia de' Signori Imperfetti per la vittoria ottenuta contro l'armi ottomane* (Venice: Pinelli, 1651). Busenello was the *protettore* of the academy, Aureli the secretary, and Minato one of the *consiglieri* (see Rosand, "L'Ovidio trasformato," LIII n. 77).

40. They would have been changed for subsequent performances in Venice too. On the impact of new prologues affixed to Venetian operas exported to Naples during the 1660s and 1670s, see Bianconi, "Scena, musica e pubblico," 21–22; also id., *Seventeenth Century*, 190, and id., "Funktionen des Operntheaters in Neapel bis 1700 und die Rolle Alessandro Scarlattis," in *Colloquium Alessandro Scarlatti: Würzburg 1975*, ed. Wolfgang Osthoff and J. Ruile-Dronke (Tutzing, 1979), 112–13. The new prologues served to transform Venetian belligerence toward the Turk into Neapolitan allegiance to the sovereign.

41. Since Cyprus was a Venetian possession, seaborne Venus was an especially appropriate mythological symbol of Venetian empire. For Venezia/Venere, see David Rosand, " 'Venetia Figurata,' " 188–90.

ably the Venetians anchored near Candia) for taking a stand as sole defenders
of the world against the Turkish barbarians:

> Heroic guests, who sit on my Cythera laden down with steel, warriors witnessing
> the errors of Ersilla, may Glory crown your locks with laurels, and with a golden
> trumpet sing your fame in resonant sound. You alone restrain the unleashed fury of
> the barbarian world. . . . I will terrify the tyrant on the throne of Byzantium with
> great-hearted pride, invincible and holy, from a floating and shining city. At the Li-
> on's roars, the grave of Leander conquered by Xerxes [i.e., the waters of the Helle-
> spont] turned back, frightened, toward the Black Sea. It feared, it trembled, that the
> magnanimous beast might drink Ottoman treachery at the spring of the Tartarean
> lair.[42]

And the prologue of Fusconi's *Argiope* (1649), written later than the rest of the
libretto (which dates from 1645), represents an allegorical conflict between
Guerra and Pace that concludes with Pace hailing Venice as her ideal resting
place:

> On my flying chariot, I made my Halcyons swiftly direct their steps here, only to
> rest until the Kingdom of the Waters was born. Clear city, chosen by the wisdom
> of Jove as a second heaven, and built for noble souls! O Fates, ignore your custom
> and spin fast the years, so that others need not have to suffer, waiting, and with a
> propitious star let fair Venice be born in the bosom of Neptune, she who with wis-
> dom and valor will be the Lady of the Sea, the glory of the world.[43]

Several prologues by Giacomo Castoreo written during the 1650s find ways
of praising Venice's peacekeeping efforts through the mouths of a variety of

---

42. "Hospiti Heroi, che sù la mia Citera / Carchi d'acciar sedete / De gl'errori d'Ersilla / Guerrieri spettatori, / V'incoroni la gloria il crin d'allori, / E con la tromba d'oro / Di voi canti la fama in suon sonoro: / D'un barbarico mondo / Voi soli raffrenate / Le furie scatenate / . . . . Sbigottirò nel soglio / Di Bizantio il Tiranno, / Con glorioso orgoglio / De petti invitti, e santi, / La Città natatrici, e folgoranti. / Del Leone a ruggiti / Il domato da Zerse / Sepolcro di Leandro / Pavido al negro mare il piè, converse; / Temè, tremò, ch'andasse / La magnanima fera / A' bever ne le fonti / De la Tartara Tana / La perfidia Ottomana" (*Ersilla*, prologue). The apostrophe to the "Venetian heroes" is fairly common. The prologue to Faustini's *Doriclea* (1645) concludes with it too, delivered by Gloria: "Di voi Veneti Heroi, / Le cui virtù sublimi / Volan dal freddo Borea à caldi Eoi, / Di voi nido e il tempio, in lui vivrete, / Ad onta di Saturnio, immortalati, / A secoli venturi, ò fortunati." It is worth remembering that 1645 was the time when political tensions with the Turk were such that

the theaters were about to close for several years.
43. "Su'l mio carro volante / Qui fei velocemente / A gli Alcioni miei drizzar le piante. / Solo per riposarmi infino a tanto, / Che nel Regno de l'Acque habbia il natale. / Chiara Città dal sen di Giove eletta, / Per Ciel secondo, e a nobil alme eretta, / Fuori del fatal'uso / De i volumi de gli anni, / Rapide o Parche homai rotate il fuso, / Perch'altri in aspettar più non s'affanni, / E con propitia stella / Nasca a Nettuno in sen Venetia bella / Che con saver, e con valor profondo / Sarà Donna del Mar, gloria del Mondo" (*Argiope*, prologue). Like *Amore innamorato* in 1642, *Argiope* is an arrangement by Fusconi of subject matter by another author (see ch. 6, n. 26, below, and Bianconi and Walker, "Dalla 'Finta pazza,'" 417 n. 156). The postponement of the production of *Argiope*—from 1645, when it was written, to 1649—may well have been owing to the politically inspired closing of the theaters, which would also account for the heavy emphasis in the later prologue on Venice's role as keeper of the peace.

divinities.[44] In that to *Eurimene* (1643), an allegory of war between Venere in a flying chariot and Marte on the ground, Venere tells Marte of Giove's decision that the Turk should be made to suffer defeat at the hands of the Venetians and urges him to stop the fighting.[45] Apollo sings a hymn of praise to Venice, haven of peace, in the prologue to *Arsinoe* (1655–56).[46] And the prologue to *Oronte* (1656) concludes with the goddess Iride exhorting members of the audience, in their capacity as defenders against the Orient, to attend to the drama.[47]

Toward the end of the 1650s, these references become even more pointed; they mention not only Venice's general attributes as bastion of peace and defender against the Turk, but specific geographical locations related to the battle for Crete and particular events. The prologue of *Tolomeo*, an anonymous text for a play with musical intermedi (1658–59), features a large number of deities associated with war: Vittoria, Vulcano, Venere, Pallade, and Marte. After a succession of specific references to Mongibello and Crete, Vittoria ends the prologue with her promise to serve the Venetian forces.[48]

The prologue of a libretto of the same year (1659), *Elena*, performed at S. Cassiano, concludes with a dialogue between Verità and Pace, which alludes to the extraordinary length of the war that has occupied Venice. (Byron referred to the War of Candia as the Iliad of Venice.)

> VERITÀ: Let the glorious Adriatic heroes hear. The time will come when the afflicted and weary Thracian, repentant in the end for his foolish pride, will beg for peace from the Great Lion.
>
> PACE: By now, in spite of Discord, my peaceful hand is dispensing olives in Adria. Indeed, it seems to me that the great Lion has arrived with his roars to frighten the moon [i.e., the crescent moon of the Turkish flag].[49]

44. Many of the texts Castoreo wrote during the 1650s were for the Teatro ai Saloni, a private theater founded by 1650 "senza alcun giro di Palchi, ma con alcuni pochi in faccia alla Scena" (Ivanovich, *Minerva*, 400). At the Saloni, performances were normally spoken, with only the prologue and intermedi set to music. Several theaters, including the Saloni, S. Salvatore, and SS. Giovanni e Paolo, seem to have specialized in politically allusive prologues.

45. "Segua ciò che destina / Il Tonante superno, / Che dell'eccelsa Monarchia d'Oriente, / Cada l'ingiusto Orgoglio / Del Hadria invitta à far scabello al soglio. / Non più guerra" (*Eurimene*, prologue).

46. "O dell'Adria ch'accoglie / Di sue glorie motrice, in sen la Pace, / Illustri Lidi, e fortunate Arene. / Dalle dorate Soglie / Dell'Oriente guerriero à voi sen viene / Il Monarca del lume, / Alle vostre vittorie, Amico Nume: / Frenate Alme sublimi / Que' bellici rigori, ond'atterite / Nella Barbara Reggia, il fiero Trace, / E pacifici udite /

D'un Arsinoe vagante i strani casi: / Ne prohibite al core, / Che frà sdegni di Marte, in reggia Scena, / Possa tall'hor, udir l'ire d'Amore" (*Arsinoe*, prologue).

47. "Veneti Eroi, che 'l frenator d'Oriente / Entro il Bosforo suo tenete à freno: / Arridi à vostre glorie il mio sereno, / Iride vi Coroni il Crin vincente.

"Quando però co i Veli, onde circonda / Il Tiranno Pangèo, l'empia Cervice / Prima v'asciugherà la Dea vittrice / Quel bel sudor, che i vostri Lauri innonda.

"Ma i Lumi avvezzi a vagheggiar sul Mare / Fra i Cipressi di Traccia i proprii Allori, / Non sdegnino mirar fra dolci amori / Le Fortune d'Oronte ancor ch'amare" (*Oronte*, prologue).

48. "A la Veneta Armata, à l'onde Egee, / In Asia, in Creta, al venerabil stuolo / Ratta mi porta obbediente volo" (*Tolomeo*, prologue).

49. VERITÀ: "Odan de l'Adria i gloriosi Eroi. / Tempo verrà ch'afflitto e stanco il Trace / Pentito al fin de folli orgogli suoi / Implorerà dal Gran Leon la

Sometimes these allusions are embedded in cleverly operatic contexts. The prologue of dall'Angelo's *Cleopatra* (1662), performed at the Teatro S. Salvatore, mixes specific political references with self-conscious comments about opera.[50] Except for Giove, all the characters are personifications of operatic elements: Poesia, Inventione, Pittura, and Musica. Giove remarks on the fact that war seems to be a constant state of affairs (it has, after all, been raging for more than a decade):

> What's this? Will the furor of haughty, tempestuous Mars always triumph? And will the happy torch of peace never shine in the bosom of fair Adria? But what peace? What peace? To arms, rage on, Venetian heroes, against the wicked Ottoman. See, I unfold my wings to join you, and bring my indignation to check this audacity. Crete is mine, let that be enough. I have come down only to lend you my thunderbolts, and just as I struck the wicked giants with them, so do I mean to reduce the Thracians to ashes.[51]

Poesia attempts to dissuade Giove from his warlike designs:

> Supreme mover, check your fury. Do not, no, do not disturb the serenity of the tranquil Venetian breast. Pray, no, do not, even for a few moments, infuse those proud hearts with bellicose spirits. . . . Behold the Venetian heroes collected in the fair circle of this new theater, who await from our music [*plettro sonoro*] sweet solace for their heavy thoughts.[52]

Poesia apparently convinces Giove to desist, at least temporarily, and to awaken Fortune in support of *Cleopatra*, opera and heroine.

A similar mixture characterizes another prologue from this same general period, that to Aureli's *Antigona* (1660). Set in the Kingdom of Music, it features

---

Pace." PACE: "In onta di Discordia omai gli ulivi / Mia Pacifica mano à l'Adria aduna. / Già, già mi par, ch'il gran Leon arrivi / Co' suoi Ruggiti à spaventar la Luna" (*Elena*, prologue). *Elena* was left unfinished by Faustini at his death and completed by Nicolò Minato for performance in 1659. See ch. 6, n. 184, below.

50. The theater had only opened in 1661. But the volume published by the Accademia degli Imperfetti in 1651 (see p. 144 and n. 39 above) was certainly connected to the group that was later active at S. Salvatore. Except for Busenello, all of the librettists represented in the book, including dall'Angelo, wrote texts for S. Salvatore.

51. "E che? sempre di Marte / Orgoglioso / Procelloso / Il furor trionferà? / Ne di pace / Lieta face / D'Adria bella nel sen risplenderà? / Ma che pace? che pace? à l'armi, / À l'ire / Contro l'empio Ottoman Veneti Eroi / Ecco dispiego il volo, / Anch'io trà voi / Porto miei sdegni à rintuzzar

l'ardire. / (*s'avanza con un volo dell'Aquila verso l'audienza*) Creta è mia, Tanto basti, A voi discendo /Sol per prestarvi i folgori Tonanti / E se già fulminai gl'empi Giganti / D'incenerir il Trace anco pretendo" (*Cleopatra*, prologue).

52. "Supremo motore / Raffrena il furore. / Del Veneto seno / Tranquillo il sereno / Non no non turbar. / Que' gl'animi alteri / Con spirti guerrieri / Per brevi momenti, / Deh no, non destar. / . . . Mira i Veneti Eroi / Raccolti in vago giro / Di Teatro novello; / Ch'attendono da noi / Con plettro sonoro, / A lor gravi pensier dolce ristoro" (*Cleopatra*, prologue). S. Salvatore may have been known as a "Teatro Novello" because it had recently been converted to opera. This may be analogous to "Teatro Nuovo," for which, see ch. 3, n. 100 above. The libretto of the inaugural opera of S. Salvatore, Giuseppe Artale's *Pasife*, also contains elaborate Venice imagery, in both prologue and epilogue.

Pace, Poesia, Musica, Furore Tacito, and Allegrezza. Pace explains her presence in this realm. The war having abated, she can turn to other duties and is bringing singers to the Kingdom of Music:

> Now that fury, drunk with human blood lies buried in the lap of sweet oblivion, I bring to your soil singing goddesses. With the audacious one chained at my feet, I passed triumphant under the Gallic sky from the Spanish kingdom, and here have folded my wings. And while I distribute olive branches, prepare immortal garlands for my tresses.[53]

In the 1670 revival the prologue had a different text, reflecting the changed political situation. The War of Candia had ended with the signing of a treaty in 1669; hence the final lines of the text were altered to read as follows:

> Janus has closed the doors, and the lethal rage of Mars rests weary in his breast. Now that Adria enjoys my longed-for olives, prepare immortal garlands for my hair.[54]

Then Musica, Poesia, and Apollo sing the praises of Pace, who responds to them.

APOLLO: This lyre, which sweetly lends its harmonious sound to the song, will expound your glories on golden strings; Pindus will bring forth laurels for your hair.

POESIA: Bind, then, the violent angry right hand of the god of arms, and I shall compose eternal hymns in your praise, and add new ornaments to your virtues.

MUSICA: I shall sing with harmonious breaths as many hymns as Poesia weaves to your fair name; and I shall spread your glories through the air.

PACE: With the major tumults of Italy calmed, and the Hispanic laurels grafted onto the fleur-de-lis through the royal wedding, you will see me cast lightning flashes of peace on the Venetian sands, to make fruitful that green and fertile soil.[55]

---

53. "Hor, che di sangue humano ebro il furore / In grembo à dolce oblio sepolto giace / Porto sul vostro suol Dive canore. / Incatenato à piedi miei l'audace. / Sotto il Gallico Ciel dal Regno Hispano / passai fastosa, hor qui raccolte hò l'ali, / E mentre porto a voi gl'Ulivi in mano, / Preparatemi al crin fregi immortali" (*Antigona*, prologue). The appearance of allegorical personifications of operatic elements was quite common during this period. A number of aesthetic points made by them, regarding such issues as their mutual relationship, are helpful in opera criticism. This statement, that peace brings singers, suggests that the war may have had something to do with the problems of the season, to which Aureli abundantly referred in his preface; see ch. 7 below.

54. "Chiuse hà Giano le porte, e al fier Gradivo / Stanche posano in sen l'ire letali. / Hor ch'Adria gode il mio bramato ulivo / Preparatemi al crin fregi immortali."

55. APOLLO: "Questa Cetra, che soave / Rende al canto il suon concorde, / Le tue glorie in auree corde / Spiegherà / Pindo lauri al tuo crin germoglierà." POESIA: "Lega pur la furibonda / Destra irata al Dio dell'armi / Che in tua lode eterni carmi / Formerò / Novi fregi à tuoi merti aggiungerò." MUSICA: "Quanti carmi al tuo bel nome / Tesserà la Poesia, / Io con fiati d'armonia / Canterò / Le tue glorie per l'Etra spargerò." PACE: "Dell'Italia placati / I tumulti maggiori, / E tai Gigli innestati / Col Reale Himeneo gli Hispani allori, / Sù le Venete arene / A fecondar quel verde suol ferace / Mi

Several years earlier, Ivanovich made his debut as a librettist with *Amor guerriero*, performed at SS. Giovanni e Paolo in 1663. The prologue, although filled with allusion, is not concerned with the details of war but, like so many earlier ones, rehearses the typical Venetian litany, as if a general reminder of Venetian superiority were needed in the face of hard times. Ivanovich's prologue is also somewhat old-fashioned in that, like some earlier ones, it takes place in a Venetian—or pre-Venetian—setting: "The scene represents a sea beach near the Adriatic lagoons, with an island in the middle, at the edge of which is seen a shell driven by two sea horses."[56] Questioned by a very skeptical Aurora, Amore foretells the story of the founding of Venice on the lagoon (an old topic, not aired in opera since the 1640s, but given a new, theatrical twist here). Ivanovich, the enthusiastic immigrant, makes use of the standard iconography.

AURORA: But tell me, why today did you exchange the shores of Amanthus for such deserted sands?

AMOR: In this marshy seaweed you will see a city that with regal foot will tame the haughty sea and extend her dominion to where you rise; and these Adriatic shores you now perceive as so forlorn will be the nest of mercy, the seat of Astraea, who will balance kingdoms on her scales; and for her wise genius [this city] will be always feared in war, and peace.

AURORA: Amore, what are you saying?

AMOR: The miracle will be worthy of eternal wonder.

AURORA: Who told you this?

AMOR: So Proteus foretold one day, singing on the sandy shores.

AURORA: I am amazed: and I foresee the Aeolian kingdoms as tributaries of the heroes to come. Let Fate, fortunate and happy indeed, write this day the victories of Adria.[57]

---

vedrete vibrar lampi di pace" (*Antigona*, preface). This is a reference to the marriage of Infanta Maria Theresa of Spain and the French king, Louis XIV, which, although it did not take place until June 1660, was planned as early as 1658 as part of the negotiations between the two nations that culminated in the Peace of the Pyrenees of late 1659. Venice hoped that once peace was concluded, France (and even Spain) might make some contribution to the Venetian campaign against the Turk. Apparently Mazarin had promised additional troops in 1659, and some French troops, under Almerigo d'Este, did fight in Candia in 1660. See Romanin, *Storia documentata*, 7: 443–44, and Cessi, *Storia della repubblica di Venezia*, 2: 202. For a more detailed chronicle of these events, see Romanin, *Storia documentata*, 7: 343–526. It was for the celebration of this same marriage in Paris that Cavalli was commissioned to compose *Ercole amante* (1662).

56.   "La scena rappresenta spiaggia di Mare intorno alle lagune Adriatiche con un'isoletta in mezzo, à piè della quale si vedrà una Conca guidata da due Cavalli marini" (*Amor guerriero*, prologue).

57.   AURORA: "Mà dimmi, da che viene, / Che d'Amatunta i lidi / Hoggi cangiasti in sì deserte arene?" AMOR: "In quest'Alghe palustri / Vedrai Città che con regal suo piede / Premendo il mar altero, / Sin là dove tu sorgi / Dilaterà l'impero, / E quest'Adriache piaggie / Ch'hor solitarie scorgi / Havrà pietà per Nido, Astrea per sede /Ch'adeguerà su la bilancia i Regni; / E per genio sagace / Sarà sempre temuta in guerra, e in Pace." AURORA: "Che parli Amor?" AMOR: "Di meraviglie eterne / Sarà degno il portento." AURORA: "A te chi 'l disse?" AMOR: "Così Protheo cantando / Sù l'arenose sponde, un dì predisse." AURORA: "Stupita io resto: & à venturi Eroi / Presagisco in tributo i Regni Eoi . / . . . Scriva il Fato / Fortunato, e lieto sì / Dell'Adria le Vittorie in questo dì" (*Amor guerriero*, prologue).

Generation after generation, Venetians never seem to have tired of hearing the mythology of their origins repeated on stage.

Despite all the allegorical representations in prologues and the selection of relevant historical or pseudo-historical themes for plot material, the connection between opera and politics may still strike us as somewhat oblique. Exotic and historically remote plots, after all, responded most immediately to a standard need for variety and spectacle in the theater; and prologues and epilogues stand by definition outside the drama proper.[58] Parallels between current events and staged action, between the exploits of actual and of operatic heroes, are not always so clear or precise.[59] Generally, Venetian opera conveyed its political message by suggestion, by implicating the knowing audience in its world of allusion as well as illusion. Its political message, the shared celebration of Venice, was imparted with the willing collusion of the spectators.

In several publications of the 1660s and later, however, the message was asserted more openly. Perhaps the most unequivocal statement of the political significance of opera occurs in the preface to a libretto by Francesco Sbarra, *L'amor della patria superiore ad ogn'altro* (1668), a bluntly didactic title reminiscent of Viennese oratorios of this period, but highly unusual for a Venetian opera.[60] The preface, signed by the Venetian printer Nicolò Pezzana and offered in praise of the author, describes Sbarra's librettistic activities and the plot of this drama in unabashedly patriotic terms. The work's aim is to instruct the audience (readers?) in the proper service of their country:

> In order to recognize the extraordinary talent and most fertile intellect of Sig. Francesco Sbarra, it is enough to glance at his works, among which the subject that he examines with the most heartfelt intensity is the greater good of the Most Serene Republic. As a most loyal subject, he has chosen the work called *L'amor della patria* . . . because he knows how to adapt himself to contemporary public concerns, con-

58. They were considered interchangeable, as revealed by the many instances in which the same prologue was used in several different operas. A particularly intriguing example is the one from *Ciro* (1654), used again for a number of operas, including *Giasone* and *Erismena* (Bologna, 1661 and 1668, Forlì, 1673; it probably also introduced the original Venetian production in 1655, since it is described in the scenario). For more on some of these interchangeable prologues, see Owen Jander, "The Prologues and Intermezzos of Alessandro Stradella," *Analecta musicologica* 7 (1969): 87–111.

59. A well-known, though non-Venetian, exception, preserved by accident, is the *Lanterna di Diogene* from Vienna; see Bianconi and Walker, "Production," 261–62. But cf. *Penelope la casta* (Venice, 1685), whose dramatis personae include, besides the main protagonists, a number of abstract figures such

as "necessità del governo" and "politica di Stato." And the moral purpose of the plot is articulated in a prologue featuring "il possibile," "l'impossibile," "il Dubbio," and "la Temerità amorosa." The overt moral message here may be associated with the particular character and aims of the theater in which the opera was performed, S. Giovanni Grisostomo; see Worsthorne, *Venetian Opera*, 44 and ch. 13, below.

60. The work was first performed in Munich in 1665, in a setting by J. K. Kerll (see Renate Brockpähler, *Handbuch zur Geschichte der Barockoper in Deutschland* [Emsdetten, 1964], 277). Listed by neither Ivanovich nor Bonlini, it was probably never performed in Venice, since it mentions neither a theater nor composer (by now these were significant omissions). We first met Sbarra as the author of a poem in honor of Benedetto Ferrari in the latter's *La maga fulminata* of 1638.

cerns already so treacherously upset by the Ottoman ferocity. He has deemed it appropriate that I (as I had already done for the *Erudite tirannide dell'interesse* of the same author) should, by means of my press, publish this one also, expanded by Signor Sbarra himself, so that, just as the most fervent zeal is passionately applied to public relief, so to the same degree everyone might understand, if they respond properly, what his own responsibilities are, and the obligation of each person to contribute with his love and actions to the breath and prosperity of his beloved homeland.

Responding to that noble stimulus propounded by this work, of the most memorable example of a complete Republic, with deeds so glorious that they are worthy of being carved in adamant in the hearts of true lovers of the revered and beloved homeland, to preserve the most precious treasure, the priceless jewel of secure liberty. The sole purpose of expressing this most devoted homage is the burning desire that it become universally impressed, sustained, and with work confirmed in all hearts, that, indeed, THE LOVE OF ONE'S COUNTRY IS SUPERIOR TO ANY OTHER. (Appendix I.30)

This rousing salute to the Serenissima only makes explicit what had been implicit in its predecessors. For all its delights, opera still had a responsibility to instruct its audience; and, being Venetian, that audience was to be made to recognize its privileged status and its obligations to the prosperous and beloved Republic.

Topical allusions and references to Venice, including such overt calls to patriotism, tended to occur within prologues during the 1660s. In the following decade, however, this was no longer the case. By 1670 the prologue had been virtually abandoned, and with it the Venetian topicality it had once contained.[61] Confirmation of this trend is provided by Camillo Contarini in his preface to *Arbace* (1667), where he criticizes the elimination of the prologue by other librettists: "They do not know how to resolve their plots except through the marriage of the characters they present, and they give birth to monstrous creatures without a head (which is the prologue, a principal part of dramas) like those Indian monsters, abridgements of nature."[62] The abandonment of the prologue signaled opera's transcendence of its earlier Venetian parochialism; it was one sure sign of the Europeanization of the genre by 1670, which was manifested, as we shall see, in other ways as well.

In his chronicle Ivanovich gave ample weight to the political function of opera. In his view, both the Bacchanalia of ancient Rome and the "trattenimenti carnovaleschi di Venezia" (i.e., opera)

---

61. Occasionally, as in Aureli's *Artaxerse* (1669), prologue material was incorporated as the first scene of the opera.
62. "Non sanno terminare i loro discioglimenti, che con le nozze de' personaggi da loro rappresentati, e partoriscono mostruosi Aborti senza capo (ch'è il Prologo, membro principale de' Drami) à guisa di quei Mostri Indiani, abbreviature di natura" (*Arbace*, preface).

are objects of extremely subtle politics, on which depend the success and abundance of the government, and through these amusements, used according to the standards of decency, the Prince gains the love of his people, who can never more easily forget their yoke than when sated or diverted by pleasures.

When the people have nothing to gnaw on, they gnaw on the reputation of the Prince, and when they have no entertainments, they can easily degenerate through idleness into schemes with very bad consequences. (Appendix II.6e)

Like the circuses of ancient Rome and the entertainments of modern courts, opera in Venice provided a diversion for the masses, a safety valve.[63] In this it was an extension of traditional Venetian social organization; like the *scuole* and the guilds, through which large segments of the disenfranchised plebeian population of Venice participated in the social and political as well as economic life of the city, the public spectacle of opera provided the disparate populace with a certain common bond. In the experience of the theater, the citizens of the Republic affirmed their allegiance to the idea of Venice.

On the more quotidian level of political fortune, opera could offer respite in times of crisis.[64] Aside from the official closing of the theaters during 1646, owing to the outbreak of the War of Candia, opera generally retained its seasonal rhythm in Venice.[65] For the duration of that lengthy conflict and during the other costly conflicts with the Ottomans that succeeded it, opera continued to offer an escape from thoughts of war. By its very existence, it represented Venice at her best. In the face of external threat, it maintained the peaceful spectacle of the Serenissima. In the face of the waning international fortunes of the Republic, opera affirmed the vitality of Venice, an ironic contrast that had been noted earlier by Francesco Pannocchieschi (nephew and coadjutor of the papal nuncio) in a "relazione sulle cose della Repubblica" (1647–52):

What astonished me was to see how people were living at that time in Venice; how that city, always full of riches and luxuries, kept itself absorbed in continual festivities, both public and private, which not only seemed inappropriate for a country

---

63. For an exhaustive consideration of the issue in Roman antiquity, see Paul Vayne, *Le Pain et le cirque: Sociologie historique d'un pluralisme politique* (Paris, 1976).

64. An anonymous libretto published in Venice in 1664, *Achille in Sciro* (on the very same subject as *La finta pazza*), confirms the notion of opera as an art of peace. The dedication to Filippo Giuliano Mazarini Mancini, duke of Nevers, signed by the printer Stefano Curti, reads, in part, as follows: "Or mentre che V. E. fà qualche pausa per la Pace, che regna in Francia dagl'Impieghi di Guerra, non dovrà disdegnare, che io venga ad offerirle un pacifico trattenimento di canto, e di poesia, quando anche il grande Achille

soleva mitigare col canto, e col suono gli ardori del suo spirito Guerriero nella ritiratezza di Sciro." The original libretto of this opera was first performed in Ferrara (1663). It names Giovanni Legrenzi as composer. Bonlini ascribes the poetry to the Marchese Ippolito Bentivoglio.

65. With the possible exception of 1651 and some years during the 1680s. In 1684 the Council of Ten prohibited all sorts of performances in Advent for the duration of the new war with the Turks. In 1699 it closed theaters "in every future year" for the novena of Christmas. See Mangini, *I teatri di Venezia*, 31.

that was at war at the time, but that would have seemed excessive even in another country that was calmer and more peaceful.[66]

All of the manifestations of *venezianità*—the evocations of the Serenissima, the actual appearance of images of Venice on the stage, the personifications of her virtues, the references to her grandeur and history in prologues and epilogues, and even the quick local allusions in the dialogue—rendered opera a very Venetian art indeed. Like the public arts of the previous century—painting, sculpture, architecture, music, and theater—opera, too, sang the litany of the myth of Venice. And like them, it in turn contributed to that myth. However crude Ivanovich's account may be, however filled with hyperbole, it is nonetheless clear that opera in Venice existed, in a fundamental way, in the service of the state. Indeed, the establishment and development of opera on the lagoon provide yet another chapter in the myth of Venice, one more manifestation of Venetian liberty and superiority—not to mention Venetian hospitality.

66. "Quello che più mi faceva restare attonito era il vedere come si vivesse in quel tempo in Venetia; come piena sempre di richezze e di lussi se ne stesse quella Città involta per lo più in continue feste sì pubbliche come private, che non solamente pareva disconvenissero ad un paese che haveva all'hora la guerra, ma che ad ogn'altro più quieto etiandio e più pacifico sembrato superflue" (quoted in Mangini, *I teatri di Venezia*, 29–30).

6

•   •   •

La nausea di chi ascolta:
The Consequences of Success

By the time the doors of the Teatro Novissimo closed in 1645, opera had established itself as a going concern in Venice. Although the Novissimo itself never reopened, the competition it had helped to inspire resumed at full tilt by 1648 among the other theaters: S. Cassiano, S. Moisè, SS. Giovanni e Paolo, and a fourth, new, theater, at SS. Apostoli.[1]

By 1650 the pattern of performances for the rest of the century had been set: an average of four new operas per year, in however many theaters were currently in operation. The number of opera houses had jumped from one to four within the first five years. The next two decades were to witness the opening of three more: after SS. Apostoli in 1648, S. Apollinare in 1651 and S. Salvatore in 1661. And another two were added during the 1670s, S. Angelo in 1676 and S. Giovanni Grisostomo in 1678, for a total of nine.[2] These statistics give an inflated impression, however, for all nine theaters never functioned simultaneously. Seldom were more than four theaters open during a single season; the more usual number was two. The market for opera in Venice, having been created from nothing in 1637, and having increased steadily over the course of its first decade, then remained fairly constant for the next fifty years or so.[3]

---

1.   Only one opera seems to have been performed in Venice in 1647 (a revival of *Deidamia* at SS. Giovanni e Paolo), but there were four in each of the following three seasons, one per theater. (The numbers are compiled from Ivanovich, *Minerva*, Bonlini, *Le glorie*, and Sartori, "Catalogo unico.") The "sixth" Venetian theater, at SS. Apostoli, according to Ivanovich, was actually two different theaters situated in private houses ("ne' Casamenti privati"), which produced operas from 1649 until 1652 and then closed: "ma come, che questi erano in apparenza: così sparvero senza speranza di riaprirsi" (*Minerva*, 399–400).

2.   This number does not include the Teatro ai Saloni from the 1650s, the one at S. Samuele, which opened in 1656, and a theater at Cannaregio opened in 1680, none of which ever actually functioned as opera houses; see Ivanovich, *Minerva*, 398–401.

3.   There were a few exceptionally busy seasons, such as 1676–77, when, according to a report in *Le Mercure galant* of August 1677, there were nine operas in five theaters (though Ivanovich lists only seven), and 1680, when ten different operas were performed in seven theaters (according to Ivanovich). The relevant passage from the French journal is given in Selfridge-Field, *Pallade veneta*, 338–40.

In a few short years, opera had become a genre whose legitimacy was conferred by its own accumulating history, by the rapid, regular, and systematic accretion of a past. As well as inspiring a new sense of confidence, however, that very history imposed a new set of problems. Opera had to continue to please; and in order to do so it needed repeatedly to surpass itself with a steady supply of new works. The curiosity-seeking carnival audience would not be satisfied with less. Writing in 1650, Pietro Paolo Bissari summarized the dilemma quite aptly:

> The city of Venice, having enjoyed approximately fifty *opere regie* in only a few years, of which few cities have seen the like, and those only with difficulty, at a wedding or on some other solemn occasion of their princes, has rendered the authors sterile and nauseated the listeners, it having become difficult to come up with things not already seen, or to make them appear more effective, with greater spectacle and display, than they ever seemed before. (Appendix I.26)

Making Histories

Bissari was neither the first nor the last to identify the problem.[4] From its very beginnings, opera in Venice had been marked by an intense awareness of itself and a determined effort to create a pedigree. This is evident in the tendency toward obsessive record-keeping that had characterized—even justified—the earliest Venetian librettos. Thus, the printer's preface to Ferrari's *La maga fulminata*, the second Venetian opera, referred to its only predecessor, the already legendary *Andromeda*, presumably as a means of sharing in its success (Appendix I.3b). And both of them were invoked in the preface to the third Venetian opera, *Delia*, by Strozzi, who, in homage to Ferrari, as we have seen, even borrowed a character from *La maga fulminata*, the witch Scarabea. Strozzi continued to keep records in his subsequent works, introducing his next libretto, *La finta pazza*, as his eighth "fatica rappresentativa," and mentioning both it and its two successors, *La finta savia* (1643) and *Romolo e Remo* (1645), in the preface to the former.[5] Not only in the prefaces, but in the texts of librettos themselves, opera's progress was being charted. As we are reminded by Armonia, a char-

4.   Already in 1642, in the preface to *Amore innamorato*, Fusconi had complained about opera audiences "who are only content with miracles and who would scorn the very harmony of heaven if they were to hear it more than once" (Appendix I.27c). And Ferrari lamented the same thing in *Il principe giardiniere* (1643) (Appendix I.4); see also his preface to *Il pastor regio* (Bologna, 1641) (Appendix I.5). Aureli complained similarly in practically every one of his librettos, especially that of *Le fatiche d'Ercole per Deianira* (1662) (Appendix I.46b). The complaint, in fact, became increasingly justified—and conventional.

5.   Such self-reference becomes standard practice. Not only are nearly all the librettos of Faustini, Aureli, and Minato sequentially numbered, but many contain up-to-date bibliographies of their authors' works.

acter in the prologue of Faustini's *Ormindo* (1644): "It has been five years already that I have shone on you from gilded stages and displayed my glories."[6]

Audiences could not fail to notice, since it was pointed out so regularly to them, that opera was getting on, was being engulfed by its own history. And they were becoming jaded, bored; they wanted novelty, and they wanted it often. Their demands placed a heavy burden on the creators of opera, who developed various strategies of response. In search of fresh plots, librettists reached out to new sources and new literary models, beyond mythology, Greek and Roman history, romance, and the pastoral to the more exotic history of the Near East and the more domestic *novella*.[7] Furthermore, they treated all of their sources with increasing freedom, adding an ever greater proportion of *invenzione*. In 1643 Busenello had briefly recounted Tacitus's version of the Poppaea story only to depart from it, concluding with laconic frankness: "But here things will be represented differently" ("Mà qui si rappresenta il fatto diverso"). Twelve years later, however, in the preface to *Statira*, he does not even bother to outline a historical version of the plot, declaring that only the names of the characters—but not their relationships—were borrowed from classical history.[8] Busenello's younger contemporary Castoreo stated the case for *invenzione* even more explicitly in the preface to his *Pericle effeminato* (1653):

> If you find something in it connected with history, know that the rest is pure invention, and therefore you will be wasting your time if you go and sift through Plutarch and Thucydides to find out whether I have strayed from the truth; because my intention is not to report a history to you but to present a tale that has nothing historical in it besides its name. It is indeed true that its principal plot is drawn from Plutarch, who writes about the passions of Pericles and Aspasia, through which he acquired the epithet effeminate; nevertheless, in fitting them into this drama I have followed my own fancy. (Appendix I.40a)

In addition to reaching out to new sources, librettists turned their attention inward, on their own art, exploiting its already established conventions with ever greater energy. Along with composers and stage designers, they found essential materials in the already proven successes of the past. Increasingly, librettos that had been used before, either in Venice or elsewhere, were revised for new Venetian performances. Usually these needed to be adapted to their

---

6. "È gia varcato un lustro / Che su palchi dorati / In te risplendo, e le mie glorie illustro" (*Ormindo* prologue, quoted in ch. 5, n. 22 above).

7. On the *Cento novelle amorose* of the Incogniti as a possible source for libretto material, see Bianconi and Walker, "Dalla 'Finta pazza,' " 422 n. 179; also Maria Gabriella Stassi, "Le novelle di Maiolino Bisaccioni tra 'favola' e 'istoria,' " in *L'arte dell'interpretare: Studi critici offerti a Giovanni Getto* (Cuneo,

1984), 291–316. For an interesting discussion of the new, freer, and more irregular kinds of plots that characterized Venetian operas of these years, see Carl Dahlhaus, "Drammaturgia dell'opera italiana," in *StOpIt*, 6 (Turin, 1988): 79–162, esp. 148–49.

8. See his *Statira* letter, quoted and discussed in Livingston, *Busenello*, 369–79, esp. 372, on the derivation of the character names.

new contexts—either modernized to suit the taste of the times or Venetianized ("Riformato all'uso di Venetia").[9] During the early 1650s there were several such revisions. *Veremonda,* by Luigi Zorsisto [Giulio Strozzi], which was performed with Cavalli's music at the Teatro SS. Giovanni e Paolo in 1653, was a doubly revised work. Not only was it imported from Naples, where it had been performed in Cavalli's setting the previous year, but it was a reworking of an earlier libretto by Cicognini, *Celio,* that had appeared in Florence in 1646.[10] Another Neapolitan libretto, *Ciro* (1653), by Giulio Cesare Sorrentino, was altered for Venetian use ("con prologo, aggiunte, imitationi, & aggiustamenti all'uso di questa città") by an unnamed poet and performed at SS. Giovanni e Paolo in 1654. In this case, Cavalli merely retouched the original score by Francesco Provenzale.[11] Adaptation became so common during the 1660s that it could be invoked falsely to mask the original authorship of a work if necessary. For some reason Minato passed off his *Seleuco* of 1666 as the revision of an anonymous Neapolitan work, though he acknowledged his authorship at a subsequent revival.[12]

While some such adaptations were completely straightforward and aboveboard, giving due credit to the original author, others went unacknowledged, masking themselves as original works. Aureli, for example, based an entire libretto, *Erismena* (1655), on Faustini's *Ormindo* (1644), even appropriating the text of one of its most striking moments, the prison scene.[13] In fact, this kind of unacknowledged modeling must have been quite common, since librettists

9. See *Ercole in Tebe. Drama per musica del Dottor G. A. Moniglia Fiorentino. Riformato all'uso di Venetia da Aurelio Aureli* (Venice: Curti & Nicolini, 1671). The meaning of "l'uso di Venetia" is not altogether clear; some authors implied that it meant cutting, or adhering to "la brevità veneta." We might say that *La finta pazza* was "de-Venetianized" for export.

10. Bianconi and Walker, "Dalla 'Finta pazza,'" identify Luigi Zorsisto as an anagrammatic pseudonym for Giulio Strozzi and demonstrate the relationship of the *Veremonda* and *Celio* librettos (445–54); they also document the connections between Neapolitan and Venetian operatic life in the early 1650s, which were chiefly the result of the activities of a group of traveling musicians. For texts of the relevant documents, see Ulisse Prota-Giurleo, *Francesco Cirillo e l'introduzione del melodramma a Napoli* (Grumo Nevano, 1952); also Bianconi, "Funktionen des Operntheaters in Neapel," 13–116.

11. See Michael F. Robinson, "Provenzale," *New Grove,* 15: 316–17. *Ciro* was revised for another Venetian performance in 1665, and still another layer of music was added, by Andrea Mattioli. Both Venetian productions were thus pasticcios. There were many more such revivals and revisions during the

1660s, most of which had originated in Venice in the first place: *Orontea* and *Giasone,* both originally from 1649, in 1666; *Dori,* from Innsbruck (1657), and *Alessandro amante,* a "rifacimento" of *Gli amori d'Alessandro magno e di Rossane* (1659), in 1667; *Eliogabalo* (a "rifacimento" of an anonymous earlier libretto) and *Seleuco* (1666) in 1668; and *Argia* (Innsbruck, 1655) and *Antigona delusa da Alceste* (1660) in 1669.

12. Since another of his works was performed in the same season at the same theater, S. Salvatore, Minato's invention of counterfeit Neapolitan origins for *Seleuco* may have been a way of making the season's offerings seem more exotic, particularly since this was the first season since 1661 in which S. Salvatore had managed to mount two productions.

13. See Ellen Rosand, "'Ormindo travestito' in 'Erismena,'" *JAMS* 28 (1975): 268–91; see also Beth Glixon, "Recitative in Seventeenth-Century Venetian Opera: Its Dramatic Function and Musical Language" (Ph.D. diss., Rutgers University, 1985), 180–81, who makes a good case for Aureli's *Le fortune di Rodope e Damira,* too, being modeled on *Ormindo.*

often took elaborate pains to deny it—or used it as a subterfuge. One scene was cut from Faustini's *Eritrea* (1652) ostensibly because it had been used elsewhere: "The elephant scene, which Your Illustrious Lordship will observe [is] mentioned, and which was the invention of the poet, has been left out because it does not suit a queen's dignity to wear clothes that, although intended for her, have been worn first by someone else" (Appendix I.35b).[14] And, only a few years later, Castoreo defended himself against plagiarism in *La guerriera spartana* (1654): "There were some who accused [the warrior] of theft because they noticed on the hem of one of her dresses a certain decoration that seemed woven at the same loom as someone else's; but let it not even be mentioned, because I could thoroughly defend it should there be need" (Appendix I.41).[15]

Along with the wholesale adaptation of old texts, librettists also appropriated and rearranged more circumscribed material from earlier librettos: scene types, dramatic procedures, and so on. Much of this material belonged to the common stock available to any potential librettist, a body of conventions in part borrowed from spoken drama, in part established by repeated use in operatic works. In most cases the reuse of such material was generalized and natural, but in some it was more specific and can qualify as outright borrowing. Such borrowing was sometimes explicit: we have seen how Faustini acknowledged lifting an episode of madness for his *Egisto* (1643), although he did not name his source (Appendix I.31a). Librettists apparently had to be careful that their borrowings were generic enough not to arouse suspicion; but as these were the very stuff of their trade, they could hardly avoid them altogether. They had to strike a balance between convention and novelty: convention enabled librettists to construct their works quickly and made them easily accessible to their audience; novelty added the spice of variety that attracted special attention.

Just as librettists relied increasingly on the adaptation of older texts, so the composer's role was frequently limited to the reworking of another composer's score to adapt it to a new set of performing conditions (as in *Ciro* mentioned above). And they too made increasing use of previously composed music—individual arias or even, as in the case of *Erismena*, whole scenes. Composers adapted to the pressures of increased demand in other ways as well. Their response, to be discussed at length in the next several chapters, is manifested by a decrease in their impact on the shaping of librettos. This in turn was balanced by greater reliance on conventional formulae for setting individual poetic structures as well as dramatic situations.

14. This is a special case; the scene probably had to be omitted for reasons of economy or space at the little Teatro S. Apollinare (see p. 171 below). Interestingly, in the libretto for the revival of the opera in 1661, references to elephants were restored (added?) in act 1, scenes 4 and 6.

15. Castoreo may have had *Veremonda* in mind, performed the previous season at SS. Giovanni e Paolo, which also featured a female warrior as the title heroine.

The balance of convention and novelty presented a special problem in the realm of scene design. The situation was complicated by the overwhelming stature of one scenographer in particular, Giacomo Torelli. Although he himself left Venice for good by 1645, he remained a looming presence for many years, having made an indelible impression on the very conception of Venetian opera. It was difficult to match Torelli's achievement, let alone surpass it. Bissari confirmed Torelli's position in the preface to *Torilda* (1648) by describing the effects of opera in the precise terms of his achievement: "Among the most often remarked upon curiosities of the modern dramas is the diversity of sets, which, pulled around or guided along wooden channels by a machine that changes them in an instant, open up new views everywhere" (Appendix I.25a).[16] Variety and speed of execution were among the chief marvels of Torelli's technique; but he was also widely praised for the verisimilitude and sheer extravagance of his conceptions.

At least one opera was specifically designed to meet the challenge of Torelli head on. In *Bradamante* (Bissari/?Cavalli, 1650), an extraneous character ("personaggio accidentale") is introduced for the express purpose of enhancing the spectacle: Bellerofonte, mounted on Pegasus, attempts to obstruct Astolfo's moonward journey on the hippogriff, but fails, falling to earth in ignominious defeat—and in a triumph of stagecraft. This "caduta di Bellerofonte," created by the scenographer Giovanni Burnacini, makes a direct (scenic) reference to Torelli's notorious and much publicized similar achievement in *Bellerofonte* several years before.[17]

Economic considerations must have affected scenography more than any other component of opera. The level of financial support that Torelli had so briefly enjoyed at the Teatro Novissimo was not easily matched elsewhere; even the queen of France had balked at the expenses incurred for *La finta pazza* in Paris.[18] Physical resources were obviously as necessary for scenic spectacle as financial ones, for the productions at two of the smaller Venetian theaters, S. Moisè and S. Apollinare, were regularly berated (by their own creators) for the inadequacy of their spectacle.[19]

Since it was so difficult to surpass Torelli's accomplishment, scenographers, even more obviously than their librettist and composer colleagues, tended to

16. See Worsthorne, *Venetian Opera*, 41–42 n. 5.

17. Bianconi suggests that Bissari himself may have played Bellerofonte ("Scena, musica e pubblico," 19), a suggestion based on a sonnet addressed to "Sig. . . . Bissari per la caduta di Bellerofonte nell'opera della sua Bradamante," in the copy of the libretto in I-Rsc, Carvalhaes 2362.

18. See Bianconi and Walker, "Dalla 'Finta pazza,' " 416 n. 152.

19. Many of the S. Moisè prefaces in particular allude to the poverty of scenic resources. Pirrotta ("Theater, Sets, and Music," *Essays*, 261–62) mentions some of the problems there. The S. Apollinare prefaces frequently complain of the same thing—for example, that of *Eupatra* (1655) (see Appendix I.36c). On the limitations of S. Apollinare, see Jane Glover, "The Teatro Sant'Apollinare and the Development of Seventeenth-Century Venetian Opera" (Ph.D. diss., Oxford University, 1975), ch. 2.

make use of conventional formulas; they borrowed and rearranged old materials. Indeed, most operas after 1650 called for a rather standard group of sets or scene types that could be reused and easily adapted to successive productions: a city, a royal palace, a courtyard, a chamber, a garden, a wood, a hellmouth (figs. 17–23).[20]

Some of the most striking scenic effects after 1650 occurred in prologues—in that of *Ciro* (1654), for example (apparently a highly effective prologue, since it was used subsequently for other works as well).[21] Architecture asserts her superiority over Poetry and Music in *Ciro* by making a spectacle of her own deconstruction, falling apart in full view of the audience, and she creates a similar spectacle of herself in the prologue to *Veremonda* (Naples, 1652).[22] Prologues, the traditional locus of aesthetic commentary from the author, were readily detached from the drama. Thus, if it were concentrated there, extravagant scenography could easily be eliminated if sufficient funds or equipment were unavailable. Despite an increased reliance on convention and the relegation of many of the most striking scenographic effects to detachable prologues after 1650, most observers continued to be struck by the visual marvels of opera for the remainder of the century.[23]

One of the most far-reaching consequences of the institutionalization of opera in the 1650s has yet to be mentioned. The needs created by intensifying

20. Pirrotta ("Theater, Sets, and Music," *Essays*, 267–70) attempts an intriguing reconstruction of the (lost) sets of *Poppea* by analogy with various designs by Torelli, illustrating the existence of generic settings. That these persisted throughout the century is indicated by the lists of settings in librettos. The characteristic scene-types of Venetian opera are enumerated and described in Claude-François Ménestrier, *Des Representations en musique anciennes et modernes* (Paris, 1681), 168–74, excerpt reprinted in *Quellentexte zur Konzeption der europäischen Oper im 17. Jahrhundert*, ed. Heinz Becker (Kassel, 1981), 85–87.

21. It introduced *Erismena* in 1655 and a revival of *Giasone* in 1666.

22. This seems to have happened as early as 1639, in the prologue to *Le nozze di Teti e di Peleo* (Persiani/Cavalli), which ends with the rubric: "qui cadde a terra il teatro." Both the *Ciro* and *Veremonda* prologues were staged by G. B. Balbi, which might account for their similarity. This was a favorite conceit, even later in the century, however. In *Il novello Giasone* (Rome, 1671), for example, the original prologue of 1649 is interrupted by an accident to the flying chariot of the Sun; Music, Poetry, and Painting are beside themselves in worried desperation when Architecture reassures them: all is under control, everything, including the accident, has been planned for the greater delight of the audience. See Bianconi, "Scena, musica e pubblico," 21. The grand master of such illusions of disaster—failed mechanisms, accidental fires on stage, floods threatening the audience—was, of course, Gianlorenzo Bernini: see Irving Lavin, *Bernini and the Unity of the Visual Arts* (New York, 1980), 1: 146–57.

23. Although a real decline is not documentable after 1650, a resurgence of interest in scenography is certainly evident toward the end of the 1670s, particularly with the opening of the Teatro S. Giovanni Grisostomo, whose productions were especially elaborate from the scenic point of view. The staging of *Nerone* (1679), for example, received an extremely detailed and enthusiastic description from the Venetian correspondent to *Le Mercure galant* (see Selfridge-Field, *Pallade veneta*, 340–44). And the whole project of the Contarini theaters at Piazzola aimed to restore scenography to the position it had enjoyed at court theaters and at the Novissimo. See Paolo Camerini, *Piazzola* (Milan, 1925), and, for descriptions of the fabulous scenic effects that were possible at Piazzola, *L'orologio del piacere che mostra l'ore del dilettevole soggiorno havuto della serenissima d'Ernest Augusto Vescovo d'Osnabruc, Duca di Branswich, Lunebergo, etc.* (Piazzola, 1685).

17. Giacomo Torelli, stage set for *Venere gelosa* (1643), 2.1–7: Città di Nasso. Engraving from *Apparati scenici* (Venice, 1644).

commercial activity, with the attendant promise of financial reward, brought into being a new kind of professional, the poet who devoted himself exclusively, willingly, and even proudly to *dramma per musica*: the librettist. We have been talking about librettists, operatic poets, all along, of course, about the various members of the Accademia degli Incogniti and about Ferrari, but in fact, until the middle of the century the authors of operatic texts were either more or less than librettists. Ferrari was librettist, composer, performer, and impresario all in one. An old-fashioned "theater man" in the style of his near contemporary Giovanni Battista Andreini, who led his own troupe of *comici*,

18. Giacomo Torelli, stage set for *Bellerofonte* (1642), 1.4–10: Regio cortile.
Engraving by Giovanni Giorgi.

and wrote and starred in his own plays, Ferrari embodies the essential link
between *commedia dell'arte* and opera.[24]

The talents of his chief competitor among the early operatic poets, Strozzi,
were more exclusively literary. But even then, libretto-writing was only one

24. Pirrotta ("Ferrari," *Enciclopedia dello spettacolo* [Rome, 1958], 5: cols. 187–88) quotes a document in which Ferrari actually describes himself as a "theater man" ("quella del teatro è stata la mia prima professione"), but in the preface to the Bologna edition of *Il pastor regio* he claims that he is primarily a musician (Appendix I.5a). On the career of Andreini, see Molinari, *La commedia dell'arte*, 145–50; also Ferdinando Taviani and Mirella Schino, *Il segreto della Commedia dell'Arte: La memoria delle compagnie italiane del XVI, XVII, e XVIII secolo* (Florence, 1982, 2d ed. 1986), 105–9. There were many other figures like Andreini in the realm of improvised theater; in fact, every troupe was led by a complete "theater person."

19. Giacomo Torelli, stage set for *Venere gelosa* (1643), 2.10–3.4:
Cortile del Re di Nasso. Engraving from *Apparati scenici* (Venice, 1644).

facet of Strozzi's literary activities; he also wrote plays, poetry both epic and
lyric, and history. The same was true, of course, of Strozzi's Incognito colleagues, who claimed to have become librettists in spite of themselves. I have
already remarked upon their disinclination to admit involvement in libretto-
writing, their disguising of their own authorship by means of standard seicento
obfuscation: pseudonyms, allusions, anonymity. Even when they did confess,
they were usually apologetic, explaining their librettistic activity as the result of
some extenuating circumstance or gratuitous act.

Debts of friendship were often cited as an excuse. Pietro Michele, the "Incognito" author of *Amore innamorato*, had apparently agreed to write the libretto
out of friendship for Loredan but refused to have anything further to do with

20. Giacomo Torelli, stage set for *Bellerofonte* (1642), 3.8–12: Sala regia.
Engraving by Giovanni Giorgi.

it, lacking the inclination "di buffoneggiare ne i Theatri."[25] The anonymous author of *Argiope* (1649), too, though a famous poet, needed the encouragement of friends in order to undertake writing the libretto; this according to Fusconi's preface:

25. This is revealed in the publisher's preface to another work by Michele, his *Rime . . . parte prima* (Venice, 1642): "La Psiche Favoletta per Musica composta sopra l'ordine d'uno scenario dattagli dall'Illustriss. Signor Gio. Francesco Loredano, a cui non ha saputo negare di farlo, essendo tra loro congiunti di tale strettezza d'Amicitia che si può agguagliare ad ogn'una delle più famose. Questa Psiche i giorni a dietro fu stampata, senza, che l'Autore lo sapesse sotto nome di Amore Innamorato, col prologo, e con altre tre o quattro scene piene di concetti di burla per allettare la plebe de gli Auditori quando si recitò; aggiuntevi da altri non havendo il Michiele inclinatione di buffoneggiare ne i Theatri. Un giorno però si lascierà vedere nell'habito suo proprio, e forse accompagnata da tre altre simili compositioni, che

21. Giacomo Torelli, stage set for *Bellerofonte* (1642), 3.1–7:
Boschetto del giardino reale. Engraving by Giovanni Giorgi.

The fabric of this tale results from the pleas of friends, dashed off rather than woven, in fourteen evenings, by the pen of that most famous swan of the Adriatic, who keeps Italian poetry alive in our century. Since he was on the verge of departure, and awaiting favorable winds for a long sea voyage, he could not apply himself to it except at moments stolen from sleep. (Appendix I.28b)[26]

---

sono la Tisbina, la Fugga di Elena, e le Nozze di Bradamante." Cf. ch. 2, p. 38 and n. 11, above; also Bianconi and Walker, "Dalla 'Finta pazza,' " 421 n. 175.

26.   Although Bonlini suggests that the author in question was again Michele, the title page of the libretto lists him simply as N.

22. Giacomo Torelli, stage set for *Venere gelosa* (1643), 3.6–10:
Campagna di Nasso. Engraving from *Apparati scenici* (Venice, 1644).

What *sprezzatura*: to knock off a libretto in fourteen sleepless nights, just to
please friends. Friendship evidently could force even non-poets to try their
hand; and if their work was criticized, they could always blame the music.[27]

27.   This was Marc'Antonio Tirabosco's tack in the preface to *Alcate* (1642): "Il veder comparire tra le più famose penne la mia, deve a ragione . . . chiamarvi alle maraviglie, poichè à me, che non fò professione di poeta, non conviene il presumere di poggiar col sù, dove le palme, e gl'allori germogliano per decorare gli Eccellenti compositori. . . . Hora mi è convenuto ubbidire alle preghiere di vero amico, à cui sono grandemente obligato, & era peccato d'ingratitudine l'oppormi alle sue giuste brame. Hò dunque pochi giorni sono, benche da sommi travagli agitato, tanto di tempo, e di respiro goduto, che applicatomi à questo drama musicale l'hò ridotto al fine col favore della contemplatione, che illustrando il mio ingegno l'ha reso atto a ricevere un picciolo raggio di quel divino spirito che vuol riscaldare ogni Poeta. Signori, [purche] l'Alcate è di già pervenuto sotto alla commune censura imploro da voi cortese un compatimento non rigoroso. . . . Haverete almeno in essa una schiettezza di dire, così richiestami per la musica."

23. Giacomo Torelli, stage set for *Venere gelosa* (1643), 2.8–9:
Inferno. Engraving from *Apparati scenici* (Venice, 1644).

Many of these authors claimed amateur status, insisting that they had written librettos merely to while away their idle hours or to ward off boredom. As Badoaro wrote (anonymously) in the preface to *Il ritorno d'Ulisse*: "the world knows that my pen fights to defeat boredom, and not to earn glory" (Appendix I.7b). In the same vein, Busenello called his published (1656) collection of librettos *Le hore ociose* (*The Idle Hours*). A few writers even used illness as an excuse, both for having indulged in libretto-writing at all and for whatever shortcomings might be found in their works.[28]

28. See Bisaccioni's preface to *Ercole in Lidia* (1645) (Appendix I.24b) and Francesco Sbarra's letter to Michel'Angelo Torcigliani introducing his *Alessandro vincitor di se stesso* (1651) (Appendix I.29b).

Even Minato, who was to become one of the most successful of all Venetian librettists, began his career by belittling his own theatrical efforts, asserting his greater commitment to his real profession, the law, and claiming that he had written his dramas during time he would otherwise have spent sleeping: "Know that I am not a poet. . . . My vocation is in the Forum; to serve him who can command me, I have stolen a few hours from sleep in order to devote them to this drama. I swear to you that the sun has never seen me with pen in hand to form characters in ink."[29]

In the same self-deprecating tone, several authors modestly insisted that they composed not for fame or riches but "per mero capriccio." The first writer actually to use the expression may have been Francesco Melosio, in the preface to *Sidonio e Dorisbe* (1642): "Be satisfied with knowing that I write out of mere whim, and that I do not want to bind myself to the strict observance of the rules."[30] The most notorious declaration of these sentiments, however, came from the pen of Giacinto Andrea Cicognini, in the preface to *Giasone* (1649): "I write out of mere whim; my whim has no other aim than to give pleasure. To bring pleasure to myself is nothing other than to accommodate the inclination and taste of those who listen or read."[31]

Cicognini's statement raises once again the issue of *il diletto* versus *l'utile* that had concerned the earlier, academic librettists. But that issue now had a new twist. Melosio, who, like the academics, was suffering the pangs of generic insecurity that characterized the early 1640s, used the phrase primarily to absolve himself of sins against literary rules. But Cicognini uses it in a more modern context, to express the pressures that were to characterize the next phase of operatic development, after 1650. His *capriccio*, though perhaps unbound by literary rules, serves another master. It is closely linked to, even determined by, audience taste.[32] Because *Giasone* was so popular (the libretto went through four printings by 1650), the phrase "mero capriccio" may have been associated with Cicognini by his contemporaries, even though he was not the first to adopt it. In the way he meant it—but also in the older, more general

29. "Sappi, ch'io non fò del Poeta. Le mie applicationi sono nel Foro: per servire a chi puote comandarmi hò rubbate alcune hore al sonno per darle à questo Drama. Ti giuro, che il Sole mai mi ha veduto con la penna alla mano per caraterizar questi inchiostri" (*Orimonte* [1650], preface).
30. "Ti basti di sapere, che io compongo per mero capriccio, e che non voglio obbligarmi alla stretta osservanza delle regole" (*Sidonio e Dorisbe*, preface).
31. "Io compongo per mero capriccio; il mio capriccio non ha altra fine, che il dilettare: L'apportar diletto appresso di me, non e altro, che l'incontrare il genio, & il gusto di chi ascolta o legge" (*Giasone*, preface).
32. This is the same point made more negatively, and indirectly, by Bissari in the passage from *Bradamante* already quoted (Appendix I.26). He blamed librettists' sterility on the audience's need to see things they had not yet seen. Audience taste was becoming increasingly exigent. Having overcome the generic insecurity of their predecessors, the second generation of librettists now had to face the problem of excesses and absurdities inspired by a jaded public. Literary rules no longer frightened them, but propriety still did.

sense of freedom from "the rules"—it became a kind of battle cry in librettists' prefaces after 1650.

Giovanni Faustini, "Librettist"

Amid the commonplaces of librettists' apologia—obligations of friendship, excuses of ill-health, and other denials of serious intentions, as well as embarrassed admissions of venal pandering to audience taste—one figure stands out. Giovanni Faustini (c. 1619–51) was the only author of his generation who confessed openly and proudly to being a professional writer of librettos, and he did this in a statement that seems pointedly intended as a response to Cicognini and to those others who declared *capriccio* rather than art to be their aim:

> I am not one of those . . . who write to satisfy their whims. I strain my pen, I confess my ambition, to see if it can raise me above the ordinary and common achievements of dull and plebeian talents. This honorable madness, which began to assault me when I had scarcely emerged from swaddling clothes and has not yet abated, forces me to the assiduous creation of various compositions. (Appendix I.33a)

These are the words of a committed professional, a man proud and passionate about what he does. Missing is the ironic and casual tone of most self-declarations, the *sprezzatura*, the excuses, self-deprecations, and false modesty shading into hypocrisy. Such a statement from a writer of *drammi per musica* could only have been possible after midcentury—that is, after opera had become securely established as a genre. It recognizes the stability of opera and the concomitant possibility of new status for its poets.

Partly because his activities are so well documented, not only by himself but by his younger brother Marco and by the printers of his librettos, we can reconstruct Faustini's career in considerable detail. Encouraged and sustained by the commercial structure of Venetian opera, as well as by the general tendency toward historical documentation, which he shared, Faustini set about his career in a self-conscious, highly professional way. Each of his librettos was published with an opus number, and nearly all of them contain prefaces and dedications that reveal his attitudes toward his work and declare his aims and ideals as a librettist. The strength of his commitment to libretto-writing is manifested not only by his pride in his work but by his gratuitous creation of librettos—that is, without specific commissions. Quite the opposite of being forced reluctantly to write librettos, Faustini could not help himself; he was the willing victim of his own *furor poeticus*.

Although still quite young when he avowed his personal commitment to libretto-writing in 1651, Faustini was speaking as a man of experience, as possibly the most successful librettist in Venice, who had already seen seven of his texts performed during the previous decade, all but one of them set to music by the leading composer of the time, Cavalli.[33] In fact, in 1651 Faustini was rather nearer the end of his career than the beginning, for he died suddenly within that year, at the age of thirty-one.[34]

But 1651 marked an important change in his status that probably encouraged his assertion of professionalism. Whether because of his commitment to the artistic integrity of his librettos or a desire to maximize his profit from them, on 19 May 1650 Faustini the librettist became an impresario. On that date he signed a contract with Zanetta Piamonte and the brothers Francesco and Giovanni Battista Ceroni, co-owners of the property, to manage the newly renovated Teatro S. Apollinare for three years, with an extension of three more, beginning the following June. Faustini agreed to undertake the work necessary to furnish the premises in accordance with their new function.[35]

The libretto in which his credo appeared, *Oristeo*, was Faustini's first work for his own theater; it marked his official debut as an impresario.[36] Some insight into the reasons for this expansion of operatic responsibility is provided by the remainder of the same preface. He wrote the libretto and its successor, he says, to discharge debts that had forced him to move (from S. Cassiano) to the Teatro S. Moisè, which, however, because of its small size, had proved unsatisfactory.[37]

> I wrote Oristeo and Rosinda, however, without my usual impetus, devoting little time to their creation, in order to free myself from the debts that inadvertently enclosed me within the confines of a theater where, if nothing else, the eye accustomed to the spaciousness of royal scenes [*scene reali*] became disillusioned by the proximity of the set. It is true that the abovementioned theater, in which Ersilla and

33. The exception was *Ersilla* (1648), supposedly set to music "da diversi," but the preface to Faustini's posthumous *Alciade* (1667) includes *Ersilda* (*sic*) among the works by Faustini set by either Cavalli or Ziani (see Appendix I.38a). Faustini's first five librettos were performed, one each season, at the Teatro S. Cassiano originally under Cavalli's and Persiani's direction, but then probably under Faustini's own. These were *La virtù de' strali d'Amore* (1642), *Egisto* (1643), *Ormindo* (1644), *Doriclea* (1645), and *Titone* (1645); the next two, *Ersilla* (1648) and *Euripo* (1649), were performed at the much smaller theater at S. Moisè.

34. This is the age given in the preface to *Alciade* (Appendix I.38a). It conflicts, however, with that given in the necrology records: 36 (I-Vas, Necrologia 1651, f. 877: "19 dicembre 1651. Il signor Zuane Faustini del quondam signor Anzolo d'anni 36 da mal maligno giorni 3.") and in the preface to *Eupatra*: 32 (Appendix I.36e).

35. "Il conduttore s'impegnava a fare tutti i lavori

necessari per attrezzare l'ambiente alla sua nuova destinazione possendo perciò in quello [loco] far quella quantità di Palchi e far recitar quelle opere che ad esso parerà e piacerà" (*b*. 194: 179). Quoted in Glover, "Sant'Apollinare," 17–18.

36. In addition to the possibility that he managed S. Cassiano after Cavalli withdrew in 1644, he may have had some administrative responsibility at S. Moisè, though Pirrotta ("The Lame Horse and the Coachman," *Essays*, 333–34) suggests that Cavalli acted as impresario there. Another librettist, Castoreo, took over the management of S. Cassiano in 1648 (25 April); see Morelli and Walker, "Tre controversie," 114.

37. The debt at S. Cassiano may have been caused by the abrupt closing of the theater in 1645 for the War of Candia—Faustini may have suffered losses like the Novissimo management. Perhaps he paid for the printing of the librettos of *Doriclea* and *Titone* and then was unable to recoup his expenses because the theater closed before the end of the season.

Euripo appeared, and in which these twins were supposed to be presented, is not dissimilar to the one I myself have built in order to cut short the sloth of the institution of my financial independence. But it is also very true that from them, as from corpses, I do not expect to gain applause, and I am reserving for happier times and more majestic theaters Eupatra, Alciade, and Meraspe, heroes who have left their embryo stage, and are almost finished. (Appendix I.33b)

The implication here is that although S. Apollinare was no larger than S. Moisè, Faustini's share of the profits would be greater because he was now not only the librettist but the impresario as well. S. Apollinare, the seventh theater to open (both Ivanovich and Bonlini agree on the numbering), was indeed quite small, with considerably fewer boxes than SS. Giovanni e Paolo and probably S. Cassiano. But the rental fee was low enough, only sixty ducats, so that Faustini's expectations of making a profit were not unreasonable.[38] Moreover, he had high hopes of moving to "more majestic theaters," presumably to increase his profits, as soon as possible.

The prefaces of two of his earlier librettos, *Egisto* (1643) and *Doriclea* (1645), already contain hints of Faustini's frustration with the limited power accorded the librettist in operatic productions. The two works are linked by a series of events whose nature we can only guess. Although performed first, *Egisto*, as we learn from its preface, was written after *Doriclea*. Faustini tells us a story that leaves numerous questions unanswered:

> In order not to let Doriclea perish, with a hasty pen I have created Egisto, which I cast into the arms of fortune. If it is not deserving of your applause, excuse the quality of its being, because having been born in but a few days, it might better be called a miscarriage than an offspring of the mind. I created it with scales in hand, and adapted it to the weakness of those who are to perform it. Theaters want machines that arouse astonishment and pleasure, and sometimes makeup, gold, and purple deceive the eyes and make deformed objects seem beautiful. If you are critical, do not abhor the madness of my Egisto as an imitation of an action that you have already seen on the stage, transferred from comic [i.e., *commedia dell'arte*] to musical drama, because the authoritative entreaties of a powerful person have compelled me to insert it in the opera, to satisfy the inclination of the performer. (Appendix I.31a)

Evidently *Doriclea* had been cancelled at the last minute and Faustini was obliged to substitute *Egisto* for it.[39] He defended himself against anticipated

---

38. S. Apollinare had only forty-eight boxes. But whereas SS. Giovanni e Paolo and S. Cassiano had many more, the rent for those theaters was considerably higher; at S. Cassiano in 1658, for instance, it was 800 ducats. See Bianconi and Walker, "Production," 223. Faustini's financial arrangements with S. Apollinare are discussed in Glover, "Sant'Apollinare," ch. 2.

39. An analogous fate had been suffered by Melosio's *Sidonio e Dorisbe* and *Orione*, the former replacing the latter, which had been written first. But the highly plausible explanation for that substitution given by Pirrotta ("The Lame Horse and the Coachman," *Essays*, 327–28), that *Orione* was too similar to other operas of the same or immediately preceding season, does not seem to serve in Faustini's case.

criticism of the new work by citing the short time he had had to complete it, and he justified his inclusion of what some might regard as a ridiculous scene, Egisto's mad scene, claiming that it was ordered by "le preghiere autorevoli di personaggio grande"—presumably some noble proprietor—in order to satisfy the whim of a singer. Although he belittles his creation as "una sconciatura" rather than "un parto dell'intelletto," he blames not himself but external demands made on him. Squeezed by the importunities of the "personaggio grande" and a singer's whim, he evidently felt that the aesthetic value of his work had been compromised.

The dedication to the Venetian nobleman Mauritio Tirelli of *Doriclea*, which was eventually staged two years later, provides further evidence of the pressures under which Faustini was working.

> I can no longer restrain, my most Excellent Sir, the generous impulses of Doriclea: impatient of remaining buried within the confines of her father's house, she is setting out to reach the goal of immortal glory. Simple-hearted and young, and guided by the blind escort of her daring, she does not fear the Alcides, who challenge her, nor heed the traps laid to impede her journey by two powerful enemies, selfish rivalry and presumptuous ignorance. . . . It is up to Your Lordship, for the affection you bear this Amazon, who uttered her first cries, one might say, in your arms, to secure her path, and to defend her reputation against the shameless ambition of certain rude versifiers, who, lacking ideas, or rather, squandering those of others, pursue the arts of slander, attempting to deface the compositions of minds better than theirs, not knowing, these magpies, the difficulty of inventing because they have never invented, and that it is, as you once said to me, a kind of philosophizing. (Appendix I.32)

Apparently, *Doriclea* had been prevented from reaching the stage originally because of some criticism of its content, perhaps by other librettists, for whom Faustini showed undisguised disdain, labeling them "rude versifiers" (*rozzi versificatori*), unworthy of being called poets. Although Faustini's remarks are permeated with bitterness, they raise the important issue of *inventione*, a quality for which he was especially noted.[40]

Invention of new plots was yet another response to the pressures of institutionalization. It was Faustini's personal solution to the problem of pleasing the jaded audience, of providing it with material it had not seen before. Unlike his contemporaries, he did not borrow his plots from mythology or history; rather, he "invented" most of them, possibly on the model of *commedia dell'arte*, incorporating elements of the pastoral and romance as well.[41]

---

40. Faustini's remarks here resemble those anti-academic comments by Ferrari in the preface to his *Il pastor regio* of 1641 (see appendix I.5a).

41. For some examples of surviving *commedia dell'arte* scenarios, which share a number of features with Faustini's librettos, see Flaminio Scala, *Il teatro delle favole rappresentative* [Venice, 1611], ed. Ferruccio Marotti (Milan, 1976); see also *Scenarios of the Commedia dell'Arte: Flaminio Scala's Il teatro delle favole rappresentative*, trans. Henry F. Salerno (New

Faustini's plots are variations on one basic pattern, what we might call the Faustini mold. Set in foreign lands, usually African, they involve characters of widely contrasting social levels, many of them borrowed from the romance tradition: knights errant, maidens in disguise, magicians. The action revolves around the romantic misadventures of two pairs of lovers of noble birth, attended by assorted comic servants—nurse, confidant, squire—who, through various complications and coincidences are separated and then reunited at the very last moment. His ability to maintain suspense up to his denouements, in fact, was highly valued by Faustini's contemporaries. It was a way of keeping the audience involved.[42]

Many of the devices that help to propel his dramas and contribute to the confusion—such as disguises, overheard conversations, misdelivered letters, and sleeping potions—were standard comic routines going back through Spanish drama and the pastoral to Roman comedy. To provide pseudo-historical backgrounds for his characters, Faustini made use of elaborate *antefatti*, which were included in the printed librettos. Originally fairly brief, these *antefatti* run to more than four tightly packed pages in some of his later librettos. They lent an aura of verisimilitude to his inventions. In addition, by varying the *antefatti*, Faustini was able to minimize the similarity of his plots.

Even though they were all cast in the same mold, Faustini's librettos satisfied the demand for novelty because they were "invented." But the mold itself soon became conventional; used in all fourteen of Faustini's *drammi per musica*, it was adopted by many subsequent librettists, who superimposed it on a wide variety of situations, historical and mythological as well as newly concocted. They stretched and varied it with additional characters and new plot twists, but the basic structure remained the same. Faustini's drive to invent, inspired by his honorable madness, provided a model for dealing with the problem of novelty. By offering a conventional plot structure that was infinitely adaptable, Faustini's librettos establish an important new stage in the development of opera.

In their poetic structure, however, Faustini's texts were not much different from those of his predecessors. Like theirs, his poetry consisted primarily of freely alternating *settenario* and *endecasillabo* verses, unrhymed or rhymed irregularly—what we would call *versi sciolti* or recitative poetry. These were interrupted occasionally by closed forms structured by a single meter (*versi misurati*) or regular rhyme scheme, usually both—that is, aria poetry. Although such closed forms were traditionally strophic, Faustini sometimes employed briefer closed passages, of three or four lines, which he repeated after a certain

---

York, 1967); and Roberto Tessari, *La commedia dell'arte nel seicento* (Florence, 1969).

42. This is a feature emphasized in the printer's preface to *Eupatra* (see Appendix I.36d).

interval as a refrain. These structured passages were usually set in aria style by composers.[43]

Although Faustini may have become an impresario partly in order to achieve artistic independence, economic considerations were apparently foremost in his mind in 1651. According to his grand plan, announced in the preface to *Oristeo*, he had no intention of remaining at S. Apollinare for the rest of his career. He projected two librettos to be performed there, the twins *Oristeo* and *Rosinda*, for which, he admitted, he did not expect to receive much applause, but only some financial rewards. As he put it, he had constructed the theater "to cut short the sloth of the institution of my financial independence" ("per decapitare l'otio della institutione del mio viver libero"), an aim reiterated in the brief preface to *Rosinda*: "I stated in the preceding Oristeo that these two dramas were composed by me in order to discharge a debt, not out of eagerness for applause" (Appendix I.34). As for his almost finished works, *Eupatra*, *Alciade*, and *Meraspe*, "heroes past the embryo stage and almost finished," he would reserve them for better times and more majestic theaters (Appendix I.33b).

As it happened, things did not proceed according to plan. For the following season Faustini projected another pair of operas, this time the "twin princesses" *Calisto* and *Eritrea*, "conceived and delivered this year" ("generate, e partorite quest'anno"). But on 19 December 1651, before either work could be produced, Faustini died. He managed to sign the dedication of *Calisto*, which had evidently been scheduled to be performed first, but *Eritrea*, in press at his death, was published posthumously, with a dedication to Marc'Antonio Corraro signed by the printer, Giacomo Batti.[44] From it, in addition to being reminded of Faustini's contribution to libretto literature, we learn something more about the difficult conditions under which he had worked:

> While a feigned death of Eritrea will delight Your Illustrious Lordship's ear, the all-too-real one of Signor Giovanni Faustini will dolefully move your soul. This celebrated man of letters died a few days ago, and after having created eleven operas, he left in press that of his beloved Eritrea. This poor queen, all beaten down by her unlucky encounters, by the extravagance of her misfortunes, has finally seen the light of day, obliged to obey that father who promised her in Calisto. There was no lack of obstacles to hinder her in her journey, besides the loss of him who, having

---

43. For an admirable recent discussion of the verse types of Italian opera, see Paolo Fabbri, "Istituti metrici e formali," in *StOpIt*, 6: 165–233. For Italian poetry in general, the standard study is W. Theodore Elwert, *Italienische Metrik* (Munich, 1968), translated as *Versificazione italiana dalle origini ai giorni nostri* (Florence, 1983); see also Mario Ramous, *La metrica* (Milan, 1984). The terms *versi sciolti* and *versi misurati*, while not used as such by these authors, em-

phasize the essential difference between recitative (unrhymed) and aria (rhymed) poetry and, for that reason, are employed here—as they are in other studies of seventeenth-century opera (see, for example, Morelli and Walker, "Migliori plettri").
44. Corraro was one of Faustini's management associates, along with Alvise Duodo; see Glover, "Sant'Apollinare," 19–22, 28.

begotten her, ought to have assisted her further. And she has lost as well the company of the virtuoso Bonifatio, who at the beginning of her journey halted both her step and her life. (Appendix I.35a)[45]

Batti's allusion to Eritrea's difficulties suggests that Faustini's problems plagued him until his death. The impression is reinforced in the preface to another posthumous libretto, that of *Eupatra*, published in 1655 by the printer Bartolomeo Ginammi, in which the librettist's premature death was attributed to overwork, he "having always dedicated his entire soul to invention, from which, through his continuous and unceasing dedication, derived the seeds of his illness, which too bitterly took his life at the age of 32 [*sic*]" (Appendix I.36e).[46]

The romantic image created by Faustini himself of the passionate librettist driven by "honorable madness" to "invent" operatic texts even beyond those required for a specific season is embroidered by the printer here. Whether his death was hastened by poetic frenzy or by financial pressures, it is clear that Faustini left behind many unpaid bills as well as unperformed works, a combination that, ironically, was to prove highly significant for the future development of opera in Venice.

Faustini's Heirs

Faustini's premature death in 1651, just at the threshold of an important new phase in the development of Venetian opera, left a vacuum, not least for Cavalli, who had relied almost exclusively on him to supply operatic texts during the previous ten years. Fortunately, however, Faustini did not die intestate. He left heirs, both literal and figurative, in whose hands his estate prospered. His brother Marco, a lawyer, assumed Giovanni's role as impresario at S. Apollinare and became one of the most important operatic powers of the next two decades; and two new poets, Minato and Aureli, together took over his artistic role as the dominant librettists in Venice, a position they shared until Minato's departure for Vienna in 1669. Even more important than his position, however, they inherited his poetic style, which through them was to become the lingua franca of the seicento libretto.

Significantly, the careers of these two librettists and Marco Faustini were linked. Aureli's first libretto was written under contract with Marco for a performance at S. Apollinare in 1652, and all but one of his next eleven texts

---

45. The meaning of "the company of the virtuoso Bonifatio" ("la compagnia del virtuoso Bonifatio") is ambiguous. It may refer to a theatrical company or perhaps to a single performer.

46. The idea of premature death from overwork evidently exercised a certain fascination; it was also cited in the case of Boretti (see Appendix IIIB.11c).

(through 1668) were commissioned by Marco as well. Minato, a close friend of Aureli's, with whom he subsequently shared the duties of impresario at S. Salvatore, also wrote for Marco Faustini, though only sporadically, in 1658 and 1659 at S. Cassiano, and in 1664 at SS. Giovanni e Paolo.

The first two librettos of Aureli, *Erginda* (1652), a failure, and *Erismena* (1655), an enormous success, reveal the influence of Giovanni Faustini most clearly. Both were based on invented plots in the Faustini mold, the latter even being modeled on a Faustini original.[47] This is particularly understandable since they were both written for Faustini's old collaborator, Cavalli. With his third libretto, *Le fortune di Rodope e Damira* (1657), however, Aureli began to develop a style of his own, finding explicit inspiration in history and mythology, and adding extra characters to the Faustini formula that helped to mask its symmetries. Although he cited several sources for the story and characters of *Rodope*, including Polidorus, Virgil, Herodotus, Strabo, "& altri Autori," Aureli firmly rejected them, indicating that the relationships between his characters would follow an independent course. History provided the *antefatti*; the poet himself devised their working out.

Aureli's subsequent librettos were all similarly structured: a historical or mythological core and ambience—provided by the Greek dramatists, Virgil, Ovid, Tacitus, even Ariosto—was elaborated and developed in accordance with operatic conventions inherited from comedy and pastoral by way of Faustini. This procedure, the embroidery of preexistent sources, seems to have been more congenial to Aureli than the freely invented Faustini model. Aureli's intellectual background was evidently quite different from that of Faustini. He was more of an academic librettist in the tradition of Busenello or Strozzi than a man of the theater like Faustini, and the rather ostentatious flaunting of history and mythology was part of his academic pose.

The separation—illustrated in the preface to *Rodope*, and in those of practically all of Aureli's subsequent librettos—between received history and invention found a more precise formulation, and possibly inspiration, in the librettos of Minato. In every one of his librettos beginning with the second, *Xerse* (1654), Minato separated historical elements ("quello che si hà dall'historia") from fictional ones ("quello che si finge"). His reliance on Faustini, like Aureli's, was strongest at the outset of his career; his first libretto, *Orimonte* (1650), was a freely composed romance in the Faustini mold. Like Aureli's *Erismena*, it was written to be set by Cavalli, and the Faustini mold may even have been the composer's idea. Like *Erginda*, though perhaps for somewhat

---

47. The evident failure of *Erginda* may be judged by its lack of subsequent performances. On the *Erismena* situation, see n. 13 above.

different reasons, Minato's *Orimonte* was a failure.[48] For his second opera, *Xerse* (1654), however, Minato adopted a different strategy, combining history with invention somewhat along the lines of Aureli's slightly later effort. *Xerse* was based on material taken from Herodotus that was embroidered upon by the librettist, a procedure that proved successful for the remainder of Minato's career, as well as for Aureli's. In the *argomento* to his next libretto, *Artemisia* (1656), Minato called his inventions "verisimili" and justified them in true academic fashion by paying tribute to Aristotle. After having outlined "quello che si hà dall'istoria," he initiated "quello che si finge" as follows: "Now, following the precepts of the master of all, Aristotle, and wishing, as he teaches, to invent on the basis of history to compose this drama, I have undertaken to imagine that. . . ."[49] Not only did a preexisting classical source underlie his drama but the very technique of elaborating that source found classical justification as well.

Aureli indulged in a similar kind of scholarly apologetics in his preface to *Medoro* (1658). After acknowledging Ariosto as the source for his subject, he further invoked the poet—and not without reason—to justify his own *invenzioni*: "Angelica, after having healed Medoro's wounds, and having secretly made him her husband, goes back with him to Cathay, her kingdom in India; but what variety of adventures she experienced in love before raising him to the throne, Ariosto left it up to another pen to write; and this affords the material for the composition of this drama, in which, with the help of realistic adventures, it is imagined that. . . ."[50]

Whether it was the result of their similar education or a more general sign of the times, the adoption of similar formulas by both Aureli and Minato signaled a new stage in the development of the Venetian libretto; the texts of the next half-century were characterized by a mixture of history and invention. The balance between the two, however, so clearly marked in their early works, became increasingly weighted in favor of invention until, by the late 1670s and 1680s, although still evoked by the titles of librettos and the names of a few characters, "l'historia" had become a mere pretense, to be ignored as much as

---

48. The libretto of *Orimonte* was admittedly weak, but there were apparently more practical reasons for its lack of success; see Morelli and Walker, "Tre controversie," 97–120.

49. "Hora seguendo i documenti del Maestro del tutto Aristotile, volendo, come egli insegna, fingere sopra l'Istoria, per comporre il presente Dramma, si è preso assunto di figurare. . . ." In the preface to *Artemisia*, however, Minato gave greater emphasis to the "invented" component: "In quel drama [*Xerse*] ti reccai qualche accidente tratto da famosissimo Au-

tore, ch'in altro Idioma lo scrisse: In questo tutto ciò, ch'io t'apporto e di mia pura inventione."

50. "Angelica dopo haver risanate le ferite a Medoro, e fattolo privatamente suo sposo, se ne ritornò con esso al Cataio suo Regno nell'India; ma qual varietà d'accidenti passasse in Amore prima d'ergerlo al Trono, fu dall'Ariosto lasciato in libertà di scriverlo ad altra penna; il che dà materia alla tessitura di questo Dramma, mentre con supposti d'accidenti verisimili si finge. . . ."

possible. Aureli himself, in fact, became one of the chief abusers of history, as well as mythology, in his later works.[51]

The use of "historical" sources initially had little effect on the Faustini formula; indeed, the librettos of Aureli and Minato continued to exploit the same dramatic structure and theatrical situations that had been conventionalized by Faustini. Their plots still centered on two pairs of lovers (attended by the requisite servants), whose separation, misunderstandings, and eventual reconciliation provided the substance of the drama. But the historical sources supplied the basis for that essential commodity, variety, as well as providing a challenge to the skill of the librettists.

Faustini's texts were rather indistinguishable from one another insofar as his invented characters tended to be generalized and interchangeable types; their names carried no particular association or expectation. Characters drawn from historical sources, on the other hand, had clear, individual identities; they brought with them well-known names, personalities, and backgrounds. The combination of these characters with the recently established conventions of operatic plots offered new theatrical possibilities, new ways for librettists to demonstrate ingenuity. By the mid 1650s audiences had come to appreciate and expect such conventions—a mad scene, a lament, a comic romp between an old nurse and a young squire—and the further complication of historical personages in those stock situations undoubtedly added a new and special appeal.

The contribution of Aureli and Minato to the Venetian libretto extended beyond dramatic structure, however, to the poetry itself. They essentially followed the style of Faustini (and his predecessors) in casting large portions of their texts in free, recitative meter, interspersed with more structured passages of poetry intended for arias, but they gradually altered the proportions, increasing the number of arias in direct response to new demands on the part of the audience and singers.

Progress in the developing genre had created a broad range of new difficulties for the makers of operas during the late 1650s and 1660s. The problems Minato and Aureli confronted were consequently somewhat different from those faced by their prolific predecessor Faustini. In addition to the familiar demand for novelty, there were two main issues: the pressure of deadlines and the increasing dominance of singers. Whereas Faustini had not lived quite long enough to complain, like Bissari, about jaded audiences, they were one of Aureli's most frequent targets. Understandably so: if Venetian audiences were jaded by 1650, they must have been absolutely surfeited by the end of that decade. Continuing at the pace of approximately four per year, the number of

---

51. Two excellent examples of Aureli's special brand of distortion are *Orfeo* (1673) and *Olimpia vendicata* (1681); see Ellen Rosand, "Orlando in Seicento Venice: The Road Not Taken," in *Opera seria as a Social Phenomenon*, ed. Michael Collins and Elise Kirk (Austin, 1984), 87–104.

old operas had swelled from something under the fifty counted by Bissari in 1650—he had exaggerated slightly—to close to ninety by 1660 (there were thirty-eight new ones introduced between 1650 and 1659). Aureli lamented this state of affairs in the preface to almost every one of his librettos, beginning with *Le fatiche d'Ercole per Deianira* in 1662: "Nowadays the people of the city of Venice have become so indifferent in their tastes for dramas that they no longer know what they want to see, nor does the intellect of the author know anymore what to invent in order to win the applause of the spectators, or to satisfy the majority (since to satisfy everyone is impossible)" (Appendix I.46b). He struck the same tone in *Gli amori d'Apollo e di Leucotoe* the following year: "I declare that the talents of our age are so capricious, and the people of Venice so difficult to satisfy, because by now they have been satiated by the performance of so many dramas, that I would not consider it a blunder to commit some blunders, as long as I were sure that these would amuse the listeners, and please those who spend [i.e., the patrons]" (Appendix I.47). And once again, in *Perseo*, two years later: "I know that the taste of the people of Venice has reached such a point that it no longer knows what it wants to see, nor do the writers know any longer what to invent to satisfy the bizarre caprice of this city" (Appendix I.48).

Similar complaints even found their way into operatic dialogue, as in the following passage from *Gli avvenimenti d'Orinda* (1659) by one of Aureli's contemporaries, Antonio Zaguri. The prologue includes a debate on aesthetics among Capriccio, Momo, Fortuna, and Inventione; in response to the idea that Capriccio might possibly invent something new, Momo replies:

Ch'egli faccia novità,	That he should create a novelty,
Ch'io lo creda, ò questo no,	That I should believe it, oh, no, indeed.
Troppo il mondo ritrovò.	Everything has been too much repeated,
Nè inventar altro si sa.	Nor does one know how to invent anything else.
Et hor suole anco la Gente	Some have even reached the point
Chiamar vecchio il Sol nascente.	Of calling old the rising sun.

As librettists struggled to alleviate the audience's boredom through new twists of plot and dramatic devices, they had also to contend with the unprecedented attention now being lavished on the singers. This difficulty was perhaps easier to resolve, although not without compromising aesthetic ideals. They could simply supply additional arias, which allowed singers to display their sheer vocal powers more obviously than recitative dialogue. Faustini himself had not been immune to pressures from singers, as we know from the preface to his *Egisto* (Appendix I.31a). But Aureli was obsessed by his audience's demand for arias, which he mentions in a number of different prefaces.[52]

---

52. See especially those of *Le fatiche d'Ercole per Deianira* and *Claudio Cesare* (see Appendix I.46 and 50).

If the steady demands of past theatrical seasons were responsible for a stultifying accumulation of old works that increasingly tested the possibilities for novelty, the unrelenting demands of present and future seasons created a problem of another kind, pressures on the resources of Venice itself for personnel. The compact, stable troupes of the early impresarios, Ferrari, Sacrati, and Cavalli, had become insufficient. The days were gone, too, when both librettist and composer lived in Venice and singers could be borrowed from San Marco. As more and more librettists, composers, and singers were required for the operatic industry, they had to be drawn from a widening geographical area. The readying of productions involving such disparate elements, which relied heavily on communication by post, became increasingly difficult, often resulting in last-minute compromises, cancellations, or replacements.

Geographical separation, difficulties with last-minute arrangements—the hiring of singers, the completion of the score—placed a severe strain on everyone concerned. Librettists, composers, and singers all operated under great constraints of time. Although Faustini had referred to his hurried creation of *Rosinda* and *Oristeo*, we know that he composed his other librettos at greater leisure, managing to complete a number of them well before they were needed. Aureli, however, seems almost always to have been working under pressure. In one instance he complained that lack of time had made him turn out an inferior work, "not a child but an abortion of the imagination,"[53] and he attributed the higher quality of a subsequent work (*Le fatiche d'Ercole*) to the unusual absence of such a deadline:

> If now and then I did not succeed in hitting the mark, know that I also did not always have the time that is required for such compositions. That this is true you will see from the consequences, since I hope that in these labors of mine dedicated to Ercole you will recognize the difference there is between writing in a hurry and composing with a tranquil mind, and at one's leisure. I confess that I have toiled harder in this than in my other dramas to answer to your liking. (Appendix I.46c)

Minato voiced similar complaints, explaining in one instance that he had worked so quickly and so close to the last minute that he had had no time to correct his libretto.[54]

The difficulties faced by this generation constituted the main challenge of Marco Faustini's career as an impresario. Although Aureli in particular is an articulate witness to the difficulties, they take on a special immediacy when viewed through the eyes of Faustini, whose job it was to overcome them.

---

53. "non dirò un parto, ma un'abhorto d'ingegno" (*Antigona*, preface). Lack of time also necessitated a shortcut, forcing him to utilize preexistent material; see p. 186 below.

54. "io involto in molt'altre occupationi ho fatica ad haver tempo di scrivere, non che di emendare" (*Mutio Scevola*, preface [1665]).

Marco Faustini, Impresario

More than any other of the period, the career of Marco Faustini epitomizes and illuminates the world of opera institutionalized. The kinds of problems he faced with his business partners, singers, librettists, and composers as the impresario of three different theaters over a period of nearly two decades (1651–68), and the solutions he devised, all with the aim of selling tickets, reflect the extent to which aesthetic questions were subject to commercial conditions. His controversies, like operatic life itself, grew more and more complicated with each succeeding season as past works continued to accumulate, making the expected novelty ever more difficult to attain. The planning of future seasons began to require more time than before; the hiring of singers, composers, and librettists, in competition with other theaters and patrons, required greater concessions to each group. Faustini's work involved a delicate balancing act among disparate, competing elements, each with its own agenda.

Faustini assumed his brother's responsibilities at S. Apollinare immediately after Giovanni's death, as can be inferred from the wording of his contract of 25 October 1655 with the owners of the theater; it was to run for ten years from June 1656, the date of expiration of Giovanni's contract. Conditions of rental were to conform to the "lease made to Sig. Giovanni Faustini his brother on 19 May 1650."[55] Marco had rights to only half of the theater, those of the other half remaining with one of the original owners, Francesco Ceroni, with whom Faustini litigated continually until 1657, when he abandoned S. Apollinare for S. Cassiano.[56]

The unpublished, unperformed librettos that Giovanni Faustini had left at his death represented a valuable property for a beginning impresario, especially one who was not a librettist himself, for in the intensely competitive theatrical world of the 1650s, new texts were not so easy to come by. Giovanni's legacy provided Marco with a stock-in-trade, enough material to tide him over for a few seasons until he could begin commissioning librettos on his own. But the legacy clearly meant more to Marco than mere operatic capital. There is evidence that his motives were emotional as well as economic, and that his career as an impresario, which began and ended with Giovanni Faustini productions,

55. "Per tutto conforme l'affittanza fatta al Sign. Zuane Faustini suo fratello ne gli atti del Sign. Alberto Mascalco notaro di questa città li 19 V 1650" (*b.* 194: 168). A large portion of this document, actually a contract with Zanetta Piamonte, proprietor of half of the theater, is quoted in Giazotto, "La guerra dei palchi," 279. The correct date of the contract is 25 October, not 21 September as Giazotto has it, or 25 December, the date given in Mangini, *I teatri di Venezia,* 68. The documents pertaining to the leasing of S. Apollinare are transcribed in Glover, "Sant'Apollinare," esp. ch. 2, "The Administration of the Teatro Sant'Apollinare," and appendix 1.

56. The documents of this litigation are found in *b.* 194: 163–69. See Mangini, *I teatri di Venezia,* 68, and Glover, "Sant'Apollinare," ch. 2.

was essentially a way of promoting the reputation of his brother. Part of his strategy was to elaborate the image of the "frenzied poet" that Giovanni himself had initiated.

Giovanni's legacy also benefited the printers of his posthumous librettos. They were probably the ones who stood to profit from sales, now that the author was no longer living. It was also in their interest to keep the Faustini myth alive, to connect the posthumous works via a romantic image of the driven genius to Faustini's past successes. It was undoubtedly for these reasons that Giovanni's entire list of operas was repeatedly invoked, by title as well as number, in each of the posthumous publications. As a result, Faustini's works survived well beyond the normal lifespan of librettos at a time when, once performed, an opera was considered old, and novelty was the single quality appreciated above all others in a libretto. But not only were Faustini's works cited again and again, his untimely death was repeatedly, and ostentatiously, lamented.

Nowhere is this more striking than in the front matter of *Eupatra* (1655), published four years after the librettist's death. The dedication is to Alvise Duodo, the recipient of previous librettos and business partner of both Marco and Giovanni;[57] it is signed by Bartolomeo Ginammi, the publisher:

> Death has no arrow that can harm those who live by their talent and die by necessity of nature. One of these is Sig. Giovanni Faustini of glorious memory, whose death we already mourned, or rather, whom we admired as he was snatched from the hands of death, and whom we applauded as wedded to immortality. Even envy has no venom to poison this glory, nor fog to dim this splendor, while even now new offspring of that most noble mind are being born, among whom is Eupatra, who cannot be called an orphan as long as her father lives in the memory of his descendants, and Your Most Illustrious Lordship is more than ever vigorous in protecting him. (Appendix I.36a)

In the preface to the reader, Ginammi amplified his evaluation with some interesting aesthetic judgments. Not only did he praise Faustini's *inventione*, but also his method of dramatic development, which saved the denouement for the very end. The passage concludes by referring once more to the author's *inventione*, to his previous twelve works, and to the untold number of treasures still awaiting performance.

> Here, finally, is the Eupatra promised four years ago, the twelfth dramatic effort of Sig. Giovanni Faustini of happy memory. If his works have won universal applause in this city and in all Italy, where they are often performed, it is not to be feared that this princess will not also receive the laurels she deserves. It will be wondrous for its invention and structure. . . . The author, as if foreseeing his untimely death,

---

57. On Alvise Duodo's relationship with the Faustini brothers, see Glover, "Sant'Apollinare," 19–22, 28.

left some pages of brief notes in his own hand, as to where certain *canzonette* belonged, which were then composed by a most capable person. Only to idiots do
those tales seem obscure that resolve in the final scenes; but connoisseurs and scholars admire them, because in such compositions even the most attentive minds must
remain in suspense, and this is what the author always practiced, not only in the
twelve works published so far, but in still others, which are being saved for future
years. (Appendix I.36b, d)

Marco managed to keep things going at S. Apollinare for several seasons
after Giovanni's death, producing a total of five operas there, one on a libretto
by his brother and two each by new librettists, Castoreo and Aureli. As for the
music, Giovanni's regular collaborator Cavalli seems to have resisted working
for Marco, who was able to secure his services for only one of the operas,
Erismena,[58] and had to rely on less experienced composers for the others:
Francesco Lucio, a veteran of a couple of seasons, for *Pericle effeminato* (1653),
and Pietro Andrea Ziani, a rank beginner, for the other three.[59]

Despite the success of *Erismena*, Marco Faustini evidently found S. Apollinare as unsatisfactory as his brother had feared it would be. He left for S.
Cassiano in 1657 (probably because of costly struggles with Ceroni, one of the
owners), signing a contract with the Tron brothers on 5 May 1657 to manage
their theater for ten years—a contract he failed to fulfill.[60] On the same day,
Marco formed a partnership, along with Corraro, Duodo, and Polifilo
Zuancarli—his associates at S. Apollinare as well—to produce operas. Because
of its size, S. Cassiano would probably have fulfilled Giovanni's hopes for "a
more majestic theater" as a showcase for his later works, but in the end only one
of them, *Elena*, ever appeared there.

For *Antioco* (1658–59) and *Elena* (1659–60), two of the three works he
produced during his brief stay at S. Cassiano, Marco was able to secure the
services of Cavalli and Minato, who had been collaborating at SS. Giovanni e
Paolo during the previous two seasons.[61] Only the first of Minato's librettos

58. Cavalli was apparently disinclined to work for
Faustini because of some negative experiences with
the latter's partner, Duodo. He expressed his dissat-
isfaction in a letter of July 1654 to Marco (*b.* 188: 14)
(see Appendix IIIA.1).

59. Lucio had two previous operas to his credit,
both written for SS. Apostoli: *Orontea* and *Gli amori
d'Alessandro e di Rossane*; see Morelli and Walker,
"Migliori plettri," CXXXII–CXXXIV. Ziani's
three operas for Faustini were *La guerriera spartana*
(1653), *Eupatra* (1654), and *Le fortune di Rodope e
Damira* (1657).

60. Contract of 5 May 1657. See Mangini, *I teatri di
Venezia*, 41; text given in *Quellentexte*, ed. Becker,
71; see also Glover, "Sant'Apollinare," 24; Giazotto,
"La guerra dei palchi," 257–58.

61. Minato's move from SS. Giovanni e Paolo to S.
Cassiano under Faustini may have been encouraged
by Aureli's move in the opposite direction, from
Faustini's service at S. Apollinare to SS. Giovanni e
Paolo. Minato alludes to this in the preface to *Antioco*
(Appendix I.42). The non–Cavalli-Minato work at
S. Cassiano, *L'incostanza trionfante ovvero il Theseo*,
actually produced first, in 1658, was a problematic
libretto by Francesco Piccoli set to music by Ziani
(see n. 78 below). The *Antioco* production is at
present the best-documented work of this period,
thanks to the survival of a production book among
Faustini's papers (in *b.* 194, unnumbered); it forms
one of the central focuses of Bianconi's and Walker's
masterful study, "Production."

was original, however; *Elena* was an arrangement or working out of a scenario left by Giovanni Faustini, another piece of his legacy. Since it had not been included in his *Oristeo* list, and since it had evidently survived in a highly unfinished state, *Elena* was presumably one of Faustini's last projects. According to Minato's dedication and note to the reader, the deceased author had left an outline of the subject, which he, Minato, had fleshed out:

> The subject of this drama was a product of the most fertile imagination of the late Sign. Giovanni Faustini of famous memory, whose virtues amazed not only the theaters of this city but even those of the most distant lands. Many sublime pens were asked, after his death, to dress it with the mantle of poetry, but for various reasons they all refused. I, however, did not know how to refuse this honor. (Appendix I.37a)

Following these conventional allusions to Faustini's reputation and death, Minato concluded with an elaborate evocation of the romance of his predecessor's existence: "I pray to heaven that the peace of his ashes not be disturbed by someone with my shortcomings who, in daring to touch his achievement, might diminish it. I declare, however, that whatever is bad in it is mine, and everything that shines with merit is his. Gentle reader, then, admire the subject, be indulgent toward the words" (Appendix I.37b).

It almost seems as though Marco kept the legacy of Giovanni's librettos in reserve, spending it parsimoniously to maintain its value, or else perhaps drawing upon it when nothing else was forthcoming. After having guarded his brother's works for five years, he probably made the *Elena* sketch available to Minato, who may have been too pressed to write a wholly new text for 1659, having already written *Antioco* for the previous season.[62] In the following year, the peripatetic Marco moved once again with his company, this time permanently, to the most majestic of all the Venetian theaters, SS. Giovanni e Paolo. Here he eventually attempted to produce the remainder of Giovanni's works.[63]

Marco's *Guerra dei teatri*

The decade of the 1660s saw a radical change in the structure of operatic politics. The 1650s had represented a period of expansion, a kind of operatic free-for-all

---

62.   Minato's editorial intervention also involved the writing of a new prologue and some new arias, *Nuovo prologo et ariette* (1659), which are found in the score (I-Vnm, It. IV, 369 [9893]).

63.   On the beginning of Faustini's connection with SS. Giovanni e Paolo, see Mangini, *I teatri di Venezia*, 59, esp. n. 11. The first dated document associating Marco with the theater is a contract with the scenographer Ippolito Mazzarini of 6 June 1660 (*b.* 194: 11). See Brunelli, "Angustie," 315. Only a preliminary draft of Faustini's original contract with the owners of the theater and a subsequent renewal, dated 23 February 1665, seem to have survived (*b.* 194: 134). See also Giazotto, "La guerra dei palchi," 266–67.

following the establishment of the genre at the end of the 1640s. The 1660s, in contrast, were a decade dominated by two theaters, one old, SS. Giovanni e Paolo, the other brand-new, the Vendramin theater of S. Salvatore at S. Luca, which opened for operatic business in 1661.[64] The competition between these theaters flavored and controlled operatic life in Venice for the next fifteen years. Despite a brief challenge in 1666, issued by the temporary resurgence of S. Cassiano and S. Moisè, their near-monopoly only began to erode in the early 1670s with the reopening of S. Moisè under new, aggressive management, which generated enormous publicity by reducing ticket prices. The monopoly was definitively broken toward the end of the decade with the opening of two new theaters, S. Angelo and S. Giovanni Grisostomo.

Although SS. Giovanni e Paolo had operated continuously since its opening in 1639 (it was the only theater to have done so), Marco Faustini's move there in 1660 initiated a new surge of activity, resulting in twelve successive two-opera seasons. These were nearly matched by the productions at S. Salvatore, which soon recovered after the spectacular failure of its inaugural opera, *Pasife*.[65] The competitive climate of these years, which focused increasingly on the rivalry between these two theaters, is attested by the theatrical gossip of the time, references in librettos and elsewhere to upsets, changes of plans, and so on. According to Aureli's preface to *Antigona* of 1660, Faustini's first season, rumor had it that there would be no performances at all at SS. Giovanni e Paolo:

> How easily the opinion of the multitude is deceived you will see this time from the results; the rumor spreading through the city of Venice that this year there were to be no performances in the theater of SS. Giovanni e Paolo prompted those in charge of the administration and patronage of the same to show you that in the brief span of this carnival not only is the theater open, but it is even staging two dramas. (Appendix I.45a)[66]

---

64.   According to Ivanovich, the Teatro S. Salvatore was the second to have opened, after S. Cassiano. Originally "fatto per recitar Commedie," it was reborn, following a fire, and began producing operas in 1661 (*Minerva*, 399). Bonlini lists it as eighth (*Le glorie*, 14). A large group of documents pertaining to this theater is found in I-Vcg, Archivio Vendramin. A number of them are utilized in Mangini, *I teatri di Venezia*, 48–55. One of them, a budget for the 1669 performance of *Argia*, is illustrated in fig. 24 (see n. 105 below). The opening of S. Salvatore must have bothered Faustini, to judge from Ziani's remarks in a letter to the impresario of 12 June 1666 (*b.* 188: 268) (Appendix IIIA.12); see Giazotto, "La guerra dei palchi," 507.

65.   The furor surrounding the premiere of *Pasife* is described in a letter of 20 February 1661 from Giovanni da Mosto to Ottavio Labia. "Fu curiosa quela

[the opera] di S. Lucca, che non pottendosi più tollerare proruppe l'auditorio in una insolenza la prima sera, che anco fu l'ultima, gettando in scena tutto quelo veniva alle mani, abbrugiando tutti l'opera [the libretto] et con gridi e batterelle fussimo sino le 8 della notte con il maggior solazzo, che mai habbi hautto. Il teatro pieno di dame fu causa che ovviò maggior male, perche in una parola meritavano di peggio. Ghe la mando [i.e., the opera's libretto] insieme con un'altra, che questa sera devesi reccitar nel teatro medemo, et stimo con simile aplauso." Quoted in Mangini, *I teatri di Venezia*, 52–53 n. 26, from Andrea da Mosto, "Uomini e cose del '600 veneziano (da un epistolario inedito)," *Rivista di Venezia* 12, no. 3 (1933): 117. The second opera referred to by da Mosto was the revival of Faustini's and Cavalli's *Eritrea*.

66.   The same rumor is also reported in *b.* 188: 375.

Apparently, however, the decision to mount a second opera was made at the last minute, since Aureli was forced to adapt his work to accommodate the resources available from the first one, *Gli avvenimenti d'Orinda* (Pietro Angelo Zaguri/P. A. Ziani): "For lack of time it proved expedient for me to adapt the drama to the sets (except for one), to the same ballets, and to some of the machines created by the Most Illustrious Sig. Zaguri" (Appendix I.45b).

That such rumors and changes in plans had more than local significance is confirmed by *Il rimino*. The issue of 13 December 1661 reported that the (evidently recent) decision of SS. Giovanni e Paolo to mount two operas would force the other theaters, namely S. Salvatore, to do likewise: "if not to surpass it, at least to keep up" ("se non di sopravanzare, almeno di caminare del pari").[67] In fact, however, S. Salvatore did not "caminare del pari" until 1666, when it managed to stage two operas for the first time since its disastrous opening season. In the following year, its attempt to "sopravanzare" took an unprecedented form. Instead of dividing the season into the customary two parts, with one opera for each, its two operas were planned as a pair, to alternate on a regular basis. Minato's *La prosperità di Elio Seiano* was to be followed—and resolved—the next evening, by his *La caduta di Elio Seiano*, both set to music by Antonio Sartorio, creating a kind of *Ring* avant la lettre. In the end, however, the plan failed; the premiere of the second opera did not take place until some two weeks after the first, owing to unspecified circumstances. It is possible that Minato's project had been publicity-inspired rather than practical in the first place.[68]

The efforts of SS. Giovanni e Paolo and S. Salvatore to maintain a regular rhythm of two productions per season involved their managements in highly competitive negotiations for singers, librettists, and composers, and the situation was complicated by competition from outside Venice. Indeed, the success of traveling companies in inspiring a taste for Venetian opera in the provinces had resulted, by the 1650s, in regular opera seasons in a number of Italian cities—Bologna, Genoa, Milan, for example—not to mention at foreign courts

67. "Gl' interessati in questi Teatri [S. Luca and Grimani], accelerano i loro preparamenti; e poi che si aspettano li due Prencipi di Bransvich, oltre il terzo Cattolico, che continua a soggiornare in questa Città, e si aspetta parimente da Fiorenza di passaggio, e ritorno in Ispruch il Sereniss. Arciduca, et Arciduchessa sua Consorte, fanno a gara li medesimi interessati, et havendo quei del Teatro di San Gio: e Paolo rissoluto rappresentare due Opere; si sforzano gl'altri di San Luca, se non di sopravanzare, almeno di caminare del pari, in modo che non guardano a qual si sia opera [= spesa]: et i medesimi di S. Gio: e Paolo, oltre l'haver fatta provisione di Musici assai stimati serventi a Prencipi, hanno fatto venire da Roma una cantatrice sopramodo stimata, non meno nel cantare, che nell'esser bella, in età di 15 in 16 anni, alla quale di Donatico hanno stipolato 150 Doppie di sopra una veste di brocato d'oro, per il viaggio 200 scudi d'argento, et il tutto fino a primi giorni di Quaresima per se, sua Madre, un Virtuoso venuto ad accompagnarlo, per un Servitore, et una Cameriera" (quoted in Matteini, *Il "Rimino,"* 91–92). An excerpt from this report is quoted in Selfridge-Field, *Pallade veneta*, 336.

68. This story, which can be gleaned from Minato's prefaces to the two librettos, dated 15 January and 3 February respectively, is recounted in Monson, "Aelius Sejanus."

in France and Austria, all of which sought out the services of the most re-
nowned singers, composers, and librettists from Venice. Personnel problems
required extreme flexibility on the part of theater managements; they had to be
prepared to arrange eleventh-hour substitutions, revisions, and even new commissions. There are numerous records of last-minute cancellations and post-
ponements during these years, and various shortcuts were developed to deal
with such situations. On some occasions, when the first opera was unsuccessful
or not ready, it was replaced by the second, and a new second opera hurriedly
prepared.[69] Aureli's *Antigona* was surely not the only second opera designed to
make use of material from the first. At least once, a missing second opera was
substituted for by repetition of the first with some of its arias changed.[70]

The competition of these years increased the value of every proven librettist, composer, and singer. Seeking to engage the best and most popular artists,
theater managers tried to avoid being outbid by one another.[71] Often they
attempted to protect themselves by extending contracts to cover more than one
season, yet they needed the flexibility to cancel them if the collaboration proved
unsuccessful. The painstaking delicacy of these negotiations, particularly with
singers, is recorded with special vividness in Faustini's papers.

Although less revealing of the impresario's relationship with composers
than with singers, the papers nevertheless indicate the kinds of compromises
Faustini was forced to accept in order to assure himself of their services. Negotiations with both Cesti and Ziani must have been quite unpleasant, though
for different reasons. Cesti, who did not write his first opera for Faustini until
1666, played hard to get, promising to provide scores and then backing out of
his promises, setting and then withdrawing conditions, which included the
hiring of certain singers.[72] Ziani, who had worked for Faustini quite regularly
since 1657 at S. Apollinare, was more difficult personally. He constantly re-
proached the impresario for esteeming him less than Cesti and Cavalli and
paying him poorly. His letters to Faustini are filled with reminders of his own
trustworthiness and the record of his past accomplishments.[73] The case of Ca-

---

69. This was the case with Cavalli's final opera,
Massenzio, which was replaced at the last minute by
a setting of the same libretto by Sartorio; see Dolfin's
letter to Johann Friedrich of 23 December 1672 (Appendix IIIB.10).
70. This was reported to have occurred in 1683 at
S. Giovanni Grisostomo: *avviso* of 6 February
(I-Vnm, It. VI, 460 [12104]); see Appendix IIIC.4.
71. This attitude is explicit in a letter of 20 September 1675 in which Nicolò Beregan expresses to
Duke Johann Friedrich his desire to hire a certain
singer, Gratianini, the moment he set foot in Venice,
before the management of any other theater could
contact him (Appendix IIIB.24). See also letter of 17

November 1675 (Appendix IIIB.25).
72. These difficulties are revealed in Cesti's correspondence with Faustini, preserved in twenty-one
letters in the Faustini documents. The letters are
listed and discussed in Schmidt, "*Tito* Commission,"
442–66. Four are transcribed in *Quellentexte*, ed.
Becker, 74–77. For transcriptions of some others,
see Giazotto, "Antonio Cesti," 496–512. See also
Brunelli, "Angustie," passim.
73. Excerpts from Ziani's correspondence with
Faustini are published in Giazotto, "La guerra dei
palchi," 465–508, appendix B. See also Brunelli,
"Angustie," passim. Two complete letters are transcribed in *Quellentexte*, ed. Becker, 78–80, both of

valli, clearly the most sought-after composer of the day, proved the most dis-
appointing of all. Cavalli was evidently reluctant to sign the contract offered
him in 1662, finally agreeing to do so on condition that Faustini accept one
rather than the two new operas he had asked for, since he lacked the time to
write a second one: "An obstacle has intervened in my affectionate agreement,
introduced by Your Lordship and not by me: because you would like two
operas, and I, for lack of time, cannot promise them to you, having also some
other interests of my own that keep me busy. . . . Rest assured that if time
permitted, I would not spare even greater effort" (Appendix IIIA.3b).[74] Faustini's frustration must have been very great in 1665 when Cavalli, ostensibly
too busy to supply another opera for SS. Giovanni e Paolo, moved to S. Salvatore, where he promptly composed two new operas, *Mutio Scevola* and *Pompeo magno*, for the seasons of 1665 and 1666.[75]

The need to produce two operas per season and the limited number of
experienced librettists available made it natural for an impresario to exploit
whatever texts he could get his hands on. In most seasons, Faustini was able to
rely on Aureli for one libretto, but he had difficulty finding an author for the
other one—Minato was available only once, providing Faustini with *Scipione
affricano* (1664), before he moved over to S. Salvatore with Cavalli. In other
seasons Faustini managed to convince a variety of noblemen and a canon to turn
author: Counts Zaguri and Nicolò Beregan in 1660 and 1661, respectively, and
Dott. Cristoforo Ivanovich in 1663.[76]

Given these conditions, it is no wonder that the legacy of Giovanni Faustini
continued to furnish performance materials during the 1660s, though it is surprising that the first Faustini revival, *Eritrea* in 1661, took place not at SS.
Giovanni e Paolo but at S. Salvatore.[77] But Faustini's librettos were now at least

---

them expressing Ziani's envy of his fellow composers. For an example, see letter of 25 July 1665 (Appendix IIIA.5).

74. From letter of 8 August 1662 (*b*. 188. 380); fac
simile in Wolfgang Osthoff, "Cavalli," in *La musica*
(Turin, 1966), 829; the document, which is somewhat damaged, is transcribed in Glover, *Cavalli*,
168–69. Cavalli tried to convince Faustini to accept
the recently performed *Ercole amante* instead of a second new opera, but evidently without success (see
also the undated document, *b*. 194: 49, transcribed in
Quellentexte, ed. Becker, 74).

75. To add insult to injury, Cavalli's *Pompeo magno*
was reported a resounding success, while the reviews
of the competing opera at SS. Giovanni e Paolo, Cesti's and Beregan's *Tito*, were mixed, according to
Ziani's letter to Faustini of 9 May 1666 (*b*. 188: 279)
(Appendix IIIA.11a). Faustini succeeded in getting

Cavalli back in 1667, for one opera, the ill-fated
Eliogabalo (contract of 29 June 1667 [*b*. 194: 50], ex-
cerpted in Brunelli, "Angustie," 334–35; see also
Glover, *Cavalli*, 28).

76. Things were evidently just as difficult at S. Salvatore, where at least three noblemen, Giuseppe Artale, Giacomo dall'Angelo, and Ippolito Bentivoglio, were pressed into service during the early
1660s. Dall'Angelo was a member of the same academy as Aureli and Minato, the Imperfetti.

77. Perhaps Minato, who was involved in the management of S. Salvatore at the time, got special permission (from Marco) for the revival. This is suggested by the printer's dedication to the second
edition of the libretto (Appendix I.35c). On the question of authors' rights, see Bianconi and Walker,
"Production," 237–39 and nn. 75–76. It is a question
that needs further investigation.

ten years old—some of them closer to twenty—and getting more antiquated every day. Not having evolved along with Venetian taste, they could no longer stand quite on their own. The problem was particularly acute because the new generation of librettists who had borrowed Faustini's plot structures and character types had themselves moved on to other things. In the late 1650s and the 1660s, as we have seen, "historical" subjects had become popular again; "invented" romance no longer appealed. Indeed, the Faustini model plot was under attack in at least one quarter already at the end of the 1650s, or so it would seem from the publisher's preface to *L'incostanza trionfante overo il Theseo* (1658), one of the most problematic operas of the period:

> With great pains, the author has avoided introducing into this drama those events that have been and are common to almost all such works. Thus you will see in it neither letters, nor portraits, nor medals, nor princes nor princesses in disguise, nor babies exchanged by nurses, nor other such professed inventions, which, even though they are presented as new and different, are always the same and can certainly no longer give pleasure. You will find instead an uninterrupted series of illusions, intrigues, and artifices that proceed naturally—or politically—and that I hope will not displease you. (Appendix I.52)[78]

More significant than the subject matter and plot devices, however, the poetic structure of librettos had changed considerably during the 1650s, with a tremendous increase in the proportion of aria to recitative verse.[79] It is no wonder, then, that Faustini's works had to be modernized if they were to succeed on stage. Many of Marco Faustini's trials and tribulations at SS. Giovanni e Paolo resulted from his intractability, his stubborn championing of his brother's reputation in the face of new stylistic requirements.

Even the very first of Faustini's librettos to be performed posthumously, *Eupatra* (1655), had needed editing, although it was only four years old.[80] New comic scenes had replaced scenes with deities—all of which functioned as intermedi—and two arias were added for one of the main characters, Irene. These changes testify to the new taste: the growing importance of comic char-

---

78. This libretto went through several editions in its first year, not because it sold out but because of rewritings, accusations of theft, and so forth. It was the opera Ziani later said he wrote over and over again. See ch. 7, n. 26.

79. Even works revived in successive years were felt to need alteration; arias were often changed, characters added or eliminated. But this was perhaps more in response to cast changes or simply an effort to make the work look newer. Sometimes new arias were even added for later performances of an opera during the same season, as indicated in second and third editions of various librettos (such as those of

Antigona [1660] and Claudio Cesare [1672], for example).

80. Technically it was the second of his operas to be performed posthumously, since Faustini died during the 1651 season, before Eritrea was produced. This is clear from the preface to the libretto and from documents presented in Beth Glixon and Jonathan Glixon, "Marco Faustini and Venetian Opera Production in the 1650s: Recent Archival Discoveries," paper delivered at a meeting of the South-Central Chapter of the American Musicological Society, Lexington, Kentucky, 1990.

acters, the decline in importance of divinities, the increase in the number of arias. Perhaps in order to enhance their value or credibility, the new arias were explained in a printer's note to the reader as adhering to the late poet's own suggestions (Appendix I. 36d).

A second printer's note informs us that special care had been taken in adding material, since Faustini had so resented having his works tampered with (they were evidently regarded as sacrosanct): "For your enjoyment, printed here are the additions to Eupatra, made by most able individuals, which [additions], however, were always loathed by the author. Nevertheless they have been arranged so that they do not detract at all from the lofty tone of the opera" (Appendix I. 36f).[81]

The problem of modernization was correspondingly greater when *Eritrea*, a nine-year-old opera, was revived at the Teatro S. Salvatore in 1661. A few added arias and scenes would not suffice. Besides a new prologue, there were changes among the comic characters—a new one was added (Trinano), another was transformed from a young lady to an old nurse (Misena), and a third underwent a name-change (from Lesbo to Florindo)—and a number of comic scenes were inserted. Several arias were added at the ends of scenes, some second strophes of arias were cut, and some strophic arias were replaced by more complex forms. Perhaps more revealing than the additions, however, were the deletions. These involved an enormous amount of recitative, several duets, and two soliloquies for one of the main characters.[82]

The differences between the two versions of *Eritrea* were so great that a new libretto, "con nuove aggiunte d'incerto autore," was published for the occasion; but in addition Faustini's original libretto was reprinted intact. This was for purposes of comparison, as we learn from a new preface, printed in both librettos.[83]

> Here, in spite of time (and she has the glory of defeating it), Eritrea once again sees the light of day. The merit of him who wrote it served as a shield to protect it from the blows of oblivion. Time may indeed have triumphed over the life of the author, but it labored in vain to eclipse the name of one who is restored to life. But because a thousand things have been added and deleted, it was proper to reprint it first in the same form in which it was performed, with great splendor, in this city, and in the form in which the author created it; and afterwards you will have, in the same

81. We know from the *Egisto* preface (quoted above) that he even resented having to tamper with them himself.
82. Actually, there were seven new comic scenes, but some of them replaced old ones. Theramene's *delirio* (2.5) was replaced by a comic scene and his soliloquy in 3.11 was simply eliminated. Trinano, under the name Vaffrino, and several of his new solo

scenes were already present in the Bologna revival of the opera in 1654 (*Eritrea* [Bologna: del Dozza, 1654]).
83. Only the date on the title page was altered, to 1662, which must have confused the chroniclers, since they all assumed that the work was actually performed at S. Apollinare in 1662, when, in fact, the theater had long been closed.

libretto,[84] the version being performed now, it having pleased the one who was responsible for it to do it this way, in order to satisfy his most kind masters, to whom he feels greatly indebted; so that the original author will not be deprived of his credit, and those who are presenting it now will be satisfied. (Appendix I.35c)[85]

The problems raised by Faustini's plan to produce another of his brother's posthumous librettos, *Medea placata*, at SS. Giovanni e Paolo in the following year were evidently even more daunting.[86] It appears that no amount of revision was sufficient to make the work viable, for it was withdrawn at the last minute, during rehearsals, for being "unpleasing to the listeners." (We can only guess the reasons for this.) It was replaced by Aureli's and Ziani's *Gli scherzi di Fortuna*, which received its premiere only about a week later, in late January.[87] This, in turn, was succeeded on 3 February by another collaboration by the same pair, *Le fatiche d'Ercole*.[88]

The withdrawal of *Medea placata* in 1662 scarcely resolved Faustini's difficulties; things deteriorated considerably in subsequent seasons. He seems to have faced something of a crisis in 1665 when Cavalli defected, along with Minato, to S. Salvatore.[89] That crisis was intensified by rumors that two dormant theaters, S. Cassiano and S. Moisè, were about to reopen, threatening to drain further the limited supply of librettists, composers, and singers. The two theaters did open, if only briefly, each producing two operas in 1666, swelling the total for that season to eight; and S. Moisè produced one more in 1667. Faustini's (probably fruitless) efforts to move the opening day of his 1666 season forward by two weeks, from the traditional St. Stephen's Day (26 December)

---

84. They ended up being two separate librettos, the reprint of 1662 and *L'Eritrea . . . Da rappresentarsi nel Novissimo Teatro di S. Salvatore, Anno 1661* (Venice: Batti, 1661).

85. Perhaps two publications were required because the opera was not performed in Faustini's theater; Marco may have insisted.

86. This libretto was never mentioned by Giovanni; but it was listed among his unperformed works in the preface to another of Giovanni's posthumous librettos, *Alciade*, published in 1667 (Appendix I.38a).

87. *Il rimino* of 17 January, 1662, report for 14 January: "fin dalla settimana passata doveva aprirsi il teatro di SS. Giovanni e Paolo, e recitarsi l'opera intitolata *Medea placata*, ma fattane la prova, e stimatasi di poco gradimento agli auditori, hanno havuto per bene gli interessati di lasciarla da parte, e provedere d'altro soggetto, per il che in ordine alli *Amori di Pirro infruttuosi*, che furono rappresentati l'anno passato, si reciteranno le nozze del medesimo [= *Gli scherzi di fortuna*]" (see Selfridge-Field, *Pallade*

veneta, 337, document no. A22).

88. Both *Gli scherzi di fortuna* and *Le fatiche d'Ercole* must have been nearly ready while *Medea placata* was in rehearsal. *Ercole* was the libretto Aureli felt leisurely about (cf. p. 180 above and appendix I.46c). These works are twice mentioned in *Il rimino* (Selfridge-Field, *Pallade veneta*, documents nos. A23 and A24).

89. Aureli too eventually moved to S. Salvatore, but only in 1670, after Minato's precipitous departure for Vienna, which resulted in a lawsuit brought against him by the Vendramin brothers for breach of the three-year contract he had signed with them in 1667. Aureli seems to have assumed Minato's role of impresario there, since he signed many of the subsequent contracts and other papers. The details of Minato's lawsuit and its aftermath can be pieced together by documents in the Vendramin archives; see especially *b.* 42 F 6/1–6 [49], ff. 28–30, 41–48; also Ellen Rosand, "Minato," *New Grove*, 12: 332; and Benedetti, "Il teatro musicale," 213–14.

to the Feast of St. Lucy (14 December), may be seen as an attempt to seize the initiative from his competitors.[90]

Faced with the prospect of intensified competition, the impresario seems to have been even more anxious than usual to exploit his fratrimony. Despite the failure of *Medea placata*, Marco planned a revival of one of Giovanni's earliest librettos, the more than twenty-year-old *Doriclea*, for the 1666 season. Perhaps hoping that the effects of age could be minimized by a fresh setting—but also because the original composer, Cavalli, was working for S. Salvatore—he commissioned Ziani to write the music.[91] The composer's reaction to the text, expressed in a letter to the impresario, provides us with a sense of just how much libretto fashions had changed since Giovanni's death:

> It seems to me that the opera is a little dry, particularly in the long soliloquies, because it is barren of *canzonette*. You will see that I have carved out a few more arias [*ariette*] than you thought necessary, in order to enliven it as much as possible, but I doubt (if it were not adorned with arias) that you would want to [have it performed?]. You know the modern practice, and such long soliloquies are loathed by everyone, so I advise you ahead of time so that you may decide for the best. I am too troubled first by Beregan's opera, which has enjoyed great success, both because it is new and welcome and because he is highly regarded; and Doriclea (it is indeed very beautiful) but it is an old opera, and its poetry has been heard before, and really I don't think it can compete with Tito. (Appendix IIIA.5a)

Although Ziani regarded the text as old-fashioned, particularly in comparison to the other opera of that season at SS. Giovanni e Paolo, Beregan's *Tito*, he nevertheless finished his setting in time for the scheduled performance. But for complex reasons having to do with theatrical politics, it was replaced at the last minute, except for the prologue, by Cesti's *Orontea*.[92] As we read in the anonymous dedication (evidently by Marco) of *Orontea*, dated 10 January 1666 [1667] (that is, quite close to the premiere):[93] "Having incurred great expense during the past nine months to present to you, magnificently staged, the drama Doriclea—written by the gifted Giovanni Faustini of high repute, and previ-

---

90. His intention is documented in a letter to him from the singer Antonio Cavagna of 14 November 1666 (*b.* 188: 37): "a me non è stata sin hora nota la premura che V. S. E. tiene di recitar a S.ta Lucia, che però farò tutti li miei sforzi per trovarmi a tempo." Giovanni Faustini had apparently tried something similar in 1651, according to Glixon and Glixon, "Marco Faustini."

91. Despite Cavalli's contract with S. Salvatore, Faustini may have asked him to revise his old score and been refused. This is suggested by references to Cavalli in several documents dealing with this commission, including two letters to Faustini from An-

tonio Cavagna, a singer with whom he was negotiating (*b.* 188: 127 and 125), and one from Ziani dated 25 July 1665 (*b.* 188: 82), which is excerpted in Giazotto, "La guerra dei palchi," 503–4, and quoted in part in Appendix IIIA.5.

92. The theatrical politics involved difficulties with singers and, possibly, competition between Cesti and Ziani. These circumstances are discussed in Schmidt, "*Tito* Commission," 457–62, and Brunelli, "Angustie," 319–22.

93. Or nearly a month after the Feast of St. Lucy that Faustini had proposed as opening day for the 1666 season.

ously performed in this city with great success during 1643 [*sic*]—new diffi-culties have been encountered that have compelled me to postpone this work for a more favorable occasion."[94] The printer was also anxious to be compen-sated for the expenses he had incurred, for two of the three acts of *Doriclea* had already been set and printed when the opera was cancelled.[95]

Burned first with *Medea placata*, then again with *Doriclea*, Marco should have realized that the Faustini myth had outlived its usefulness; but he did not. Whether he was blinded by fraternal piety or merely desperate for new librettos, the fiasco with *Doriclea* did not discourage him from scheduling produc-tions of two more of his brother's librettos in 1667: *Alciade* and *Meraspe*.[96] These were the two works (besides *Eupatra*) that Giovanni had mentioned in his *Oristeo* preface of 1651 as being nearly ready, and for which he had been awaiting "more propitious occasions and a vaster theater" (Appendix I.33b).

SS. Giovanni e Paolo was certainly vaster than S. Apollinare, but the season of 1666 turned out to be anything but propitious. In a letter of October 1666 to the agent of one of the singers with whom he was negotiating for the fol-lowing season (and who had apparently insulted him by proposing two other operas, Cesti's *Alessandro* and *Argia*), Faustini finally acknowledged explicitly his sense of responsibility to his brother's memory.

> Both operas [*Alciade* and *Meraspe*] are by Sig. Giovanni Faustini of happy mem-ory, my brother, who died in 1651 at the young age of 30 years [*sic*], having pub-lished and produced 14 operas, all set to music by Signor Cavalli and Signor Ziani, and who was admirable in invention, and from which all these men who have up to now produced operas in this city have stolen the beautiful ideas, which are per-formed almost every year in the principal musical theaters of Italy; whence Your Illustrious Lordship may judge if I am about to abandon the production of those, which were left by him as favorites and promised in his publications in order to present Argia and Alessandro, operas already produced and seen in Venice; . . . the first, Alciade, was left . . . in all perfection; the second, called Il tiranno humiliato d'Amore, less perfect. It would be indecent to alter its beautiful subject in any part; I had the most illustrious Beregano do the first act,[97] and since he could not continue, I gave the second and third to a most capable individual, who entered very well into the spirit of the [work], and thus the opera will be admirable in every respect. I have been too long-winded in this part, but I shall be forgiven because I am too in-

94. From Schmidt, "*Tito* Commission," 460.

95. This whole story is detailed in Brunelli, "An-gustie," 321. The printer's complaint is found in *b*. 194: 78–80ᵛ. For some idea of the tightness of print-ing schedules for librettos, see Massi's letter to Jo-hann Friedrich of 27 January 1672 [1673] (Appendix IIIB.17).

96. Apparently *Alciade* was initially planned for the 1666 season; see Ziani's letter to Faustini of 28 No-vember 1665 (*b*. 188: 354) (Appendix IIIA.10).

97. There are several references in Faustini's earlier

correspondence to Beregan's alterations of the *Mer-aspe* libretto. Evidently *Meraspe*, like *Elena*, had sur-vived in the form of a scenario that needed to be fleshed out with poetry. In any case it was apparently given to several authors to elaborate. Cesti was to set text revised by Beregan. After he had resigned his commission, Pallavicino was apparently engaged to replace him. But the opera did not please the singers; see below. Documents concerning *Meraspe* include *b*. 188: 163 and 294–99.

volved in producing the works of a brother of mine, which have been exalted to the highest degree by everyone who has heard them, and for the production of which I took up the theater. (Appendix IIIA.15)[98]

The preface to *Alciade*, signed by the printers, Francesco Nicolini and Steffano Curti, contains the fullest elaboration of the myth we have yet encountered, emphasizing all of the traditional points—*inventione*, the number of works, the untimely death—and includes a complete and chronologically accurate bibliography, attribution of all the musical settings, as well as some critical evaluation of the works, culled, apparently, from previous prefaces of Faustini librettos, especially that of *Eupatra*:

> In his earliest youth, Signor Giovanni Faustini, for his own pleasure, devoted his talent to musical dramatic compositions, in which he proved remarkable, especially for his invention. And, in the course of only nine years (having been carried off too prematurely by death in 1651, his thirty-second year) there were staged in the theaters of this city to great acclaim La virtù de'strali d'Amore, Egisto, Ormindo, Titone, Doriclea, Ersilda, Euripo, Oristeo, Rosinda, Calisto, Eritrea, and after his death also Eupatra, then Elena rapita da Teseo, dressed with the mantle of poetry by a sublime artist [i.e., Minato], all set to music by either Signor Francesco Cavalli, most worthy organist of the Most Serene Republic, or Signor Don Pietro Andrea Zianni, presently chapel master of Her Majesty the Empress; they satisfied not only the taste of this city, especially discerning from having heard so many similar performances, but of many of the other major cities of Italy, in which time after time they were performed to unstinting applause; furthermore, their many and various inventions have served, their origins forgotten, to adorn and enrich other compositions.[99] Three works of this artist still remain: Medea placata, Alciade, and Meraspe, overo il tiranno humiliato d'Amore. This year, at the most noble Grimani theater, first Alciade and then Meraspe will appear, promised by the author in his publications in the year 1651, when he passed to another life. (Appendix I.38a)[100]

It seems that *Alciade* was finally performed in 1667, sharing the stage with Cesti's and Apolloni's *Dori*. *Meraspe*, however, which had needed more revision than *Alciade* in the first place, according to Faustini (Appendix III.A14), was postponed until the following season.

98. Like *Alciade*, which was planned for 1666 but not performed until 1667, *Meraspe* was initially planned for one season (1667) but postponed until the next (1668), when it was unsuccessful; see Brunelli, "Angustie," 334–40. *Alessandro* may refer to *La magnanimità d'Alessandro*, which had been performed in Innsbruck in 1662 (see Appendix IIIA.13). This was not the only time a suggestion for a replacement for a Faustini libretto was offered. Moniglia's *Semiramide* was proposed instead of *Meraspe* in letters from the singer Donati to Faustini of 5 and 27 July 1667 (b. 188: 172, 174).

99. This presumably means that they served as material for other librettos, which Marco had also claimed (Appendix IIIA.14: "hanno rubato l'inventioni")—such as Aureli's *Erismena* and *Rodope e Damira*. They had, in fact, entered the mainstream of operatic convention.

100. Note the similarity of the positive aspects listed in the remainder of this preface (Appendix I.38b) to the points made in the preface to *Theseo* (Appendix I.52), and also to the complaints Giovanni Faustini himself voiced in his preface to *Egisto* (Appendix I.31a). The problems raised by reviving *Alciade* must have been similar to those encountered with Nicola Coresi, husband of the Roman singer Antonia Coresi, regarding *Meraspe* the following year; see Appendix IIIA.17.

The unsigned preface of *Meraspe*, dated 12 December 1667, instead of giving final voice to the Faustini myth, acknowledged the strain of upholding it:

> The present drama was left unfinished by the late Signor Giovanni Faustini, since he composed only two acts of it, but poor in arias [*ariette*], and the greater part in recitative style, as was the custom at that time; whence, to adapt it to modern usage, the efforts of more than one pen were necessary, though without altering the subject at all, since the scenario was completely finished by the author, as was the prologue. In the poetry, however, a few things by the author himself will be mixed in, which were necessary to insert in order to give meaning to the title of the work. (Appendix I.39)[101]

The "other pens," as we have seen, included that of Nicolò Beregan. It is clear that in the end the recitative had not been altered enough, because the singers complained about it. In letters of June 1667 they criticized the "long boring speeches . . . which in Venice need to be avoided" ("gran dicerie. . . che a Venezia bisogna sfuggirle") and "the scenes that are so long that the same characters remain forever on the stage" ("le scene così lunghe che li medesimi personaggi stanno sempre in scena").[102]

Although *Meraspe* finally reached the stage in late 1667, its appearance hardly represented a victory for Marco. In fact, it was the last step before his defeat: the negotiations over the opera marked the impresario's final scene. On 15 December, just a few days after the *Meraspe* premiere, he signed over all his rights and obligations to Carlo and Vincenzo Grimani, the owners of the theater for whom he had worked.[103] He left operatic life as his brother had left life itself: suddenly, and deeply in debt. Originally his source of inspiration and success, Giovanni's librettos had become a liability that helped to precipitate Marco's downfall.

The very same conditions that had contributed to the flourishing of Marco Faustini's career in the first place ultimately led to his abrupt retirement. When he stepped into the breach to rescue his brother's finances and literary reputation in 1651, Venetian opera had just reached an important milestone: it had achieved the status of a genre in its own right. But it would not stand still. The business of opera had undergone tremendous change since Marco's debut as impresario. What had begun as a relatively small-scale operation had blossomed into a much more complex endeavor. Expenses at the tiny Teatro S. Apollinare had been comparatively low, particularly because of the low rent, and were more than covered by the income from box rental. But, although both S.

---

101. Obviously the libretto contained some of the original Faustini poetry, but not much. An old prologue was considered acceptable since prologues were by now anachronistic and obsolete anyhow.
102. Letters of 13 and 4 June 1667 (*b.* 188: 164 and 163); see Appendix IIIA.17a and ch. 8, n. 70, below.

103. According to this document (*b.* 188: 199–200), dated 15 December 1667 (see Brunelli, "Angustie," 340, and Appendix IIIA.22), Faustini ceded his entire interest in SS. Giovanni e Paolo to the Grimani brothers.

Cassiano and SS. Giovanni e Paolo were much larger and had more boxes, increasing expenses, particularly for singers' fees, were not as easily recouped by box rental.[104]

The mounting of an operatic spectacle had assumed a degree of complication that Marco Faustini could not have foreseen at the outset of his career. At that time he was, operatically speaking, a rich man, with several librettos in hand, a composer accustomed to their style and tied to him by debts of friendship, and a financially profitable arrangement with the owners of the theater. By 1667, however, his store of librettos was exhausted, his composers were reluctant to commit themselves, and his singers were scattered all over Italy and making contractual demands that he could no longer meet.

In terms of absolute cost, operatic expenses had more than doubled during the period of Faustini's activity. Although we have figures for neither S. Apollinare in 1651 nor SS. Giovanni e Paolo in 1667, we can extrapolate from some figures available for other seasons (fig. 24). We know, for example, that in 1669 the total cost of a production at S. Salvatore was 62,966 Venetian lire, nearly twice that of *Antioco* at S. Cassiano ten years earlier, which in turn was twice that of the second production at S. Cassiano in 1638, where a small company of six, including composer, librettist, and singers, all serving multiple functions, shouldered the entire responsibility of presenting *La maga fulminata* for 2,000 scudi (or 19,200 Venetian lire).[105]

The business of opera was clearly much more expensive now; but increased cost was not the only consequence of operatic overdevelopment. It affected the very fabric of the art. Most significant, new exigencies, the result of institu-

---

104.   Most boxes at S. Apollinare rented for twenty ducats, while the more numerous ones at S. Cassiano went for twenty-five ducats, which should have yielded a much greater profit. But Bianconi and Walker ("Production," 222–23) suggest that for S. Cassiano, at least, profits were eroded by Faustini's contract with the Tron family, whereby he was required to pay the costs of readying the theater for opera.

105.   The cost of *La maga fulminata* is mentioned in the preface to the libretto (Appendix I.3b). The information for S. Salvatore comes from a sheet of accounts in I-Vcg, Archivio Vendramin, Teatro S. Salvatore, *b.* 42 F 6/1–6 [49], no. 20, 13 April 1669 (fig. 24). Conversion rates for Venetian currency, derived from information in the Faustini papers, are as follows: *lira* = 20 soldi; *ducat* = 6 lire, 4 soldi; *scudo* = 14 lire; *doble* = 28 lire; *cecchino* = 17 lire. See N. Papadopoli-Aldobrandini, *Le monete di Venezia descritte ed illustrate* (Venice, 1907), 3: 267–356 (1646–

59); also Bianconi and Walker, "Production," appendix 2, "Monetary Systems," which seeks to determine the relationship between Venetian currency values and those of Rome and Modena of the same period. Inflation could not have explained the geometric rise in expenses, since it was relatively low during this period. This is indicated by various comparative figures, such as the salary for the first violinist, which rose modestly from 17 lire in 1658 to 18.12 lire in 1665 (see *Antioco* and *Ciro* payment records in *b.* 194: *Antioco* account book, unnumbered, and 286). On the economic situation in Venice during this period, see *Crisis and Change in the Venetian Economy in the 16th and 17th Centuries*, ed., Brian Pullan (London, 1968); id., *Aspetti e cause della decadenza economica veneziana nel secolo XVII* (Venice and Rome, 1961); and Domenico Sella, *Commerci e industrie a Venezia nel secolo XVII* (Venice and Rome, 1961).

24. Accounts for *Argia* (13 April 1669), Teatro Vendramin at S. Salvatore.
Venice, Casa Goldoni.

tionalization, altered the relationship among the makers of opera that had characterized the 1640s and 1650s, increasing their independence from one another and creating a new hierarchy, in which, finally, the singer came out on top. The growing separation of the tasks of librettist, composer, scene designer, and performer—a division of labor making possible something like mass production—had a profound effect on the nature of the operatic work.

7

$\bullet$ $\bullet$ $\bullet$

I compositori scenici:
Librettist and Composer

Marco Faustini's failure was intrinsic to the system of opera production that had nourished him. The institutionalization of opera had initiated a chain reaction. The increased demand for new works intensified the pressures on a limited pool of opera makers, whose expansion required the exploitation of additional (including foreign) suppliers, which in turn created difficulties of communication and coordination at every stage in the preparation of a production: at conception, composition, and rehearsal. Conception was impeded by the fact that the libretto was often written before the cast had been assembled, making it difficult for the poet to decide on the number and importance of the various characters. Composition suffered from the geographical distance between librettist and composer, who often resided in different cities and therefore could not work together;[1] furthermore, like librettists, composers did not always know their casts in advance and were unable to tailor their music accordingly. Finally, the rehearsal period became increasingly difficult since, in addition to providing the opportunity for the normal ironing out of staging problems, it had to allow for many alterations involving text and music that would formerly have been taken care of earlier, at the stage of composition or even conception.

One of the significant results of institutionalization, then, was a change in the relationship among the makers of operas, among librettist, composer, and performers. Originally part of a single impetus, the three functions grew increasingly separate and independent of one another. This growing independence, even as it reflected the development of opera, in turn had its own impact on that development.

---

1. One of the most revealing documents we have of the kind of interaction that took place between librettist and composer during this period has survived precisely because of the distance that separated them: Ivanovich's letter of 26 June 1673 to Giovanni Maria Pagliardi, concerning their collaboration on *Lismaco*. The letter is given in Appendix II.5.

Collaborative Talents

In Ferrari's tiny troupe, whose *Andromeda* and *La maga fulminata* had been the first operas in Venice, librettist, composer, and performers were closely linked—by geographical proximity, background, and common goal. Ferrari, being a musician himself, although he did not actually compose the music for either opera, was certainly sensitive to the requirements of music, and the collaboration between him and Manelli must have been worked out on an intimate, daily basis. Both text and music must also have been precisely fashioned to suit the abilities of the singers in the company. The multiple talents and responsibilities of the various members of the troupe—Ferrari, as we know, played the theorbo in the orchestra, and Manelli sang—bridged the boundaries not only between text and music but between creation and performance as well.

The relationship between librettist and composer was of course closer still in those subsequent operas for which Ferrari served as both: *Armida* (1639), *Il pastor regio* (1640), *La ninfa avara* (1641), and *Il principe giardiniere* (1644). Unfortunately, we are unable to evaluate the results, since none of these scores have survived.[2] Although a number of composers began their operatic careers as singers, including Manelli, Cesti, and Boretti,[3] few of them combined Ferrari's publicly recognized "multiplici virtù," which suggested comparison to "un mostro diversamente simile alla chimera,"[4] and made him an ideal maker of operas. But he considered himself primarily a musician rather than a poet, claiming that his most important attribute as a writer was knowing what kind of poetry was best suited to musical setting.[5] To the extent that the two can be

2.   An example of Ferrari's dual efforts in the chamber music field, his *Musiche e poesie varie*, vol. 3 (1641), has survived, but it has not yet been scrutinized from this perspective.

3.   Cesti's first operatic role may have been as either Egeo or Dema in the Florentine performance of Cavalli's *Giasone* in 1650; he also appeared in a performance in Lucca in the same year. See Lorenzo Bianconi, "Cesti," *DBI* 24 (Rome, 1980): 283; also Francesco Sbarra's letter to Michel'Angelo Torcigliani, printed as a preface to his *Alessandro vincitor di se stesso* (1651) (partly reproduced in Appendix I.29). Giovanni Antonio Boretti (not Guido Antonio, who appeared in *Andromeda* in 1637) performed in Ziani's and Aureli's *Le fortune di Rodope e Damira* in Turin in 1662; see Rosand, "Boretti."

4.   The expression comes from Fusconi's prefatory letter in Ferrari's *Argomento e scenario del principe giardiniero* (1643). Composer-librettists were definitely a rare breed. After Ferrari, no such figure appeared in connection with Venetian opera until Romolo Pignatta, whose *Asmiro re di Corinto* was performed at

the Teatro SS. Giovanni e Paolo in 1696 (see Magini, "Indagini," 425). Among the few others, active elsewhere, were two singers, both castratos: Giovanni Andrea Angelini Bontempi, who wrote both words and music of his *Paride* (Dresden, 1662) (see Colin Timms, "Bontempi," *New Grove*, 3: 37–38), and Francesco Antonio Pistocchi. Because of his diverse talents, Pistocchi was considered an ideal operatic poet by the Arcadian critic Pier Jacopo Martello (see his *Della tragedia antica e moderna* [Rome, 1715], "Sessione quinta," in Piero Weiss, "Pier Jacopo Martello on Opera [1715]: An Annotated Translation," *MQ* 66 [1980]: 378–403, esp. 386 and n. 8). The Roman theater manager Filippo Acciaiuoli is supposed to have written both words and music of the opera *Chi è cagion del suo mal pianga se stesso* (Rome, 1682); see Thomas Walker, "Acciaiuoli," *New Grove*, 1: 33–34.

5.   As he declared in his preface to the Bologna edition of *Il pastor regio* in 1641: "I don't care about being a poet, but I profess myself to be a good musician, and to know what kind of poetry is best suited to music" (Appendix I.5a).

separated, then, the composer in Ferrari clearly held sway over the poet. His self-evaluation reveals his attitude toward the relative importance and stature of music and text, at least in his own works. That attitude, the subservience of text to music, or of the librettist to the composer, is reflected more generally, though only fleetingly, in the operas of his time.

Indeed, several early composers of Venetian opera, although they may not have shared Ferrari's poetic skills, exercised control over their poets in various ways. The most striking example, of course, is Monteverdi, whose influence on the texts of his operas was fundamental. His famous lessons to Giulio Strozzi, revealed in letters he wrote concerning their collaboration on *La finta pazza Licori*, involved dramatic issues as fundamental as plot structure, characterization, and verisimilitude.[6] Monteverdi also instructed his other poets in the art of libretto-writing, although our evidence for this is somewhat more indirect. One of them, the anonymous author of *Le nozze d'Enea*, confessed to having made a number of changes in his text in order to suit Monteverdi's style: "I have shunned remote thoughts and concepts and rather been attentive to the affections, as Signor Monteverdi wishes, and in order to please him I have also changed and omitted many of the things I had originally included" (Appendix I.9g). Another, Badoaro, gained his education in retrospect, claiming that he hardly recognized his *Ritorno d'Ulisse* in Monteverdi's setting because of the many changes made by the composer.[7]

To be sure, Monteverdi, like Ferrari, represents a special case, though in a different way. His long experience and many successes had earned him a reputation as the greatest opera composer in Italy. He was credited by at least one seventeenth-century observer as having been the moving force behind the development of opera in Venice, although his participation in the Venetian opera scene was delayed somewhat, as we have already noted.[8] Furthermore, Monteverdi's commitment to the ideals of the *seconda prattica* placed him in a special position with regard to words. In order to investigate fully the power of his music to communicate feeling through text, Monteverdi essentially had to create the text himself, often using what was provided by the poet as a skeleton to be fleshed out with repetitions, cuts, emphases, and so on (this will be examined further in chapter 9).[9]

---

6.   This correspondence is discussed more fully in ch. 11 below.

7.   Badoaro made this confession in the letter to the composer that prefaces one of the manuscript librettos of *Il ritorno d'Ulisse*, quoted in Appendix I.7c.

8.   See ch. 1, pp. 15–17 and n. 19, above.

9.   For Monteverdi's need to create his own text to compensate for inadequacies in the poetry, see Gary Tomlinson, "Madrigal, Monody, and Monteverdi's *via naturale alla immitatione*," *JAMS* 34 (1981): 60–108. A more positive view of Monteverdi's intention is offered in Ellen Rosand, "Monteverdi's Mimetic Art: *L'incoronazione di Poppea*," *Cambridge Opera Journal* 1 (1989): 113–37.

Close working relationships seem also to have existed between other early composers and their librettists. Cavalli, for example, exercising his prerogative as impresario in some cases and in others his position as the most important and respected opera composer in Venice after Monteverdi, personally commissioned or arranged for many poets to write for him: these included Persiani, Busenello, Faustini, Melosio, Minato, and Aureli.[10] They, in turn, knowing the composer for whom they were writing, could fashion their texts to suit him. Indeed, the scores of a number of Cavalli's operas reveal that the music actually took shape along with the text—much as we imagine the Ferrari-Manelli creations to have emerged. Several, including *Veremonda* (1653), *Xerse* (1654), *Statira* (1655), and *Artemisia* (1656), preserve earlier versions of the text than those in the printed librettos, whose development out of those earlier versions can be traced in the scores themselves.[11]

In a more general way, Cavalli's long-term working relationship with Giovanni Faustini, which produced at least ten operas, must have influenced the poet's style. Faustini's lengthy affective monologues in *versi sciolti* punctuated by refrains may well have been written to suit Cavalli's gifts as a composer of expressive recitative. Furthermore, Faustini's practice (though hardly his alone) of postponing resolution of his complex plots until the final scene, immediately preceded, even triggered, by a protagonist's lament, may have developed in response to Cavalli's skill at composing affective laments in a mixed recitative-aria style.

The librettos of Cavalli's only other steady collaborator, Minato—who may have been coerced by the composer into writing texts for him[12]—were in various respects modeled on those of Faustini; he too punctuated lengthy monologues by refrains and wrote short strophic texts to be set as arias as well as extended lament texts. The composer indicated his appreciation of Minato in his response to Marco Faustini's request for new works in 1662. In a letter to the impresario of 8 August (Appendix IIIA.3), he explained that he had decided to abandon operatic composition altogether, but that Minato's insistence had persuaded him to change his mind.[13]

10.   Busenello in fact seems to have written differently for Monteverdi than he did for Cavalli (see ch. 9). For Melosio's relationship to Cavalli, see Pirrotta, "The Lame Horse and the Coachman," *Essays*, 331–34; for that of Faustini, Minato, and Aureli, see below. Cesti's relationship with Beregan, the author of several of his librettos, is documented in a series of letters from the composer; for an example, see below, n. 72.
11.   See Jeffery, "Autograph Manuscripts," 262. The process of alteration is particularly clear in the aria "D'Ermosilla giovinetta" in *Statira* (I-Vnm, It.

IV, 372 [9896], f. 17 libretto, p. 30) (Jeffery, 227). See also the opening aria of *Xerse* (I-Vnm, It. IV, 374 [9898], ff. 1–2ᵛ) and the second ending of *Hipermestra* (I-Vnm, It. IV, 362 [9886], ff. 134–37). The accidental nature of the preservation of these—or any—scores suggests that similar documentation must have existed in others. For *Artemisia*, see below, p. 218 and n. 69.
12.   Minato's "Sappi, ch'io non fò del Poeta . . . " (*Orimonte* preface, quoted above, ch. 6, p. 168, n. 29) may suggest some sort of mild coercion.
13.   For Cavalli's collaborations with Minato, see

While Cavalli's impact on Minato's texts can only be inferred, his specific influence on a third librettist, Aureli, is documented. The young Aureli consciously modeled *Erismena* (1655), his second libretto, on the style of Cavalli's regular librettist, the recently deceased Faustini, even borrowing a lengthy passage from Faustini's *Ormindo*. The borrowing, from an opera Cavalli had set to music more than a decade earlier, was certainly the composer's idea, since he used his old music, a particularly moving lament dialogue, in the new context. *Erismena* became one of the most successful operas of the entire century.[14]

Cavalli was the last (possibly the only) composer of the period to wield power as an impresario. The rapidly increasing complexity of the operatic scene must have made that role unbearable to him, for he gave it up quite early in his operatic career, choosing to work under contract, first with Bortolo Castoreo and others at S. Cassiano, then with Giovanni Faustini at S. Apollinare and with Marco Faustini at S. Cassiano and SS. Giovanni e Paolo, and finally with Minato at S. Salvatore.[15] Even after he renounced his managerial responsibilities, his reputation was sufficient to assure his continued aesthetic control over his subsequent works, but his early shift from employer to employee was one sign of more general adjustments in the operatic hierarchy, of the decline in the composer's comparative status with respect to the librettist—and soon the singer.

Three special individuals—Ferrari, the composer-librettist, Monteverdi, the "creator of opera," and Cavalli, the dean of Venetian opera composers and its leading businessman[16]—maintained the power of the composer somewhat artificially. Competing forces gradually undermined that power, however. Perhaps this change was part of what Ferrari had in mind when he complained so poignantly, already in 1643, that he felt obsolete:

> Although a veteran of scenic compositions, I am distressed by the refinement of the century, its factions torment me, but virtue, in the end, is a sun that, despite the clouds of passion surrounding it, never ceases to shine. These days musical theaters attract the most melodious swans; and sirens yearn to be angelic instead

---

Edward Raymond Rutschman, "The Minato-Cavalli Operas: The Search for Structure in Libretto and Solo Scene" (Ph.D. diss., University of Washington, 1979); also id., "Minato and the Venetian Opera Libretto," *CM* 27 (1982): 84–91; and Martha Clinkscale, "Pier Francesco Cavalli's *Xerse*" (Ph.D. diss., University of Minnesota, 1970).

14. Cf. above, ch. 6, p. 157 and n. 13. The only other Cavalli setting of an Aureli libretto, *Eliogabalo*, was never performed. It was the last work scheduled by Marco Faustini for SS. Giovanni e Paolo. For the possibility that the work was canceled because the

music was considered too old-fashioned, see ch. 8 below.

15. Cavalli's career as impresario at S. Cassiano, which lasted from 1638 (contract signed 14 April) until 1644 (document signed 4 June), is outlined and documented in Morelli and Walker, "Tre controversie," 97–120. He seems also to have acted in a managerial capacity at S. Moisè, where his *Amore innamorato* was produced in 1642 (see Pirrotta, "The Lame Horse and the Coachman," *Essays*, 333–34).

16. Cavalli's considerable business dealings are detailed in Glover, *Cavalli*, ch. 1, and Morelli and Walker, "Tre Controversie."

of maritime. . . . With your usual kindness, forgive the defects of my *Giardiniere*, of my music, and of my theorbo. (Appendix I.4)

The death of Monteverdi, Cavalli's withdrawal from managerial duties, and Ferrari's lament about the changing order of things, all of which occurred around the same time, mark a shift. During the course of the 1640s, the various mechanisms of propaganda used to stimulate the growth of opera in Venice, in particular the printing press, focused with increasing exclusivity on the new professional librettist.

As printed scenarios, librettos, and reports of performances make increasingly clear, the librettist was considered "l'auttore." It was his text that was immortalized through print—usually, as we know, at his own expense (Appendix II.6bb)—and his name that was associated with the opera in the mind of the public. He was usually the recipient of any laudatory sonnets printed in the libretto, though an occasional singer or composer might be eulogized in the same way (often by the librettist himself). The librettist's preeminence, even as late as 1671, was recognized in the following praise of Nicolò Beregan:

> The opera of Sig. Nicola [i.e., *Heraclio*] is so beautiful that it never becomes tedious. So lofty is its governing idea that Sig. Nicola has been deified in that theater [SS. Giovanni e Paolo], where without his say-so no new production will be undertaken, and if he invents new worlds of exquisiteness, everyone will converge to admire him, since there is really no one comparable to him in invention, magnificence, and summit [*Piramide*] of imagination. (Appendix IIIB.6)[17]

It was also the poor librettist who had to bear the brunt of the public's fickleness, to respond to the taste for novelty, and to produce a constant stream of texts rapidly, on demand.[18] Librettists often compounded their responsibility and control over operatic productions by assuming the duties of impresario—as both investors and organizers. Indeed, unlike the composers, Cavalli being a temporary exception, most of the early librettists, including Ferrari, Faustini, Minato, Aureli, Beregan, and Pietro Dolfin, were involved in theater management as well.[19]

17. "Piramide," literally "pyramid," which might be translated as "glory," was Beregan's nickname.
18. The pressures on librettists are amply documented in various letters to Johann Friedrich from his secretary Massi. In one (Appendix IIIB.23) he detailed the many problems faced by Pietro Dolfin in trying to put on one of his operas at SS. Giovanni e Paolo, and concluded that he "would never counsel a friend of his to produce operas in Venice." Even though their works were performed regularly, unless they belonged to the patrician class, librettists apparently had trouble making ends meet. In another

letter (Appendix IIIB.1), Massi asked Johann Friedrich for some extra funds to sustain Aureli in his time of need.
19. Among other librettists involved as impresarios were Bortolo Castoreo (author of *Armidoro* [1651] for S. Cassiano) and at least some of the Incogniti, such as Badoaro (at the Novissimo). Marco Faustini, as we know, was not a librettist, but Vincenzo Grimani, one of the brothers who took over his responsibilities at SS. Giovanni e Paolo, was. Santurini, impresario at S. Moisè, began his theatrical career as a scenographer. The next important

Obviously, composers did not completely lose their influence on the work, even in the eyes of the public. And their names were often included on the title pages of librettos or mentioned in prefaces, almost always in positive, if rather conventional, terms: the composer, variously called the Apollo (Monteverdi, Cavalli, Sartorio, Boretti) or the Amphion (Cavalli, Ziani) of the century, or else the Sun (Monteverdi and Cavalli) or the Moon (Sacrati), often covered or minimized the imperfections, enlivened the inanimate corpse, or sweetened the bitterness of the libretto;[20] or he may have honored, enriched, ennobled, adorned, illustrated, or otherwise favored it.

Composers, as well as scene designers, costumers, and singers—the most obvious creators of pure spectacle—were presumably mentioned in the hope that their names would attract the crowds and thus guarantee the commercial success of an opera.[21] To that end, various flattering biographical details were occasionally supplied, such as the fact that a composer served one or another princely patron. But in more than half the librettos printed between 1637 and 1675, composers' names did not appear at all. We have seen that Giovanni Faustini completed a number of librettos for which no specific productions had yet been planned. They were written for performances in the indefinite future, in a theater and with a cast and composer as yet unknown. Although Faustini was especially industrious, the dissociation between libretto and eventual setting was becoming increasingly characteristic of opera. Librettists, under pressure to produce works quickly, and assured of a steady market, began to write and print texts ahead of time, often before all of the other arrangements for a production could be concluded.

Librettists' Tribulations

Geographical separation, difficulties with last-minute arrangements—the hiring of singers, the completion of the score—all this placed a severe strain on everyone concerned in operatic production. If in many cases librettos were written before composers had been engaged to set them, in others librettists had to write their texts with composers breathing down their necks. Both situations were symptoms of the same disease: the lack of coordination between supply and demand that resulted from the institutionalization of opera.

---

composer to function in the capacity of impresario after Cavalli seems to have been Antonio Vivaldi. Librettists sometimes performed the functions of impresarios in the eighteenth and nineteenth centuries. See John Rosselli, *The Opera Industry in Italy from Cimarosa to Verdi: The Role of the Impresario* (Cambridge, 1984).

20. See, for example, the prefaces of *Amore in-namorato*, *Bellerofonte*, *Erismena*, and *Antigona*. The famous comparison of Monteverdi's sun to Sacrati's moon occurs in the preface to Badoaro's *Ulisse errante* (1644) (Appendix I.8l).

21. It is thus perhaps somewhat surprising, given his reputation at the time, that Monteverdi's name is nowhere mentioned in the *Poppea* scenario—but then again, neither is Busenello's.

Time was sometimes so short that composers were forced to begin setting librettos before they had been completed, presumably without even having read the whole text. A number of librettists remarked defensively on the conditions that forced such piecemeal settings. One (Francesco Sbarra) complained publicly to a friend that because of illness and the pressures of a deadline for performance, he had to send his text off immediately to be set (by Cesti):

> Because I didn't have even the minimum time necessary to check it over, I had to allow it to be placed under the notes in the very same form in which I sketched it. Furthermore, since it ended up being too long for the music, it had to be shortened, and consequently it can only have been mangled; and they tell me that they had to print it in that form. (Appendix I.29c)

And he begged his friend to see to it that the libretto was corrected before being printed:

> I appeal to Your Lordship to do me the favor of checking this work and altering it as you see fit before it is printed. . . . You will find many errors of language, numerous weaknesses and harshnesses in the poetry, and in the humor an infinity of our local idioms that are unsuitable elsewhere, in addition to many dissonances caused by the shortening of the work. (Appendix I.29d)[22]

Perhaps the most vivid description of piecemeal composition was that by the librettist of *Hipsicratea* (1660), Giovanni Maria Milcetti:

> This work was written in Badia delle Carceri and from there sent, page by page, to Murano, whereupon it was immediately structured into scenes. Anyone who knows the distances between the two places will not be surprised by the differences in poetic structure and words between the printed libretto and the opera performed in the theater, because, in effect, even before the poetry was finished and organized it was already being set to music, and the *sinfonie* were already being sung. (Appendix I.53a)[23]

As usual, rhetoric mixes with reality in these complaints. Like the librettists' common disavowal of serious commitment to writing, the excuse of "l'angustia del tempo" was part of their characteristically apologetic preemptive strategy. In an amusing variation on this approach, a few authors admitted to inordinately long gestation periods for their librettos. Matteo Noris's first libretto, *Zenobia* (1666), for example, took him four years to write, while Be-

---

22. *Alessandro vincitor di se stesso* (1651), "Lettera dell'autore al signor Michel'Angelo Torcigliani." According to the same letter, Sbarra designed his work for a specific troupe, Cesti's, which he had seen in Lucca (see Appendix I. 29a); therefore he wrote the correct number of parts—not always possible for a librettist to do.

23. Milcetti may have been writing from Carceri, a town in the Basso Veneto near Este. It is not clear to what "la Badia delle Carceri" refers.

regan claimed that his second libretto, *Tito* (1666), took five.[24] The seriousness of long-term commitment was evidently deemed as admirable as the *sprezzatura* of speedy composition.

Whether or not they wrote under pressure of time, librettists had to be ready to make changes in their texts, either at the request of the composer or in response to the requirements of a particular performance. It is quite clear from a variety of evidence that it was only during the rehearsal period that an opera took its final (though not necessarily permanent) shape. The librettist as well as the composer was expected to attend rehearsals in order to accommodate these alterations. In one instance the author of *Adone* (1639), Paolo Vendramin, wrote to the composer, Manelli, explaining that he could not be present for the rehearsals, and charged him with the responsibility of overseeing the production: "It will be up to you to lend it that study and that diligence that I could not, and which is required when producing an opera in Venice."[25] In another instance, the librettist Francesco Piccoli "being unable to assist in the completion . . . nor in the alterations, indeed changes, required by the staging" of his *L'incostanza trionfante overo il Theseo* (1658), it was necessary to engage another librettist for the final changes.[26]

In a note at the end of his *Hipsicratea* (1660), the author Milcetti asked the composer Don Pietro Molinari to add some arias to his text because he was unavailable for final alterations:

> Since distance does not allow me to be around to see to the needs of my drama, I am happy that Your Lordship will insert the songs [*canzonette*] that you describe. I beg you to mark them in the margins with a star or with double commas, as is the custom. I say this because I do not like to dress what is mine in others' ornaments; thus I will be extremely glad if the difference is clear. (Appendix I.53b)[27]

24. "Sono anni quattro in circa, che hò delineato questo, mio parto. . . . Fino ad ora si è nascosto per non lasciarsi vedere cosi imperfetto, e deforme, & al presente arroscisse anco sù la candidezza de fogli. E si conosce senza senno nel comparire su le publiche Scene" (*Zenobia*, preface); "Dio voglia . . . che questo Drama, composto nello spatio d'un lustro, ancorche concepito da Elefante, non sortisca una vita da Efemera" (*Tito*, preface). *Tito*, which Beregan must have begun sometime around 1661, was still not ready to be set to music by 12 July 1665, but that was six full months before it was scheduled to be performed; see Cesti's letter to Beregan in Giazotto, "Cesti," 499.

25. "Toccherà a lei di darli quello studio, e quella diligenza, che io non hò potuto, e che merita il far recitare un'Opera à Venezia" (*Adone*, preface, 6). Vendramin had legal reasons for not coming to Venice at the time; see Arthur Livingston, "Una scappatella di Polo Vendramin e un sonetto di Gian Francesco Busenello," *Fanfulla della Domenica*, 24

September 1911, and Bianconi and Walker, "Dalla 'Finta pazza,' " 422 n. 178.

26. "non potendo egli assistere alla perfettione dell'Opera ne' alle alterationi, anzi diversificationi necessitate dalla pratica della Scena" (*Theseo*, publisher's preface). This production was particularly difficult. It was the one Ziani complained about having had to revise ten times ("un Teseo fatto e rifatto dieci volte" [b. 188: 268]; also "un Teseo fatto e rifatto" [b. 188: 255]). The problems obviously did not begin at the rehearsals, but much earlier. They are evident, but can be unraveled only with difficulty, in the prefaces to the various versions of the libretto published during the inaugural season.

27. Evidently the composer wrote the extra text too. Milcetti seems unusually moralistic in his discomfort at parading the poetry of another author as his own; more likely, he was worried about ruining his reputation, particularly if the new text proved inferior.

Composers must often have been required to add text, particularly for arias. In sending his libretto *Lismaco* to its composer, Giovanni Maria Pagliardi, Ivanovich encouraged him to make whatever changes he thought necessary:

> If you find some emotion [*affetto*] in the recitative that can be reduced to a *cavata*, don't hesitate to do so, since anything that stands out unexpectedly is pleasing. As far as the number of *ariette* is concerned, to be arranged with their *sinfonie*, use your discretion, with due attention to the brevity that is so important here [in Venice]. (Appendix II.5b)

The numerous textual alterations that occurred either at the time of setting to music or during rehearsals created a special problem at the publication stage. If printed librettos, like their less expensive predecessors the scenarios, were to be of use to the audience in the theater, they had to correspond to the work being performed on stage. This was rendered difficult by the length of librettos—too long to be printed in the period, at most a matter of a few days, between rehearsals and premiere. As it was, librettos often did not come off the press until the very last minute.[28] Printers compensated for this difficulty by devising various methods of incorporating last-minute alterations. In fact, the frequency and extent of such changes is confirmed by the development of standard techniques for indicating them: the use of *virgolette*, which could be added on the printer's copy of the manuscript even at the last minute before typesetting, and brief stop-press additions, which could be set at the bottom of pages that had already been printed.

At first, at least, *virgolette* gave the clearest message: they indicated text that was not sung. I have already mentioned one of the earliest uses, that in the 1640 print of Rinuccini's *Arianna*, which followed the revival of Monteverdi's opera in that year. Although they were unexplained, the *virgolette* were placed next to passages that were obviously cut in the revival (nearly all of the choruses, as well as some of the dialogue)—those passages, in fact, that would have been anachronistic in Venice. The printer—and probably Monteverdi too—had edited the text according to Venetian usage ("secondo l'uso di Venezia"), without acknowledging as much.[29] At first it was usually recitative that was cut, but as the century wore on *virgolette* tended to appear next to second strophes of arias as well.[30] Although they retained their original function throughout the cen-

---

28. A letter from Massi to Duke Johann Friedrich, dated 27 January 1672 [1673], indicates that the libretto of *Massenzio* was not ready until 3 A.M. on the morning of the premiere (Appendix IIIB.17). Printers could run into trouble if they began publishing too soon, as in the case of *Doriclea*; see ch. 6, pp. 192–93, above.

29. "L'uso di Venezia," or "brevità veneta" (mentioned in the preface to *Pasife* as well as elsewhere)

was one of the most frequent reasons given for cutting; others included adapting a play for sung rather than spoken performance (as in *La finta savia* and *Torilda* [see n. 33 below]) and just plain fear of boring the audience ["per levare il tedio"]).

30. It is difficult to draw chronological conclusions from the practice of cutting second strophes, however, since many second editions of librettos of the same period *add* strophes to arias.

tury, *virgolette* were also increasingly used to distinguish material added to a libretto by another hand.[31]

For more complicated situations, and when time did not allow for *virgolette*, librettists used the preface to explain discrepancies or else resorted to stop-press additions. Since these affected only a single page of type, they could presumably be produced at the very last minute, conceivably even on the day of the performance, even though librettos were stitched (though not bound). A note in the preface to Aureli's *Gl'amori infrutuosi di Pirro* (1661), for example, explained that the libretto had been printed too soon to incorporate *virgolette*.[32] The tightness of schedule is nicely illustrated by another Aureli libretto, *La costanza di Rosmonda* (1659), in which *virgolette* appear in the second and third acts only. A last-minute postscript explains the discrepancy: the first act had been printed before cuts were made so it appeared without *virgolette*, whereas the other two acts had been printed late enough to incorporate them (Appendix I.44a). Of course, we have no idea which lines of act 1 were affected; we know only that some were cut.

What postscripts lacked in specificity, however, they made up in flexibility, for they could convey many different kinds of information about a variety of last-minute changes, and not just cuts. Most important, they often justified such changes, thus providing valuable insight into aesthetic and practical considerations affecting opera production. At the end of his *Delia* (1639), for example, Strozzi informs the reader that his text has been altered by the composer, Manelli: "So that your eyes will agree with your ears, know, exquisite reader, that in representing the work more than three hundred lines have been omitted, in order not to abuse your courtesy" (Appendix I.15i). And then he proceeds to justify the cuts: "It is necessary that the poet abandon his ornaments, that is, his digressions and episodes, to make way for the singers' ornaments. Do not, therefore, fault the performers for doing what they have done the better to serve you" (Appendix I.15j). In one of his later librettos, *La finta savia* (1643), Strozzi again explains that the unusually lengthy text has been cut because it was too long for musical setting, having been written to be performed without music as well (Appendix I.18a).[33]

31. As in *Hipsicratea*, mentioned above; *virgolette* were also used to differentiate the various hands in *Ciro* (1653–54), which was revised twice, and *La schiava fortunata* (1674), originally by Moniglia and Cesti, with new music by Marc'Antonio Ziani and new text, possibly, by Giulio Cesare Corradi (according to Ivanovich), among other instances.

32. "[P]er non arrecarti tedio con la longhezza, si tralasciano molti versi, che per essere già stati stampati non s'hanno potuto segnar con i punti, onde ti prego a supplire con la velocità dello sguardo nella lettura" (*Gl'amori infrutuosi di Pirro*, preface).

33. Perhaps surprisingly, in view of the qualms of the academic librettists discussed in ch. 2, Bissari's *Torilda* (1648) was one of the few other librettos that offered the option of spoken performance (according to a stop-press addition at the end of the 1648 libretto: "le Virgole poste nel margine segnano quel, che si può tralasciare in Recita musicale, come per altra Recita serve l'opera intiera").

Although some changes clearly occurred when the composer initially set the text to music and may have been justified by aesthetic considerations, many more must have been made at the last minute in response to specific performance conditions. In *Veremonda* (1653), for instance, several lines were added in a scene of the second act: "Since, owing to the distance of the Fort of Calpe, Zelamina and Zaida couldn't be understood, they have been made to come outside to speak, and then, having seen Delio, in respect for Giacutte, to go back in until he leaves. As a consequence, the following lines in the middle of act 2, scene 8, must be altered and added."[34]

Whereas librettist and composer had to make these small adjustments on the spot, some changes were effected simply by a new direction to the singer (with perhaps a record of it left in the libretto), as in *La costanza di Rosmonda* (1659): "In act 1, scene 14, where it says 'Clitennestra recites in a balcony,' it was thought better to have her appear on the stage in order to make her visible to the eyes of everyone, especially those seated in the boxes" (Appendix I.44b).

The preface to Aureli's *Claudio Cesare* (1672), finally, summarizes quite effectively the kinds of changes that took place during rehearsals and the typical librettist's attitude toward them:

> After the libretto was printed and the opera rehearsed on stage, it was decided to cut various superfluous parts of it; therefore, you are urged kindly to pass over various lines and certain scenes, which for greater brevity have been cut, since we did not have the opportunity of doing so, the libretto already having been printed. Below you will also find three aria texts that have been changed; all of this information is given so that only what is read will be sung, thus bringing greater delight to the audience. You will appreciate the difficulties that composers [*compositori*, meaning composers and librettists] face today in satisfying not only the strange tastes of this city, but also the extravagant whims of the performers [*i Signori Musici recitanti*]. (Appendix I.50b–c)

Composers' Obligations

The kinds of alterations that so preoccupied librettists were of less concern to composers; or at least their concern was less obvious. One reason for this difference was sociological. Librettists, however inadequate, casual, or amateurish they claimed to be, were educated in and practiced *lettere*: they were writers, whose words laid traditional claim to immortality, especially since the invention of the printing press, and whose capabilities were judged by well-

---

34. "Perche, per la lontananza della Fortezza di Calpe, Zelamina, & Zaida non potevano esser intese, si fanno uscir fuori à parlare, e poi, veduto Delio, per rispetto di Giacutte, ritornar dentro, fin ch'egli parta. Però, si devono mutare, & aggiungere questi Versi nel mezzo della Scena Ottava dell'Atto Secondo." This information is provided in a note at the end of the libretto, probably by the producer, Balbi, who signed the preface. The four added lines are also given in the note.

established critical criteria. Composers, on the other hand, no matter how intelligent and well educated—and whatever the higher claims of music as theory—were essentially artisans, practitioners of a trade, for hire. Theirs was a service profession. Last-minute modifications determined by the demands of a patron, an occasion, or a particular performance site were a traditional part of their job. Such changes were, of course, more fundamental to the structure of librettos than of scores: they involved adding or subtracting characters, eliminating precious lines of poetry, metaphors, special turns of plot, and other such *invenzioni*. For composers the changes were minimal: a transposition here, an aria there.

Librettists might have been more relaxed had their works remained as ephemeral as opera scores or performances. It was the act of printing the libretto per se—a sign and consequence of institutionalization, as we have seen—that stimulated these writers' anxiety and caused them to express their concern so openly. Their professional identities (as well as their material profits) were embodied in the published work.

Librettos enjoyed an independent existence as printed texts. Scores did not; they were working documents, tied to the facts and moments of performance. Whereas it was to the librettist's advantage to distinguish between the composition and rehearsal stage in the development of his text, such a distinction was hardly relevant to the composer, for whom the two stages merged in the normal process of composition. Indeed, composition was not considered complete until the work had been readied for performance; the composer's presence at rehearsals was an integral part of his contract. This is clearly set forth in Cavalli's contract of 24 July 1658 with Marco Faustini at S. Cassiano, which stipulates that, in addition to providing one opera per year for three years himself ("con la diligenza et Virtù sua propria"), he "be present at all the rehearsals that are needed, and also to change parts, alter, cut, and add whatever is necessary in the music in the service of the opera" (Appendix IIIA.2).[35]

Although composers' scores are never as explicit as printed librettos in distinguishing between the stages of composition—between what took place before and what took place during rehearsals—they often record something of the composer's process, his methods of shaping and continually modifying his musical setting as he moved toward performance or even from one perfor-

---

35. The contract is given in full in *Quellentexte*, ed. Becker, 72. Cavalli's responsibilities were laid out in essentially the same way nearly ten years later in his final contract with Faustini, of 29 June 1667 (b. 194: 50): "dovendo assister alle prove et occorrendo anco aggiunger, alterare, et levare quelle cose, che fossero necessarie, et occorressero conforme alla sodisfazione d'esso Sig. Faustini, al quale doverano restare l'originali" (i.e., the score and parts). This was the contract for the ill-fated *Eliogabalo*. Here it is clearly spelled out that the composer did not have the rights to his score (cf. ch. 6, n. 77, above); also Bianconi and Walker, "Production," 237 n. 72. This contract is partially transcribed in Brunelli, "Angustie," 334–35.

mance to the next. Printed librettos, by their very fixity, help to shape speculation about the meanings of the scores to which they are connected. Differences between libretto and score might indicate that the score either represents a modification for a subsequent performance or an earlier stage of the libretto, which later was revised for publication by the poet; or again, the score might represent a later version that the poet could not or would not adopt for his published text.

These differences could, of course, have originated at the composition stage. Even during the early years of intimate collaboration, composers did not always set the poet's text exactly. We have already referred to important differences between Monteverdi's and Badoaro's versions of *Il ritorno d'Ulisse*. The scores of Monteverdi's *L'incoronazione di Poppea*, too, diverge considerably not only from Busenello's printed text and the several extant manuscript versions of the libretto but from the scenario as well.[36]

A number of Cavalli's scores are quite different from their printed librettos. Strophic texts are set non-strophically, both as arias and recitatives, refrain lines are added, and, of course, passages of text omitted. Such differences, however, probably more reflect the temporal relationship between extant score and printed libretto than any aesthetic question. These discrepancies would probably have disappeared if the libretto could have been printed late enough to include all last-minute alterations. On the other hand, they also reveal the kinds of changes Cavalli and, presumably, other composers normally made as they worked from a manuscript libretto, changes that might subsequently be incorporated in printed librettos. In the case of librettos printed before the works were performed, we can usually assume that most differences from the score reflect composers' changes. But if they were printed afterwards, as in Busenello's *Delle hore ociose*, which contains all of his librettos, we must also consider that the librettist may have revised his text in the interim, and that his original text, or one closer to it, is represented in the music.[37]

Since composers presumably had less of a stake in a precisely finished product than did librettists, and since it was part of their job to make continual adjustments and changes up to the last minute, many of the indignities librettists complained about were simply matters of course to them. Piecemeal composition, for example, which might have prevented librettists from editing or polishing their works to their own literary satisfaction, was more the rule than the exception for composers. They reported the receipt and dispatching of

36. But, since we know that both scores are late, their differences from the librettos might have reflected changes made well after Monteverdi's death. On these differences, see Curtis, preface to *L'incoronazione di Poppea*, and id., "*La Poppea impasticciata*"; also Rosand, "Monteverdi's Mimetic Art," and id., "Seneca."

37. Curtis, however, argues that Busenello's print is probably closest to his original text (preface to *L'incoronazione di Poppea*).

single acts or groups of scenes of librettos and scores with apparent equanimity. Thus Ziani, writing to Faustini on 2 August 1665 about the ill-fated *Doriclea* (whose last-minute cancellation we have already discussed), reported that he had just sent him the music of act 1, but was awaiting the arrival of act 2 of the libretto so that he could begin to set it.[38] And Cesti exhibited similar nonchalance when he wrote on 21 June 1665 to Beregan, whose *Tito* he had been contracted to set, urging him to send act 1 as soon as it was ready, without waiting until the entire work was completed.[39] He made the same request again on 12 July. He must have received the text (and set it) by 2 August, when he reacted enthusiastically to the arrival of act 2 in another letter to Beregan: "I received the second act; it is beautiful, beautiful, beautiful."[40]

Composers' piecemeal settings routinely found their way to the singers (or impresario) in the same fashion. Cavalli sent the first act of his *Hipermestra* to Florence ahead of the others.[41] Cesti and Ziani both refer often to having sent off a single act or several scenes with the promise of the rest in due course. In a letter of 20 December 1666, Cesti writes that he has just mailed half of act 2 of *Tito* and hopes that act 1 has arrived, although it lacks the opening *sinfonia* ("la Sinfonia avanti s'alzi la tenda"), which he will write after having finished the opera "because it isn't so urgent at the moment" ("per non essere presentemente di tanta necessità").[42] Although piecemeal setting may not have bothered composers, it seems (reassuringly) to have had a negative effect on some singers, who were frustrated in their attempt to understand their parts. As we shall see, Nicola Coresi complained that he had received the wrong impression of his role in *Meraspe* from the excerpt he had been sent originally;[43] and Catterin'Angela Botteghi asked to see the whole libretto of the same opera so that she could understand better how to interpret her role.[44]

Composers may have taken piecemeal composition for granted, but they were not altogether insensitive to the time pressures that plagued librettists. Ziani lost no opportunity of reminding Faustini how he had saved the day by writing *Annibale in Capua* in five (or six) days.[45] Speed was his trademark, a characteristic both he and, apparently, his critics emphasized, though obviously

---

38. Letter from Vienna (*b.* 188: 75) partially transcribed in Giazotto, "La guerra dei palchi," 504–5.
39. Letter from Innsbruck (*b.* 188: 119): "Quando havesse all'ordine tanto basterebbe mandarmi il 1° Atto" (Giazotto, "Cesti," 499).
40. "Ho ricevuto il 2° Atto bellissimo, bellissimo, bellissimo." Letter from Innsbruck (*b.* 188: 76–80); see Giazotto, "Cesti," 501.
41. According to letters from Atto Melani quoted in Lorenzo Bianconi, "Caletti," *DBI* 16 (Rome, 1973): 692 (I-Fas, Archivio Mediceo del Principato, F. 5452, cc. 747–48, and F. 5453, cc. 595–96).

42. Letter to Beregan (*b.* 194: 138); see Schmidt, "*Tito* Commission," 459, and Giazotto, "Cesti," 507. In the end, the sinfonia, in three parts, was pieced together from several of his earlier operas; see Schmidt, 459 n. 49.
43. Letter from Rome, 13 August 1667 (*b.* 188: 166); see Brunelli, "Angustie," 337; also ch. 8 below.
44. Letter from Florence, 27 August 1667 (*b.* 188: 170); see Brunelli, "Angustie," 339.
45. Letters of 25 July 1665 (*b.* 188: 82) and 9 May and 10 July 1666 (*b.* 188: 279, 269); transcribed in *Quellentexte*, ed. Becker, 78–79.

for opposite purposes. Ziani regarded his facility ("solita facilità") as an inimitable quality,[46] which he invoked ironically in a request to Faustini for payment ("I write quickly but am paid slowly") as well as to counter criticism of his works: "If my arias are, have been, and will have been good, for the theater as well as for church, all of them pass under the same rush in the making."[47] He imputed to the envy of his competitors the accusation of his having written *Alciade* while in transit from Innsbruck to Venice, yet he himself described some music he was sending to Faustini as "another piece of an opera completed by me in transit."[48]

Ziani was especially famous (or infamous) for his speed, but other composers could work just as quickly when necessary—though they and their supporters did not hesitate to exaggerate such feats. Sartorio, for example, was reported to have set Bussani's *Massenzio* in thirteen days, although it probably took him closer to a month.[49] Whereas Sartorio survived the pressure and even profited from it in enhanced reputation, not all composers were so resilient. One of them, Giovanni Antonio Boretti, reportedly even died from the anxieties of readying an opera for production: "Poor Gio Ant Borretti . . . died yesterday after two weeks of sickness caused by readying his opera for production" (Appendix IIIB.11c).[50]

Although they were often at the mercy of circumstances beyond their control, composers, like their librettist colleagues, recognized the difference between working at leisure and under pressure. Cesti, for example, who complained about having to compose five acts of *Il pomo d'oro* in six weeks, wrote

46. "Non so se le fatiche continue di questo Paese di tal uno, apporterà a lei pregiudizio se pure la prestezza del operare del Ziani non dasse motivo ad altri d'imitarlo e superarlo." Letter of 10 July 1666 (*b.* 188: 269); transcribed in *Quellentexte*, ed. Becker, 79.

47. "Il mio scrivere è presto, ma son tardi pagato. . . . Se le mie arie sono, sono state e saranno state buone sì per teatro come per le chiese tutte passano soto alla medema fretta nell'operatione." Letter of 9 May 1666 (*b.* 188: 279); transcribed in *Quellentexte*, ed. Becker, 78.

48. "Bugiardi e maligni sono quelli che tassano Alciade fatto per viaggio (che non è vero però) ma se fosse stato fatto anco sopra alle zangole gli farei un presente della sedia e a suo dispetto farò sempre buona riuscita" (ibid.). "Gli mando un altro pezzo d'opera fatto da me in viaggio." Letter of 3 November 1665 from Innsbruck (*b.* 188: 226), not included in Giazotto's inventory but identified as Ziani's in Schmidt, "*Tito* Commission," 459 n. 47.

49. He actually composed it between 23 December 1672 and 25 January 1673. The date of completion is established by a letter of 20 January 1672 [1673] from Dolfin to Duke Johann Friedrich (Appendix

IIIB.16). The letter reports that the premiere of *Massenzio* was scheduled for the following Wednesday. Since 20 January was a Friday in 1673, the following Wednesday would have been 25 January. According to the same author, writing on 23 December, Sartorio began writing the opera on that date (Appendix IIIB.10); Dolfin subsequently reported that it had taken Sartorio only thirteen days to complete the work (letter of 3 February 1673, Appendix IIIB.18).

50. It is not clear whether Boretti's problems were caused by *Claudio Cesare* or *Domitiano*, or both, since they seem to have been intended for the same season; the dedications of both librettos are dated 27 December 1672, but Bonlini lists *Claudio Cesare* for 1672 (along with *Adelaide*) and *Domitiano* alone for 1673. A second edition of the latter libretto, however, alludes to difficulties with the season: "In quest'anno gl'accidenti han variato gl'ordini nelle Rappresentationi del Drama; onde la mia debolezza non ti comparirà sù la Scena, colpo del caso, che in ogni cosa ne hà parte," confirming that *Domitiano* was the fatal work. Furthermore, it was plagued with difficulties created by a poor cast (see Appendix IIIB.13).

appreciatively to his librettist Beregan about being able to take his time over *Tito*, working at the relaxed pace of one act per month: "When one can enjoy the benefit of time, things come out much better."[51] In the event, however, he did not finish the opera any too soon—in fact, not until 17 January, less than a month before the premiere at SS. Giovanni e Paolo.[52]

The main source of trouble for composers, as for librettists, was the time it took to negotiate with the singers. It is clear that casts were often not fully assembled until well after the librettist and composer would have had to begin work. Librettists could still manage with a fairly general notion of the cast; some idea as to the number and relative importance of the singers would suffice for an initial draft of the text, which could be modified later. Giovanni Faustini, we remember, had sketched a number of librettos without knowing who would perform (or even set) them. It was unthinkable, however, for a composer to begin work before he knew at least the ranges of the voices for which he was writing. In the early days of the stable, continuous companies of Ferrari-Manelli, Cavalli-Faustini, and Sacrati, this was not a problem, and there were even periods of stability later in the century, when casts carried over from one season to the next.

But last-minute hiring and cast changes were increasingly the rule.[53] Composing *Alciade* (1666), Ziani had to make several decisions on his own ("in order not to lose time") because Faustini had not informed him of the cast in time. He wrote the role of the boatman (*Nocchiero*) for the bass singer (who otherwise had a very small part and could evidently double here) and Lerilda for a soprano (of which Faustini had several to choose from). And he asked for information on the voice for the "Vecchia" Clipea in act 3, not indicated by Faustini, having assigned it, in the interim, to the soprano who also played Idiotea—and who, he said, had not appeared on stage for a while (Appendix IIIA.10). Even in parts that had been cast, however, he was forced to make a number of alterations in response to last-minute substitutions or even careless assumptions: octave

---

51. "Quando si gode il benefizio del tempo, le cose riescon molto meglio." Letter of 16 August 1665 (*b*. 188: 88–89), transcribed in Giazotto, "Cesti," 503–4; the contents of this letter are summarized in Schmidt, "*Tito* Commission," 456. While Giazotto claims that this letter was addressed to Faustini, Schmidt assumes, more convincingly, that the recipient was Beregan.

52. Letter of 17 January 1666 (*b*. 188: 305, 344). The dedication of the libretto was signed 13 February 1666; see Schmidt, "*Tito* Commission," 460. From Ziani's letters to Faustini of 3 April and 9 May 1666 (*b*. 188: 255–56ᵛ, 279–80) we learn that the music and the performers of *Tito* had been well enough

received, but that the libretto had been criticized, and that Faustini's profits had not been particularly high. These letters are summarized in Schmidt, "*Tito* Commission," 462–63, and partially transcribed in Giazotto, "La guerra dei palchi," 506. For the letter of 9 May, see Appendix IIIA.11.

53. This is documented repeatedly in the Faustini papers as well as in the correspondence of Duke Johann Friedrich's Venetian agents. See, for example, the letter of 30 December 1672 from Dolfin in which he mentions the possibility that his singer, Lucretia, might have had to learn a part in two days (Appendix IIIB.11a).

transposition of one role (Guerra) from baritone to alto, and transposition a fourth or fifth lower to suit the alto performer of the messenger (*Nuntio Messo*) in *Doriclea*, which he had originally scored for soprano.[54]

Cesti, too, repeatedly requested information about the intended singers for his *Tito*, at one point asking specifically who would sing the hunter (*Cacciator*) in the final scene of act 2, "because there is no indication."[55] At another point he made a revealing suggestion of his own, that instead of two sopranos and a contralto, it would be better to have a lower voice, either tenor or baritone, "because in the most beautiful scenes diversity of voices seems much better, and if the scene between Domitiano and Berenice, as it is, scored for two sopranos, were sung by two different voice parts, it would stand out marvelously, and I am taking into account that with the two Amorini there will be nine sopranos."[56]

The information requested by both Ziani and Cesti evidently concerned minor roles, many of which involved decisions about doubling. Clearly the major roles would have been assigned earlier. Normally, casts were decided upon several months before the beginning of a season—usually by August—with singers scheduled to arrive in Venice, parts learned, by mid November at the latest—that is, about six weeks before the premiere, when rehearsals began.[57] The planning of special stage effects and the construction of machinery

---

54. Letter of 3 November 1665 (*b.* 188: 226). Ziani had written nearly the entire role of Euristo in *Akiade* for soprano, not realizing that the singer was an alto. He finished it in the proper range and presumably altered the part already written (Appendix IIIA.11). Changes like these are reflected in a number of scores in the Contarini collection, especially *Poppea*, *Calisto*, and *Xerse*, though they may just as easily be for revivals as for last-minute cast changes. There is some confusion about this letter. Giazotto fails to mention it but lists another one, of 13 December 1665 (*b.* 194: 116), which he says concerns the types of voices to be used for *Doriclea* ("La guerra dei palchi," 507).

55. "perche non v'è alcun segno" (letter of 16 August 1665 [*b.* 188: 88–89]); see Giazotto, "Cesti," 504, and the discussion in Schmidt, "*Tito* Commission," 455–56.

56. "perche nelle scene più belle paria molto meglio la diversità delle voci, e se la scena fra Domitiano e Berenice, come è fatta in duoi soprani, fosse cantata con due parti diverse, spiccherebbe a meraviglia; e considero che saranno con li duoi Amorini in numero 9 soprani." Letter to Beregan of 2 August 1665 (*b.* 188: 76–80); see Giazotto, "Cesti," 501. The contents of this letter are discussed in Schmidt, "The *Tito* Commission," 452–53.

57. This timetable is generally supported by the Faustini correspondence with singers. For example, according to a letter from her husband Nicola, dated 27 August 1667, Antonia Coresi (or Tonina) knew her part well enough to go on stage the very next day: "sa la parte in maniera che ancora per lei si potrebbe andar domani in scena" (*b.* 188: 166; in Brunelli, "Angustie," 338). Many reports from Venice document that rehearsals were taking place during November. "Qua si va concertando le opere," writes Massi, for example, in a letter to Johann Friedrich, 28 November 1670 (vol. 4, no. 627, f. 216). A particularly late contract was the one signed by Faustini with Pietro Lucini on 11 November 1665 (*b.* 194: 53; see Brunelli, "Angustie," 325; also Schmidt, "*Tito* Commission," 458 n. 46). The panic expressed in Alvise Duodo's letter to Faustini of 5 November 1658 is understandable. He reports that the costumes are not being worked on, what musicians there are have not received their parts, and "God knows an opera can't be performed in this form." And he reminds Faustini that, to top it all off, one of the principal parts has not even been assigned yet; nor has anything been heard from the Roman contralto to whom thirty scudi have already been advanced (*b.* 188: 19–20); text in Bianconi and Walker, "Production," 224 n. 47.

probably began before the singers arrived—in October.[58] But there were often troublesome exceptions. Long-distance negotiations with at least one singer, the much-sought-after castrato Ciecolino (Antonio Rivani), were still in progress on 17 November 1670, a mere month before the season was to begin.[59] Two years later the same difficult singer did not arrive in Venice until late December, after the season had started, "tardi per recitare," but not too late to appear in at least some performances.[60]

Although negotiations with singers often concluded surprisingly close to the beginning of the season, there was apparently considerable flexibility with respect to the actual date of opening night for a work. Traditionally, of course, the season coincided with Carnival, which began the day after Christmas, and most opera houses opened as close to that time as possible. We noted earlier how Marco Faustini tried to move the opening day of SS. Giovanni e Paolo forward by some two weeks in 1666 in order to seize the advantage from his competition.[61] Later in the century, openings in early December or even late November were not uncommon, particularly in years when Carnival was unusually short.[62] Theater managers could hardly be blamed for wanting to squeeze more performances into a season.

58.   Letter from Massi to Johann Friedrich, 5 October 1670 (vol. 4, no. 627, f. 200): "Si va ogni giorno più fissamente pensando all'opera, si assoldano musici, e si va inventando nuove mutanze nell'ordine del Theatro. Tengono che in quest'anno si vedranno cose fuori dell'ordinario." Contracts with scene designers were often the first to be signed. Faustini signed one with Gasparo Mauro on 8 March 1665 for *Tito* and *Doriclea* (*b.* 188: 109), transcribed in Schmidt, "*Tito* Commission," 444 n. 9, and a month later, on 8 April 1665, he signed a three-year contract with Horatio Franchi in which the latter agreed to produce costumes for two operas per year at the annual salary of 800 ducats (the figure is comparatively high because Franchi was required to supply the materials himself [*b.* 194: 42]). But negotiations with a few singers for the same season were concluded even earlier: contracts with Nicola Coresi and Sebastian Cioni were dated 17 February and 7 March 1665, respectively. See Schmidt, "*Tito* Commission," 445 n. 11.
59.   Letter from Massi, 17 November 1670 (vol. 4, no. 627, f. 211ᵛ): "sono qui cominciate le comedie a San Samuele, e qua Cecolino al quale hanno offerte dobble 250; ma lui non vuol recitare se non sono almeno 300." Ciecolino, or Ciccolino, had been employed by the duke of Savoy since 1668, when he precipitously left the service of Queen Christina in Rome. During the 1650s his patron was Cardinal Gian Carlo de' Medici of Florence. See Rosselli, "From Princely Service," 7.

60.   See letters from Massi of 9 December 1672 (Appendix IIIB.8), 30 December 1672 (IIIB.11b), and 13 January 1673 (IIIB.15). Late arrivals were obviously not uncommon, as illustrated by the case of a Signor Clemente, whose late arrival forced Aureli to carve a new role out of existing text in an opera that had already been cast: "per essere il Signor Clemente arrivato in tempo ch'erano già dispensate le parti del Drama, m'è convenuto inserirlo nell'uno, e nell'altro al meglio, che hà potuto permettere la brevità del tempo; havendo havuto un solo riguardo, di non privarti del godimento della voce di un Virtuoso si insigne" (*Gl'amori infrutuosi di Pirro*, preface). This singer may have been the Antonio Clementi who played Berecintia in *Ercole in Tebe* in Florence in 1661 (see Robert Lamar Weaver and Norma Wright Weaver, *A Chronology of Music in the Florentine Theater, 1590–1750* [Detroit, 1978], 131), or else Clemente Hader (see Bianconi and Walker, "Production," 277).
61.   It should be reiterated, perhaps, that competition was especially fierce in 1666, with four theaters planning productions rather than the more usual two.
62.   Such was the case in 1672–73, according to several documents in the Johann Friedrich correspondence. See, for example, Massi's letter of 28 October 1672 (vol. 4, no. 627, f. 303): "Comincieranno le opere avanti il tempo, perche il Carnevale venturo sarà breve"; also 29 November (f. 287): "Si allestiscono li Teatri per le opere, quali principieranno per

In any case, since the opening date was not strictly fixed, it could be postponed if the opera were not ready yet; if the problem concerned the second opera of the season, the first could continue until the second was ready, or else an opera from a previous season could be substituted at the last minute. All of these situations actually occurred. Composers were announced and changed (*Argiope*);[63] a new libretto and setting, or just a new setting, commissioned at the last minute (*Eliogabalo*, *Massenzio*);[64] or an old opera substituted (*Orontea* for *Doriclea*).[65]

Naturally the most intense pressure occurred during the rehearsal period, when a libretto, along with the score, took its final shape. Many operas were reportedly revised and readied for performance in a matter of days: twelve days proved adequate to prepare *Annibale in Capua* for performance in 1661 (twice as long as the five [or six] it took Ziani to write it, as he never tired of saying), ten for a revival of Cesti's *Orontea* in 1666, and a record eight for his *Dori* in 1667.[66] Printed librettos and manuscript scores both reveal the kinds of changes that would have taken place during rehearsals, or else during the run of the work. The cast of Faustini's and Cavalli's *Calisto*, for example, gained a character, a crude peasant (*Bifolco*), at the last minute (or at least after the libretto had been printed and the score copied). Bifolco appears in three scenes, twice alone and once with another character, in acts 2 and 3. Faustini refers to these scenes in a note to the reader as "superimposed on the original structure of the story to delight you,"[67] and Cavalli's score accounts for the addition with the rubric:

---

tempo per esser corto il carnevale." See also manuscript *avvisi* in I-Vnm, It. VI, 459 [12103], of 21 November 1682 (Appendix IIIC.1) and 5 December 1682 (Appendix IIIC.2), which indicate that the traditional opening day was anticipated for the benefit of the duke of Mantua, an important patron; but another report, from 11 December 1683 (It. VI, 460 [12104]), indicates that the operas were not always ready when opening day was pushed forward too far (Appendix IIIC.5).

63. The preface to *Argiope* promised two composers, Rovetta and Leardini (Appendix I.28c), but a stop-press addition on the last page of the volume, p. 96, announced that in the end, Rovetta did not contribute (Appendix I.28d). The production of *Argiope* was delayed by several years, as we have seen, possibly as a result of the War of Candia.

64. Cavalli's setting of Bussani's *Massenzio* was scrapped at rehearsal and Sartorio commissioned to provide a new setting (letter of 23 December 1672 from Dolfin to Johann Friedrich [Appendix IIIB.10]). The case of *Eliogabalo* was somewhat different. Cavalli's setting of Aureli's original libretto, intended for the season of 1668 at SS. Giovanni e Paolo, was canceled at the last minute, in part because of Faustini's difficulties with the Grimani

brothers. They commissioned Aureli to write a new libretto on the same subject, to be set to music by Boretti, which was performed that same season, 1668. In a contract with Marco Faustini of 10 October 1667, Aureli agreed to "adjust certain things in *Eliogabalo*," which suggests that he was not the original author (*b.* 194: 31; transcribed in Brunelli, "Angustie," 335), a fact that he himself confirms in the dedication to the second *Eliogabalo* signed 10 January 1667 [1668] (Appendix I.49).

65. The substitution is specifically documented in the note to the reader of *Orontea*, signed 10 January 1666 (see ch. 6, pp. 192–93, above). The note is translated in Schmidt, "Tito Commission," 460.

66. Apparently the revival of *Dori* in Florence in 1661 took only four days to prepare; see Carl B. Schmidt, "Antonio Cesti's La Dori," *RIM* 10 (1975): 460; also id., "Tito Commission," 463 n. 55; the relevant letter from Cesti is quoted in John W. Hill, "Le relazioni di Antonio Cesti con la corte e i teatri di Firenze," *RIM* 11 (1976): 27.

67. "inestate nella Favola per dilettarti fuori della sua tessitura." The "diletto" was probably provided by some stage business performed by the country bumpkin. The added text is given at the end of the libretto, on pp. 76–82.

"Qui và la Scena del Bifolco," though no music is provided.[68] Conversely, the cast of Cavalli's and Minato's *Artemisia* was modified by reduction sometime after the music was written, but before the libretto was printed. The score, mostly autograph, has music for a character called Cleante, who does not appear in the libretto, and it actually illustrates how the reduction was achieved. In three places, music for Cleante has been crossed out and the text distributed to other characters in the opera.[69] The fact that Cleante never made it into the printed libretto and that the score is one of Cavalli's composing scores rather than a fair copy suggests a relatively early date for the modification.[70]

Dramatic coherence, what there was of it, was increasingly at the mercy of such exigencies. A curious extreme was surely reached in 1676 when Giulio Cesare Corradi, the librettist of *Germanico sul Reno*, claimed to have added a scene for an Orfeo, not listed in the cast and totally extraneous to the plot, in order to exhibit the talents not of a singer but of a special violinist.[71] But once again, the incorporation of such late arrivals, motivated by the usual desire to appeal to the audience, exacted a toll principally on the librettists. The required changes were often substantial enough to interfere with whatever dramatic continuity or balance their original texts may have aspired to. To composers the cost was negligible. Musical modifications were usually relatively minor and had little if any effect on the opera as a whole.

We return then to the social distinction between librettist and composer and their different claims, aspirations, and functions with respect to *dramma per musica*. Librettists were deeply concerned with the dramatic coherence and literary integrity of their work, as we have seen in the elaborate strategies they developed for preserving it or compensating for its absence. Composers could not possibly have felt the same way. Their scores could never have aspired to the objective wholeness of librettos; their music was doubly contingent: on their librettists and on their performers. Musical coherence independent of ei-

68. I-Vnm, It. IV, 353 (9877), ff. 59 and 101ᵛ.

69. I-Vnm, It. IV 352 [9876], ff. 18ᵛ–19, 42ᵛ–44, and 67–68ᵛ. See Jeffery, "Autograph Manuscripts," 238–39.

70. Much earlier, that is, than the adjustment Aureli had to make in his and Ziani's *Gl'amori infrutuosi di Pirro* (1661), mentioned in n. 60 above. Additions to casts during the run of an opera were apparently not that uncommon, as indicated by the following *avviso* of 2 January 1683 [1684] (I-Vnm, It. IV, 460 [12104]): "Si proseguiscono le recite nelle quattro enumerati Teatri, et in quello di SS. Giovanni e Paolo vi si è accresciuto un personaggio con nuove aggiunte, e canzonette. Superando però il vanto di tutti quello di San Luca per le esquisite voci."

71. "Ti prego pure à non far riflessione sopra l'Orfeo di Stige nel fine del Atto Secondo, accessorio solo introdotto per farti sentire un famoso Suonatore da Violino" (*Germanico sul Reno*, preface). This suggests the beginning of an increased emphasis on virtuoso instrumentalists, which Harris Saunders sees as a special feature of later seventeenth-century opera in Venice ("The Teatro Grimani di San Giovanni Grisostomo: The Interaction of Family Interests and Opera in Venice," paper read at the annual meeting of the American Musicological Society, New Orleans, 1987).

ther was an anachronism and an impossibility. Indeed, once the formerly unified activity of producing an opera had disintegrated into an amalgam of specialized tasks, the subservience of the composer in the operatic hierarchy became still clearer.

The kinds of alterations composers were called upon to make during rehearsals or in preparation for revivals, to adapt their works to new performers
or to the requirements of a new theater or audience, remained central to their
profession. But because of institutionalization and the consequent logistical
problems raised by geographical separation and competing patronage, these
alterations could not always be made by the original composers. Cesti, for
example, instructed Beregan to arrange for Rovettino to fulfill his rehearsal
obligations—namely, "to cut, add, change, or do whatever else was necessary
in the music"—since he could not come to Venice for the premiere of his *Tito*,
owing to commitments to his employer in Vienna.[72] And Ziani, although he
referred on several occasions to his obligatory presence in Venice for the rehearsals of his work, assuring Faustini at one point that he would not "leave
Venice until the whole score has been furnished and accommodated,"[73] later
gave him rather grudging permission to engage someone else for the task.[74]

Given the nature and extent of some of the changes that took place at
rehearsals—new arias, cuts, transpositions, rearrangements, even whole new
roles—which might have been supplied by someone other than the original
composer, many of these works would certainly qualify as pasticcios. But they
were not the first such cooperative ventures. Multiple authorship may not have
become a necessity until the pressures of institutionalization made it so, but it
had been a reality, even a positive feature considered worthy of advertising,
well before then.

Some early Venetian operas were specifically designed and promoted as
pasticcios. *La finta savia* (1643), for example, proudly boasted the music of
four different composers: Laurenzi, Crivelli, Merula, and Ferrari (Appendix
I.18b).[75] Many of the operas we have already mentioned ended up as pasticcios,
either by design or by accident. *Argiope* (1649), as we have seen, was touted as

72. Letter of 6 December 1665 to Beregan (b. 194:
145, 156): "Occorrendo poi di levare, aggiungere,
mutare e qualsivoglia altra cosa nella musica io prego
V.S. Ill.ᵐᵃ a far supplire al Signor Rovettino . . . che
mi dichiaro sodisfattissimo sapendo che m'ha voluto
sempre bene et ha favorito altre volte il mio poco
talento" (see Giazotto, "Cesti," 506–7).
73. "Non partirò di Venetia se non la vederò del
tutto fornita & acumodata." Letter of 2 August 1665
(b. 188: 75); Giazotto, "La guerra dei palchi," 504–5.
74. "Che io habbi per male, che altri mettino le

mani in mia absenza nelle mie opere non ci penso
niente, perchè per commodità della scena non si può
di meno." Letter of 10 July 1666 (b. 188: 269); Giazotto, "La guerra dei palchi," 507.
75. There were actually six composers involved,
including Alessandro Leardini and Vincenzo Tozzi.
See Osthoff, "Laurenzi," 175. For an extended discussion and schematic indication of the distribution
of the text of *La finta savia* among these six composers, see Magini, "Indagini," 540–45.

a pasticcio manqué;[76] Faustini's revival of Cesti's *Orontea* became a pasticcio in effect when it was prefaced by Ziani's new setting of the prologue to *Doriclea*.[77] And Cavalli's *Giasone* became part of an overt pasticcio when it appeared in Rome as *Il novello Giasone* in 1671 with some music by Stradella. Indeed, nearly every work that was revived, either in Venice or elsewhere, in the original composer's absence, or after his death, was a pasticcio. The most famous of these, at least in the versions that have come down to us, is Monteverdi's *L'incoronazione di Poppea*, the only modern "classic" of Venetian opera. Both extant scores, which probably reflect the Naples revival of 1651, contain music that Monteverdi could not have written. The only disagreement in this case is over the amount of original music still remaining.[78]

But that is not a meaningful question for operatic music of this period. Unlike that of the libretto, the sanctity of the operatic score was a concept virtually unknown and irrelevant in seicento Venice. Although it is difficult to judge from our distance, the replacement of one composer by another does not seem to have created a problem of stylistic incongruity either for contemporary audiences or for the composers themselves. Operas were increasingly bound by musico-dramatic conventions, making substitution of composers relatively easy.[79]

Because their professional stature and livelihood depended on it, librettists emphatically claimed and numbered their texts, carefully keeping track of their careers and burnishing their reputations. Composers, however, as they continued, often anonymously, to fulfill their multiple functions, increasingly disappeared behind their creations, leaving the singers to represent them.

---

76. See n. 63 above.

77. See above, ch. 6, p. 192 and n. 92.

78. Curtis finds considerable evidence, notational as well as musical, of the intervention of composers younger than Monteverdi in the score of *Poppea*; see "*La Poppea impasticciata*."

79. It is worth emphasizing that individual styles emerged quite late among opera composers, particularly in comparison with the sixteenth-century madrigalists. The strength and demands of operatic conventions undoubtedly helped to thwart such development. Equally significant, perhaps, is the fact that because opera scores were not published, they did not circulate, and were thus not available to be scrutinized. The music remained ephemeral, tied to the moment of its performance. The printing press did not serve these composers as it did both their madrigalist predecessors and their literary colleagues, the librettists.

8

◆　　◆　　◆

I più canori cigni e le suavissime sirene:
The Singers

An opera did not exist independent of its singers, either at its conception or its performance; they were its spokesmen, its true publicists. The singers mediated between opera and its audience. Transforming a private arrangement into a public spectacle, they transported the operatic product to the consumers.

In companies like Ferrari's or Sacrati's, singers were well known to composer and librettist from the very beginning of a project. Their roles, like costumes, were cut to measure in advance, fitted during rehearsals, and displayed at the performance. Composers themselves even used the tailoring metaphor to characterize their work. "I made the part to his measure" ("Holli fato la parte a suo dosso") was the way Sacrati described his composition of the title role of *Bellerofonte*, written for Michele Grasseschi.[1] We know too that Monteverdi's conception of the character of Licori in his aborted *La finta pazza Licori* was very much conditioned by the abilities of the singer he envisioned in the role, Margherita Basile. Whatever adjustments were found necessary during rehearsals took place behind the scenes, quietly, within the close professional family that together produced the work. Most of them would have gone unrecorded in librettos, since the early librettos were usually not issued until after the performance and could thus have incorporated the changes. The other chief documentary evidence of such changes, letters between the makers of operas, were of course unnecessary when a troupe lived and worked in such close proximity. Such alterations moved out into the open, as it were, only when practical conditions of institutionalization forced them there, when the original partnership among the makers of operas had begun to dissolve into the division of labor described in the previous pages.

1. Letter of 26 October 1641 (I-Fas, Fondo Mediceo del Principato, F. 5421, c. 516), quoted in Magini, "Indagini," 517. Other letters in Sartori, "Un fantomatico compositore," 798, and Alessandro Ademollo, *I primi fasti della musica italiana a Parigi (1645–1662)* (Milan, [1884]), 99–105. For more on Grasseschi's career in Florence, see Weaver and Weaver, *Florentine Theater*, entries for 1657, 1658, 1660, and 1661.

At the same time as singers became divorced from the original act of composition, they also became the increasing focus of public attention; and this required ever greater efforts on the part of composer and librettist to enhance their stature, to show them off to best advantage, even if it meant compromising their own aesthetic values. From a position of equality (or even less) in the original operatic partnership, singers rose to a position of undisputed preeminence. Once representatives of the art, they became its very embodiment. Paradoxically, the separation of the singers from the actual creation of the work eventually resulted in an increase in their final impact on it—or at least the visibility of their impact. Their growing influence, external as well as internal, can be measured in terms as diverse as salaries, contract negotiations, audience attention, and, of greatest aesthetic significance, changing ratio of aria to recitative.

The Wages of Singing

Some measure of the relative importance of the various contributors to the operatic enterprise is offered by a comparison of their earnings. The figures reflect the hierarchy at any given time, and compared over a substantial period, they reveal significant shifts in that hierarchy as well. The few documents we have for this period—two theater budgets, several contracts, and some references in correspondence—relate especially to composers and singers; information on librettists' earnings, which were based primarily on libretto sales and thus independent of theater budgets, is more difficult to come by.[2] Composers were evidently paid at different rates, depending on their reputation. Thus Cavalli's fee was unusually high. He received 400 ducats from Faustini for *Antioco* (1658) and *Elena* (1659), and 450 ten years later for *Eliogabalo*.[3] To be sure, in 1658 Cavalli was practically at the apex of his career: in addition to holding the prestigious position of organist at San Marco, he was the best-known composer of opera not only in Venice, whose theaters he had supplied regularly for twenty years, but in all of Italy. His Venetian works had been performed throughout the Italian peninsula, and he had fulfilled at least two

---

2.   The earnings of librettists were augmented by the largesse of dedicatees; see Bianconi and Walker, "Production, " 238 n. 75. Aureli signed a contract with Faustini to adjust the text of *Eliogabalo* for Cavalli, agreeing to divide the gift he received for the dedication with Faustini; and since Faustini was paying printing and binding costs, he would also receive half of the profits from sales. This must have been exceptional, since it had to be spelled out in a contract (*b.* 194: 31; transcribed in Brunelli, "Angustie," 335). In 1686 dedication gifts for three operas (paid to both composer and librettist) cost Duke Ernst August 266 Thalers, equivalent to the cost of employing the duke's ten Venetian gondoliers for a month (Bianconi and Walker, "Production," 269 n. 150).

3.   See the Cavalli-Faustini contracts, Appendix IIIA.2–4.

"foreign" commissions: *Orione* for Milan (1653) and *Hipermestra* (1654, performed 1658) for Florence.

Other composers were paid considerably less. Ziani, for example, earned only 50 ducats for *Annibale in Capua* in 1660, even though this was his fifth opera for Faustini. And he complained later in a letter to the impresario that it was 70 ducats lower than normal.[4] His fee rose considerably in the following years—to 200 ducats for *Amor guerriero* in 1663 and *Doriclea* in 1666—but it remained much lower than Cavalli's usual fee, which he resentfully noted in the same letter as 100 *dobles*. Granting that Cavalli's fee was justified by his reputation, Ziani nevertheless regarded his own poor salary as an insult. He was even more irritated, however, by the disparity between his salary and those of the singers: "If you pay singers 150 and 100 *dobles* [=440–660 ducats] apiece, why shouldn't a famous composer, who is the prime vehicle for putting on an opera, be given at least as much or only slightly less?" (Appendix IIIA.5c).[5] Ziani also complained that he was paid less well than Cesti. As for Cesti, we do not know how much he actually received for his Venetian operas, but he himself noted jealously that he earned less than Cavalli.[6]

High as it may have been for a composer, Cavalli's fee nevertheless compared unfavorably with those of the singers. In 1666 a salary of 300 scudi (or 450 ducats, exactly Cavalli's fee) was considered standard for an average female singer,[7] but most singers' salaries were higher. The best-paid singer in *Antioco*, for example, "Signora Girolama," received 750 ducats, nearly twice as much as the composer,[8] while several others earned only slightly less than he did (only one earned much less, 50 ducats).[9] Naturally singers were paid according to their rank or importance in the opera, but the wide discrepancies in their earnings also depended in part on geographical considerations. Most were imported from outside Venice, and their fees were calculated to include traveling and living expenses. Thus, Signora Girolama's 750 ducats included round-trip

4. Letter of 25 July 1665 (*b.* 188: 82), Appendix IIIA.5b; excerpted in Giazotto, "La guerra dei palchi," 503–4. His low salary may reflect the fact that he was otherwise unemployed and possibly desperate, having left his position as *maestro di cappella* at Bergamo in 1659.

5. See Bianconi and Walker, "Production," 225 n. 50. In bringing up this comparison, Ziani notices a certain inequity in the hierarchy. If anything, though, he has underestimated singers' salaries for this period. On his appreciation of Cavalli, see his letter of 9 May 1666 (Appendix IIIA.11b).

6. Letter of 21 June 1665 (*b.* 188: 119, 137); partially transcribed in Giazotto, "Cesti," 498–99: "mi

vedro costretto di dover poi pubblicare molta maggiore la ricognizione ad esempio del Signor Cavalli."

7. See Brunelli, "Angustie," 327. Letter from Carlo Mazzini to Faustini (*b.* 194: 144): "non è dovere che loro vadino se non hanno 300 scudi per una, sì come si costuma a dare ad ogni benche ordinaria virtuosa."

8. The "prima donna" of *Elena*, Lucietta Gombo detta Widmann, earned 650 ducats; see her contract with Faustini, dated 18 July 1659 (*b.* 194: 10); transcribed in Brunelli, "Angustie," 314. The figures for *Antioco* are drawn from Faustini's account book in *b.* 194: unnumbered.

9. See Bianconi and Walker, "Production," 224.

travel between Rome and Venice; a singer from Turin was paid slightly more than one from Milan; and the singer who earned only 50 ducats was a Venetian.[10]

Salary was obviously a matter of prestige, among singers as well as between singers and composers. Apparently, singers borrowed from certain establishments were paid more than others. In one revealing instance, a singer agreed to take a lower salary as long as he could say that he had earned a higher one, "in deference to the prince he serves" ("in riguardo al principe che serve").[11] Singers' fees seem to have varied from theater to theater, too, and were probably inflated as the result of competition among the various houses. S. Salvatore apparently paid more than SS. Giovanni e Paolo and often succeeded thereby in luring singers away from the older establishment. In 1665 a singer at the latter (Cavagna) complained to Faustini that another (Ciecolino) was earning more at S. Salvatore than he was at SS. Giovanni e Paolo; Cavagna was eventually offered even more than that by S. Salvatore, but affirmed his loyalty to Faustini by agreeing to accept the same fee he had earned in 1662.[12]

These figures indicate that in the 1660s singers were generally considered on a par with the most important composer of the time: exceptional ones were paid more, ordinary ones about the same or perhaps slightly less. But this parity did not last. Although the composer's fee—at least Cavalli's—remained fairly constant over the decade 1658–68, those of the singers rose substantially. If Signora Girolama earned almost twice as much as the composer already in 1658, another, Giulia Masotti, one of the most sought-after singers of the period, earned four times as much in 1666 (at SS. Giovanni e Paolo), and nearly six times as much in 1669 (at S. Salvatore).[13] Cavagna, who had earned 350 ducats in 1658,

10.   Girolama's contract is spelled out in *b.* 188: 22 (see Rosselli, "From Princely Service," 25 n. 86). Her salary also included living expenses, but not lodging, while in Venice, which was calculated in addition; Cavagna, from Turin, received 350 ducats, Manni, from Milan, 332. The Venetian was Antonio Formenti. The comparative figures are sometimes misleading since it was not always clear when fees included traveling expenses and when they did not. Moreover, the currencies in which fees are quoted, even within the same document, are not always the same, nor are the conversion rates always given. In general, I have adopted the conversion rates listed in ch. 6, n. 105, above.

11.   The singer was the castrato Rascarini, according to another castrato and fellow employee of the duke of Savoy, Giovanni Antonio Cavagna or Cavagnino (letter to Faustini of 27 June 1665 [*b.* 188: 117]).

12.   Letter of 3 April 1665 (*b.* 188: 98–99). As we remember, 1665–66 was a particularly difficult year for Faustini, in part because of competition from S. Salvatore. Cavagna seems to have been part of the problem. In both 1666 and 1667 he played off his obligations to his patron, the duke of Savoy, against his contract with SS. Giovanni e Paolo; see Rosselli, "From Princely Service," 7, 9–10, esp. n. 32.

13.   In 1666 the figure was 380 *doble*, or 1,600 ducats, not including living expenses; for living quarters Giulia had her choice of Faustini's or Giovanni Grimani's house. Her contract with Faustini (*b.* 194: 110) is transcribed in Brunelli, "Angustie," 332. In 1669 it was 15,920 lire (about 2,500 ducats or 1,200 scudi). This figure may have included 200 scudi for traveling expenses (see I-Vcg, Archivio Vendramin, cited in ch. 6, n. 105, above). The figures in the Vendramin archives are especially confusing; some are clearly in ducats, others in *doppie* or *doble*.

considered 600 ducats too little in 1665.[14] And Ciecolino, whose salary of 150 *doppie* (more than 600 ducats) had been considered enviably high in 1665, was offered 250 in 1670, but refused to sing for less than 300, or twice as much as his salary four years before.[15] In addition to increasing in proportion to other expenditures, then, singers' salaries, unlike those of composers, evidently kept rising with their reputations. They must have continued their disproportionate escalation, since twenty years later the prima donna Margherita Salicola earned 500 *doppie*, or 19,000 lire, for her performance in *Penelope la casta* (1685).[16] This figure, we should note, equaled the total cost of producing *La maga fulminata*, the second Venetian opera, in 1638.[17]

Their comparatively high and rapidly rising salaries only confirm what is clear from other evidence—namely, that the singers had come to be regarded as the most important members of the operatic hierarchy. Impresarios devoted a major portion of their energies to securing casts, dispatching agents to attend performances all over Italy to report on particularly outstanding singers. By the late 1660s it was understood that a singer could make or break an entire season, almost regardless of the opera being performed. That point is brought home rather explicitly in a report to Faustini from one of his agents, the librettist Pietro Dolfin, who had attended a performance in Verona by Anna Venturi, a singer Faustini had recently engaged:

> The opera pleased me in all its aspects (considering that I was in Verona), but Signora Anna, in the part of Romilda displeased me so greatly that she became insupportable, not only to me but to everyone who was with me, and they encouraged her every time she came on stage with everyone present greeting her every time she came on stage with what one might call a beating with the cackles they made during her trills and *cadenze*. She is so odious that she alone is enough to cause an opera to fail, and so disgraceful that the other singer from Mantua and [the one called] Orsetta seem like angels. (Appendix IIIA.9)[18]

14. See letter of 3 April 1665 (*b.* 188: 98–99) mentioned in n. 12 above.

15. Letter from Massi to Johann Friedrich, 17 November 1670 (vol. 4, no. 627, f. 211ᵛ): "è qua Ciecolino al quale hanno offerte dobble 250, ma lui non vuol recitare se non sono almeno 300."

16. Bianconi and Walker, "Production," 276. We do not know what happened to composers' salaries in this period. The last documented salary for Cavalli is 450 in ducats in 1668 at SS. Giovanni e Paolo (Appendix IIIA.4).

17. The figure given for *La maga fulminata* was 2,000 scudi (Appendix I.3b). Although we do not have precise figures for inflation, we do know that ticket prices remained the same throughout this period, and that the salaries of the instrumentalists did not change appreciably; see ch. 6, n. 105, above.

18. See Brunelli, "Angustie," 325–26. There were many complaints about Anna Venturi, who was the wife of the tenor, Carlo Righenzi. Sebastiano Cioni, another singer, accused her of singing out of tune, insisting that she did not fit in any company of virtuosi, and predicting that Cavagnino, supposedly hired to sing with her, "resterà molto scandalizzato quando si vedrà a petto una donna tale" (*b.* 188: 129–30). Marc'Antonio Cornaro, one of Faustini's chief associates and agents, assured him that she would never make it in Venice: "certo certo non farà riuscita in Venezia" (letter of 6 November 1665 [*b.* 188: 207]).

And he concluded, naturally, by strongly urging Faustini not to hire her. Evidently, it was her trills and cadenzas that bothered Dolfin the most. In the end, Faustini received so many complaints about her that he broke their contract, settling accounts with her in two installments.[19]

Singers were frequently credited with primary responsibility for the outcome of an opera.[20] Poor singing was reportedly responsible for the failure of *Domitiano* (Noris/Boretti), an opera otherwise praised for the superior quality of its text and music, at SS. Giovanni e Paolo in 1673, while what was considered by some to be an inferior work of the same season at S. Salvatore, *Orfeo* by Aureli and Sartorio, was apparently rescued by an excellent cast, according to one account:

> Last night, the 30th of December, the opera at SS. Giovanni e Paolo, entitled *Domitiano* by Noris, opened, which was truly staged superbly, in a beautiful production, but so poor in singers that it is pitiful; aside from Signora Giulia [Masotti], no one can sing; to such a sorry state has opera in Venice been reduced. It's true that the S. Lucca [i.e., S. Salvatore] management, despite a ragged opera of Aureli's called *Orfeo*, because it has better singers, will triumph over the SS. Giovanni-Paolisti. (Appendix IIIB.13)

The particular stars were Gratianini, who made such a good impression that he was given the title role in the second opera of the season, *Massenzio*,[21] and Tonina, "marvelous of voice, exquisite, clever, and attractive for a Roman" ("di voce meravigliosa esquisita, furba, et attrattiva per esser Romana").[22] In fact, the failure of *Domitiano*, which in addition to its poor cast may have owed something to the death of its composer, Boretti, during the rehearsal period, was catastrophic for SS. Giovanni e Paolo: Grimani reportedly lost 3,000 lire that season. To make matters worse, one of the singers employed by the theater was shot and killed while riding in a gondola with four or five of his fellow singers.[23]

Actually, neither the verdict on the singers of *Orfeo* nor that on the opera as a whole was unanimous. One report described "Tonina," who played Euridice, as "divina," but the other singers as merely "ascoltabili"; one of them, a certain Pia, had so deteriorated since the previous year, particularly in the "crudeness" of her voice, that she made no impression at all.[24] Another report

19. On 7 February and 1 March 1666 (*b.* 194: 113; *b.* 188: 353).
20. According to a letter from Dolfin to Johann Friedrich of 19 December 1670 (vol. 2, no. 625, f. 409), the singers saved S. Salvatore from bankruptcy: "se la copia d'esquisiti cantanti non la sostenasse si sarebbe sin hora chiuso il Teatro."
21. Gratianini was the singer Beregan would be so anxious to hire for S. Salvatore in 1675 (Appendix

IIIB.24); see the letter from Dolfin to Johann Friedrich, 20 January 1672 [1673] (Appendix IIIB.16a).
22. Tonina is Antonia Coresi. Letter from Massi, 16 December 1672 (Appendix IIIB.9).
23. Letter from Massi to Johann Friedrich, 10 February 1673 (Appendix IIIB.21).
24. Letter from Dolfin, 23 December 1672 (Appendix IIIB.10).

noted the unfortunate absence of two singers, Lucretia and the castrato Lassi.[25] And still another (prejudiced) report criticized "the singer of Signor Leonardo Loredano," who replaced Lucretia for the third soprano role (Euridice's maidservant?) as "insoportabile."[26] As far as the opera itself was concerned, several accounts were quite positive, one of them considering it praiseworthy despite the fact that it was written by Aureli.[27]

The Prima Donna

The most impressive index of the singers' growing stature was their increasing influence on the works they sang. Roles had always had to be adjusted to fit their ranges and to show off their particular vocal strengths. But singers eventually became responsible for more profound changes that involved dramatic structure and even undermined the verisimilar balance and pacing that had been so carefully achieved between action and contemplation, between kinesis and stasis. Their gradual accrual of power is documented in their correspondence with impresarios, in remarks of librettists, and, most important, in the operas themselves.

Although the big jump in their earnings did not occur until the third decade of operatic activity in Venice, singers had manifested their influence on opera much earlier, actually after only the first few seasons. Composers, accustomed from the beginning to altering their scores to suit, seem to have taken their subservience to singers for granted; librettists, apparently, did not. On the contrary, in the absence of more direct documentation, their complaints about having to satisfy singers' whims are one of our chief sources of information on the subject.

A very early indictment of singer-power came from Ferrari on the occasion of a revival of his *Il pastor regio* in Bologna in 1641:

> Having to present my Maga fulminata and Pastor regio at Sig. Guastavillani's theater in Bologna, it was necessary, to please my friends and because of the whims of some of the singers, who are never satisfied, to add and cut some things from the works; thus you should not be surprised if you find them to be quite different from their first printing in Venice. (Appendix I.5b)[28]

---

25. Letter from Dolfin to Johann Friedrich, 30 December 1672 (Appendix IIIB.12).

26. "La putta protetta" of Signor Leonardo Loredan is mentioned in Dolfin's letters of 23 December 1672 and 20 January 1673 (Appendix IIIB.10 and 16). He expressed the fear that she would "spoil the other apples."

27. Letter from Massi of 27 January 1672 [1673] (Appendix IIIB.17).

28. Singers' exigencies may have been partly responsible for the changes perpetrated on *La finta pazza* when it was revived in Piacenza in 1644, about which Strozzi complained in the preface to his reprint of the same year (Appendix I.16e).

Giovanni Faustini, too, we recall, lamented the inordinate influence of singers quite early in his career—in his second libretto, *Egisto*, of 1643 (Appendix I.31a). Although Ferrari did not indicate precisely the kinds of changes his singers wanted, beyond the addition and cutting of unnamed passages, Faustini was quite specific. He had to add a mad scene for his protagonist. In his case, the reasons were clear: *La finta pazza*, the operatic hit of 1641, had made mad scenes de rigueur in any work that wished to compete with it.

The elevation of the mad scene to such importance in the early 1640s was in no small measure owing to the protagonist of the original mad scene, Anna Renzi, the singer who has appropriately been called the first diva of the Italian operatic stage.[29] It exemplifies the impact of the singer beyond the confines of the single work, an impact that extended to the establishment of a convention and, ultimately, to the development of opera itself.

The career of Anna Renzi, while symptomatic of maturing opera in seventeenth-century Venice, was also quite unusual. Although she was but the first of a long line of star singers, she was uniquely implicated in the development of the genre itself. (I have already touched upon her significance in chapter 4.) Renzi was created, in part, by the press; her undoubtedly extraordinary performances were aggrandized by Incognito publicity as part of their general, successful campaign to establish opera as a going concern in Venice. Owing to this, we know exactly which Venetian operas she appeared in and which roles she sang; more significant, we know a good deal about her voice and personality, her art of singing as it was viewed by her contemporaries—and even her appearance (fig. 25).

She began her career in Rome, performing in operas at the house of the French ambassador, and was brought to Venice late in 1640 to create the role of Deidamia in *La finta pazza*, the inaugural opera at the Novissimo. We first learn about her presence in Venice from the libretto of that opera, an Incognito publication of 1641, whose author, Giulio Strozzi, describes her rather conventionally as "a sweet siren who gently ravishes the souls and pleases the eyes and ears of the listeners" (Appendix I.16c). The city of Venice, Strozzi continues, should be forever grateful to Francesco Sacrati, composer and musical director of *La finta pazza*, for having brought Renzi from Rome. Indeed, Sacrati undoubtedly composed the role of Deidamia specifically for Renzi, fitting it to her particular talents as he did for other singers. Renzi's powers were extolled further and somewhat more explicitly in the *Cannocchiale per la finta pazza* of the same year, in which she was praised for being "as valorous in action as she is

29.   Sartori, La prima diva della lirica italiana: Anna Renzi." For Renzi's career, see also Bianconi and Walker, "Dalla 'Finta pazza,' " 417–18; Thomas Walker, "Anna Renzi," *New Grove*, 15: 745–46; and Sergio Durante, "Il cantante: Aspetti e problemi della professione," *StOpIt*, 4 (Turin, 1987): 361–64.

ANNA RENTIA ROMANA

★

Intima si cantum simulat præcordia mulcet,
Ipsam animam sensim si canit Anna rapit.

Jacobus Pecinus Venetus faciebat Ven:

25. Portrait of Anna Renzi, from *Le glorie della signora Anna Renzi romana*
(Venice: 1644). Venice, Fondazione Scientifica Querini Stampalia.

excellent in music" (Appendix I.17e). She starred in subsequent productions at the Novissimo and SS. Giovanni e Paolo, most notably, from our point of view, as Ottavia in *L'incoronazione di Poppea* in 1643.[30]

We would know very little more about her were it not for a special volume published in her honor in 1644, yet another product of the Incognito press. *Le glorie della signora Anna Renzi* (fig. 26) is by Giulio Strozzi and is dedicated to Filiberto Laurenzi, Renzi's teacher ("Chirone della Signora Anna").[31] It features a large number of encomiastic poems by various authors, many of them represented only by their initials or academic names, but identifiable as Incogniti.[32] The poems describe her performances in various roles. One of them, an "idilio," much longer than the others, narrates her career, opera by opera, in rich detail, concluding with a vivid description of her portrayal of Ottavia in *L'incoronazione di Poppea*.[33]

The most revealing part of the book, however, is the lengthy laudatory essay by Strozzi himself that opens the volume. Filled with enthusiasm for her style of singing, Strozzi's observations are extraordinarily informative, especially in comparison to the usually perfunctory remarks about singers found in similar volumes—most of them earlier, such as those dedicated to Isabella Trevisan, Leonora Baroni, and others[34]—and to the comments found in libretto prefaces. Most descriptions of singers involve single adjectives and adverbs, strung together in a variety of lengths. The preface to *Andromeda*, for example, set a standard for variety of single-adverb description of the singers: they sang "mirabilmente," "divinamente," "squisitamente," "egregiamente," "gentilissimamente," "celestamente," "gratiosamente," and "soavissimamente."

In terms quite unlike those of conventional flattery, Strozzi describes Renzi's actions on stage, the movements of her body, arms, face, and voice, with the attentiveness of a stage director. Interestingly, he begins by remarking on the passion and verisimilitude of her acting and diction:

30. At the Novissimo, Renzi played Archimene in *Bellerofonte* (1642), Deidamia in *Deidamia* (1644), and a leading role (Rodopea?) in *Ercole in Lidia* (1645), in which she was admired by John Evelyn. At SS. Giovanni e Paolo, she was Aretusa in *La finta savia* (1643) and starred in *Torilda* (1648) and *Argiope* (1649). In *Poppea* and *La finta savia* she was joined by Anna Valeri, as Poppea and Aventina; see Osthoff, "Laurenzi," 174–75. Other singers in *La finta savia* included Stefano Costa as Numitore, and "Corbacchio," or Rabacchio. Osthoff ("Neue Beobachtungen," 135–37) suggests that Renzi also sang the role of Ottavia in the Naples production of *Poppea*, a role that was expanded by the addition of a new solo scene; but documentary evidence for her presence in Naples is lacking.

31. Laurenzi's mythological title comes from a poem addressed to him by Francesco Maria Gigante at the end of the Strozzi volume. Laurenzi's career is outlined in Osthoff, "Laurenzi," 173–94, and, more recently, in Magini, "Indagini," 514–53.

32. The authors represented in this volume are identified, some more accurately than others, in Sartori, "La prima diva"; see also Osthoff, "Laurenzi," 177.

33. This text is given in ch. 12 below. A number of the shorter poems in the volume are addressed to her in the role of Ottavia.

34. See, for example, the *Applausi poetici alle glorie della Signora Leonora Baroni* (Rome: Costazuti, 1639, 1641) and *Echi poetici all'armonia musicale della signora Isabella Trevisani romana* (Bologna: Ferroni, 1648).

LE
GLORIE
Della Signora
ANNA RENZI
ROMANA.

IN VENETIA, M.DC.XLIV.

Appreſſo Gio: Batiſta Surian. Con Licenza de'Sup.

26. *Le glorie della signora Anna Renzi romana* (Venice, 1644), title page.
Venice, Fondazione Scientifica Querini Stampalia.

> The action that gives soul, spirit, and existence to things must be governed by the movements of the body, by gestures, by the face and by the voice, now raising it, now lowering it, becoming enraged and immediately becoming calm again; at times speaking hurriedly, at others slowly, moving the body now in one, now in another direction, drawing in the arms, and extending them, laughing and crying, now with little, now with much agitation of the hands. Our Signora Anna is endowed with such lifelike expression that her responses and speeches seem not memorized but born at the very moment. In sum, she transforms herself completely into the person she represents, and seems now a Thalia full of comic gaiety, now a Melpomene rich in tragic majesty. (Appendix II.2a)

Only then does Strozzi arrive at her vocal qualities—obviously in service to her acting, a contributory aspect of her theatrical presence. He enriches his description with some rare practical advice on the care of the voice, which reveals the extent of his own experience with singers: "She has a fluent tongue, smooth pronunciation, not affected, not rapid, a full, sonorous voice, not harsh, not hoarse, nor one that offends you with excessive subtlety; which arises from the temperament of the chest and throat, for which good voice much warmth is needed to expand the passages, and enough humidity to soften it and make it tender" (Appendix II.2b).[35] The specifics of her vocal technique come next, along with appreciation of her resilient professionalism, her ability to create her role anew night after night: "She has felicitous passages, a lively trill, both double and *rinforzato*, and it has befallen her to have to bear the full weight of an opera no fewer than twenty-six times, repeating it virtually every evening, without losing even a single carat of her theatrical and most perfect voice" (Appendix II.2c). Strozzi then moves to a consideration of Renzi's mind, and her off-stage personality:

> I have considered, aside from her physiognomy, that in her that maxim holds true according to which for the formation of a sublime spirit these things are needed, namely, great intellect, much imagination, and a good memory, as if these three things were not contradictory and did not stand in natural opposition when found in the same subject: all gifts of generous nature, who only rarely knows how to unite these three qualities, as if in a republic, no one holding the majority. Signora Anna, of melancholy temperament by nature, is a woman of few words, but those are appropriate, sensible, and worthy for her beautiful sayings, of the reward of praise. (Appendix II.2d)

Finally, he describes her way of studying human behavior as a means of understanding and portraying characters: "She silently observes the actions of others, and when she is called upon to represent them, helped by her sanguine temperament and bile, which fires her (without which men cannot undertake great things), shows the spirit and valor learned by studying and observing.

---

35. Giulio Strozzi's experience with singers must have been nourished by his relationship with Barbara Strozzi, the chamber singer and composer whom he adopted, and whose career he encouraged in many different ways. See Rosand, "Barbara Strozzi," esp. 257–58.

Whence the heavens were propitious in providing her with such an admirable and singular intelligence" (Appendix II.2e).

This description offers a convincing portrait of a consummate singing actress, one who clearly imposed her own personality on the roles she sang. Renzi was the kind of singer who, in addition to realizing Strozzi's model of the ideal performer, almost certainly would have appealed to Monteverdi, notorious for his concern with singers' interpretation of his roles. The chief evidence for that concern is a series of letters of 1627 to Alessandro Striggio the Younger, focused on *La finta pazza Licori*, a libretto by Giulio Strozzi.[36] Indeed, Strozzi's appreciation of dramatic singing, expressed so eloquently in his encomium to Anna Renzi, may have been part of Monteverdi's legacy to him.

Renzi and the Novissimo flourished together; their successes were closely linked, the one nourishing the other. But her influence lasted well beyond the Novissimo years. She appeared regularly at SS. Giovanni e Paolo until 1649.[37] And after two brief periods in Innsbruck and one in Genoa, she returned to Venice to sing for Marco Faustini at S. Apollinare in 1655 and at S. Cassiano in 1657.[38] At S. Cassiano, as Damira in Aureli's and Ziani's *Le fortune di Rodope e Damira*, Renzi closed her memorable Venetian career as she had opened it, portraying a "finta pazza."

All of Renzi's roles were clearly tailor-made for her by composers and librettists intimately acquainted with her abilities. Her presence was intrinsic to the works she sang, her special talents part of their conception. She was active at a time when mutuality in operatic creation was still possible, when text, musical setting, and performance were inextricably linked from the start. Renzi's connections with the composers and librettists who wrote for her were unusually close. Sacrati evidently knew her in Rome before he engaged her for the Novissimo; Laurenzi was her teacher well before he composed her role in *La finta savia*;[39] Busenello and Fusconi were her friends, the latter even serving as the executor of her will.[40] She was the dedicatee of several publications, including Fusconi's libretto of *Argiope*,[41] yet a further affirmation of her close ties with the makers of operas.

---

36. These letters are discussed in ch. 11 below.

37. Her last documented performance at SS. Giovanni e Paolo was in *Argiope*, in 1649.

38. She sang in the Genoese productions of *Cesare amante* and *Torilda* in 1653; see Bianconi and Walker, "Dalla 'Finta pazza,' " 442 n. 257. Renzi's appearance in *Eupatra* at S. Apollinare in 1655 has recently been documented by Glixon and Glixon, "Marco Faustini."

39. She had already performed in Laurenzi's *Il favorito del principe* in Rome in 1640; see Magini, "Indagini stilistiche," 515–16.

40. I-Vas, Notarile, Testamenti chiusi, atti Beaciani Francesco, test. n. 69; see Bianconi and Walker, "Dalla 'Finta pazza,' " 417 n. 157.

41. The dedication was dated 1645 (Appendix I.28). Another work dedicated to Renzi was *Canzonette amorose a doi, e tre voci per cantar' sopra il clavicembalo, o tiorba del Signor Horatio Tarditi, raccolte d'Alessandro Vincenti dedicate alla molto illustre, e virtuosissima signora la Signora Anna Renzi* (Venice: Vincenti, 1642). Her name was undoubtedly invoked chiefly as a means of attracting special attention to the volume.

Fortunately, the music for four of Renzi's roles has survived, representing the work of four different composers: that of Deidamia from Sacrati's *La finta pazza*, Ottavia from Monteverdi's *L'incoronazione di Poppea*, Aretusa from Laurenzi's *La finta savia*, and Damira from Ziani's *Le fortune di Rodope e Damira*.[42] From that music and from Strozzi's description of her singing, it is clear that Renzi's vocal style was not primarily showy or virtuosic—though she certainly possessed flexibility of voice. Her roles called for dramatic intensity above all. Her interpretations, then, would have enhanced the effect of opera as drama; opera was not yet the vehicle of vocal pyrotechnics it was soon to become. And yet, for all that she evidently lived her role, became her character, this first prima donna could not help but focus attention on the performer per se. If, as a public representative of the Novissimo company, she shared the responsibility of having helped to establish opera as a genre, she also shared the responsibility for its subsequent development, in particular the meteoric rise of the virtuoso.

Renzi's career essentially established the model of the prima donna (and *primo uomo*), in which the character becomes the vehicle for the singer. As she was with "la finta pazza," so other singers too became associated with particular kinds of roles. The hunchback stutterer featured in several operas between *Torilda* (1648) and *Erginda* (1652) may well have been played by the same singer.[43] Carlo Righenzi, a famous "buffo" tenor, who sang the role of Gelone in *Orontea* in Venice in 1666, created similar roles in other operas.[44] And there are many records of librettists as well as composers having conceived of certain roles, even whole operas, with specific singers in mind. Thus in 1673 Dolfin

42.   Fourteen of Laurenzi's arias from *La finta savia*, a pasticcio, have survived—because they were published in *Arie a una voce . . . dal Sig. Filiberto Laurenti* (Venice: Magni, 1643). They include nine for Aretusa. See Osthoff, "Laurenzi," 173–94.

43.   The best-known hunchback stutterer in opera was probably Demo in *Giasone* (1649). The singer may have been Girolamo Antignati, who is identified as the stutterer in one edition of *la Torilda, Drama per i moderni teatri* (Venice: Valvasense, 1648). This particular print concludes with seven pages of "Applausi dispensati in recita musicale della Torilda" (114–20). Antignati, in the role of Nuto, the stutterer, is one of the singers honored by poetry. For some later character-actor associations, see Bianconi and Walker, "Production," 249, esp. n. 104; also appendix 1. For a list of singers compiled from Francesco Caffi's unfinished "Storia della musica teatrale," see Worsthorne, *Venetian Opera*, appendix 4. The cast lists for the Teatro S. Giovanni Grisostomo, showing a number of regulars, which are also based on Caffi's manuscript, are recorded in Saunders, "The Repertoire," appendix F; in appendix G, Saun-

ders provides an alphabetical index of singers, derived largely from those lists.

44.   Righenzi, tenor, and sometime poet and impresario, may have appeared in Ferrara in *Egisto* in 1648 (cf. Bianconi and Walker, "Dalla 'Finta pazza,' " 401 and n. 101); he was certainly active as an impresario in Bologna, where he signed several librettos, including that of *La virtù de' strali d'Amore* (1648); he sang in a number of operas in Florence from 1657 to 1663, including *Il potestà di Colognole* (1657), *Il pazzo per forza* (1658), *La serva nobile* (1660), *Ercole in Tebe* (1661), and *Erismena* (1661). He also appeared in Milan in *Crispo* (20 December 1663), *La farsa musicale* (9 February 1664), and *Xerse* (5 August 1665), and in Turin in *Xerse* (1667). He was responsible for the revisions of the text of at least one opera performed in Verona, Minato's and Cavalli's *Xerse* (1665) (in which his wife had made such a poor impression on Dolfin; see n. 18 above). He also acted as an agent for Marco Faustini during the 1660s (there are communications from him in *b.* 188 and *b.* 194).

reported that he had been so impressed by the performance of a particular singer, Gratianini, that he was inspired to write a libretto especially to accommodate him.[45] Singers even took on public associations with their roles, often becoming known by the characters' names (as had, traditionally, *commedia dell'arte* actors). Anna Maria Sardelli was called Campaspe, the role she played in *Alessandro vincitor di se stesso* (Venice, 1651); Giulia Masotti was La Dori, after her role in Cesti's eponymous opera (Venice, 1663, 1667, and 1671); and Giovanni Francesco Grossi was regularly called Siface after his appearance in that role in a Roman production of *Scipione affricano* (Minato/Cavalli) in 1671.[46]

The publicity surrounding Anna Renzi may represent something of a special case, forming part of a more general campaign on the part of the Incogniti, but the kind of singer-worship implicit in Strozzi's *Le glorie della Signora Anna Renzi* reached exaggerated proportions by the 1670s and 1680s, when "Applausi," usually broadsides containing celebratory poems, were literally showered on the prima donna at curtain calls. This procedure is vividly described by the Parisian diplomat Saint-Disdier, a keen observer of Venetian society: "The partisans of these admirable singers have quantities of sonnets printed in their honor, and during the applause that these singers inspire, they shower thousands of them from the heights of Paradise, filling the loges and parterre."[47]

Like Anna Renzi, subsequent prima donnas enjoyed close relationships with librettists, composers, and impresarios, but they were generally of a more idiosyncratic and personal nature. Such relationships were encouraged by the long-standing practice whereby singers traveling to Venice, along with their entourages—including relatives and servants—were customarily lodged at the house of the impresario or theater owner. Arrangements like these were usually spelled out in singers' contracts, as in that between Faustini and Giulia Masotti in 1666.[48] Such temporary arrangements evolved into more permanent ones, in

45. Letter of 3 February 1673 (Appendix IIIB.18). Gratianini played the title role in *Massenzio* (Bussani/Sartorio) at S. Salvatore and also performed in *Orfeo* in the same season at the same theater (see Appendix IIIB.16a). This was the same singer that Beregan later wrote about so enthusiastically to Johann Friedrich, expressing his desire to hire him before any other management could get its hands on him (letters of 20 September and 17 November 1675, Appendix IIIB.24, 25).
46. See Michael Tilmouth, "Grossi," *New Grove*, 7: 743–44.
47. "Les Partisans de ces admirables Chanteuses font imprimer quantité de Sonnets à leur louange, et parmy les acclamations qu'elles s'attirent en chantant, ils en sement des milliers du haut du Paradis, et en remplissent les Loges, et le Parterre" (Saint-Disdier, *La Ville et la République de Venise*, 423

[*Quellentexte*, ed. Becker, 85]). A manuscript of one such "Applauso" by Pietro Dolfin for Tonina Coresi, who played Euridice in Sartorio's *Orfeo* (1672), is preserved in the Hannover documents (vol. 2, no. 625, f. 443): "Il merito della Sig.^ra Tonina Coresi che nell opra dell'Orfeo rappresenta la parte d'Euridice Sonnetto Venetiano gettato l'ultima recita dà palchi dà chi puo l'A.V. imaginarsi." For an indication of the nature and number of such broadsides in late seventeenth-century Italy, particularly Rome, see Lowell Lindgren and Carl B. Schmidt, "A Collection of 137 Broadsides Concerning Theatre in Late Seventeenth-Century Italy: An Annotated Catalogue," *Harvard Library Bulletin* 28 (1980): 185–233.
48. See n. 13 above. The contract (*b.* 194: 110) is summarized in Brunelli, "Angustie," 332 . The item in question is no. 3: "Haverà essa Sig.^ra Giulia l'alloggio e le spese del vitto, o in casa di detto Sig.

which singers actually became part of the households of their aristocratic patrons, who vied with one another for such prized possessions—another phenomenon deemed worthy of mention by Saint-Disdier:

> When a new young woman appears in Venice to sing at the opera, the principal noblemen make it a point of honor to become her protector, especially if she sings very well, and they spare nothing to that end. A Cornaro is arguing over one of them with the duke of Mantua, and he finally wins her. Victory belongs to him who offers the richest presents, even though the charms of her voice are not accompanied by those of beauty.[49]

Patrons acted as agents for their charges, negotiating contracts as well as providing for their other immediate needs. In the case of particularly young singers, their protectors sometimes arranged for additional vocal training. Their ties were so close that a singer was often referred to by the name of her patron.

The various ramifications of these relationships are illustrated by the case of Lucretia "Dolfin," a singer who came to live in the house of the librettist/impresario Pietro Dolfin sometime in the 1669–70 season. Referring to her variously as "my pupil" (*mia allieva*), "my new singer" (*mia nuova cantatrice*), or even "the child of my house" (*la putta di mia casa*), Dolfin took complete charge of her career. He exercised strict control over her contracts, refusing to allow her to sing in one instance because the part offered was smaller than those she was accustomed to, and in another because the other members of the cast were not of sufficient calibre.[50]

That Dolfin's interest in Lucretia exceeded the purely professional is evident from a story involving Nicolò Beregan, another aristocratic librettist and frequent patron of singers. It is told in one of those letters to Duke Johann Friedrich of Brunswick and Lüneburg from which we have been quoting:

> This most noble sphere [of women] is admirably adorned by the most beautiful young singer that Signor Pietro [Dolfin] keeps under his wing. She, having achieved excellence from continued study and from her most sonorous voice, is the beloved idol of the same Signor Pietro, whose jealousy is amazing. That lusty old wolf, our own Signor Nicola, has already eyed her, but Signor Pietro, who is nervous, won't have him around. Having become aware of this, Signor Nicola, in order to spite

---

Faustini, overo in casa Grimani, secondo la sodisfattione di lei, e ciò per il tempo che si trattenerà in Venetia."

49. "Dés qu'il paroist à Venise une nouvelle fille pour chanter à l'Opera, les principaux Nobles se font un poinct d'honneur d'en estre les Maistres, si elle chante fort bien, et ils n'épargnent rien pour en venir à bout: un Cornaro en disputa une avec le Duc de Mantoue, et l'emporta en fin, c'estoit à qui luy feroit de plus riches presens, bien que les charmes de sa

voix ne fussent pas accompagnez de tous ceux de la beauté" (*La Ville et la République de Venise*, 423 [*Quellentexte*, ed. Becker, 85]). The various kinds of patronage enjoyed by singers of this period are discussed in Rosselli, "From Princely Service," esp. 7–12.

50. According to letters from Dolfin and Beregan to Johann Friedrich, of 23 and 30 December 1672 respectively (Appendix IIIB.10, 13). See n. 26 above.

Signor Pietro while he was writing the drama for SS. Giovanni e Paolo, tried to insinuate himself into that theater, and he was so successful that he managed to get
himself appointed librettist for this year. Signor Pietro, who had already composed
the drama, was stuck, and had to put up with the jest of Signor Nicola, who, working quickly on the Grimani brothers, succeeded in officially obliging Signor Pietro
to make available for the season, along with other famous singers, his own sweet-
heart. Whence Signor Nicola is happy because with this pretext he is obliged to
graze with his eyes in the theater, and even to insinuate himself into it, if possible.
But the other one saw through this amorous trickery and resolved not to leave his
beloved, not even for a moment. Thus, if Your Lordship is in Venice for carnival,
you will enjoy watching two dramas at the same time, one in music, the other in
prose, one with the actions in silent pantomime, the other with notes and voices.
Thus between these two farces you will have double pleasure, seeing feigned passions represented in the one, real love in the other. (Appendix IIIB.3)[51]

Thus were the public and personal dimensions of operatic life in Venice
confused, to the amusement of avid observers. Indeed, opera seems to have
offered itself as an appropriate model for comprehending reality. This account
suggests the degree to which opera had taken hold of the Venetian imagination.
In terms of our present discourse, the story illustrates the power of the virtuoso;
for in this case, a singer—unwittingly, to be sure—actually determined the
choice of a libretto for a particular season.

Primi uomini ed altre

It was more customary for prima donnas (and *primi uomini*) to wield their power
more directly. Even during Anna Renzi's generation, singers had begun to exert
their influence in specific ways that overlapped the responsibilities of their partners in operatic creation. Sometimes this was actually encouraged by the
librettist—and condoned by the composer. As early as 1640, a rubric in the
margin of Ferrari's libretto for *Il pastor regio* gave a singer permission to insert
an aria "at her pleasure";[52] a singer in *Artemisia* (Minato/Cavalli, 1656) was
directed to change a certain aria every night;[53] and in *La costanza di Rosmonda*
(Aureli/Rovettino, 1659), a singer was invited to insert "un aria francese."[54]

---

51.   Dolfin seems in fact to have been displaced as
librettist by Beregan, whose *Heraclio*, set to music by
Ziani, was the second opera of the 1670–71 season at
SS. Giovanni e Paolo (the first was *Semiramide*
[Moniglia-Noris/Ziani]).   Dolfin's   *Ermengarda*,
which had been performed in 1669–70 with Sartorio's music, was his last libretto for the Grimani
brothers. He discusses *Ermengarda* in a letter to Johann Friedrich of 26 December 1669 (see Appendix
IIIB.2).
52.   *Il pastor regio* (Venice: Bariletti, 1640), 21: "Qui

canta la fanciulla [Psitide] un aria a bene placito."
53.   *Artemisia* (Venice: Giuliani, 1656), 3.9, p. 58,
next to Erillo's aria, "Chiedete, e sperate": "quest'aria ogni sera sarà variata."
54.   *La costanza di Rosmonda* (Venice: Valvasense,
1659), 1.1, for the slave, Vespino. His introductory
recitative, which ends "Nel linguaggio natio [clearly
French] vo procurar almeno / La fatica addolcir col
canto mio," is followed by the rubric "Quivi zap-
pando la terra canta un'aria francese." It was apparently not that unusual for an "aria francese" to be

Since neither text nor music was provided, in all three of these cases the singer was evidently expected to supply the aria from his or her own personal repertoire. This practice of inserting arias ad libitum, sporadic at first, reached a climax toward 1700 with the so-called *arie di baule* (literally, baggage arias) so ridiculed by Benedetto Marcello in *Il teatro alla moda*.

On other occasions the impact of the singers extended well beyond the insertion of songs, to impinge upon the turf of composer, librettist, and even impresario. It could influence such matters as the choice of the opera to be performed, the cast, the composer,[55] the dramatic structure of the libretto—length of scenes, proportion of aria to recitative—as well as the size (and shape) of their own individual parts. Evidence of performers' attempts to exert their influence permeates the correspondence between Marco Faustini and the various singers with whom he negotiated contracts. Singers frequently expressed interest in the other members of prospective casts, making suggestions for inclusions as well as exclusions. Sebastiano Cioni, for example, refused to appear with Anna Venturi because she sang out of tune;[56] Giuseppe Donati hoped that Gabrielli had not been engaged, because of personal incompatibility: "his personality doesn't mesh with mine because I want to live in peace and quiet and don't want fights or dissension and that requires agreement and not malice and envy."[57] Another singer would not sign a contract because the rest of the cast was poor;[58] while two others refused to appear together because they shared a protector.[59]

One of Faustini's regular singers, the castrato Antonio Cavagna, was particularly exigent about his participation in the 1666 season. Having looked over the part he was scheduled to sing, possibly that of Artabano in *Doriclea*, he did not hesitate to request two additional arias. Furthermore, he informed Faustini peremptorily that he expected to sing in Roman pitch (i.e., a whole tone lower than Venetian pitch): "I intend to sing with the instruments tuned to Roman

---

inserted by a comic character. For a similar rubric in a Roman edition of Minato's *La prosperità di Elio Seiano* (1672), for which the text and music of the piece have actually been reconstructed, see Monson, "Aelius Sejanus," 19–21.

55.   Cesti claimed at least once that a certain singer had agreed to participate in a production only if he, Cesti, wrote the music (see letter to Beregan of 12 July 1665 discussed in Schmidt, "*Tito* Commission," 451; text given in Giazotto, "Cesti," 499: "il signor D. Giulio s'era disposto di recitar nell'opera, col solo riguardo ch'io vi facevo la musica mentre per altro egli mostravasi lontanissimo da questi impegni"). In another instance a singer (Formenti) and the prince of Bavaria, his patron, were reportedly willing to agree

to a contract only because Sartorio would be writing the music (letter from Dolfin to Johann Friedrich, 15 April 1672; see Appendix IIIB.7).

56.   Letter of 6 November 1665 (see Appendix IIIA.8).

57.   "Il suo umore non si confa punto con il mio perche voglio vivere quieto e non voglio liti ne discordie perche ciò ricerca unione e non malignità et invidie" (letter of 5 July 1667; in Brunelli, "Angustie," 339, mentioned below, n. 68]).

58.   Letter of 17 October 1665 (see Appendix IIIA.6).

59.   Documented in Massi's letter of 20 October 1673 (see Appendix IIIB.22).

pitch [*al giusto tono di Roma*] and not as I did in *Statira*, in *Teseo*, and in other works, because it is better for my voice, and I say it now so that no one will complain about it later" (Appendix IIIA.6).[60] In a subsequent reference to his role, Cavagna complained about the incoherence of one of the arias, refusing to sing it unless it was reset by the composer: "As for the *arietta* 'Dolce foco,' it isn't very good to sing because it is very mannered and beggarly, and unless you get him [the composer] to write new music for it I won't sing it at all" (Appendix IIIA.7). He was concerned, too, about his role in *Alciade*, originally scheduled for the 1666 season, but postponed until 1667. He objected to his costume and to potential comparison with the stars of the production; he also complained about the range of one of his arias:

> Only two things frighten me: one, to have to sing with the mask of a Moor, something I no longer do, and which I didn't understand until after I read the third act; the other, to have to sing between two angels, Signora Antonia and Signora Giulia. The *canzonetta* that you enclosed, excuse me, but who wrote it? It is for contralto, not for soprano, and is very different from Signor Ziani's style, so I will be content with singing the duet and that Signora Giulia sing her song alone. (Appendix IIIA.16)[61]

"La Signora Giulia," to whom Cavagna referred, was the same Vincenza Giulia Masotti whose salary was so high in 1669 and who was distinguished as the only competent singer in *Domitiano*.[62] Praised by another singer, Nicola Coresi, as "the most superb woman in the world,"[63] and much sought after by Faustini and other impresarios, she was constantly wary of her status: her part had to be the largest in the opera, even if there were two major female roles. It was actually written into her contract that she have "la parte prima" and that she be able to examine her parts before agreeing to do them.[64] Because the former stipulation could not be fulfilled in the case of *Alciade* (another prima donna, Antonia Coresi, having already been engaged for the other major female role), Masotti's agent suggested substituting a different opera!

60. Among other things, this letter, of 17 October 1665 (*b.* 188: 212), informs us that Cavagna sang in *Statira* (Busenello/Cavalli, 1655) and *Teseo* (Piccoli/Ziani, 1658), which we would not otherwise know. An earlier letter, of 10 October (*b.* 188:211), suggests that Cavagna's role in *Doriclea* was Artabano, a king. But kings were rarely portrayed by castratos; in Cavalli's setting Artabano was a tenor.
61. This may refer to the aria he sent back for rewriting; see below. (The role in question was probably that of Megaristo, Alciade's servant.)
62. See Beregan's letter of 30 December 1672

(Appendix IIIB.13); also Dolfin's of 30 December (Appendix IIIB.12), and Massi's of 9 and 16 December (Appendix IIIB.8, 9).
63. "la più superba donna che sia al mondo" (letter of 19 October 1665 [*b.* 194: 48]).
64. She had to promise not to allow the scores out of her hands in Rome (*b.* 194: 109, item 6): "Che per accertarsi d'essere favorita delle prime parti vuol vedere avanti di partir di Roma tutte due l'opere che si hanno da rappresentare, assicurando però che non saranno vedute, ne usciranno dalle sue mani" (from Brunelli, "Angustie," 331).

> She told me that an excellent solution would be to present Argia or Alessandro instead, and that when it was resolved to present Argia, Signora Giulia would agree that Apolloni, the author of the opera, could add and cut all the scenes that he wished. . . .I say only that changing the opera would dispel all doubts about the part, all the more since Signora Giulia is very inclined toward it, having the example of what happened in Rosilena. (Appendix IIIA.13)[65]

In the end, of course, she got more than she asked for, when the opera in which she had achieved her greatest success, *Dori*—rather than either *Argia* or *Alessandro*, which she had suggested—was revived at the last minute.[66] She must have repeated her earlier success in *Dori* since the opera was revived for her yet again, in 1671.[67]

Not all singers wanted large parts, however. Giuseppe Donati agreed to sing the title role in *Meraspe*, but asked that it not be too difficult. He also suggested as a possible substitute for *Meraspe*, in case Faustini was looking for one, Cesti's *Semiramide*.[68] When his role arrived, he found it too high and asked permission to have it adjusted, though in a faintly apologetic tone, repeatedly assuring Faustini that he would do nothing without the composer's permission:

> It has to be altered in some places so as not to spoil the composition; without [the original composer's] agreement, I will not touch it; but since it is a thing of little importance, I believe he will be satisfied, it being necessary only at cadences that I make sure the voice part remains fixed and, even without moving the basso continuo, that it does not relinquish its normal harmony. But without his approval I don't intend to put my hands where they don't belong. (Appendix IIIA.18)

Of all the operas cast by Faustini, *Meraspe* seems to have caused the most trouble. Donati was not the only one who tried to discourage Faustini from producing it.[69] The tenor Nicola Coresi, husband of the much more sought-

---

65. Faustini's angry response to Giulia's implied criticism of his brother's librettos is preserved in the draft of a letter (*b.* 188: 294–95) already quoted (see Appendix IIIA.14). Apparently *Rosilena* (Aureli/Rovettino), the "new" opera in which Giulia had appeared several seasons earlier (1663), had been a failure, whereas she had been a great success in *Dori*, a revival, in the same season (*b.* 188: 345).

66. Readied for performance in only eight days (according to the publisher's preface, dated 16 January 1667), it shared the season with *Alciade*, replacing *Meraspe*, which was postponed to the following season (see ch. 6, p. 194, above).

67. See letter from Massi to Johann Friedrich, 26 December 1670 (Appendix IIIB.5). This third revival evidently cemented her connection with the opera, since she was subsequently called by the nickname "La Dori" (see Appendix IIIB.9).

68. Letters from Rome of 5 and 27 July 1667 (*b.* 188: 172, 174). It is interesting to note how fre-

quently substitutes were being proposed for Giovanni Faustini's librettos (see ch. 6, n. 98 above). Apparently Faustini did consider *Semiramide*, but fruitlessly, as indicated by the preface to the work that was performed instead, a revival of *Giasone* (1666): "Ti preparavo la Semiramide Opera del Signor Moniglia, ma questa gran Regina . . . non ha per adesso volsuto arischiarsi fin dall'Asia trasportarsi Pelegrina nell'Adria col seguito d'infinite disaventure." *Semiramide*, though in a setting by Ziani, was eventually performed in 1670–71, unsuccessfully, according to a letter from Massi to Johann Friedrich, 12 December 1670 (vol. 4, no. 627, f. 217): "Si e principiato a recitar a S. Zuanipolo la Semiramide, opera non riuscita, e poco lodata, ancor che li musici siano esquisiti." In this case, apparently, unlike *Orfeo*, good singers could not save a poor opera.

69. In a letter of 4 June 1667 (*b.* 188: 163); see Brunelli, "Angustie," 336 n. 53.

after Roman singer Antonia Coresi, also attempted to talk Faustini into a substitution. When Faustini refused, he suggested alterations in the structure of the
libretto, specifically the shortening of some scenes: "And if you are absolutely
resolved to do *Meraspe*, at least let it be altered, as you once promised me, so
that those scenes are cut which are so long that the same characters remain on
stage forever."[70]

Coresi continued his criticism of the libretto in a subsequent letter, invoking
the concept of "Venetian brevity": "It seems to me that to begin with there are
long dull speeches [*gran dicerie*], as in the fourth scene of the second act where
it says 'Piange Olinda,' which is the kind of boring speech that can never sound
beautiful, and that, as you know, must be shunned in Venice" (Appendix
IIIA.17a).[71] He then proceeded to attack the music:

> In the second scene of act three there is a song [*canzona*] that begins "Ride il core,"
> which is worthless, having already been seen by the best musicians of Rome. Your
> Lordship should have it changed or else I will, my chief purpose being that my wife
> bring herself honor this year; however, she must be satisfied that the part is altered
> where necessary, and thus Your Lordship will be well served and we satisfied. (Ap-
> pendix IIIA.17b)

He concluded by asking Faustini to have Cavalli alter one of his wife's arias to
the specifications of her range: "Please do me the favor of presenting the enclosed to Sig. Francesco Cavalli, to whom I indicate my wife's range so that he
can accommodate her" (Appendix IIIA.17c).[72]

In a subsequent letter, Coresi again asked to have the aria "Ride il core"
rewritten (by Pallavicino this time), preferring, he said, to have all the music by
the same composer rather than having it done in Rome.[73] But this time Faustini
responded that Pallavicino was out of town and asked Coresi to have a new
piece supplied of his own choice.[74] Finally, in another letter, Coresi questioned
rather unsubtly the completeness—that is, the size—of his wife's part: "In act
3 she has nothing but the second and third scenes, so that it seems impossible
to me that there is nothing more. You should check to see if you haven't left
out a scene, because she ends with that duet that says 'Vincerai, vincerò,' and
then the *canzonetta* that concludes the opera" (Appendix IIIA.21).

70. "E se ella assolutamente risolve di fare il
Meraspe, almeno faccia accomodare, conforme una
volta mi disse, e non vi sieno quelle scene così lunghe
che li medesimi personaggi stanno sempre in scena"
(letter of 4 June 1667 [*b*. 188: 163]).

71. Coresi's criticisms are very much like Ziani's
regarding *Doriclea* (Appendix IIIA.5), which probably referred to monologues like Doriclea's in 3.1.
The monologue is illustrated in ch. 12 below (example 80).

72. Brunelli, "Angustie," 336, n. 54. Coresi was
mistaken about the composer of *Meraspe*; it was Pal-

lavicino rather than Cavalli, a mistake he corrected in
a subsequent letter. Cavalli actually did sign a contract with Faustini only ten days later, on 23 June
1667, to write an opera for the 1667 season, to be
present at rehearsals, and to make the necessary additions, alterations, and cuts, but the opera was to be
Eliogabalo (*b*. 194: 50); Brunelli, "Angustie," 334; see
ch. 7, n. 35, above.

73. Letter of 30 July 1667 (*b*. 188: 165). He seems
not to have appreciated the fact that many operas
were pasticcios!

74. Letter of 6 August 1667 (*b*. 188: 168).

The comments of the solicitous husband were not always negative, however. He was apparently quite taken with the first act of his wife's part in *Massenzio* in 1673, according to a report by Dolfin (Appendix IIIB.11c). Nor was Coresi's concern unselfishly limited to his wife's roles. Indeed, he continually complained about the size and content of his own, clearly secondary, parts as well. When Faustini attempted to alleviate one complaint by adding the prologue to his role in *Meraspe*, Coresi refused it: "Regarding the prologue that Your Excellency sends me, there are four short words; however, I pray you with all my heart not to make me do it, because, not having ever done a prologue, I don't want to start now, and besides, this is a part that anyone can do" (Appendix IIIA.15).[75] He was thoroughly insulted by the part Faustini sent him the following year, and promptly returned it with a petulant note, explaining that he never would have accepted it had he known how small it was going to be:

> I received the part of Caristo, which I send back to Your Excellency because it is not a part to send someone like me . . . and if I accepted the part last year it was because you showed me only a single scene, but now that I have seen the whole thing, I have discovered how little you esteem me. If you show this part around Venice, you will see that it is a part to be given to the lowest of musicians. (Appendix IIIA.19)

Two weeks later, having cooled off slightly, Coresi explained further some of his objections to the part. As it turned out, it was not so much its small size as the fact that it lacked an aria: "I have always told you that I don't care to perform if I do not have a part worthy of me, and for a part to be worthy it is not enough that it have poetry of high quality, since even a thousand lines of brilliant repartee would not make a good part, something you either don't know or don't care to know, if they didn't include a bit of song."[76]

In 1667 it was predictable that any role without an aria, even a minor role, would be difficult to cast. Ever since the beginning of opera in Venice, but especially after 1650, the value of arias—and their proportion with respect to recitative—had been rising steadily. As early as 1645, Faustini had added arias (among other things) to his *Doriclea*, and every new version of an old opera had to display at least some new arias.[77]

---

75. Letter of 3 November 1666; Brunelli, "Angustie," 333–34. Two weeks later, when he agreed to do it after all, he admitted that he just had not wanted to bother changing costume (letter of 17 November 1666 [*b*. 188: 36]).

76. Letter of 27 August 1667 from Rome (*b*. 188: 166); Brunelli, "Angustie," 338. *Meraspe*, as we know, was more than a decade old, and so undoubt-

edly had many fewer arias than singers expected by 1667. Cf. Appendix IIIA.5a for Ziani's comments on this subject.

77. See ch. 6, pp. 188–90, above on *Eritrea* and *Eupatra*. Occasionally only second strophes were added, although at other times, second strophes were cut; see ch. 7, n. 30, above.

Librettists deplored this increase because it tended to trivialize their poetry and undermine the integrity of their dramas; and they were quick to place the blame on a combination of public taste and singers' whim. Aureli summed it up with a characteristic pun in the preface to his *Le fatiche d'Ercole per Deianira* of 1662: "I know I have expended more than one breath in claiming that I write out of mere whim, and to obey him who commands me, and not out of ambition to immortalize myself with those works, which, in being composed entirely in music, have no foundation other than air [*l'aria*]" (Appendix I.46a). The public is the scapegoat in Aureli's more explicit preface to *Claudio Cesare* ten years later: "I present to you my Claudio, richer in songs and *ariette* than in incident. It is enough to say that it is a *dramma per musica*. What can be done? If these days the whim of Venice wishes it thus, I shall try to satisfy their taste" (Appendix I.50a). But Aureli as well as other librettists regularly blamed the singers too, as in this epilogue to the same libretto: "Have sympathy for the difficulty composers face these days in being able to satisfy not only the numerous strange whims of this city, but also the moods of the singers" (Appendix I.50c).

Singing and/or Acting

Aureli's complaints were symptomatic of criticism of the time; by the late seventeenth century, opera was generally regarded as having drowned in a flood of *canzonette*. But it was a flood that had begun much earlier, whose origins were in a sense implicit in the genre from the very beginning. The development of opera in Venice relied on the approval of an unusually heterogeneous audience; it was easy for such an audience to focus on the singers as the most obvious representatives of the genre—which had been encouraged by the early publicity surrounding Anna Renzi. And focus on the singers was guaranteed by arias that served as a kind of musical spotlight, as show-stoppers that allowed singers to stand still and demonstrate their vocal prowess to an admiring, responsive audience.

I am speaking here about a different kind of singer from Anna Renzi, one defined essentially by voice rather than by acting abilities. During the earlier history of opera, a dichotomy was recognized between singers who acted and actors who sang. The first Orfeos, Jacopo Peri and Francesco Rasi, were of the former type. The first Arianna, Virginia Andrea Ramponi, was of the latter. The dichotomy—and the possibility of interchange—is explicit in the case of Monteverdi's *Arianna*: although eventually performed by an actress, the title role had been conceived for a singer. The anonymous author of *Il corago*, writing probably in the 1630s, confronted the issue directly:

> Above all, to be a good singing actor, one must also be a good speaking actor, from which we have seen that some who had particular grace in reciting were marvelous when they also knew how to sing. On this subject, some question whether one should choose a not bad musician who is a perfect actor or an excellent musician who has little or no talent for acting, the case being that excellent singers, no matter how cold their acting, gave greater pleasure to those few who know a great deal about music, whereas the normal theater audience received greater satisfaction from perfect actors with mediocre voices and musical ability. Therefore, since the composer has to distribute the parts appropriately and use everyone to perfection, he will try to imitate as far as possible the excellent singers, but putting those who are bloodless and stiff at reciting in parts that are not very active and surrounding them by many stage props, as in clouds and other machines in the air, where not much expressive movement or acting ability is required. (Appendix II.1e)

Once again, Anna Renzi offers a standard of measurement. Although she had effectively initiated the age of the prima donna, appreciation of her performances had emphasized her abilities as an actress. She was a singer who found most vivid expression in the *stile recitativo*. Her style—*recitando* rather than *cantando*—was predicated on the centrality of recitative, of dramatic verisimilitude. It is difficult to think of her having demanded more arias; indeed, she established her reputation in operas that had relatively few of them. But operatic style changed around her. After the middle of the century she was undoubtedly still making the same impression, but she was singing more arias. Her younger contemporaries and successors benefitted from her achievement and stature, though they did not share her background and training. Whereas she had put herself at the service of the drama, they were more self-centered, exigent, and ornamental. Their arias resembled the scenic distraction that the author of *Il corago* had recommended as compensation for poor or unconvincing actors. Arias focused the audience's attention on the singers—attention stimulated by, and in turn causing, a variety of off-stage intrigues.

The rapid increase in the number and size of arias—which began to gather momentum during the course of the 1650s, accelerated during the 1660s, and culminated in the following two decades—is the most obvious sign of the ascent of the singer, *qua* singer, to first place in the operatic hierarchy. Originally merely the mouthpiece of the librettist and composer, the singer gradually wrested control of opera from their hands. In order to satisfy performers' demands for arias, librettists were forced to rewrite their dramas. Composers had to accommodate to these demands either by writing extra arias or by seeing other composers called in to do so, their music being cut and replaced to satisfy the whims of the singers. By the end of the century, the original relationship among the makers of opera had been thoroughly transformed. For their adoring audience, the singers had grown to personify opera itself.

9

• • •

Gran dicerie e canzonette: Recitative and Aria

As the geographical and creative separation between composers and librettists increased, the language of their communication with one another became, by necessity, more explicit and efficient. Librettists' texts differentiated more clearly between aria and recitative verse and composers' responses became more predictable. Aria and recitative attained their own distinct, and mutually exclusive, identities.

The Florentine Background

At the beginning of its development, operatic poetry was relatively undifferentiated. The first librettists, borrowing from the pastoral, chose *versi sciolti* for their dramas, a meter characterized by freely alternating *settenario* and *endecasillabo* lines, unrhymed or rhymed irregularly. Lacking formal restraints or conditions, the pastoral meter suited the open-ended *stile recitativo* devised by the Florentine composers for the clear and immediate communication of dramatic poetry in music. The *stile recitativo* was relatively unencumbered by textural, harmonic, or melodic responsibilities. It could thus aspire to the condition of speech, ebbing and flowing in response to the changing emotional temperature of a dramatic text. Governed by the form and sense of poetry rather than by principles of musical structure, it was an effective means of communication that did not strain verisimilitude.

The musico-dramatic continuity promoted by *versi sciolti* was occasionally interrupted by an unusual textual passage that attracted special attention to itself by virtue of its structure: a succession of tightly rhymed lines, perhaps, or a passage in a new meter. Inspired by some unusual event or emotion in the drama, such passages frequently gained further emphasis (and greater differentiation from their context) through immediate repetition of their distinctive verse structure, thereby producing a strophic form. Self-contained forms like these suggested a contrast in musical setting, a more closed, structured treatment in which the freedom of speech would yield to the control of musical form. But any kind of musical structure, especially strophic repetition, interrupted the dramatic continuity and undermined the verisimilitude that the *stile recitativo* had been developed to sustain. The use of the same music for two different passages of text was inimical to a style in which music sought to respond directly, newly, and uniquely to specific words. It broke the illusion of spontaneity: people did not speak in strophes, or in rhyme, or in meter, let alone in melody—at least not under ordinary circumstances.[1]

But not all circumstances in opera were ordinary. Some explicitly called for music. In addition to dialogue, operas (like plays) contained songs, choruses, and dances. For such occasions, musical organization was not merely possible; it was necessary. There were other instances, too, not so obvious, in which organized music was more effective than ordinary speech for projecting character and situation: moments of great emotional intensity—elation or despair—often needed a special outlet, the heightened emphasis provided by song.[2]

Formal music, then, might temporarily slow the dramatic action by stepping outside its flow, but by that very separateness it could also serve the action by summarizing, punctuating, or commenting on it; or it could carry the action on a new level, that of music rather than speech, as songs and choruses. Early librettists reserved textual formality for just such occasions: where it could contribute directly to the drama without seriously disrupting or undermining its verisimilitude.[3]

1.   Caccini implicitly recognized the aesthetic contradiction embodied in strophic settings when he defended the "arie" in his *Le nuove musiche* not for their expressive verisimilitude but for their pleasing qualities, terming them good for relieving depression ("per sollevamento tal volta degli animi oppressi"). The contradiction is spelled out in *Il corago*, the treatise already mentioned on the production of theatrical spectacles, operatic and spoken, dating from about 1630. Its anonymous author mentions lack of verisimilitude as one of the chief inconveniences ("incomodità") of arias (Appendix II. 1a).

2.   In ch. 5 of his *Trattato della musica scenica* (1640) (*De'trattati di musica* [Florence: A. F. Gori, 1763], 2), part 2, "La commozione d'affetto in scena richiede il canto, e non il parlare quieto," Giovanni Battista Doni argues that certain vehement emotions require musical expression because even in speech such emotions cause the voice to be heightened in a way that approaches song: "Ma che gli affetti veementi siano potenti incentivi della Musica, e che dove si rappresentano in Scena, ivi massimamente si richiegga la melodia, da quello si può conoscere, che natural-mente sospendendo la voce, come si fa ne' lamenti, minacce, giubbili, ed altre umane passioni, ci avviciniamo al canto." In chs. 10 ("Che la Musica Scenica si può perfezionare assai") and 11 (". . . In che differisca lo stile Recitativo dal Rappresentativo, ed Espressivo"), Doni speaks of the necessity of variety in dramatic music and argues that, although verisimilitude of expression is necessary (the style closest to speech), so is beauty (a more songlike style). His three styles of theatrical music, the narrative, the expressive, and the madrigalistic, are discussed in Hanning, *Of Poetry and Music's Power*, 72–73.

3.   On the function of formal music in early opera, see Pirrotta, *Music and Theatre*, ch. 6 ("Early Opera and Aria"), 269; also id., "Monteverdi and the Problems of Opera," *Essays*, 249–50. Pirrotta developed a special critical vocabulary that elegantly isolates and distinguishes three ways of thinking about the music of early opera. "Recitar cantando" (sung recitation), an expression frequently used by the early theorists of opera themselves, refers to their basic intention to imitate speech in song, Doni's *stile recitativo*. The reverse, "cantar recitando" (singing in a

The composer's response to the librettist's formal hints depended, of course, on his interpretation of their function. If actual songs or choruses were indicated, he usually chose aria style, a measured, lyrical setting that unfolded according to musical rules. In more ambiguous cases he might try to minimize, undermine, or counteract their static implications by using a declamatory vocal style or writing a strophic recitative only loosely structured by means of a repeated bass; or else he could use a combination of styles, reserving lyricism perhaps just for the conclusion of such a passage. Finally, he might choose to ignore the librettist's formal hints altogether, or, conversely, to impose a formal structure where the libretto had none, in response to his own interpretation of the drama.

The composer's confirmations of the librettist's formal structures, even if they resulted in more highly organized music, were as consonant with the precepts of the *stile rappresentativo* as was open-ended recitative. Both kinds of response were governed by the words; the aim of both was the same: to interpret, reflect, or project the drama through its poetry. The *stile rappresentativo* of the Florentines, then, actually covered a wide spectrum of music, ranging from free, speech-imitating recitative to more formal, self-contained, and musical moments. This wide spectrum eventually separated into recitative and aria.

Closed forms, for solo as well as chorus, internal as well as external to the drama, were built into opera from the very start. Orpheus, the quintessential operatic hero, sang his way into Hades, proving that music could promote action. To be sure, singing was his natural mode of expression. Yet even for him librettists and composers distinguished between speech and song. He achieved his goal specifically through a formally organized song: Rinuccini's "Funeste piaggie" comprises three irregular stanzas linked by a refrain set lyrically by Peri; Striggio's "Possente spirto" is a six-strophe text in *terza rima*, which Monteverdi cast as an increasingly elaborate series of strophic variations. Despite—or actually because of—their form, Orfeo's songs satisfied the requirements of verisimilitude.

Even in operas not featuring musicians, however, music per se could serve the drama. Songs were a frequent ingredient of early opera, as they had been in the pastoral. Nymphs and shepherds could sing in musical plays because they sang in nature. Likewise, divinities could express themselves in any form they chose; their songs actually helped to distinguish them from ordinary mortals.

---

recitational manner) refers essentially to non-operatic music with representational or dramatic intentions, e.g., Caccini's "madrigali." Finally, the fanciful "cantar cantando" (singing in a singing man-

ner) describes those operatic moments that do not pretend to be speech at all but assert themselves as song—Orfeo's "Vi ricorda o boschi ombrosi," for example.

Verisimilitude was not an issue for the inhabitants of Olympus or Arcadia.[4] Yet, even more realistic opera plots concerned with human characters, such as *Arianna* in Mantua and those involving biblical and chivalric heroes introduced in Rome during the 1620s and 1630s, contained a variety of closed forms. These were mostly choruses and dances, though there were some solo songs as well — especially for servants and other minor characters, but occasionally also for protagonists. If they did not always serve specific dramatic functions as songs, they at least did not interrupt the action.[5]

Venetian Conservatism

By 1640, Roman librettos distinguished quite clearly between aria and recitative verse; they contained numerous closed forms (suggesting musical interruptions), especially strophic ones, in a wide variety of meters. By comparison, early Venetian librettos are remarkably undifferentiated in poetic style and exceptionally poor in arias. The first two Venetian librettos, Ferrari's *Andromeda* and *La maga fulminata*, contain very few hints of anything but recitative. Interruptions of the open-ended recitative style in *Andromeda* are limited to five strophic texts, all but one for chorus (i.e., structurally external to the dramatic narrative), and a few rhymed quatrains or otherwise patterned metric arrangements for Venere and Astrea that suggest some kind of closed setting. In *La maga fulminata* the number of such indications is somewhat greater, particularly in connection with the comic nurse, Scarabea. Her speeches are quite highly organized in meter and rhyme, lending them a sing-song quality that tends to emphasize their humor. In addition, strophic texts are provided for several characters, including the god Mercurio and the enchanted mortal Pallante. While strophic arrangements of *settenario* and *endecasillabo* lines are the most common formal signals, both librettos also contain individually closed sections marked by unusual metric organizations involving regular successions or alternations of short and long lines, many of them in *versi misurati*.[6]

---

4. This is another point made explicit in *Il corago*; see Appendix II.1b.

5. The author of *Il corago* assumes the appropriateness of singing for comic characters when he suggests that their music imitate as closely as possible the vulgar inflections characteristic of their speech (Appendix II.1d). On operatic songs, see Pirrotta, *Music and Theatre*, 273–75. Murata, *Operas for the Papal Court, 1631–1668*, 185–86, mentions three different, characteristic arias in *Sant'Alessio* (1632), which introduce, summarize, and divert dramatic

action without interrupting it. She discusses Roman aria texts in general on 179–80, and 184–88; see also Silke Leopold, " 'Quelle bazzicature poetiche, appellate ariette': Dichtungsformen in der frühen italienischen Oper (1600–1640)," *Hamburger Jahrbuch für Musikwissenschaft* 3 (1978): 101–41.

6. For example, Scarabea's solo scene, 1.4, is marked by three passages of alternating rhyming lines of four and ten syllables interspersed with more usual *versi sciolti*.

In light of the progress toward integration of music and drama in the works of his predecessors to the south, Ferrari's reticence toward closed forms is somewhat surprising. Lacking Manelli's settings, we cannot be sure, but the musical highlights of both operas seem to have been the choruses—or "madrigali," as they were called in the descriptions published soon after the works were performed. Apparently, the question of verisimilitude, rendered less urgent through experience in Florence and Rome, was still an issue in Venice. Perhaps this was because of the wider social range of the opera audience there, an audience that may have been less willing and able than its courtly counterparts in central Italy to suspend disbelief for entertainment's sake.[7]

Elaborate scenery and, of course, mythological plots should have helped to diffuse the need for strict verisimilitude or at least have expanded its limits. But, as I suggested earlier, perhaps even more than for the aristocratic Medici and Gonzaga audiences, satisfied by implicit connections between opera and classical drama, for Venetian *hoi polloi* identification with the actions on stage was a prerequisite for the appreciation—and success—of a work. Plays with songs, *commedie*, had been the usual fare of Venetian audiences during the early years of the century, and they provided the standard for verisimilitude in its early operas.

The absence of firm poetic distinctions between recitative and aria (and the limited number of arias) in early Venetian librettos may also be the result of another, quite opposite, influence, that of the academic librettists, who, as we have seen, took control of opera in Venice during its crucial formative period— the first decade. It was they who felt the pressures of classical precedent most strongly; and, aside from Ferrari's first two librettos, it is their texts that adhere most closely to notions of propriety that frequent arias would have violated. To be sure, whereas the problem of verisimilitude was attenuated considerably in mythological or magical contexts, it was especially troublesome in librettos that dealt with more realistic, historical subjects—subjects that the academic librettists introduced quite deliberately in their attempts to emulate the classical dramatists.[8]

---

7. The author of *Il corago* expresses his faith in the effect of repeated exposure to opera on the ability of the audience to suspend disbelief: "con il tempo il popolo s'avvezzarebbe a gustar ogni cosa rappresentata in musica" (p. 64).

8. This was another problem anticipated by the anonymous author of *Il corago*, who advised the would-be musical dramatist to choose subject matter distant from the present, either from mythology or biblical history (Appendix II.1c).

Monteverdi and His Collaborators

Among the academics, perhaps the most ascetic of all early Venetian librettists when it came to arias was Giacomo Badoaro. His initial entry into the operatic field, *Il ritorno d'Ulisse*, was written for Monteverdi and performed in 1640.[9] It is cast primarily in *versi sciolti* and provides few clues as to where a composer might have halted the recitative flow to write an aria. We are at an advantage here, however, with respect to Ferrari's librettos, because we have Monteverdi's score, which, while fundamentally in recitative, is surprisingly rich in lyrical moments—though these do not always qualify as full arias. The inspiration for these moments can usually be traced to subtle formal hints in the libretto, passages of text that are more highly organized than those around them. Quatrains or sestets may be structured by means of regular rhyme or repeated meter: a group of four *settenari*, perhaps, or a succession of six regularly rhymed alternating *settenari* and *endecasillabi*. While such metric organization suggests musical closure, it does not insist upon it—in fact, the rhyme is never that tight; sometimes a group of *endecasillabi* remains ambiguous because the rhymes are so far apart. Badoaro almost never used *versi misurati*, which would automatically distinguish themselves from recitative poetry. However subtle the librettist's formal suggestions might have been, Monteverdi nearly always capitalized on them.

Only on three occasions are Badoaro's formal hints unambiguous. His libretto contains three strophic texts, which Monteverdi set as strophic variation arias. Badoaro's conservative use of strophic form, in only these three instances, confirms his belief in the need for verisimilitude. Each of the three texts—and, by extension, Monteverdi's aria settings—is dramatically justified. In each case, the formal structure enhances the drama rather than undermining it. Melanto, a simple servant girl flirting with her lover, sings the first of them; the second is sung by Minerva, a goddess in disguise—and therefore doubly exempt from normal rules of behavior; and Iro, the parasite, a ridiculous comic character whose appetite is as peculiar as his manner of speech, sings the third.

Although Monteverdi's score is filled with lyrical, or arioso, expansions, the composer nevertheless seems to have wanted more structure than the libretto provided, and often edited Badoaro's text accordingly. His intervention is notable in three of the most intensely emotional moments of the drama, all of them marked by the presence of refrains. In one of them, in act 1, scene 9, where Ulisse finally recognizes that he has returned to Ithaca, Monteverdi converted

---

9.   This date is discussed in ch. 3, n. 36 above.

an exceedingly amorphous text into what almost amounts to a strophic aria, utilizing two irregularly spaced refrain lines (italicized) to mark the opening and closing of each strophe. Badoaro's text reads as follows (example 1):

O fortunato Ulisse,	*O happy Ulysses*
Fuggi del tuo dolor	Flee from the old error
L'antico error;	Of your sorrow;
Lascia il pianto,	Let be your weeping:
Dolce canto	A sweet song
Dal tuo cor lieto disserra;	Unleash from your glad heart;
Non si disperi più mortale in terra:	*Let mortals of this earth cease from despairing.*
O fortunato Ulisse.	*O happy Ulysses.*
Dolce vicenda si può soffrir,	Sweet vicissitudes one may suffer—
Hor diletto, hor martir, hor pace,	Now delight, now martyrdom, now peace,
hor guerra,	now war;
Non si disperi più mortale in terra.[10]	*Let mortals of this earth cease from despairing.*

Monteverdi expanded the two refrain lines enormously through textual and musical repetition so that they take up most of the aria; then, despite their unequal length, he treated the penultimate line of each "strophe" similarly, using the same extended melisma for "lieto" and "guerra." Inspired by Badoaro's refrain as well as by the expressive content of Ulisse's words, which actually invite song ("dolce canto . . . disserra"), Monteverdi's lyrical setting effectively changes not only the weight but the form of the text.

In another highly dramatic moment toward the end of the opera (3.8), where Ericlea wrestles with herself about revealing Ulisse's identity to Penelope, Monteverdi turned an irregular, 24-line text into a refrain form comprising four unequal sections of nine, four, five, and six lines, each closing with a *sententia* of self-justification (italicized) (example 2):

(1) Ericlea, che vuoi far,	Ericlea, what will you do,
Vuoi tacer ò parlar?	Will you be silent, or speak?
Se parli tu consoli,	If you speak, you will bring comfort,
Obbedisci se tacci	You obey if you are silent.
Sei tenuta à servir	You are compelled to serve,
Obbligata ad'amar	Obliged to love.
Vuoi tacer, ò parlar?	Will you be silent, or speak?
Ma ceda l'obbedienza alla pietà,[11]	But let obedience yield to pity.
Non si dee sempre dir ciò, che si sà.	*We must not always tell that which we know.*
RITORNELLO	RITORNELLO

10. The texts of *Il ritorno d'Ulisse* are taken from what appears to be the oldest of the nine surviving manuscript librettos, I-Vmc 564. These manuscripts (seven are listed in Osthoff, "Zu den Quellen," 69) reveal a number of metric irregularities. The libretto readings often differ from those in the manuscript score (A-Wn 18763). This particular aria text comes at the end of 1.8 in I-Vmc 564.

11. Note the slightly different readings in libretto and score.

(2) Medicar chi languisce, o che diletto	To minister to him who languishes, oh, what delight!
Mà che ingiurie, e dispetto	But what injury, what spite,
Scoprir gli altrui pensier	To disclose another's thoughts;
Bella cosa tal volta è un bel tacer.	*At times silence is golden.*
(3) È ferità crudele	It is ferocious cruelty
Il poter con parole	To be able with words
Consolar chi si duole, e non lo far;	To comfort the grieving, and not do it;
Mà del pentirsi al fin	But repentance, in the end
Assai lunge è il tacer più che il parlar.	*Far longer from silence than from speaking lasts.*
RITORNELLO	RITORNELLO
(4) Del secreto tacciuto	A fine secret wrapped in silence
Tosto scoprir si può,	Can always be disclosed later;
Una sol volta detto	Once said,
Celarlo non potrò.	Hide it I can no more.
Ericlea, che farai, taccerai tù,	Ericlea, what will you do, will you be silent?
Che in somma un bel tacer scritto non fù.[12]	*For, in sum, silence is not a law.*
RITORNELLO	RITORNELLO

By adding a ritornello after sections 1, 3, and 4, and setting each final sententious line to the same highly expanded music, the composer intensified the formal implications—and the affect—of Ericlea's monologue. The music concretely marks her progress from her initial vow of silence (sections 1 and 2), through ambivalence (section 3), to her decision to speak. As in Ulisse's aria, but by different means, Monteverdi superimposed a kind of strophic structure on the text and, far from sacrificing affective intensity, he increased it. The absence of a confirming ritornello after the second "refrain" (line 13) and consequent telescoping of sections 2 and 3 creates a sense of urgency that matches Ericlea's ambivalence.

Monteverdi's most impressive intervention, one that involved extensive text editing as well as reweighting, occurs in the very first scene of the opera, where he completely restructured Penelope's opening lament. He took a diffuse text of no fewer than 125 lines, in four uneven sections, that wandered rather aimlessly from topic to topic, and transformed it into a tripartite recitative of slowly building intensity, utilizing two irregular refrains provided by the librettist as structural pillars of the powerfully dramatic form. Intensified by the composer's restructuring, Penelope's torment resonates throughout the entire opera.[13]

Although written expressly for Monteverdi, Badoaro's libretto clearly did not completely satisfy the composer's lyrical impulse, his yearning for texts to set lyrically. In fact, as we have already noted, Monteverdi's alterations—

---

12. Note the slightly different readings in libretto and score.

13. See *Tutte le opere di Claudio Monteverdi*, ed. Gian Francesco Malipiero (Asolo, 1926–42), 12: 14–22.

which, in addition to those already mentioned, involved a variety of repetitions, single-line expansions, the creation of refrains, cuts, and so on—rendered the text virtually unrecognizable to its original author, or so Badoaro admiringly reported in a letter attached to one of the contemporary manuscript copies of the libretto.

> To the Most Illustrious and most Reverend Signor Claudio Monte Verde Great Master of Music: Not in order to compete with those talented men who, in recent years have publicized their compositions in the Venetian theaters, but to stimulate the imagination of Your Lordship to make known to this city that in warming the affections there is a great difference between a real sun and a painted one, I initially dedicated myself to compose the Return of Ulysses. . . . Now, having seen the opera performed ten times, always before the same [large] audience of the city, I can positively and heartily affirm that my Ulysses is more obligated to Your Lordship than the real Ulysses was to the always charming Minerva. . . . We admire with the greatest astonishment those rich ideas of yours, not without some perturbation, because I can no longer recognize this work as mine. (Appendix I.7a, c)

Monteverdi's powerful brand of editing is set into relief by comparison with an opera contemporary with *Il ritorno d'Ulisse*, Sacrati's setting of Strozzi's *La finta pazza*. To be sure, of the latter two collaborators, the librettist rather than the composer was the more experienced and more self-confident; certainly *La finta pazza* is a more effective and skillful text than *Il ritorno d'Ulisse*. It is also considerably richer in explicit invitations to lyricism, containing eleven formal texts, all but two of them strophic, many utilizing *versi misurati*, and nearly all of them dramatically explicable as actual songs.[14]

Whatever the reason, Sacrati seems to have accepted Strozzi's text quite willingly, satisfied to follow the libretto's lyrical implications without creating his own closed forms. He did sidestep Strozzi's structural directive in one case, however, setting each of the two quatrains (strophes) of Deidamia's aria "Verga tiranna ignobile" to different music, thereby creating an AB aria instead of a strophic one; and in two other instances (Achille's aria "Felicissimo giorno" in 1.3 and the Eunuch's "Serva, serva chi vuole" in 2.10) he restructured Strozzi's text slightly by bringing back the opening line (or lines) later in the form, creating a miniature ABA in the first instance and a rondo in the second (the composer's repetitions are in italics):

---

14. These figures are based on the original edition of the libretto (Venice, 1641). The recently uncovered score, which coincides with the libretto published in connection with a performance in Piacenza in 1644, has a few additional arias.

(1) Felicissimo giorno   Oh, most happy day,
    Se le nubi squarciate   If the clearing mists
    Di queste spoglie ingrate   Of these ungrateful clothes
    Faccia Acchille ad Acchille il suo ritorno.   Allow Acchille to return to himself,
    Felicissimo giorno.   *Oh, most happy day.*

(2) Serva, serva, chi vuole,   Let him who wishes be a servant,
    Ch'io non hò voglie ignobili,   For I have no such ignoble
      ed ancelle: and housemaidenly desires.
    Fuggono insin le Stelle   Even the stars flee
    Per non servir il Sole.   So as not to serve the sun.
    Serva, serva chi vuole,   *Let him who wishes be a servant,*
    Ch'io non hò voglie ignobili,   *For I have no such ignoble*
      ed ancelle: *and housemaidenly desires.*
    O che gentil solazzo   Oh, what gentle consolation
    Haver poco salario, e 'l padron pazzo.   To have a low salary and a mad master.
    Serva, serva chi vuole,   *Let him who wishes be a servant,*
    Ch'io non hò voglie ignobili,   *For I have no such ignoble*
      ed ancelle.[15]   *and housemaidenly desires.*

As for Strozzi's recitative verse, Sacrati emphasized a fair number of lines and couplets by arioso treatment, many of them significant with respect to the meaning of the work. In act 2, scene 2, for example, a particularly pregnant speech within an exchange between Ulisse and Acchille, although formally rather neutral, is nevertheless set lyrically. In response to Acchille's question as to whether he thinks that a young lover can change his affections and his beloved when he wishes, Ulisse responds:

Questo nò, no 'l dirò mai,   This, no, I'll never say it,
In amor io son costante,   In love I am constant,
Fede eterna le giurai,   I swore eternal faith
E morrò fedele amante.   And I'll die a faithful lover.

The exchange involves Ulisse's fidelity, and is probably an allusion to his role in *Il ritorno d'Ulisse* of the previous season.

In another instance, a six-line passage of Deidamia's in 3.2 that refers pointedly to matters outside the drama itself, namely to the theater management, is also set lyrically:

In vece d'herbe, e fiori, hoggi mi dà   In lieu of herbs, and flowers, today
E stecchi, e spine, e lappole[16]   Your paternity vouchsafes me
Vostra paternità?   Sticks and thorns and cockleburs?
Che padri ingannatori,   What deceiving fathers,
Pieni d'insidie, e trappole,   Full of wiles and traps,
Vivono in quest'età?   Has this age begotten?

15. The musical settings for these and other texts cited from *La finta pazza* may be found in *La finta pazza*, ed. Bianconi.

16. Lappoli was the leaser of the Teatro Novissimo (see ch. 4 above).

Aria style, finally, is used to set a particular passage directed to the audience by
the Eunuch in 3.3 (example 3):

[RECIT]:	Io non son buono	I am not able
	A ricordarlo al padre.	To remind her father of it.
[ARIA]:	Mà s'altri, che mi ascolta,	But if anyone who can hear me
	In sè sperimentato,	Has himself experienced,
	O ne congiunti suoi	Or has any relatives who have,
	Havesse alcun segreto	Any secret way
	Da sanar la pazzia,	To cure madness,
	L'impresti à Deidamia.	Let him lend it to Deidamia.

Other, briefer passages elicit lyrical treatment because of their emotional content. These include Acchille's plea to Deidamia for forgiveness at the end of a
speech in 3.4 ("Perdona, tu, perdona"), and Deidamia's acceptance of his hand
later in the same scene ("Caro pegno di fede").

Such passages are neither as elaborate nor as frequent as Monteverdi's arioso
expansions in *Il ritorno d'Ulisse*; furthermore, Sacrati ignores a number of formal
hints—such as the four sestets at the end of act 1, and various rhymed couplets
and quatrains, and lengthy sequences of *settenari*—that Monteverdi would have
pounced on as excuses for musical elaboration or structure. *La finta pazza*
contains extended passages of straight recitative setting of *versi sciolti* uninterrupted by lyricism that nevertheless reveal in Sacrati a powerful musical imagination at work. It must be said that poet and composer were more compatible
in *La finta pazza* than in *Il ritorno d'Ulisse*.

Monteverdi's next librettist, Busenello, less conservative than Badoaro, as
well as more experienced in the art of libretto-writing, seems to have produced
a more satisfactory text.[17] Although *L'incoronazione di Poppea* also needed many
alterations, to judge from the printed libretto, it seems to have provided Monteverdi with what he lacked in *Il ritorno d'Ulisse*—namely, multiple occasions for
lyrical expansion. In addition to thirteen strophic texts, most of them for secondary characters, and all of them arias in Monteverdi's score, the libretto of
Poppea contains a large number of prominent couplets and quatrains. Monteverdi almost always set these lyrically, sometimes splitting them line by line,
sometimes treating them as a whole ("Poppea sta di buon core," end of 1.10),
and sometimes turning them into miniature ABA arias by repeating the first
line at the end as a refrain ("E pur io torno" [1.1]; "O felice Drusilla" [3.1]). In

17.   But see Rosand, "Seneca," for some general examples of incompatibility between the two. Gary
Tomlinson, *Monteverdi and the End of the Renaissance*
(Berkeley and Los Angeles, 1987), 216 and n. 3, argues that Monteverdi took more liberties with
Busenello's text than with Badoaro's. But, although
there are many fascinating differences between the
scores and the librettos of *Poppea*, including the
manuscripts as well as Busenello's printed text, none
of them quite equals Monteverdi's radical restructuring of Penelope's lament. I discuss some of these
alterations in "Monteverdi's Mimetic Art."

L'incoronazione di Poppea, as in *Il ritorno d'Ulisse*, Monteverdi left almost no suggestion for musical structuring or lyrical expansion unexploited; but in the libretto of *Poppea* there were more of them.[18]

Poppea, even more than *Il ritorno*, depends on lyricism; it owes its affective impact to distinctions between speech and song. Whether fleeting emotional outburst or fully considered pleading, song lies at the heart of the work, touching all the characters and all the situations. Nino Pirrotta regards the unusual abundance of song in *Poppea* as evidence of relaxed standards of verisimilitude, which he ascribes to the fact that the characters are carried away by love.[19] In fact, very little of the lyrical expansion in *Poppea* is actually formal, and thus "unnatural." Predictably, most of the strophic arias are songs sung by comic characters, the repetition and patterning enhancing the humorous effect; those that are not (and even some of those that are) are treated as quite free strophic variations, which minimizes their repetitiveness. And in most cases, whether comic or serious, the structure contributes to the development of the drama.[20] Monteverdi's song, a correlative of heightened passion, emerges from and fades back into speech quite naturally, feelingly. *Poppea* is especially lyrical, airy (*arioso*), but not especially formal.

Busenello and Cavalli

Busenello's distinctions between aria and recitative are not totally unambiguous; but Monteverdi could read them, or at least he did read them, the way he wanted to. Beyond the arias, Busenello's text provided Monteverdi with the kind of structure and imagery that stimulated his musical imagination. Given what we know of the composer, and in the context of the deficiencies of *Il ritorno d'Ulisse*, it is likely that the text of *Poppea* was constructed to Montever-

---

18.   The question of authenticity has been raised repeatedly with reference to *Poppea*, most notably by Walker ("Errori") and Curtis ("*La Poppea impasticciata*"). Their skepticism is chiefly based on the fact that the two scores were copied in conjunction with a revival (or revivals) that took place well after Monteverdi's death, and that both of them contain obvious alterations, including transpositions as well as, probably, newly composed music. Both scores certainly contain music that Monteverdi did not write, most notably the final duet "Pur ti miro" and, in the Naples score, some new music for Ottavia. But, until more convincing documentary evidence becomes available, I will maintain my belief in the essential authenticity of the work as a whole—with minor exceptions—which rests on stylistic characteristics that distinguish *Poppea* from the music of any other known composer. These include an attitude toward

text-setting that marks Monteverdi's works in all genres. Indeed, it is my contention that Monteverdi's treatment of Busenello's text in particular (but also Badoaro's) is the natural culmination of his experience in writing madrigals, an experience that no other known opera composer of the time shared. Monteverdi's unique attitude toward the text, in fact, renders his Venetian operas atypical. Although they had great significance in establishing the genre on a firm footing, they are not strongly implicated in its future development.

19.   Pirrotta, "Monteverdi and the Problems of Opera," *Essays*, 252–53.

20.   See, for example, Poppea's self-comforting refrain "Per me guereggia Amor" (1.4); Drusilla's ironically exuberant "Felice cor mio" (2.10) and "O felice Drusilla" (3.1); Arnalta's sleepy lullaby (2.12). See Rosand, "Monteverdi's Mimetic Art."

di's specifications, or at least with his tendency toward mimetic musical expansion in mind. This is particularly clear from a comparison with Busenello's two previous librettos, written for Cavalli, *Gli amori d'Apollo e di Dafne* (1640) and, especially, *Didone* (1641). The feature that chiefly distinguishes *Didone* from *Poppea* is its many strophic texts and few independent quatrains. In practically every scene of the earlier libretto, the free succession of *versi sciolti* yields to organization in the form of strophes, usually three or four, but sometimes as many as eight (eleven in one case!), comprising from three to eight lines each, which are set off from the surrounding text by their more regular meter and/or rhyme scheme.

In *Didone*, then, Busenello established strophicism as the clearest and most frequent closed form for opera. But its musical implications remained ambiguous for a number of years. The distinctions between the strophic forms and the surrounding poetry are not all equally sharp. While a number of strophes utilize meters that contrast strongly with the predominant *versi sciolti*, such as *quinari* or *ottonari*—*versi misurati*—others are cast in the characteristic meters of recitative—*settenario* and *endecasillabo*—though in more structured patterns: typically a quatrain of *settenari* followed by a hendecasyllabic couplet. In some cases the strophes fail to create a strong metrical effect because their rhymes lack prominence. They may be too far apart, as in a succession of rhyming hendecasyllabic verses, or they may be counteracted by an opposing or simply non-confirming metrical structure; or else the rhyme may be restricted to the closing couplet, with the remaining text unrhymed, much like the standard recitative verse.

The formal units created by these strophes, some of them more insistent than others, always suggested some change in musical language, a closed rather than open-ended setting that would reflect, through musical repetition, the specially structured text. But since such musical repetition, whether in aria, recitative, or mixed style, generally threatened the illusion of dramatic continuity and verisimilitude, it could be used only rarely, and in specific circumstances.

Busenello's sensitivity to the implications of strophic form is revealed by the occasions on which he employed it. Nearly all of the twenty-six strophic texts in *Didone* are dramatically justified in one of the standard ways. A number of them are for gods, traditionally exempted from the laws governing human behavior; several others are for essentially comic or ironic characters (Sinon Greco, the ladies-in-waiting), who speak in clichés, and whose unwanted advice falls quite naturally into rhyme; and three of them are for the boy Ascanio, who may be thought of as not yet having learned the rules of adult behavior or whose youth is projected in his rhythmic, singsong speech. Busenello's serious characters fall into patterned rhythm and rhyme only in spite of themselves, when self-control has failed owing to some kind of extraordinary pressure: fear of death, abandonment, or madness. In general, then, the librettist is quite conservative in his demands on the composer. His strophic forms suggest some special musical structuring, but not indiscriminately, and not necessarily in the form of an aria, as we can see from Cavalli's score.

If Busenello is conservative, Cavalli is downright reactionary in his respect for verisimilitude. To compensate, however, he penetrates more deeply into the drama, finding justification for musical expansion on psychological grounds. Of the twenty-six strophic texts in Busenello's libretto, Cavalli set only twelve as strophic arias; he set eight as strophic recitative, four with mixed treatment—part recitative, part aria—and ignored or changed the strophic form altogether in two. The libretto has only one non-strophic closed form, a series of *quinari sdruccioli* for Ecuba's invocation, which Cavalli set as an aria.[21] With his thirteen arias in the whole opera, Cavalli exploited fewer than half of the opportunities provided in the libretto for formal music.

Perhaps the most eloquent illustration of Cavalli's attitude toward verisimilitude and toward Busenello's textual directives—his basic disinclination to confirm strophic structure in music—is provided by an example in which he changed compositional styles, from recitative to aria, within the same strophic form. In act 3, scene 6, the gods have just informed Enea that he must leave Carthage. He knows that he is obliged to obey them, although he is reluctant to abandon his beloved Didone. Busenello provides him with a text consisting of seven strophes of six hendecasyllabic lines each, with the rhyme scheme *abbacc*, in which Enea expresses his bitter conflict between his love for Didone and the realization that the gods' command is law (example 4). He articulates that conflict most explicitly in the third strophe:

Fierissimo contrasto, aspro conflitto;	Most savage contention, bitter conflict!
Amor m'induce ai pianti a viva forza,	Love leads me with brute force to weep,
Honor trova le lagrime, e le sforza	Honor meets the tears and compels them
A' soffocarsi in mezo il core afflitto.	To be stifled within the afflicted heart.
Son pianta combattuta da due venti,	I am a plant shaken by opposing winds,
E vengon da due inferni i miei tormenti.	And from opposing hells come all my torments.

Cavalli set the first four strophes, in which Enea gives voice to his torment, in expressive recitative style. Although they share general harmonic shape, the four strophes vary in length, are supported by different bass lines, move to different internal cadential goals, and exhibit remarkably different rhythmic and melodic profiles.[22] The most abrupt change, however, occurs at the fifth stro-

---

21. A second strophe is added later in the score, however (I-Vnm, It. IV, 355 [9879], ff. 33ᵛ-34).

22. For a compelling discussion of this piece, see Glixon, "Recitative," 121–24.

phe, where recitative yields to aria. It is at this point that Enea's thoughts shift from himself and his own conflict to his beloved Didone, whom he addresses gently:

Dormi, cara Didone, il Ciel cortese	Sleep, dear Dido; may kind Heaven
Non ti faccia sognar l'andata mia,	Keep you from dreaming of my going.
Il corpo in Nave, e l'alma à te s'invia,	Though my body be embarked, my soul makes its way to you.
Non sien mai spente le mie voglie accese,	My kindled desires will never be extinguished.
Ite sotto al guancial del mio tesoro,	Go beneath the pillow of my treasure,
O miei sospiri, e dite, ch'io mi moro.	O my sighs, and proclaim that I am dying!

Cavalli set this strophe and the next as a kind of lullaby in lyrical aria style; clearly responding to a change in the mood of Busenello's text, he himself supplies, through music, an emotional climax to the turmoil expressed in the previous recitative strophes. Even the two aria strophes are not treated in a strictly strophic manner, however, although they share many features. Nor is aria style maintained consistently throughout them; the penultimate line of each is set as recitative, which overflows into the final lyrical line. In fact, the second strophe builds on the first in many ways, but its whole structure is more continuous and its phrases are more closely related, producing a greater sense of growth from one to the next. This second strophe is also more final than the first, containing a lengthy ritardando and cadence in the subdominant just before the recitative line. Melodic restraint and balance in the first strophe rather fittingly convey Enea's feelings, his tender sorrow, his hesitancy, his fear of disturbing Didone's repose and of her awakening, perhaps to thwart his resolution. Full of self-doubt, he is most concerned with reassuring her. He speaks louder and more forcefully in the next strophe as he becomes stronger in his resolve. Now he is more passionately concerned with himself, with expressing his own suffering. The more sustained buildup of musical tension and affect of the second strophe heightens the opposition between desire and destiny.[23] In the final strophe, he returns once more to the basic conflict—and to recitative style—as he bids his beloved *addio*.

The form of Busenello's text alone, then, does not allow us to predict Cavalli's response. Indeed, text meaning—or, rather, dramatic context—far outweighs rhyme scheme, meter, or any other formal device as the chief determinant of his style. Nowhere is this clearer than in the recitative itself, from which Cavalli occasionally extracted lines for lyrical setting purely on the basis of their meaning: emotional outbursts, resolute conclusions or summaries, statements of intention could all incite his lyrical imagination. In many cases

---

23.   See Ellen Rosand, "Comic Contrast and Dramatic Continuity: Observations on the Form and Function of Aria in the Operas of Francesco Cavalli," *MR* 37 (1976): 98–102.

these passages take on a culminative structural function when they occur at the ends of scenes or action segments. Unlike Monteverdi, however, Cavalli does not seem to have been seeking excuses for lyricism; he flatly rejected some obvious opportunities, maintaining a powerful commitment to recitative even within closed forms.

Indeed, despite *Didone*'s much larger number of strophic texts, its center of gravity—unlike that of *Poppea*—lies not in the arias or in arioso but in the recitative. The first act in particular, arguably the highpoint of Cavalli's accomplishments in this style, provides a lesson in recitative expression that other composers, even Monteverdi, rarely matched.[24] Only infrequently interrupted by arias—and then less interrupted than intensified—the dramatic thread is sustained essentially by recitative, now narrative, now heightened by feeling, which even intrudes, as we have seen, into the arias themselves. The mutuality of text and music in the recitative of *Didone* is almost matched in the arias, which rarely move beyond straightforward text presentation into musical elaboration. Typically, the setting is line for line, with any repetition or musical expansion saved for the end. In fact, there is often more "music" in the recitative than in the arias, more of the composer's art.

The small proportion of Busenello's strophic texts set completely as arias is a reflection of Cavalli's attitude toward verisimilitude. It also confirms the fact that, in 1641, strophic texts did not necessarily require aria setting. Indeed, aside from distinctions in meter and rhyme, librettists had not yet developed specific, unambiguous poetic signs for arias—as opposed to strophic recitative or mixed style; nor were such signs yet necessary. In opera of the early 1640s, strophic recitative or a mixed recitative-aria style was still a viable response to a strophic text, as it had been since the beginning of the century—a strategy designed to limit or minimize undramatic stasis. The choice was still primarily the composer's. It was only with the increased emphasis on the singer—and the aria—that the librettist's language gradually acquired greater specificity.

Cavalli and Faustini

An important step in that direction was taken by Cavalli's next—and probably most important—librettist, Giovanni Faustini. Undoubtedly encouraged by the composer, with whom he collaborated steadily and exclusively for a decade, Faustini developed more explicit and more varied ways of indicating closed forms and suggesting a change from recitative to aria style. In addition to

24. Sacrati's recitative in *La finta pazza* is occasionally comparable, particularly in some of the more expressive passages such as those in the dialogue between Deidamia and her nurse in 2.4 (see *La finta pazza*, ed. Bianconi).

strophic arrangements, Faustini's texts included numerous passages marked off by refrains as well as individual sections of highly metrical, rhymed texts forming individual poetic stanzas. Cavalli's response was generally more predictable than it had been in *Didone*.

Faustini's formal signals were not only clearer and more varied than Busenello's; they were also more numerous, but not because he was any less bound by verisimilitude than his colleague. On the contrary, he expressed his commitment to verisimilitude by stretching its boundaries, developing additional pretexts, new ways of justifying formal music. His librettos are constructed with a view to rendering song more natural. If his lack of academic background proved an advantage in this connection, it was because it permitted him to move beyond classical and mythological sources for his librettos, to create characters and situations that were not weighted down by responsibilities inherited from the past. He was free to create an imaginary new world in which fictional behavior—speaking in song—was more plausible.

Faustini exercised his freedom of invention by imbuing his characters with qualities, and his plots with incidents, that translated well into formal music—comic servants pontificating or spewing clichés, expansive, self-indulgent heroes and heroines easily carried away by love (and grief), and plots revolving around disguise, which encouraged, even required, participants to behave or think unrealistically—unlike themselves. Furthermore, to stimulate their inclination to musical expression, Faustini presented many of his characters in solo scenes, thereby releasing them from the necessity of realistic communication with their fellow actors. It was easier for an audience to accept the singing of soliloquies, of inner thoughts, than to accept sung communication between two characters. Finally, Faustini constructed texts that were formal and dramatic at the same time, that served the needs of music and action simultaneously.

His librettos contain far fewer strophic forms than Busenello's; but these are at once more standardized and more clearly differentiated from their recitative surroundings—and this by virtue not of meter but of rhyme. They usually consist of three six-line strophes that, although utilizing the preferred recitative meter—the standard seven- and eleven-syllable lines—are tightly rhymed, normally closing with a couplet. Most significant for their translation into music, successive strophes frequently share a concluding refrain (it occasionally opens the strophe as well) that emphasizes even further their isolation from their context. Cavalli, in response to their greater formal clarity and standardization, was much more consistent than before in setting them as lyrical arias. In *Ormindo* (1644), for example, Cavalli set twelve of the fourteen strophic texts as arias and only two as recitative. But the score has many more than twelve arias. Indeed, strophic texts comprise only about half of the total number of closed forms in a typical Faustini libretto. Most of the others are articulated by means of refrains.

Refrains were an important component of Faustini's attempt to stretch verisimilitude. Comprising either single or multiple lines, they could promote continuity as well as closure: a refrain might recur within a recitative text for dramatic reasons, for emphasis, only temporarily interrupting the recitative flow; or it might enclose a static form. Refrains recur effectively and affectively in a wide range of situations throughout the libretto of *Ormindo*. While Cavalli invariably marked their recurrence musically, his treatment varied, depending on their form or dramatic context. If his response to strophic texts had become conventionalized, with refrains he continued to exercise his composer's freedom. The drama was still in his hands.

In *Ormindo*, Faustini often used a single-line refrain to isolate a tight rhyming quatrain or cinquain—*abba, abaa,* or *abbaa*—within a lengthy section of recitative verse. In Cavalli's setting, some of these brief texts become miniature tripartite arias, while others shade into the recitative background. In act 1, scene 8, for example, he makes a little ABA aria out of Erisbe's simple quatrain responding to Ormindo's protestations of love (refrains italicized) (example 5):

Fortunato mio cor,	*Fortunate is my heart,*
Con diluvii di gioie	With floods of joy
Tempra l'incendio tuo benigno amor.	Your benign love tempers its flames.
Fortunato mio cor.	*Fortunate is my heart.*

He gives additional prominence to the single-line refrain through extensive repetition of its text and music and by the addition of strings to the continuo accompaniment. Similar quatrains for Melide (a lady-in-waiting) and Erice (the nurse) in act 1, scene 5, however, are treated as simple recitative, with just a hint of extra musical expression given to the refrain line (example 6a, b):

MELIDE: *Frena il cordoglio, frena.*	*Cease your sorrow, cease.*
Mercè d'Amore ancora	Thanks to Love
Vedrò cangiata in gioia	Will I see all your suffering
ogni tua pena,	transformed to joy.
Frena il cordoglio, frena.	*Cease your sorrow, cease.*
ERICE: *Rasserena la fronte,*	*Calm your brow.*
Ancora Amida ancora	Amida once more, once more
Cancellerà co' baci i sprezzi,	Will cancel his scorn and insults
e l'onte.	with his kisses.
Rasserena la fronte.	*Calm your brow.*

Cavalli evidently regarded these formal hints as an excuse rather than a command for lyrical emphasis. His settings clearly depended on larger dramatic considerations. In the first example, lyrical expansion of Erisbe's protestation of love to Ormindo is particularly appropriate because it needs to be overheard by her other lover, Amida; in the second and third examples, Melide and Erice are merely encouraging their mistress, Sicle, not to lose hope.

In the case of lengthier refrains—of four and five lines—Faustini's message may be louder, but Cavalli's response is just as independent. Indeed, although in these cases he invariably set the refrain lyrically—to impart the emphasis Faustini called for—Cavalli's treatment still depends primarily on his own interpretation of the drama. In act 1, scene 7, for example, a five-line refrain encloses a highly structured seven-line text for Erisbe (example 7):

Se nel sen di giovanetti	*Though from youthful hearts alone*
L'alma mia	*Does my soul*
Sol desia di trar diletti,	*Desire to find pleasure,*
Vecchio Rè	*An old king*
Per marito il Ciel mi diè.	*For a husband did Heaven give me.*
Famelica, e digiuna	Famished and starved
Di dolcezze veraci,	For true sweetness,
Con sospiri interotti	With interrupted sighs
Passo le triste notti,	I spend sad nights,
Satia di freddi, e di sciapiti baci	Sated with cold and wasted kisses,
Pasco sol di desio l'avide brame,	My eager yearnings feed only on desire,
E à mensa Real moro di fame.	And at a royal table I die of hunger.
Se nel sen . . .	*Though from . . .*

Cavalli expanded the refrain considerably by means of text repetition and melismatic extension, dividing it into two distinct sections with contrasting music for its final couplet, music that is then repeated and further expanded in a lengthy ritornello. Alone, Cavalli's setting of this five-line text has all the earmarks of a bipartite aria. It recurs intact as a refrain, complete with ritornello, creating a fully rounded ABA structure with recitative B section; lyrical expansion weights the refrain more heavily than the B section, whose text is heard only once. This emphasis is particularly appropriate since the refrain effectively encapsulates Erisbe's predicament, the incompatibility of her youthful yearnings with her marriage to an aged husband, a conflict that lends plausibility to her subsequent behavior.

But the composer does not always emphasize the refrain at the expense of the enclosed text. In act 1, scene 5, a four-line refrain, itself including a refrain, encloses five lines of equally structured text for Sicle (example 8):

Chi, chi mi toglie al die	*Who, who will deliver me from this existence,*
Carnefice pietoso	*What merciful executioner*
De le sciagure mie?	*Of my misfortunes?*
Chi, chi mi toglie al die.	*Who, who will deliver me from this existence.*

Angoscie aspre, ed acerbe,	Harsh and bitter anguish,
Se tanto fiere siete,	If you are so savage,
Perche non m'uccidete?	Why do you not kill me?
De la sua vita priva	Deprived of her life,
Non viva più la misera, non viva.	Let the unhappy one no longer live.
Chi, chi mi toglie al die . . .[25]	*Who, who will deliver me . . .*

Cavalli's setting is much more continuous; he distinguishes his refrain from the enclosed text chiefly by meter, not by affective intensity, which continues to build in the central section. The return of the refrain thus becomes the climax of the whole passage, imparting a sense of continuity rather than contrast, and creating a form that, despite—because of?—its closure, convincingly portrays Sicle's increasing desperation over her betrayal by Amida. Closure is reinforced in two different ways in these two examples: in the first by expansion of the refrain itself, in the second by the building of the middle section toward culmination in the refrain. In both cases formal closure suited or enhanced the dramatic situation. In neither was it the form of the text alone that determined the musical treatment.

Musical closure was not a necessary consequence of all refrains, however. For a text for Erisbe's aged husband Hariadeno in act 1, scene 9, in which a two-line refrain encloses nine rhyming *settenari*, Cavalli provided an undifferentiated recitative setting, emphasizing neither the refrain nor the highly structured central section. An aria was possible here, but the composer did not deem lyricism appropriate to the dramatic situation. Perhaps he wished to minimize sympathy for Hariadeno, to enhance his characterization as a cold old man. Drama rather than form must have been the chief motivating factor, since Cavalli set a number of texts less highly structured than this one as arias. In act 3, scene 13, he wrote an aria to a simple seven-line text, five *settenari* followed by a hendecasyllabic couplet, without refrain, obviously because of its dramatic position: it serves as an emotional release for Ormindo, who joyfully recognizes Hariadeno as his long-lost father.

Cavalli was more likely to accept Faustini's formal cues under certain conditions. Monologue scenes, for example, which often end with strophic texts, frequently display other hints for closure such as a refrain or a metrical passage of text. Lyricism and formality are justified in these instances, or at least mitigated, as we have already said, by the understanding that the character is voicing his thoughts to himself—and only incidentally to the audience—rather than to his fellow actors. The monologue situation seems to have encouraged Cavalli to set such texts lyrically, thereby producing a lyrical crescendo that culminated in the strophic aria.

25. Cf. ch. 10, p. 298.

Melide's monologue in 2.5, for example, comprises two sections, a six-line passage of *versi sciolti* and three six-line strophes of *ottonari* with refrain, calling for recitative and aria setting, respectively. Indeed, the recitative text prepares that of the aria. In it Melide reflects that she, too, wishes to love, but has decided not to, since Cupid is so cruel (example 9):

Volevo amar anch'io,	I, too, should have wished to love;
Ma vedo, che chi serve	But I see that whoever serves
Amore, ingiusto Dio,	Love, O unjust gods,
Riceve in guiderdon doglie proterve,	Is rewarded by ferocious pains;
Onde il cor sbigottito	Whence this dumbfounded heart
Di non innamorarsi hà stabilito.	Has determined never to love.

She then addresses her aria to the god of love himself:

Tendi l'arco à tuo volere . . .	Use your bow as you will . . .

Rather than treating the opening six lines as recitative, however, Cavalli, taking advantage of their closed rhyme scheme, *ababcc*, set them in duple-meter aria style, actually rounding out the form by bringing back the musical material developed in lines 1–2 for line 6 and for a concluding sinfonia. The lyrical setting of this section is clearly not required by the meaning or form of the text, but it provides an effective musical springboard for the following strophic aria, which, although in a different meter, is in the same key.

Although quite rudimentary in form, this little scene prefigures the later operatic *scena*, which, after a lengthy period of expansion, ultimately solidified in the cantabile-cabaletta convention of nineteenth-century Italian opera. A position is taken at the beginning of the scene and expounded or amplified at the end: an opening aria launches a topic that the closing aria discharges. Paired arias like these, usually separated by a recitative passage that developed the argument of the first aria and precipitated the second, were particularly common for Faustini's secondary characters; they became a staple for the protagonists only later in the century.[26]

Like Monteverdi, Cavalli would change or reorganize text when it suited his purposes. Nowhere in *Ormindo* is the composer's independence of the libretto more powerfully demonstrated than in the dialogue aria at the climax of the opera, just before the resolution of the plot (in act 3, scene 12).[27] The two

26. Escalating lyrical sequences like this, which are quite common in *Ormindo*, are discussed in ch. 10 below. The various sections of these scenes were sometimes linked musically, not only by key but even by shared motivic material. For some slightly later examples, see Harold S. Powers, "L'Erismena travestita," in *Studies in Music History: Essays for Oliver Strunk*, ed. Harold S. Powers (Princeton, 1968), 293–97. And see id., " 'La solita forma' and 'The Uses of Convention,' " *AcM* 59 (1987): 65–90, on the cantabile-cabaletta convention in later opera, particularly Verdi.

27. This aria is discussed and illustrated in Rosand, " 'Ormindo travestito,' " 268–91.

characters involved are the protagonists Ormindo and Erisbe, illicit lovers who, while attempting to flee the kingdom of Erisbe's husband Hariadeno (the fact that he is also Ormindo's father is as yet unknown), have been captured, imprisoned, and poisoned by the king's soldiers, and are now awaiting the poison's fatal effect. No aria is signaled here by the librettist, who has provided an irregular text, structured only by a single recurrence of Ormindo's two-line refrain, "Non ti doler d'Amore, / Non l'oltraggiar mio Core" (example 10):

ERISBE: Ah questo è l'Himeneo,
    Che ci promise d'Amatunta il Dio?
    Son queste le sue faci,
    Ch'arder doveano intorno à nostri letti,
    Per infiammarci maggiormente i petti?
    O di superbo, e dispietato Nume,
    Traditrice natura, empio costume.

Is this the marriage
We were promised by the Cyprian god?
Are these his torches
That should have burned around our beds
To further inflame our hearts?
Oh, of haughty and unfeeling god
Deceitful nature, wicked custom.

ORMINDO: *Non ti doler d'Amore,*
    Non l'oltraggiar mio Core,
    Querelati del Cielo
    Contro di noi d'hostilità ripieno,
    Ei fè l'aere sereno
    Per negarci il fuggir, divenir fosco
    Egli crudel ci preparò quel tosco.
    Non ti doler d'Amore,
    Non l'oltraggiar mio Core.
    Sua mercede godrem gioia infinita
    Ne' felici giardini,
    Di veraci riposi unichi nidi,
    Spiriti uniti eternamente, e fidi.

Do not blame Love,
Do not offend him, my beloved.
Complain to Heaven
That is filled with hostility against us.
It is he who made the air,
To deny us flight, become murky,
He, cruel one, prepared for us that poison.
Do not blame Love,
Do not offend him, my beloved.
As his reward we shall taste infinite joy
In the happy gardens,
Of true rest, the only shelter,
Spirits united and true for eternity.

ERISBE: Sì, sì, che questa notte
    In virtude d'Amore à le nostre alme
    Aprirà un dì lucente
    Perpetuo, e permanente.

Yes, yes, this night
Thanks to Love, to our souls
Shall open up a shining day
Perpetual, and permanent.

[ORMINDO *Non ti doler d'Amore,*
    Non l'oltraggiar mio Core.]

[*Do not blame Love,*
Do not offend him, my beloved.]

ERISBE: L'ombra, ch'hor vela il mondo,
    Se terrore produce
    A noi partorirà stato giocondo
    Contro il costume suo madre di luce.

The shadow that now veils the earth
Although generating terror,
Will create for us a state of joy,
Becoming, contrary to its nature, the mother
    of light.

[ORMINDO *Non ti doler d'Amore,*
    Non l'oltraggiar mio Core.]

[*Do not blame Love,*
Do not offend him, my beloved.]

ERISBE: Ma temo ohimè ben mio
    Che nel varcar di Lete,
    Non spegna in te l'ardor l'acqua d'oblio.

But I fear, alas, my beloved
That in passing through Lethe
The waters of forgetfulness may extinguish
    your passion.

Cavalli molded this text into a lengthy, three-part ostinato aria, each part containing a statement by Erisbe followed by Ormindo's refrain. While the librettist repeats Ormindo's refrain only once, within Ormindo's single speech, interspersed with five lines of recitative, Cavalli uses it twice again (bracketed here) to comfort Erisbe during her speech, integrating it into her lament by using the same ostinato figure to accompany it. Moreover, he expands these lines extensively by means of internal text repetitions. The ostinato, which has acquired enormous momentum through its persistence, almost uninterrupted, through thirty-two lines of text, terminates abruptly as Erisbe feels the first effects of the poison, and Cavalli shifts to recitative for her three final lines — and from a diatonic to a chromatic accompaniment. Extra word repetitions and aria setting were not suggested by this text. Cavalli the dramatist modified the libretto to create a much larger and more highly structured form than that provided by Faustini, a form that expresses with great intensity the lovers' increasing closeness as death approaches.

Despite the greater specificity and range of Faustini's formal cues, in particular the standardized strophic forms that evoked consistent aria treatment from the composer, *Ormindo* is remarkably rich in instances of the composer exercising his stylistic prerogative: in his treatment of refrains, in his use of lyricism within recitative, and in his expansion and rearrangement of text. Recitative and aria styles still mix freely, and some of the most expressive passages in the score are those particularly Cavallian efflorescences, the arioso expansions of single lines or couplets within passages of text that were clearly intended as recitative. The freedom granted by the librettist and exercised by the composer here was reduced considerably by the middle of the century, as the distinction between aria and recitative became more absolute.[28] That distinction was strengthened as the formal structure of aria texts became increasingly confirmed by their meaning and dramatic function, and eventually their position within the scene. A new stage in this development is represented by Cicognini's and Cavalli's *Giasone* of 1649, one of the most popular and, consequently, most influential operas of the entire century.

Cavalli and Cicognini

Giacinto Andrea Cicognini's background and career differed as much from those of his contemporaries as did his librettos. Educated in Florence rather than Venice, he was well versed in the tradition of Spanish *comedias*, of which he produced several adaptations and translations.[29] And he was fully established as

28. The variety of Faustini's affective refrains, one important source of that freedom, eventually bore formal fruit in the da capo aria. See ch. 10 below.

29. For Cicognini, see Robert Lamar Weaver, "Cicognini," *New Grove*, 4: 390; Morelli and Walker, "Migliori plettri," CXXXIV–CXXXV; and M. Vi-

the author of a number of prose dramas before entering the world of opera toward the end of his literary career. Two of his librettos, *Giasone* and *Gli amori d'Alessandro magno e di Rossane*, even led an independent existence as prose dramas; in the former case, the libretto was the source of the play, while in the latter the relationship was reversed.[30] Cicognini's librettos are more varied, more individualized, and poetically more sophisticated than those of his Venetian contemporaries. They stand out especially for their mixture of comic and serious characters—even the permeation of serious elements by comedy—and for the dramatic impact of the poetry itself. Although *versi sciolti* still form the basis of his poetic language, Cicognini employed a much greater variety of meters throughout his text, primarily in the arias, but also in recitative for dramatic purposes.

The most famous scene in *Giasone* is Medea's invocation of the spirits of the Underworld at the end of the first act. Standing as the prototype of all subsequent operatic incantations, it illustrates the ways in which Cicognini used poetry for dramatic contrast. The variety of accent produced by the changing meters (two symmetrical groups of *quinari sdruccioli*, each closing with a *tronco* [A: 12 lines], followed by a group of mixed *settenari* and *endecasillabi* [B: 11 lines], then an irregular mixture of two-, three-, four-, five-, seven-, and eleven-syllable lines, variously accented [C], and finally ten *quaternari tronchi* [D]) combined with free rhyme irregularly interspersed with couplets, and the contrast between *sdruccioli*, *piano*, and *tronco* verse-endings creates a scene of remarkable energy (example 11):

[A] Dell'Antro magico   Of this magic cavern,
    Stridenti Cardini   You creaking hinges,
    Il varco apritemi,   Open wide for me.
    E frà le tenebre   And into the darkness
    Del negro Ospitio   Of the black hospice
    Lassate me.   Let me go.
    Sù l'Ara orribile   On the horrible altar
    Del lago Stigio   Of the Stygian lake
    I fochi splendino,   Let the flames rise,
    E sù ne mandino   And send forth
    Fumi, che turbino   Clouds of smoke to obscure
    La luce al Sol: The light of the sun.
[B] Dall'abbruciate glebe   From your fiery globes,
    Gran Monarca dell'Ombre intento   Great monarch of the shades, listen care-
        ascoltami,   fully!
    E se i dardi d'Amor già mai ti punsero,   And if Love's darts have ever struck you,
    Adempi ò Rè de i sotterranei popoli,   Fulfill, O King of the Underworld,
    L'amoroso desio, che 'l cor mi stimola,   The amorous desire that quickens my heart,
    E tutto Averno alla bell'opra uniscasi;   And let all Hades join in the fair deed.

gilante, "Giacinto Andrea Cicognini," *DBI*, 25 (Rome, 1981): 428–31.

30. See Anna Amalie Abert, *Claudio Monteverdi und das musikalische Drama* (Lippstadt, 1954), 156–63.

I Mostri formidabili,	Let the horrendous monsters,
Del bel Vello di Frisso,	Fierce, untiring guardians
Sentinelle feroci infaticabili,	Of Phrixos's lovely fleece
Per potenza d'Abisso	Through the powers of the abyss
Si rendono a Giasone oggi domabili.	Be subdued by Jason today.
[C] Dall'arsa Dite	From fiery Dis
(Quante portate	(Oh, how many
Serpi alla fronte)	Serpents you bear on your brow)
Furie venite,	Furies, come,
E di Pluto gl'Imperi a me svelate.	And reveal to me Pluto's kingdom!
Già questa verga io scoto	I already sway this wand,
Già percoto	Already the earth
Il suol col piè:	Quakes beneath our feet.
Orridi	Horrible
Demoni,	Demons,
Spiriti	Spirits of
D'Erebo,	Erebus,
Volate a me:	Fly to me!
Cosi indarno vi chiamo?	Do I call you in vain?
Quai strepiti,	What clamor,
Quai sibili,	What hissing,
Non lascian penetrar nel cieco baratro	Prevents my terrible words
Le mie voci terribili?	From penetrating into the blind chasm?
Dalla sabbia	From the shore
Di Cocito	Of Cocytus
Tutta rabbia	All the furies
Quà v'invito,	I summon here.
Al mio soglio,	To my throne
Quà, vi voglio,	I order you.
A che si tarda più?	Why do you still tarry?
Numi Tartarei, sù, sù, sù, sù;	Spirits of Tartarus, up, up, up, up!
. . .	. . .
[D] Si, si, si,	Yes, yes, yes,
Vincerà	My king
Il mio Rè,	Will conquer.
Al suo prò	For him
Deità	The deity
Di la giù	Of the Underworld
Pugnerà;	Will fight.
Si, si, si	Yes, yes, yes,
Vincerà,	He will conquer,
Vincerà.	He will conquer.

Such verses imperiously demanded to be matched in the musical setting, and Cavalli responded effectively to the poet's cues with music that reinforces the metric individuality of the scene. In restricting the melody to repeated notes and simple triadic figures following precisely the accentuation of the text, the composer powerfully projects the intensity of Medea's invocation. It is worth noting here that the composer distinguishes individual metric sections of the text from one another and that part of his setting—the first twelve lines—clearly qualifies as a closed form or aria, though it is not particularly lyrical.

More generally speaking, Cicognini controls meter and rhyme with particular skill to distinguish clearly between recitative and aria verse. Indeed, the contrast between the two types of poetry is much cleaner in *Giasone* than in any of Faustini's (or Busenello's) librettos. Strophicism is by far Cicognini's preferred method of indicating an aria, characterizing more than two-thirds (seventeen of twenty-four) of the closed forms in the work; and Cavalli set virtually all of Cicognini's strophic texts as arias. All seven of the non-strophic arias, like those of Faustini, are based upon sections of text that stand out because of their special meter and rhyme—like the opening section of Medea's incantation scene already mentioned. But their independent setting is assured—or at least strongly suggested—by their highly individualized meter and unusual length: several of them comprise as many as ten or eleven lines.

Cicognini's strophic texts as well are unusually long. Rather than the characteristic Faustinian six lines, most of Cicognini's strophes range between eight and ten lines. Furthermore, they are extremely varied: hardly any two forms share the same meter or rhyme.[31] The variety is achieved not only through the choice of a different meter for virtually every text but through the metric changes within individual texts themselves. Whereas some arias are in a single meter, relying on the rhyme scheme to articulate their form, others combine lines of very different meters, sometimes as many as five or six in a single strophe. Delfa's aria in 3.10, for example, utilizes four meters and a variety of accentuation patterns and verse endings, which produces a distinctly off-balance (comic?) effect (example 12):[32]

31. With respect to metric variety, Cicognini was atypical of his generation (though at least one of his older contemporaries, Bartolini, considered it an important feature of dramatic poetry; see Appendix I.21). Poets of the late seventeenth and early eighteenth centuries tended to use much greater variety than those of Cicognini's generation. See, for example, Ivanovich's letter to Pagliardi of 1673, in which he specifically mentions the metric variety in his *Lismaco*: "Hò adoperato varietà di metri; a finche campeggino nella loro bizzarria gli andamenti della sua musica" (letter of 26 June 1673, Appendix II.5a). See, more generally, the directives in Martello's *Della tragedia antica e moderna*, trans. Weiss, "Pier Jacopo Martello on Opera," 395–96. The positive effect of metric variety on the musical setting of dramatic poetry was recognized at the beginning of the

seventeenth century as well. See Alessandro Guidotti's preface to Cavalieri's *La rappresentatione di anima e di corpo*: "Conviene . . . che [il Poema] sia . . . pieno di versetti, non solamente di sette sillabe, ma di cinque e di otto, et alle volte in sdruccioli, e con le rime vicini per la vaghezza della musica, fa grazioso effetto." Doni, too, acknowledged the advantages of such variety, distinguishing between "versi lunghi" (that is, *endecasillabi*), "versi mezzani" (or *settenari*), and "versi piccoli" (*quinari* or *quatternari*). See his *Trattato della musica scenica*, ch. 7, p. 18; see also Leopold, " 'Quelle bazzicature poetiche,' " passim.

32. Cicognini also uses metric regularity for specific dramatic effect, as in Giasone's presentation aria "Delizie contenti" in 1.2; the piece is elegantly analyzed in Bianconi, *Seventeenth Century*, 206.

È follia	It is madness
Frà gl'Amori	To sow jealousy
Seminar la Gelosia,	Between lovers,
Per raccoglier al fin' rabbie, e rancori,	Only to reap anger and bitterness in the end.
Consolar sol' ne può	Only the lover we hold in our arms
Quel ben' che in sen ci stà.	Can bring comfort.
La Gioia, che passò,	Joy that is passed
In fumo, in ombra, in nulla se ne và;	Goes up in smoke, in shadow, in nothing.
Chi vuol sbandir dal cor' doglia,	Whoever wishes to banish woe and anguish
e martello	from his heart,
Lasci amar, ami ogn'un, goda 'l	Should let himself love, love everyone,
più bello.	and enjoy the best.

Cavalli's setting underscores the irregular structure of the text by sticking quite closely to it, creating an aria that is comically erratic and unpredictable, particularly in its phrase structure. The pattering musical rhythm exactly translates that of the text, from which the unassuming melody, consisting primarily of repeated notes and mincing half-steps, does not detract. Only at the final line does the voice finally cease its patter, the bass now taking over for a characteristic conclusive flourish. Although Cavalli has followed the text precisely, almost slavishly, until this point, he expands the aria at the end, slowing the vocal part down for the last line, which contains the main message of the aria.

In contrast to Faustini's exploitation of refrain forms, only three of Cicognini's arias—one of them strophic—are marked by a refrain—apparently too few for Cavalli, who created several refrain forms himself by repeating first lines of arias at the end.[33] Cicognini hardly used refrains in his recitative either; but when he did their message seems clear: Cavalli regarded them all as invitations to lyrical setting. And he found plenty of other opportunities for arioso expansion—within and increasingly at the ends of speeches. Significantly, the most extended arioso passages are reserved for Egeo and, especially, Isifile, the two principals whose love remains unrequited for most of the opera and who therefore have less to sing about and are more prone to emotional excess seeking or requiring an outlet than the other characters.

In keeping with a rather old-fashioned conception of verisimilitude, Cicognini distributed his arias quite unevenly among the cast. The four principals, Giasone, Medea, Isifile, and Egeo, sing very few—only one or at the most two each—all of them specially justified by the dramatic circumstances. (And this despite the fact that established legend was left far behind in this plot, the

33. These include Alinda's non-strophic aria "Quanti soldati" in 2.12, Egeo's strophic aria "Perch'io torni à penar" in 3.6, and Isifile's non-strophic "Gioite, gioite" in 3.7. The libretto has a third non-strophic refrain aria in 1.2 (Giasone's "Amor tutto è pietà"), but it was replaced in the score by the strophic aria "Delizie contenti" mentioned above. Cicognini tended to use inexact refrains somewhat more frequently at the ends of strophes.

traditional names of the characters notwithstanding). This contrasts markedly with the large number of arias given to the secondary characters: five for the old nurse Delfa, and three each for Alinda and Oreste. Confirmation, perhaps, of a kind of abstract taste for arias is provided by Rosminda, a gardener, who seems to have been introduced solely for the purpose of singing an aria in 1.3—and possibly to provide cover for the set change required for Medea's appearance in her throne room in 1.4.[34]

Cicognini's decisions were determined by considerations of verisimilitude not only in the distribution of arias, but in their dramatic function and placement within scenes. With the exception of three or four, all the arias take place out of earshot of the other characters—either in solo scenes or when the other character in the scene is asleep;[35] or else they are specifically used, as arias, to enhance a dramatic situation or a characterization. For example, Giasone's first appearance in the opera is marked by an expansive aria that conveys, economically and operatically—both to the audience and to his lieutenant Ercole— Medea's power over him. Ercole, responding to his captain's "aria as aria" as evidence of irrationality, urges him to return to his senses.

In placing most of his arias at the beginnings of scenes, Cicognini exploits their natural potential for emphasis: to set up a situation against which other characters (or the same character in a monologue) can react. In the few instances, usually comic monologues, where he places them at the ends of scenes, they are more static, summarizing the action that has occurred and marking the singer's exit.[36] Of course the dynamics of the two kinds of scenes are very different from one another, and the variety of aria placement corresponds to larger dramatic considerations. Arias can be propulsive at beginnings of scenes but not at ends. Giasone's scene-opener, in addition to characterizing his position within the plot, sets the whole drama in motion, beginning to build anticipation for the appearance of the legendary Medea two scenes later. Monologue scenes that close with arias are usually external to the plot; they are intended not to further the action but to develop characterization, to let the audience in on the character's thoughts.[37]

Cicognini distinguished more clearly between aria and recitative than any previous librettist, reinforcing that distinction by comfortable, appropriate

---

34. Rosmina has a second aria in the Vienna score of *Giasone*; perhaps she was one of those singers for whom a part had to be expanded at the last minute.

35. Cicognini must have enjoyed sleep as a pretext for song, since he used it twice in *Giasone*, in 2.2 and 3.3 (as well as in *Orontea*).

36. There are only three such arias in *Giasone*, all sung by comic characters: Delfa in 1.13, Oreste in

3.2, and Delfa again in 3.10. Medea closes the first act with what might be regarded as an exit aria (section D of her monologue discussed above).

37. Several scenes in *Giasone* end with brief arioso passages, whose lyrical setting is intended to mark the texts for future attention—in the very next scene; see "Alla nave" (2.6) and "Adoriamoci in sogno" (3.2).

placement within the drama, and provided the opportunity for greater musical variety in his arias. But Cavalli still asserted his privileges as a musical dramatist in the usual ways: by imposing his own form on arias and, even more characteristically, by exercising his option of setting recitative text lyrically for affective purposes.

The composer's ultimate control over the librettist's form is especially striking in the opening scene of act 3, for Oreste and Delfa, confidant and nurse of Isifile and Medea respectively, who represent opposite sides in their mistresses' tug-of-war for Giasone. Their dialogue is organized in three strophes of four successive *ottonari sdruccioli*, two strophes for Oreste enclosing one for Delfa. Although formally parallel, the three stanzas do not share the same mood. Oreste's opening strophe, in which he comments lyrically on the beauty of the shadowy night, is countered by Delfa, who punctures his lyrical effusion by denigrating the shadow as temporary and fleeting, offering the non-sequitur that she would find the embraces of a lovable husband more delightful. Her response causes an abrupt change in Oreste's tone as he defensively strikes back at her, hoping to disqualify himself as an object of her desires (example 13):

ORESTE: Nel boschetto, ove odor spirano, Vaghi fiori, e 'l suol ricamano,	In this wood where lovely flowers Breathe out their scents and embroider the ground,
Ove l'Aure intorno aggirano, A posar l'ombre ne chiamano;	Where gentle breezes waft, The shade beckons us to repose.
DELFA: L'ombra a me non è giovevolle, Ch'è fugace, e vana, è instabile, Più che l'ombra, è dilettevole Abbracciar marito amabile.	Shade does not please me, is fleeting, useless, and fickle. More than shade, it is delightful To embrace a palpable body.
ORESTE: Nel bramar sei larga, e calida, Fiacca, e scarsa è mia cupidine, E Pigmea mia forza invalida, Polifema è tua libidine.	Your passion is ravenous and hot, Weak and scarce is my desire. And pygmy are my feeble powers, Polyphemous your libido.

Despite their different moods, Cavalli set both of Oreste's strophes to the same music; at least in the first strophe that music hews closely to the meaning of the text. Three sequential phrases of ascending eighth-notes in 5/4 meter set the first three parallel lines; but for the fourth line, appropriate to its meaning—rest after action ("A posar l'ombre ne chiamano")—Cavalli counteracts the parallelism, almost wilfully doubling the note values as the melody descends from its peak to cadence on its low point. The result is a rather asymmetrical, but nicely shaped, strophe that ignores the text form as it follows, literally, its meaning.

Delfa's strophe, though it is in the same form, is set to different music, but with equal attention to text meaning. Here Cavalli's treatment is again sequential, with three of the four parallel lines set syllabically to repeated quarter notes; it is the second line of this strophe that evoked a contrasting setting from him, in this case an acceleration rather than deceleration, to elaborate, wide-ranging melismatic motion in sixteenth-notes for literal portrayal of the words: "Ch'è fugace, e vana, è instabile." These are the subtle adjustments that contribute so much to the effective matching of music and text that characterizes this opera.

To serve the drama, Cavalli not only suppressed or overrode textual regularity; for the same purpose he occasionally did the opposite and regularized Cicognini's poetry. One of the best examples of this procedure occurs in the duet between Giasone and Medea in 3.2. The scene, entirely in recitative meter, is laid out almost symmetrically for the two characters. Following an opening quatrain for Medea, set in rather lyrical, well-shaped recitative style by the composer, each of the lovers has a three-line stanza, which Cavalli set in a parallel, if not exactly strophic, manner, again in a kind of arioso style. The lovers then join voices for a brief duet, which is followed by two passages of text, the first for Medea, the second for Giasone. These, although they begin similarly, are of unequal length and dissimilar form (example 14):

MEDEA: Dormi stanco Giasone,
    E del mio cor, che gl'occhi tuo[i]
      rapiro,
    Stan le palpebre tue cara prigione.
	Sleep, weary Jason,
	And for my heart, which your eyes have
	    ravished,
	Let your eyelids be the sweet prison.

GIASONE: Dormi ch'io dormi, ò bella,
    E mentre i sensi miei consegno al sonno,
    Oggi per te Giason vantar si puole,
    D'haver l'alma trà l'ombre, e'in braccio
      il sole.
	Sleep while I sleep, my beauty,
	And while my senses are consigned to sleep,
	Today, because of you, Jason can boast
	That he has his soul in the shadows and the sun
	    in his arms.

Cavalli transforms this text into a kind of reciprocal refrain-enclosed lullaby, setting the two lovers' statements to similar ("strophic") music, despite their different texts. Taking advantage of the parallelism of the opening lines, he turns them into refrains, which he brings back at the end of each strophe, compensating for the differences in their texts—essentially Giasone's extra line—in a freer, strongly text-interpretative central section where the formal disparity passes virtually unnoticed. Cavalli's molding of this lullaby into the climax of a wonderfully symmetrical scene owes its impetus, perhaps, to Cicognini's word choice; but it is the composer who increased the mutuality of the lovers by making them closer in music than they are in words.

Cicognini's Legacy

For the Arcadian critics bent on the reform of Italian literature at the end of the seventeenth century, Cicognini's *Giasone* was a crucial work. According to Giovanni Maria Crescimbeni, one of their chief spokesmen, the author of *Giasone* was worthy of both praise and blame: praise for having created the first and most perfect drama in existence ("il primo, e il più perfetto Dramma, che si trovi"), and blame for having opened the floodgates to all kinds of abuses, the mixing of genres, the abandonment of linguistic elegance and purity, and, through the introduction of arias, the destruction of verisimilitude in drama.

> Around the middle of that century, Giacinto Andrea Cicognini . . . introduced drama [as opposed to *favole pastorali*] with his *Giasone*, which, to tell the truth, is the first and the most perfect drama there is; and with it he brought the end of acting, and consequently, of true and good comedy as well as tragedy. Since to stimulate to a greater degree with novelty the jaded taste of the spectators, equally nauseated by the vileness of comic things and the seriousness of tragic ones, the inventor of drama united them, mixing kings and heroes and other illustrious personages with buffoons and servants and the lowest men with unheard of monstrousness. This concoction of characters was the reason for the complete ruin of the rules of poetry, which went so far into disuse that not even locution was considered, which, forced to serve music, lost its purity, and became filled with idiocies. The careful deployment of figures that ennobles oratory was neglected, and language was restricted to terms of common speech, which is more appropriate for music; and finally the series of those short meters, commonly called *ariette*, which with a generous hand are sprinkled over the scenes, and the overwhelming impropriety of having characters speak in song completely removed from the compositions the power of the affections, and the means of moving them in the listeners. (Appendix II.7)[38]

Although Crescimbeni admits his ignorance of the period immediately preceding Cicognini's work and fails to appreciate Cicognini's connections to an already burgeoning operatic tradition, the focus of his attention on *Giasone* is symptomatic of its historical position. He was not wrong in ascribing special importance to the work: even from our vantage point it appears to stand at an important crossroads in the history of opera. It is, of course, unlikely that any single work (out of so many) could have had the impact Crescimbeni ascribes to *Giasone*. But the opera was clearly a symbol of the times; and its extraordinary popularity allowed it to represent those times quite legitimately.[39]

38. Francesco Saverio Quadrio and Stefano Arteaga, among others, followed Crescimbeni's lead in blaming Cicognini for all these things, although some of them had access to more material than he did. Quadrio ascribed to *Giasone* "tutte le circostanze di drami, che poi furono seguitati." See William C. Holmes, "Giacinto Andrea Cicognini's and Antonio Cesti's *Orontea* (1649)," in *New Looks at Italian Op-*

era: Essays in Honor of Donald J. Grout, ed. William Austin (Ithaca, N.Y., 1968), 118–19.

39. It was probably the most frequently performed opera of the entire seventeenth century. In addition to records of performances throughout Italy provided by librettos published between 1649 and 1690 (this last under the title *Medea in Colco*), its popularity is attested by the survival of at least nine manuscript

In *Giasone* the definitive separation of aria and recitative was finally achieved. Cicognini's standard means of distinguishing them persisted until the end of the century: strophicism and/or *versi misurati* meant aria; *versi sciolti*, recitative. The distinction was reinforced by clarified dramatic functions for arias: to promote action (the incantation aria; the lullaby), to comment on action and philosophize on life (the comic arias), and to express intense feeling (Giasone's opening love song; Egeo's lament).

Despite these general features, however, Cicognini's arias do not seem predictable either in form or function because they arise so naturally out of the drama. Clear as his signals are, the only formal feature shared by most of his arias is their strophicism. Otherwise, each one of them is unique: in a different meter, with a different rhyme scheme, and an altogether different shape, conferred by highly irregular line lengths. And, clear as their dramatic function is, each emerges from its context in its individual way, for its own purpose, strictly in accordance with verisimilitude. No two characters are presented in the same way. Each scene, each action segment, each act unfolds musically in its own particular fashion.

The special strengths of *Giasone*, and its significance as a model, lie in the balance it embodies. The clear signals of the librettist are perfectly matched by the composer's response, achieved both without recourse to rigid formula and without excessive strain on verisimilitude. The musical drama is shaped by an appreciation, shared by the poet and composer, of the distinctions between speech and song. *Giasone* is an ideal *dramma per musica*, in which both elements of the now-historic compromise have equal weight—mutually justifying each other. *Giasone* also offered a model for operatic conventions of a more general kind, presenting traditional scene-types with a naturalness rarely matched in its successors. We shall have occasion to consider this aspect of the opera in detail in chapters 11 and 12. Literally, then, *Giasone* represented a brief moment of equilibrium in the history of opera: at once the endpoint of a process of generic maturation and the beginning of a new stage in which, now fully legitimized, and aided and abetted by the rising influence of the singer, *musica* would eventually subjugate *dramma*.

Paradoxically, perhaps, the very inventive freshness of *Giasone* was both the source of its popular success and the cause of its eventual indictment by the Arcadians. Although it was itself carefully constructed so as not to disrupt verisimilitude, either in the arias or in the mixing of comic and serious elements,

---

scores dispersed in various European libraries—far more than for any other seventeenth-century opera. For a survey of these sources, see Bianconi, "Caletti," 692, and Thomas Walker, "Cavalli," *New*

Grove, 4: 32. Crescimbeni may in fact have known the work in one of its later, more aria-filled incarnations.

it spawned imitations that were less observant. The decadence deplored by Crescimbeni is in fact much better exemplified by one of those imitations, *Alessandro vincitor di se stesso* (Venice, 1651), which was specifically modeled on *Giasone*, by two operatic neophytes, Francesco Sbarra and Antonio Cesti.[40] Often cited by modern historians as marking the definitive breakdown of operatic verisimilitude by having initiated the invasion of the aria, *Alessandro* is far better known for the preface to its libretto than for anything else. In fact, its score was misattributed to Cavalli until relatively recently.[41] In confronting the crucial issue of verisimilitude in his preface, Sbarra acknowledged that arias are unsuitable for serious characters such as Alessandro and Aristotile, but he justified them on the basis of operatic necessity: "if recitative were not interrupted by such jokes, opera would cause more annoyance than delight" (Appendix I.29f).

But, as the libretto itself illustrates, abuse of verisimilitude runs much deeper than the mere misbehavior of Sbarra's heroes. Admittedly, the distribution of the arias is atypical. Not only does Alessandro sing five "ariette" and Aristotile two—out of a total of some thirty closed forms—but another principal, Efestione, sings seven, while Apelle, a character who could easily—and humorously—have sung more, has only one. By focusing on Aristotile's and Alessandro's few "ariette," however, Sbarra obscured the real abuses of verisimilitude in his work, abuses that reveal his lack of experience as a librettist and his misunderstanding of the model represented by *Giasone*. Sbarra's misconception has to do with the function of arias in the drama. For it is not so much *that* Alessandro and Aristotile sing arias, but *when* they do so, and *why*. Most of their arias, as well as some sung by other characters, are wholly unjustified dramatically.

Alessandro bears signs of inconsistency, both in the librettist's method of signaling closed forms and in the composer's response, an inconsistency born of confusion over the purpose of such forms. Indeed, it is that confusion, dressed as purposeful, that is described in Sbarra's preface. Although it has a somewhat greater number of arias than other operas of the same time (some thirty-odd), many more of their texts are formally ambiguous. Only eight—fewer than one-fourth—are strophic, a much smaller proportion than in Cicognini's librettos, and the others fall into surprisingly many patterns, hardly any two of them alike. They range from as few as four to as many as thirteen lines in a variety of meters and rhyme schemes, and only a few of them utilize

40. The modeling is alluded to in Sbarra's preface (Appendix I.29a-b).
41. The correct attribution was first proposed by Pirrotta in "Tre capitoli su Cesti." It was reasserted in 1960 by Osthoff, "Antonio Cestis 'Alessandro vincitor di se stesso,'" 13–43. The misattribution stemmed from the usual source, Ivanovich.

refrains. Particularly in the case of the shorter texts, it is often difficult to know whether to regard them as aria signals at all, although the composer obviously took them that way.

The dramatic function of these texts does little to reinforce their formal significance or clarify their message to the composer. Indeed, they often seem to contradict the implicit conventions of verisimilitude altogether. Invitations to lyrical expansion are reserved for neither commentary, contemplation, nor highly emotional expression, but occur almost indiscriminately, even in the midst of conversations.

For example, the dialogue between Efestione and Alessandro in act 1, scene 5, is cast in a succession of tightly rhymed, highly metrical passages; the text form suggests aria setting but the dramatic situation does not.

[ALESS.] Godo che la fortuna	I am happy that Fortune,
Emula di me stesso a' merti tuoi	Emulating me, has to your merits
Voti gli Erarii suoi.	Devoted her treasures.
Mà dove, dov'è	But where, where is
La gemma si bella,	The lovely gem
Che provida stella	That a provident star
In dono ti diè?	Gifted you with?
Mà dove, dov'è?	But where, where is it?
[EFEST.] Sù presti	Come, quick,
S'appresti,	Let it be readied,
Conducasi quà.	Let it be led here.
Discopra	Let the rare beauty
Quest'opra	Of this work
Sua rara beltà.	Be revealed.

And then later in the same scene:

[EFEST.] Di Gemma così grande,	Of so great a gem
Di cui maggior non è	That none greater exists
Da l'Occaso agli Eoi.	From West to East.
Solo degni ne son gli Erarij tuoi.	Only your treasures are worthy.
Deh mi conceda la tua bontà,	Pray let your kindness grant
Ch'io depositi là	That I deposit there
Questa mia ricca preda.	My rich booty.
[ALESS.] Tua virtù	Your virtue
Non hà più,	Needs only
Che bramare	To desire,
Impetrare	To beseech.
Tutto può,	It is all-powerful,
Quanto chiede Efestion negar non sò.	What Efestion requests I cannot deny.

Cesti set the first dialogue and the last passage in aria style in response to clear signals from the poet. But such treatment renders the interaction between the characters extremely unnatural and stilted. Sbarra's lack of discrimination here is exacerbated by Cesti's faithful setting (example 15). The libretto contains a number of other instances of one character addressing another in aria. They include Cina's midscene strophic address to Alessandro in 1.3; Aristotile's, also strophic, to Alessandro in 1.4; and his non-strophic closing address at the end of the same scene, which, although it might have served to mark his exit, fails to do so because he remains on stage.

Sbarra's blurring of textual-formal distinctions between action and contemplation licensed Cesti to exploit the slightest formal cue to justify lyrical expansion, regardless of the dramatic situation. In act 1, scene 6, for example, the inappropriateness of Alessandro's aria is more the fault of the composer than the librettist. The text is a quatrain addressed to Campaspe:

Tua bellezza è celeste,	Your beauty is celestial,
Caduca esser non può, non può morire;	It cannot be ephemeral, cannot die.
Che della morte il gelo	For the ice of death
Trionfa della Terra, e non del Cielo.	Prevails on Earth, not in Heaven.

Although this is not as unequivocally formal as the previously quoted text—its only regularity is a rhyming final couplet—Cesti confirms closure by setting it as an elaborate, florid, and highly expanded aria (example 16).

Cesti set most of Sbarra's metrical texts lyrically, no matter how short, but he weighted some more heavily than others through the use of string accompaniment, instrumental ritornellos, and repetition of music and text, thereby emphasizing their separation from the recitative context, their "aria" character. In other instances, however, the lyricism is more fleeting—and more acceptable from the point of view of verisimilitude. Emerging suddenly from the recitative context, it disappears back into it with minimum impact; the composer runs straight through the text, only once, as if it were recitative, with no musical elaboration at all.

Even when separation from the dramatic context is specifically legitimized, both by the particular situation and the text form, as in most of the strophic arias, Cesti adhered closely to the structure of the poetry. Such adherence often yields an effective mixing and juxtaposition of styles, "alla Cavalli." In Fidalpa's aria in act 2, scene 7, for instance, the composer breaks the nine-line text into three sections—aria-recitative-aria—thereby retaining flexibility of text portrayal, even within an aria. The variety of Cesti's responses to Sbarra's signals for closure would seem to require a richer descriptive terminology; *aria* alone does not suffice. Such terms as *arioso*, *mezz'aria*, and *arietta* are useful here to distinguish between lyrical passages that are integrated within recitative, short arias that are musically undeveloped, and light "singsong" arias that are based on strongly metrical texts.[42]

Sbarra's numerous metrically distinct texts, almost all of which Cesti set lyrically, may have assured sufficient relief from musical tedium, but at great cost to the drama. By depriving arias of their traditional—and purposely limited—functions as songs or as vehicles of emotional release, and thus flattening the distinctions between them and recitative, Sbarra and Cesti actually deprived *dramma per musica* of one of the chief sources of its strength. Aristotile and Alessandro indeed did not act like heroes. They could not behave properly in public because they did not know the difference between speech and song, knowledge that any comic servant or Venetian audience was fully privy to.

In marked contrast to *Giasone*, *Alessandro* seems to have failed at its first performance.[43] It would be reassuring to be able to ascribe that failure to its shortcomings as a music drama, to the tastes of a discriminating audience; but unfortunately evidence for such discrimination is lacking. Indeed, despite its problematic character, the work was revived at least six times during the 1650s.[44] But it remained an anomaly. The librettists and composers of the second half of the century—including Cesti, and even Sbarra—eventually found more effective ways of incorporating additional arias into their operas: they did so not by abusing verisimilitude but by expanding the opportunities for justified song. Rather than depriving arias of their dramatic function, Cicognini's heirs altered the dramaturgy of their librettos to accommodate more of them, developing structural as well as dramatic conventions to shield them—in monologues and dreams, at entrances and exits. It was the crystallization of these conventions, originally inspired by the requirements of verisimilitude, and the attempts to circumvent or vary them, that eventually led to the decline lamented by Crescimbeni.

---

42. The term *mezz'aria* was used by Domenico Mazzocchi to refer to measured or songlike sections within or at the ends of recitative passages in his *La catena d'Adone* (Rome, 1626); see Nino Pirrotta, "Falsirena and the Earliest Cavatina," *Essays*, 340 and n. 11. The similarity of Marazzoli's conception of "mezz'Arie . . . che rompono il tedio del recitativo" and Sbarra's *ariette*, which provide the same service, is striking. In general, writers of this period seem to use *arietta* as a synonym for our *aria*. For a modern attempt at an analytically useful definition of *arietta*, see Beth Glixon's review of Drammaturgia musicale veneta, vols. 4, 6, 12, 18, 24, 26, *CM* 39 (1985): 82 n. 15. Glixon proposes the term to distinguish "librettist-generated" periods of lyrical recitative, marked by odd groups of *versi misurati*, from those

initiated by the composer himself without a formal signal from the libretto.

43. It is to Benedetto Ferrari that we owe the information that *Alessandro* was unsuccessful—if we can believe him. He wrote to Ottavio Orsucci, a nobleman in Lucca, on 3 April 1651, that he had received "bad reports" of the music of "Allessandro" (letter in I–La); see Bianconi and Walker, "Dalla 'Finta pazza,'" 431: "La rilatione poi, ch'ella mi scrive, essersi havuta da Venetia dell'Allessandro qui s'è havuta ad un'altra maniera cioè, che non ha ricevuto applauso nissuno, che la musica non ha valuto niente, se non che della poesia non ne dicono male."

44. For a complete list of revivals, which occurred in various Italian cities as well as Munich, see Sartori, "Primo tentativo."

10

• • •

Il diletto: Aria, Drama, and the
Emergence of Formal Conventions

By the middle of the century the basic outlines of *dramma per musica* had been firmly established. Librettists and composers could now exuberantly explore and extend its implications. The era of the academic librettists had virtually ended, and with the death of Faustini and Cicognini by 1651, most of the old guard had disappeared, leaving a new generation in charge, a generation inspired perhaps even more by the promise of financial or commercial success than by any special aesthetic aims. The leading poets of these years were Minato and Aureli, both of whom made their operatic debuts around 1650. The old composers, too, were gone. Ferrari, Manelli, Sacrati, and Monteverdi belonged to the past. Soon they would be replaced by younger composers less closely associated with the values of the *seconda prattica*: Cesti, Ziani, Pallavicino, Sartorio. Only Cavalli bridged the eras; a conservative, he continued to adhere to his original principles in the face of change all around him. Nevertheless, his renown as an opera composer increased well into the 1660s, exceeding that of any other in his lifetime. Only at the very end of his career, in the 1670s, did his style come to be regarded as hopelessly old-fashioned.

By midcentury, too, the main musical elements of opera—aria and recitative—had been clearly defined in both form and function. They had achieved a large measure of musical independence from each other: closure had become definitively associated with lyricism; librettists' signals and composers' responses had become clear and predictable, if not yet thoroughly conventionalized. The common indication for an aria in a libretto was a group of strophes (eventually two) in *versi misurati*; some kinds of non-strophic texts, often involving refrains, had also emerged as aria signals. By 1650, not all arias were strophic, but virtually all strophic texts were set as arias.[1]

---

1. There were, of course, exceptions. One of the old-fashioned aspects of Cavalli's *Eliogabalo* (1668) was the number of times he chose recitative or stro-phic variation rather than straightforward aria style for the strophic texts.

Closed forms had also become more numerous, their average number per opera more than doubling, from about a dozen in 1640 to around twenty-five a decade later.[2] And they continued to increase: most operas of the 1670s contained sixty arias or more. Obviously, as more and more of an opera became devoted to closed forms, these assumed increasing weight—musical, dramatic, and expressive. Their dramatic function gradually expanded to include more frequent affective outbursts and even, on occasion, conversation. The arias themselves changed accordingly: their dimensions expanded; they assumed new formal configurations and greater musical complexity. But they remained closely linked to the drama. Formal conventions emerged in response to— almost as a by-product of—specific dramatic needs.

This makes arias difficult to categorize formally. It is almost as if composers and librettists, reacting anew to each dramatic situation within the most general of guidelines, invented as they went along. Every solution was a fresh one, every formal configuration a response to dramatic necessity. Yet some categorization does seem possible. Critics have attempted it, but they have usually come up with categories insufficiently useful, either because they are incommensurable (Worsthorne's *strophic* and *da capo*) or too minutely descriptive (Hjelmborg's *rondo-refrain* and *rondo–da capo*, etc.).[3] The challenge is to find a taxonomy that is not too restrictive, one that reveals persistent or emerging formal patterns while allowing for the central place of dramatic function as the original inspiration for them. The subheadings in this chapter suggest the dimensions of the difficulty: "The Bipartite Aria," "The Exit Convention and the Bipartite Aria," "Tripartite Forms," "Refrain in Recitative," "Da Capo Refrain Arias," "Coherence in Da Capo and Da Capo Refrain Arias," "Contrast in Da Capo Forms," and "Static Da Capo Arias." The distinctions are further clouded by the fact that most of the subsections consider the same issues: the effect of textual form and meaning on musical setting, the musical relationship of refrain to its context, whether recitative or aria. One basic theme, however, serves both to link and to clarify these subdivisions: the fundamental relationship of all of this music to the needs of the drama. Beyond that, a general chronological trend is evident. After a period of formal experimentation involving a variety of refrain forms, composers came increasingly to confirm expectation, resulting in the emergence of the bipartite and, eventually, the da capo aria.

2. Some early operas had considerably fewer than a dozen: there were only three closed forms in the libretto of *Il ritorno d'Ulisse* and only five in *Andromeda*.

3. Worsthorne, *Venetian Opera*, 58. Bjørn Hjelmborg, "Aspects of the Aria in the Early Operas of Francesco Cavalli," in *Natalicia musicologica Knud Jeppesen septuagenario collegis oblata*, ed. Bjørn Hjelm-borg and Søren Sørensen (Copenhagen, 1962), 174–80. In the past I myself have used a typology based on dramatic mode, dividing arias into comic, serious, and lament. See Ellen Rosand, "Aria in the Early Operas of Francesco Cavalli" (Ph.D. diss., New York University, 1971); also id., "Comic Contrast," 92–105.

Strophic form was the umbrella for most midcentury arias. Composers no longer exercised the option of setting individual strophes to different music; on the contrary, exact musical repetition became so commonplace that only a single strophe of music was necessary. Many scores do not even provide the texts for subsequent strophes, let alone the music, leaving it to the performers to extract them from the libretto.[4] (Presumably, an aria could be lengthened or shortened at will simply by adding or subtracting strophes.) These single strophes were themselves variously organized, depending on the dramatic function of the individual aria. Often they ended with a sententious summary line or couplet in a distinctive meter (example 17, text p. 285 below) which could either be varied in subsequent strophes, repeated as a refrain, exactly (example 18, text, p. 286 below), or slightly modified (examples 19, 20, texts, p. 287 below). Such texts suggested a bipartite, or AB, musical setting, reflecting the poet's distinction between the refrain or *sententia* and the preceding lines. Sometimes, rather than just closing each stanza, the refrain appeared at the beginning as well (examples 29–44, text pp. 300–318 below). In such cases a tripartite, or ABA, setting was suggested.

Of course, the effect of both AB and ABA arrangements changed with the addition of subsequent strophes. Librettists assumed that all of their strophes would be set. This was not a problem with bipartite organization, which simply replicated itself, retaining its original proportions, AB CB DB, and so on. But a tripartite strophic aria risked becoming unwieldy by placing undue emphasis on the refrain material: ABA ACA ADA. For this reason, librettists modified the form in one of three ways: (1) by changing the refrain from stanza to stanza (ABA, CDC, EFE, example 29, text, p. 300 below); (2) by replacing the opening refrain in all stanzas after the first (ABA CDA EFA, examples 28 and 30, pp. 299 and 301 below); or (3) by omitting the opening refrain in all stanzas after the first (ABA CA DA, example 31, p. 302 below).[5] The first two types ended up being essentially the same musically, despite their poetic distinctions, since composers followed the normal rules of strophic structure in setting them: ignoring the fact that the first lines of all strophes were different, they set them

---

4. Sometimes last-minute addenda to librettos contained extra strophes for arias. See, for example, the one published in connection with *Medoro* (1658) in *Medoro*, ed. Morelli and Walker, CXCIV–V. Evidence from a number of the Contarini manuscripts indicates that strophes subsequent to the first were regularly cut during rehearsals. On the other hand, as we know, strophes were often added in rehearsals as well. Directions such as "si fa la seconda stroffa" or "questa stroffa non si fa" are common. Also, second strophes are sometimes crossed out.

5. The form resulting from the first of these prac-

tices might be called *strophic da capo*; Hjelmborg ("Aspects of the Aria," 179) has termed the other two *da capo refrain* and *rondo refrain* respectively. He does not mention the first option, perhaps because musically it would be treated in the same way as the second; composers regularly set a changing refrain as if it were a repeated one. There is another permutation of the rondo-refrain form, practiced exclusively by Minato, in which the lines of the initial refrain (A) are reversed when they return (C), so that the musical form suggested is more like ABC DC EC (for an example of this arrangement, see n. 35 below).

to the same music. The third type invited greater variety, with greater contrast between refrain and strophe. Reduced to a single stanza, these were the arias that most closely resembled the later da capo aria. However their musical realizations may have differed, all three variants belong to the formal category of da capo refrain, as distinct from the plain da capo aria (or single stanza enclosed by a refrain).

To use the expression *da capo* in connection with any aria written before 1650 is to risk the charge of using anachronistic terminology. The term refers more accurately to a form that, though it developed in the second half of the seventeenth century, did not reach its peak until the early years of the eighteenth. Pirrotta has warned against applying the term to ternary forms that "lack an exact repetition of opening music, a full and stereotyped repetition of words, and a clear division into sections."[6] Indeed, at least until the 1680s, tripartite or ABA structure was more commonly found as a subcategory of strophic form than as an independent structure. Still, the fact remains: these tripartite strophes, though they may have lacked one or more of the defining characteristics of "classic" da capo form, did share at least one of those characteristics, and the most prominent one: the return to opening material, the "da capo." The dramatic function of such return and composers' methods of dealing with it may differ for the miniature forms and the fully developed ones, but they are equally significant for both. These shared concerns, which transcend specific musical differences in dimensions or proportions, are emphasized by — and, indeed, justify — the use of the term *da capo* avant la lettre, particularly in connection with strophic refrain forms. We must bear in mind, however, that the "classic" da capo form acquired its defining features gradually, and from a number of diverse sources, not simply from refrain-enclosed strophes but from particular kinds of refrains with a particular dramatic function.

6. Pirrotta, "The Lame Horse and the Coachman," *Essays*, 459, n. 26. Hjelmborg, too, recommends reserving *da capo* for arias "in which the dimensions and internal organization of the da capo section are sufficiently developed to make the part appear as a self-contained unit, almost as an aria strophe in itself, further accompanied by orchestra and followed by a ritornello, whereas the cases when the repeated section only appears precisely as a section within the strophe relying on the other sections for support could be called simply ternary aba forms" ("Aspects of the Aria," 180). But, as we shall see, there are many degrees of independence between refrains and the rest of a setting for which the designation *da capo* seems appropriate, particularly since the *da capo* rubric is actually used. Powers, "Erismena," 307–9, accepts neither Pirrotta's nor Hjelm-

borg's definition, refusing to grant da capo status to any aria that is not an exit aria, even if it displays generous proportions, an elaborate instrumental accompaniment, and an exact return of a distinct refrain. Rather than attempt a restrictive definition, Saunders has distinguished usefully between da capo design and form, the latter associated with a particular, standardized tonal plan that developed in the final decade of the seventeenth century (see id., "Repertoire," 185–97). A good example of an early da capo aria complete with identifying rubric that meets Pirrotta's and Hjelmborg's criteria (but not those of Powers) is Corinta's "Udite amanti" from *Oristeo* (Faustini/Cavalli, 1651), 1.6 [=1.7] (see facsimile in Italian Opera, 1640–1770, ed. Howard Mayer Brown [New York, 1982] [henceforth cited as Garland facs.] 62: ff. 22–22ᵛ).

Both the bipartite and tripartite forms eventually flowered into showcases for the composer's and singer's art, but their earliest manifestations were hardly distinguishable, musically, from recitative. Like recitative, they initially responded to particular dramatic needs, developing into fully standardized formal types only after the middle of the century. Furthermore, as we shall see, both types of aria can be linked to a particular convention of recitative poetry, the one-line aphorism, which was introduced by Busenello, exploited and popularized by Faustini, and institutionalized in the librettos of Aureli and Minato.

The Bipartite Aria

First to emerge as a form in its own right, the bipartite aria developed from attentive, recitative-like setting of text that followed the poetry line by line, precisely mirroring its metrical and rhyme structure without developing or emphasizing any single idea. This procedure is evident in Acchille's short speech at the beginning of 1.3 of *La finta pazza* (Strozzi/Sacrati, 1641) (example 17):

Ombra di timore,	No shadow of fear
Non mi turba il petto;	Disturbs my bosom.
Nembo di sospetto	No cloud of suspicion
Non mi scuote il core.	Shakes my heart.
Non può vero valor perder sue tempre.	True valor cannot its temper lose.
In ogni habito Acchille, Acchille è sempre.	Under any guise Achilles is ever Achilles.

Sacrati's setting, completely straightforward and syllabic, in duple meter, is only marginally more highly organized than normal recitative. Each of its first two parallel phrases (setting lines 1–2 and 3–4) is followed by an instrumental echo, for two violins and continuo; and a slight flourish at the end, involving repetition of part of the final line of text, promotes closure (even though the passage ends in the relative minor). Sacrati's music responds to the text on three different levels: it matches its form, a sequence of four *senari* culminating in two *endecasillabi*, rhyming *abbacc*, a kind of organization that was typically (though not here) duplicated in a succession of strophes; it underlines the self-affirmation of its closing line; finally, it heightens its dramatic function as Acchille's first utterance in the opera.[7] While it would be difficult to consider Acchille's brief speech an aria, particularly in the absence of subsequent strophes, it does illustrate the kind of austerity of text-setting that characterizes the earliest Venetian arias.

---

7. This is an early presentation aria; see p. 314 below.

Most composers, however, propelled by their own natural impulse toward closure, would have taken greater advantage of the metric distinction of Acchille's closing couplet, emphasizing it by a change of meter, key, and/or melodic style, and capping it with a ritornello based on the same musical material—a kind of non-verbal reiteration of the text. Such treatment was encouraged when the final line or couplet carried a distinctive meaning, in the form of an epigram or aphorism. When such a line or couplet recurs as a refrain in successive strophes, the emphasis takes on even greater formal weight. But the effect is not merely formal; reiteration serves a rhetorical purpose by calling repeated attention to the already emphatic message of the refrain.

In responding to the combination of formal and rhetorical distinctions in such texts, composers wrote arias that were essentially bipartite; that is, they differentiated clearly between the refrain or epitomizing moral (the B section) and the rest of the text (A). To reinforce general distinctions of meter and melodic style, they often changed the accompanimental forces, from bare continuo to string tutti. And they sometimes called further attention to the change of style in mid aria, heightening the effect of the refrain or moral by setting the line immediately preceding it as recitative (as in example 20 below).

In Cavalli's earliest arias, the distinction between the A and B sections is often quite sharp. Sometimes, as in Jarba's "O benefico Dio" from *Didone* (Busenello/Cavalli, 1641) 3.10, the refrain is the only part of a closed form he set lyrically (example 18):

O' benefico Dio,	O beneficent God,
O' dator delle gratie, e de favori,	O giver of mercy and of favors,
Felicità mi doni,	You grant me happiness
Che soprafà	That overwhelms
L'humanità;	Humanity:
Chi più lieto di me nel mondo fia,	*Who shall be happier in this world than I,*
Se Didon finalmente sarà mia.	*If Dido at last is to be mine.*
O' secreti profondi,	Oh deepest secrets,
Non arrivati dal pensiero humano;	Unapproachable by the human mind;
Per contemplarli	To contemplate them
Forza non hà	Humanity lacks
L'humanità;	The power;
Chi più lieto di me . . .[8]	*Who shall be happier . . .*

Here the lyrical setting, seconded by a related five-measure ritornello, emphasizes Jarba's incredulous happiness at the possibility that Didone will be his, despite his fears to the contrary. Conversely, and more remarkably, Cavalli occasionally distinguished a refrain from the body of a strophe by setting it alone in recitative style. The refrain in another of Jarba's arias, "Rivolgo altrove

---

8.   All refrains are henceforth italicized.

il piede" (2.2), is a cry of distress whose affect is more powerfully projected by irregular recitative than it would have been by metrical lyricism (example 19):

Rivolgo altrove il piede,	I turn my steps elsewhere,
E'l cor mio resta qui.	And my heart remains here.
D'aita, e di mercede	The day of succor and mercy
Veder non spero il di.	I do not hope to see.
Insanabile mal m'opprime il core,	*Incurable malady oppresses my heart;*
Son disperato, e pur nutrisco amore.	*I am despairing, yet I nourish love.*
Derelitto, ramingo	Derelict, wandering,
Didone, ahi dove andrò,	O Dido, where alas shall I go?
Lagrimoso, e solingo	Tearful and solitary
Le selci ammolirò;	I shall soften the very stones,
Dirà pur sempre agonizando il core	*And my agonizing heart will ever say,*
Son disperato, e pur nutrisco amore.	*I am despairing, yet I nourish love.*

The mere change of style is enough to call attention to the refrain.

Typically, however, the contrast was more subtle and did not involve a change in style. Among numerous early examples of the standard, straightforward bipartite aria, a characteristic one is Erino's "Stolto chi fà d'un crine" from *La virtù de' strali d'Amore* (Faustini/Cavalli, 1642) 1.9 (example 20):

Stolto chi fà d'un crine	Foolish the man who of a tress
A la sua libertà laccio, e catena;	Makes a noose, a chain to his freedom:
D'una infida Sirena	Loving the impious, killing beauty
Amando l'empio bello, ed homicida,	Of a faithless siren,
Che mentre l'alma affida	Who, while he entrusts to her his soul,
Gl'appresta eterne, e misere ruine:	Prepares for him eternal, pitiful ruin:
Amor è un precipitio, e morte alfine.	*Love is a precipice, and death in the end.*
Sfortunato quel piede,	Unfortunate the foot
Che errando và per l'amoroso impero,	That wanders over love's empire,
In cui scacciato il vero	Wherein, truth having been banished,
Sol la bugia s'annida, e il tradimento,	Only lies and treachery make their nest,
La perfidia, il tormento,	Perfidiousness, and torment,
Il lungo affaticar senza mercede:	And long, thankless labor:
Amor è fele al core, e non ha fede.	*Love is bile to the heart, and it is faithless.*
[+ two more strophes]	

Consisting of four seven-line strophes that conclude with a sententious inexact refrain, its text form is somewhat irregular in that meter and rhyme fail to confirm one another completely. This may be why Cavalli chose to treat the first six lines in a speechlike manner. He set the refrain apart from the rest, however, by a shift to triple meter and disjunct musical material suggested by its imagery. The line stands out by virtue of its distinctive "precipitio" motive, which provides the subject for the following ritornello. The refrain music is unequivocally text-inspired, but by the first strophe only; it fits the subsequent refrains much less well.

The balance between the two sections of this aria is more equal than the distribution of its text would suggest. The distinctive music of the B section, particularly as reinforced by its echoing ritornello, compensates for its comparative brevity. The tendency to alter the proportions of a textual form for dramatic purposes increased markedly during the course of the century. Indeed, rather than merely balancing the longer texts of A sections, B sections eventually outweighed them (as in example 22 below). Usually, the emphasis on B involved repetition of its music and text. The two statements generally occurred on different tonal levels, the second returning the piece to the tonic. In such cases the resultant form might more properly be identified as ABB′ rather than AB. This extended bipartite aria was the predominant type.[9]

The repetition of B material was occasionally only partial. More frequently, however, repetition involved the complete B section, particularly when that section comprised a complete refrain. In an aria for Dema from *Egisto* (Faustini/Cavalli, 1643), "Piacque à me sempre più" (2.8), the B section is repeated not only as a whole but in parts as well, thereby emphasizing the message of the refrain quite thoroughly (example 21):

Piacque à me sempre più	I always loved lovely youth
La vaga gioventù d'ogn'altra etade;	More than any other age;
Sempre quella beltade	Ever that beauty
Mi porse più contento,	Gave me more pleasure
Che non havea ruvido pelo al mento.	Than any rough-bearded chin.
Chi hà provato il mio amor	*She who has felt my love,*
mi dice errai?	*will she say I erred?*
Non credo un sì, non credo udir giamai.	*I scarcely think I'll ever hear a "yes."*
Labro lanoso à me	A woolly lip has never
Un sol bacio non diè, che mi ricordi,	Given me a single kiss, that I remember.
Ben con desiri ingordi	Instead, with ravenous desire,
Io volsi ambrosie care	I have preferred ever to sip
Da guancie tenerelle ogn'or succhiare.	Precious ambrosia from tender cheeks.
Chi hà provato . . .	*She who has felt . . .*
[+ one more strophe]	

Extensive and irregular repetition of B material here gives a greater sense of harmonic closure than usual; B′ actually contracts the material of B, but the two sections are harmonically almost identical: they both move from relative major to tonic, though only B′ remains there. Repetition in this case performs a formal as well as expressive function. Not only does it emphasize the message

9. Alfred Lorenz christened this form the "Seicento Aria" (*Alessandro Scarlattis Jugendoper* [Augsburg, 1927], 1: 213–18).

of the refrain, but it serves to ground the piece strongly in the tonic. In the most elaborate ABB' arias, particularly after the middle of the century, expansion was inspired as much by musical considerations—the desire to establish harmonic closure—as by rhetorical ones.

Despite their differing proportions, dimensions, and musical style, all five of the foregoing examples illustrate the development of the bipartite aria out of the recitative aesthetic. They show how the composer's attempt to enhance the shape and meaning of certain kinds of texts led to the bipartite form. But the direct relationship between recitative procedures and this form is demonstrated even more vividly by considering a characteristic practice within recitative poetry itself: the use of the epigrammatic arioso. The impetus behind the form and the procedure is the same: a desire to focus attention toward climax at the end.

Aphoristic tag lines were not exclusively associated with formal poetry. In librettos of the 1640s they often occurred at the end of recitative speeches, sometimes coinciding with the end of a scene and the departure of the speaker. Composers (occasionally Monteverdi, primarily Cavalli) tended to set such lines lyrically, in arioso style, repeating them and thereby emphasizing their punctuating function—and their meaning.[10] Both function and meaning were often further enhanced, like equivalent mottos in arias, by a ritornello or sinfonia based on the same material.[11]

Recitatives culminating in epigrams continued to be used well past the middle of the century, not merely for punctuation but more consistently for exits. Both Minato and Aureli favored them. *Erismena* (Aureli/Cavalli, 1655) contains many, of widely varying lengths. Act 1, scene 10, for example, ends

---

10.   There are several such passages in *La finta pazza*, usually comprising more than one line of text, which perform a punctuating function without necessarily ending a scene. Faustini's librettos are a particularly rich source of examples. The *locus classicus* for this procedure was identified by Pirrotta in a Roman opera, Mazzocchi's and Tronsarelli's *La catena d'Adone* (1626). Pirrotta regards passages like these as ancestors of the cavata, and, eventually, the cavatina. Such passages were extracted (i.e., *cavate*) from recitative poetry for lyrical setting. See Pirrotta, "Falsirena," *Essays*, 340 and n. 15; also Powers, "Erismena," 280; and, more recently and conclusively, Fabbri, "Istituti metrici e formali," 180–85, and Colin Timms, "The Cavata at the Time of Vivaldi," in *Nuovi studi vivaldiani* (Florence, 1988), 451–77. In using the term in his letter to Pagliardi (Appendix II.5b), Ivanovich gives a clear idea of the purpose of such excavations: to underline a particular passage of text ("Se poi ritrovasse qualche affetto nel recitativo, che si possa ridurre in una cavata, non tralasci di farlo, che vien gradito qualche risalto improviso"). The term "cavata" is actually found in some opera scores of this period, where it seems to refer to arias based on very short, metrically closed texts lacking refrains or any other kind of formal indication (see the Vienna score of Sartorio's *Orfeo* [1673], discussed in Rosand, "L'Ovidio trasformato," XXXIII). One such piece is illustrated in ch. 11 below (example 51).

11.   In *Ormindo* 3.9, for example, an extended recitative by Mirinda ends with an arioso line followed by a related sinfonia but no exit (f. 157^v). Cavalli even transformed one such final line from *Ormindo* (3.11) into an arioso duet (ff. 163^v-164). The terms *sinfonia* and *ritornello* are not quite used synonymously in opera scores of this period. The former is usually reserved for independent introductory movements (overtures) or single instrumental movements within the drama that accompany some action, while the latter refers to an instrumental refrain separating the strophes of an aria.

with a seven-line exit recitative for Idraspe, which culminates in a sexually allusive aphoristic couplet, set lyrically by the composer:

Amor Nume bendato	The blindfold god of love
Che di foco novel nutre mia speme	That has renewed my flame for this fair stranger,
I perigli non vede, e non li teme.	He does not see, and therefore fears no danger.
De passati successi	Those forgotten affections,
La memoria hò perduta, e sappi amico,	I bequeath to Armenia, too well finding,
Che à l'amorose brame	That amorous desire
Un cibo sol non trasse mai la fame.[12]	Does for its thirst more than one draught require.

Occasionally, the exit function rather than the meaning seems to have inspired the lyrical setting of a recitative line or couplet, as in the case of Argippo's scene-closing arioso from *Erismena* 1.3:

Lodato il Cielo? anch'io piagato un dì	Praised be to Heaven! I, too, once wounded,
Torno in Corte a mirar chi mi ferì.	Return to court to see the one who wounded me.

Such punctuating ariosos eventually became functionally and literally linked to the exit aria.[13]

The link is nicely illustrated in two examples from *Erismena*. They involve comparison between two versions of the score, the original of 1655 [1656] and a revision dating from sometime before 1670.[14] In one instance an exit aria by one comic character (Alcesta) replaces an exit arioso by another (Flerida) who has been eliminated from the revised scene. The text of aria and arioso are equivalent; both comment on the preceding action, but the aria is, naturally, more emphatic (and gives the character more opportunity for humor). In the other instance (from 1.10), an exit arioso in the earlier version is followed in the later one by an exit aria for the same character, expostulating or expanding upon the sentiment of the arioso. Here the culminating effect is intensified and reinforced, rather than replaced.[15]

---

12.   See Powers, "Erismena," 286, for discussion of the revision of this passage in 1670. The translations from *Erismena* are taken from the text of the seventeenth-century English score, which may have come from the library of Samuel Pepys, and may have been the "Italian opera in musicque, the first that had been in England of this kind" that John Evelyn saw on 5 January 1674. See Winton Dean, "Review of Erismena," *MT* 108 (1967): 636. Since it was a singing translation, the English is not always exactly equivalent to the Italian, as in line 5 here. But it makes perfect sense in the context of the opera as a whole.

13.   See, for example, Aceste's closing speech in *Argia*, 3.3 (Garland facs., 3: ff. 115ᵛ–116). There are numerous instances in *Scipione affricano*: for Scipione in 2.11 (Garland facs., 5: f. 78); for Ericlea in 3.4

(Garland facs., 5: f. 102); and for Sofonisba in 3.10 (Garland facs., 5: f. 112ᵛ). See also *Adelaide* 1.1 and 1.2 (Garland facs., 8: ff. 8 and 12 respectively). The procedure of arioso punctuation was still in use as late as *Giustino* (Beregan/Legrenzi, 1683); see Glixon, "Recitative," 379–85.

14.   On the dating of the scores of *Erismena*, see Powers, "Erismena," 271–72.

15.   The exit aria is in ABA rather than the more characteristic ABB form, a distinction discussed below (see Powers, "Erismena," 277–93). There are numerous examples among other operas that were revised over a period of years of the replacement of an exit recitative or arioso *sententia* by an aria. Compare, for example, the Venice and Modena scores of *Le fortune di Rodope e Damira*, 1.13. In *Scipione affricano* 3.11, an exit recitative for Scipione in the li-

In fact, the intensification of a sententious arioso by following it with an exit aria was quite common, even much earlier than the *Erismena* revision. Such sequences of lyrical events were particularly characteristic of comic soliloquies in Cavalli's Faustini settings. In these scenes, the music matched the drama: the buildup of momentum toward exit was confirmed by increased musical intensity and structure.[16]

The Exit Convention and the Bipartite Aria

Although ABB' arias did not always coincide with a character's departure, at least not until well after 1650, the two levels of action, musical and dramatic, meshed well. When associated with exits, the arias enhanced them even further. In addition, the echoing ritornellos commonly generated by both aria and epigrammatic arioso facilitated the business of exiting; perhaps arioso expansions and arias were even inserted in some cases to justify the interpolation of such instrumental passages.[17]

During the 1650s and 1660s, bipartite arias gravitated increasingly to the ends of scenes. The growing interest of Venetian audiences in the singers and their self-exhibition in arias must have been partially responsible for this tendency to save the best for last. Once a conventional function and position had been found for them, however, such arias were freed from the austerity of recitative-style setting. Accordingly, the close correspondence of music and text that characterized the earliest examples yielded to more expansive musical treatment. Although musical expansion affected entire arias, it was still the B section—the refrain or aphorism—that displayed the greatest freedom; compositional inventiveness further enhanced its exit function. But expansion could still serve a dramatic purpose beyond that: within an aria it could contribute to characterization or to the shaping of a conflict.

In *Erismena*, the text of the heroine's "Comincia à respirar" (1.12) comprises two unequal sections, of four and two lines. The aria is a soliloquy in which Erismena tries to feel hopeful over her quest to recover her faithless lover; she exhorts herself to optimism in the refrain, which summarizes the import of the text: "Courage, courage, my heart. Shake off all your griefs, bid sorrow adieu" (example 22):

---

bretto has been transformed in the score into a strophic aria through the addition of several lines of text (Garland facs., 5: ff. 113ᵛ-114ᵛ).

16. There are many examples of such increasing musical momentum in *Egisto*, *Ormindo*, and *Doriclea*. See p. 297 below.

17. This may not have been strictly necessary, since unattached instrumental music is not completely unknown in these scores. See, for example, the unattached exit Sinfonia at the end of *Scipione affricano* I, 4 (Garland facs., 5: f. 13ᵛ).

Comincia à respirar	Be cheerful, O my heart,
Più giocondo ò mio cor l'aure vitali,	And let your joys trample your suffering under.
Satie di fulminar	Fortune will sheathe her dart
Spera veder un dì l'ire fatali:	And angry Jove will one day cease his thunder.
Vivi lieto sù sù,	*Courage, courage, my heart.*
Ridi in mezo del duol, non pensar più.	*Shake off all your griefs, bid sorrow adieu.*
[+ one more strophe]	

Cavalli's setting more than compensates for the unequal length of the two sections through the usual means of expansion of B: a change of meter, the addition of strings to the continuo accompaniment, new motivic material, extension by means of instrumental echoes between phrases, repetition of the text as a whole, and a concluding ritornello based on its distinctive material. All serve to emphasize the epitomizing function of the refrain, thereby imparting the affective essence of Aureli's text. The A section consists of two subsections, the first moving from the tonic, D minor, to the dominant, A, the second remaining in the relative major, F. With slightly unusual symmetry, the two B sections mirror one another, the first moving from tonic to subdominant, the second in the opposite direction. All the standard related keys are touched in this aria, but their sequence produces a somewhat atypical harmonic structure. The composer's emphasis on the refrain lends depth to the characterization, suggesting energy and self-control, qualities that will help Erismena achieve her objective of regaining Idraspe's affections.

The flourishing of the bipartite aria was essentially a musical phenomenon. The librettist could call for musical repetition by writing a refrain, or he could suggest musical contrast by juxtaposing strongly contrasting meters; but the repetition and expansion of the B section in AB arias were up to the composer.

Despite its conventionality, the ABB' aria never became completely divorced from its origins as a dramatic procedure for emphasizing a tag line. That is, if a text lacked an epigrammatic close worthy of emphasis, the composer did not feel compelled to write an ABB' aria. This is illustrated in an unusual aria from *Argia* (Apolloni/Cesti, 1669). Feraspe's "Aurette vezzose" (1.2) contains a four-line refrain of which Cesti repeats only the first two lines—those most essential to the meaning of the text—to different music (example 23):

Aurette vezzose,	Delightful breezes,
Foriere del giorno	Harbingers of dawn,
Ch'errate d'intorno	That flit about
Con ali di rose,	On rose-scented wings,
Volgetevi à mè;	*Turn to me*
E dite dov'è	*And say where is*
Coleì, che desia	*She, who covets*
Il mio Regno, il mio cor, l'anima mia.	*My kingdom, my heart, my soul.*

Stellanti zaffiri,	Starry sapphires
Ch'i mali influite,	That influence wrongs,
Se mai compatite	If ever you pity
D'un'alma i sospiri,	A sighing soul,
Volgetevi à mè . . .[18]	*Turn to me . . .*

Furthermore, the ritornello is not based upon the B section, as we would expect, but upon A. The musical form of this aria interestingly overlaps that of the poetry. The first two phrases of the A section encompass the whole first sentence of text (lines 1–5), including the first line of the refrain, and move from the tonic, A minor, through the relative major to the dominant; the third phrase of A treats the second line of the refrain, line 6, twice, and closes on the relative major. The B section sets the last two lines of the text, 7–8, expanding them somewhat by means of sequential repetition, and also ends on the relative major. The final section of the aria (C) repeats lines 5–6, running them together for the first time, to completely new music. In fact, then, although the text form clearly suggested a normal bipartite aria, Cesti wrote a tripartite one, choosing to emphasize the indirect question ("say where is she") in the middle of the stanza rather than the hendecasyllable at the end. That is, he emphasized the sense of the text over its form, ignoring the conventional refrain structure.

In some late bipartite arias the composer's liberty took a more aggressive turn. Reaching beyond extreme elaboration and variation, it extended to the writing of new music for the second B section. While such expansion often tended to increase the forward momentum of these arias, and was thus an extension of the ABB impetus, it also ran roughshod over the librettist's text by creating ABC forms out of AB material. In Flavia's "Cieca Dea la tua possanza" from *Eliogabalo* (Aureli/Boretti, 1668) 1.19, for example, Boretti repeated the text of B (lines 3 and 4) to music that is different—and not only harmonically, which would be expected, but also rhythmically and melodically (example 24):

Cieca Dea la tua possanza	Blind goddess, your power
Non m'afflige, e non m'atterra;	Does not afflict me, does not prostrate me;
Con usbergo di costanza	Shielded by constancy,
Armo il sen per farti guerra.	I arm my breast to wage war against you.
[+ one more strophe]	

B' begins to resemble B only at the final melisma on *guerra*, but the melisma is expanded sequentially the second time over a harmonic structure drawn from the end of A, of which it sounds like an embellished variant. Despite its text,

---

18. This aria comes from the Venice 1669 score but was probably also part of the original setting for Innsbruck (1655).

then, B′ actually shares as much with A as it does with B, and the ritornello strengthens the unified effect: a composite of A (mm. 1–5) and B′ (mm. 16–19). Boretti created a rounded aria whose form was not suggested by Aureli's text.[19]

Ziani treated a number of aria texts in *Le fortune di Rodope e Damira* (Aureli/ Ziani, 1657) with similar freedom. Lerino's "Voglio un giorno innamorarmi" (2.7) is built on a six-line stanza, the last two lines of which form a refrain (example 25):

Voglio un giorno innamorarmi	Some day I should like to fall in love,
Donne belle, mà però	Beauteous ladies, but only
Con tal patto, che lasciarmi	On one condition, that I won't let you
Lusingar da voi non vò.	Flatter me.
Sò, che amando tradite, e scaltre ogn'hora	*I know that, as you love, you betray, and, ever wily,*
Voi la fate sù gli occhi à chi v'adora.	*You play your game in full view of him who adores you.*
Far le morte, o spasimate	To play dead, or yearning,
Con me nulla gioverà,	Will gain you nothing with me,
Perche l'arti vostre usate	For your much-used artifices
Mi son note un tempo fà.	Were known to me long ago.
Sò, che amando . . .	*I know that, as you love . . .*

The composer did not emphasize the refrain in the conventional way. Instead, he first repeated the music of lines 3–4, which had closed in the relative minor, this time ending it on the tonic; then he proceeded with the refrain, repeating only its last line extensively in the normal way and carrying forward its motive to the following ritornello. Rather than bipartite, the form might be described as a miniature ABB′CC′. It seems as if Ziani's musical conception needed two additional lines of text before the refrain.

Rodope's aria "Luci belle, se bramate" (1.8), another six-line strophic form with a distinct refrain, is also expanded in the middle (the music of lines 3–4 transposed and extended), and again only the final line of the refrain is repeated, after which its material is taken up in the ritornello; the form, once more, is ABB′CC′, or even ABB′CDD′ (example 26):

Luci belle, se bramate	Beauteous eyes, if you desire
Di saper quant'io v'adori,	To know how much I love you,
Osservatelo a gl'ardori,	Read it in the ardor
Che nel sen voi mi vibrate.	Which you have kindled in my breast.
E direte, che in amarvi	*And you shall say that, loving you,*
Posso struggermi ben, mà non lasciarvi.	*I may well consume myself, but never leave you.*

---

19.   Boretti had no obvious dramatic reason for modifying the librettist's form. There are several examples of this same kind of modification in Sartorio's *Orfeo*.

Lumi cari se volete	Beloved eyes, if you wish
Penetrar i miei martiri,	To penetrate my martyrdom,
Dicerneteli à i sospiri,	Discern it in the sighs
Che dal cor uscir vedete,	You see issuing from my heart.
E direte . . .[20]	*And you shall say . . .*

Both arias represent a departure from the ABB′ form, with its heavy emphasis on B; they allow the illusion of through-composition despite the text. The illusion is enhanced in the second aria by the motivic relationship between A and B, which disappears with the varied repetition of B.

This kind of textually unjustified expansion and variation, inspired as it may have been in certain instances by dramatic considerations, was a general sign of the loosening of the bonds between music and text. There were other signs as well, including the inappropriate application of melismatic decorations and the emancipation of ritornellos from their arias.[21] But it was also a function of the flexibility of the bipartite form itself, of the essential compatibility of that form with dramatic progress, its ability to disappear or become subsumed in a natural action. Even when reiterated strophically, the ABB′ form was decisive, active, progressive; an action could be taken during its course. And even if it did not mark a character's exit, it could still maintain forward momentum, allowing the stage action to continue after just a brief punctuation.

Tripartite Forms

But progress toward resolution was not always dramatically appropriate or necessary. Situations characterized by obsession or indecision, where conflict remained unresolved, were often more effectively portrayed by formal backtracking than by movement toward a goal. Accordingly, some non-strophic forms, as well as the individual stanzas of strophic ones, were enclosed by refrains. In non-strophic contexts, such refrains, whether long or short, epigrammatic quatrains or single-line exclamations, tended to promote closure merely by marking off the segments of text between them.

Far from automatically signaling arias, though, such refrains in operas of the 1640s and early 1650s were utilized primarily and most effectively as intensification of recitative, interrupting passages of free dialogue unpredictably with emotional outbursts. It was only after the middle of the century that they became regularly associated with more tightly structured poetry, and that lyrical setting of the whole became standard procedure. The refrain per se, like the

20.   Rodope's strophes are interlaced with strophes for Nigrane.
21.   Ziani is frequently guilty of inappropriate melismas, including one on *meno* in Damira's aria from

Rodope, 2.1. The emancipation of ritornellos from their arias is particularly striking in Lucio's *Medoro* (see Morelli and Walker, "Migliori plettri," CLII–III).

aphoristic tag line, was essentially an affective device inspired by the drama. Stimulated by an excess of feeling—why else would a character say the same thing more than once?—its very recurrence invited musical emphasis, and, in the context of recitative, this emphasis involved a change or contrast in musical style, usually a lyrical expansion—or else, if the context was already lyrical, a recitative outburst. Such refrains gained special power from their unpredictability; usually unprepared by the intervening recitative, they gave the impression of arising naturally out of a character's emotional overflow. Composers were free to expand upon refrains in a recitative context precisely because the refrains seemed to spring directly from feelings rather than reason. In arias, however, refrains could have a stultifying effect. Predictability compromised or diluted their dramatic immediacy, artifice weakened their direct link to the emotions of the character. The difficulty was compounded, of course, by strophic form. Accordingly, until the middle of the century the ABA form was less common for arias than the ABB'. Afterwards, particularly in their non-strophic guise, ABA forms increased in frequency and size, eventually supplanting bipartite structure as well as strophicism itself to become the dominant form for opera for the next hundred years: the da capo aria.[22]

Like the bipartite aria, then, the da capo aria had its roots in the recitative style, specifically in the use of the enclosing refrain.[23] The kinship as well as the contrast between the two procedures—refrain in recitative and refrain-enclosed arias—is clearly illustrated in the early collaborations between Faustini and Cavalli. More than any other works of the period, theirs exploited the refrain as an affective-structural device in aria and recitative alike.

Refrain in Recitative

Faustini's lengthy recitative passages were periodically marked by refrains of one or more lines that stood apart from the rest because of their meter or rhyme, and also, usually, because of their affective intensity. Their impact, however, depended primarily on their recurrence, sometimes as many as three or four times in a scene, which Cavalli enhanced through the usual means: shift of meter, repetition of text, musical expansion, change of musical style, addition of string accompaniment, and often the attachment of a ritornello based on the same material.

A number of speeches in *Ormindo* (1644) are articulated by refrains. In Nerillo's monologue in act 1, scene 3, a symmetrical, three-line moralizing

---

22. The proportion of tripartite strophic arias in a few randomly chosen operas is as follows: *Xerse* (1654) 16/37; *Erismena* (1655) 5/29; *Eliogabalo* (1668) 24/52; *Orfeo* (1673) 33/50. Some tripartite strophes replaced bipartite ones in the revision of *Argia*. The forms of most of the added arias in operas that were revised were tripartite rather than bipartite.

23. On this point, see Powers, "Erismena," 309.

refrain encloses a lengthy passage of recitative in *versi sciolti* that develops the moral of the refrain: "Oh, wise is he who knows how to flee woman's beauty" (example 27):

O sagace chi sà	*Oh, wise is he who knows how*
Fuggir, come il suo peggio	*To flee, as his bane,*
La donnesca beltà.	*Woman's beauty.*
Beltà mentita, e vana,	A beauty false and vain
Che per far lacci à cori	That to tie hearts
Và rubando i capelli	Goes around stealing hair
A teschi infraciditi entro gl'avelli:	From moldering skulls in their tombs.
Ma che parlo de' morti,	But why am I speaking of dead men,
Se con vezzi lascivi	When, with lascivious simpering,
Pela spietatamente insino i vivi?	It robs without pity even the living?
O sagace chi sà . . .	*Oh, wise is he . . .*

Cavalli distinguished the refrain by setting it in a highly elaborate aria style, expanding and reworking the text by repeating individual words and lines and finally going through the whole text a second time with varied music. Melismatic sixteenth-note scale passages interpret *fuggir* each time it occurs; strings briefly echo various vocal phrases, concluding the refrain with a more substantial echolike ritornello based on the *fuggir* motive. The second refrain statement, exactly like the first, ushers in the first of two arias in the scene in a sequence of escalating lyricism of the kind we have already remarked upon in connection with the sententious arioso. This increasingly lyrical organization was characteristic first of comic monologues and later of serious ones.[24]

It was a function of comic characters to make moralistic generalizations on behalf of their masters, directed as much to the audience as to the characters on stage. The very artificiality of repetition helped to distance the remarks from the immediacy of the drama and focused them more directly toward the audience. It was different for serious characters, who needed special license to repeat themselves or express themselves formally. Excessive passion was virtually their only justification. For them, refrains within recitative offered an opportunity for lyrical expression without the limitations of formal aria. Indeed, Cavalli and Faustini seem to have been particularly interested in the refrain as an affective device in serious contexts, in the power of refrains to project passion.

In *Ormindo* they exploited that power in conjunction with one character in particular: the abandoned princess Sicle, whose feigned death stimulates the reawakening of her lover's affection and the symmetrical resolution of the plot.

24. Example 21 above is part of such a scene. It is the second of two arias separated by a recitative passage. A particularly effective example for a serious character is Sofonisba's soliloquy from Cavalli's *Scipione affricano* 2.9, illustrated below in example 91.

Unlike the other main characters, Sicle sings no arias (she is the most serious of all the lovers, the most steadfast in her faith); but her passionate recitatives are frequently punctuated by refrains, some of them quite lengthy. Her extended speeches in 1.5 are interrupted at various junctures by three successive refrains of differing length and intensity. In the previous chapter we saw how Cavalli specially emphasized the last of them, a quatrain itself enclosed by a refrain, by means of a lyrical setting that involved word repetition, dissonance, syncopation, sequence, and other standard affective techniques (cf. example 8):

> *Chi, chi mi toglie al die*
> *Carnefice pietoso*
> *De le sciagure mie?*
> *Chi, chi mi toglie al die.*
> Angoscie aspre, ed acerbe,
> Se tanto fiere siete,
> Perche non m'uccidete?
> De la sua vita priva
> Non viva più la misera, non viva.
> *Chi, chi mi toglie al die . . .*[25]

The five lines that separate the two appearances of the refrain are treated as straight recitative, but do not stand apart musically from the refrain. On the contrary, as Cavalli set them, they lead powerfully to its return, their close on the dominant awaiting the refrain to reassert the tonic. The effect of the whole is cumulative; the second cry of despair, "Who, who will deliver me from this existence!" is the culmination of the entire passage. Forward motion rather than retrospection is promoted by the recurrence; the second statement of the refrain seems more powerful than the first for having been anticipated by it.

What is more, each of these individual refrains might almost be thought of as a miniature ABA aria. In fact, the structure of this "refrain within a refrain" exemplifies the affective inspiration of refrains in general. It also illustrates an important distinction between two refrain types: the passionate exclamatory line and the more expansive multiple-line statement, a distinction to which we shall return. It seems quite natural, given the emotional temperature of the refrain text to begin with, that it should inspire its own single-line refrain, which itself is required to resolve a half-cadence. Sicle's four-line refrain does not seem artificially structured or dramatically stagnant. It forms a single, emotionally inspired lyrical gesture.

It was a small step from the lyrical refrain in recitative to the da capo aria. All that was still missing was the formal integration of the intervening text and music. But composers had to work harder in arias to match the intensity that

---

25.   See ch. 9, pp. 263–64, example 8; translation there.

could be achieved by refrains in a recitative context. They had to infuse the aria form with progressive energy to counteract the static effect of return.

Da Capo Refrain Arias

The earliest ABA arias, most of them comic, were not unlike their bipartite counterparts in their proximity to the recitative style. Their texts were generally set syllabically, straight through from beginning to end; their refrains, usually of the single-line exclamatory variety, rarely received special musical treatment. Any musical distinctions between A and B were usually inspired by textual distinctions, such as a shift in meter. In fact, librettists often assured musical continuity by linking the refrain to either or both ends of the intervening text by rhyme as well as meter. Frequently only the presence of a ritornello based on the refrain material served to emphasize the refrain above the rest of the text. Occasionally, though, the return of the refrain was amplified through repetition, resulting in an ABA' rather than ABA form.

A characteristic early example is Mercurio's aria from act 3, scene 9 of *La virtù de' strali d'Amore* (example 28):

Donne, s'amar volete	*Ladies, if love is your desire,*
Venite quì, correte,	*Come hither, run:*
Con gli strali d'amor v'impiagherò;	I will wound you with Love's darts;
Ma da chi più vezzosa	But she who has the fairest,
Hà la bocca amorosa	Most loving lips
In premio del mio colpo un bacio io vuò.	Must reward my deed with a kiss.
Donne s'amar volete	*Ladies, if love is your desire,*
Venite quì, correte.	*Come hither, run.*
Da colei, che più belle	From her, whose eyes
Le luci ha de le stelle	Are lovelier than the stars,
Un lascivetto sguardo io chiedo sol;	I only demand a lascivious glance;
Ma s'alcuna donare	But if any of you will give
Mi vuol cose più rare,	Something more rare,
Accetterò ciò, che donar me vuol;	I shall accept whatever you wish to give me;
Donne, s'amar volete	*Ladies, if love is your desire . . .*
Venite quì, correte.	
[+ one more strophe]	

In this ditty, addressed directly to the ladies in the audience, and distinctly outside the dramatic action, the text is set straight through like recitative, syllabic and unheightened. The refrain is continuous with the rest, lacking any thematic, harmonic, or metric distinction. Although an abrupt harmonic juxtaposition signals its return, only a single extra word repetition, a slight bow in the direction of closure, differentiates the second statement from the first. The stanza is followed by a ritornello loosely based on a motive taken from the refrain, specifically that setting the words *Venite quì,* the climax of the text; but even this relationship serves no particularly emphatic function, since the refrain itself is so little distinguished from the rest of the music.

The breezy, recitative-like rapidity with which Cavalli dispatched this text, refrain and all, is appropriate because it contributes to the comic effect of the aria. The musical setting promotes verbal intelligibility and makes only limited vocal demands on the singer, who was probably chosen as much for his histrionic as for his vocal abilities.[26] Further, it responds directly to the poetry, which makes no metric distinction between the refrain and the rest of the text. The composer did little more than transcribe the poetic structure into musical notation. The text virtually sings (=speaks) itself.

Other early da capo refrain arias are more complicated (and more interesting). Some display greater contrast between sections and greater emphasis on the refrain. In Melloe's aria "Voglio provar anch'io, che cosa è Amor" from *Doriclea* (Faustini/Cavalli, 1645) 3.4, a distinction between the refrain and the B section is suggested by the meter of the text (example 29):

Voglio provar anch'io, che cosa è Amor	*I, too, wish to experience what love is.*
Ogni donzella	Every damsel
Sciocca m'appella,	Says I'm silly
Perch'à un sembiante	Because I never gave my heart
Di vago amante	To the countenance
Mai diedi il cor.	Of a fair lover.
Voglio provar anch'io, che cosa è Amor.	*I, too, wish to experience what love is.*
Ciascuna ama mi dice, amare io vò,	*Everyone loves, they tell me, and I wish to too.*
Voglio, che sia	I wish that
L'anima mia,	My soul,
Il mio diletto	My delight
Un giovanetto,	Be a youth
Che scieglierò.	Whom I will choose.
Ciascuna ama mi dice, amare io vò.	*Everyone loves, they tell me . . .*
[+ one more strophe][27]	

The composer marked the librettist's distinction through a change of meter and by the imposition in the B section of sequential patterning in response to the repeated accents of the five short lines; B is further developed in the ritornello, a relationship that, although it inverts the standard da capo connection between ritornello and refrain, is at least musically appropriate for this particular aria, the B material being more distinctive than that of the refrain. As in Mercurio's aria, undifferentiated syllabic treatment is appropriate here because of the nature of

26.   Cf. *Il corago* (Appendix II.1d). The simplicity of the comic style is undoubtedly also intended to suggest popular music; see Pirrotta, *Music and Theatre*, 279.

27.   This scene ends with a recitative that closes with an arioso punchline summarizing the affect of the aria, a reversal of the escalating lyricism from arioso to aria link described above; it is a good example of one solution to the problem of large-scale scene-structure, discussed further in ch. 11.

the text—the humorous musings of the amorous servant girl Melloe shared with the audience.

Given the importance of the words and the possibility that they were sung by actors rather than singers, it is perhaps not surprising that comic da capo arias, like comic arias in general, continued to be musically modest well into the second half of the century. Often, however, composers' attention to the words yielded more distinctive musical material as they attempted more actively to translate the text into musical imagery. In Eumene's "La bellezza è un don fugace" from *Xerse* (Minato/Cavalli, 1654) 2.8, the "fleetingness of beauty" is portrayed by a sixteenth-note refrain motive that seems to spirit the words away (example 30):

La bellezza è un don fugace,	*Beauty is a fleeting gift,*
Che si perde in pochi dì	Which is lost in a few days.
Il suo sereno,	Its clear sky
Come baleno	As in a flash
Tosto fuggì.	Has come and gone.
Chi s'accese, e ne languì	Whoever was ignited by it, and languished of it
Speri pur nel tempo edace.	May as well place his hopes in ravenous time.
La bellezza è un don fugace.	*Beauty is a fleeting gift.*
L'alterezza d'un bel volto	*The haughtiness of a lovely face*
Si castiga con l'età,	Is punished by age;
Il fresco, il verde	All that's fresh and green
Tosto disperde	Soon loses
Fior di beltà.	The bloom of beauty
E struggendo ogn'hor si và	And is ever consuming itself,
Come al vento esposta face	Like a torch exposed to the wind.
La bellezza è un don fugace.	*Beauty is a fleeting gift.*

Beginning with two sixteenth notes to a syllable, increasing to four and finally to twelve, the refrain material spills over into the B section for four of its six lines, following the sentence structure. The two final lines of B are set separately, to new, more appropriate, slower-moving material geared to the word *languì*, finally coming to a stop on a half-note. The return of the refrain reasserts the message of the text all the more forcefully after the slowdown. The refrain material, which is the message of the text translated into music, permeates the entire aria: strophe, accompaniment, and, of course, ritornello. Despite the greater musical interest of Eumene's aria, it shares with Mercurio's and Melloe's the straight-through setting and the small dimensions that help to project the words clearly and are appropriate to the economical, matter-of-fact expression of a comic character.

In serious contexts, however, it was often more appropriate for the composer to linger over the whole text, particularly the refrain, and to distinguish it even more strongly from the rest of the text. Such treatment was especially suitable when the message was more affective than literal, when the purpose of the aria was to communicate feeling rather than information or opinion, and when the text was an integral part of the drama rather than external to it, sung by a protagonist rather than a stock figure. In such situations, the music remains closely tied to the words, but asserts its own momentum. The composer used the text more expressively; rather than transcribing the poetic structure or translating the words, he now interpreted the feelings behind them. In these cases, the dimensions of the music far exceed those suggested by the text. Words are repeated, emphasized, dwelled upon, and heightened to convey the emotion that generated them.

Eurinda's "Udite amanti, udite" from *Doriclea* 1.5 is one of the most fully developed, musically satisfying da capo refrain arias of the period.[28] Eurinda is not a comic character, but one of the noble protagonists, a member of the standard amorous quartet. Although she directs her song to the audience (or to those of it who are lovers), she does not preach to them, but, rather, describes her own feelings. Overcome by her love, she bursts into formal lyricism, an unusual mode of expression for a protagonist in 1645; but her passion justifies the arioso-style expansion of the text (example 31):

Udite amanti, udite,	*Hear, lovers, hear:*
Trà le schiere d'amor	*In Love's ranks*
Non si trova del mio più lieto cor?	*No heart is happier than mine.*
Dolce fiamma il sen m'accende,	A sweet flame kindles my bosom,
È diletto il mio martoro,	My martyrdom is sheer delight;
Cieco Dio co' strali d'oro	The blind god with his golden darts
Mi saetta, e non m'offende.	Pierces me, yet hurts me not.
Che dite voi, che dite	*What say you, what do you say,*
Trà le schiere d'amor	*In love's ranks*
Si può trovar del mio più lieto cor?	*Can there be a happier heart than mine?*
Del mio foco io son l'ardore,	I am the love of my lover,
Chi m'avvinse avvinto giace,	My captor captured lies,
Non mi rode il duol vorace,	Devouring pain gnaws not at me,
Tutto manna assaggio amore.	Love is manna to my taste.
Che dite voi . . .	*What say you . . .*

This text is actually somewhat irregular for a da capo refrain aria; it fails to conform to any of the standard modifications of da capo refrain form. The opening tercet does not return, but is replaced by a variant, which concludes both stanzas. The composer confirmed the poetic structure, the contrast between the seven- and eleven-syllable refrain and the *ottonario* B sections, with his own metric contrast, a shift from triple to duple meter. Beyond that, how-

28.   The aria occurs in 1.6 of the score. It is a rondo-refrain aria (according to Hjelmborg's categories) similar in form to "Ombra mai fù" from *Xerse* (example 42 below).

ever, refrain and B sections are closely linked, by harmonic structure and thematic material. Both are generated by the same opening interval, the descending fifth, E to A, and both are expanded musically. In addition to elaborate, lengthy melismas, on *cor* in the refrain and *strali* and *saetta* in the first B section—none of them particularly expressive of the words—expansion is achieved through repetition of varying textual units: words, phrases, whole lines.

The unusual musical expansion is a function of the composer's long-range dramatic plan, an aspect of characterization. In contrast to Doriclea, the other female lead, Eurinda, is easily carried away by her emotions. She frequently expresses herself in aria style, whereas Doriclea hardly ever does.[29] This particular aria acts as a kind of presentation piece for Eurinda; its elaboration exemplifies her flighty, fickle character. It is, furthermore, ironically appropriate. The unrestrained passion for Farnace expressed here sets into ironic relief her behavior in the very next scene, when, with no preparation whatsoever, she becomes enamored of another man. The musical abundance seems to serve multiple dramatic functions in addition to providing satisfaction for its own sake.

Da capo refrain arias for comic characters did not undergo much development during the century. The features that characterized their earliest manifestations—economical, syllabic setting to ensure text clarity, and minimal musical expansion—remained as appropriate after 1650 as before. Whatever musical expansion such arias displayed, as a result of exaggeration of musical gestures or excessively literal representation of text, tended to enhance their comic effect. The conditions under which comic characters sang their arias did not change either, since they persisted in performing their conventional functions of commentary on and parody of the action.

Da capo refrain arias for serious characters, on the other hand, developed considerably. They became more frequent as librettists found new excuses for them, and they became more standardized in form. In creating additional aria situations, serious or dramatic, librettists nevertheless continued to ensure minimal disruption of dramatic flow. Formal structures continued to support dramatic function. And composers developed new techniques to enhance drama within the increasingly conventionalized formal schemes. In some instances, greater musical coherence between refrain and enclosed text helped to minimize

---

29. The propensity toward formal lyricism may have been a standard means of characterization for Faustini. A similar contrast marks the heroines of *Ormindo* (Erisbe and Sicle) and of *Rosinda* (Nerea and Rosinda); but it is also true of Ottavia and Poppea in *L'incoronazione di Poppea* and Medea and Isifile in *Giasone*. Perhaps it was always thought of as a way to differentiate between the two leading ladies.

the artificiality of return. In others, return itself assumed a specific dramatic function, which an increased contrast between sections helped to emphasize.

Coherence in Da Capo and Da Capo Refrain Arias

In the librettos of both Minato and Aureli, da capo arias for serious characters were of two distinct types, largely determined by their dramatic function.[30] The more common type initially featured single-line refrains associated with multiple stanzas (modified in one of the standard ways), with which they were often linked by meter or rhyme. Less frequently, until later in the century, the refrains were longer and enclosed single stanzas, from which they were usually poetically more distinct, creating a form that resembled the prototypical baroque da capo aria in most important respects.[31] The two types occasionally overlapped; that is, some arias with short refrains were not strophic, and some strophic arias had long refrains.

The length of the refrain, however, was directly related to the dramatic function of the aria. By and large, those with short refrains were more immediately responsive to, and more deeply imbedded in, the ongoing action. The refrains themselves were usually highly impassioned, indignant or angry outbursts, or rhetorical questions, whether addressed outward to other characters or inward by the characters to themselves. They resembled Faustini's recitative (arioso) refrains in their affective intensity and apparent spontaneity, but were associated with more formalized texts.[32] Such arias usually began abruptly in response to a specific action or event; they often concluded a scene or action-segment and were followed by the character's exit. Or else they opened solo scenes that presented a character responding to an action that had recently taken place. *Xerse* has a number of such arias with opening lines like "Che barbara pietà" (immediate response to an action), "Và, speranza" (self-exhortation), "Morirò: volete più," "Lasciatemi morire" (more considered response), or "Dammi, Amor, la libertà." Arias with longer refrains were usually associated with more static situations, where emotions were more controlled or had not yet been ignited. Declarative rather than participatory, they were more likely to initiate or set the stage for an action than to respond to one, and they often marked entrances rather than exits.[33]

In both types of aria the return of the refrain might strain verisimilitude. The risk, however, was attenuated in the longer refrain arias by their more

---

30. Comic da capos shared the same forms, but not the accompanying dramatic distinctions.

31. One of the most crucial defining characteristics of the mature da capo form is a dramatic one, and depends on the acceptance of exact return as dramatically appropriate. There was a distinction in dramatic function almost from the outset between short refrain forms, which were usually integrated within the action, and more fully developed da capo arias, which were in some sense external (see below).

32. Cf. Sicle's "Chi mi toglie al die" from *Ormindo* (example 8 above).

33. The opposite became true later, of course.

external function, while the shorter refrains were often dramatically justified by their affect, which could well be intensified by return, as long as it did not seem programmed or artificial. Composers and librettists could intensify the affective impact of return by making it seem natural. One way of achieving this was to integrate the returning refrain with the B section so that it seemed necessary, even inevitable, rather than redundant.

Integration is achieved quite effectively in most of the abovementioned arias from *Xerse*. In Amastre's "Morirò: volete più" (2.13), she reacts to the accumulated frustration of being repeatedly ignored by her beloved Xerse. Integration is encouraged by the meter and rhyme scheme of the text (example 32):

Morirò: volete più?	*I will die: do you want more?*
Stelle crude al mio martir	Cruel stars, if your rays
S'il mio duolo a raddolcir	Don't have the power
Vostri rai non han virtù.	To soothe my torment's pain,
Morirò: volete più?	*I will die: do you want more?*
Se tradita è la mia fè	If my faith is betrayed,
Se non posso haver mercè	If I can't have mercy
Di costante servitù	From loyal servitude,
Morirò: volete più?	*I will die: do you want more?*

Cavalli set it straight through, linking the refrain to the B section through phrase structure (the first phrase spans lines 1–2), harmony (the refrain lands on the dominant, which is resolved to the tonic only at the end of the first phrase), and motivic material (the rhythm of the refrain, with its initial upbeat, persists throughout the strophe). The link between the end of the B section and the returning refrain is, if anything, even tighter. An expanded and transposed variant of the refrain completes a rising sequence of upbeat phrases that began in the strophe with line 3 on G♯, proceeded to line 4 on B, and finally to the refrain on high G, which provides the climax of the aria, ending strongly on the relative major. The refrain in fact does not return at its original pitch until a phrase later, where, acting as the fourth and final member of the sequence begun with line 3, it resolves the aria to the tonic. Cavalli followed the librettist's lead by treating the entire text of five strictly rhymed *ottonari tronchi* as a unit. The refrain provides both the generative idea and the climax of the aria.[34]

Meter and rhyme scheme were not the only inducements to musical continuity. Sometimes the meaning of a text actually depended on the incorporation of the refrain at the end as well as the beginning, so that its recurrence did not seem like a repeat at all, but rather the culmination of the aria. Such is the effect of Romilda's self-exhorting "Amante non è," which she sings at her exit

34. This was originally one of those strophic rondo-refrain arias, ABA CA. The composer evidently chose to cut the librettist's second strophe, which could not have followed from his setting of the refrain.

in 2.15. Minato integrated the refrain line into the strophe by inverting the syntax at the end: "He is not a [true] lover, / Who yields to the fury. . . . He who fears pain / Is not a [true] lover" (example 33):

Amante non è	*He is not a lover*
Chi cede al furor	Who yields to the fury
D'irata Fortuna,	Of irate Fortune:
Tutto quel, che Pluto aduna	The most perfidious punishment
Più perfido rigor	That Pluto assembles
Non vince il mio core,	Cannot conquer my heart,
Non turba mia fè,	Nor disturb my faith.
Chi teme il dolore,	He who fears pain
Amante non è.[35]	*Is not a lover.*

The composer brilliantly paralleled this integration with his own musical anastrophe. Prefaced by an independent ritornello, as befits its rather considered, philosophical tone, the brief refrain presents a motive (strictly derived from the text rhythm) that, although repeated sequentially at the outset of line 2, quickly disintegrates into more varied rhythmic and melodic patterns inspired by individual words. The text and music of the two final lines, the refrain and its predecessor—which form a paired couplet with the two preceding lines—are heard twice, as in a typical ABB′ expansion, first beginning and ending on the dominant, then beginning on the dominant and reaching the tonic with a slight flourish that restores the music of the original refrain as the inevitable, sequential climax of the line. The musical development of the aria is linear; it moves naturally and inexorably from refrain to refrain without doubling back.

The integration of refrain and B section illustrated in these two examples from *Xerse* helps to counteract the natural regressiveness of the da capo. In both instances, musical integration was encouraged by the librettist, although the particular means of achieving it was up to the composer. There are numerous examples, however, in which the composer's contribution stands out because it seems to go beyond the librettist's indications, using them merely as a starting point for much greater integration and expansion.

35.   The form of this text resembles Minato's characteristic inversion of the returning refrain of tripartite arias, mentioned in n. 5 above. The inversion of the refrain in the following text suggests new music, producing a form that is more rondolike than either strophic or da capo.

> S'Amor vuol così,
> Che far ti poss' io,
> Dolente cor mio?
> Non ti giovano i sospiri,
> Senza frutto è 'l lagrimar
> Non osserva i tuoi martiri,
> Non sí piega al tuo penar

> La beltà che ti ferì.
> Dolente cor mio,
> Che far ti poss' io,
> S'Amor vuol così?

> Hai nemica la fortuna
> Getta al vento la tua fè,
> Non aver speranza alcuna
> D'ottener pietà, mercè,
> Fin che durano i tuoi dì,
> Dolente cor mio . . .
> (Artemisia, 2.1)

In Miralba's aria "Non dovevi innamorarti" from *Medoro* (Aureli/Lucio, 1658) 2.14, the musical coherence far exceeds that of the text, whose sole suggestion of integration is the (conventional) rhyme between the final line of the strophe and the returning refrain (example 34):

Non dovevi innamorarti,	*You should not have fallen in love,*
Infelice mio cor, se non volevi	O my unhappy heart, if you were unwilling
Sentir d'Amor le pene:	To feel the pangs of Love:
Stolto sei, se le catene	Foolish are you, if you think
Credi sciorti e liberarti:	You can loosen your bonds and free yourself:
Non dovevi innamorarti!	*You should not have fallen in love.*
Soffri in pace i tuoi martiri,	*Suffer in peace your martyrdom,*
Che sei nato al penar, e di Cupido	For you were born to suffer, and to Cupid
Fatto sei scherzo, e gioco:	You are but a whim, a toy.
Tormentati in mezo al foco	Your breath shall ever be
Saran sempre i tuoi respiri.	Tormented amidst the flames.
Soffri in pace i tuoi martiri.	*Suffer in peace your martyrdom.*

Musical integration is achieved initially by the persistence into the B section of the refrain's initial, steady eighth-note motion and upbeat phrase beginnings. This general connection is reinforced by a specific one, a kind of musical rhyme emphasizing the textual rhyme between the end of B and the refrain. The composer set the two rhyming syllables (the *rar* in *innamorarti* and *liberarti*) to elaborate, highly rhythmic, and very similar melismas. The relationship is highlighted in several ways. To begin with, the last two lines of the strophe are repeated in a second key (E-A, A-D), which entails repetition of the melisma on *liberarti*. Then the refrain is also repeated, first in the dominant, then in the tonic. Not only is the melisma thus also heard twice in the refrain, but each time it is expanded to double its original length. By returning first on the dominant and then on the tonic, and by expanding the original melisma, the refrain sounds less like a repetition than a new development of earlier material: its own and that of the B section. It is worth noting that a second statement of the refrain was not required by the tonal structure of the B section, which ended firmly in the tonic. But a preliminary statement in the dominant sets up the final statement in the tonic as a bigger climax; the refrain acts like a large authentic cadence. In Miralba's aria, Lucio went beyond the normal means of integrating refrain and B section to establish a strong thematic relationship between the sections. Although that relationship may have been suggested by the closing rhyme of Aureli's text, it was the composer's choice to exploit it as the source of forward momentum in the aria.

There are some da capo arias in which integration is so complete that the distinction between refrain and B section is virtually obliterated, the refrain supplying all of the musical material for the aria (we observed something like this in example 31 above). The technique is particularly appropriate when the refrain line actually provides the subject matter for the whole text.

Orfeo's "Cerco pace e mi fà guerra" from *Orfeo* (Aureli/Sartorio, 1673) 1.13 is an effective example of what might be called the monothematic da capo. It literally demonstrates the permeation of a whole aria by the affect of its refrain (example 35):

Cerco pace e mi fà guerra	*I seek peace but am warred against*
Gelosia co 'l Dio d'Amor.	*By jealousy and the god of Love.*
Cinto l'un d'acceso telo	*The one, armed with a burning dart,*
Porta il foco, e l'altra il gelo,	*Carries fire, the other frost,*
Per far breccia in questo cor.	*To make a breach in my heart.*
Cerco pace . . .	*I seek peace . . .*
La bellezza à far rapine	*Beauty taught even*
Si à Giove anco insegnò.	*Jove to be a ravisher.*
Non han freno accese voglie,	*Once enflamed, cupidity is unbridled,*
E più bella, ch'è la moglie	*And the lovelier the wife,*
Il sospetto anco è maggior.	*The greater the suspicion.*
Cerco pace . . .	*I seek peace . . .*

Orfeo's unremitting jealousy generates an incessant running sixteenth-note continuo accompaniment, which, pitted against a smoother, slower-moving vocal line, gives concrete expression to jealousy's power to undermine Orfeo's peace. It is the meaning of the two-line refrain ("I seek peace but am warred against by jealousy") that is embodied throughout the aria by the bass motion, which never stops. The refrain and B section are separated by half-note pauses at either end, but the return of the refrain is nonetheless heard rather as a continuation of the B section than a reprise of earlier material.

Although the methods and results differed, integration of refrain and B section in all of the preceding examples entailed some recomposition and expansion at the recurrence of the refrain. Sometimes it was minimal, just an extra cadential repetition, either to provide closing punctuation or to restore the tonic if the refrain had originally ended elsewhere (as in examples 28 and 32, respectively). Sometimes it involved more extensive repetition of the whole refrain, rendered necessary by its own initial instability (examples 30 and 33). The refrain itself might return in a new key and then be repeated in its original key, sometimes additionally extended to produce a more satisfactory cadence (example 34). In the most effective examples, the final repetition of the refrain gained expressive power—and finality—for having been anticipated by such a transposed statement of itself: that is, by seeming to resolve or stabilize its preceding statement or acting as the culminating member of a sequence (examples 32 and 33).

Sometimes, however, as we have seen, recomposition was much more extensive—and more gratuitous. In Miralba's aria, Lucio's expansion of the refrain went well beyond harmonic or structural necessity into the realm of expression. A number of refrains in other arias from *Medoro* are similarly expanded. In Miralba's final aria in the opera, "Respira mio core" (3.16), the extensive elaboration of A′ is clearly justified by affective considerations. Expansion in both of Miralba's arias, like that in an increasing number of others, smacks as well of deference to the singer. Virtuosic display is not the least of its justifications.[36]

While recomposition through expansion was one effective means of overcoming the static effects of da capo return, composers explored a number of other paths to the same end. Sometimes they ignored the presence of the textual refrain altogether, as in Amastre's "Speranze fermate" from *Xerse* 2.1 (example 36):

Speranze fermate;	*Ye hopes, remain!*
Sì tosto fuggite?	So soon do you flee?
Ancora non sete	You are not yet
Speranze tradite.	Hopes betrayed.
Voi dunque m'havete	Do you then harbor
Si poca pietate?	So little pity toward me?
Speranze fermate.	*Ye hopes, remain!*
Pensieri sperate;	*Ye thoughts, have hope!*
Sì presto temete?	So quickly you fear?
Ancora ingannati	You are not yet
Pensieri non sete.	Thoughts deceived.
Già d'esser sprezzati	You are wrong to swear
A torto giurate.	You are disdained,
Pensieri sperate.	*Ye thoughts, have hope!*

Here Cavalli altered the form of Minato's text by bringing back the refrain, not with its original music, but attached to the preceding line and set to entirely new music, which he repeated, thereby actually transforming a da capo text into a bipartite aria. The hopes have indeed fled![37]

In Seleuco's "Tardanza noiosa" from *Seleuco* (Minato/Sartorio, 1666) 1.7, the musical return of the refrain is postponed by transposed reiteration of interior lines of the strophe involving some new musical material (example 37):

36. The aria may be found in *Medoro*, ed. Morelli and Walker, ff. 89ᵛ-90ᵛ.
37. In ignoring or bypassing the librettist's direc- tives, Cavalli's setting of this text resembles Ziani's treatment of the two bipartite texts from *Rodope e Damira* illustrated above in examples 25 and 26.

> *Tardanza noiosa*   *Troublesome lateness,*
> Molesta dimora.   Annoying delay:
> A un alma ch'adora   To a soul in love
> Sei sempre penosa.   You are always painful,
> *Tardanza noiosa.*   *Troublesome lateness.*
>
> *Non gode non posa*   *Unable to enjoy or to rest*
> Chi aspetta il suo bene,   Is he who awaits his beloved;
> Rinforzi le pene   You aggravate his pain
> Con sferza dogliosa   With your hurtful rebuke,
> *Tardanza noiosa.*   *Troublesome lateness.*

When the "tardy" refrain text finally does return, it is set to new music that elaborates material introduced in the expanded B section, only with its final cadence, an open descending fifth, recapitulating the opening refrain.

The return of a refrain could also be disguised by beginning it differently or recapitulating it only in part, starting from within the refrain rather than at the beginning.[38] Most often, however, returning refrains were embellished or re-composed at the end, for the reasons outlined above: to fulfill large-dimension harmonic requirements and for purely expressive or formal ones. The expansion of A' in da capo arias is of course analogous to that of B' in bipartite arias, and, despite the difference in form, the results were similar. In both, the expansion lent the aria as a whole a sense of forward propulsion, often culminating in the character's exit from the stage.

Contrast in Da Capo Forms

We have emphasized composers' and librettists' efforts to integrate the da capo refrain into an ongoing, overarching structure. On the other hand, as we have already observed, the da capo form was often chosen expressly for its naturally static effect, for dramatic situations that required backtracking. Such situations benefited from emphasis on the refrain's independence rather than integration, and from its exact repetition rather than its progressive, climactic expansion. The large, static da capo arias almost never involved elaboration of the refrain, but merely called for its repetition by means of the rubric *da capo*. In such cases, musical contrast was more appropriate than integration because it focused greater attention on the returning refrain. We are coming closer to the textbook da capo form.

In Aldimira's aria from *Erismena* 3.12, musical contrast, inspired by the meaning of the poetry, intensifies the impact of the refrain's return. Aldimira is responding to an order to leave. She refuses emphatically and directly: "Ch'io

---

38.   As in Rodope's aria, "Si vedrà," from *Rodope e Damira* 3.1 (I–Vnm, It. IV, 450 [9974], ff. 82–82ᵛ) and Antioco's lament, "Per pietà," from *Seleuco* 3.7 (I–Vnm, It. IV, 454 [9978], ff. 91–93. Minato's refrain reversals (see n. 35 above) encourage disguises like these.

parta? non posso," a line that initiates and then concludes a non-strophic aria consisting of eight *senari* (example 38):

Ch'io parta? non posso.	*That I depart? I cannot.*
In prima conviene	First it would be necessary
Il nodo spezzar	To break the knot
Di quelle catene,	Of those chains
Che mi fan restar	That make me stay.
In vano à l'andar	The foot is moved
Il piede vien mosso,	In vain to leave.
Ch'io parta? non posso.	*That I depart? I cannot.*

In response to its emphatic suddenness, Cavalli set the refrain line as recitative, changing to triple meter for the six lines that follow, during which Aldimira explains why it is she cannot leave. The contrast between the refrain and the rest of the text—and the naturalness of the aria style here—is heightened by their harmonic relationship. The refrain is in harmonic limbo; it stops suddenly on a C triad, which becomes, only in retrospect, the dominant of the aria's key. The middle section is itself rather unstable, moving from F to C minor and finally to B♭, where the refrain comes in, again concluding on the dominant, leaving the continuo to effect a quick resolution to the tonic. Not only is the relationship of refrain to B section exceedingly natural and appropriate to the text, but the central section itself, with its breathlessly repeated sequences, overlapped cadences, and intensifying momentum, communicates Aldimira's overwrought emotional state admirably, creating momentum that strengthens her resolution not to leave. Here the contrast of the refrain clearly functions as a dramatic element.[39]

Aldimira's affirmation of her unwillingness to depart is essential to the action; her refrain gains conviction from the emphasis conferred by a distinctive, contrasting setting. But the decision was largely the composer's. Nothing in the text requires contrast. On the contrary, it is structurally continuous. Often, however, the text of a da capo aria insists upon musical contrast between refrain and B section. One of the most obvious instances involves the portrayal of a character's indecision or internal conflict.

In Rodope's "Rendetemi il mio ben stelle fatali" (*Le fortune di Rodope e Damira* 3.8), another non-strophic text, musical contrast effectively portrays her ambivalence toward her lover, Nigrane. That ambivalence is built into the text. Rodope's love for Nigrane conflicts with her desire for vengeance. She wishes to harden her heart against him, but, as the return of the refrain tells us, she cannot (example 39):

---

39. Except for its regularity, this text is quite like some of the recitative-refrain texts of Faustini and even Minato. There are several in *Xerse*, including Romilda's "L'amerò, non fia vero," in 2.5.

Rendetemi il mio ben stelle fatali:	*Return to me my love, O fateful stars!*
Fate che l'impietà	Cause the impiousness
D'un Rè barbaro e amante,	Of a barbarous and loving king
Alimenti in un istante	To nourish instantly,
Nelle viscere mie la crudeltà,	Cruelty within my viscera
Sin che morte gli tronchi i dì vitali.	Until death cut short his living days.
Rendetemi il mio ben stelle fatali.[40]	*Return to me my love . . .*

In the refrain, triple meter, minor tonality, heavily accented appoggiaturas, string echoes, melismatic extensions, and affective text repetition all help to portray the intensity of Rodope's longing for Nigrane, while in the B section a shift to duple meter, D major, steady eighth-note motion, syllabic text-setting, and short, symmetrical phrases attempt to communicate her anger. Although the effect of B is perhaps a little too bright and jaunty to portray anger, it nevertheless communicates a different mood from that of A.[41]

Sectional contrast is inspired in other instances more by the imagery of a da capo text than by its dramatic function. In Elisa's strophic aria from *Mutio Scevola* (Minato/Cavalli, 1664) 1.13, poetic structure and imagery dictated the distinctive musical setting of the refrain. In this statement of principle, inspired by repeated attempts on her honor, Elisa asserts her steadfastness in metaphoric terms that suggested a series of pictorial images to the composer (example 40):

Fermo scoglio è la mia fede,	*A firm rock is my faith,*
Agitata,	Agitated,
Flagellata	Flagellated
Dal furor d'onda spumante	By the fury of frothy wave,
Più costante nulla cede:	Yet more constant, nothing yields:
Fermo scoglio è la mia fede.	*A firm rock is my faith.*
Vivo alloro è la mia fede,	*A living laurel is my faith,*
Ch'il suo verde	Whose green
Mai non perde	Never fades
D'Aquilon al fiato acuto,	In the face of northern blast,
Nè canuto	Nor is seen
Mai si vede.	Ever hoary.
Vivo alloro è la mia fede.	*A living laurel is my faith.*

The refrain is set to a syncopated, falling fourth motive, depicting the *fermo scoglio* by its rocklike reiterated rhythm and gravitational motion. The second and third lines inspire agitated, ascending eighth-note patterns, *furor* in the

---

40. This aria, from the Modena score (MS I-Mo Mus. F. 1301), appears in neither the Venice score nor the libretto. It is one of seven added arias in that score, nearly all of them tripartite exit arias. A similar example, Damira's "Vendicar spero" (3.10), is less effective. It is much shorter and its contrast much weaker, perhaps because the text form is so continuous. Although this aria does not appear in the Venice libretto, it is inserted in the Venice score. It is

not strophic in either score but that does not mean that a second strophe was not sung or at least initially intended. As we know, the scores often fail to indicate second strophes that are provided by the libretto.

41. This is actually a rather unsuccessful aria, one of a number by Ziani. He understood that a contrast was warranted but chose the wrong affect. Perhaps it was one of those arias he wrote while traveling.

fourth line a descending sixteenth-note figure, *onda spumante* a syncopation, and *costante* the conventional long notes in the voice part accompanied by a running bass. The return of the refrain with its pictorial motive reinforces the message of the aria; the refrain is self-referential, embodying its own meaning. It both states and represents the imperviousness of Elisa's faith to the furious assaults of her enemies.

A madrigalistic response to text yielded an even greater distinction between the poetically continuous refrain and B section of Angelica's much more elaborate non-strophic aria "La mia mente è un vasto Egeo" from *Medoro* (3.11). As in Elisa's aria, the text is a metaphoric distillation of intense emotion delivered while the character is alone on stage, but the refrain and B section stand in sharper opposition: the refrain depicts an untroubled, peaceful seascape that is threatened in the B section by the pirate, Fortune (example 41):

La mia mente è un vasto Egeo	*My mind is a vast Aegean*
Dove ondeggiano i pensieri;	*Wherein my thoughts toss about like waves;*
E, Pirata, la Fortuna	And the pirate Fortune
Contro me sventure aduna	Rallies misfortunes against me,
Acciò resti vil troffeo	That I may be the vile trophy
De' suoi colpi crudi, e fieri.	Of her rude, fierce blows.
La mia mente è un vasto Egeo . . .	*My mind is a vast Aegean . . .*

Sixteenth-note melismas repeated at the same pitch level initially portray the vast calm of the Aegean of Angelica's mind; the melismas are then literally transformed into the waves of that sea, dissipating into a more concrete, sequential three-note figure (eighth plus two sixteenths) in a two-beat pattern that breaks irregularly against the prevailing three-beat meter before culminating in a final sixteenth-note flourish at the cadence. The B section, marked by a shift to duple meter, is equally pictorial, its contrasting material beginning with an angular, syncopated, broken-chord figure representing piratical Fortune, whose cruel blows have destroyed Angelica's innocent, floating thoughts. The entire B section is repeated and varied before closing in the relative minor, which leads to a literal reprise of the refrain, indicated by the rubric *da capo*. Unlike Elisa's refrain, however, whose return emphasized its own meaning, Angelica's seems gratuitous, unmotivated except by the contrasting mood and imagery of the text.

Musical contrast in these last two arias was generated not by the dramatic function of their texts but by their imagery. The metaphoric nature of both texts removes them from the realm of action to that of contemplation—or self-contemplation. Unlike Aldimira and Rodope, Elisa and Angelica are not even expressing their emotion directly, but describing their feelings, commenting on them with a certain aesthetic detachment. This kind of distillation of emotion becomes commonplace in later da capo arias. Indeed, both Elisa's and

Angelica's texts, refined somewhat, might easily have come from a libretto by Metastasio.

These two arias affirm the connection between the single-line refrain aria and the more fully developed da capo. The form of Elisa's aria is like many of the refrain forms discussed earlier: it is strophic, it has a single-line refrain, its dimensions are small, and the A material is not repeated exactly—there is an extra cadential flourish at the end.[42] But like Angelica's aria, a full da capo with identifying rubric, Elisa's contrasting textual imagery inspired musical contrast rather than continuity between refrain and B section, and as a result the sections are clearly distinguished from one another. What links Elisa's and Angelica's arias is their sense of standing outside the action, whereas, as we have seen, so many da capo refrain arias are fully integrated within it.

In none of the four arias with contrasting refrains that we have considered, from *Erismena*, *Rodope*, *Mutio*, and *Medoro*, does the poetic form alone determine the contrast. Rather, their imagery and dramatic function, far more compelling than their structure, dictate the musical setting. Composers' choices, prompted by the librettists, were, as always, motivated by the need to integrate the arias within the dramatic fabric, to make the music serve the drama.

Static Da Capo Arias

Poetic form had a more exclusive and abstract impact on musical form in da capo arias with longer refrains. For one thing, the longer refrains were always metrically distinct from their surrounding text and thus did not lend themselves to musical integration. For another, these arias did not usually require integration within a dramatic fabric because they were designed to function outside it. Arias with longer refrains were reserved for situations in which formality was appropriate. The refrains merely emphasized their formality. The form of these arias matched their function. Statuesque, objective, they offered the composer greater freedom of expression than was available to him in the more dramatically relevant arias with short refrains, freedom to indulge in musical expansion and development of various kinds. Not incidentally, nearly all of these arias were non-strophic. Rare before 1650, they increased in number during the second half of the century, as librettists developed more occasions for them. Eventually, every protagonist was introduced by one, a presentation aria. And others found their way into librettos disguised as songs of one kind or another.

Possibly the most memorable of all presentation arias from this period is Xerse's "Ombra mai fù," which opens *Xerse*.[43] The text, made famous by

---

42. Might we call it an "arietta"? It certainly lacks what Pirrotta would term a "full and stereotyped" repetition of words (cf. above, p. 284 and n. 6).

43. It is preceded by an introductory recitative in the Paris version of the score (F-Pn MS 42, 2.312, p. 7), a bow to the growing convention of recitative-aria pairing.

Handel's subsequent setting, comprises a four-line refrain in *quinari*, which encloses two six-line strophes of *settenari* and *endecasillabi*.[44] The refrain extols the plane tree, whose special qualities are appreciated more specifically in the two strophes (example 42):

Ombra mai fù	*Never was shade*
Di vegetabile	*Of vegetable*
Cara, & amabile,	*More dear & amiable,*
Soave più.	*More sweet.*
Bei smeraldi crescenti,	Lovely growing emeralds,
Frondi tenere, e belle,	Tender, beautiful branches,
Di turbini, ò procelle,	May the importunate torments
Importuni tormenti.	Of whirlwinds or storms
Non v'affligano mai la cara pace,	Never afflict your precious peace,
Ne giunga a profanarvi Austro rapace.	Nor rapacious southern gale profane you.
Mai con rustica scure	May injurious peasant
Bifolco ingiurioso	Never cut a leafy branch
Tronchi ramo frondoso,	With his crude axe;
E se reciso pure	And if one should be severed,
Fia, che ne resti alcuno, in stral cangiato,	May it remain, changed into a dart,
O lo scocchi Diana, ò 'l Dio bendato.	To be hurled by Diana, or by the
	blindfolded god.
Ombra mai fù . . .	*Never was shade . . .*

Cavalli's music is appropriately formal and expansive. He set the refrain (A) twice, basically straight through, first moving to the dominant, then back to the tonic, D major, with string accompaniment throughout; and he followed it with an instrumental ritornello. Although their scoring is different—continuo instead of strings—and they are generally more elaborate, with more expressive text interpretation involving word repetitions and melismatic extensions, the strophes (B) resemble the refrain in a number of ways: in their tonality (D major), meter (triple), and general melodic motion. Likewise harmonically self-sufficient, they do not require the refrain for closure. Indeed, the independence of the two sections seems to be confirmed by the rubric *aria* at the head of the first strophe in the Venice score, suggesting that Cavalli (or his copyist) thought of the refrain and strophes as two separate pieces. On the other hand, their relationship is also stressed by a linking ritornello, based on the refrain, which appears at the end of A and after the first strophe of B, though perhaps not after the second.[45] The refrain then returns, exactly as it was, followed by its ritornello.[46]

44. On the influence of Cavalli's and Bononcini's settings of the opera on Handel, see Harold S. Powers, "Il Serse trasformato," *MQ* 47 (1961): 481–92; 48 (1962): 73–92.

45. The ritornello was crossed out in the Venice score (ff. 2ᵛ-3) which is almost entirely autograph.
46. Surprisingly, Cavalli did not use the da capo rubric to indicate the return of the refrain.

Many presentation arias are cast in similarly expansive da capo form, with lengthy refrains, but "Ombra mai fù" is atypical in several respects. The formal boundaries between its refrain and strophe(s) are more clearly articulated than most, by a ritornello and by the harmonic self-sufficiency of each of them. Yet the two sections are quite similar in character, so much so that the same ritornello can be used after each. Usually composers tended to emphasize the formal distinction between refrain and strophe more strongly by contrasting their musical material, but they made them harmonically interdependent so that the return of the refrain is at least tonally necessary for the completion of the aria. The special qualities of Xerse's aria are undoubtedly the result of its special dramatic function. It not only presents him as the hero of this opera, but by associating him indelibly with one of his best-known attributes—the plane tree—it identifies him as the historical Xerxes. The stiltedness of the expanded da capo form perfectly matches the iconic situation.

Medoro's non-strophic aria "O luce serena" in *Medoro* (1.8) is more typical of the formal da capos used for the presentation of protagonists.[47] Angelica has been anxiously awaiting Medoro's return from battle; in this aria, he presents himself to his beloved. The four-line refrain is distinguished by meter and closed rhyme scheme from the rest of the text, although it does share its rhyme (not its meter) with the line preceding its return. And there is also a distinction in tone. The refrain is more abstract, an apostrophe, whereas the middle section is more urgent, an active engagement of the beloved (a contrast that parallels the one in "Ombra mai fù") (example 43):

O luce serena	*O serene light*
Del cielo d'amor,	*Of the heaven of love,*
O dolce mia pena,	*O my sweet sorrow,*
O luminoso ardor.	*O luminous ardor.*
Fuor di mè,	Beside myself,
Tutto in tè,	Wholly in you,
Trasformato in un respiro,	Transformed into a breath,
Volo, ò bella in un sospiro	I fly, O beauty, in a sigh
A bearmi nel tuo cor.	To bless myself in your heart.
O luce serena . . .	*O serene light . . .*

Lucio emphasized the contrast in structure and tone between the sections with highly contrasting music. The refrain unfolds slowly, line by line, in a stately manner, hovering over the D-major tonic chord for the first twenty measures; leisurely repetition of words, phrases, and lines of text and the string echoes of each vocal phrase help to prolong the ethereal effect of harmonic stasis. A single

---

47. Although we have already met Medoro in passing in scene 2, this is his first aria in the opera.

move to the dominant, as the final line concludes, provides the harmonic climax; the refrain resolves to the tonic during the repetition of its final phrase, which links the two formerly separated phrases setting lines 3 and 4, the whole falling into characteristic ABB' form.

A shift to duple meter and an implied modulation to the dominant mark the onset of the B section, which is, characteristically, accompanied only by continuo.[48] In contrast to the harmonic stasis of the refrain, the B section avoids asserting any key at all until its final cadence in G (IV), although its steady eighth-note motion does let up briefly to cadence on E minor before resuming its sequential propulsion toward the end. (It immediately transforms the refrain tonic, D, into the dominant of G, though postponing confirmation of G as its tonic until the end.) Like the refrain, the B section is also a miniature ABB' form; its final phrase, which sets the last three lines of text, undergoes the usual transposed repetition. The return of the refrain is necessary from a harmonic point of view, and it restores the placidity of the scene as well as the tonic, grounding the emotional intensity expressed in the middle section. This aria is a presentation of Medoro and an extravagant declaration of his love for Angelica—to which she responds in kind. It stands as an appropriately static portal to the ensuing action, during which their love will undergo severe testing before its final reaffirmation at the happy end.[49]

Aside from presentation, there were numerous individual situations in which the static, elaborate da capo aria functioned with particular efficacy. Usually, the preparation of an action rather than a response is involved. Aldimira's "Vaghe stelle" in *Erismena* (2.7) has a specific purpose, which its elaborate da capo structure helps to fulfill. Like Xerse's "Ombra mai fù" and Medoro's "O luce serena," it serves as a prelude to a dramatic action and thus stands apart. But it goes farther than either of those arias in being designed to initiate that action: to rouse the sleeping Erismena, disguised as Erineo, with whom Aldimira has fallen in love. As such it benefits from musical elaboration, which can only increase its impact on the sleeper. The composer, evidently relishing the opportunity for expansion encouraged by its dramatic purpose, filled the aria with some of the most expressive music in the opera. As in "Ombra mai fù," the refrain is metrically distinct from the B section. In sense, too, the two sections parallel those of "Ombra mai fù." The refrain is an apostrophe, an abstract, metaphoric invocation, while the central section is more

48.   The contrast also apparently involved a tempo change, to judge from the adagio rubric. Perhaps the tempo marking is supposed to counteract a natural tendency to speed things up in response to the smaller note values of B.

49.   It may in turn (or also) be a musical response to Angelica's aria in the previous scene. See Morelli and Walker, "Migliori plettri," CLI.

direct, more urgent and more mundane, abandoning metaphor for literalism: Erismena's "stars" become mere "eyes" (example 44):

Vaghe stelle,	*Stars transcendent,*
Luci belle	*Lights resplendent,*
Non dormite.	*Why thus sleep ye?*
Aprite il sereno	Display the serene
De vostri begli occhi,	Of your beauteous eyes,
Lasciate, che scocchi	Let love play his part
In questo mio seno	On this stage of my heart,
Amore i suoi dardi,	Shoot hither his shafts
	and fix here his dart.
Bei lucidi sguardi	Ye splendors so clear,
I lumi deh aprite.	Unveil and appear.
Vaghe stelle . . .	*Stars transcendent . . .*

Cavalli's setting is unusually free and expressive, contributing to the passionate tone of Aldimira's address. The piece is proclaimed a formal aria by an opening ritornello, which also announces (typically) the main thematic material of the refrain, and which later returns to separate the refrain from the middle section of the aria. The three-line refrain is expanded considerably, both musically and textually, not only by means of the opening and closing ritornello (which, though textless, has the rhetorical function of emphasizing the words of the refrain), but by repetition of the text as a whole, which introduces a new motive before cadencing with the original one; the extra repetition also serves to solidify a return to the tonic, temporarily left for the dominant at the end of the first statement. (Text is repeated to increase the dimensions and weight of this aria, possibly because Aldimira was the prima donna.) The three-line refrain is thus actually heard four times, twice with and twice without words; three times with the same music, once with new music. The refrain returns verbatim, though without the introductory ritornello, at the end of the aria.

Emphasis on the refrain is predictable, but the composer's expansion of the central section of the aria is perhaps less so. Textually already twice as long as the refrain, it becomes even longer and heavier through repetition of individual lines, melismatic extension, interruption by ritornello (after the first two lines), and, finally, through threefold reiteration of its final line, each time on a different scale-degree (C, A, G), which lends urgency to Aldimira's plea. In Cavalli's setting, the text reads:

> Deh, deh aprite, aprite
> Deh, deh aprite, aprite
> bei lucidi sguardi
> i lumi deh aprite
> deh lucidi sguardi
> i lumi deh aprite

—the momentum increasing through modulation and through the addition of string accompaniment.

Although, as in "Ombra mai fù," the refrain and middle section are not particularly contrasting musically—they share meter, melodic style, overall harmonic structure, and even the string accompaniment—each is harmonically complete and thus independent of the other. Here, however, the composer provides an added expressive touch by unexpectedly eliding the end of the strophe with the returning refrain, thereby emphasizing the naturalness of the recurrence.

These expanded da capo arias seem to share very little with the recitative-like refrain forms with which our discussion began. From the retrospect of subsequent operatic history, the larger forms seem more "progressive": nonstrophic, with longer, tonally closed refrains that were not recomposed but repeated (as indicated by rubric), and with clear formal boundaries, their distinguishing characteristics became the conventions of the mature da capo form of the early eighteenth century.

It is important to recognize, however, that the differences between the two types represented more than a chronological development from the early 1640s to the mid 1650s. This is made clear by a comparison of the expanded da capo arias with other pieces contemporary with them, even those within the same operas—for example *Xerse*, *Medoro*, and *Erismena*. These arias stand out as exceptionally large and fully developed even within their own specific contexts. Nor did da capo arias increase in size all at once. Musical expansion remained exceptional well into the final decades of the century, in bipartite as well as da capo arias.

As I have suggested, the elaborate da capo arias, no less than their more austere counterparts, developed in response to specific dramatic situations. The shorter refrain forms were invariably integrated within the dramatic fabric; musical continuity between sections and recomposition of the refrain often contributed to that integration. The more statuesque forms served their function by being external, outside the drama; that function was enhanced by expansive musical treatment and strong formal articulations between sections.

Elaborate arias, during which the increasingly powerful singers could command the stage for extended periods, obviously pleased them and their adoring public more than shorter, more modest ones and might have proliferated for that reason alone. But the ultimate ascendancy of the larger forms was a function as well of modifications in the dramaturgy of librettos. In addition to all of the standard justifications for arias, librettists developed clear dramaturgical conventions for their use, at entrances and, increasingly, at exits. These conventions in turn absolved librettists and composers of the necessity of fitting each aria into a specific dramatic context—the general supplanted the specific—and eventually freed composers to indulge their musical inclinations.

As the total number of arias increased during the 1650s and 1660s, so did the proportion of da capo to bipartite arias, but more gradually. In operas of the 1650s, da capo arias constituted less than one-third of the total; by the 1660s the proportion was about equal; and by the late 1670s the bipartite aria was virtually obsolete.[50] The gradual disappearance of the bipartite aria and of the shorter, more spontaneous da capo refrain forms at once reflected and affected changing concepts of dramatic structure. The accumulating energy of both the bipartite and the continuous, affective da capo refrain arias, which suited them so well to integration within ongoing action, became less necessary as the dramaturgy of librettos accommodated arias through a conventionalized scene structure built expressly to contain them.

From the early recitative-like closeness of music and text, which tended to keep them functioning within a fluid dramatic framework and restricted their musical elaboration to brief, text-inspired moments, arias expanded to take up increasing amounts of operatic space and time; they eventually absorbed much of the expressive responsibility formerly exercised by recitative and arioso. Musical expansion, originally text-inspired and quite irregular, gradually settled into more conventional schemes of repetition involving whole sections of text, particularly the refrain, though not always to the same music. The conventions of formal structure as well as dramaturgy increasingly outweighed the requirements of any individual dramatic situation.

The conventional occasions for arias developed by earlier librettists and composers—the public situations that called for formal songs and comic commentary and the private ones that lent conviction to the formal expression of intense passion as thought rather than speech—remained in use throughout the century. But these were increasingly supplemented by others, most notably that of direct address between characters on stage, a mode of communication that required a real stretch of imagination to be believed; that dilemma was only partly eased by the conventions of entrance and exit that were superimposed on all of these situations.[51]

The greater number and more conventionalized placement of arias had a significant effect on their dramatic responsibility and musical treatment. In

50. In the inaugural opera for the Teatro S. Giovanni Grisostomo in 1678, *Vespasiano* (Corradi/Pallavicino), only five of the fifty-two arias were not da capos. See Saunders, "Repertoire," 186.

51. One of the first operas in which characters conversed in aria was *Alessandro vincitor di se stesso* (1651); see ch. 9 above. The practice became increasingly common. Sometimes this was achieved rather cleverly. For instance, on two occasions in *Seleuco* (3.1 and 2.14) one character supplies the refrain to another's strophes.

order to fulfill the expanded role of the aria in characterization, and for purposes of musical variety, librettists and composers began to focus on a single, specific affect or emotion in each aria, portraying the multiple facets of a character seriatim, one at a time, over the course of several arias. Such distribution and concentration of affect provided substance enough for the increased number of arias sung by each character, often more than ten in a single opera.[52] Inspired by a particular word or phrase, the affect was usually embodied in the refrain, which increasingly supplied the central musical idea of the aria that was then developed in some way in the B section and emphatically reiterated in an elaborate da capo. These, of course, were the arias of the affections of late baroque opera satirized so effectively by Marcello and others.

The da capo aria not only gradually supplanted the bipartite aria. In its most fully developed and expanded form it eventually replaced the convention of strophicism, which, though often problematic from the point of view of verisimilitude, had been fundamental to the definition of aria from the very beginning of operatic history. With the da capo aria, librettists still maintained some measure of control over composers' settings. At the same time, however, the form provided the singers with an official, sanctioned opportunity to exercise their own freedom by ornamenting the returning refrain. The abandonment of the strophic structure in favor of the da capo is a final sign of the singer's arrival to claim center stage.

52. The highest number of arias for a single character in *Medoro* (1658) is five for Angelica; in *Eliogabalo* (1668) the title hero has nine; in *Orfeo* (1673) Euridice sings ten.

11

• • •

Le convenienze teatrali:
The Conventions of *Dramma per musica*

In constructing their operas, librettists and composers drew upon a large and varied body of conventions, in part derived from the traditions of spoken theater and in part newly developed in response to the exigencies of the operatic genre itself. The availability of a stock of readily adaptable formulae was essential to the proliferation of opera in Venice; enabling supply to keep up with growing demand, it was prerequisite to institutionalization. Through such conventions the genre, in effect, identified itself to its audience. The knowing recognition and appreciation of conventions was a crucial aspect of the experience of opera. In every dimension of construction, in each of its constituent parts, large and small, opera was fabricated out of formulaic units—from the most general to the most specific level of structure, from its overall shape to the individual musical style for a particular text.

Once established, some of the most general structural conventions remained fairly constant throughout the century, while others, more specifically musico-dramatic, changed in response to the developing genre. On the largest scale, the three-act format, after some initial uncertainty, became standard for operatic plots. Although the material of those plots shifted from an emphasis on mythology to romance and increasingly fictionalized history, a conventional structure based on the Faustini formula emerged quite early in the 1640s: two pairs of lovers, surrounded by a variety of comic characters, whose adventures involved separation and eventual reunion. That formula provided subsequent librettists with the basis for variation and invention.

Within this standardized framework, other conventions served to articulate the larger structure. The first act was usually prefaced by a prologue declared by mythological or allegorical characters, providing the occasion for special scenic display. Operas commonly began with an instrumental movement, a sinfonia (sometimes such a movement opened each of the acts), and the first two acts normally concluded with a *ballo* of some kind. The individual acts could vary in length and number of scenes, with first acts generally longest and third acts shortest.

The distribution of the action was also predictable. Act 1 presented the basic situation, including the subplots, and ended in confusion. Act 2 further complicated the confusion, which reached its apex at some point during the third act and resolved near the end, even as late as the final scene. These structural conventions quite naturally carried with them musical expectations as well. The emotional climax in the third act was usually marked by a lament, the reconciliation of lovers at the end by a duet.

Within each individual act, the audience expected a dramatic structure built up in groups of scenes: the number of actors on stage would increase to a certain point, when a break occurred, with a change of setting and characters, comic interludes often bridging the gaps between successive scene-groups or sets. All of these conventions could be manipulated and varied; resolution could be postponed, for example, or a further plot complication introduced unexpectedly. But the effect of such manipulation was predicated on the assumption of a normative structure and dramatic development familiar to the audience.

Beyond such general assumptions about operatic structure, the audience would also have expected the characters to relate to one another in established ways and to behave according to type. In addition to the usual confrontations, conflicts, and love scenes between members of the same class, there were obligatory scenes that involved mixed social classes: the nurse giving advice to her charge or the squire complaining to his master. Each of the principals was normally introduced by a presentation aria of some kind, and they could each also be counted on for a soliloquy at some major turning point later in the opera. Comic soliloquies, on the other hand, tended to occur between sets to allow for changes of scenery.

The audience's expectations also extended to visual aspects of the performance. It anticipated scenic variety, contrast between outdoor and indoor settings of different kinds: a courtyard, a landscape, an armed camp, a chamber, a forest, the Underworld. And, of course, it also expected elaborate costumes. Deviations from the norm were bound to produce a reaction—and to require comment and explanation.[1]

Among conventional scene-types, the lament, the mad scene, the ghost or Underworld scene, and the sleep scene were borrowed directly from the traditions of spoken theater, from comedy and the pastoral, two of opera's chief

---

1. The conventional stage-sets are neatly categorized in Claude-François Ménestrier, *Des Representations en musique anciennes et modernes* (Paris, 1681), 168–74 (*Quellentexte*, ed. Becker, 86–87). They include the heavenly, the sacred, the military, the maritime, the royal, the historical, the magical, and the academic. On the last category in particular, see n. 23 below.

literary ancestors. Adapted to the new genre, these theatrical conventions in turn became associated with specifically musical ones: the lament with an aria based on the descending tetrachord, the Underworld with arias featuring *versi sdruccioli*, and the sleep scene, quite naturally, with the lullaby. Inherited character types, too, assumed conventional musical associations: the roles of the heroes were usually sung by soprano and alto castrati, the heroines by female sopranos; basses sang the parts of old men, whereas nurses were usually played by tenors *travestiti*. Further, the utterances of comic characters were distinguished from those of serious characters by special musical treatment of their texts, particularly in the arias. And the discourse of the gods was distinguished from human communication by its greater virtuosity, its vocal flights.

Convention also determined the composer's deployment of his musical resources. Certain kinds of texts or dramatic moments became associated with specific kinds of music: the reading of letters usually called for specially organized recitative;[2] aggressive, combative texts prompted imitations of trumpets (eventually real trumpets);[3] highly expressive aria texts and even an occasional recitative passage (usually one per opera) were often distinguished by string accompaniment rather than just the usual continuo.

Some conventions were restricted to the works of a single librettist and therefore might better be termed personal stylistic traits—the twenty-scene act, for instance, was a trademark of Minato. Others, such as the mad scene, were particularly strong within a limited timespan—the early 1640s, in this case—suggesting that they may have been inspired by one another. And still others, such as the closing love duet, might have been the result of practical considerations—economic or even physical limitations that rendered elaborate mythological endings unfeasible.[4] Finally, certain conventional character-types, such as the stutterer, or musical genres, like the lament, may have received their original impetus from the talents of a particular singer or composer.[5] Regardless of their origins, however, most of these conventions, more or less modified,

---

2. Beth Glixon discussed the convention of the letter in "The Letter-Writing Scene," a paper delivered at the annual meeting of the American Musicological Society, Philadelphia, 1984.

3. See Tarr and Walker, " 'Bellici carmi,' " 143–203.

4. The operas produced in S. Moisè and S. Apollinare were undoubtedly affected by the small dimensions of those theaters—both stages and auditoriums—to which librettists often alluded in their prefaces. See, for example, Faustini's remarks in the preface to *Oristeo* (Appendix I.33b) and elsewhere. Also Melosio's remarks in the preface to *Sidonio e Dorisbe* (quoted in Pirrotta, "The Lame Horse

and the Coachman," *Essays*, 326). But the general economic conditions under which all theaters operated would have tended to inspire cost-cutting adjustments in productions, particularly in view of increasing expenditures for singers.

5. On the possible influence of performers on their roles, see ch. 8, pp. 233–35 above; also Bianconi and Walker, "Production," 249. The laments of Cavalli, present from his first to his final opera, are surely the musical highpoints of his scores, a claim that cannot be made for those few surviving scores of his contemporaries. Ziani's laments, for example, seem quite perfunctory.

were ultimately absorbed within the generalized style recognizable as that of "Venetian"—eventually Italian—opera, a single rubric that subsumed the efforts of particular librettists, composers, scenographers, and even singers. Individual stylistic distinctions between composers or librettists faded into the background as the shared conventions of the genre fell into place.

Particularly after the middle of the century, every opera was a patchwork of conventions stitched together more or less tightly and confidently. Some tend to show their seams, while others, because of the particular skills of librettist and composer, manage more successfully to present the appearance of a uniform fabric. Even these, however, unravel quite readily to reveal their constituent parts.

Surely no single Venetian opera lends itself more appropriately to scrutiny of this kind than that standard-bearer of midcentury style, *Giasone*. We have already noted (chapter 9) the extraordinary popular success of the work and recognized its place at the crossroads of operatic developments. Besides representing a moment of equilibrium, an ideal balance between *dramma* and *musica*, *Giasone* offers a model of operatic conventions. Its success, in fact, like that of *La finta pazza* before it, can be ascribed more to the effective exploitation of conventions than to any particular originality; that is, to the skill with which it utilized and highlighted a full range of operatic conventions that were already familiar to its audience.

The Comic Aria

Essentially based on the Faustini model, *Giasone* features a typical cast of characters, who perform the functions and express themselves in the language appropriate to their several classes. The comic characters in particular, considerably more numerous here than usual, illustrate one of the oldest and most stable of operatic conventions: the comic aria style. A distinctive style for comic arias, in fact, based on a combination of textual and musical features, had been established in the very first Venetian operas and persisted throughout the century. We have already explored and illustrated some aspects of this style in chapters 9 and 10.

Comic arias depended for their effect on being in some sense artificially formal statements, either songs that served within the drama as props, like drinking songs or lullabies, or else cliché complaints or advice, ostensibly addressed to fellow actors, but effectively directed to the audience. Their texts usually comprised two or more strophes of *versi misurati*, generally *senari* or *ottonari*, which often contained refrains of one or more lines, either within the strophes or enclosing them. The strophic form itself, of course, although antithetical to dramatic progress and thus inappropriate for many dramatic situations, was essential to the song, distinguishing it from other more natural modes of communication and thereby underlining its nature.

Beyond reinforcing strophic texts with strophic music, composers emphasized the strongly metrical structure of individual comic strophes by marking grammatical articulations as well as formal patterns—rhymes, metric parallels and contrasts—and by setting the refrain lines clearly apart from the rest of the text. And, since much of the humor of comic texts lay in details of language—odd turns of phrase, puns, alliteration—as well as meaning, composers generally adopted a simple, almost speechlike style in which such verbal play would be clearly audible: speedily delivered syllabic text-setting within a narrow range involving many repeated notes, homophonic texture, short, often separated, repeated musical phrases based on text-phrases, and text-derived rhythmic patterns. In addition, comic arias were often marked by exaggeration of various kinds: excessively literal text-painting, sharp and frequent musical contrasts, and overly extended sequences or repetitions.

Such music—normally not requiring extraordinary breath control, particularly well-developed high and low registers, or vocal flexibility—allowed for an unusual freedom of stage movement. In fact, certain of these musical features—such as the short, separated phrases, which were often linked to one another by instrumental echoes—even actively encouraged comic stage business. It is worth emphasizing, once again, the suitability of such music for performance by skillful actors rather than trained singers.[6]

The comic arias in *Giasone* display typical characteristics of the type. One of them, sung by Medea's old nurse Delfa, "È follia" (illustrated above in chapter 9 [example 12]), is marked by a mincing, stepwise, highly repetitious melody, strictly syllabic text-setting, short, clipped phrases, and a strong contrast between strophe and refrain. Like most of the other comic arias in the opera, it is part of a lyric scene, the second of two arias separated by a recitative passage. Comic arias by other composers, as well as later ones by Cavalli himself, share many of the same features, particularly the sense of text-generated music, although one or another aspect may be emphasized, depending on the particular dramatic situation or text at hand. Exaggeration and contrast, always in the service of text clarity, remain constant features of the comic style. They are fundamental to an aria like Alceo's "Io pensavo innamorarmi" from *Argia* (Apolloni/Cesti, 1669) 2.5, where speechlike, syllabic text-setting in a small range alternates back and forth with wildly extended, sequentially struc-

---

6. Some comic roles, however, were clearly played by extremely skilled singers: for example, that of the bass, Chirone, in Sartorio's *Orfeo*, which is filled with coloratura passages.

tured melismas (example 45). A similar contrast is found in Clitarco's "Fier tiranno" from *Ercole in Tebe* (Moniglia/Boretti, 1670) 1.13 combined with other typical comic features (example 46). Here short sequential phrases separated by instrumental echoes move in steady eighth notes, setting the text syllabically; suddenly, near the very end of the final refrain, that steady motion explodes in an enormous (four-measure) sixteenth-note melisma on *tiranno*, a word whose previous three settings, in syllabic eighth notes, leave the listener unprepared for the final expansion.

Finally, rapid text delivery is deliberately exaggerated in Erinda's "S'io potessi ritornar" from *Orfeo* (Aureli/Sartorio, 1673) 1.4, where the continuous eighth-note motion in the voice, hardly pausing for breath, is intensified by the relentless continuo accompaniment that matches the voice note for note, even urging it on at the ends of phrases (example 47).[7]

The examples are countless. There were comic arias like these in every opera from the 1640s until the end of the century, when comic characters were finally expunged from operatic plots—only to reappear, however, in the intermezzi of the early eighteenth century, with the same musical characteristics. But although they remained musically recognizable, such arias became somewhat less distinctive as the century progressed, owing largely to the proliferation of arias for serious characters. In their attempts to differentiate serious arias from one another and to strengthen the portrayal of affect in them, composers adopted some of the most characteristic features of comic arias.

Two arias from Sartorio's *Orfeo* illustrate the point. In Autonoe's "Qual spirto dannato" (1.5) exaggerated repetition and literal text interpretation portray the central image of the text, *girando*, which represents the character's hopeless wandering (example 51 below). In Euridice's "Non sò dir" (1.17) similarly literal text interpretation as well as abrupt contrast between syllabic and melismatic motion are directed more generally toward displaying that character's power—dramatic as well as vocal (example 48).

Sometimes the adoption of comic features seems more explicit and deliberate. In Atamante's "Nascer grande, ohimè che giova" from Cesti's *Argia* (1.5), for example, the use of comic characteristics—in particular, strong and abrupt contrast between syllabic and melismatic text setting, short, motivic phrases, metric shifts, and literal text interpretation (especially of *scherzo* and *gioco*)—tends, effectively, to undermine the seriousness of the king's amorous dilemma: that he cannot bear to marry beneath his station (example 49).[8] And, in another instance, in *Adelaide* (Dolfin/Sartorio, 1672) 1.11, an aria in simple

---

7. Example 30, "La bellezza è un don fugace," discussed in ch. 10 above, is another good instance of speed and patterning.

8. The use of an inappropriate style of speech (or song) for dramatic purposes is an important resource in mad scenes. See pp. 359–60 below.

syllabic style, with many repeated notes and strictly motivic structure, is part of Duke Annone's disguise as a shepherd—he expresses himself very differently, in a much more elaborate style, when he is alone (example 50).

Comic arias, like the characters who sang them, did not undergo significant development over the course of the century. Clarity of text presentation remained their primary objective, and musical expansion, accordingly, was kept to a minimum—or else comically exaggerated beyond sense. But they nevertheless served an important and continuing function in the evolution of the operatic genre. Their negligible affective responsibilities encouraged composers to experiment with their form, and those experiments bore fruit in the context of serious arias.

Composers' experiments with comic style exceeded the boundaries of individual arias to affect entire scenes. Comic scenes, expanding upon the idea of contrast that formed such an important ingredient of individual comic arias, were the first to display a succession of two arias linked by recitative. We already noted that Delfa's aria "È follia" (chapter 9, example 12) belongs to such a scene; and the same is true of several of the other comic arias discussed in earlier chapters.[9] Such successions eventually found their fuller realization in the obligatory operatic *scene* for protagonists. But whereas successive arias in a comic context required no greater justification than any individual aria—they simply intensified the comic effect—serious characters, at least initially, needed a specific excuse for repeated or sustained lyrical expression.

The large-scale musical structure of early comic scenes, like their dramatic structure, is negligible. Delfa's little scene (3.10), for instance, displays only the most rudimentary coherence. The two arias, one a brief bipartite stanza (almost too short even to be called an aria), the other (illustrated in example 12) a more extended strophic bipartite form, in different meters and keys, D minor and G major respectively, are linked by a recitative passage that begins immediately in the key of the second aria, where it cadences twelve measures later. But aside from distinctions of key, meter, and formal structure, the two arias are quite similar. They share the same sort of text treatment, the same restricted range of melodic motion, the same patter rhythm; in short, the same affect. There is no dramatic progress from one to the next, and no need for it. This was true even in more elaborate contexts, where arias were longer and where there were more elements in the scene than just the basic pair of arias and connecting recitative—*sinfonie*, arioso passages, independent refrains.

Serious scenes of the composite type, however, were structurally more complex and more strictly integrated, dramatically as well as musically. Au-

---

9. Delfa's scene is not as elaborately lyrical as some earlier composite comic scenes, such as those of Dema in *Egisto* (example 21) or Melloe in *Doriclea* (example 29).

tonoe's *scena* (*Orfeo* 1.5) (example 51), for instance, the second aria of which I
have already mentioned, opens with a brief aria expressing her generally sad
state. The aria is cast in expanded bipartite form by Sartorio, who divides the
six-line text in half and expands the second half through a combination of
irregular repetition and affective melismatic extension on *tormento*. Autonoe
explains the reasons for her sadness in the ensuing recitative, which culminates
in an angry outburst against her fate. The recitative also accomplishes the rather
radical harmonic transition from A minor, the key of the first aria, to B minor,
the key of the second. The second aria, half the length of the first, is no less
effective. Autonoe now announces the specific means whereby she hopes to
overcome her dejection—her intention to pursue her faithless lover, "traveling,
searching" (*girando, cercando*), until she finds him again. The generalized sadness
expressed in the first aria is particularized in the following recitative and chan-
neled in the much more energetic second aria. The musical contrasts between
the arias, not only of key but of meter and text treatment as well, animate the
dramatic structure. Autonoe's scene is a clear albeit distant ancestor of the
cavatina-cabaletta.[10]

The Trumpet Aria

Other arias in *Giasone* are conventional in a different sense; rather than portraying character, they exploit conventional topics or textual imagery. Act 2,
scene 12, between Alinda and Besso (who happen also to be comic characters),
illustrates several important and long-lasting conventions of this kind. One of
them, the so-called trumpet aria, is invoked twice in the same scene, first in
Alinda's aria "Quanti soldati" and later in her duet with Besso, "Non più
guerra."[11] Both aria and duet exploit the literal imitation of text characteristic
of comic arias, but the imitation is more specific and it leads to an aria type that
transcends social class (examples 52 and 53).

Although the trumpet aria established itself as an operatic type sometime
during the 1640s, its roots go back much further. It derived from a madrigalistic
attitude toward poetry inherited from the sixteenth century and dramatically
developed by Monteverdi; in particular, it grew directly out of Monteverdi's
stile concitato, his legendary excited or warlike style.[12] Clearly demonstrated in

10. The second aria, labeled "cavata" in the Viennese score (A-Wn 17940), is actually followed by
a brief recitative, linking it to the following scene
(see Rosand, "L'Ovidio trasformato," XLVII).
There were other large scenes for protagonists with
many elements, including accompanied recitative;
see Doriclea's lament in ch. 12 below.
11. "So-called" because trumpets themselves were

not actually used in them until the 1670s. See Tarr
and Walker, " 'Bellici carmi,' " 159–73.
12. The *stile concitato*, described by Monteverdi in
the preface to his *Madrigali guerrieri et amorosi* (Book
8) and exemplified most explicitly in works such as
the *Combattimento di Tancredi e Clorinda* and "Hor che
'l ciel e la terra," was an important demonstration of
the composer's conception of imitation as it evolved

operas of the 1640s by Sacrati and Cavalli as well as those by Monteverdi himself, the madrigalistic origins of the trumpet aria found their fullest realization in the eighteenth century, in such arias as that opening Handel's *Orlando*, Zoroastro's stirring "Lascia Amor e segui Marte."

In the earliest Venetian operas, even the most fleeting references to war within recitative dialogue were usually marked by brief, but obvious, trumpet imitations. Trumpets themselves were occasionally mentioned, as in a passage from *La finta pazza*, "Suona d'intorno la fiera tromba," a reference to the Trojan War that is central to the plot—although any word alluding to armed conflict would have done as well, such as *battaglia* or *guerra* (example 54). But the war was just as likely to be metaphorical as actual, amorous as military, especially in Monteverdi's operas. In *L'incoronazione di Poppea*, for example, the *stile concitato* is inspired in one instance by a figurative reference to the war of love[13] and in another by an actual conflict, but one of wills rather than armies.[14]

In *Il ritorno d'Ulisse* the references to war are more literal. One of them, in the mock-serious duel between Iro and Ulisse (3.10), culminates in a battle symphony (called "La Lotta") based on a much more extended, and literal, trumpet imitation that accompanies the duel itself.[15] Imitative battle music like this was quite common in Cavalli's operas too, often written in the trumpet key of D.[16] Other operas included literal alarums (*all'armi*). At the end of act 1 of *Doriclea* (Faustini/Cavalli, 1645), for example, Venus calls her Cupids to arms in an extended refrain aria based on a trumpet theme, a theme echoed by them in their subsequent four-part chorus (example 55).[17]

Without much apparent fanfare, the brief, transient trumpet imitations soon developed into full-fledged arias. By the time of *Giasone*, at least one such aria was de rigueur in every opera. But although actual battles became increasingly thematic in opera plots, especially those based on history, Monteverdian ambiguity continued to affect later trumpet arias as well: war was interpreted in its broadest sense. In *Giasone*, a war of love provoked Alinda's and Besso's military

in his late works. On the relationship of Monteverdi's warlike style to the poetry of Marino, see Gary Tomlinson, "Music and the Claims of Text," *Critical Inquiry* 8 (1982): 585–88, and id., *Monteverdi*, 202–14.

13. In Poppea's aria "Speranza tu mi vai" (1.5) a vivid trumpet figure is heard several times in association with the refrain "Per me guerreggia Amor" and thus becomes thematic of the aria. *Tutte le opere di Claudio Monteverdi*, ed. Malipiero, 13: 40–41.
14. At the end of the pivotal confrontation between Seneca and Nerone (1.9); Malipiero ed., 13: 80–83.
15. See Malipiero ed., 12: 145–46.
16. *Le nozze di Teti e di Peleo* has a "chiamata" in

1.5; *Didone* a "passata dell'armata" at the end of act 1 as well as a "caccia" in act 3. A declaration of enemy surrender in *Erismena* (1.14) is heralded by a trumpet imitation, and there are two such movements in *Elena*. a "lotta" accompanying a fight—like the one in *Il ritorno d'Ulisse*—and a "tocco" (1.16). There are numerous others as well, in *Pompeo*, *Scipione*, *Argia*, and elsewhere. See Glover, *Cavalli*, 110, and Tarr and Walker, " 'Bellici Carmi.' " Cavalli's *La virtù de' strali d'Amore* contains an entire battle scene in accompanied recitative utilizing the *stile concitato* (3.14).
17. *Doriclea* exhibits several other instances of the *stile concitato*—including one in a lament, illustrated in example 80 and discussed in ch. 12 below.

duet, although Alinda's initial trumpet aria was inspired by Besso's appearance as a member of Giasone's army.

During the second half of the century, in fact, trumpet style was adopted for the expression of an even greater variety of emotions, from joy, where the pomp of trumpet figuration would add to the celebratory effect, to revenge, which often evoked images of combat. Rodope's vengeance aria in *Le fortune di Rodope e Damira* (Aureli/Ziani, 1657) 2.15, for example, an expression of her aggressive feelings toward Creonte, makes extensive use of the trumpet style (example 56). Some operas, especially those featuring repeated battles, contained numerous trumpet imitations, in recitatives as well as arias and instrumental movements. In *Medoro* (Aureli/Lucio, 1658), which revolves around the theme of military conquest, there are trumpet imitations in several *sinfonie*, one aria, and throughout the recitative, setting every military allusion. And there are four different trumpet arias in addition to recitative trumpet imitations in *Totila* (Noris/Legrenzi, 1677), a military drama of a different, more conventional, kind.[18]

As with comic arias, the stylistic distinctions between composers' settings of trumpet arias were overshadowed by their similarities. But developments within the trumpet aria tended to reflect developments within operatic style in general. Thus, in contrast to the somewhat shapeless refrain-aria from *Doriclea* already mentioned (example 55), a trumpet aria of the 1660s or 1670s was likely to be accompanied by strings and cast in highly expanded da capo form, with a contrasting B section. The contrast usually involved silence of the accompanying instruments and a change from triadic to stepwise motion in the voice part. The opening aria of *Adelaide* is a typical instance (example 57).

The presence of trumpet-style arias in so many early operas might seem difficult to reconcile with the historical fact that the trumpet itself did not appear regularly in opera orchestras until the early 1670s. However, the imitation of trumpets by strings was very much in keeping with the aesthetic of Venetian opera. Such imitation was an illusion that would have been appreciated as such by an audience, like any other illusion.[19] Indeed, the introduction of the trumpet

18. *Concitato* trumpet imitations in *Medoro* are unusually numerous (see Morelli and Walker, "Migliori plettri," CLIII). Cf. for example, *Medoro,* ed. Morelli and Walker, 19–20 ("Alla pugna, alla battaglia") and 108 ("Di strage di guerra"). For *Totila,* see arias in 1.3 ("Arda Roma," Garland facs., ff. 5ᵛ-7ᵛ); 2.8 ("Pugnando, atterando," ff. 47ᵛ-48ᵛ); 3.3 ("Snodate i fremiti," ff. 68ᵛ-70ᵛ); and 3.5 ("Il mondo festeggi," ff. 97-98, an aria with trumpet obbligato).

19. The audience apparently appreciated one particular singer's imitation of the trumpet, according

to Pierre d'Ortigue de Vaumorière (*Lettres,* 5th ed. [Brussels, 1709], 2: 214): "Il y a une celebre Chanteuse que l'on appelle la Margarita [Salicola], qui joüe un Rôle d'une force et d'une beauté inconcevable; c'est dans un tems qu'elle paroît furieuse, et qu'elle entre dans une espece de délire. Elle croit voir que la Terre abîme sous ses pieds, que l'Enfer s'ouvre pour l'engloutir, et toute la Ville de Rome paroît en armes pour la punir de ses crimes. Les Démons l'épouvantent par leurs cris, elle entend des Trompettes, des Tymballes et des Tambours dans les airs; et non seulement elle exprime par son chant les differentes

itself seems to have had little substantial effect on either the frequency or structure of the arias. Nor did it affect the choice of key, since most trumpet arias were in D major in any case. This suggests that the tonal association may have been important, whether or not a trumpet was actually involved. In some later arias, however, composers exploited the trumpet more fully by pitting it against the voice in concertato style.[20]

The trumpet aria embodies a particular kind of relationship between music and text that had broad implications for the future development of opera. It exemplifies the transformation of a pictorial approach to words developed in the sixteenth-century madrigal into the baroque aria of the affections. Although more easily identified as a type than other arias, because it exploited a well-established equation of an external image and internal feeling, the trumpet aria was only one of an increasing number of arias on various topics, expressing distinct affects that were prompted by specific textual images.

Those images, which emerge from even a cursory look at any single opera of the 1650s, 1660s, or 1670s, were the same ones that had attracted the attention of the madrigalists and that had inspired earlier opera composers to flights of arioso fancy when they occurred in recitative dialogue. They included highly charged words that invite some kind of literal interpretation (or representation) in music, either by means of sound itself or by some sort of visual equivalent: verbs describing physical action or emotional expression, like *fermare*, *fuggire*, *rubare*, *sospirare*, *piangere*, *volare*, *vibrare*, *cantare*, *ballare*; nouns like *gelosia*, *vendetta*, *speranza*, *catene*, *lacci*, *aurette*, *zeffiretti*; and adjectives like *costante*, *variabile*, *miserabile*—all of them with strong affective resonance. These words called forth conventional or predictable musical images or representations, rhythmic, melodic, and textural, which were developed to infuse entire arias with their affect. This eventually produced arias expressing such varied emotions as jealousy, fear, anger, happiness, uncertainty, constancy, confusion, and despair—in short, arias of the affections.[21]

Few of the arias in any single affective category were quite as similar to one another as trumpet arias. Other kinds of arias left greater leeway for individual

---

manieres dont son esprit est agité, mais elle imite même si parfaitement le son des Trompettes, que l'on s'imagine entendre ces instrumens de guerre, lors même que l'on n'entend que sa voix" (quoted in *Quellentexte*, ed. Becker, 100; also Helmut Christian Wolff, *Die venezianische Oper in der zweiten Hälfte des 17. Jahrhunderts* [Berlin, 1937], 163 n. 91). It is worth noting that Salicola's trumpet imitation occurs in the context of a mad scene (cf. n. 62 below). Practically the same words are used by Chassebras de Cramailles to describe Salicola's performance in Pallavicino's *Il re infante* in the *Mercure de France* of Feb-

ruary 1683; the passage is quoted in Tarr and Walker, " 'Bellici carmi,' " 166.

20. See, for instance, *Flora* (Bonis/M. A. Ziani, Sartorio, 1681) and *Giustino* (Beregan/Legrenzi, 1683); examples in Tarr and Walker, " 'Bellici carmi,' " 168–71.

21. Some of these images are discussed in Olga Termini, "The Transformation of Madrigalisms in Venetian Operas of the Later Seventeenth Century," *MR* 39 (1973): 4–21. On literal representation in Monteverdi, see Rosand, "Monteverdi's Mimetic Art."

composers to assert their own personal styles. Some composers, too, were more skilled than others at capturing the affect of a particular text or developing a single motive into a full aria; and some made more forceful distinctions between aria types than others. By the 1670s, however, most arias in any one affective category bore a sufficient family resemblance to be easily identified by an audience; and affective counterparts for most arias in any one opera could be found in any other. A particularly striking illustration is provided by two jealousy arias, one from Sartorio's *Orfeo*, the other from Legrenzi's *Totila* (examples 35 and 58). In both arias *gelosia* is the operative concept; that emotion, or, rather, the undermining and pervasive effect of that emotion on the peace of mind of the character, is embodied in a running bass against a slower-moving vocal line; it is a bass whose steady progress in short, harmonically articulated but uninterrupted phrases never falters; which never confirms the phrase structure of the voice part, but consistently overlaps it, persisting steadily from the beginning to the end of the aria. Jealousy is ever present; it is permanent.[22]

The Music Scene

Alinda's and Besso's scene is the locus of yet another of the operatic conventions in *Giasone*, what we might call a topical convention: the topic is music. One of the most humorous exchanges in the scene consists of a series of allusions to music and to singing. They are completely gratuitous, without the slightest relevance to the plot (example 59). Although it is treated with dispatch here, in just a few lines of recitative and appropriate musical expansion, culminating in the duet "Non più guerra" (example 53 above), the topic of music—and song as song—is exploited extensively in many operas of this period.

Songs, as we know, although frequently interpolated in spoken drama, acquired a special significance within the context of opera as a kind of test of the basic premise of the genre: the distinction between speech and song. Whereas the earliest librettists and composers tended to introduce songs quite self-consciously in their operas, often specifically as excuses for formal music, their successors continued to enjoy the song as a special convention well into the second half of the century, when the standards of operatic verisimilitude had long since yielded to accommodate the formal aria as a normal means of communication. Song may have justified musical organization and expansion in

---

22. The fact that the two arias share the same tonality, F major, may be coincidental; on the other hand, it may suggest a connection between tonality and affect. Also coincidentally, perhaps, the bass of Legrenzi's ritornello exactly replicates the melodic line of Sartorio's aria.

early opera, but it became an excuse later for other kinds of liberties: for more elaborate arias or for scenic extravagances involving several arias in succession. Many operas featured singers as characters and found opportunities for elaborate scenes involving musical performance in the plot itself.[23]

Seleuco (Minato/Sartorio, 1666) contains a particularly effective music scene in which the court singer attempts to find the proper song to suit the mood of the love-sick hero Antioco. He begins two unsuitable ones, finally succeeding on the third try. The composer, of course, capitalizes on the conceit of beginnings and interruptions. And the scene reaches an appropriately self-conscious climax when Antioco literally repeats all three strophes of the song that pleases him as a sign of his approbation (example 60).[24] Another effective exploitation of the music scene is one in Aureli's and Sartorio's *Orfeo* that takes place in Orfeo's music room (2.13). Here Achille explains that he is studying music and, when asked to sing, sits down at the harpsichord to accompany himself in an aria, "Cupido, fra le piante." The conceit is carried even further as Achille's audience, noticing a peculiar intensity in his song, begins to suspect that his aria is not merely a ditty about love but an expression of his actual feelings.[25]

Songs, sung by "singers," were often different from normal arias: they could be more elaborate and more expansive, such as those sung by Chirone, Acchille's music teacher; or more repetitive, such as the one in example 60; or else they could be longer, like Miralba's song in *Medoro* (Aureli/Lucio, 1658) 2.5, which comprises three rather than the normal two strophes—the third, however, being quite realistically interrupted as the string on Miralba's lute breaks.[26] Songs also tend to call for special accompanying instruments played by the singers themselves, like Miralba's lute and Acchille's harpsichord, or like the theorbo used by the nurse Nisbe to accompany her lullaby in *Eliogabalo* (Aureli/Boretti, 1668) 1.11. Formal irregularities, such as breaking off in the middle, often emphasize the artificiality of these songs, helping to distinguish them from "normal" arias. Indeed, most songs are conceived with a special awareness of the conventions of aria, and they are specifically constructed to extend or counteract those conventions.

---

23. This topos had scenographic implications as well. It falls in Ménestrier's category of "academic" scene: "Les [Decorations] Academiques sont les Bibliotheques, les cabinets des Sçavans avec des Livres et des Instrumens de Mathematique, un cabinet d'antiques, une Ecole de peinture, etc" (*Representations en musique anciennes et modernes*, 173–74 [*Quellentexte*, ed. Becker, 87]).

24. This scene bears a striking resemblance to those cantatas by Cesti and Barbara Strozzi that concern themselves with the appropriateness of various songs

to different moods. See Rosand, "Barbara Strozzi," 271 and n. 97; Bianconi, "Il cinquecento e il seicento," 355–56; and Murata, "Singing about Singing," 374–82.

25. See *Orfeo*, ed. Rosand, 95–96.

26. The composer inexplicably fails to do justice to Aureli's text here; he sets the third strophe to new music, thereby missing the opportunity of interrupting an already established tune. See *Medoro*, ed. Morelli and Walker, 91–94.

The Love Duet

One final operatic convention illustrated in Alinda's and Besso's fertile scene is the love duet. "Non più guerra" (example 53), literally embodying its text, provides a harmonious resolution to the preceding flirtatious repartee, the *guerra* of the scene. The duet, or aria for two, was a natural musical impulse, a readily available resource for composers of vocal chamber music, but one whose viability in opera was open to question. Indeed, as Badoaro had been quick to point out in his apology for opera in 1644, not only was it thoroughly unrealistic for "men to conduct their most important business in song," but it was equally absurd that, "speaking together they should spontaneously find themselves saying the same things" (Appendix I.8j).

The only reasonable occasion for a duet under these circumstances was one in which the characters were somehow united in their sentiments; and there was no more natural or powerful bonding agent than the spell of love. Indeed, love not only sanctioned characters singing together but in turn was confirmed by their harmony. The duet, then, as an expression of amorous accord, had a particular dramatic function. In the context of the shape of librettos of the 1640s, it assumed a structural function as well: to mark closure. For the reconciliation of Faustini's lovers was usually postponed until the final scene, and the cementing love duets were usually saved to emphasize that moment. Unanimity was usually further enhanced by the practice of casting the protagonists, both male and female, as sopranos, so that their duets could involve literal intertwining, even occasional unison encounters.

Duets, of course, could occur earlier in a drama, and they could also involve characters who were not lovers, but in such cases they usually served some other, more specific, dramatic purpose. Even then, however, they often exploited the appropriateness of the duet as a symbol of amorous agreement.[27] One such duet in *L'incoronazione di Poppea*, between Nerone and Lucano in the middle of act 2, serves to underscore an important theme of the opera. Monteverdi adopts the conventional form of lovers' communication to establish an erotic effect in this scene. By celebrating Seneca's death with the texture, procedures, and affect of a love duet devoted to an appreciation of Poppea's beauty, the composer underlines the opera's libertine message.[28]

Whether or not duets occurred earlier in the drama, for lovers or other characters, it was only the exceptional seventeenth-century Venetian opera that failed to close with at least one duet—or two, one for each pair of lovers;

27. One of the atypical (and old-fashioned) features of *Il ritorno d'Ulisse* is that it contains a number of duets that are not strictly love duets: the one between Ulisse and Telemaco, for instance.

28. Although its effect is quite lascivious, the duet does not legitimate the interpretation of this scene perpetrated by at least one notorious stage director as a debauched homosexual orgy.

sometimes the four would join forces for a closing quartet. This particular convention seems to have become established quite early in the 1640s. It co-incided with the movement away from mythological plots, which concluded with elaborate supernatural scenes, toward more exclusively human dramas. The intimate duet ending is appropriate to the more personal opera plots of the 1640s. On the other hand, like those plots themselves, it also may have been encouraged by practical limitations that made choruses—and supernatural scenes—too expensive or difficult to produce.

The transition is illustrated by several operas of the early 1640s that seem to combine both traditions. *Gli amori d'Apollo e di Dafne* (Busenello/Cavalli, 1640) ends with a mythological duet—between Apollo and Pan—while the libretto of *Le nozze d'Enea* (Anon./Monteverdi, 1641) has a love duet in the penultimate scene but actually closes with the typical supernatural chorus. In this respect it is similar to *Il ritorno d'Ulisse*, whose libretto also closes with a mythological finale, but whose score ends sooner, with the preceding love duet. (Perhaps the same was true of the score of *Le nozze d'Enea*, which is lost.)

L'incoronazione di Poppea, too, originally concluded with a mythological scene with final chorus. It is now generally agreed that the present, notorious final love duet, "Pur ti miro," with text by Ferrari, was introduced into the original finale sometime after its first performance, possibly during a revival; certainly the music is not by Monteverdi. It may have been specifically moti-vated by the limited stage equipment (and cast) available for such a revival. But it seems more likely that it was added because by the time the opera was revived, whether in 1651 or earlier, a final love duet had become de rigueur, a necessary sign of closure.[29]

The duet may even have been added during the initial run of the opera, as happened in a work of the previous season, *La virtù de' strali d'Amore*, the first collaboration of Faustini and Cavalli. That opera, too, had originally ended with a mythological finale preceded by a scene of reconciliation for the pro-tagonists. But although in the libretto the penultimate scene closes with an aria,

29.   The revival in question is the only documented one, in Naples (1651). But the work may also have been revived earlier, perhaps in Bologna under the auspices of Ferrari or Sacrati or both. In the Naples score of *Poppea*, the complete mythological finale precedes "Pur ti miro." Most of that finale was never copied in the Venice score, however, and the part that was, namely a recitative for Amore and an aria for Venere, is crossed out (see *L'incoronazione di Poppea*, facs., ff. 104-105ᵛ). On Ferrari's authorship of the text of the duet, see Chiarelli, " 'L'incoronazione di Poppea,' " 150-51. Magini ("Le monodie di Benedetto Ferrari," 281–90, and "Indagini," 478–

511) suggests, on stylistic grounds, that Ferrari may also have written the music. Most recently, and on the basis of the newly discovered score of *La finta pazza*, Curtis (preface to *L'incoronazione di Poppea*) has proposed Francesco Sacrati as the composer of the problematic duet. Probably the most judicious evaluation of the situation, however, is Bianconi's (*Seventeenth Century*, 194–96), who, adding Laurenzi to the list of possible composers, along with Cavalli, as well as Ferrari and Sacrati, concludes that the question cannot be answered with certainty given the present state of research. For my views on the subject, see ch. 9, n. 18 above.

it is followed in the score by a love duet that was evidently inserted after the libretto was printed. If the mythological finale of *Virtù* was cut, as was that of *Poppea* in at least one performance, both operas would have concluded with love duets that, besides being late additions, were quite similar in style and message (example 61).[30]

The conventionality of the love duet was naturally not limited to its dramatic placement; it extended to its text and musical setting as well. Texts were usually quite short—sometimes only a line or two—and used essentially the same images. The endings of Aureli's two *Eliogabalo* librettos of 1668, one set by Cavalli, the other by Boretti, illustrate the range of duet texts. Cavalli's text, set as a quartet, reads as follows:

Pur ti stringo,	Yet I hold you,
Pur t'annodo	Yet I clasp you.
Meco il fato	Fate no more,
Idol caro	My darling idol,
Crudo avaro non è più.	Is a cruel miser with me.
Tant'è la gioia quant'il duolo fù.	Joy is as great as sorrow was.

Boretti's text, set as a duet, is shorter:

Al ferir	In wounding
Occhi veraci	True eyes
Sia campo il letto e dolci strali i baci.	Let bed the field, and kisses the sweet arrows be.

The first of these bears a strong resemblance to, among other closing-duet texts, that of *Poppea*.[31] The similarity, although notable, merely illustrates the conventionality of the poetry, the dependence of librettists on formulas. Indeed, unlike that of the rest of an opera, the text of the final duet had little importance. The opera was essentially over. The musical message of duet texture itself was sufficient to convey the resolution of the dramatic situation.

Even more than in the conventional aria types, and with even rarer exceptions, stylistic similarities among composers' settings of these duets predominate over any individual differences. In fact, it is difficult to point to any significant differences at all.[32] Duets suffered built-in musical limitations imposed by their similar affect. But although stylistic choices may have been restricted,

---

30.　Both the aria and duet at the end of *Virtù* make use of ostinato-like bass patterns not unlike that of "Pur ti miro."

31.　"Pur ti miro, pur ti godo, / Pur ti stringo, pur t'annodo, / Più non peno, più non moro, / O mia vita, o mio tesoro. / Io son tua, tuo son io, / Speme mia, dillo dì, / Tu sei pur l'idol mio, / Sì mio ben, sì mio cor, mia vita sì." The text is almost exactly the same as that in the final scene of Ferrari's *Il pastor regio* (Bologna, 1641).

32.　Although the love duet from *Poppea* is practically the only one that I know of to be based on a strict ostinato pattern (another is that of Melanto and Eurimaco in *Il ritorno d'Ulisse* 1.2 [Malipiero ed., 12: 31–33]), it would perhaps not be so unique if some of Ferrari's operatic duets were to be found. It closely resembles a trio in *La finta pazza* (see Bianconi, *Seventeenth Century*, 195).

expression was not. Frequently accompanied by strings, and in triple meter, love duets often involved considerable expansion of text through repetition and melismatic extension. The repetition was usually threefold, one statement for each voice followed by one for both together. In addition to repetition of individual words and lines in successive musical phrases, opening lines were sometimes repeated at the end to create a da capo form. Duets usually began with brief motivic exchanges or longer imitative passages that culminated in parallel movement in thirds and sixths enriched by suspensions and resolving into unisons. Interdependence of lines, perfect consonance, and ultimate union: these were all qualities that represented quite literally the relationship between reconciled lovers. The most eloquent confirmation of the conventionality of the closing duet is provided by a series of examples, chosen almost at random, from operas spanning several decades and representing the work of a variety of composers. Despite their different authors and disparate dates, they are virtually interchangeable (example 62 a–d).

Seen against the convention of the closing love duet, which was well established by the middle of the century, the ending of *Giasone* gains special impact as a kind of ironic transformation. It, too, presents the coming together of formerly opposing forces in two duets, each for two high voices. The first, for Isifile and Giasone, is followed by a second, not, as expected, for Medea and Egeo but for Medea and Isifile, two erstwhile rivals in love. This permutation of the convention, playing on expectations both dramatic and vocal, surely delighted an audience of 1650.

Sleep

One of the most pervasive conventions in *Giasone* is a dramatic device borrowed from spoken drama: the sleep scene. Isifile and Giasone each fall asleep twice and Medea once, for different purposes, not always crucial to the plot. Like all such dramatic conventions, sleep was an abnormal state of consciousness that facilitated the suspension of disbelief and thereby encouraged musical expression. It did so triply: for the singer of the provoking lullaby, for the sleeper, who could dream out loud, and for the on-stage observer, who could express himself as if alone.

Beyond its general loosening effect on verisimilitude, sleep functioned in a variety of specific ways as a plot device, in comedy as well as in opera. A sleeping character is vulnerable—to assassination, to rape, to penetration of disguise, and to involuntary disclosures via dreams. (In act 1, scene 14, Isifile, dreaming, describes Giasone's departure from Corinth, a scene that took place before the opera began; in act 2, scene 2, her sleeping encourages her servant

Oreste to attempt a rape—titillating the audience, no doubt, with the threat of class crossing;[33] in act 3, scene 17, Egeo attempts to murder the sleeping Giasone, but is prevented from doing so by Isifile.) Furthermore, a sleeping character (or one feigning sleep) can stimulate a companion (lover) to disclose his innermost feelings, thinking he is unheard. (Believing Medea to be asleep, Giasone declares his love to Isifile, which declaration, although only feigned at the time, persuades Medea to demand her rival's death.) Sleep was used in a variety of dramatic situations, but its musical associations were fairly limited. These were chiefly the prefatory lullaby (sung either by the eventual sleeper or by a companion), the dream (which could involve some special musical, in addition to dramatic, extravagance), and the miming of the action of falling asleep itself.

By 1650 the sleep convention already sported a lengthy operatic pedigree. It had been used in *La finta pazza*, that prodigious repository of conventions, to trigger the resolution by encouraging Achille to express his love for Deidamia; and again in *Il ritorno d'Ulisse*, where Ulisse is transported to Ithaca while asleep so that he will be unaware of the divine intervention on his behalf. A more striking example is that in *L'incoronazione di Poppea*, where Poppea's sleep facilitates the precipitating action of the denouement, Ottone's attempt on her life. This scene is especially interesting and significant from the musical point of view because it provides a concrete example of what Monteverdi called "music suggesting sleep," thereby demonstrating his conception of musical imitation.[34] Music imitates sleep in two different ways here. First, it depicts Poppea's drowsiness: her words and musical line become halting, interrupted by rests, and she then acknowledges her sleepiness in a descending line that sinks gradually to the bottom of her range, whereupon she falls asleep (example 63). Her nurse Arnalta's soporific lullaby then imitates sleep itself, or actually assures it, by different musical means: repetitive, circular melody within a restricted range, abnormally long-held notes at cadences, and harmonic oscillations would provoke a yawn from anyone, whether on-stage or in the audience.[35]

As with so many of the conventions, Monteverdi's musical realization was prophetic for the future development of opera. Lullabies continued to display the circular, repetitive motion appropriate to them, and the act of falling asleep (or fainting) continued to be treated mimetically, even by later composers who did not share Monteverdi's conception of imitation. In fact, some even ex-

33. Orestes, the prince of Mycenae, is cast in a comic role here, a typically Venetian *inventione*.
34. Monteverdi's expression "armonie imitanti il sonno" occurs in a letter to Alessandro Striggio of 24 May 1627, concerning *La finta pazza Licori* (*Lettere*, ed. de' Paoli, 251).
35. Malipiero ed., 13: 184–87.

tended their treatment of sleep to the moment of awakening as well. These scenes are not always essential to the plot. Isifile's second one, for example, merely provides the occasion for the diverting attempted rape by Oreste. But they all share features with Monteverdi's scene. Isifile falls asleep very much as Poppea did, although her fatigue seems to come on more suddenly, during a short monologue at the end of act 2, scene 1 (example 64):

Alinda troppo vana,	Too heedlessly Alinda
Seconda il genio, e la sua voglia insana;	Follows her mindless moods and fancies.
Oimè non posso più,	Alas, I cannot bear it any longer;
Perche manchin li spiriti,	My senses are failing,
Manca l'anima al seno,	My heart weakens in my breast,
Vacilla il piede, e a forza di stanchezza	My footsteps falter, and with sheer weariness
Trabocco sul terreno.	I fall upon the ground.

After an abrupt harmonic shift, the last five lines of text are set to a gradually descending chromatic melody interspersed with some long rests and articulated by a final upward leap before resolving down to a cadence. Medea's and Giasone's joint lullaby "Dormi, dormi" (example 14), on the other hand, although it is somewhat repetitive in rhythm, and perhaps exaggeratedly sequential, does not quite match the intensely soporific quality of Arnalta's.

The range of possibilities and functions (and the persistence of mimetic devices) offered by the sleep convention is illustrated by two sleep scenes separated by more than a decade: one from *Orontea* (Cicognini/Cesti, 1656), the other from *Ercole in Tebe* (Moniglia/Boretti, 1671) (examples 65 and 66). In *Orontea* 2.4, Alidoro, overcome by his confusion and his apparently unrequited love for Silandra, faints. Cesti's setting realistically disintegrates into short phrases, interrupted, chromatically descending, though leaping up for a brief final gasp before sinking with Alidoro into unconsciousness—the voice leaving the bass to cadence alone. In his unconscious state, which lasts for three scenes, Alidoro is first prey to having his pocket picked by Gelone, then oblivious audience to Orontea's declaration of love and to her (redundant) lullaby, and finally the unknowing recipient of a letter, which she leaves in his possession. He then awakens gradually, with ever longer, and rhythmically and melodically more active, phrases, to find Orontea's letter, which provides enough material to propel the rest of the plot. Like Monteverdi, Cesti responded mimetically to the action of falling asleep and even awakening, but his setting of Orontea's lullaby lacks the hypnotic effect of Arnalta's. Cesti's natural inclination toward bel canto, his talent for writing fluid, well-shaped melodies, overcomes his sensitivity to the dramatic situation.[36] Despite the greater dra-

36. See Antonio Cesti, *Orontea*, ed. William Holmes, Wellesley Edition 11 (Wellesley, Mass., 1973), 164–66.

matic complexity and greater number of elements in this scene, the items of musical interest are essentially the same as those in Poppea's sleep scene.

Boretti's scene, on the other hand, contains several new elements. When the despondent Megera falls asleep near the end of act 2, she dreams of Ercole's victory in the Underworld. Upon awakening, she realizes it was a dream, but vows to be hopeful anyway. Boretti's depiction of drowsiness is considerably less convincing than Cesti's. It comes on suddenly, after Megera has sung an extended, virtuosic (exhausting?) arioso with trumpet imitations. In recitative she acknowledges the growing effects of a sweet lethargy, but she resists long enough to sing what amounts to a lullaby to herself (accompanied by strings), more elaborate than Arnalta's, but sharing some of the same repetitive features, including the prominent imperfect cadences. She sleeps during a *ballo* and then awakens rather abruptly to sing an optimistic aria about the outcome of Ercole's trip to the Underworld, "Festeggia, o core."[37] Here, aside from changing Megera's mood, the sleep scene serves primarily as an excuse for several arias. The mimetic aspect, with respect to *Poppea* and *Orontea*, is reduced in favor of musical elaboration.

The convention of sleep challenged the librettist more than the composer: it was up to him to find new ways of incorporating such scenes into his drama, a challenge he met with varying success. But the particular dramatic function of the sleep scene had a limited effect on the music. In some librettos, sleep seems to serve no significant dramatic purpose whatsoever (the librettist was unsuccessful in integrating it into the drama), though it may have inspired more than one kind of musical elaboration, as in the Boretti example. At the other extreme, the scene may have been pivotal to the drama, but was completely passed over by the composer.[38]

In later operas, the emphasis seems to have shifted from concentration on the act of falling asleep and on sleep as an occasion for special, unwitnessed action to emphasis on its more imaginative and inspiring results, dreams. Portrayed in special ways by composers, dreams precipitate important actions in a number of operas of the 1670s. An ingenious and effective use of the dream provides one of the musical and dramatic highpoints of Aureli's and Sartorio's *Orfeo*. Orfeo, having exhausted himself in lamenting Euridice's death, falls asleep (3.4), whereupon Euridice's ghost appears, as in a dream, urging him to seek her in Hades. Sartorio forgoes the opportunity to mime musically Orfeo's falling asleep, but he does exploit Euridice's spectral appearance for special musical effects. These include some extremely elaborate coloratura passages, a

---

37. Garland facs., 6: f. 78ʳ.
38. In *Annibale in Capua*, for example, Ziani ig-nored the possibilities of imitation offered by the hero's sleep aria in 1.13.

lengthy (if misplaced) lament accompanied by strings, and an evanescent ending on an imperfect cadence that marks Euridice's disappearance just before Orfeo awakens.[39]

Invocation

Of all the conventions in *Giasone*, the most celebrated is Medea's incantation scene, in which she invokes the powers of darkness to aid Giasone in his quest for the Golden Fleece. We discussed the special poetry of this scene and illustrated its setting in chapter 9 (example 11). Since Medea's magical powers are intrinsic to her persona, any treatment of the Medea legend would have whetted an audience's appetite for a scene in which those powers were exhibited. *Giasone* did not disappoint. Medea's incantation scene, closing the first act, is one of the most powerful in the opera.

The scene of infernal invocation (the "ombra" scene) differs from other music-theatrical conventions in several important ways. For one, it was associated with a special verse form, the short line—either *quaternario*, *quinario*, or *senario*—with a *sdrucciolo* ending, an association, like the scene-type itself, inherited from spoken drama. Fundamental to its identity as a convention, this distinctive meter not only affected the musical setting of invocations but distinguished them from the rest of an operatic text. In addition to its meter, the invocation also involved a distinctive scenic dimension, requiring an infernal or magical setting of its own. In fact, the convention may have originated in part as an excuse for scenic contrast in the early operas. Finally, such scenes often included choruses, either alone or interacting with the soloist.

Although it did not initiate the convention,[40] Medea's incantation probably did more than any other to assure the persistence of such scenes throughout the century. A real tour de force for the prima donna, it was also the centerpiece of the drama: Medea's invocation of the infernal spirits enables Giasone to capture the Golden Fleece and frees him to return to his homeland with her, thereby exacerbating the crisis with his abandoned wife, Isifile, which forms the substance of the opera.

Related scenes appeared with some consistency in the operas that followed *Giasone*. But as an action the invocation was not as pervasive as other dramatic conventions, primarily because it resisted variation. While the affect of invocation was occasionally employed metaphorically, literal invocation scenes

---

39. See ch. 13 below. This scene is discussed in Rosand, "L'Ovidio trasformato," XXXVII and XLI–XLII.

40. Such scenes occur at least as early as *La virtù de' strali d'Amore* (Faustini/Cavalli, 1642).

were difficult to integrate into most dramas. Unless they were built into the libretto via its source—as in *Giasone* or the operas based on the Hercules legend—they tended to be extraneous, serving merely as a pretext for scenic display.[41] Both the difficulty of integration and the importance of the scenic dimension are reflected in the placement of invocation scenes within these operas. Whether for solo voice, chorus, or both, like Medea's scene they often appear, intermedio-like, at the ends of acts, where they lead directly into the entr'acte *balli*; or else they occur in prologues.[42] Significantly, too, these scenes were often omitted in revivals, a commentary on their peripheral dramatic function as well as, presumably, the extravagance of their scenic demands.[43]

Nonetheless, the invocation scene seems to have outlasted all of the other musico-dramatic conventions of this period, persisting well beyond the seventeenth into the eighteenth and even nineteenth centuries. But it hardly developed at all; it remained insensitive to stylistic change. Because of its strong metric associations, the invocation imposed greater strictures on composers than any of the other dramatic conventions. While this rigidity may have limited its usefulness, it also contributed something to its effect: unchanging and thus increasingly primitive in its power, its very stylistic anomaly evoked a sense of dark antiquity. That chthonic power is particularly evident in the two best-known invocation scenes of later centuries, those in Gluck's *Orfeo ed Euridice* and Verdi's *Un ballo in maschera*.[44]

Although primarily associated with the actual invocation of the Underworld, *versi sdruccioli* were also used when Hell or the world of darkness was invoked figuratively, out of jealousy, fury, or some other strong emotion. In *Giasone*, Medea employs them not only in her incantation but later as well, in the aria "L'armi apprestatemi" (3.9), in which she calls upon the Furies to lend her their arms so that she can punish the faithless Giasone.[45] *Versi sdruccioli* also appear in Ecuba's aria from *Didone* (1.7), in which she invokes the spectre of Hell as she seeks to purge herself of her weak, lamenting emotions (example 67):

---

41.   As well as in *La virtù* and *Giasone*, actual invocations involving scenic transformations—so-called *ombra* scenes—may be found, among other places, in *Rosinda* (Faustini/Cavalli, 1651, a chorus) and *Ercole in Tebe* (Aureli/Boretti, 1670, 3.6 in Pluto's realm).
42.   Like that of *Giasone*, the (more extraneous) incantation in *Tito* occurs at the end of act 1. In *Rosinda*, both the prologue and the final scene of act 1 are infernal.

43.   *Xerse* 1.2, an Underworld scene, is omitted in the Paris score of the opera, written in conjunction with the Paris production of 1662.
44.   On *Un ballo in maschera*, in particular, see Frits Noske, *The Signifier and the Signified: Studies in the Operas of Mozart and Verdi* (The Hague, 1977), ch. 8, esp. 197–99.
45.   This text is not set in any of the surviving scores of the opera.

Tremulo spirito	Tremulous spirit,
Flebile, e languido	Plaintive and languid,
Escimi subito.	Leave me forthwith.
Vadasi l'anima,	Let my soul depart
Ch'Erebo torbido	For gloomy Erebus
Cupido aspettala.	That hungrily awaits it.
Povero Priamo	Unhappy Priam,
Scordati d'Ecuba	Forget Hecuba,
Vedova misera.	Pitiful widow.
Causano l'ultimo	Cause of the ultimate
Horrido essitio	Horrid calamity
Paride, & Elena.	Are Paris and Helen.

And they are used in Sesto's aria "Ciecche tenebre" from *Pompeo magno* (Minato/Cavalli, 1666) 2.16, in which he calls upon darkness to hide him as he attempts to enter his beloved Issicratea's room unseen:

Ciecche tenebre	Blind shades
Apprestatemi	Lend me
Denso vel	A thick veil,
Ocultatemi	Hide me
Anco al Ciel.	Even from Heaven.
D'ombre tacite	Let murky darkness
Pur mi celino	Hide me
Foschi horror;	With its silent shadows,
Ne mai svellino	And never eradicate
Quest'Amor.	This love.

Along the same lines, *sdrucciolo* passages, carrying with them their symbolic connection to irrational or demonic force, also form an important ingredient of mad scenes and laments.

The conventional effect of such scenes, as we have noted, depended primarily on their use of verses with the *sdrucciolo* ending. Distinguished from the other verse endings, the abrupt *tronco* and the gentler *piano*, which call for accents on the final and penultimate syllables respectively, the *sdrucciolo*, exemplified by the word itself, is more awkward, receiving an accent on the antepenultimate syllable. Considered ugly and boorish by sixteenth-century poetic theorists, *versi sdruccioli* coincide in these operas not only with invocation but generally with texts associated with the darker elements of life: with the uncivilized, the demonic, magic, and also, on occasion, the comically rustic. Inherited (with its associations) from the pastoral, in particular the eclogue, the *sdrucciolo* apparently appealed to something quite fundamental in human experience. It persisted for a long time and in several languages, not only in Italian but in German as well. Its basis was evidently in the affective impact of the accent itself.[46]

One of the most extended uses of *versi sdruccioli* in an opera of the period occurs in *Calisto* (Faustini/Cavalli, 1651), where it conjures the rustic or satyric world of Arcadia. The pattern pervades all of the dialogue (including an aria) of two characters, Satirino and Pane, both members of a lower, less rational order, half man, half beast.[47] The meter lends to their utterances a rhythmic awkwardness that is exacerbated by erratic melody, monotonous harmonic motion, and irregular phrase structure. But the effect of their distinctive metric language is particularly striking in the scenes they share with other, more evolved characters, as in this one between Satirino and the nymph Linfea (1.13) (example 68):

SATIRINO: Io son, io son d'origine	I am, I am of origin
Quasi divina, e nobile,	Almost divine and noble;
Ben tù villana, e rustica	But boorish and rustic your birth
Nata esser dei trà gl'Asini,	Surely was, amongst the asses,
O da parenti simili.	Or some like parents.
Sò perche mi repudia	I know why your
L'ingorda tua libidine,	Greedy libido rejects me,
Perche Garzone semplice	Because I'm a simple fellow
Mal buono à gl'essercitij	With little skill in the ways
Di Cupido, e di Venere,	Of Cupid and Venus.
Ancor crescente, e picciola	Still growing and dainty
Porto la coda tenera.	Is the tender tail I bear.
LINFEA: *Ne le mandre ad amar và*	*Go take your love to the flocks,*
Aspetto ferino.	Fierce-looking one,
Fanciullo caprino	Goat-child.
Che Narciso,	What a Narcissus!
Che bel viso,	What a pretty face!
Vuol goder la mia beltà,	He would enjoy my beauty.
Ne le mandre ad'amar và.	*Go take your love to the flocks.*

Clearly, not every opera could support a full incantation scene, but most had a *sdrucciolo* aria of some kind.[48] Like the texts themselves, the musical

46.   The persistence of the association between the *sdrucciolo* and the Underworld is considered in Wolfgang Osthoff, "Musica e versificazione: Funzioni del verso poetico nell'opera italiana," in *La drammaturgia musicale*, ed. Lorenzo Bianconi (Bologna, 1986), 126–32, esp. 126–27. See also id., "Händels 'Largo' als Musik des goldenen Zeitalters," *AMw* 30 (1973): 177–81; and Noske, *Signifier*. It is worth noting that while in demonic contexts the *versi sdruccioli* are inevitably short, in rustic contexts they are longer: sometimes *ottonari*, more often *endecasillabi*. For the origins and use of the *endecasillabo sdrucciolo*, see Elwert, *Versificazione italiana*, esp. paragraphs 10, 119, and 120. On the pastoral associations in particular,

see Leopold, " 'Quelle bazzicature poetiche,' " 113–19; and id., "Madrigali sulle egloghe sdruccole di Iacopo Sannazaro," *RIM* 14 (1979): 75–127, esp. 75–80. On the use of *versi sdruccioli* for low characters, see the remarks of the author of *Le nozze d'Enea* (Appendix I.9f).

47.   The characters appear, alone and together, in a large number of scenes, including the three closing scenes of act 1 (13–15) and the four closing scenes of act 2 (11–14), both scene groups culminating in *balli*.

48.   Most operas have more than one text in *versi sdruccioli*. See, for example, *Adelaide* 1.14: "Numi tartarei / Stiggia Proserpina" (Garland facs., 8: f. 36ᵛ), a bipartite aria prompted by love; and *Totila*

settings were virtually interchangeable. More than in the case of any other aria type, the librettist controlled the composer's response. The musical settings of these texts are dominated by a characteristic dactylic rhythm, to which all other stylistic elements are subservient. The aria "O voi dell'Erebo" from *Annibale in Capua* (Beregan/Ziani, 1661) is typical (example 69). Melodic and harmonic subservience is evident in the large number of repeated notes, the triadic and sequential leaps, the rigidly regular, emphatic cadences, and the often widely separated phrases. Occasionally some melodic or harmonic expression intensifies the affect projected by the dominant rhythm. Ecuba's aria mixes chromaticism with its chordal melody (example 67 above) and Medea's invocation gains momentum by powerful harmonic motion (example 11 in chapter 9). But in general, the domination of the rhythm gives the sense that the character is being ruled by an urgent force over which he or she has no control. The impact of the *sdrucciolo* is equivalent to that of trumpet figuration in "trumpet" arias. Both originally represented a specific dramatic situation or emotion, and the significance of both broadened to accommodate an affective component: the concrete representation of the irrational in one case, of emotional conflict in the other. Such equation of inner feeling and outward sign is characteristic of the mechanism through which music conveyed emotion during this period.

Madness

With Medea's incantation as its centerpiece, *Giasone* set a memorable standard for scenes of invocation; without actually establishing the convention, it articulated it for the future. *Giasone* honored other conventions by indirection, satisfying expectation through parody. The mad scene, for example, which had received its definitive operatic shape nearly a decade earlier, in *La finta pazza*, seems absent from *Giasone*, but as we shall see, that absence is only apparent.

Temporary madness, feigned or real, had a long literary heritage. Undoubtedly owing its inspiration to Canto 24 of Ariosto's *Orlando furioso*, perhaps the most celebrated portrayal of madness in Italian literature, the topos became a favorite tour de force for some of the most famous actors (or, more often, actresses) in the *commedia dell'arte* troupes;[49] but it held special, if fairly

---

3.17: "Apri, omai le tue voragini" (Garland facs., 9: ff. 84^v-85^v), also a bipartite aria, inspired by despair. *Versi sdruccioli* are also used briefly but effectively in Publicola's first mad scene (1.11) (Garland facs., 9: f. 15).

49.   The earliest known example was *La pazzia d'Isabella*, performed by (and named for) Isabella Andreini with the Gelosi troupe in Florence in 1589. The tradition of mad scenes in the *commedia dell'arte*

and its relationship to early opera are treated at length in Maria Paola Borsetta, "Teatro dell'arte e teatro d'opera nella prima metà del seicento" (Tesi di laurea, Bologna University, 1986). For a thorough treatment of the influence of both written and improvised comedy on the development of the operatic mad scene, see Fabbri, "Alle origini." See also id., *Monteverdi*, 263, in which Andreini's *La pazzia d'Isabella* (1589) and *La pazzia di Scappino* by Francesco

obvious, implications for *dramma per musica*, justifying the use of music in a very specific sense. Madness freed characters from the decorum of normal behavior, allowing them to do whatever they pleased—even to sing.

But mere singing was not enough to project madness, particularly in an operatic context where everyone sang. In spoken drama, mad characters gained credibility by what they said as well as how they said it: by speaking irrationally, disconnectedly, and inappropriately, by voicing delusions—as well as by behaving unreasonably, dressing peculiarly, moving abnormally.[50] The musical setting of such texts would not automatically have produced convincing operatic madmen, however. Such characters had to break the accepted rules of their own language, music; they had to sing abnormally, erratically. Unlike the rules and norms of speech, which might depend on genre or theme, those of musical expression changed with changes in style. A mad scene of the 1640s might not share specific musical features with one of the 1720s or 1840s.[51]

As with so many other operatic conventions, we owe the critical as well as musical articulation of the issue of madness to Monteverdi, who was the first composer to attempt self-consciously—his characteristic mode of operation—to portray it in opera. He recorded his ideas on the subject in a famous series of letters of 1627 concerning an opera on which he was working with Giulio Strozzi, *La finta pazza Licori*, their first collaboration and Strozzi's first opera libretto.[52]

In advising Strozzi about the kind of text he wanted, Monteverdi was particularly concerned with the character of Licori, the "finta pazza" herself, and especially with her madness. His suggestions involved matters ranging from the disposition of the action and when and how often Licori appeared, to the actual poetry and topics of her discourse.

Gabrielli (1618) are cited in connection with Monteverdi's *La finta pazza Licori*.

50. Molinari, *La commedia dell'arte*, 121, describes the madness of the *comici dell'arte* as a "sonno della ragione, [che] si manifesta come discorso assurdo, un discorso cioè in cui, salva restando la struttura grammaticale e sintattica, saltano invece quei nessi e quelle norme di ordine logico che presiedono alla generazione del discorso verbale." A description of Isabella Andreini's interpretation of "la pazzia d'Isabella" by the Medici court chronicler Giuseppe Pavoni (*Diario . . . delle feste nelle solennissime nozze delli serenissimi sposi il sig. duca Ferdinando Medici e la sig. donna Christina di Lorena* [Bologna: Rossi, 1589]) is more precise in isolating the "mad" qualities of the performance, in particular her speaking in foreign languages, singing, and imitating the accents of other members of the company, which he characterizes as "tutti fuor di proposito." He describes her as "scorrendo per la

Cittade, fermando hor questo, & hora quello, e parlando hora in Spagnuolo, hora in Greco, hora in Italiano, & molti altri linguaggi . . . & tra le altre cose si mise à parlar Francese, & à cantar certe canzonette pure alla francese. . . . Si mise poi ad imitare li linguaggi di tutti li suoi comici" (quoted in Flaminio Scala, *Il teatro delle favole rappresentative* [Venice: Pulciani, 1611], Marotti ed., LXXV).

51. It was only when musical rules were firm enough or clear enough that breaking them could have an effect. On this subject, see Rosand, "Operatic Madness." On madness in later opera, see Giovanni Morelli, "La scena di follia nella 'Lucia di Lammermoor': Sintomi, fra mitologia della paura e mitologia della libertà," in *La drammaturgia musicale*, ed. Lorenzo Bianconi (Bologna, 1986), 411–32.

52. This correspondence is discussed in Tomlinson, "Twice Bitten, Thrice Shy," 303–11, as well as in Fabbri, "Alle origini."

I have no intention of failing . . . to confer with him [Strozzi] and (as is my habit) to see that this gentleman enriches it [the libretto] . . . with varied, novel and diverse scenes. . . . This I shall explain according to my judgment, in order to see whether he can improve it with other novelties [besides madness], such as additional characters, so that the crazy girl is not seen so frequently in action. . . .

In my opinion she has very good speeches in two or three places, but in two others it seems to me that she could have better material—not so much on account of the poetry, as of the originality. I must also insist on his rearranging Aminto's lines, when the girl is fast asleep, for I would like him to speak as if he had not enough voice to be able to wake her up. This consideration—the need to speak in a low voice—will give me a chance to introduce to the senses a new kind of music, different from what has gone before. (22 May 1627)[53]

Strozzi was evidently quick to make the specific changes requested: "He . . . admits that as far as the part of Licori is concerned, he will make her come in later, and not in almost every scene, yet he will see to it that she always expresses new ideas and actions" (5 June 1627).

For the portrayal of Licori's madness, Monteverdi placed special emphasis on the clarity of the text presentation, the variety of the emotional expression, and the rapidity with which different emotions succeeded one another, as well as on the gestures:

Each time she comes on stage, she can always produce new moods and fresh changes of music, as indeed of gestures. (22 May)

Whenever she is about to come on stage, she has to introduce fresh delights and new inventions. (24 May)

It will now be up to Signora Margherita [Basile] to become a brave soldier, timid and bold by turns, mastering perfectly the appropriate gestures herself . . . because I am constantly aiming to have lively imitations in the music, gestures, and tempi take place behind the scene. . . . The changes between the vigorous, noisy harmonies and the gentle suave ones will take place suddenly so that the words will really come through well. (10 July)

He had earlier expressed his concern about the casting of the main role, urging that

because of its variety of moods . . . [it] not fall into the hands of a woman who cannot play first a man and then a woman, with lively gestures and distinct emotions. (7 May)

---

53.   All of these letters were written to Alessandro Striggio, the Younger, during a three-month period in 1627, from May through July. Texts may be found in *Lettere*, ed. de' Paoli. Unless otherwise indicated, the translations are from *The Letters of Claudio Monteverdi*, ed. Stevens.

His most striking formulation, however, regards the special setting of Licori's text, for which he advocated a distinctive treatment of individual words as disembodied, disconnected entities rather than parts of sentences:

> Since the imitation of such feigned madness must take into account only the present and not the past or future, it must therefore be based on the single word and not on the sense of the phrase; when, therefore, war is mentioned, it will be necessary to imitate war, when peace, peace, when death, death, and so on. And because the transformations and their imitation happen in the shortest space of time, the person who takes the principal part, which should arouse both laughter and compassion, must be a woman who can lay aside every sort of imitation except that dictated by the word she is uttering. (7 May)[54]

In addition to affording a view of the general style of the work, Monteverdi occasionally describes the action in considerable detail:

> In three places I certainly think the effects will come off well; first when the camp is being set up, the sounds and noises heard behind the scenes and exactly echoing her words should . . . prove quite successful; secondly, when she pretends to be dead; and thirdly, when she pretends to be asleep, for here it is necessary to bring in music suggesting sleep. In some other places, however, because the words cannot mimic either gestures or noises or any other kind of imitative idea that might suggest itself, I am afraid the previous and following passages might seem weak. (24 May)

For unknown reasons, *La finta pazza Licori* was never performed. It was probably never even completed.[55] But Monteverdi's ideas left deep traces in other

---

54. "perchè la immitatione di tal finta pazzia dovendo aver la consideratione solo che nel presente e non nel passato e nel futuro, per conseguenza la imitatione dovendo aver il suo appoggiamento sopra alla parola et non sopra al senso della clausula, quando dunque parlerà di guerra bisognerà inmitar di guerra, quando di pace pace, quando di morte di morte, et va seguitando, et perchè le transformationi si faranno in brevissimo spatio, et le immitationi; chi dunque averà da dire tal principalissima parte che move al riso et alla compassione, sarà necessario che tal Donna lassi da parte ogni altra Immitatione che la presentanea che gli somministrerà la parola che haverà da dire" (*Lettere*, ed. de' Paoli, p. 244; my translation). The meaning of this passage has caused considerable discussion. Whereas most writers, including myself, have interpreted it specifically with regard to Monteverdi's portrayal of madness (see Rosand, "Monteverdi's Mimetic Art," 135 and n. 25, and Bianconi, "Il cinquecento e il seicento," 353–54), Tomlinson has seen in it confirmation of his view of Monteverdi's late style as excessively focused on individual words at the expense of whole lines or sentences ("Madrigal," 101–2—a view Tomlinson revised somewhat in *Monteverdi*, 205–6).

55. An early version of Strozzi's text, in dialogue form, may have been performed in the Palazzo Mocenigo sometime before June 1627, as suggested by Monteverdi's letter to Striggio of 5 June 1627: "Giulio Strozzi . . . having been urged by me very insistently to do me the honor of adapting *La finta pazza Licori* to my way of thinking . . . willingly offered his services, confessing that in writing this play he did not achieve the degree of perfection he had in mind, but wrote it in dialogue to provide entertainment at a musical evening which a certain Most Illustrious Signor Mocenigo, my Lord, had arranged to give. I, visualizing its presentation with some by no means straightforward rearrangement, did not want to set it to music." This information seems to conflict with that in an earlier letter, of 7 May 1627, in which Monteverdi claimed that *La finta pazza* had been "so far neither set to music, nor printed, nor ever acted on the stage." Perhaps the performance in the Palazzo Mocenigo was a spoken one. In any case, Strozzi's three-act libretto, which he revised for Monteverdi, was never performed. The tortured history of this project is unraveled in Tomlinson, "Twice Bitten, Thrice Shy."

works: in Sacrati's *La finta pazza* and the mad scenes it inspired,[56] and in his own *Il ritorno d'Ulisse in patria*.

Clearly, a number of the most important features of the *Licori* libretto found their way into Strozzi's second *La finta pazza*, the libretto set by Sacrati in 1641. Although Deidamia has only one real mad scene, at the end of act 2 (scene 10), it is central to the plot and carefully prepared well beforehand. Also it is quite long. The idea of feigning madness begins to take shape in Deidamia's poignant monologue of act 2, scene 6; it is carried further in the discussion between Giove and Vittoria (2.7); is previewed by the defeated cavalier's call to the gods of the Underworld, which seems as if it will become a mad scene (2.8); is described by Diomede in a conversation with the Eunuch (2.9); and finally culminates in Deidamia's appearance at the very end of the second act (2.10).[57] In the mad scene proper, Deidamia speaks repeatedly of war and also of death (cf. Monteverdi's letter of 7 May); she shifts rapidly from topic to topic as she pretends to rave (ibid.); and she feigns sleep, which encourages Acchille (= Aminto) to speak softly to her (cf. letter of 22 May). She also gestures wildly, as she herself says at the end of one speech, when she decides to stop talking: "What the tongue would say, let gesture do."[58] Finally, though her ultimate aim is a serious one, Deidamia's madness has a healthy admixture of the comic in it. Her disconnected, erratic discourse ranges freely over many topics and includes under the mask of madness, as we saw in chapter 4, a number of apposite allusions to her surroundings, the theater, the production itself.

All subsequent mad scenes reveal a kinship with Deidamia's, even if they were not directly modeled on it. Their common elements include rapidly shifting subject matter, tone, rhythms, and rhyme patterns; frequent exclamations; expressions of violence, often in the context of repeated references to war (*bellicosa pazzia*), associated with trumpet imitations, and to Hell, usually marked by the conventional *versi sdruccioli*; identification with mythological characters; delusions regarding the perversity of nature; reference to imaginary physical ailments or danger; incursions of abnormal speech—screaming, crying, laughing, singing; allusions to dance; and sudden, unexpected requests for songs.[59]

---

56.   These included *Didone* (Cavalli/Busenello) and *La ninfa avara* (Ferrari) in 1641, and *Egisto* (Cavalli/Faustini) in 1643.

57.   The postponement of Deidamia's mad scene to the end of act 2 may reflect Monteverdi's suggestion to Strozzi about limiting Licori's appearances as a madwoman (letter of 22 May, quoted above).

58.   "Quel che diria la lingua esprime il gesto." Anna Renzi's gestures in the role were remarked upon several times; see the poetry in her honor and the *Cannocchiale*, cited above in ch. 8. For another interpretation of *gesto*, see n. 65 below. Note also the reference to gesture in the description of madness in

the preface to Strozzi's *La finta savia* (1643): "a questo furore soprafatte le sibille facevano varie mutanze di voce, e diversi strani movimenti della persona come le descrive Virgilio nel sesto della divina Eneide."

59.   Deidamia's request for a song from the Eunuch—who is present in the scene—is the occasion for a host of comic puns and double entendres (see ch. 4 above). The similar phrases in which a song is requested in both Jarba's (*Didone*) and Lilla's (*La ninfa avara*) mad scenes: "Cantami un poco in tuono d'effaut / S'è più bella l'Arcadia o il Calicut," and "Meritevole sei / Ch'in tuon d'F, fa ut, / Ti canti in un l'Arcadia, il Calicut," suggested to Pirrotta that

Occasionally, the madness terminates after a deep (or pretended) sleep (see below), a resolution that, like the topos itself, was probably inspired by *Orlando furioso*.

In several instances, the effect of the mad behavior is heightened by being described beforehand. In *La finta pazza*, Diomede's description leads directly to Deidamia's entrance:

Da tante amare doglie	By so many bitter woes
Soprafatta la giovine dolente	Overcome, the sorrowing girl
Languì, tremò, sudò	Languished, trembled, perspired,
Inferocì, girò	Grew wild, turned
Gl'occhi insieme, e la mente,	Her eyes about, and her thoughts,
E con diluvio di querele atroci	And with a deluge of hideous laments
Versò l'affanno, e vomitò l'ingegno.	Poured out her grief and vomited her wits.
Uscita fuor da le paterne stanze,	Issuing forth from the paternal chambers,
Per le piazze di Sciro	She makes of Skyros's public places
Del suo furor insano	The woeful, dolorous scene
Fa scena lagrimevole, e funesta.	Of her insane fury.

Not only do such descriptions whet the appetite of the audience, but they alert the audience (and the critic) to the things they should notice; they call attention to the skill of the poet—and anticipate that of the actress. In *Egisto* (Faustini/ Cavalli, 1643), Cinea's description of the hero's madness, which occurs between his two mad scenes, provides a particularly detailed and accurate forecast of the second one, emphasizing its most important elements: Egisto's fury, his uneven ranting and raving, his irregular, improper language, his sighs and sudden laughter, and his scandalous song ("Io son Cupido").

Signor l'hospite Egisto	My lord, our host Aegistus's
L'intelletto hà travolto,	Intellect is overturned.
E' divenuto stolto,	He has become a dolt.
Hor di furor ripieno	Now filled with fury
La Campagna trascorre,	He runs about the countryside;
Hor s'arresta, e discorre	Now he stops and addresses
A sterpi, à tronchi, à venti	Bushes, tree trunks, the winds
Con vari, e impropri accenti,	With various inappropriate exclamations;
Hor tace, e bieco mira,	Now he falls silent and looks grim,
Nè conosce mirando,	Nor, looking, recognizes;
Hor geme, & hor sospira	Now he moans, and now he sighs;
Hor ride, e và cantando	Now he laughs and goes about singing
Sciocche, e immodeste rime,	Foolish and immodest rhymes,
E talvolta di Clori il nome esprime.[60]	And on occasion utters Clori's name.

---

both were derived from the same specific source, possibly from *Licori* ("The Lame Horse and the Coachman," *Essays*, 328 and n. 11). The imagery is shared, as well, by the second strophe of a song in *La finta pazza*: "Fare il basso . . . ," which mentions "gamma-ut." Musical references, while particularly apposite in the operatic context, were a common in-

gredient in spoken mad scenes as well (see, for example, the description of Giuseppe Pavoni quoted in n. 50 above).

60. This passage identifies many of the same elements as Ariosto's description of Orlando's actions. It also resembles those of the various "pazzie d'Isabella." See Borsetta, "Teatro dell'arte," 140–49.

Monteverdi's descriptions as well as those of Diomede and Cinea promise striking musical effects in the portrayal of madness. And indeed, each of these early mad scenes fulfills expectation by exaggerating or perverting what might be regarded as a normal narrative sequence or language of communication. Strikingly, all of them embody Monteverdi's program, at least to some degree.[61]

Sacrati's music for Deidamia is dominated by obsessive arpeggios and martial rhythms, clear allusions to trumpet fanfares that qualify as literal imitations of the predominating battle and hunt imagery in the text.[62] Although the arpeggios are primarily on G, A, and C, the imitation of trumpets is finally carried to a literal extreme when they occur in the trumpet tonality of D major.[63] The association is established even before Deidamia's entrance in the canonic fanfare duet between Diomede and the Eunuch announcing her appearance, which she then echoes (examples 70a and b). These aggressive arpeggios, which also occur independently of hunt imagery in this mad scene as well as others, would seem to represent the soul at war with itself. They occasionally yield to music that is more characteristic of Deidamia's former (sane) mode of address: lengthy successions of repeated notes or softer melodic lines that rise or fall gradually, in stepwise motion. These are usually inspired by some particularly poignant phrase of text, such as that leading into an aria near the end of the scene: "Ah so ben io / Qual di racchiuso pianto al mesto core / Fa lago il mio dolore" ("Ah, well I know how holding my tears back will make a lake of my suffering") (example 70j). The prevailing duple meter of her recitation is interrupted twice, first for a short arioso passage calling special attention to three particularly scurrilous lines of text: "Giacer io volea teco, / E lasciar il mio Giove, ch'ogni notte stà meco" ("I wanted to lie with you and leave my Jove, who stays with me every night") (example 70g), the change back to duple meter likewise emphasizing the conclusion of this passage: "Ma stanco dal lunghissimo camino, / Ch'ei fa dal Cielo in terra, / Mi riesce sovente il gran tonante /Un sonnacchioso Amante" ("But tired out from the long journey that

61. These mad scenes, with special emphasis on that of Egisto, are discussed by Giovanni Morelli, *Scompiglio e lamento (simmetrie dell'incostanza e incostanza delle simmetrie): "L'Egisto" di Faustini e Cavalli*, Gran Teatro La Fenice, Opere-Concerti-Balletti, 1981–82 (Venice, 1982), 605–12, 618.

62. Wolfgang Osthoff, "La musica della pazzia nella 'Finta pazza' di Francesco Sacrati," in *L'opera fra Venezia e Parigi* (papers read at a conference held at the Fondazione Giorgio Cini, September 1985) (in press), 3, points to a traditional association between the hunt ("la caccia"), or hunting cries and fanfares, and madness.

63. The tonality of this scene, in general, emphasizing sharp keys, contrasts with a predominance of flat keys in the other scenes in which Deidamia appears. Osthoff, "La musica della pazzia," 17–18, finds a correlation between tonal spheres and Deidamia's various moods, and he relates those spheres, such as C minor for Deidamia's sleep scene, to the use of tonality in other operas. In *Poppea*, for example, Arnalta's lullaby is in C minor; and in *Il ritorno d'Ulisse*, Ulisse awakens in the same key. Osthoff suggests that this may be what Monteverdi meant by "armonie imitanti il sonno" (see n. 34 above).

he makes from heaven to earth, the great thunderer often turns out to be a sluggish lover"). The second interruption occurs near the end of the scene, in a short aria accompanied by strings, a kind of parody of a lament that invokes the powers of the Underworld in the conventional *versi sdruccioli* (example 70k).

Extremes of Deidamia's range—at either end of the staff—are exploited, sometimes within a very short span. This usually can be understood as literal, even simplistic, text imitation of the kind Monteverdi advocated for madness.[64] For example, a sudden dip to the low tessitura accompanies the phrases "soldato dormiglione" ("sleepy soldier") and "tacete, homai, tacete" ("be still, now, be still") and an octave descent interprets the distance—or lack of it—expressed in the line "destati ch'il nemico di qui poco è lontano" ("Wake up, for the enemy is near") (example 70f). For the phrase "Ma stanco dal lunghissimo camino / ch'ei fa dal cielo in terra," Sacrati moves to a melodic high point on F for *cielo*, from which he descends rapidly a ninth, by means of an extended, rhythmicized melisma, to low E on *terra* (example 70g). Later in the scene, in an amusing and academically allusive passage, Deidamia literally silences herself in response to the line "A stride quiete, dunque" with an octave leap from C down to middle C, where she remains, appropriately, through "Alla muta, alla muta" (example 70h):

Non si può più parlare,	One can no longer speak.
Ogn'un, a quel ch'io sento,	Everyone, I gather,
Hoggi mi vuol glosare,	Wants to gloss me today,
Mi vuol far' il comento,	Wants to comment on me.
A stride quiete, dunque	To silent shouts, therefore,
Ad intendersi a cenni,	And gestured understandings.
Alla muta, alla muta	Mum! Mum!
Pronta man', occhio presto,	Nimble the hand, quick the eye!
Quel che diria la lingua, esprima il gesto.[65]	What the tongue would say, let gesture do!

Deidamia's concluding aria, the lament-parody (example 70k), inspired by two quatrains of rhymed *settenari sdruccioli*, displays several concrete imitations. Contrast of high and low tessituras literally portrays the contrast between "alti papaveri" ("high poppies") and "sozzi cadaveri" ("loathsome corpses"). And the phrase "resto immobile" ("I remain immobile") is communicated by an unchanging harmony for two measures in contrast to the half- and quarter-measure changes before and after it. Sacrati imposed an interesting and unexpected musical contrast on the two similar quatrains of this text. For the first one, in duple meter, a rhythmically sequential, diatonic melodic line moves

---

64. Going a bit further, Osthoff ("La musica della pazzia," 9) interprets these leaps as evidence that Deidamia is "playing now a woman, now a man," in response to Monteverdi's directive for Licori.

65. *Gesto* here may refer to the octave leap itself. See Osthoff, "La musica della pazzia," 8. Cf. n. 59 above.

repeatedly to a high point on F before leaping to the low point, D, on *cadaveri*. It contrasts strongly with the more affective setting of the second quatrain, in triple meter, in which the melody ascends chromatically and sequentially to its own highpoint (which is actually lower than that of the first strophe) before gently descending to the tonic. In one final literal imitation at the end of the scene, Deidamia screams as she is forcibly removed from the stage in chains. The kind of literal imitation counseled by Monteverdi, then, illuminates the most outstanding features of Deidamia's mad music: the evocation of war (or hunt) by means of arpeggios and martial rhythms and the use of schizophrenic tessituras an octave apart in response to individual words or phrases implying distance, direction, or dynamics.

In comparison to *La finta pazza*, Cavalli's first attempt to portray operatic madness, in *Didone*, is somewhat pallid, perhaps because it was accomplished in such a hurry.[66] But in his second essay, in *Egisto*, he carried Monteverdi's ideas abut literal imitation and contrast considerably further than had Sacrati. Egisto's madness is more extensive than Deidamia's, occupying two lengthy scenes, the first (3.5) a monologue, the second (3.9) performed, like Diadamia's mad scene, in public. Egisto's texts are also more highly structured than Deidamia's. In addition to frequent incursions of *versi sdruccioli*, they contain several refrains and a large number of rhyming couplets. Furthermore, perhaps because Egisto's madness is real rather than feigned, Faustini's poetry itself exhibits greater affective contrast; in particular it places greater emphasis on the emotion of love, which is repeatedly juxtaposed against war and anger. Having called such explicit attention to these scenes in his preface, as we have noted several times, it is apparent that Faustini lavished special care on them.

Largely in response to the richer text, Cavalli's musical realization is more varied; it makes use of a larger vocabulary of musical gestures involving rhythm and harmony as well as melody. And Cavalli worked with his text more actively than Sacrati, repeating many more words and phrases to increase affective intensity. In general, Cavalli's music is more mobile than Sacrati's; it contains more sequential repetition, more rhythmic patterning, and more dissonance. As a result, Egisto projects a more authentic confusion than Deidamia does—but, we must recall, hers was only feigned. (See example 71 a and b.)

Martial fanfares play an important role here too, but they usually respond more exclusively to Underworld references in *versi sdruccioli* and are juxtaposed more forcibly with other kinds of melody and rhythm; these include lengthy single-note reiterations that tend to culminate in furious *stile concitato* climaxes,

---

66.   On the last-minute addition of these mad scenes, see Rosand, "Opera Scenario," 341–42, and ch. 5, pp. 122–23, above.

and conjunct lines that ascend or descend gradually, often creating strong dissonances against the bass.

Wide melodic leaps between phrases emphasize the discontinuity of discourse and frequent exclamations, whereas those within phrases are more directly inspired by individual words, such as the leap of a ninth on *aspri* in "Udite, prego, udite aspri, e maggiori" ("Listen [you leaves] to my bitter and great [pains]) (mm. 37–41). Rhythmic contrasts, such as juxtapositions of disparate note values, also respond to specific text cues: the phrase "Non mi nega l'inferno / La sospirata moglie, / Più caro seno accoglie / La mia donna incostante" ("Hell does not deny me my hoped-for wife, but welcomes my unfaithful lady more warmly"), for example, is set to a sequence of almost uninterrupted eighth notes that brakes abruptly for an extended whole-note cadence on [*inco*]-*stante*, a literal rendering, in rhythmic terms, of inconstancy (mm. 42–48). In another passage, comprising two parallel phrases of text, rhythmic discontinuity between affective long-note syncopations and *stile concitato* sixteenth notes stresses the conflict between the expansive, emotional first line and the angry tension of the second two (mm. 68–80).

Ah cor malvagio, ah core	Ah, wicked heart, ah, heart!
Fuori di questo petto,	Leave this breast!
Che non vò dar ricetto à un traditore;	For I will not give shelter to a traitor.
Ah cor malvagio, ah core	Ah, wicked heart, ah, heart!
Esci via, via, che tardi,	Go, leave, leave, why do you tarry?
Over spegni quel foco onde ancor ardi.	Or else extinguish the flame
	that still consumes you.

Beyond these contrasts, Egisto's recitative is interrupted more than once by arialike sections characterized by faster, more regular bass motion and more self-contained melody; while a few of them are based on textually distinct passages, such as a lengthy sequence of *quinari* (at "Io son Cupido" in 3.9, example 71b[3]), others are inspired by a change of direction or tone in the text (at "Amor sospendi i vanni" and "Aprite il varco, aprite," example 71a, mm. 81–93 and 107–34). This kind of musical contrast gives the impression of the mad Egisto speaking temporarily in another voice, an effect that communicates the sense—or non-sense—of the text.

In addition to rather obvious and brief imitations of actions—such as laughter, sighs, and so on—Cavalli's setting includes some more subtle, intellectualized imitative effects. One of the most striking is a triple-meter arioso passage near the opening of Egisto's second scene, setting a three-line passage of text:

Hor ch'il mondo è in scompiglio	Now that the world's in disarray,
O popoli di Dite	O ye subjects of Pluto,
Di guerreggiar con Giove io vi consiglio.	I advise you to wage war on Jove.

Here the characteristic D-major fanfare inspired specifically by the image of conflict between Heaven and Hell becomes literally (rhythmically, metrically) out of joint, at war with itself, through a powerful hemiola on the word *guerreggiar* (example 71b[2]).[67]

As with Deidamia's mad music, behind the mad scenes in *Egisto* clearly lies Monteverdi's prescription for the projection of madness: literal imitation and abrupt contrast are both fundamental to Cavalli's treatment. Because of his own special musical and dramatic gifts, however, in particular the mobility of his word-sensitive style, and possibly because of the structural variety of Faustini's text, the impact of literal imitation is diluted by a greater reliance on contrasts and discontinuities—on communication of text rather than strict imitation. The effect of irrationality is projected not so much by a succession of unrelated imitations (or images) as by an accumulation of contrasts.

Despite the effectiveness of these mad scenes and the resonance in them of Monteverdi's ideas, the fullest realization of those ideas is found, not surprisingly, in a work by Monteverdi himself. The opening scene of the third act of *Il ritorno d'Ulisse* is a monologue for the parasite Iro, who laments his hunger. Although this is not strictly speaking a mad scene, Iro's fear of starvation, comic at first, becomes increasingly exaggerated and irrational until, in a radical reversal of mode, it leads him abruptly to take his own life. A strange comic character who suddenly shifts modes to achieve a kind of heroic status at the end, Iro evokes a disturbing mixture of laughter and compassion, precisely the combination of affects Monteverdi sought from Licori. Monteverdi evidently used Iro's scene to test this combination, since it was he and Badoaro who added its tragic conclusion; in Homer the parasite has nothing more to say after he has been defeated by Ulysses (example 72).[68]

Monteverdi's music for this monologue shares many features with the mad music of Sacrati and Cavalli, including wide leaps, *stile concitato* trumpet imitations, and dance elements. What is especially striking about this scene, however, is the extent to which Monteverdi breaks up and stretches out the text, attaching musical images almost at random to individual words. Cavalli fre-

---

67. See Cesti's *Tito* (I-Vnm, It. IV, 459 [9983], f. 11ᵛ), for another mimetic setting of "scompiglio"; see also Isifile's reference to thoughts that "scompiglian la mente" (*Giasone* 1.14). Osthoff, "La finta pazza," 6–7, 14, makes a great deal of this idea, likening it to Hamlet's "time out of joint."

68. Like the Licori of Monteverdi's letters, Iro, too, talks of war and death, and each topic is symbolized by a single image: "m'abbatte," and "estinti." The full example is given in Malipiero ed., 12: 170–76. Iro is discussed more fully in Rosand, "Iro," 141–64; see also id., "Operatic Madness."

quently repeated words and lines, but he always did so to enhance textual meaning; Monteverdi's repetitions are so extensive that they tend almost to obliterate the text, replacing it with musical images.[69]

His isolation of and fixation on individual words goes far beyond anything we have seen in either Sacrati or Cavalli. Monteverdi thought nothing of repeating a single word or phrase as many as eleven times (*l'ho distrutta*, example 72a—in this case admittedly to an appropriate musical figure). While the choice of words to repeat is usually justified rhetorically—*ah* (six times), *rida* and *m'abbatte* (four times each), *mai* (seven times)—the appropriateness of the particular musical association is not always immediately evident. Even as it decontextualizes the word itself, however, the musical image increases its psychological effect. Monteverdi repeats Iro's desperate textual refrain "chi lo consola" ("who will console [the starving man]") numerous times, setting it to an extended, outwardly incongruous triple-meter arioso over a *ciaccona* bass (example 72b, c). But the musical image itself, a protracted, regular dance, actually offers temporary consolation: the reassurance of a calm, patterned oasis within the frenetic, sputtering context of the monologue as a whole. Iro asks for comfort and he literally gets it, however briefly, from the composer. Monteverdi's fragmented treatment may fracture the sense of Iro's discourse, but it thereby heightens its instability—and poignancy.

Monteverdi's literal imitations, too, are far more exaggerated than Cavalli's. Iro's opening whine on a single pitch seems extended almost infinitely, its exaggerated length measured out and intensified by an eighth-note ostinato figure in the bass (example 72d). The word *estinti*, repeated three times to a strangely disjunct sequence of descending thirds separated by several interruptive rests, finally extinguishes itself (example 72e). *M'abbatte* pits two overlapping five-beat melodic figures in the voice and bass against a six-beat measure—the three patterns literally beat against one another, causing considerable conflict (example 72f). And Monteverdi's laugh (example 72g), unlike Cavalli's, is so extreme, so exaggerated and stylized that it turns itself from musical imitation to singer's trill to actual laugh: Monteverdi enacts the transformation of music into mimetic gesture.

Whether because the developing musical style suited them less well or because of the dramatic limitations of the convention itself, mad scenes receded somewhat in prominence during the second half of the century.[70] The flash fire

69.   Repetition here deprives Iro's text of its sense. This is particularly evident from a comparison of Monteverdi's text treatment elsewhere, where he clearly repeats words to increase meaning. Cf., for example, Seneca's suicide monologue or Poppea's "Per me guerreggia" aria in *L'incoronazione di Poppea*.

70.   Later librettos in which madness plays a central role are not too numerous. They include, among others, *Il pazzo politico* (Castoreo, 1659); *Coriolano o*

of the early 1640s, when every new opera had its mad scene, rapidly died down, to be refueled only occasionally. One such occasion was the final appearance on the Venetian stage of the original "finta pazza," Anna Renzi, as Damira in Aureli's and Ziani's *Le fortune di Rodope e Damira* (1657). In that opera Damira feigns madness in order to reclaim her husband from the clutches of the courtesan Rodope. Surely the audience must have recalled the triumph of Renzi's now legendary debut and recognized in Damira's shrewd gesture the recreation of that earlier success. In convention was the memory of theatrical history. And Renzi's own reenactment of the convention reemphasizes the importance of the connection between mad scenes and the prima donnas who created them, a connection that was fundamental also to the persistence of the convention in *commedia dell'arte*.

Madness may have relinquished its prominence on the operatic stage after the early 1640s, but it remained potently dormant, retaining a strong hold on the imaginations of librettists and composers—and presumably on those of audiences as well. Indeed, the (apparent) absence of a mad scene in the plot of *Giasone* is corrected by the characters themselves: they deliberately create one. Giasone seizes on the topos to protect himself, using it as a screen for Isifile's behavior. Her madness, he explains, has caused her to appropriate the events of Medea's life as her own. (The audience is aware, of course, that the lives of the two women are in fact remarkably parallel: each is a queen, each is the mother of twins sired by Giasone.) It is an explanation that Medea readily believes because such delusions are the common coin of operatic madness. In this case, the character herself does not feign madness; it is feigned for her. Making further use of the convention, Giasone prepares the audience for Isifile's appearance by a vivid, Monteverdian description of her mad behavior, a familiar preparatory procedure:

Or s'allegra, or si duole,	Now she rejoices, now she sorrows,
Or ride, or piange,	Now she laughs, now she cries,
Or s'umilia, or s'adira,	Now she humbles herself, now takes offense,
Conforme alla cagion per cui delira.	According to the occasions of her ravings.

La pazzia in trono (Ivanovich, 1669); and *Caligola delirante* (Gisberti, 1672), none of whose scores has survived. See also Aureli's *Gli amori d'Apollo e di Leucotoe* (1663), and Moniglia's *Il pazzo per forza* (1682) and *L'Incoronazione di Dario* (1685). The convention plays a subsidiary, even purely comic, role in many other works, however. In Minato's *Pompeo magno* (2.12), madness provides a screen for an aside from the librettist to the audience (or to the later historian). The "mad" old lady Atrea, pretending to be a gypsy, reads the palm of Delfo the page, from which the audience learns (or is reminded) that the singer of Delfo's role had been a star singer in his youth (more than twenty years earlier) when he had played leading roles in *Poppea*, *Narciso ed Ecco immortalati*, and *Ciro*: "Ne gl'Anni più fioriti / Con gloria tua gl'Adriaci Eroi t'udirò / Rappresentar Narciso, / Finger Nerone, e Ciro. / Hor ch'il tempo ti sparge il crin d'argenti, / Qui fai rider le Genti." This would have been particularly amusing since Delfo was supposedly an adolescent page. Minato, however, may have had his facts wrong: the line mentioning Narciso is omitted in Cavalli's setting. This is reminiscent of Deidamia's "real" talk about the Teatro Novissimo in the guise of madness.

When Isifile finally appears, only Medea believes she is mad. The other characters on stage, and the audience, know otherwise. But she fools them. After playing the scene out, Isifile unexpectedly fulfills Giasone's characterization of her: she becomes mad with anger. Affirming the implicit connection between emotional excess and madness, she erupts in a furious assault on Medea and Giasone, to the obvious delight of both of her audiences—on stage and in the theater. Cavalli could hardly resist the opportunity provided by the libretto. He seconded Cicognini's impulse by extremely literal treatment of Giasone's description of Isifile's state, and by the use of the *stile concitato* to project the violence of her climactic explosion (example 73).

Monteverdi's influence can still be felt in this brief passage—Cavalli carried the standard to the end of his career—though its power is considerably diminished. But operatic style was changing, and with it the concept of normalcy against which Monteverdi had measured his interpretation of madness. The effects of the literal, isolating imitation and abrupt contrast he developed could only portray madness within a context that was highly word-oriented, where text interpretation was fundamental to the style itself. Focusing on individual words was, of course, normal in this music, but they were regarded as parts of phrases or sentences and emphasized for their contextual meaning. The sense of a word normally affected an entire musical phrase rather than just the setting of itself. Decontextualizing or objectifying the single word, a process carried to an extreme in Iro's monologue, was thus abnormal: it upset the reason and structure of conventional discourse. But it had enormous expressive impact: musical obsession assumed psychological dimensions.

The portrayal of madness was achieved, then, by straining the boundaries of the normal. It provided an excuse for the composer (and the singer) to exhibit his (her) prowess, to display his (her) raw technique unencumbered by large-scale dramatic or structural concerns. In so doing, the composer called attention to crucial elements of his style. The mad music of the 1640s worked because it exploited the extreme text-orientation of the period. But as operatic style evolved, other features began to take priority. As I have repeatedly emphasized, the intimate, word-oriented rapport between text and music that characterized early *dramma per musica* gradually yielded to a more generalized, formal relationship, one determined by more exclusively musical considerations. The development can be measured in the treatment of mad scenes.

The mad scenes of the later seventeenth century are musically quite different from their predecessors, despite common elements in their texts, their exploitation of a similar framework of references—mythology, the Underworld, *versi sdruccioli*, battle imagery. Rather than by obsessive adherence to individual words and to word-painting techniques, the rapid emotional changes characteristic of madness are portrayed by the unexpected and the inappropriate on a larger scale—by formal or affective improprieties: by unpredictable juxtapositions of recitative and aria or of arias of wildly contrasting moods or irregular form; by the totally inappropriate setting of a particular text; or by recourse to music and text that are unsuitable to the dramatic situation at hand.

Thus, in her first mad scene in *Le fortune di Rodope e Damira* (1657, 2.10), Damira sings an ironically extravagant aria to celebrate the forthcoming marriage of her husband and her rival. But after they have shared her enthusiasm in a brief duet, she abruptly calls a halt to their celebration with a suddenly contrasting arioso setting of a single word, *fermate*, which is followed by a bitterly accusatory recitative. By these contrasts, appropriate for a mad character, she manages to keep her would-be betrayers off balance and increasingly to undermine their resolve (example 74). And later in the same act, Damira bursts unexpectedly into a jubilant aria in response to the news of her own death. The aria should inform her husband and servant that she is not dead at all but, since they do not recognize her, its inappropriately celebratory tone merely reinforces their conviction that she is mad.

In *Helena rapita* (Aureli/Freschi, 1677), the arias of the feigned madwoman Euristene are inappropriate in another way. The mood of their music directly counteracts the sense of their words. The trivial, sing-song settings of both "Sù le rive d'Acheronte," an evocation of Hell and a lover's desperation, and "Se non fuggi amante insano," an angry, violent attack on her betrayer, Paride, madly belie their texts (examples 75a, b).

Finally, in *Totila* (Noris/Legrenzi, 1677), the mad Publicola not only lapses into a succession of contrasting arioso passages that emerge too suddenly out of recitative, but he sings two mad love songs that are strikingly inappropriate to his tragic situation (examples 76a, b).

In all these cases, the portrayal of madness exploits and subverts the assumptions of stylistic decorum on which it builds. If the appropriate match of style and situation, of setting and affect, represents a normative aesthetic of mid-seicento opera, inappropriateness becomes, de facto, the proper expression of the abnormal. Mismatch is right for madness. The convention of the mad scene, in other words, depends upon a set of prior accepted stylistic conventions against which it can, in its perverseness, be gauged.

12

• • •

Il lamento: The Fusion of Music and Drama

The lament was different from the other operatic conventions. It came to opera as an entity in its own right, with distinct definition and a generic integrity of its own, first purely literary, then musical as well. Its pre-operatic existence was an exceptionally long one, stretching from Greek tragedy and Ovid's *Heroides* to *Orlando furioso* and *Gerusalemme liberata*; its context was narrative, its function dramatic. Throughout its history the lament asserted its independence, standing somewhat apart from its situation. An emotional climax followed by resolution of whatever action was involved, it was a soliloquy, a moment of particularly intense expression for the protagonist, the affective crux of a narrative structure. Poets called special attention to laments, distinguishing them from their narrative contexts by special formal means combined with particularly expressive rhetoric and affective imagery.

As a result of its affective intensity and formal distinction, the lament had also acquired a musical identity by the time it was appropriated for the operatic stage. Lament texts had especially attracted composers of the sixteenth century who were preoccupied with the translation of poetic affect into musical language; the strongest emotions cried out most loudly for musical expression. And the response is reflected in numerous polyphonic and monodic settings of laments from epic poetry.[1]

As a clear demonstration of music's power to move the affections, the lament embodied the operatic ideal; and it found its proper place as the emo-

---

1. These include settings of laments of Orlando, Isabella, Bradamante, Olimpia, and Fiordiligi from *Orlando furioso*, and of Armida, Tancredi, and others from *Gerusalemme liberata*, by composers such as Stefano Rossetti and Antonio Barré in the sixteenth century, and Giaches de Wert, Antonio Cifra, and Monteverdi later. See Alfred Einstein, *The Italian Madrigal* (Princeton, 1949), 2: 208, 3: 564–75. For an exhaustive list of madrigal settings of texts from *Or-* *lando furioso*, including the laments, see Maria Antonella Balsano and James Haar, "L'Ariosto in musica," in *L'Ariosto: La musica, i musicisti*, ed. Maria Antonella Balsano (Florence, 1981), 47–88. For a list of Tasso settings, see Antonio Vassalli, "Il Tasso in musica e la trasmissione dei testi," in *Tasso: La musica, i musicisti*, ed. Maria Antonella Balsano and Thomas Walker (Florence, 1988), 59–90.

tional core of opera early in the history of the new genre, in fact, in the very first operas in Florence.[2] But it was Monteverdi in Mantua who realized its full implications. Specifically, his "Lament of Arianna" and the later "Lament of the Nymph" articulate the poles of its development. The latter was never operatic and the former was best known out of its operatic context—an indication of the generic independence of the lament in comparison to other operatic conventions.

The Recitative Model

The lament from Monteverdi's *Arianna* attracted particular attention the very first time it was heard, at the inaugural performance of the opera in 1608.[3] Not only did it elicit special mention in descriptions of the performance, it evoked the compliment of emulation by a number of composers in their own laments of Arianna printed in monody books beginning in 1613.[4] Monteverdi himself encouraged circulation of the lament, which he regarded highly, by extracting it from the opera for publication in three different forms: as a five-voice madrigal in 1614, as a monody in 1623, and as a contrafactum of the madrigal in 1640.[5]

In its parallel operatic and monodic contexts, Arianna's lament was a *dimostrazione* of Monteverdi's art, offering him the ideal vehicle for the expression of emotions too intense to be merely spoken. Monteverdi's music, perfectly matching the rhetoric of Rinuccini's 79-line text, responds with creative sympathy to the vicissitudes of Arianna's passion.[6] Five unequal but increasingly

2. Rinuccini's first two librettos, *Dafne* and *Euridice*, both contain prominent lament texts, Apollo's "Non curi la mia pianta, o fiamma, o gelo" and Orfeo's "Non piango, e non sospiro" respectively; and those texts inspired particularly expressive music from the composers who set them, Peri, Caccini, and Marco Gagliano (in 1608).

3. See the comments of Follino, *Compendio* (Mantua, 1608), quoted in Solerti, *Gli albori*, 2: 145. A passage from Follino's remarks is quoted on p. 384 below.

4. Monodic settings of Rinuccini's text were published by Severo Bonini (1613) and Francesco Costa (1626). Pellegrino Possenti's "Pianto d'Arianna" (1623) is a setting of a text by Giambattista Marino, evidently inspired by Rinuccini's example. In addition to these laments of Arianna, Monteverdi's inspired a large number of monodic laments for other characters as well, including Olympia, Dido, Apollo, Jason, Orpheus, Erminia, and the Virgin Mary. See Nigel Fortune, "Monteverdi and the 'Seconda Prattica,' " in *The New Monteverdi Companion*, ed. Denis Arnold and Nigel Fortune (London, 1985),

192–94. See also Ellen Rosand, "The Descending Tetrachord: An Emblem of Lament," *MQ* 55 (1979): 346–59, esp. 347–48. Facsimiles of many of these monodies, including the three laments of Arianna, are available in *Italian Secular Song, 1606–1636*, ed. Gary Tomlinson (New York, 1986). Monteverdi's example also inspired a number of polyphonic laments of Arianna, by, among other composers, Giulio Cesare Antonelli, Antonio Il Verso, and Claudio Pari.

5. *Il sesto libro de madrigali* (Venice, 1614); *Lamento d'Arianna . . . con due Lettere Amorose in genere rappresentativo* (Venice, 1623); and "Iam moriar fili," in *Selva morale e spirituale* (Venice, 1640). For the differences between these settings and for the significance of the lament for Monteverdi, see Tomlinson, "Madrigal," esp. 80–108.

6. The text as it occurs in Rinuccini's libretto of *Arianna* is given in Solerti, *Gli albori*, 2: 175–78. This text was altered in the monodic print, in the madrigal, and in the several extant manuscript versions of the lament; see Tomlinson, "Madrigal," 87–88 n. 41.

intense musical sections, separated by choral commentary (not present in either the monodic or madrigal arrangements), chart the abandoned heroine's jagged emotional shifts from desperation to anger to fear to self-pity to attempts at understanding, and finally to desolation and recognition of the excesses, and futility, of her own emotion.

Arianna's lament derives its structure from a variety of elements, both textual and musical: refrains, recurrent rising and falling of intensity, shifting between sections of opposition and coordination of voice and bass line, and sequences and other literary and musical patterns. The principal source of its extraordinary affective power lies in Monteverdi's projection of Arianna's thoughts through flexible control of these elements in unpredictable combinations of contrast and recurrence. The lament is self-contained, but it is not closed: it is not an aria. Arias, being fixed, predetermined musical structures, were inappropriate to the expression of the uncontrolled passion of a lament. The structure of Arianna's lament develops out of the internal exigencies of its text; no superimposed form determines its shape.

The *Arianna* lament operated as a paradigm for close to half a century. Its impact extended south to Rome and north to Venice, where it continued to affect the composition of laments in both monody books and operas into the 1650s.[7] Operatic laments, perhaps influenced by the wide circulation of monody books with their laments clearly labeled, were identified as such quite early in Venetian scores and librettos. Scenarios mention them frequently by name; scores indicate them with rubrics. Apparently everyone knew what was meant by *lamento*. Always a response to unrequited love, whether the cause was death or merely infidelity, a lament could occur anywhere in an opera. Operas usually contained several, often for different characters, dispersed freely through the three acts, although one was invariably reserved for the protagonist, to be sung at the climactic moment just before the denouement. Like the lament of Arianna, most operatic laments were much more than individual numbers; they usually comprised entire scenes in which the protagonist confronted both the crux of the drama and the audience with all of her/his musical and dramatic powers.[8]

7. The most famous acknowledgment of that influence was Severo Bonini's observation, made some thirty years after his own setting, that no house with a cembalo or theorbo lacked a copy of Arianna's lament (*Discorsi e regole sopra la musica* [1640], ed. Leila Galleni Luisi [Cremona, 1975], 110). On the influence of Arianna's lament in Rome, see Margaret Murata, "The Recitative Soliloquy," *JAMS* 32 (1978): 45–73. To be sure, Arianna's lament was not the only work operating as a model; its own literary antecedents and its musical successors exerted independent influence as well.

8. Bianconi offers a fine discussion of the operatic lament in *Seventeenth Century*, 204–19 . He suggests (218) that the choice of subject matter for librettos may have been influenced by the potential they offered for such laments, which he originally dubbed "la scena madre" (translated unfortunately as "tearjerker," 209).

In writing their laments, librettists and composers in Venice were clearly responding to the model of *Arianna*. This is evident from Monteverdi's own Venetian laments—notably those of Ottavia in *Poppea*—but it is especially striking in the early laments of Cavalli.[9] His first opera, *Le nozze di Teti e di Peleo* (1639), on a libretto by Orazio Persiani, contains three lament monologues for Teti, the first two in response to Peleo's apparent drowning (2.2 and 2.7), the third to his presumed infidelity (3.6). Typically, the texts are long—ninety, fifty, and fifty-seven lines respectively—and cast in the standard meters of recitative. Also typically, they share certain features that distinguish them from their recitative context. The *versi sciolti* are interrupted in various ways, by extended blocks of *settenari* or *versi sdruccioli*, for example, or successions of rhymed couplets, or, as in the act 3 lament, by a recurrent refrain. Furthermore, in addition to particularly vivid, often violent, imagery, they all make use of standard rhetorical devices for intensification: alliteration ("il tuo morbo è mortale irremediabile"), enumeration ("muta, languente, e pallida"), anaphora ("ai sospiri, ai singhiozzi, à gli urli, ai gemiti"; "qual furia, qual tormento, qual fierezza"). Finally, they all fall *Arianna*-like into multiple sections that mark the vicissitudes typical of a lamenting heroine in extremis.

Cavalli's settings of these texts reveal the expressive power of his recitative style, in part perhaps learned from Monteverdi, but in greater part uniquely his own. Of Teti's three laments, the text of the last is the most tightly structured, a structure provided by a varied refrain ("Pietà, misericordia, . . .") that recurs irregularly four times, and by a lengthy succession of *endecasillabi sdruccioli* filling the four central sections (thirty- four lines) of the monologue, which are framed by two sections of *versi piani*.[10]

(1)	Pure orecchi sentiste, occhi vedeste,	Yet you have heard, ears, you have seen, eyes,
	Quel che mirare, & ascoltar mi calse,	That which I had to see and hear.
	Tetide or più non lice,	Thetis, now may you no longer
	Al tuo buon genitore,	Deny credence to your good father,
	Negar credenza, & adular te stessa,	Nor deceive yourself:
	Il tuo Consorte infido,	Your faithless consort,
	Quel che per nume adori,	Whom you worship as a god,
	D'altra Amante gioisce,	Rejoices in another lover,
	E tù gelosa ti distruggi, e mori!	And you, jealous, destroy yourself and die!
(2)	Il tuo morbo è mortale irremediabile!	Your illness is mortal, irremediable!
	Già ti senti mancar gli ultimi spiriti,	Already you feel your last spirits failing.

9.   Tomlinson has argued that Monteverdi's later laments suffer in comparison with that of Arianna, showing the strain of applying or matching a musical conception based on one kind of text to a very different style of poetry. See Tomlinson, "Madrigal," 97–104, and id., "Music and the Claims of Text," esp. 585–89.

10.   Magini analyzes Teti's first lament in "Indagini," 294–302.

Ecco già muta, e già languente, e pallida,

Behold, already mute, and already
languishing and pale,

Spiri dal freddo sen gli estremi aneliti,

You exhale your last breath from your cold
bosom.

Prima, che tragittare il varco orribile,
All'officcio primier richiama l'anima,
E per attimo breve, e momentaneo,
Sciogli misera omai, sciogli le redine,
Ai sospiri ai singhiozzi, à gli urli, ai gemiti,

Before traveling across the dread passage,
Recall your soul to its first office,
And for a brief and transient moment
Loosen, unhappy one, loosen the reins
Of your sighs, your sobs, your shouts, your
moans:

Pietà, misericordia amor terribile,

Pity, mercy, O terrible love!

(3) L'orrida gelosia rimanda all'erebo,
Non voler, che mi strazi, e che m'estermini
Il suo veneno gelido, e pestifero,
Non basta, che m'uccida, e che m'esanimi,

This horrid jealousy send back to Erebus:
Ask not its icy, pestiferous venom
To rack and exterminate me.
Is it not enough that your fierce, unwonted
blaze

Il tuo si fero inusitato incendio!
Pietà, misericordia amor terribile;

Kills me and robs me of my soul!
Pity, mercy, O terrible love!

(4) Mà qual furia d'Averno ora inabissami!
Qual tormento d'abisso ora imperversami!
Qual fierezza m'inaspera, e m'invipera!
Sento intorno al mio cor serpenti, & aspidi!
A stracciarmi, a sbranarmi, aprir le fauci
Oimè veggio cento Idre, e cento Cerberi,

But what Fury of Avernus now engulfs me!
What abysmal torment now rages at me!
What savagery embitters me, enrages me!
I feel round my heart serpents and asps!
Rending me, devouring me, their jaws agape,
Alas, I see a hundred Hydras, a hundred
Cerberuses!

Pietà, misericordia o mostri indomiti.

Pity, mercy, O untamed monsters!

(5) [Un portento fierissimo mi sviscera,
Un flagello durissimo mi lacera,
Mà quanti in un sol punto il cor mi
stracciano,
Oimè con cento sferze, e cento fulmini,

[A most cruel portent eviscerates me,
A scourge most harsh lacerates me.
But how many together tear at my heart!

Alas, with a hundred whips and a hundred
lightning bolts

Le man di Briareo l'alma m'opprimono,
Il grave sasso à me rinunzia Sisifo,
Perch'io m'aggiri con dolor perpetuo,
Non più vuole Ission la rota volgere;
Et è l'Augel vorace, e spietatissimo,
Di Titio nò, mà del mio cor famelico,
Pietà misericordia, o Pluto, o Demoni.]

Briareus's hands oppress my soul.
His weighty stone Sisyphus yields to me.
That I may circle in perpetual grief,
Ixion desists from turning the wheel.
And the voracious, most unpitying bird
Hungers not after Tityus, but after my heart.
Pity, mercy, O Pluto, O Demons!]

(6) Mà folle io pietà spero,
Dalla stessa impietade,
Perche da ferro la mercè, ch'io bramo
Timida non ricerco!
Si si ferro letale,
Termini de miei giorni il fil vitale;
Mà che l'aspro martoro:
Che vivendo sopporto,
Non finirà s'invendicata io moro:
Convien, che pera in dispietata guisa,

But I am mad to hope for pity
From pitilessness itself.
Why not timidly seek from the sword
The mercy I crave?
Yes, yes, let the lethal sword
Cut the vital thread of my days.
But the harsh martyrdom
I bear while living
Will not end if I die unavenged.
It is meet that in pitiless fashion

L'uccisore, e l'uccisa,	The slayer and the slain should perish.
Mirerà questa riva	This tearful, sorrowful
Lagrimevole, e mesta,	Shore shall witness
Tragedia miserabile, e funesta.	A pitiable, dolorous tragedy.

Although the dramatic progression in the text is not as clear as that in Arianna's lament, the individual sections articulate distinctly contrasting moods. Teti moves from jealous disbelief through self-pity, minimizing of the offense, and violent anger, to a desire for death—and revenge—which follows a sudden about-face that occurs during a moment of sober self-reflection ("Ma folle io pietà spero"), the traditional signal for closure of a lament.[11]

Cavalli's setting projects Teti's changing moods through contrasts in harmony, rhythm, and melody reflecting the text on levels of syntax and meaning. His music matches the rhetoric of individual poetic lines and phrases as well as the dramatic shape of the monologue as a whole, Teti's progression from irrational fury to reasoned (if desperate) calm (example 77). That progression is anchored and sealed by Cavalli's use of a single unifying tonality to bind the entire monologue, which begins and ends firmly on C. And, although it moves elsewhere—never too far—during its course, to G, D, and E♭, it touches the tonic periodically, at the outset of each refrain and at other important junctures. Further large-scale formal and expressive articulation is provided by Cavalli's distinctive setting of the refrain, a setting whose strong profile, with its motivic rhythm, specially jagged melody, and central dissonance reinforces the sense of obsession underscored by the refrain idea (mm. 38–42, 54–58, 67–71).

Cavalli's matching of music to the affective form and content of the poetry involves flexible control and coordination of all of the musical elements at his disposal. His melody varies from virtually none at all (successions of repeated notes, at the top, bottom, or middle of the range, as in mm. 15–16 or 62–63), through extreme linearity (ascending or descending, as in mm. 22–29), to intense disjuncture (mm. 59–60). Rhythm, too, runs the gamut from smooth, speechlike successions to obsessive patterning and rapid, percussive accentuation. And harmony ranges from smoothly consonant and functional to erratic, unpredictable (though always text-inspired) juxtapositions and dissonance.

This represents Cavalli's prototypical recitative-lament style and the style of his Venetian contemporaries as well. Librettists tended to supply such lament monologues consistently, at least during the 1640s. And composers continued to set them in a similar manner, emphasizing the sectionality and the refrain (if there was one) by similar musical means.[12]

11.   On sectionalism in laments, see Murata, "Recitative Soliloquy."
12.   In addition to Penelope's lament from *Il ritorno* *d'Ulisse* and the two well-known laments of Ottavia from *L'incoronazione di Poppea*, examples may be found in Sacrati's *La finta pazza* as well as in many of

The Strophic Lament

Not all lament texts were constructed of irregular *versi sciolti*, however. From 1640 on an increasing number were strophic, calling for musical treatment that was more highly organized. Although they did not yet necessarily imply lyrical setting, neither did strophic texts lend themselves to the kind of unrestrained passionate freedom that characterizes Arianna's lament; they made more specific formal demands. On the surface, at least, they seem an inappropriate vehicle for the kind of expressive intensity generated by a lament.

Nevertheless, Cavalli's second opera, *Gli amori d'Apollo e di Dafne* (1640), contains one such text—comprising nine four-line strophes—for Apollo's lament, which occurs in the expected place, just before the denouement (3.3), after Dafne's transformation. It is one of more than thirty strophic texts in Busenello's libretto, but its setting is unique.[13] Like Procri's recitative lament earlier in the opera, it—or part of it (strophes 3–5)—bears a generic designation in the score.

If strophic structure itself seems a limitation on expression, this is compounded in the poetry of Apollo's lament by the absence of the kind of rhetorical intensity that characterized lament monologues like Arianna's and Teti's—the patterns, enumerations, alliterations. Nevertheless, Cavalli managed to create an extremely effective lament from this text. Rather than restricting him, the strophic structure seems actually to have inspired him to discover a style that would serve him well, and his followers also, for the remainder of his career. Instead of treating the entire text strophically or ignoring the structure altogether, two obvious options, Cavalli chose to vary his treatment of the individual strophes. He set the first two in recitative style, the next three as a strophic aria based on the descending tetrachord ostinato (to be discussed presently), strophes 6–8 in recitative again, and strophe 9 as a new aria, the stylistic distinctions reflecting distinctions in expressive content among the strophes (example 78):

Ohimè, che miro? ohimè dunque in alloro	Alas, what do I see? Alas, into a laurel
Ti cangi, ò Dafne, e mentre in rami, e in frondi	You are transformed, O Daphne, and as in branches and leaves
Le belle membra oltredivine ascondi,	You hide your more than divine limbs,
Povero tronco chiude il mio thesoro.	A poor trunk encloses my treasure.
Qual senso humano, ò qual Celeste ingegno	What human sense, or what celestial mind
A' sì profondo arcano arrivò mai?	Ever imagined so deep a mystery?
Veggo d'un viso arboreggiare i rai,	I see the rays of a face arbored,
Trovo il mio foco trasformato in legno.	I find my beloved transformed into wood.

Cavalli's early operas, including *Gli amori d'Apollo e di Dafne*, *Didone*, and *La virtù de' strali d'Amore*.

13. Magini discusses this lament at considerable length in "Indagini," 318–28.

Misero Apollo i tuoi trionfi hor vanta
Di crear giorno, ove le luci giri,
Puoi sol cangiato in vento de' sospiri
Bacciar le foglie all'odorata pianta.

Miserable Apollo, now vaunt your triumphs
Of creating day by turning the lights.
Only changed into the breeze of sighs
Can you kiss the leaves of the perfumed plant.

Sgorghino homai con dolorosi uffici
Dai languid'occhi miei lagrime amare,
Vadino in doppio fonte ad irrigare
D'un Lauro le dolcissime radici.

Let bitter tears gush forth with doleful office
From my languid eyes,
Let them in a double stream irrigate
The sweet roots of a laurel.

Era meglio per me, che fuggitiva,
Ma bella oltre le belle io ti vedessi,
Che con sciapiti, e non giocondi amplessi
Un'arbore abbracciar sù questa riva.

It was better for me that fleeing,
But surpassingly beautiful, I had seen you,
Than with numb and unjoyous arms
To embrace a tree on this shore.

Giove, crea novo lume, io più non voglio
Esser chiamato il Sole, e dentro all'onde
Delle lagrime mie calde, e profonde
Immergo il caro, e de miei rai mi spoglio.

Jove, you create new light. I no longer wish
To be called the Sun, and in the waves
Of my warm, deep tears
I immerse my chariot and abandon my rays.

Spezza tu la mia sfera, ò tu l'aggira,
Al Zodiaco per me puoi dir à Dio;
De pianti in Mar novo Nettun son'io,
Suona agonie la mia lugubre lira.

Break my sphere, or you turn it.
To the Zodiac you can say farewell for me.
Of laments in the sea am I the new Neptune.
My lugubrious lyre sounds my agonies.

A' te ricorro omnipotente Amore,
Al mio gran mal le medicine appresta;
Di questo alloro un ramoscello inesta
Con incalmo divin sopra il mio core.

To you I turn, omnipotent Cupid,
Lend medicine for my great illness;
Attach a branch of this laurel
With divine graft to my heart.

Così, lauro mio bello, e peregrino,
Horto sarà il mio petto ai rami tuoi,
Sarà con union dolce tra noi,
La mia divinitade il tuo giardino.

Thus, my beautiful and rare laurel,
My heart will be orchard to your branches.
With sweet union between us
My divinity will be your garden.

Strophes 1 and 2 present Apollo's initial startled reaction to Dafne's transformation. By strophe 3 the original shock has worn off. He becomes more introspective and self-pitying, concerned with his own feelings and fate; and the abrupt change from highly emotional recitative to the lyrical aria underscores the change in focus of his concern. His mood then remains constant through strophe 4, self-involved and pitying. In the fifth strophe he finally reaches an awareness of his own responsibility: his unrelenting advances drove Dafne to her fate. He would be better off had he not pursued her but rather admired her from afar. At least she would still be alive. The change in direction of Apollo's address, from outward railing against fate to introspective self-pity, is typical of laments—we noted a similar change in Teti's. But the association of that change with a change in musical style, from recitative to aria, is new here. And it will persist in subsequent laments. The lyricism provides a kind of parenthesis, a cushion or shelter for Apollo's externalization of his inner emotions or thoughts; it allows him to speak to himself. Significantly, the designation *lamento* is reserved for this most introspective portion of the text.

After the fifth strophe, Apollo becomes more excited again, his thoughts more desperate, less rational; he looks toward the future, passionately vowing to renounce his identity as sun god; and Cavalli once again turned to the more erratic, excited recitative language of strophes 1 and 2. But Apollo's excitement is spent by the end of the eighth strophe; in strophe 9 he expresses his final acceptance of his fate, resolving to place his relationship with Dafne on a spiritual level. Cavalli set this last strophe apart from the rest of the text in a lively, measured style. Moreover, he increased its weight in proportion to that of the other strophes by repeating its entire text and music, thereby providing a suitably stable conclusion for the changing, unstable aria-recitative.

Cavalli's treatment of this text is remarkable for a number of things, in particular for the abandonment of strophicism for dramatic purposes: of the nine strophes, only the third through fifth—the ostinato-aria strophes—are treated strophically; nor did he even mark a division between the recitative strophes. But the composer's most significant decision was to use the descending tetrachord as the organizing principle of the aria setting strophes 3–5, the section identified as the *lamento* in the score.

The Descending Tetrachord: An Emblem of Lament

And here we return once again to Monteverdi, the inevitable *eminence grise*, and to his second lament-paradigm, the "Lament of the Nymph." Just as Cavalli modeled his recitative laments on the Monteverdi-Rinuccini "Lament of Arianna," so, too, he must have had that other Monteverdi-Rinuccini model in mind—published only two years before, in Monteverdi's Eighth Book of madrigals—when he chose to use the descending tetrachord in connection with Busenello's strophic lament of Apollo. Monteverdi's madrigal displays several distinctive features that may have suggested it as a model to Cavalli. Not only is it built on the descending tetrachord ostinato, but it is based on a strophic text whose formal outlines are virtually obliterated by Monteverdi's setting.

The "Lament of the Nymph," *in genere rappresentativo*, is a dramatic scene in which a shepherds' chorus frames and comments on the nymph's plaint— they sing four strophes in all, while she sings six, to completely different music.[14] Although the formal outlines of their strophes are marked by cadences,

14. *Tutte le opere di Claudio Monteverdi*, ed. Malipiero, 8: 288–93.

hers are obscured by Monteverdi's setting, specifically through his use of the minor descending tetrachord ostinato as a means of organization. Possessed of a strongly articulated shape and affect, the ostinato substitutes for or superimposes itself on Rinuccini's strophes. As a result, the strophic structure of the text yields to the musical structure of its setting, a musical structure that by its special nature encourages free expression rather than inhibiting it, and thus contributes directly to the affective intensity of the piece.

Monteverdi's lament was only one of a number of works of the period based on the descending minor tetrachord ostinato. Various aria books published during the 1630s contain pieces that utilize the pattern, at least one of them specifically called a lament.[15] Whether the association of affect and pattern was Monteverdi's idea in the first place—which would be difficult to prove, however attractive the notion—the eloquence of his setting helps to reveal those features inherent in the tetrachord pattern that rendered it particularly suitable for laments.

Its most significant, potentially affective features are its strength and perceptibility. Unlike other, older ostinato basses such as the romanesca or ruggiero, the descending tetrachord is short; and it is strongly directional harmonically, moving inexorably, with stepwise melody and steady, unarticulated rhythm, from tonic to dominant, either through a modal succession of root position triads or a more tonal progression involving two first inversion triads. The tonic itself is structurally ambiguous, functioning either as the beginning of a new pattern or the ending of an old one. The powerful harmonic direction and structural ambiguity of the pattern encourage contradiction in the voice part. Denial of its tonal implications through suspensions, or of its formal structure by phrase overlap and syncopation, creates tension appropriate to the affect of lament. Two other features of the tetrachord contribute to its expressive potential. Its strongly minor configuration, emphasizing two of the most crucial degrees of the mode, invokes the full range of somber affects traditionally associated with minor since the Renaissance; and in its unremitting descent, its gravity, the pattern offers an analogue of obsession and depression—perceptible as the expression of unrelieved suffering.

In the "Lament of the Nymph," the descending tetrachord ostinato supplants the effect of strophic repetition with its own formal implications, implications that contribute to the affect of lament rather than detracting from it. The strength of the earlier lament texts, the *Arianna*-style recitatives, was their

---

15.   Some of these are listed in Rosand, "Descending Tetrachord," 352 and n. 16. For examples by Sances, Pesenti, and Fontei, see *Italian Secular Song*, ed. Tomlinson, vols. 6–7. The tetrachord was not restricted to the north of Italy. A number of Roman cantatas, by such composers as Loreto Vittori and Giacomo Carissimi, also contain arias based on the pattern.

passionate unpredictability and irregularity, their independence of formal indications or strictures, their openness of rhyme and meter, and their concentration of rhetorical expression. Monteverdi, and Cavalli after him, replaced these features with a musical technique that allowed freedom and unpredictability even in a strophic context, even in an aria. Musico-textual rhetoric was replaced by a purely musical sign.

Monteverdi masked the textual symmetries in the nymph's plaint essentially by rewriting Rinuccini's poetry, breaking it up and rearranging it. He then subjected it to musical manipulation by exploiting the ambiguities of the ostinato and its potential for creating tension against a freely moving voice part. Cavalli's methods in Apollo's lament (strophes 3–5) are similar but less radical. He, too, rewrote his librettist's poetry to supply the rhetorical intensification missing in the original, but without seriously disturbing its strophic form. In fact, judging from his treatment of the text alone, he seems to have emphasized its strophicism by treating all three strophes similarly: he added an affective repetition in the first line and repeated the entire fourth line, providing the occasion for musical repetition at the end of each strophe. But his expansion of the text actually enabled him to create a surprisingly asymmetrical structure for each strophe, one that is dramatic and progressive: line 1 is broken up into two unequal phrases (of four and five measures respectively)—facilitated by internal word repetitions; line 2 is set to a six-measure phrase, line 3 to seven measures, line 4 to eight measures (3 + 5), and its repetition to nine measures (3 + 6). This expressive expansion is achieved through the judicious use of melismas within a generally syllabic context, most of them text-inspired, combined with free treatment of the descending tetrachord. Indeed, unlike Monteverdi, who treated it as an unwavering ostinato throughout his piece, Cavalli played with the tetrachord, extending it, modulating with it to the relative major, and finally abandoning it completely after its fourth statement.

The unpredictably expanded phrases of the vocal line combine with the unexpected, gradual departure from the ostinato to create a sense of instability well suited to lamentation. Furthermore, rather than sacrificing the power inherent in the ostinato, its abandonment actually intensifies the effect of its return at the beginning of each new strophe, a return that emphasizes its emblematic obsessiveness: it is always there and cannot be forgotten. By his treatment of the tetrachord, Cavalli managed to create highly expressive individual strophes. At the same time, the bass pattern enabled him to turn to his advantage the seemingly recalcitrant strophic succession of the poetry.

According to the rubric in Cavalli's score, Apollo's lament actually begins only with the third stanza of Busenello's text and presumably ends after the fifth; that is, it is a strophic aria based on the descending tetrachord. The change in textual expression that marks the onset of the lament, Apollo's shift from spontaneous outward reaction to more considered, inward self-pity, similar to the more fleeting vicissitudes within recitative laments, is equivalent to the standard (later) distinction between active recitative and contemplative aria. In this respect, Apollo's lament is quite forward-looking; it offers an early instance of the conventional lament-aria based on the tetrachord. It is forward-looking in another respect as well: although the lament ends with the final tetrachord strophe, Apollo's monologue continues, with two more strophes of recitative followed by what is essentially a second (non-strophic) aria that contrasts emphatically with the earlier one. Apollo's monologue, then, is also an early instance of the pairing of two contrasting arias bridged by recitative. Despite its continuous strophic coherence, this is in effect a *scena* of the type that was to become more common as increasing weight was given to the arias.

Through his use of the descending tetrachord in Apollo's lament, Cavalli found a means of maintaining expressive openness within the confines of a strophic text. It was a discovery well suited to his temperament as a musical dramatist, and one that he continued to exploit. Given the prevailing attitude toward dramatic verisimilitude in opera of the 1640s, of which he was the leading advocate, Cavalli must have found it difficult to set laments as formal arias. Even though the extreme emotional state of the character might have justified some artificiality of expression, the superimposition of a closed, predetermined musical structure on such an essentially spontaneous situation would have hindered the communication of emotion. The descending tetrachord ostinato provided an ideal means for setting the lament apart from its context and at the same time maintaining its intense emotional power. Whatever loss of spontaneity such patterning entailed was more than compensated for by the affective implications of the tetrachord itself: by its intrinsic, emblematic meaning.

The most convincing evidence for that meaning, however, comes not from arias like Apollo's lament or the "Lament of the Nymph," where the pattern clearly served an important structural function, but from recitative laments where the pattern was structurally gratuitous. An early instance, perhaps the earliest, occurs in Sacrati's standard-setting *La finta pazza* (2.6), where Deidamia sings a recitative lament with a refrain based on the descending tetrachord (example 79). The text of her lament is much shorter than those we have discussed, a mere twenty lines; and it does not present a succession of contrasting moods, but rather a single angry and ironic mood that culminates twice in a climactic cry of self-exhortation: "Sù, sù senno ingegnoso, Rendimi il caro sposo."

Ardisci, animo, ardisci:	Be bold, my soul, be bold:
Osa, mio cor, che temi?	Be daring, my heart, what do you fear?
Temi quel, che di grande,	Do you fear that which so great,
Di grande, e d'impensato,	So great and unexpected,
Ne' tuoi perigli estremi,	In your extreme danger
Ti suggerisce un consiglier fidato?	A trusted counselor advises you?
S'il precipitio miri,	If you are looking at the precipice,
Se la ruina aspetti,	If you are awaiting ruin,
Sgombra, sgombra i rispetti,	Banish, banish all respect,
Adempi i tuoi desiri,	Fulfill your desires,
Vergogna non t'arresti,	Let shame not stop you.
Troppo udisti, e vedesti;	You heard and saw too much.
Sù, sù senno ingegnoso,	*Come, come resourceful spirit,*
Rendimi il caro sposo.	*Return to me my beloved husband.*
Arti, industrie, discorsi, oh Dio, che spero,	Arts, diligence, discourses, O God, let me hope,
Fissatevi quì meco,	Join with me here
Per destar à pietade, un crudo, un fiero,	To arouse to pity a cruel, a proud man,
Un fuggitivo Greco;	A Greek fugitive.
Sù, sù senno ingegnoso,	*Come, come resourceful spirit,*
Rendimi il caro sposo.	*Return to me my beloved husband.*

The single mood is portrayed musically with some of the same techniques Cavalli had used in Teti's lament. Many repeated notes followed by sudden large leaps, arpeggios, accented dissonance between bass and voice, exploitation of extremes of range within a single phrase, and syncopation are all closely geared to the expression of the text. All musical contrasts are subsumed, however, under the single most striking one, ushered in by the refrain; involving a change from duple to triple meter for its second line and a movement into aria style, the intensity of the refrain is heightened by repetition of the text and by the presence of the descending tetrachord in the bass, heard twice, with which the voice part, dissonant in itself, conflicts, rhythmically and harmonically. Although two statements hardly constitute an ostinato, the expressive intention of the tetrachord refrain is unmistakable. Subsequent practice confirms what is only hinted at here.

The tetrachord ostinato plays a much greater role within some of Cavalli's recitative laments as a means of emphasizing a characteristic change of mood. Doriclea's lengthy, multipartite recitative lament, for example (in *Doriclea* 3.1), contains at its center a brief, but weighty, lyrical section based on the tetrachord, marking her shift from impatient anger at herself to a plea to the heavens that her prayers be carried to her imprisoned husband. Although its text consists of only four lines (out of a total of forty-eight), the lyrical section is both emphatic and self-contained. In addition to beginning and ending firmly on the tonic, D minor, it is distinguished from its recitative surroundings by an instrumental frame: statements of the tetrachord in the strings provide an introduction and epilogue. It is thus essentially an aria, prepared expressively and tonally by the recitative that precedes it (example 80).

Despite the expressive weight of this aria, there is no letdown in the remainder of the monologue. On the contrary, intensity is maintained as Doriclea angrily resorts to *stile concitato* recitative—a favorite technique familiar from the laments of Arianna and Sacrati's Deidamia—at first accompanied by continuo alone, but then intensified by strings as it gains momentum with Doriclea's vision of her imprisoned husband. Her return to reality ("che vaneggio")—the conventional reversal—is marked by a cessation of the string accompaniment, but it comes back again, calmer now, in sustained tones, as she sinks exhaustedly—and typically, for a lamenting character—into a deep sleep.[16]

In this scene, temporary tetrachord-aria style is just part of the panoply of expressive techniques used for the development of the internal psychological drama of the character. But it stands alone as a calm center of stability, setting up or preparing the way for the more active, excited outbursts to follow. It thus lends shape to the soliloquy as a whole. The structure of the text is very different, but the effect is analogous to that of Apollo's monologue: a recitative lament that encloses an independent tetrachord aria. Doriclea's lament, like Apollo's, gains expressive power from a fusion of two very different, originally separate, affective modes or techniques: unbridled recitative and ostinato aria style. And their juxtaposition increases the effect of each. The intensity of recitative becomes all the more expressive as it breaks free from the restraints of measured aria style, and the restraint of aria style in turn earns tension from having succeeded in reining in an emotional outburst. In some of the most powerful laments of the period, the two styles thus work with and against one another.

In *Giasone*, the paradigmatic midcentury opera and model of convention, this kind of stylistic compromise reached its climax. The text of the last of Isifile's three laments (3.21), like that of other recitative laments, consists of an extended series of seven- and eleven-syllable verses, sixty-seven in all, very few of them rhymed. It has fewer sections than usual, however—only three. In the first (thirty-seven lines), Isifile hurls an accusatory, angry, ironic diatribe at Giasone, her betrayer; in the second (only eight lines), she pleads with the

---

16. The use of accompanied recitative, exceedingly sparse in these operas, is always dramatically or affectively significant. Here the strings seem to represent first Doriclea's magical vision of her husband in danger, then her increasing sleepiness: the effects of an outside (supernatural) power. Accompanied recitative is used similarly in Sartorio's *Orfeo*, for Euridice's speech from the Underworld (or rather, Or-

feo's dream of Euridice's speech). Sleep, in these operas, is a conventional consequence of any extreme emotional exertion. Deidamia, we remember, slept after her mad scene in *La finta pazza*. But it is inappropriate after Orfeo's lament in 1673 (see ch. 13 below). Doriclea's lament is discussed in Magini, "Indagini," 339–50.

assembled company—the queen and her companions—to come to her aid against Giasone; and in the final section (twenty-two lines), she bids them all farewell (example 81).

Like Doriclea's aria oasis, Isifile's (mm. 71–121) coincides with a shift in the object of her attention, in this case from Giasone to the assembled company. And likewise, a change of key and an instrumental declaration of the tetrachord announce that change of focus, insulating Isifile's new remarks from the heat of her previous passion (if only temporarily), as if setting them in quotation marks or in another voice. The sense of formality provided by the tetrachord bass, particularly its heavy accentuation, lends an appropriately solemn tone to her address to the queen as well as a sense of self-control to Isifile's words. But the self-control quickly dissipates; the aria is short-lived. Unlike Doriclea's, it is incomplete, interrupted for no obvious formal reason nine lines before the end of the textual unit; there Cavalli's setting takes on a life of its own, suddenly breaking into highly charged, affective recitative style, a change that effectively captures the overflowing violence of Isifile's imagery:

Assistino à i martiri	Let the children witness
Della madre Tradita,	Their betrayed mother's martyrdom,
E che ad ogni ferita	Let them drink the blood
Che imprimerà nel mio pudico petto	From every wound
Bevino quelli il sangue mio stillante,	Inflicted on my chaste bosom
Acciò ch'ei trapassando	So that it will course
Nelle lor pure vene, in lor s'incarni,	In their veins,
Onde il lor seno in qualche parte sia	And they will be
Tomba Innocente, all'Innocenza mia.	The innocent tomb of my innocence.

By her sudden burst of recitative, Isifile emphatically frees herself from the constraints of the descending tetrachord, which had been holding her in check, helping her to maintain decorum. She is now carried away by her own rhetoric, in an excess of emotion that the music portrays even more emphatically than the text.

After Isifile's unexpected recitative outburst, another significant musical contrast initiates the final section (mm. 137–72), a contrast suggested by yet another change in the focus of her attention, from passionate self-justification to a generalized leave-taking. Following her calm farewell, the lament concludes with one further passionate outburst as Isifile admits she still loves Giasone.

Within Isifile's lament, as in Doriclea's, the lyrical section (or aria) stands out as the affective center, the musical focus, providing the springboard for the dramatic climax. And it is prepared, like an aria, by the preceding recitative. But whereas Doriclea's aria is self-contained, Isifile's does not end; rather, it explodes suddenly and unpredictably into the climax. The use of the tetrachord aria style in *Giasone* is the more effective; it reveals a composer self-confidently striking out on his own rather than strictly following the librettist's structure. But in both cases the effect is predicated on the musical weight and contrast provided by the tetrachord pattern, and on its innate affective implications.

Isifile's monologue was among the last of Cavalli's great recitative-laments. Stylistic developments in opera after the middle of the century, in particular the increasing dichotomy of aria and recitative, rendered such fluid compromise obsolete. The multiple, kaleidoscopic contrasts that so eloquently portrayed the vicissitudes of the lamenting Arianna and her successors were gradually reduced to one, the contrast between preparatory recitative and lengthy, weighty aria. By the mid 1650s, virtually all laments were arias, many of them strophic. Lyricism had gradually absorbed all of the expressive responsibility it had formerly shared, via the tetrachord, with recitative.

Graphic documentation of the process of reduction is provided by a series of revisions of Isifile's lament. *Giasone*, as we know, enjoyed an unusually long life, being revived quite regularly until the end of the century. Each time it was edited or modernized for a new performance, arias were added and recitative was cut. Although the lament endured as long as the opera itself, the opening recitative portion underwent a succession of cuts until, in the *Novello Giasone*, a version edited by Antonio Stradella for a production in Rome in 1671, it was radically reduced, from seventy-one to a mere eleven measures. The original proportions were reversed; from an extended recitative with a central lyrical section, it had become essentially a tetrachord aria prefaced by a brief, standard recitative introduction and followed by an expressive recitative epilogue, reduced from fifty to nineteen measures (the sections marked VI = DE, mm. 12–70, 115–36, and 147–63 in example 81, were cut).[17]

By virtue of its formal and affective implications, the descending tetrachord ostinato facilitated the transition from lament recitative to lament aria as the conventional operatic procedure. Being infinitely expandable, the pattern was suitable for lyrical passages of various lengths, brief inserts within recitative or full aria strophes. Whether in the context of recitative or aria, the tetrachord lent to the lament a sharp, distinctive profile, particularly when reinforced by the host of secondary attributes associated with it: triple meter, slow tempo, and string accompaniment (in addition to syncopation, suspensions, and phrase overlap encouraged by the ostinato pattern itself). These were all independently expressive techniques whose special effect depended in part on their being used only rarely—though always together—at particularly dramatic moments dur-

17.   The libretto of *Il novello Giasone* was published in Rome in 1671. Stradella's edited score is in I-Rsc. There were several stages in this evolution, as reflected in librettos printed between 1650 and 1673; but Stradella's version had the least amount of recitative.

ing the course of an opera. String accompaniment, in fact, had a particular association with lament that extended at least as far back as *Arianna*.[18] The combined use of these secondary features in conjunction with the tetrachord helped to mark the lament as the most important moment in the opera.

Interestingly, these attributes were considered as much a part of the lament convention as the tetrachord itself, and even sometimes served as substitutes for it. Generic designations for laments in Venetian scores often included reference to one or more of them. *Lamento con violini* occurs more than once; and sometimes the attributes alone were sufficient to signify the genre—laments often bear the indication *adagio* or just *con viole* or *con violini*. In one exceptional instance the rubric *con le viole* even appears in a libretto, next to what was obviously intended as a lament text.[19]

The Lament Aria: Variations on a Theme

Although the association between the descending tetrachord and the lament was based on expressive qualities intrinsic to the tetrachord itself, it was only through repeated use, primarily in the operas of Cavalli, that the combination became thoroughly conventionalized. But that repeated use was far from mechanical. Cavalli's treatment of the tetrachord remained extremely varied throughout his career—a testimony both to his compositional skill and to the power of the convention (example 82). As we have noticed, he tended to treat the tetrachord more freely than Monteverdi did in the "Lament of the Nymph." Only Rosinda's lament in *Rosinda*, 3.5 utilizes the basic descending tetrachord in a single key throughout. Usually, if he chose the simple pattern, he varied it through modulation or combined it with another related pattern; or else he completely abandoned it during the course of the lament (as in that of Apollo). More commonly, the pattern itself underwent modification: it was inverted (*Hipermestra* 3.12), chromaticized (*Egisto* 2.6), arpeggiated (*Eliogabalo* 1.16), or otherwise embellished melodically or rhythmically. Occasionally Cavalli treated the tetrachord with even greater freedom, utilizing its aura, its implications, rather than the pattern itself: in some laments he exploited the harmony or the possibilities of phrase overlap suggested by the tetrachord, or the affective language, the suspensions and syncopations associated with it, but without any discernible bass configuration (*Artemisia* 2.12). Finally, in a few instances,

18. According to Follino's description, Arianna's lament was accompanied by violas and violins ("viole et violini") (*Compendio*, quoted in Solerti, *Gli albori*, 2: 145). For the possible source of the string accompaniment of Arianna's lament in the intermedio tradition of the sixteenth century, see Tomlinson, *Monteverdi*, 138; see also Weaver, "Sixteenth-Century Instrumentation," 363–78; and Rosand, "Descending Tetrachord," nn. 12, 20.

19. *Veremonda l'amazzone di Aragona* (Venice: Giuliani, 1652) by Luigi Zorzisto [Giulio Strozzi] (2.7), 83–84.

specific tetrachord reference was relegated solely to the ominous announcement of the opening ritornello (*Artemisia* 3.19).

Cavalli's varied treatments of the pattern often highlight one of its affective attributes in particular: the obscuring of formal boundaries by means of ambiguities between phrase and strophe endings (*Ciro* 2.9), the ambiguity of the cadence (*Statira* 3.4 and 3.10), or the potential for extremely extended vocal phrases (*Rosinda* 3.5). The specific relevance of all of these features to the lament affect is demonstrated by Ciro's lament from *Ciro* (3.15), "Negatemi respiri" (example 83). Here syncopation, phrase extension, and a repeatedly interrupted vocal line converge to portray Ciro's labored breathing under emotional stress, a translation of the central image of the text. The tetrachord enables Cavalli to imitate an action.[20]

Monteverdi's two laments may have defined the stylistic boundaries of the convention, but it was Cavalli's repeated, continuous exploration, extension, and refinement of that definition over the course of his 25-year career that assured its permanent status in opera. Cavalli's natural inclination toward variety and toward realizing the implications of the tetrachord, in recitative as well as in aria, kept the convention alive as the climactic moment that audiences repeatedly anticipated. Their anticipation was rewarded not by something tired and predictable but by something always new.

The laments of Cavalli's contemporaries and immediate successors tended to show continuing variety. Although most were now arias, they remained distinctive in text form as well as musical setting. Many were non-strophic, in contrast to the growing number of strophic forms that characterized all other kinds of arias. And most, strophic and non-strophic alike, were treated more freely than other arias. They were usually more sectional, incorporating recitative passages or some other kind of contrast; they usually involved more repetition of text and more melismas—that is, greater musical expansion; and they were often integrated within a larger musical-dramatic context. Whether introduced by recitatives, linked to other arias, or just very long in themselves, many laments continued to comprise entire scenes. Most significant, they continued to represent the musico-dramatic high point of the opera.

In their use of the tetrachord, these laments run the gamut from unwavering strictness to a flexibility in which the merest allusion to the pattern is a sufficient reminder of its original function and meaning. Nor does the style of the moment seem to have especially influenced the choice. Selino's lament from Cesti's *Argia* (1669) 3.18 offers a particularly effective example of the strict type.

20. Another lament with an interrupted vocal line is Xerse's "Lasciatemi morire" (from *Xerse* 3.19). Many lament texts emphasize words related to breathing: *sospir, respir, spirare, esalare*, which are enhanced by halting delivery over a steady descending tetrachord.

Here a chromatic version of the tetrachord recurs twenty-one times under a constantly unfolding, repeatedly overlapping, seemingly unfettered, and consequently highly expressive vocal line (example 84).[21] Other, somewhat less effective examples of strict tetrachord use occur in two works by Carlo Grossi, *Romilda* (1659; 3.15, diatonic tetrachord) and *Artaxerse* (1669; 3.11, a chromatic tetrachord) (examples 85 and 86).[22]

Freer treatment of the tetrachord, however—or at least strict treatment of a freer paraphrase of the pattern—was more common during this period. Nigrane's lament from Ziani's *Le fortune di Rodope e Damira* (1657) 3.4, for example, is strictly based on a version of the pattern that is so varied and extended that its repetitions are barely perceptible, leaving Ziani to rely on rather small-scale rhythmic and harmonic conflicts of bass and voice rather than the more forceful structural overlaps that derive from opposition to a strongly articulated—and strongly perceptible—pattern (example 87). The conflict is weakened by the particular structure of the bass itself, which consists of twelve measures divided into two similar, but unequal, sections, the first of which seems to end too early and the second too late. The forward motion of the bass is impeded also by too many cadences—three: a half-cadence in m. 4 and full cadences in mm. 8 and 12, all of them confirmed by the violin parts above. Its tonal impact, overemphasized by the too-frequent cadences, is nevertheless contradictory and ambiguous in its combination of strong F major with several insistent chromatic inflections. Rather than somehow compensating for or counteracting the awkwardly sectional bass, the vocal line confirms the short subphrases with subphrases of its own. These are created by a very rigid, undramatic treatment of the text, in which nearly all clauses are repeated, some of them several times, to sequential music, whether they are particularly expressive or not. As a result, affective emphasis is completely lacking, both in the presentation of the text and in the piece as a whole. The effect can be appreciated by reading the text as presented in Ziani's setting (in brackets):

Rodope dove sei [dove sei, dove sei],   *Rodope, where are you* [where are you, where are you]
Pria ch'alla morte [pria ch'alla morte]   Ere I to death [ere I to death] do go,
  io vada,

E svenato [e svenato] al suol cada   And gored [and gored] to the ground do fall
[E svenato, e svenato al suol cada]   [And gored, and gored to the ground do fall],

21. Cesti seems to have been fond of the pattern, for he used it in diatonic form nearly as strictly in Silandra's lament from *Orontea* (1666) (2.8). But he could use it freely with at least equal success (as in *Tito*, below). The *Argia* lament is taken from the Venetian score (I-Vnm, It. IV, 391 [9915]), which apparently reflects the revival of 1669. But, according to comparison of the two librettos, the lament was the same in 1669 as it had been in 1655.

22. The lament in *Artaxerse* represents a rather late use of the strict tetrachord ostinato, although Sartorio's *Orfeo* of 1673 also contains one, in Euridice's lament (3.4). The pattern seems to have died out in Venetian opera after the 1670s, but it can still be discerned at the opening of a lamentlike aria, "A morire, a morir," from Pollarolo's *Irene* (1695), act 4, scene 9.

Almen quest'occhi [almen quest'occhi] miei	May these eyes at least [these eyes at least] of mine
Ti potessero dar [ti potessero dar] l'ultimo guardo [l'ultimo guardo]	Upon you cast [upon you cast] their last gaze [their last gaze],
Per bearmi nel foco [per bearmi nel foco] in cui [in cui] tutt'ardo	That I may rejoice in the flame [that I may rejoice in the flame] in which [in which] I burn.
Che contento o mia vita [contento o mia vita] all'hor [all'hor] morrei	For happy, O my life [happy, O my life], I then [I then] should die.
Rodope dove sei? [dove sei, dove sei, Rodope, dove sei?]	*Rodope, where are you?* [where are you, where are you, Rodope, where are you?]

With only a few exceptions—the refrain line, perhaps, and "all'hor" in line 7—the repetitions fail to heighten the natural rhetorical emphasis in the text. The result is a lament that seems aimless, short-breathed, and ineffectual.

Far more expressive is Polemone's lament from Cesti's *Tito* (1666) 3.8, which, however, is built on a bass whose relationship to the tetrachord is virtually nonexistent (example 88). Cesti did not tie himself down to an ostinato as Ziani did; his bass is much freer and more generative than Ziani's. Differences are immediately apparent in the opening ritornello, which is the same length as Ziani's. In contrast to Ziani's three cadences within twelve measures, Cesti has only one, at the end. Until then, Cesti studiously avoids cadences with the help of the string parts, whose continuously overlapping suspensions maintain harmonic intensity throughout.

Cesti's voice part enters before the cadence rather than coinciding with it as Ziani's does. Although Cesti's voice and bass phrases do not dovetail any more than Ziani's do, the string parts overlap them both, urging the piece forward. Furthermore, because they work together, voice and bass produce strong, propulsive syncopations against the strings, particularly toward the end of the lament (mm. 55–64). Cesti's vocal line is more singable than Ziani's, too, moving primarily by step, with an occasional expressive leap. Although its subphrases are equally short, they build syntactically to climaxes. Despite the absence of affective opposition between voice and bass, phrase extension is made possible by the freer bass—voice and bass together stretch phrases through syncopation and by invoking the deceptive cadence (mm. 67–80).

The difference between these two laments is epitomized by a comparison of the text presentation of the two composers. Cesti also repeated text, but in a manner that underscores rather than distorting its natural emphasis. And when his repetition creates melodic patterns, they are shorter, more motivic, and used for affective reiteration rather than sequence, as building blocks to a climax rather than going nowhere:

Berenice [Berenice] ove [ove, ove] sei,	Berenice [Berenice], where [where, where] are you?
Dove, dove t'ascondi?	Where, where do you hide,
Luce de gl'occhi miei	Light of my eyes?
[Berenice ove sei?]	[Berenice, where are you?]
Marmi o voi che nel candore	O ye marbles that in candor
Pareggiate la mia fè	Match my faith,
Palesate [palesate, palesate] il mio sol, dite dov'è [dite dov'è, dov'è, dov'è, dite dov'è].	Reveal [reveal, reveal] my sun, say where it is [say where it is, where it is, where it is, say where it is].
[Palesate il mio sol, dite dov'è, dite dov'è, dov'è, dov'è, dite dov'è.]	[Reveal my sun, say where it is, say where it is, where it is, where it is, say where it is.]

Clearly the success of these endeavors depended on the composer, not on the lament convention itself. The convention was flexible enough to allow a composer to make his own decisions. His choices were still numerous. A free adaptation of the tetrachord pattern, while sacrificing the obsessive impact of ostinato repetition, allowed him greater flexibility of expression. He could, of course, still depend on the value of the implied, underlying (but absent) tetrachord as a sign, while drawing freely upon its conventional affective concomitants, syncopation, suspensions, and phrase overlap.

But sometimes composers used the stylistic conventions of the lament too superficially, in combination with other features that tended to counteract them, producing a conflict that seriously weakened the identity of the genre. Some of the laments that utilize the tetrachord merely as a vague point of reference rather than a structural feature fail to project the intended affect. That is, despite the use of individual conventional accoutrements (such as string accompaniment and tetrachord reference), they display a misunderstanding or misuse of the convention itself.

In Leucotoe's lament from Rovettino's *Gli amori d' Apollo e di Leucotoe* (1663) 3.11, duple meter, excessive rhythmic activity and melodic sequence, and predominantly major tonality undermine the expressive intention of the text and contradict the tetrachord and string accompaniment references (example 89). A similar miscalculation weakens the impact of Domitiano's lament from Boretti's *Eliogabalo* (1668) 2.11, where repeated allusions to the chromatic tetrachord, string accompaniment, and the minor key are insufficient to counteract the trivial effect of rapid rhythmic activity and short patterned phrases, both in the opening section in duple meter and the closing triple-meter section (example 90). These examples fail to fulfill their potential as laments because of conflicting affects. Reference to the tetrachord and string accompaniment may have been necessary, but obviously they were not sufficient to constitute a lament.

They needed the confirmation of a slow tempo, minor key, suspensions, and expansive text-setting.

The convention was exploited in a variety of ways throughout the century, with more or less full understanding of its implications. For a final affirmation of the power of the convention, we return once more to Cavalli: to one of his late operas, *Scipione affricano* (1664). One of the most moving scenes, Sofonisba's soliloquy (2.8), consisting of a recitative and an aria, derives its power precisely from not being a lament.[23] In fact, that is its point: it is intentionally a non-lament that can be understood only against the background of pieces that are laments (example 91).

In her opening recitative, a highly affective discourse that makes use of the usual expressive techniques of repeated notes, dissonance against the bass, and a gradually ascending line interrupted by a few extreme leaps against descending chromatic motion in the bass, Sofonisba, the wife of the imprisoned Siface, explains that she must keep her sorrows to herself lest her situation deteriorate even further. She begins very much as Ottavia does in her first lament in *Poppea*, with the words "Di misera regina. . . ." The recitative concludes in an arioso that makes the same point, though with added emphasis through lyricism, affective harmony and melody, and repetition of text.

The following aria, then, is not a lament but an invocation of nature, of the "verdi herbette rugiadose" ("green dewy grass"), which Sofonisba calls upon to lament in her stead: "S'io non possò dir ohimè, lagrimate voi per me." The continuo aria (not string-accompanied) in duple meter (not triple), with a walking bass and syllabic, stepwise melody, contrasts strongly with what a lament would be—intentionally. But the walking bass (which subtly refers to the tetrachord in its descending stepwise motion), the melody (which creates dissonance against the bass through a series of accented appoggiaturas), and the harmony (particularly the cross relation in the refrain, heard twice, and the overall minor tonality) lend a poignant mood to the piece that tends to counteract the lively tempo and syllabic text-setting. In not being a lament, and in emphatically abjuring its most obvious conventional associations, this aria nonetheless draws upon all of the affective power of the lament. Denied on the surface, the lament affect animates this aria from within, peering out from behind Sofonisba's mask.

As an operatic convention, the lament combines features of all of the conventions we have discussed so far. Like madness and sleep, and often associated

---

23. Sofonisba is the "prima donna." The "seconda donna," Ericlea, has a lament aria in the proper place in the third act (3.17). It may be found in Garland facs., 58, ff. 127–29. It is curious that the entire text of Sofonisba's scene is placed within *virgolette* in the libretto. What a pity if the original Venetian audience never heard it!

with them, it was a theatrical device that enhanced the verisimilitude essential to opera. Lamenting characters, only slightly more responsible than mad or sleeping ones, were released from the bonds of decorous behavior by the intensity of their feelings, which verged on—and often culminated in—madness. Like the trumpet aria or the *sdrucciolo* aria, too, the lament was associated with a particular musical technique. And like the love duet it developed a precise structural and dramatic function, usually occurring at the point of maximum complication, just before the resolution of the plot. But the lament surpassed all the other conventions in its impact. From the very outset it had a stronger identity, one that was both musical and dramatic, and, indeed, was actually defined by the combination of those two elements. And its identity was reaffirmed and solidified, not only in opera but in the monody and aria books that developed symbiotically alongside, influencing and in turn being influenced by operatic developments. The lament did not require a context in order to be recognized—it could (and did) exist independently of opera.

We have traced the evolution of the operatic lament from one Monteverdian archetype to the other, from the *Arianna*-type sectional recitative to the "Lament of the Nymph"-type tetrachord-aria (with or without recitative introduction); but the evolution was not strictly linear. Aria and recitative laments coexist in many operas of the 1640s and 1650s, and an occasional recitative lament may be found as late as the 1660s.[24] However erratic its evolution from recitative to aria, the lament was a microcosm of operatic developments in general, of the growing preference for static summary and distillation of feelings over action. The increasing proportion of aria to recitative displayed by Isifile's lament from 1650 to 1671 reflects, succinctly, the change of proportion in opera as a whole during the same period.

With all of its development, however, the lament remained remarkably standardized for quite some time. An aria style that was viable for a lament in 1640 (in *Gli amori d'Apollo e di Dafne*), hard on the heels of Venetian opera's beginnings, was deemed suitable for the same purpose thirty years later (in *Il novello Giasone*). Although it seems to have disappeared temporarily from Venetian (or by now Italian) opera after the 1670s, the genre lasted much longer elsewhere—witness Purcell's classic setting of Dido's lament and the abundance of tetrachord laments in the dramatic music of Handel and Bach.[25] The longevity of the genre must be ascribed at least in part to the specificity of its musical characteristics, what we might call its musical formula, the descending tetrachord and its concomitants. Musical associations so much more specific

24.   Examples of recitative lament texts are found in *Cleopatra* (Giacomo dall'Angelo/Castrovillari, 1662) 3.11 and 16, but both of them contain measured aria-like passages.

25.   Significantly, most of these adhere to the original formula much more rigidly than the operatic laments of the seventeenth century. The further away from its origins, the heavier the weight of accumulated convention, it would seem.

than those for any other dramatic convention undoubtedly helped to preserve the lament from stylistic change, to promote a certain conservatism. Further, the fact that the musical formula itself had an intrinsic relationship to the specific affect of the lament made the connection all the more natural, inevitable, and permanent.

In some later operas the tetrachord-aria lament seems to have assumed the role of an intentional, self-conscious archaism. This is suggested by the contrast between its characteristic white-note notation—typical meters are 3/1 or 3/2— and the increasingly pervasive quarter-note values of the music in the rest of the opera. As operatic style changed around it, the increasingly anachronistic lament served as a poignant reminder of old musico-dramatic values, of the way music had once embodied the affect of a text.

The intrinsic connection between the drama and music of the lament was certainly one reason for the longevity of the genre. Another may be its association with performers. From its origins as an operatic highpoint, the lament was associated with its singer, perhaps because it was the affective center or core of the main role(s). Singers' reputations were often connected to laments; they were praised for their skill at lamentation. And with the rise in their importance within the operatic collaboration, they may have helped to sustain the genre.[26]

Much of the reportage surrounding *Arianna* concerned the performance of the famous lament: "The lament that Ariadne . . . sang on the rock . . . was performed with so much feeling and in such a pathetic manner that not a single listener remained unmoved, nor did a single lady fail to shed some small tear at her plaint."[27] The singer was Virginia Andreini, a *comica ordinaria* known by the stage name Florinda, who at the last minute replaced the tragically deceased young singer Caterina Martinelli, for whom Monteverdi had conceived the part. Andreini's performance was immortalized by Giambattista Marino (*Adone*, 7.88), who compared it to those of the most famous singer of the day, Adriana Basile:

Tal forse intenerir col dolce canto	Thus perhaps with her sweet song
Suol la bella Adriana i duri affetti	The lovely Adriana is wont to melt harsh sentiments,
E con la voce e con la vista intanto	While with her voice and with her look
Gir per due strade a saettare i petti;	She takes two paths to pierce men's breasts;
E in tal guisa Florinda udisti, o Manto,	Thus, Mantua, did you hear Florinda,
Là ne' teatri de' tuoi regi tetti	There in the theaters beneath your royal roofs,
D'Adrianna spiegar gli aspri martiri	Expounding Ariadne's harsh martyrdoms
E trar da mille cor mille sospiri.	And drawing from a thousand hearts a thousand sighs.

26. That laments were still the focus of audience attention in 1673 is confirmed in a passage from Ivanovich's letter to Pagliardi of 26 June (Appendix II.5a). It will be on the various laments in his *Lismaco*, he writes, "a' quali sarà dirizzata principalmente la curiosità." The existence of laments for several protagonists in a number of operas, sometimes with scant dramatic justification, suggests that they may have provided a special arena for competition among singers.

27. Follino, *Compendio*, quoted in Solerti, *Gli albori*, 2: 145. But see also, with a more generous quotation from Follino, Fabbri, *Monteverdi*, 133–34.

The first Venetian prima donna, Anna Renzi, too, was particularly acclaimed for her performances of laments. Several sonnets in the volume of encomiastic poetry addressed to her by Giulio Strozzi refer to her powers of persuasion in that mode:

Nella Scena Real forma sonori
I mesti accenti suoi, canoro il pianto,
E col finto languir ben desta in tanto
In noi verace duol, vivaci ardori.[28]

On the regal stage she sonorously forms
Her mournful accents, singing her plaint,
And with pretended sorrow the while awakes
In us authentic grief, living desires.

Among other roles, her lamenting Ottavia in Monteverdi's *L'incoronazione di Poppea* elicited special praise.

Non è Ottavia, che lagrime diffonde
Esule, esposta a le spumose arene;
È un mostro, che con note alte, e profonde
Acrescer và lo stuol de le Sirene.[29]

It is not Ottavia shedding her tears,
Exiled, exposed on foamy shores;
It is a monster, who, with notes high and deep
Augments the company of the Sirens.

The most specific description of her performance of Ottavia's lament occurs in a passage from the anonymous *Idillio* in Strozzi's volume that provides a running commentary on all of her roles.

Poi cominciasti afflitta
Tue querele Canore
Con tua voce divina,
Disprezzata Regina,
E seguendo il lamento
Facevi di dolore
Stillar in pianto, e sospirar Amore.
Sò ben'io, che se vero
Fosse stato il cordoglio,
E l'historia funesta,
Alla tua voce mesta,
Alle dolci parole, ai cari detti.
Si come i nostri petti
Colmaro di pietade, ah sò ben'io,
Neron s'havrebbe fatto humile, e pio.[30]

Then, afflicted, you intoned
Your melodious complaints
With your voice divine,
O spurned queen,
And continuing your lament
You forced Love
To burst into tears and sigh.
Well do I know that,
Had the grief been true,
And the dolorous tale,
Hearing your mournful voice,
Your sweet words, your endearing expressions,
Just as they filled our breasts
With pity, ah, well do I know that
Nero would have been rendered humble
and compassionate.

Surely few descriptions of a lamenting protagonist, however, could rival in vividness and realism of detail this one in a letter to the duke of Brunswick from his secretary, Francesco Massi:

[The Rangoni maiden, jealous of her protector's attentions to another prima donna] . . . had resolved never to sing again, when, encouraged by friends of the marquis

28. *Le glorie della Signora Anna Renzi romana* (Venice: Surian, 1644), 25. The reference is to one of her performances at the Grimani theater.
29. Ibid., 28, sonnet by Benedetto Ferrari: "Per la Signora Anna Renzi Romana . . . rappresentante Ottavia ripudiata, e comessa all'onde entr'uno schifo."
30. Ibid., 37–38. Two words have been corrected here: *seguendo* replaces *seguenao* in line 5, and *stato* replaces *stattu* in line 9.

[Rangoni, her protector], right in the midst of a conversation she began to sing a lament, precisely made to measure for her, of most beautiful poetry and most perfect music. Now whoever did not witness that scene cannot know what it is to transform oneself in song. She moved around, and, as the nature of the lament required, prayed, emoted, called her betrayer beloved; gently she persuaded him, looked at him, and exuded passion from her eyes, cried with tears of trust, protested that her heart was the altar where the fire of an immense affection always burned, that he was the king of the entire realm of her thoughts, that therefore he shouldn't abandon her. She followed with desperate actions, with great violence, and so much so that she seemed actually to be an enraged Fury; naming at one point her rival, she turned her eyes to heaven and exclaimed, "Ah, ah, let her be cursed!" She returned then with her heart to the beginning [*a segno*], and blaming for her fate more the wrath of destiny than the inconstancy of her lover, finished the lament and fainted. (Appendix IIIB.22b)[31]

This description closely follows the narrative progress of the lament itself, through vicissitudes of passion familiar from the many laments we have examined. Text and music both can almost be reconstructed from the description. Prayers, persuasion, penetrating looks, tears, desperation, and fury (*stile concitato?*) lead to the exclamatory climax ("ahi, ahi, che sia maledetta!" perhaps in recitative), which is followed by a pulling back ("dal segno," a return to the opening), an awareness of futility, and a final generalized diatribe against fate, culminating in a faint. Although this lament is surely an aria "cut to measure," the stages of feeling described are very much like those of the paradigmatic recitative lament of Arianna. The stylistic dichotomy that separated recitative and aria-laments was less important than the similarity of affect that linked them.

Massi's description not only recreates the narrative progress of the lament; it provides a vivid sense of the affective intensity of its performance. No matter that the stage for this production was a private *salotto* rather than one of Venice's public theaters, or that the singer-protagonist played not a fictional character in historical garb but herself. The fate she lamented was her own. Her lament declared its generic independence of opera. Its verisimilitude transcended art, asserting a powerful connection to life. No other operatic convention had the power to do so much.

31. This lament elicited an equally vivid response on the part of the lady's competitor: an arietta deprecating jealousy, as Massi goes on to report (Appendix IIIB.22c).

13

• • •

Il ritorno d'Orfeo: The Decline of a Tradition

Orpheus, the mythic musician of Thrace, who charmed men, gods, savage beasts, the very rocks with his song, was the quintessential operatic hero. His story was an explicit demonstration of the power of music, an operatic archetype. Orpheus, most celebrated of mythological musicians, specifically harnessed the rhetorical powers of music for dramatic ends, to persuade the god of the Underworld to release Eurydice from the bonds of death; and it was this dramatic application that accounted for his special appeal. Rendering the Orpheus myth in music represented one of the great challenges to librettists and composers—from Rinuccini and Peri to Cocteau and Stravinsky—a test of their own powers of musical persuasion.

Although not officially the first operatic hero, having been preceded in that role by his father Apollo several years before,[1] Orpheus was certainly the most important. In 1600 in Florence, as spokesman for Rinuccini and Peri in *Euridice*, he forcefully asserted the propriety of sung drama. Soon afterwards, in 1607, under his own name, he carried the operatic message to Mantua for Striggio and Monteverdi; and in 1647 he appeared in Paris in Francesco Buti's and Luigi Rossi's *Orfeo*, to confirm the arrival of the genre beyond the Alps.[2] It is thus perhaps somewhat surprising that in Venice opera had been in existence for some thirty-five years before Orpheus made his debut there. Evidently his presence had not been strictly necessary for the establishment of opera in Venice; the legitimacy of *dramma per musica* had been achieved through other means.

---

1. In *Dafne*, a libretto by Rinuccini, set to music by Peri and Jacopo Corsi. On this opera, see especially William Porter, "Peri's and Corsi's 'Dafne': Some New Discoveries and Observations," *JAMS* 18 (1965): 170–96; and Hanning, "Glorious Apollo," 485–513.

2. *Orfeo* by Francesco Buti and Luigi Rossi (1647) was the first Italian opera written expressly for Paris.

Orpheus also may have appeared in Rome in 1619 in *La morte d'Orfeo* by Stefano Landi, but not as a musical hero. For a discussion of Orpheus's various operatic personae in the seventeenth century and their classical sources, which included Ovid, *Metamorphoses* 10–11 and Virgil, *Georgics* 4.453–527, see Rosand, "L'Ovidio trasformato," IX–XVII.

Indeed, mythology in general, the chief source for operatic subject matter in Florence and Rome (and later in Paris), had quickly relinquished that role in Venice to romance and history. After the first few seasons, the gods were permanently relegated to the sidelines—retained along with allegorical person-ifications in prologues and intermedi, primarily as an excuse for spectacle.

By the time he finally appeared in Venice during the 1670s, then, Orpheus was redundant, even superannuated. His main claim to operatic fame, the spe-cial ability to translate music into action, was by then taken for granted. Through repeated practice it had become common to all operatic heroes, what-ever their lineage. Opera, which had once depended on the Orphic exemplum for its verisimilitude, was now fully sustained by the power of convention.

Nor was the Thracian musician merely superfluous. Compounding the ignominy of his redundance in 1673, Orpheus became a Venetian casualty, a victim of operatic success. The conventions that had developed during the initial decade of operatic activity in Venice—that had been deployed so naturally and effectively in *Giasone* in 1649, and that were exploited repeatedly in sub-sequent years by every librettist and composer working on the lagoon—exacted their toll on the operatic hero: they succeeded in depriving him of his unique birthright, his heroic status. Orpheus's loss of stature in Venice was not merely symbolic. It was actually dramatized on the stage of the Teatro S. Salvatore, in *Orfeo* of Aureli and Sartorio.

The unheralded return of Orpheus in 1673 did not signal any particular revival of interest in mythology—no such interest is reflected in other operas of the time. Yet it was hardly a casual event. No audience could have been un-aware of Orpheus's mythic musical powers, and no librettist or composer could have ignored his operatic pedigree. He carried it with him wherever he went, daring librettists and composers to come to terms with it. A century later Orpheus would stand for the rebirth of opera in Gluck's and Calzabigi's setting of his story. In 1673, as well, he evoked an inevitable, if tacit, comparison with his own past, an implicit confrontation with the original ideals of opera. He had in effect always been waiting in the wings, ready to reappear when needed, either as an actor or as an observer of his own art.

Aureli, accustomed to weaving fantasy around a kernel of *historia*, per-formed his usual operation on the Orpheus myth, using it as the basis of a conventional Venetian plot in the Faustini mold. To obtain the standard double pair of lovers, he added Aristeo (a legitimate addition adopted from Virgil's version of the myth),[3] who competes with Orfeo for Euridice's affections, and

---

3. Aristaeus, who also appeared in the Orpheus operas of Buti/Rossi (1647) and Offenbach (1858), played an important role in the earliest dramatic ren-dering of the Orpheus myth, Angelo Poliziano's *Fabula d'Orfeo* (1480). On the significance of Poli-ziano's *Orfeo* for the development of opera, see Pir-rotta, *Music and Theatre*, ch. 1, "Orpheus, Singer of *Strambotti*."

Autonoe, who loves Aristeo (her spouse in Greek mythology). Comic relief comes from the conventional nurse (Eurinda, serving Euridice) and squire (Orillo, serving Orfeo); and a subplot is provided by the actions of Achille, Chirone, Ercole, and Esculapio (Orfeo's brother and the only one bearing even the slightest relationship to the main plot), who are exploited for a variety of conventional purposes. Achilles, as we recall from (inter alia) *La finta pazza*, was sent into hiding by his mother, Thetis, to protect him against his fate in the Trojan War. In Aureli's *Orfeo*, his legendary musical studies with the centaur Chirone provide an excuse for the introduction of a conventional singing scene.

In addition to the extra personnel, who help to turn this story into a typical Venetian libretto—they also include the gods Pluto, Tetide, and Bacco—the events of the myth itself are distorted and rearranged. But Aureli's *invenzione* goes well beyond mere *dimostrazione*. The operatic implications of the myth charge his emphases and omissions with special significance. They cannot but comment on the state of opera in 1673. The most basic events of the myth are: the death of Eurydice from a snakebite; Orpheus's desperation and determination to rescue her from the clutches of death; his plea to the Underworld, a test of his powers as a poet and musician—the quintessentially operatic action; her restoration; her second death; and, finally, his renunciation of womankind. All these are present in Aureli's text, but each is purposely perverted. The poet managed to incorporate some of the most important operatic conventions of the day, at the same time as he systematically reduced the stature of Orpheus as hero.

Euridice dies from the snakebite while being chased by Orfeo's rival, Aristeo. But this ostensibly crucial event hardly precipitates all of the action of the drama: since it does not take place until the end of Act 2, it is as much the result of previous actions as the cause of subsequent ones. Indeed, it occurs only after Orfeo himself has attempted to kill Euridice out of jealousy, has actually threatened to pursue her to Hades for the purpose of doing so—an ironic anticipation and inversion of his traditional course of action—and has subsequently enlisted his servant Orillo to accomplish the deed.

Hypocritically, then, and rather weakly, Orfeo laments her loss, which he had himself tried to engineer, but the emotional drain of lamentation tires him and he falls asleep (sleep scene). He eventually does follow Euridice to Hades, but only after she herself has urged it on him in a dream (invocation scene), during which she sings a passionate lament (descending tetrachord aria). He wins her release, but the prayer, which counts as his most singular act of musical heroism, is never heard. It occurs off stage, between scenes, out of earshot of the audience—who learn of it only from Pluto's report: "Orpheus, you have won. Your sonorous song has placated the furies and softened hell." ("Orfeo, vincesti. Il canto tuo sonoro / Placcò le furie e raddolcì l'Inferno"

[3.13]). (To increase the irony of the omission, Sartorio's setting of this report is extremely elaborate and florid, as if Pluto rather than Orpheus were the legendary singer.) On their return to earth, despite all Euridice's warnings and pleas, Orfeo insists upon looking back at her. At her second death, he does finally sing an impassioned lament, but no sooner has he finished than he launches into a strongly contrasting aria in which he happily renounces all womankind (cantabile-cabaletta combination; use of comic style for incongruity). Whereas in the myth his renunciation is filled with bitter passion, eventually culminating in his own violent death, here it becomes the subject of a comic aria.

By expunging, inverting, or parodying all of the scenes in which Orpheus had traditionally proven his mythic valor, Aureli dissuades us from recognizing him as the hero of this opera. Euridice, in fact, is clearly the more heroic of the two. In addition to planning her own rescue from the Underworld, she remains steadfast in her love for Orfeo and adamant in her respect for the law and her adherence to Pluto's decree.[4]

Nor is the audience encouraged either by Aureli or Sartorio to appreciate Orfeo as a musician. Every other character seems to have usurped his traditional musical functions. Achille rather than Orfeo is the "singer" of the opera (he sings a song in Orfeo's music room); Euridice sings the tetrachord lament we would have expected from him; and in describing to the audience Orfeo's triumph over the Furies, Pluto actually sings Orfeo's elaborate Underworld prayer.

The mythological operatic hero has been transformed into a jealous Venetian husband, a character whom anyone in the audience would have recognized easily enough. Orpheus's altered identity, his demotion to Everyman, is acknowledged by the titles affixed to revivals of the opera: *Orfeo o sia Amore spesso inganna* (Brunswick, 1690) and *Orfeo a torto geloso* (Bologna, 1695).[5] Although audiences must have appreciated the ironies of the once-heroic musician's transformation and enjoyed the role played in it by their favorite operatic conven-

---

4. Although representing a reversal in terms of the myth, the treatment of Eurydice here resembles that in many earlier Venetian librettos in which the heroism of women was exalted over that of men, emphasizing their moral superiority. Those that immediately come to mind are Erismena and Doriclea, but there were many others. Indeed, the heroic treatment of women in Venetian opera is a topic worthy of further investigation. Within the growing literature on seventeenth-century Italian feminism, see, for example, Ginevra Conti Odorisio, *Donna e società nel seicento* (Rome, 1979), esp. ch. 5, "La Storia. La donna colta e la donna forte. Il mito delle Amazzoni."

5. The revivals of *Orfeo* are listed in Sartori, "Primo tentativo." Orpheus's demotion is enhanced by his absence from the final three scenes of the opera; the *lieto fine* is accomplished without him. Aureli's refusal to conclude the opera with the conventional reunion of both pairs of lovers provides yet another ironic twist. In adhering closely to this one aspect of the myth, Aureli has provided his audience with yet another unexpected novelty. Having prepared them throughout the opera to expect details of the myth to be altered in the service of Venetian conventions, he surprises them by failing to end the opera conventionally.

tions, the transformation itself was symbolic of something they probably could not fully have appreciated, at least not all of them. It represented the erosion of operatic decorum. In surrendering his heritage and sinking to the level of the audience, Orpheus personified the decline that the Arcadians were soon to ascribe to Cicognini's influence. Like Orpheus, opera, too, had lost its stature.

Il volgo tumultuario

The conditions that contributed to the fall of Orpheus in 1673 were reflected in other developments as well. In the very next year, the two-theater monopoly that had dominated operatic activities for more than a decade was broken. Newly revitalized, the Teatro S. Moisè, which had unsuccessfully threatened the monopoly some years earlier (in 1666), entered into competition with SS. Giovanni e Paolo and S. Salvatore. And the S. Moisè's new manager, Francesco Santurini, incurred the enmity of his competitors by reducing the price of admission. The change was lamented by Ivanovich, among others.[6] He regarded it as undermining the level of operatic entertainment, and alluded to it passionately several times during the course of his "Memorie teatrali" before devoting an entire chapter to a discussion of its deleterious effects.[7] In Ivanovich's view, reduced ticket prices, besides limiting the funds available for operatic productions and therefore diminishing their grandeur, lowered the social level of the audience to include ignorant and disruptive crowds.[8]

Santurini's move, strongly opposed by the other theater managements, met with great popular success.[9] Despite the notoriously small size of S. Moisè, the price reduction was so profitable that it encouraged him to seek the usual patrician support for the construction of a new, larger theater, where he could expand the practice. The first new opera house in nearly three decades, the Teatro S. Angelo opened for business in 1677.[10] The new theater was still relatively small, but its modern facilities and central location combined with the reduced price of admission attracted a large audience, forcing the competing theaters to lower their prices as well—S. Salvatore in 1677, SS. Giovanni e Paolo in 1680.[11]

6. This was big operatic news, as indicated by the fact that it is mentioned repeatedly in reports from Venice to the duke of Brunswick (Appendix IIIB.12 and 16b). The other theaters evidently felt the competition, as indicated by a remark in the *avviso* of 30 January 1683 (Appendix IIIC.3).

7. For earlier allusions, some of them quite thinly veiled, see Appendix II.6l, m, and v.

8. See Appendix II.6x.

9. As reported in several letters from Massi to the duke of Brunswick; see Appendix IIIB.14 and 15.

10. Until 1677 the Teatro S. Apollinare, con-

structed in 1650, had been the newest opera house. The Teatro S. Samuele had been constructed more recently, in 1655, but for the purpose of spoken drama rather than opera. See Mangini, *I teatri di Venezia*, 70.

11. The whole story is related by Ivanovich (Appendix II.6x, y): "Profits at the door, the basis of the business investment, instead of growing are diminishing, evidently endangering the continuation of this noble entertainment. The low price eliminates the possibility of maintaining the customary splendor, allows entry to the ignorant and riotous multi-

Although other factors were certainly involved, perhaps the most significant result of Santurini's move was the opening in 1678 of yet another new theater, the Teatro S. Giovanni Grisostomo (Figs. 27, 28), by the most important theatrical entrepreneurs of the period, the brothers Grimani, proprietors of SS. Giovanni e Paolo (and of the prose theater of S. Samuele as well). While these shrewd businessmen eventually bowed to competition by reducing the price of admission to their older opera house, they retained the traditional higher price for their new one, thus asserting its social distinction. It was clearly their aim to maintain a certain decorum. Larger, better equipped, and more magnificent than any other theater of the seventeenth century, the Teatro S. Giovanni Grisostomo eventually became a symbol of the restoration of decorum to Venetian opera as a whole.[12]

The decline of operatic standards could not be ascribed exclusively to the influence of the "volgo tumultuario." As Ivanovich explained when he returned to the subject, the causes ("abusi correnti") were intrinsic to the works themselves and to the system that nourished them. Commercial considerations and the rule of the marketplace had so eroded the ethics of librettists that they

---

tudes, and causes those virtuous works performed no less for delight than for profit to lose their decorum. The first year in which musical dramas appeared in Venice was 1637. The price of a ticket, which served as passport to the theater, was set at the reasonable sum of four lire. That lasted unchanged, no matter what misfortunes affected the various theaters, until 1674, and would be the same today if in that year Francesco Santurini, having at his disposal the Teatro S. Moisè, which he had rented at an advantageous fee that included sets and materials supplied the previous season through the generosity of an academy, and with a mediocre company of singers, had not violated the integrity of custom by lowering ticket prices to a quarter of a ducat [= two lire]. This novelty was a universal success; whereupon, enriched by his profits, and seeing himself prevented from continuing at the S. Moisè, he decided to build the Teatro Sant'Angelo with the help of donations for boxes, and to charge the same admission fee in 1677. . . . Examples of novelty are willingly embraced when they have beneficial results. A drop of more than half in their receipts was detrimental to those competing theaters used to counting on the usual fee of four lire, with the result that the famous Teatro SS. Giovanni e Paolo, after forty years of charging a decorous price of admission, reduced its ticket prices in 1679, and, following its example, San Salvatore and San Cassiano did the same in 1680, leaving only the new Teatro S. Giovanni Grisostomo charging the old rates." See also Mangini, I teatri di Venezia, 45.

The price differential was very well known, to judge from the remarks from Le Mercure galant quoted in n. 12 below. According to a description in the March 1683 issue of the French journal, the Teatro S. Angelo contained five rows of boxes, with twenty-nine boxes in a row. The slightly larger S. Cassiano, SS. Giovanni e Paolo, and S. Salvatore had the same number of rows with thirty-one, thirty-two, and thirty-three boxes per row respectively. S. Apollinare had only three rows of fifteen boxes each. The relevant passages from Le Mercure galant, by Chassebras de Cremailles (remarks later collected and published by Vaumorière, Lettres), are quoted in Mangini, I teatri di Venezia, passim; see also Worsthorne, Venetian Opera, ch. 3, and Saunders, "Repertoire," nn. 1.22 and 1.25.
12.   On the Teatro S. Giovanni Grisostomo, in addition to Saunders, "Repertoire," see Mangini, I teatri di Venezia, 77–83. The new theater made a special impression on foreign observers, to judge from the reports of Cremailles [and Tessin] in Le Mercure galant, April 1679, 75–94, quoted in Selfridge-Field, Pallade veneta, 341–42: "Quant au Théâtre de S. Jean Christome, fait cette année mesme, il a remporté le prix sur tous les autres, tant pour sa somptuosité que pour la simphonie, musiciens, décorations, et machines. Ce n'est que de l'or au dehors des loges. Le dedans est tapissé de velours de damas, et des plus riches etofes qui se fassent à Venise." See also the issue of 20 February 1683, 230–309, signed by Chassebras de Cremailles (Selfridge-Field, Pallade veneta, 346–52).

27. Teatro S. Giovanni Grisostomo. Engraving from Vincenzo Maria Coronelli, *Venezia festeggiante* . . . (Venice, 1709). Venice, Biblioteca del Civico Museo Correr.

regularly stooped to plagiarism of all kinds, even trampling on the bonds of friendship in the process: "They steal not only the cleverest incidents but *ariette* and whole lines of poetry too, by using the pretense of friendship, the artifice of ostensible familiarity, nor is there any longer a secure path to trust."[13] Plagiarism had been a cause for concern for some time, and the "borrowing" of individual scenes was commonplace. The transfer of whole arias from one work to another, a more recent phenomenon, was a somewhat different matter, however. It was acknowledged only occasionally, as in the printer's prefaces to *Argia* (1669) and *Antigona* (1670):

13. Ivanovich's most stinging criticisms, including this one, are found at the end of his essay in a response to the Marchese Obizzi of Ferrara, who had written him a letter on the history of opera in Venice (Appendix II.6hh–jj).

28. Entrance ticket for the Teatro S. Giovanni Grisostomo. Venice, Biblioteca del
Civico Museo Correr (Cod. Cicogna 2991/II).

You will notice a few arias heard on another occasion; but because it is known that
they were taken from this drama they have been left in, because they are both few
and of singular exquisiteness. (Appendix I.55)
If you recognize the beauty of some of Ziani's ariettas that you have heard before,
either in Venice or in the Imperial Court, understand that everything was done with
the single aim of pleasing you more. (Appendix I.51)

But the practice was clearly more widespread. We recall that by the 1660s
singers were being permitted, if not encouraged, to bring their own arias with
them. The very fact that wholesale lifting of musical and textual materials could
occur at all is in itself symptomatic of the decline of the genre: it assumed the
conventionality of the arias, trading on their loss of musico-dramatic specificity.

As a further cause of generic erosion, Ivanovich cited librettists' mistreat-
ment of their sources, the lacerations, distortions, and anachronisms perpetrated by them in their attempts to create something new:

> With indiscreet freedom they begin to make mincemeat of the libretto, and with the caprice of those few who pretend to set universal standards, they lacerate, they displace, they decompose the model, they jostle the invention, they deform the disposition, and make the locution worse, so that what is exposed in public is a deformed product, like the statue in Athens. Passing now to a consideration of the success of such works, and what one can expect from a composition distorted by so many alterations, no scruple is attached to anachronisms; no defect seen if the history or fable is changed. (Appendix II.6ii)

Ivanovich's final attack was multipronged. Moving to the question of decorum of genre and language, he decried in rapid succession the lowering of tone, the confusion of serious and comic elements, the destruction of linguistic propriety, the domination of the arias, and, perhaps most significant of all, the elimination of emotion: "It is considered a small error that the same style is used for the heroic and the ridiculous; that the pathetic element, which is the soul of the drama, is restricted, that the *ariette* take the place of the necessary recitative" (Appendix II.6jj).

Ivanovich's remarks acquire substance from their relevance to Aureli's and Sartorio's *Orfeo*. They can even be read as a critical response to that work insofar as it represents all works of the period. As we have seen, many of the key moments of *Orfeo* involved familiar techniques and scene-types (not demonstrably the result of plagiarism but rather of convention): the sleep scene, the ghost scene, the scene in the music room, the lament on the descending tetrachord. The source of *Orfeo* was certainly mistreated; deconstructed, rearranged, and deformed, it was subjected to numerous anachronisms.[14] Furthermore, the opera was virtually defined by its mixture of the heroic and the ridiculous. The validity of Ivanovich's remarks is confirmed by *Orfeo*, and they in turn affirm the representative nature of Sartorio's and Aureli's work.

In Defense of Decorum

The professed aim of Ivanovich's book, as we learn from the dedication, was to glorify his aristocratic patrons, the Grimani brothers, "whose theaters are admired by the whole world" (Appendix II.6a). With their magnificent theaters and generous profusion of gold, these "true Apollos . . . allow the most elevated meters and the most exquisite voices to be heard" (Appendix II.6b). They will prevent any further erosion of decorum. Their theatrical abilities are all the more powerful for being inherited, as Ivanovich recognized in ascribing to their "great progenitors" the responsibility for having resurrected theaters equal in

14. Aureli actually apologized for showing Achilles and Hercules together even though they lived at different times, hardly the most striking anachronism in this particular libretto; see Rosand, "L'Ovidio trasformato," XXVII.

splendor to those of ancient Rome (Appendix II.6c). The Grimani, of course, in the person of their illustrious uncle, Giovanni, had been responsible for the founding of the theater at SS. Giovanni e Paolo in 1639, one of the earliest and grandest opera houses in Venice. And the family had been active in the affairs of a number of other theaters as well, most recently, as Ivanovich emphasized, with the erection of the magnificent new Teatro S. Giovanni Grisostomo, which merits a special celebratory sonnet just after the dedicatory message.[15]

After the dedication and sonnet, Ivanovich continued to compliment his patrons during the course of the volume, although somewhat more obliquely. His concern with decorum and ticket prices, for example, turns into an implicit tribute to their high standards and lofty aims. They alone refused to descend to the level of cheap competition by lowering prices (Appendix II.6y). And in the chapter entitled "The Number of Theaters There Were and Are at Present in Venice and the Date of Their Founding" (Appendix II.6o), his description of S. Giovanni Grisostomo is more elaborate than that of the other theaters, containing a number of flattering, if gratuitous, details: "The eleventh [theater], at San Giovanni Grisostomo, [was] erected with admirable speed in the year 1678 by Giovanni Carlo and the Abbot Vincenzo, the Grimani brothers, Antonio's sons, nephews and heirs of the abovementioned Giovanni, who thus showed that they had inherited his magnificence as well as his virtuosic genius, making the nobility of lineage and spirit all the more conspicuous" (Appendix II.6r).[16]

Ivanovich's special appreciation of the Grimani brothers and of their new theater for maintaining aesthetic standards may have been the obligatory response of a courtier to his patrons and therefore rather rhetorical. His relationship with the family, after all, had been a long one; it went back at least to 1663, when he wrote the libretto of *Amor guerriero* for SS. Giovanni e Paolo, which was then under the direction of the brothers' uncle, Giovanni (d. 1663). But his respect for them and their new theater was not misplaced. For the Grimani brothers, at S. Giovanni Grisostomo, were eventually instrumental in promoting the "reform" that Ivanovich's criticism of "abusi correnti" implicitly called for. The older of the two brothers, Giovanni Carlo, was a statesman and diplomat with many connections in Rome. His interests were strongly academic, and he was an important patron of the arts and of men of letters. In 1691, at his home in Venice, aided by the family's young secretary, Apostolo Zeno, Gio-

---

15. The sonnet is entitled: "Nella maravigliosa nuova erezione del Teatro Grimano a San Giovanni Grisostomo." For a discussion of the importance of the Grimani family as patrons of opera, see Saunders, "Repertoire," ch. 1: "The Grimani Brothers as Theatrical Entrepreneurs." The Grimani also took over the lease of Teatro S. Salvatore for ten years, begin-

ning in 1687, but the arrangement lasted for only two years. See ibid., 26 and n. 1.96, and Mangini, *I teatri di Venezia*, 54.

16. Rather than emphasizing the Grimani's earlier theaters, Ivanovich merely quoted Martinioni on the erection of SS. Giovanni e Paolo and S. Samuele by Giovanni Grimani (Appendix II.6n).

vanni Carlo founded the Accademia degli Animosi, which became incorporated as a colony of the Roman Arcadian academy in 1698.[17]

The relationship of Arcadian literary theory to the reform of opera at the end of the seventeenth century has been the subject of much scholarly attention. The Arcadians themselves were to spill considerable ink over the topic of opera, as the most visible and popular manifestation of the general decadence in Italian literature that they wished to reform. Their widely publicized views on the reasons for the decline and the sources of salvation, exemplified by the remarks of Crescimbeni quoted earlier, and by those of other writers, eventually succeeded in promoting a restoration of literary standards to the "decadent" genre.[18]

Giovanni Carlo Grimani, then, represented a direct link between opera in Venice and the impending Arcadian reform. Indeed, so-called reform librettos made their first Venetian appearance on the stage of S. Giovanni Grisostomo shortly after 1690.[19] But even before 1691, when the Accademia degli Animosi began to exercise a classicizing effect on the repertory of S. Giovanni Grisostomo, the predilection of the Grimani brothers for a stricter sense of decorum was manifested at that theater in various ways: in its high entrance fee, and consequent cultivation of a particularly aristocratic audience, and in productions that were not only consistently more elaborately staged but generally more elevated in tone than those of other theaters, eschewing the sexual explicitness that characterized many operas of the 1680s.[20] The contrast is particularly vivid between the two Grimani theaters. The older SS. Giovanni e Paolo, with reduced prices, continued to employ professional librettists like Aureli, and to perform such patently decadent works as *Alcibiade* (1680) and *Dionisio ovvero la virtù trionfante del vizio* (1681). In the newer theater, on the other hand, ancient Roman themes predominated, and librettists were increasingly drawn from the higher reaches of society. Conceivably the Grimani brothers were intentionally exploiting both ends of the market, depending on

17.   On the Animosi and its relationship to the Roman Arcadians, including relevant bibliography, see Saunders, "Repertoire," ch. 2, nn. 6, 7.
18.   On Arcadian opera criticism, see ibid., ch. 4; also Freeman, *Opera without Drama*, ch. 1. Although Freeman includes extensive translations of Arcadian writings, their usefulness is limited by their inaccuracy and the absence of the original texts.
19.   These include such works as Adriano Morselli's *L'incoronazione di Serse* (1691) and *Ibraim sultano* (1692), both based on French models (by Corneille and Racine, respectively), as well as Domenico David's notorious *La forza della virtù* (1693), which

inspired a spirited defense from members of the Accademia degli Animosi and which was once, prematurely, dubbed "the first reform libretto" (by Nathaniel Burt, "Opera in Arcadia," *MQ* 41 [1955]: 145–70). For a comprehensive recent view of the position of the Arcadians on opera reform, see Renato di Benedetto, "Poetiche e polemiche," *StOpIt*, 6 (Turin, 1988): 3–76, esp. 16–30.
20.   This sexual explicitness was a manifestation of the "vizio di Venere" attributed to Venetian society by one commentator of this period. See Bianconi and Walker, "Production," 267.

large lower-class audiences in one theater to support their extravagances in the other.[21]

The exalted image of the Teatro S. Giovanni Grisostomo persisted well into the eighteenth century. It was apparently the only opera house in Venice to resist the general invasion of comic intermezzi that began early in the century, a resistance that inspired the second historian of opera, Carlo Bonlini, to praise its uncompromisingly high standards: "At S. Giovanni Grisostomo [comic intermezzi] were never allowed, that majestic theater having always tried to maintain decorous restraint in all things."[22] And it was the site of a regular series of important *opere serie*—with librettos by such well-known reformers as Zeno, Domenico David, Girolamo Frigimelica Roberti, and Francesco Silvani—from the end of the seventeenth century until 1747, when it ceased to function as an opera house.[23]

In identifying with the accomplishments of the Accademia degli Animosi and in bringing their ideals into the opera house for the purpose of promoting operatic reform, Giovanni Carlo Grimani was reviving an old relationship between opera and the academy. Half a century earlier, we recall, another academy, the Incogniti, had exercised comparable influence on the genre. Its voluminous aesthetic discussions in opera librettos and elsewhere had established the premises for the development of the genre. They had aired the fundamental questions of verisimilitude, linguistic decorum, and adherence to Aristotelian principles, justifying all sorts of evasions and improprieties on the basis of modern taste; and they had invoked precedents drawn from a wide range of historical sources. It was the very improprieties they so avidly defended that, when naturally extended, became the abuses that the Arcadians, invoking their own precedents drawn from the tradition of French classicism, were to condemn and seek to correct. Seicento opera in Venice, then, was bracketed by the activities of two academies, both claiming special influence by virtue of their elaborate propaganda networks.[24]

21.   Several S. Giovanni Grisostomo librettos were published anonymously, suggesting a parallel to the situation in the 1640s when various aristocratic Incogniti withheld their names from libretto publications. These included a few probably by Grimani himself, such as *Elmiro re di Corinto* (1687), set by Pallavicino, *Orazio* (1688), set by Tosi, and *Agrippina* (1710), set by Handel; see Saunders, "Repertoire," 29.

22.   "A S. Gio Grisostomo [gl'intermedi comici] non sono mai stati ammessi, avendo sempre quel Maestoso Teatro cercato in tutto di mantenere un decoroso contegno" ([Bonlini], *Le glorie della poesia e della musica*, 149–50).

23.   On the closing of the theater, see Saunders,

"Repertoire," 26 n. 1.95. Frigimelica Roberti, one of the most important and austere of the neoclassicizing librettists, composed all eleven of his librettos for S. Giovanni Grisostomo (ibid., 78–79; Frigimelica Roberti's librettos are listed on 88). See also Karl Leich, *Girolamo Frigimelica Robertis Libretti (1694–1708): Ein Beitrag insbesondere zur Geschichte des Opernlibrettos in Venedig*, Schriften zur Musik 26 (Munich, 1972).

24.   Saunders ("Repertoire," 79) has argued quite convincingly that it was the academy's active propaganda apparatus that was responsible for the inordinate influence of Zeno and the Arcadians, as opposed to that of other writers such as Frigimelica Roberti, on the reform of opera.

Ivanovich's History and Criticism

Ivanovich may have dedicated his *Minerva al tavolino* to the Grimani brothers and paid them various compliments during the course of his narrative, but his intention in writing the volume—and his achievement—was much grander than mere flattery of a patron. His object was historical: to provide a documented catalogue raisonné of operas performed in Venice, and to supply a historical framework that would help to explain it:

> The introduction of musical dramas took place, as we have already said, in the year 1637 under the Dogate of Francesco Erizzo, and in a time when the Republic enjoyed a most tranquil peace. It is therefore an obligation that so virtuous and delightful an entertainment, introduced in our own day, be registered with precision in all of its worthiest details, so that the memory of it shall not end with the sound of its instruments and voices (as occurred with the tragedies and other theatrical spectacles of Rome, for which there was no one with diligence equal to ours to inform posterity, which now lives in the dark about them), and so that it shall not remain buried among the shadows when the lights that illuminated it are extinguished. So worthy a memory, which challenged the greatest talents to produce the most curious and noble creations that ever appeared to human sight, deserves to be granted immortality, so that the merit of their virtue shall forever stand as an example and stimulus to those who feel inclined to practice it for its greater glory. Thus these "Memorie teatrali di Venezia" are followed by a general catalogue in which, for each work from the year 1637 to the present year, 1681, distinct and accurate mention will be made of the year, the theater, the title of the drama, the name of the author, and that of the composer. (Appendix II.6dd)

Ivanovich, however, like all good historians, was also a critic. He could not refrain from evaluating his material even as he set it down. To this tendency of his we owe the first official, sustained criticism of Venetian opera. But his critical remarks, in particular his repeated references to the decay that had affected the genre, have a familiar ring. For instance:

> The theater was originally, and would now still be, of great benefit if its original decorum had been preserved, if abuses had not occurred, and if imaginations were tempered with more worthy sentiments. (Appendix II.6cc)

In the early years of operatic activity in Venice, the poetry

> was not weighed down by as many concerns as it is at present. Any story was possible, every plot was appreciated, every phrase admired, as in all genres when they are new. These days it is thought a great miracle to encounter the most bizarre and uncommon inventions, structures, and elocutions, so spoiled and exacting have tastes become from being exposed to the sweetest delicacies of virtue. (Appendix II.6bb)

And again:

> In the beginning theaters were not ruled by prices, since discretion and honesty carried some weight and the labors of the artists were better appreciated and tolerated; whereas at present taste has become so exigent that decay has replaced growth. Furthermore, instead of the former profits, debts are incurred because of the excessive payment to singers. At the beginning two exquisite voices, a small number of delightful arias, and a few scene changes sufficed to satisfy the curiosity [of the audience]. Now, one objects if one hears a voice that is not up to European standards; one expects every scene to be accompanied by a change of setting, and that the machines be brought in from another world. (Appendix II.6u)

And finally:

> The . . . success of an opera, whether good or ill, depends on a thousand accidents based for the most part on the extravagant play of ridiculous Fortune, and which usually goes hand in hand with the verdict of the rabble. (Appendix II.6w)

Ivanovich's comments echo concerns, even language, we have already encountered, both among earlier critics of opera, primarily librettists of some thirty years before, and among later ones, like Crescimbeni. Indeed, Ivanovich's observations take their place within a critical tradition as old as Venetian opera itself. It is a tradition that developed along with opera in Venice as a necessary corollary to its self-confirmation as a genre, a genre characterized by intense self-consciousness, by recognition of its own conventions and compromises, and by a keen awareness of its audience—their tastes, prejudices, and expectations.

In lamenting its decline, then, Ivanovich was repeating a recurrent critical theme of the later seventeenth century, one that had concerned even those librettists most guilty of the abuses he decried. His articulation of issues and values familiar from the past affirms the continuity of the tradition of opera in Venice. That continuity was one of its most significant features, manifested most obviously in the persistence of conventions and in the frequent revivals of old works. It was simultaneously maintained and documented in printed librettos, whose very existence was symptomatic of the idiosyncratic economic and social structure of opera in Venice. In addition to advertising and promoting individual works, printed librettos became permanently available as documents, sources of historical information, preservers of conventions, and as potential candidates for revival or *rifacimento*.

Ivanovich acknowledged their function as reminders and inspiration when he justified the three indices that conclude his catalogue:

> The first [index] will be of all the titles of the dramas, and it will be useful for those who compose, to know them in order to avoid [repeating] them, or to vary the choice of the actions of the protagonist, as illustrated by Hercules, with various titles, Alexander, and Pompey. The second will be of all the names of the authors

who have composed them. The third of all the names of the composers of the music. These indices will be useful to many who have the spirit and talent to undertake with virtuous effort the career in a field so laudably trod by the first and foremost pens of the literary republic. (Appendix II.6ee)[25]

Ivanovich himself, as we have seen, had certainly acquired his knowledge of the history of opera as well as of the views of his predecessors by reading the librettos he catalogued. He urged his readers to do the same, promising that they would gain a more accurate appreciation of their quality than that provided by their reputations, which were often based entirely on extraliterary circumstances:

> Varied are the causes, and strange the events that accompany dramas on the stage, each one of which is sufficient to earn or to deny applause for the author. Already some dramas of great merit have been observed to be thwarted by bad luck, to the great surprise of those who professed themselves knowledgeable about such things, either because the choice of singers was only ordinary, or because of weak music, lack of machines, imperfection of sets, or poverty of costumes, all circumstances beyond the author's control, and nonetheless all of them injurious to his success. On the other hand, some dramas filled with the most monstrous defects, intolerable for their structure and their elocution, have been favored in the competition, either because of a special voice heard again, or for music of unusual meter, or for a machine of eccentric invention. In sum, it would seem that destiny, for the most part, favors those of least merit. From the reading of the dramas cited in the catalogue of the present "Memorie," it will now be possible for those skilled writers who have employed their talents nobly to hope to win from the objective judgment of posterity the praise they deserve; better than the present situation where it is denied to them because of the natural inclination to envy the fame of outstanding men while they live and to praise them only when they are dead. (Appendix II.6gg)

Tradition and Revival

The Venetian tradition consciously sustained itself in a variety of ways. Librettists' prefaces sometimes read like litanies or operatic curricula vitae. Most revivals and *rifacimenti* were clearly (and proudly) acknowledged as such, even on the title pages.[26] Such revivals and *rifacimenti* may well have been motivated by a shortage of new librettos or new subjects, but, rather than suffering for being derivative or unoriginal, they apparently claimed special status by virtue of pedigree, by the very fact of having had a past.

25. See also the passage from *Minerva*, ch. 19, 423: "onde in ogni tempo apparisca il merito della Virtù ad esempio, ed eccitamento di chi n'avrà genio d'esercitarla à sua maggior gloria" (Appendix II.6dd).

26. Sometimes the citation of earlier performances or sources was obviously intended to increase the impact of the work, as in the Faustini revivals already discussed, like *Eritrea* of 1661. See also the revivals of *Ciro* (1665), *Orontea* (1666), *Giasone* (1666), *Dori* (1667), *Alessandro amante* (1667), a "rifacimento" of *Gli amori d'Alessandro magno, e di Rossane* (1651), *Seleuco* (1668), *Semiramide* and *Ercole in Tebe* (1670), *Dori* (1671), previously heard in 1663 and 1667, and *Scipione affricano* (1678).

Many revivals involved the new setting of an old text. Scores, it must not be forgotten, were not published and so were less readily available than librettos. But old music was often reused as well, if it could be found. This is clear from a complaint regarding the difficulty encountered both in locating and in adjusting the original music of Cesti's *Dori* for a revival in 1667.[27] Since the work had been performed as recently as four years earlier at S. Salvatore, presumably the problem was not overwhelming. And since the previous performance had not been the first, there were probably multiple scores in circulation.[28] The difficulty must have been immeasurably greater in 1683, however, when Cesti's nearly thirty-year-old *Orontea* was revived at SS. Giovanni e Paolo: "At SS. Giovanni e Paolo they are rehearsing another new opera called *Orontea*, which, it is hoped, despite the fact that it was performed here years ago, will be successful, since it has quite a lot of humor and is the work of the reliable pen of Cesti."[29] Interestingly, although the reporter of this occasion expressed some concern about the antiquated nature of the score, he was reassured by Cesti's reputation, as well as by the humor in the libretto. Clearly, the underlying assumption here was one of stylistic continuity. While some operas underwent considerable alteration that involved aspects of dramaturgy, others could be brought up to date merely by the addition of new arias and sometimes, as we saw with *Giasone*, the excision of recitative passages as well.[30]

The relative stability of opera in seventeenth-century Venice, maintained through the persistence of powerful musical and dramatic conventions, is underscored by a comparison with a non-Venetian opera that was revived in Venice thirty years after its first performance, Monteverdi's *Arianna*. Modern, not to say pathbreaking, in the Mantua of 1608, the work was a complete

27.   "Si è incontrato molte difficoltà così nel trovare l'originale della musica, come nell'aggiustarlo" (*La Dori overo lo schiavo reggio Dramma per musica da rappresentarsi nel Nobilissimo Teatro Grimano di SS. Giovanni e Paolo L'Anno 1667* [Venice: Nicolini & Curti], preface).

28.   This is an assumption confirmed by the comparatively large number of scores still extant. On the sources of *Dori*, see Carl B. Schmidt, " 'La Dori' di Antonio Cesti: Sussidi bibliografici," *RIM* 11 (1976): 197–229, esp. 211–13 on the scores.

29.   "A SS Giovanni e Paolo si fanno le prove d'altro nuovo Dramma chiamato l'Orontea che sperasi non ostante che anni sono fù esso qui rappresentato riuscirà di comune sodisfatione il havere assai del ridicolo et essere compositione dell'accreditata penna del Cesti" (*avviso* of 13 February 1683, I-Vnm, It. VI, 460 [12104], Mercuri o Gazette settimanali). The original setting of Cicognini's libretto, in 1649, was the work of Francesco Lucio (see n. 31 below).

30.   On the modifications to *Erismena* of 1655 for a production in 1670, which were quite substantial, see Powers, "Erismena," 259–324; see also id., "Il *Mutio* tramutato*, Part I: Sources and Libretto," in *Venezia e il melodramma nel seicento*, ed. Maria Teresa Muraro (Florence, 1976), 227–58. A number of other operas that were revived over several decades lend themselves well to the study of revisions. These include Cesti's *Orontea*, *Dori* (the subject of exhaustive study by Carl B. Schmidt: "Antonio Cesti's *La Dori*: A Study of Sources, Performance Traditions, and Musical Style," *RIM* 10 [1975]: 455–98, and " 'La Dori' di Antonio Cesti: Sussidi bibliografici"), and *Argia*. Even those operas revived within a few years of their first performance, however, such as Ziani's *Antigona delusa da Alceste* or *Le fortune di Rodope e Damira*, reveal interesting changes that affect the proportion of recitative and aria, the structure of dramatic units, and even the portrayal of character.

anachronism in the Venice of 1640. The alterations made in the libretto, such as the elimination of choruses, could not possibly have brought it into line with contemporary Venetian practice. Only Monteverdi's enormous reputation at the time could have sustained *Arianna* in Venice. In its new context—surrounded by such works as Strozzi's and Manelli's *Delia*, Busenello's and Cavalli's *Gli amori d'Apollo e di Dafne*, or Ferrari's *Il pastor regio*, and especially Monteverdi's own, only slightly later *Il ritorno d'Ulisse* and *L'incoronazione di Poppea*—*Arianna* must have stood out as an anomaly, constructed for a different kind of audience at a very different phase in the evolution of opera. The libretto of *Orontea*, however, performed in 1649, 1666, and 1683—even with much of the same music—could remain essentially unchanged.[31]

Indeed, the preservation and appreciation of their own tradition by the Venetian public, and the availability of old music, are wonderfully illustrated in the prologue to a revival of Cesti's *Argia* in 1669. It is set in a library of musical scores, a variation on the scene in the music room. These Apollo, Piacere, and three Muses remove one after another from the shelves to evaluate them for possible performance and to sing arias from them, including one from the more than ten-year-old *Hipermestra* (Cavalli/Moniglia, 1658).[32]

It was this very continuity, self-consciously developed and maintained, that constituted and confirmed the generic identity of Venetian opera. Regularity of demand, dependability of economic support, and predictability of audience, all of these features, unique to seventeenth-century Venice, had combined to sustain the establishment of the new, distinct, and permanent art form, one that carried within itself all the premises of its future development. Once firmly established—in fact, even before then—opera began to spread from its Venetian matrix. The Febiarmonici, always on the move, transported it up and down the

31. The *Orontea* librettos are discussed in Holmes, "Giacinto Andrea Cicognini's and Antonio Cesti's *Orontea*," 108. Morelli and Walker convincingly ascribe the first (1649) setting of Cicognini's libretto, a score that is now lost, to Francesco Lucio ("Migliori plettri," CXXXIV–CXL). Cesti's setting was the second, composed for Innsbruck in 1656 and revived in Venice in 1683.
32. The two other scores from which arias were sung seem to have been more recent, however. They were *Fabio Massimo* and *Il ratto delle Sabine*, which, according to Apollo, "d'un istessa penna ambi son parti." The latter may refer to a work by Draghi and Minato that was not performed until four years later in Vienna. But Minato's preface to that work indicates that it had originally been written for Venice. As for *Fabio Massimo*, the title does not correspond to

any known Venetian opera or any work by Draghi and Minato; but perhaps Fabio Massimo refers to a prominent character in another opera, such as *L'amor della patria superiore ad ogn'altro* (Sbarra/Kerll, Munich, 1665), or *Marcello in Siracusa* (Noris/Boretti, Venice, 1670). Since the music for this prologue has not survived, and since the texts of the borrowed arias are not given in the libretto, we cannot be sure which arias were actually sung, although several are described in some detail in the libretto by the second muse: the one from *Fabio Massimo* is a love song sung by Fabio "a Regia donzella"; and one of the two from *Il ratto delle Sabine* is sung by Mirena and Heraclea, the other by Romolo "ch'assalito ad un tempo dal Tracio Nume, e dal Bambin di Gnido, Teme il Guerriero Dio men di Cupido."

peninsula for occasional performances, beginning as early as 1640 in Bologna. Eventually, stable theaters, with their own regular repertories, mostly borrowed from Venice, began to emerge in centers like Florence, Milan, Bologna, Genoa, Rome, Naples, and Palermo, none of them remotely resembling Venice in their social structure.[33] But by then opera had been fully formed; it no longer required the nurture of the Venetian hothouse environment.

What had been worked out by the middle of the century in Venice had become permanent. Yet it was never taken for granted. The issues that both challenged and inspired generic definition—questions of verisimilitude, distinctions between speech and song, propriety of style and language, play with illusion and reality in the three dimensions of music, words, and setting—were repeatedly addressed and resolved, in Venice and elsewhere, throughout the seventeenth century and beyond.

Orpheus's Venetian appearance in 1673 confirms the persistent relevance of these issues. As the character with the most legitimate claim to musical speech and action, his antiheroism in Venice is a direct challenge to operatic verisimilitude. His refusal to accept his role, to be himself, reaffirms the vitality of the operatic paradox. His subsequent appearances elsewhere, in other guises, under other conditions, would revive the same basic issues. From Gluck's and Calzabigi's eighteenth-century Vienna to Offenbach's nineteenth-century Parisian Underworld to Harrison Birtwistle's twentieth-century Thatcherized Britain, he boldly proclaimed his identity, raising and resolving anew the question of the legitimacy of opera.

Although Venice maintained its position as the major operatic center of Italy to the end of the eighteenth century, with the largest number of active theaters, by the end of the seventeenth it had yielded its operatic hegemony. New works were regularly being created elsewhere. But Venice left a permanent imprint on the genre. Responsive and relevant, exploiting the ambiguous power of multiple means of expression combined, the genre that so fascinated audiences in Venice, that was so effectively nourished by the Venetian climate, still lives. The creative ambiguity that was formally recognized and concretized

33. The situation is somewhat more complicated. Courtly patronage persisted in Medici Florence, for example. Also there had been operatic activity before the Febiarmonici in Florence. This situation is outlined in Bianconi, *Seventeenth Century*, 190–204. The diffusion of Venetian opera through Italy is discussed in Bianconi and Walker, "Dalla 'Finta pazza.' " For Florence, see Weaver and Weaver, *Florentine Theater*; for Naples, Bianconi, "Funktionen des Operntheaters in Neapel"; for Turin, see the various studies of Mercedes Viale Ferrero, including "Repliche a Torino di alcuni melodrammi veneziani e loro caratteristiche," in *Venezia e il melodramma nel seicento*, ed. Maria Teresa Muraro (Florence, 1976), 145–72; for Bologna, see Corrado Ricci, *I teatri di Bologna* (Bologna, 1888); for Rome, Alessandro Ademollo, *I teatri di Roma nel secolo decimosettimo* (Rome, 1888), and Per Bjurström, *Feast and Theater in Queen Christina's Rome* (Stockholm, 1966); for Genoa, see Remo Giazotto, *La musica a Genova nella vita pubblica e privata dal XIII al XVIII secolo* (Genoa, 1951), and Ivaldi, "Gli Adorno," 87–152.

by terminological consensus in the acceptance of *dramma per musica* in midseventeenth-century Venice has continued to animate opera. The same self-questioning, self-assertion, and self-definition are inherent in virtually every subsequent descriptive subtitle affixed to the genre: *opera seria, opera buffa, tragédie lyrique,* grand opera, melodrama, *azione teatrale, dramma lirico, Musiktheater,* even *Gesamtkunstwerk*—all recapitulate the aesthetic issues first elaborated in the opera workshop of seventeenth-century Venice.

Appendix I: Librettos

◆   ◆   ◆

1. Pio Enea degli Obizzi, *Ermiona* (Padua: Frambotto, 1638)

Giravano d'intorno intorno cinque file di loggie l'una sopraposta all'altra con parapetti avanti à balaustri di marmo, distinguevano gli Spazi commodi à sedeci spettatori alcuni tramezi, che terminavano nella parte esteriore à forgia di colonne, dove si sporgevano in fuore braccia di legno innargentate, che sostenevano i doppieri, ch'illuminavano il Teatro. Le due più alte, e più lontane file erano ripiene di cittadinanza, nella terza sedevano i signori Scolari, e i nobili stranieri, il secondo come luogo più degno era dei Sig. Rettori e de' Nobili veneti, e nel primo se ne stavano le gentildonne, e i principali gentilhuomini della città. (description by Nicolò Enea Bartolini, p. 8)

2. Benedetto Ferrari, *Andromeda* (Bariletti, 6 May 1637)

a. A Gloria de' Signori Musici ch'al numero di sei (coll'Autore collegati) hanno con gran magnificenza, ed' esquisitezza, à tutte loro spese, e di qualche consideratione, rappresentata l'Andromeda, e per gusto non meno, di chi non l'hà veduta, hò stimato cosa convenevole il farne un breve racconto in questa forma.

b. Sparita la Tenda si vide la Scena tutta mare; con una lontananza così artifitiosa d'acque, e di scogli, che la naturalezza, di quella (ancor che finta) movea dubbio a' Riguardanti, se veramente fossero in un Teatro, ò in una spiaggia di mare effettiva. (printer's preface, pp. 5–6)

3. Ferrari, *La maga fulminata* (Bariletti, 6 February 1638)

a. E' da lei stata goduta, & applaudita nel Theatro; non fia per dispiacerle nel Gabinetto. Bella Dama alletta in publico, diletta in privato. Già presentai all'Eccellenza Vostra canorii tributi della mia riverente servitù; hora glieli porgo poetici; perch'io voglio, ch'il mio ossequio verso di lei gareggi di durabilità con gli anni; e (se mi fosse concesso) lo vorrei addottare per figlio all'Eternità. (dedication)

b. Se l'Andromeda, del Signor Benedetto Ferrari l'anno adietro rappresentata in Musica dilettò in estremo, il presente Anno, la sua Maga fulminata hà fulminato gli animi di meraviglia. Non contento d'haver addolcite l'onde dell'Adria col non più inteso suono della sua dolcissima Tiorba, con i concerti delicatissimi di doi volumi di Musica da lui fatti stampare, n hà voluto anco far d'oro questo clima con i caratteri oscuri d'una penna. A me toccò di dare alle Stampe la sua Andromeda, resto honorato non meno della sua Maga, laquale è stata prima stampata ne' cori, che sù le carte. Accoglietela, Lettori, come nobilissimo parto uscito da Autore insigne, quale hà potuto del suo, e con quello di cinque soli Musici Compagni con spesa, non più, di due mila scudi, rapir gli animi à gli Ascoltanti colla reale rappresentatione di quella; operationi simili à Prencipi costano infinito danaro. In oltre, ove s'è trovato à tempi nostri privato Virtuoso, à cui sia dato l'animo, di porre le mani in tali funtioni, e riuscirne con honore, come hà fatto egli la cui gloria, e de' Compagni, il grido universale della Serenissima Città di Venetia applaude? Accogliete non meno intanto l'intentione mia, qual'è di giovarvi, e dilettarvi, col porgervi in dono, col mezo delle mie Stampe, le fatiche illustri, di così nobile Virtuoso, e col discrivervi la musicale rappresentatione, dell'Opera, la quale seguitò in questa guisa. (printer's preface, p. 5)

4. FERRARI, *Il principe giardiniero* (Salis, 30 December 1643)
Argomento e scenario

Benche veterano nei Scenici Componimenti, la finezza del secolo m'afflige, la partialità mi tormenta; mà la Virtù finalmente è un Sole, che per nubi di passione, ch'ella habbia intorno non cessa di risplendere. Hoggidì l'Orchestre musicali atterriscono i più canori Cigni; e le Sirene vi si bramano angeliche, ne più maritime. . . . Colla solita vostra benignità scusate i difetti del mio Giardiniero, della mia Musica, e della mia Tiorba. (preface, p. 4)

5. FERRARI, *Il pastor regio* (Bologna: Monti & Zenero, 18 May 1641)

a. Io più per gusto di servire chi comandare mi poteva che per capriccio di poetare, fabbricai per musica cinque opere rappresentate tutte con Apparato Regio su le famose piagge dell'Adriatico ove per emularmi sono poi suscitate più Opere, che involontari quali, s'altro di buon non hanno, non hanno almeno, com'alcuni, il crine posticcio, d'argomento tolto alle carte Greche o Latine ne il viso bellettato di concetti stiracchiati o delle frasi pedagoghe. Non mi curo d'essere Poeta, ma profeso d'esser buon Musico, e di conoscere quale Poesia meglio alla musica s'adatti. S'io prendo una Tiorba in mano, sento d'havere una qualità, che mi può rendere singolare, e tanto mi basta.

b. Dovendosi nel Teatro dell'Ill. Sig. Guastavillani in Bologna rappresentarsi in musica la mia Maga Fulminata, e il mio Pastor Regio, mi convenne, à compiacimento de gl'amici & per il ghiribizzo d'alcuni Musici, che mai si contentano, aggiungere, e levare qualche cosa all'Opra, onde non ti maravigliare se le troverai alquanto varie dalla prima lor impressione di Venetia. (preface)

6. OTTAVIO RINUCCINI, *Arianna* (Venice: Bariletti, 1640)

a. Hora dunque che l'Arianna, Componimento, che fra' Drammatici hà riportati i primi vanti da' Theatri Italiani, ritorna à veder le Scene in Venetia, per opra del Signor Claudio Monte Verdi, celebratissimo Apollo del secolo, e prima Intelligenza del Cielo armonico, prendo occasione di non tenerle i miei più lungamente celati; ma con offerirla al Nome di V.S. di manifestargli al Mondo per mezzo della sua nuova ristampa. (printer's dedication, pp. 5–6)

b. Sonetto del Signor Benedetto Ferrari dalla Tiorba al Sig. Claudio Monteverdi Oracolo della Musica:

> Questo bel Monte sempre verde, e molle
> Orna dell'ampia terra ogni confine;
> Non di pompe selvagge onusto il crine,
> Ma di glorie canore al Cielo estolle.
>
> È di lui men famoso Ischia che bolle,
> E fiamme scaglia da le nevi alpine;
> Meraviglie gentili, e peregrine!
> Vile appò lui è de le muse il colle.
>
> Non per altro esce il Sol dall'orizonte,
> Che per furar à le sue cime belle
> Raggi da farsi un diadema al fronte;
>
> S'avvien che Aegra i figli rinovelle,
> Colla sola armonia di questo Monte
> Foran possenti ad'espugnar le stelle. (pp. 8–9)

7. [GIACOMO BADOARO], *Il ritorno d'Ulisse in patria* (MS libretto [1640])

a. L'Auttore Al molt'Ill^re et molto Reverendo Sig^r. Claudio Monte Verde Gran Maestro di

Musica: Non per farmi concorrente di quelli ingegni, che ne gli anni adesso hanno publicato le loro compositioni ne Veneti Teatri, mà per eccitare la virtù di V.S. a far conoscer a questa Città che nel calore degl'affetti vi è gran differenza da un sol vero à un sol dipinto. Mi diedi da principio a compore il ritorno d'Ulisse in Patria le amabilissime lusinghi delli Ill^mi Sig^ri Pietro Loredano et Gasparo Malipiero. . . .

b. Ad ogni modo il mondo sà che la mia penna combatte per vincer l'otio e non per guadagnar gloria.

c. Hora veduta à rappresentar l'opera dieci volte sempre con eguale concorso della Città convengo affermativamente, et vivamente affermare, che il mio Ulisse è più obbligato a V.S. che non fu il vero Ulisse alla sempre Gratiosa Minerva. . . . Ammiriamo con grandissima maraviglia i concetti cosi pieni, non senza qualche conturbatione, mentre non sò più conoscere per mia quest'opera. (author's prefatory letter, I-Vmc, Cod. Cicogna 546, transcribed in Wolfgang Osthoff, "Zu den Quellen von Monteverdis *Ritorno di Ulisse in patria*," *Studien zur Musikwissenschaft* 23 [1956]: 73–74)

8. [BADOARO] L'assicurato academico Incognito, *Ulisse errante* (Pinelli, 1644)

a. Al Signor Michel'Angelo Torcigliani: . . . Feci già molti anni rappresentare il ritorno d'Ulisse in Patria, Dramma cavato di punto da Homero, e raccordato per ottimo da Aristotile nella sua Poetica, e pur'anco all'hora udij abbaiar qualche cane, ma io non fui però tardo à risentirmene co' sassi alle mani. Hora fò vedere l'Ulisse Errante, ch'è in sostanza dodici libri dell'Odissea d'Homero: in parte hò diminuiti gli Episodii, in parte hò aggrandito il soggetto con inventioni per quanto mi parve il bisogno, non dilungandomi però nell'essenza dalla rappresentata Historia.

b. Se dirà alcuno, che non era soggetto da portarsi in Scena, io dirò di sì, sperando che tosto udito che l'habbia, sia per cangiarsi d'opinione. Se dirà, che sono più Attioni, io dirò, che l'hò detto prima di lui, e ciò potrassi agevolmente vedere nelle divisioni di esse, che à questo effetto io gliele mando quì occluse. In riguardo agli accidenti, che occorrono viaggiando ad Ulisse, sono, è vero, più attioni; ma in riguardo alla intentione del Viatore, che è di girne in Patria, non è che una sola. (pp. 6–7)

c. La Favola . . . vuol esser'*una unius*. Una dunque è la mia Favola, perche d'unità materiale è sempre Ulisse, d'Unità formale è sempre errore: nè i molti errori fanno molte favole, ma molte parti di favola, che la costitusicono attione tutta una, e grande, come ricerca Aristotele.

d. Se queste ragioni piaccino, s'accettino: se nò, dicasi c'hò voluto rappresentare gli accidenti più gravi, occorsi ad Ulisse nel gir'in Patria. Quelli, che di propria inventione si fabricano i soggetti, fanno ottimamente à camminare con la puntuale osservatione delle regole; poiche stando ad essi la eletta, prudentemente operano, se vanno con la commune: ma chi s'obliga all'Individuo d'una Historia non puo assumerla senza la particolarità di quegli accidenti, che necessariamente la accompagna. (pp. 7–8)

e. Quest'Opera portava necessariamente l'uscir delle regole, io non lo tengo per errore, e s'altri pur vuole, ch'egli sia, sarà errore di voluntà, non d'inavvertenza. . . .

f. Se vorrà affermar un bell'Ingegno . . . che il soggetto è più da Epopeia, che da Tragedia, io le dico, che chi vorrà leggerlo in Epopeia anderà nell'Odissea d'Homero, e chi vorrà sentirlo in Tragedia, venirà nel Theatro dell'Illustrissimo Signor Giovanni Grimani, dove in poco tempo, e con minor fatica lo vedrà più pomposo comparire sopra le Scene. (pp. 9–10)

g. Per il tempo, che deve misurare il soggetto, vollero alcuni concedere otto hore, e non più, altri un giro di Sole, alcuni due giorni, altri tre, e pure queste incerte regole non sono state sempre osservate da Eschilo, da Euripide, e da Sofocle, mentre in alcuni loro soggetti scorrono i mesi, e gli anni; altri dissero, che bastava assai, che la Favola potesse essere abbracciata da un riflesso di memoria senza fatica, & a quest'opinione io potrei appigliarmi. Non sono poi permanenti i Precetti della Poetica, perche le Mutationi de' Secoli fanno nascer la diversità del comporre.

h. . . . la Tragedia ne' suoi primi giorni era recitata dal Poeta solo tinto il volto delle vinaccie; dipoi v'introdussero i Personaggi, e le Maschere, indi vi aggiunsero i Chori, la Musica, i Suoni, le mutationi de Scena, in luogo de' Chori i Balli, e forse per l'avvenire col cambiare dell'età vedranno i nostri Posteri introdotte nuove forme.

i. Erano in queste detestate una volta le variationi di loco, & al presente per dare sodisfattione all'occhio, pare precetto ciò che all'hora era prohibito, inventandosi ogni giorno maggior numero di cambiamenti di Scene;

j. niente si cura al presente per accrescer diletto agli Spettatori il dar luogo a qualche inverisimile, che non diturpi la Attione: onde vedemo, che per dar più tempo alle Mutationi delle Scene, habbiamo introdotta la musica, nella quale non possiamo fuggire un'inverosimile, che gli huomini trattino i loro più importanti negotij cantando; in oltre per godere ne' Theatri ogni sorte di Musica, si costumano concerti a due, tre, e più, dove nasce un'altro inverisimile, che essi favellando insieme possano impensatamente incontrarsi à dire le medesime cose. Non è dunque maraviglia, se obligandoci noi al diletto del Genio presente, ci siamo con ragione slontanati dall'antiche regole. (pp. 10–12)

k. In ogni tempo si è veduta aperta la strada dell'inventare, non tenendo noi altro obligo circa i precetti degli Antichi, che di saperli. (p. 13)

l. Fù il Ritorno d'Ulisse in Patria decorato dalla Musica del Signor Claudio Monteverde soggetto di tutta fama, e perpetuità di nome, hora mancherà questo condimento; poiche è andato il Gran Maestro ad intuonar la Musica degli Angeli à Dio. Si goderanno in sua vece le gloriose fatiche del Signor Francesco Sacrati, e ben'era di dovere, che per veder gli splendori di questa Luna, tramontasse prima quel Sole. (author's prefatory letter, pp. 16–17)

m. La prova mi fà conoscer per vero, che spesso i favori accrescono l'ardire in chi li riceve; Io hebbi dalla mano dell'Auttore l'Ulisse Errante con privilegiata auttorità di farlo stampare in grande con le figure doppò fornite le recite, & ciò intrapresi per haver occasione di mostrar al mondo quelle fatiche, che hò io incontrate per ben servire à questi Cavalieri.

n. . . . è nato in mè nuovo ardire di farla anco stampar in questa forma per incontrar la sodisfatione di quelli, che godono più simili cose, quando sieno accompagnate dalla lettura. (Torelli's preface, pp. 19–20)

9. Anon., *Argomento et scenario delle nozze d'Enea in Lavinia* (printer not named, 1640)
Lettera dell'auttore ad alcuni suoi amici:

a. Già s'avicina il finir dell'anno, che fù la prima volta recitata la bellissima Tragedia del ritorno d'Ulisse in patria del nostro Illustrissimo, & virtuosissimo amico. (p. 1)

b. Ma come sia vero, che la Tragedia d'esito lugubre sia migliore dell'altra, non è però, ch'anco questa [tragedia "di lieto fine"] non sia atta all'eccitamento delle passioni; partorendo ella poi il diletto maggiore, il quale se non è il fin principale, come l'utile dovuto alla Poesia, deve tuttavia dal Poeta esser molto ricercato; massime così richiedendo la conditione de tempi, à quali si sono sempre li Poeti grandemente accomodati.

c. . . . Io per accomodarmi al gusto corrente, mi son eletto più tosto Tragedia di lieto fine, ch'altrimenti, aggiungendosi che dovendo ella cantarsi, e non semplicemente esser recitata più mi parve propria in si fatto modo, non già, ch'io non sappi ch'anticamente anco le malinconiche tragedie erano cantate, e per lo meno la parte corica, ma certo è, che un tal uso s'andò tralasciando, in modo, ch'anco alle liete parve che la melodica fosse restata solo per un così fatto estrinseco ornamento. (pp. 4–5)

d. Quant'al loco dove per me havrei eletta una Città, ò una parte d'essa come fanno li buoni tragici & amici antichi, e moderni, per dilettar nondimeno li spettatori con le variationi mi son preso una poca parte del Latio picciola portione d'Italia, perche si mostri or in Reggia, or in boscareccia, & in altro modo, che portano l'occasioni. Ma quanto al tempo non hò voluto dipartirmi dalla Regola tante volte commandata, dal maestro del vero sapere, che statuisce alla Tragedia lo spatio d'una giornata, ò poco più. (p. 6)

e. Mi son servito di costui [Numano, nominato da Virgilio forte] come di persona giocosa, non trovando nell'Autore altri più à proposito, & sapendo l'umore di molti Spettatori, a' quali più piacciono così fatti scherzi, che le cose serie, come vediamo l'Iro dell'amico haver maravigliosamente dilettato, al qual genere di personaggio io veramente in altra Tragedia non havrei dato luogo.

f. Et così per accomodarmi alle persone, & à gli affetti, che devono da loro esprimersi, mi son servito di più metri di versi, com' à dire dando lo sdrucciole [sic] à persone basse, & il breve, e tronco ad adirati, ben sapendo che gli buoni tragici toscani non hanno usato altro, che l'epmsillabo [sic], Endeca sillabo, & tal volta il pentasillabo, se bene, c'havendo gli antichi Greci, & Latini nelle lor Tragedie adoperati, oltre il Iambo, il trimeno, tetrameno, & altri, io non sò perchànoi sia prohibito almeno ne così il essiliabo [sic], & optosillabo: oltre che alle Tragedie musicali si deve quella licenza, che non hanno l'altre semplicemente rappresentate. (pp. 18–19)

g. Io [ho] schifati li pensieri & concetti tolti di lontano, & più tosto atteso à gli affetti, come vuole il Signor Monteverde, al quale per compiacere hò anco mutate, & lasciate molte cose di quelle, ch'io havea poste prima. (pp. 19–20)

h. Il Coro poi era parte integrale delle vecchie Tragedie, entrando non solo come personaggio, mà cantando principalmente tra Atto; e Atto con gesti, e saltationi, e con quei cosi fatti gemiti, & eiulati. Mà nelle moderne è fatto men considerabile, vedendosi in alcune per poco più, che per partimento de gli Atti. Io come hò introdotti anco più Cori nel mezo de medesimi Atti, cosi non me ne son valso nel fine di loro,

i. perch'essendo cantata tutta la Tragedia, cantando anco il Coro riuscirebbe di troppo tedio, onde per appagar più li Spettatori con le variationi si sono introdotti balli, in certo modo dalla favola scaturienti, come ancora gli antichi Cori ballavano al canto del tetrametro; verso appropriatissimo à moti del corpo.

j. Et se bene modernamente si usa il divider anco le cose recitate in tre Atti, à me è più piacciuto il far ciò in cinque, perche con più posate possano li Spettatori respirare dalla fatica della mente in tener dietro ad una serie d'accidenti rappresentati, al qual fine fù ritrovato un così fatto spartimento. Et anco per accomodar almeno in apparenza il tempo dell'imitatione à quella della cosa imitata. Perciòche essendo lo spatio dell'attione un giorno, tanto à punto parerebbe, che dovesse durar la rappresentatione, mà perchè ciò riuscirebbe con troppo incommodo, & tedio de Spettatori, perciò si divide la medesima attione in Atti, perche trà l'uno, e l'altro si presupponga correr più tempo di quello, che corre, si che in tutto si giunga allo spatio della giornata. (pp. 21–22)

k. Prende il medesimo Himeneo occasione di ritoccar l'origine, & grandezza di Roma . . . & poi il nascimento della nostra Venetia, non certo di soverchio lontano, & con sforzato stiramento, essendo che questa nobilissima Città all'hora cominciò, che si vide cader Roma sotto il giogo de Barbari, li quali invadendo l'Italia, spinsero molti suoi abitanti non mica ignobili per sottrarsi al loro furore à ricoverare in queste Lacune, dando in sì fatto modo principio alla Città . . . che co'l valore di nostri padri pervenne alla grandezza, in cui la miriamo. (author's prefatory letter, pp. 23–24)

l. Himeneo . . . con Venere, & Giunone . . . congiunge li Sposi felici presagiendo di tal maritaggio le grandezze di Roma, & la nascita, & maraviglia della Città di Venetia. Qui restando terminata l'opera. (scenario, p. 36)

10. GIAN FRANCESCO BUSENELLO, *Gli amori di Apollo e di Dafne* (1640), *Delle hore ociose* (Giuliani, 1656)

Le altre cose nel presente Drama sono Episodii intrecciati nel modo che vederai; & se per aventura qualche ingegno considerasse divisa l'unità della Favola per la duplicità degl'Amori, cioè d'Apollo, e Dafne; di Titone, e dell'Aurora; di Cefalo, e di Procri, si compiaccia raccordarsi, che queste intrecciature non disfanno l'unità; mà l'adornano, e si rammenti, che il Cavalier Guarino nel Pastor Fido non pretese duplicità d'Amori, cioè trà Mirtillo, & Amarilli, e trà Silvio, e

Dorinda; ma fece, che gli Amori di Dorinda, e di Silvio servissero d'ornamento alla Favola sua. (argomento, pp. 6–7)

11. BUSENELLO, *Didone* (1641), *Delle hore ociose* (Giuliani, 1656)

a. Quest'Opera sente delle opinioni moderne. Non è fatta al prescritto delle Antiche regole: mà all'usanza Spagnuola rappresenta gl'anni, & non le hore.

b. . . . E perche secondo le buone Dottrine è lecito ai Poeti non solo alterare le Favole, mà le Istorie ancora: Didone prende per marito Iarba. E se fù Anacronismo famoso in Virgilio, che Didone non per Sicheo suo Marito, mà per Enea perdesse la vita, potranno tollerare i grandi ingegni, che quì segua un matrimonio diverso e dalle favole, e dalle Istorie. Chi scrive sodisfa al genio, e per schiffar il fine tragico della morte di Didone sì e introdotto l'accasamento predetto con Iarba. Quì non occorre rammemorare agl'huomini intendenti come i Poeti migliori habbiano rappresentate le cose à modo loro, sono aperti i Libri, & non è forestiera in questo Mondo la eruditione. (argomento, pp. 3–4)

12. BUSENELLO, *La prosperità infelice di Giulio Cesare ditattore* (?1646), *Delle hore ociose* (Giuliani, 1656)

a. Se gli Atti sono cinque, e non trè, rammentati, che tutti i Drami antichi, e particolarmente le Tragedie di Seneca sono distinte in cinque Atti. Nè ti paia strano la mutatione de' luoghi, perche chi scrive non crede far peccato se scrive à modo suo.

b. E chi gode di farsi schiavo delle regole antiche habbia le sue sodisfattioni in Plenilunio. . . .

c. Bisogna in qualche parte dilettare i gusti correnti, ricordandoti sempre della lode, che diede Tacito à Seneca, cioè che haveva un' ingegno fatto à posta per i gusti di quei tempi. (preface, pp. 3–4)

d. Qui gl'Anni vederete / Epilogati in hore, . . . / Chi fia mai, che dissenta / Se una notte canora à voi discopre / Di mille giorni l'occorrenze, e l'opre? / . . . Et io per apportar diletto à voi / Discepoli d'Alcide, anzi Maestri, / Con arte lusinghiera / Più d'un anno hò racchiuso entro una sera: / Senza adoprare ò Corridori, ò Navi, / Senza seggio mutar discoprirete / Thessaglia, Lesbo, il Faro, Egitto, e Roma. (prologue)

e.

LIBERTÀ: Verso l'Eccelse cime / Dell'Olimpo sublime, / Mal trattata da Roma io mi rivolgo, / Perchè chiari preveggo i danni miei, / Nè sò quando il destin mandarà i giorni, / Che in terra ad habitar sicura io torni.

NETTUNO: Fermati Libertà, / Tuo soggiorno sarà / Una Cittade gloriosa, e grande, / Che Vergine, & invitta / L'onda per base havrà, per tetto il Cielo. / Quivi tu vederai / Diviso in mille teste / L'unico dell' Impero, / Venetia sarà detta / Questa Città suprema e trionfante, / Che renderà famose / Le Adriatiche sponde; / Ristretto de stupori, / Ritratto delle sfere, / Epilogo del Mondo, / Ricco Empireo dell'arti, / Compendio di Natura, / E del grand'Universo abbreviatura. / Forte, libera, giusta, / Nel Zodiaco politico vedrassi / Tre segni illuminar d'ogni staggione, / La Vergine, la Libra, ed'il Leone.

LIBERTÀ: E quanto mi consoli, ò qual decoro / Tu m'accresci ò Nettuno, / Mà almen veder potessi / Trà gl'essemplari dell'eterne Idee, / Di Città più Celeste, che terrena / L'abozzo eccelso, e l'immortal figura.

NETTUNO: Mira colà che Giove / Di sua Divinità nell'ombra estende / Una picciola forma / Di Venetia felice, / E mira come à prova / Le folgoran d'intorno / Lampi divini, & ella / Di sereno à se stessa / Nel suo lucido cerchio / Nota il Sol d'otioso, e di sovverchio.

LIBERTÀ: O beata magione, / Ciel terreno à togati Semidei, / Tu regnerai sull'acque / E sarà del tuo Impero, / Recinto la Natura, e ronda il Sole.

NETTUNO: Libertà, senti, ascolta / Fatidico Nettun ciò che predice / Di quà à secoli molti, /Tu canterai le lodi, & io gl'applausi / Di VENETIA immortal in stil giocondo /Nel TEATRO GRIMAN famoso al Mondo.

CORO: Viva VENETIA, viva, / Ogni penna descriva / Del suo nome le glorie, / De suoi gesti l'historie, / Et il Destino ingemmi le Corone / Al suo generosissimo LEONE. (final scene, pp. 62–64)

13. BUSENELLO, *Statira* (Giuliani, 18 January 1655)

a. Haverei scritto più diffusamente in questo Drama, & uniti gli spiriti à sollevare à qualche grado lo stile, se la commandata brevità, e la proprietà della Scena me ne havessero data licenza. Altro è comporre una Oda, overo un Sonetto, ove è permesso l'entusiasmo al pensiero, e l'estasi all'ingegno nell'eccitare gli aculei dolci à gl'orecchi, & il brillo lascivo nel cuore con l'inventione d'una chiusa blandiente, & spiritosa; altro è comporre un Drama, ove i Personaggi han correggii, parlano familiarmente, e se la vena troppo s'inalza perde il decoro, & la vera proprietà. (dedication, pp. 6–7)

b. . . . dovendo io scrivere et havendo scritto poesia che deve essere cantata e che le misure e i numeri, le desinenze e le assillabazioni riguardano la musica, le strofe, le antistrophe e gl'epodi dei greci qui non vengono in taglio.

c. E posto anche che le poesie degl'antichi greci fossero cantate, come altri vuole, e che Homero medesimo fosse il poeta e il musico delle sue proprie canzoni, altri era quella musica dalla nostra.

d. . . . La introduzione delle azioni in musica nei teatri, che sia inventata dagl'antichi o da' moderni trovata, io non voglio farmene giudice. (author's MS letter to Giovanni Grimani "nell'occasione di rassegnarli il dramma intitolato la Statira," January 1656; excerpted in Arthur Livingston, *La vita veneziana nelle opere di Gian Francesco Busenello* [Venice, 1913], 371–79)

14. GIULIO STROZZI, *Erotilla, tragedia di Giulio Strozzi, Saggio Primo, Terza impressione* (Alberti, 1621)

a. Mà che hanno da fare le Tragedie colle nozze? Nel vero la disconvenevolezza sarebbe grande, se la mia non fosse una di quelle Tragedie, alle quali è lecito di terminare con fine allegro, e di lasciare à bocca dolce gl'uditori. . . .

b. Nè voglio, che altri per Tragicomedia me la battezzi, percioche questi mostrarebbe di non intender la forza di tal voce, nè di sapere in qual senso l'habbiano usata gli Antichi. Poiche Tragicomedia dissero à quelle Comedie solamente, nelle quali frammetevano alcun personaggio più nobile, e tragico, come Heroe, o Dio, mà non chiamarono mai con tal nome quelle Tragedie, le quali in allegrezza fecero terminare.

c. E vero, che queste tali secondo le regole di Aristotile paiono meno perfette, mà secondo il gusto di hoggidì, che è regola d'ogni regola, sono con maggior avidità ricevute, e con maggior patienza ascoltate. (preface, p. 8)

15. STROZZI, *Delia* (Pinelli, 20 January 1639)
Argomento e scenario (5 November 1638)

a. Perche i sublimi ingegni di V.S. e del Signor Alfonso Rivarola non possono filosofare intorno alle machine, s'io non discuopro loro quello, che vado alla giornata operando con la penna, le invio il ristretto della mia Delia. (scenario, dedication, p. 3)

b. Mà perche . . . non hò operato à caso nella struttura di questa favola, le dirò ancora l'allusione di lei. I figliuoli del Sole . . . sono i miseri mortali, sottoposti al gastigo di lui, per l'alterigia, & arditezza loro. I Ciclopi significano i vapori malvagi. . . . Il Sole saetta i Ciclopi, cioè que' perniciosi vapori . . . e fà cessar il male. . . . [Il Sole si finge] Pastor d'Admeto, cioè del Prencipe prudente, il quale coopera con mezzi opportuni alla nostra salvezza. . . . Si può tutta questa compositione, à guisa de' Sacri Poemi, spiritualmente applicare all'Anima nostra, che desidera di congiungersi con Dio, dal quale è ricevuta in gloria. (pp. 22–24)

c. [Il] Signor Giovanni Grimani . . . [ha] eletta [*La Delia*] ad esser la prima [opera], che comparisca in quel nobilissimo Teatro, ch'egli in questa Città di Venetia, nello spatio di pochi giorni, hà con tanta grandezza d'animo fatto nascere, per così dire, per dover durar molti anni à solo beneficio della Musica; E'n vero mi sono parse le pietre unirsi da se stesse, quasi invitate dall'armonia di novelli Anfioni; con sì poca fatica è sorto da' fondamenti quell'ampio, e sicuro Teatro, nel quale ancora intendo, che si destina di recitare quest'anno una segnalata fatica del Signor Benedetto Ferrari, poiche senza servirsi delle parole, ò concetti del Tasso, hà composta, & ornata insieme di Musica una nuova Armida, che sarà come sono state l'altre due degli anni andati, la maraviglia delle Scene, venendo hoggi tanto nobilitata dalle Machine di Vostra Signoria, e del Signor Alfonso, & honorata, (come sarà primieramente la Delia) dalle voci d'alcuni de' più canori Cigni della nostra Italia. Le mando per fine il numero de' personaggi che formano la mia Delia. (scenario, pp. 25–27)

d. M'era scordato di dirle, come il Signor Francesco Mannelli Romano, che vestì di Musica, com'ella sà, con molto applauso l'Andromeda, e la Maga Fulminata del Signor Benedetto Ferrari, hà questa volta mostrato un eccesso del suo affetto, & un sommo del suo valore in honorar la mia Delia. Io sò quel, che mi dico: stupirà Venetia in sentir à qual segno arrivi lo studio fatto in quest'Opera dal Signor Mannelli; Hà un'imitatione di parole mirabile, un'armonia propria, varia, e dilettevole: in somma, come esca alle stampe questa fatica, si conoscerà, se ho parlato per interesse, ò più tosto defraudato al vero. (scenario postscript, p. 27)

e. Ho partita con qualche metodo l'opera in tre azzioni. Division commune di tutte le cose: principio, mezzo, e fine. Gli antichi formavano cinque, perchè vi frammettevano il canto. Questa ch'è tutta canto, non hà dibisogno di tante posate.

f. Ho introdotto qui l'Hilaredo de' Greci, e questi sarà il giocoso Ermafrodito, personaggio nuovo che tra la severità del Tragico, e la facetia del Comico campeggia molto bene sù le nostre Scene.

g. D'un paio d'hore mi sono preso licenza: Non sò s'Aristotile, ò Aristarco me le farà buone.

h. . . . . Abbozzai la Delia nelle ritiratezze del passato Gontagio, per sollievo dell'animo, e per tributo di riverenza à gran Principe, nelle cui nozze io mi credeva di pubblicarla. Non seguì per mia negligenza. (libretto preface, pp. 6–7)

i. Accioche tù accordi gli occhi con l'orecchie, sappi, o esquisito lettore, che nel rapresentarla si sono levati dall'opera più di 300. versi, e questo per non abusar della tua cortesia.

j. Egli è dover, ch'il Poeta lasci le sue gorghe, che sono le digressioni, e gli episodi, per dar luogo ai passaggi de' Signori Musici. Onde non attribuire tù ad errore de' recitanti quello, c'hanno fatto per meglio servirti. (libretto postscript, p. 80)

16. STROZZI, *La finta pazza* (Surian, 14 January 1641)

a. Questa è l'ottava fatica rapresentativa, che mi trovo haver fatta; cinque delle quali hanno di già più volte passeggiate le Scene, e' n questa m'è riuscito assai felicemente lo sciorre più d'un nodo di lei senza magia, e senza ricorrere a gli aiuti sopranaturali, e divini.

b. Non ti ridere dell'humiltà del nome, nè della qualità della materia, impercioche ho voluto tenermi basso con l'inscrittione, e stretto con l'invito, per corrispondere senza altitonanza di titoli nel rimanente molto meglio alla poca aspettatione dell'Opera. (p. 5)

c. Supplisce alla povertà de' miei concetti il tesoro della Musica del Sig. Francesco Sacrati Parmigiano, il quale maravigliosamente hà saputo con le sue armonie adornar i miei versi e con la stessa meraviglia hà potuto ancora metter insieme un nobilissimo Choro di tanti esquisitissimi Cigni d'Italia; e sin dal Tebro nel maggior rigor d'un' horrida stagione hà condotta sù l'Adria una suavissima Sirena, che dolcemente rapisce gli animi, & alletta gli occhi, e l'orecchie degli ascoltanti. Dalla diligenza del Sig. Sacrati deve riconoscere la Città di Venetia il favore della virtuosissima Signora ANNA. (preface, p. 6)

seconda impressione, 1641

d. . . . dall'avidità de' Lettori di quest' opera à metterla due volte in un mese sotto il torchio; tanto applauso ha ricevuto dalle lingue universali La Finta Pazza nel Teatro Novissimo della Città di Venetia, ov'ella, con regale apparato è stata in 17. giorni dodici volte rappresentata. (printer's afterword, p. 96)

terza impressione, 1644

e. Venni volentiere à questa Terza impressione della vera Finta Pazza, perchè ho veduto, ch'alcuni musici di fortuna l'hanno variamente fatta ristampar altrove, e la vanno rapresentando, come cosa loro. L'Autore poco se ne cura, & havrebbe caro di poter ringratiar Iddio, ch'i suoi componimenti gli fussero migliorati. Onde ne farai tù il giuditio della lettura dell'una, e dell'altra, e quando tu non ci scorga miglioramento, dirai, se tanto è piaciuta alterata, ch'haverebbe fatto nel suo vero essere: quando pure in bocca della signora Anna Renzi, con la musica del signor Sacrati, e con le macchine del Signor Torelli fece stupire una Venetia. (preface)

17. *Il cannocchiale per la finta pazza, dilineato da M[aiolino] B[isaccioni] C[onte] di G[enova]* (Surian, 1641)

a. Io considerava questi giorni, che la compositione del Sig Giulio Strozzi della Finta Pazza, le macchine ritrovate dal Sig. Iacomo Torelli, e la Musica orditavi sopra dal Sig. Francesco Sacrati, eran'un Cielo degno d'esser contemplato da tutti, ma così lontano à gran parte dalle genti, che era un toglier il pregio à tanti, che sono concorsi à si nobile fattura, se non si faceva commodo ad ognuno di vederla, & ammirare, fù stampato il Scenario, e fù pur anco stampata l'Opera, ma le macchine, e gli habiti, e le comparse restavano lontane dalla vista delle genti, e però non lodate. (preface, pp. 3–4)

b. Godano con gli occhi sù queste carte anco gli esteri più remoti, e ritirati, quello di c'hanno goduto gli occhi, e gli orecchi in questa Città, che in ogni sua parte eccede i confini delle meraviglie.

c. Sono stati parti d'anni altrove i theatri aperti, & un solo hà fatto celebre un popolo, e memorabile per un secolo. Venetia n'ha veduti e goduti di quattro ad un tratto emuli fra di loro e di Metri, e di arte scenica, e di Musiche, e d'apparati, e di Macchine;

d. l'ultimo de' quali [Teatri], che per appunto è stato detto il Novissimo hà passato ogni credenza, poichè nello spatio di sei mesi è stato da i fondamenti alzato, e perfettionato con l'assistenza sì per la fabrica d'esso, come per quello ch'appartiene alle Scene, e alle Macchine del Sig. Iacomo Torelli da Fano: il quale venuto per essercitare i suoi talenti dediti alla militia in servigio di questi [*sic*] Augusto Senato, impatiente dell'otio, hà dato à divedere quanto ei vaglia d'ingegno. (pp. 6–7)

e.[La finta pazza] fù la Signora Anna Renzi Romana, Giovane così valorosa nell'attione, come eccelente nella Musica; così allegra nel finger la pazzia, come savia nel saperla imitare, e modesta in tutti i suoi modi. (p. 8)

f. Si dilettò con meraviglia chiunque v'andò ad essere spettatore, nè contento d'una e due volte, vi ritornò la terza e la quarta, e più ancora.

g. Riempita quanto più era capace l'orchestra di spettatori, che impatienti attendevano il moto della tela; fù dato principio ad una sinfonia di non men dotta, che soavemente toccati Instromenti, doppo la quale s'alzò con indicibile prestezza la Cortina. (p. 9)

h. Gli uditori dimenticatisi d'essere in Venetia. . . . L'occhio non havea quasi dove terminar lo sguardo, e quel breve spatio d'una scena sapea mentire un immenso dell'onde, e del mondo. (p. 10)

i. Cominciò il giovanetto, qual era un valorosissimo cantarino da Pistoia, à cantare si delicatamente, che gli animi de gli ascoltanti quasi che usciti dalle porte de gli orecchi si sollevarono a quell'altezza per assistere al godere di tanta dolcezza. (p. 12)

j. Era questi [Achille] un giovanetto castrato venuto da Roma (com'anco tutti gli altri Musici condotti da varie parti) di vago aspetto sì che sembrava un'Amazzone, c'havesse misti i spiriti guerrieri con le delicatezze feminili. (pp. 22–23)

k. L'ingannar il senso dell'occhio è il difficile dell'optica, ma il far poner in dubbio, se la pittura sia scultura, non è tiro, se non da eccelente pittore. (p. 39)

l. Non terminò il desiderio nel popolo di rivederla, onde quante volte fù replicata, altre tante fù di numerosa gente ripieno il luogo, e sempre molti hebbero da biasimare la propria pigritia d'esser andati ad occupare i luoghi, dovendo partire senza trovar dove accomodarsi, nè il lungo tratto da gli ultimi giorni Carnovaleschi a i Paschali hà fatto cessar nella Città il desiderio di riveder opra così pregiata, e pure non è cosa più facile ne i popoli, che la domesticanza, ond'è stato necessario, di riaprir di nuovo il Theatro, e più volte rappresentarla, per lo che la fama sparsane alle Città d'Italia nel convitar gli esteri a sì dilettevole spettacolo è stato cagione, che Venetia fuor del uso già dieci giorni prima veda l'abondanza del popolo, che suol concorrere alla divotione, & alla Sollennità che si celebra dell'Ascensione. (*Cannocchiale*, pp. 54–55)

18. STROZZI, *La finta savia* (Leni e Vecellio, 1 January 1643)

a. Molti Versi si tralascieranno per la lunghezza dell'Opera fabricata dall'Autore per poterla anco rappresentare senza Canto. (preface, p. 9)

b. La Musica di questo Drama è per la maggior parte compositione esquisita del Signor Filiberto Laurenzi. . . . Il Signor Crivelli hà maestrevolmente favorite alcune delle mie Scene, ed alcun'altre sono state honorate dal Signor Merula, ed altre finalmente nobilitate dal Signor Benedetto Ferrari: E perche l'operatione lodi i facitori, habbiamo ad ogni Scena posto il nome dell'Autor della Musica. (pp. 184–85)

c. Questi Drami son Poemi imperfetti: e l'uno contiene una Historia Greca, e l'altro una Latina: L'uno mira alla distruttione di Troia, l'altro accenna la futura fondatione di Roma, che negli anni venturi, à Dio piacendo, andiamo apparecchiando. . . . Il vero nome della Finta Savia fù Anthusa, che noi per leggiadria diverso, habbiamo in Aretusa cangiato: e' l nome di Anthusa fù il terzo nome della Città di Roma. . . . Il secondo nome di Roma era d'Amarillide tratto dagli Amori d'Ilia, e di Marte, che nel futuro Drama di Romolo, e di Remo saranno da me spiegati. (Afterword, p. 188)

19. VINCENZO NOLFI, *Il Bellerofonte* (Surian, 1642)
Argomento et scenario (Surian, 1642)

a. Il Teatro Novissimo che l'anno passato nella rappresentatione Musicale della Finta Pazza del Signor Giulio Strozzi si rese degno del favore, e de gl'applausi della Città hà per il presente preparato altro Drama, pur Musicale, da chi per ogni sua conditione gli giova di sperare dovergli esser conservato, se non migliorato il suo Posto; è questi il Bellerofonte opera del Signor Vicenzo Nolfi Gentilhuomo di Fano, e leggiadrissimo Poeta di questo secolo, fatica alla verità è egli di pochi mesi, senza, che habbi havuto tempo di stagionarsi, & appena d'essere in fretta in fretta ricorso, di che riderebbe forse Oratio, e pure se si concedi Entusiasmo la Poesia, puote la divinità figliare anco in istanti le perfettioni. Sarà il giudicio dell'Orchestra, à chi con volontà infinitamente divota il Signor Nolfi l'invicta, & da questi Signori Interessati non s'è ommesso al Certo per le loro forze quanto à gl'apparati numero alcuno per incontrare la sua sodisfattione, e 'l suo gusto; doverà in ogni caso esser gradito il lor desiderio almeno, è l'animo, che per servir al suo merito da loro obligata, e singolarmente rive[ri]to paragoni di altissime qualità, non hanno atterito in Cimento. (scenario, preface, pp. 3–4)

b. Se nelle Scene, e Macchine, che io ho ordinato per rappresentarti, ò curioso, non rintraccierai quella perfettione, e vaghezza, che meriti, e che bisognerebbe come necessitosamente poste in virtuosa emulatione d'altri Celebri, e nobilissimi Teatri in così gloriosa Patria, condona, che ha preponderato in me il desiderio di dilettarti alla cognitione del debole mio talento.

Gradisci cortese il poco, che posso offrirti con la relatione al molto che bramo; le imperfettioni sono infinite, lo confesso, ne mi lascio adulare dalla premura con che altri havesse procurato forse di servirsi di cose da me prima inventate, stabilite, e dirò ancora conferite; quali elle si sieno sono certo parto semplice del mio ingegno.

Il sito del Teatro Novissimo non può farti concorrer formalmente le cose, l'angustia di esso toglierebbe il poter perfettamente operare anco à singolar architetto.

Sia questo ancora appresso di tè motivo di scusa, e compatimento.

Coprirà in gran modo le mie debolezze il pennello del Signor Domenico Bruni Bresciano, che con la sua ordinaria felicità s'è adoperato nelle Scene. (scenario, pp. 4–5, note by Giacomo Torelli)

c. Tu perdi il tempo, ò Lettore se con la Poetica dello Stagirita in mano vai rintracciando gl'errori di quest'Opera, perch'io confesso à la libera, che nel comporla non ho voluto osservare altri precetti, che i sentimenti dell'inventore de gl'apparati. . . .

d. Questo è un genere di Poema, che ritornato alla primiera natura del Drama quant'al canto, mà ridotto quanto al resto à diversa coltura, secondo il compiacimento del secolo da gl'ingegni de nostri tempi, non riconosce hoggi più ne Epicarme per Padre, ne Sicilia per patria, ne Aristotile per Legislatore.

e. Tutte l'usanze si mutano, e piacciono le novità anco depravate, disse lo Scaligero in proposito dell'Anfitrione di Plauto. S'hoggi vivessero i Crati, gl'Aristofani, i Terentij cangerebbero forse pensiero.

f. Delli due fini, che insegnò Oratio non è rimasto alla poesia, che il diletto; in questa età non han bisogno gl'huomini di imparare il vivere del mondo con gl'altrui componimenti.

g. Ma il punto stà, che ne anche questo ritroverai ne presenti fogli, perche la favola ruvinosa per l'antichità è stata ristaurata dalla mia penna sul modello Dramatico nell'angustia di brevissimo tempo in ordine à ricevere la perfettione dalla bellezza delle macchine, & apparati Teatrali. (libretto, preface, pp. 3–5)

h. Più cose, dopo la Stampa del Scenario, hanno nell'Opera alteratione, & riforma, onde se nel numero delle Scene, ò in qualche parte dell'introdotto [sic] in esse troverai dall'uno all'altra alcuna diversità non ti mettere al critico di primo tratto; ricevi ogni cosa di buon occhio, mentre s'hà per solo fine il tuo minor tedio, e maggior diletto. (libretto, postscript, p. 129)

20. NOLFI, *Bellerofonte*, *Descrittione de gli apparati del Bellerofonte di Giulio del Colle* (printer not named, 1642)

a. Non hanno le qualità, e conditioni della Città di Venetia titolo proprio, e corrispondente, eccedendo elle ogni voce, & epiteto col quale possi ingrandirsi cosa di mondo, se pur quell'uno non se gli adegua di emula dell'Antica Roma, o pure Roma Antica alla nostra età rediviva; in fatti habbisi riguardo alla maestà del Dominio, alla gravità del governo, alla prudenza, e virtù de Cittadini, alla magnificenza de publici, e privati edificii, & a tante altre marche di nobiltà, & eccelenza troverassi al paraggio ben aggiustata la nominanza. Se ben poi il sito singolare, e miracoloso rende Superiore Venetia a Roma, & ad ogn'altr'opera di mano humana, e fà confessarla fattura di Divinità.

Solo ne' Spettacoli, è penso sin a quest'hora, che con gli Teatri famosi temporari de Scauti, e de Curioni non habbi havuto uguaglianza Venetia, ma di ciò militava in causa, che la Republica di Roma instituta col fine delle guerre, e degl'acquisti, havendo per massima politica i giuochi atletici, e sanguinolenti, come quelli, che usavano i suoi Cittadini alla ferocia militare, e gli rendevano liberi da certi sensi di pietà, e di tenerezza che vanno quasi all'huomo congeniti applicatamente vi s'impiegava; ma altri sono i fini, e gli instituti di questa Serenissima Patria drizzati solo alla conservatione del proprio, al ben publico, & alla sicurezza de soggetti, quali con Leggi santissime, e veramente Cristiane regge, e governa; ne se pure impugna spada di guerra è ella in modo alcuno ambitiosa, ed ingiusta; ma sempre, o che difende i proprij Stati insidiati, od'assaliti, o che solleva li amici oppressi dalle libidini inique de grandi.

Quanto a spettacoli Scenici, ammaestramenti degl'huomini, e che con verace norma di vivere gli pongono al sentiero della virtù, ha pure in questi ultimi anni dato a divedere poter con apparati, e rappresentationi affatto reali far, ch'arrossi l'antico Latio; armonia di paradiso, apparenze, e macchine di meraviglia, comparse d'habiti pomposissime, e queste in Teatri molteplici, con operati quasi incredibili. (p. 8)

b. Il Teatro Novissimo, eretto da doi Anni in quà, hà fatto veramente stupori, & tra' singolari hà meritato, e conseguito gli applausi. Hà egli rappresentato il presente anno il Bellerofonte Drama del Signor Vicenzo Nolfi da Fano, e perche per tanti riguardi è egli degno di minuta descrittione delle cose introdotte in esso hò preso, se ben imperfettamente, il pensiero di farla. (p. 9)

c. L'Innocenza . . . [fu] rappresentata da un soprano di Parma con molta proprietà. . . . Rappresentava [la Giustizia] un valorosissimo Castrato di Roma, che con voce soavissima, e delicata con gesto nobile, e maestoso accrebbe gran cumulo d'applausi al notissimo valor suo . . . rappresentò con infinita sua lode questa deità [Nettuno] un tenore di Parma . . . Paristide [fu] rappresentato da un tenor di Pistoia di soavissima voce . . . Sosteneva questo personaggio [il Re] un virtuosissimo basso di Siena che riuscì per ogni parte in quest'attione degno di lode . . . Signora Giulia Saus Paolelli Romana . . . [rappresentò] la regina Anthia . . . non s'inoltra con descrittioni la penna poiche da tre anni in quà ha questa Patria con l'honore del suo soggiorno bastevol cognitione de suoi talenti, e quel favor divoto che alla sua prima venuta rubbarno dolcemente i suoi sembianti, e rare virtù à gl'animi più nobili, e qualificati tanto va prendendo per giornata d'alteratione, che posso dire gl'affeti sollevarsi in ammirationi, e quasi toccar dell'adoratoni i confini . . . un castrato di Parma d'alta virtù [rappresentò] Delfiride la nodrice; Pallade e Diana [furono rappresentati da] due soprani castrati di gran valore. Melistea Dama di corte [venne] rappresentata da un castrato di Pistoia di molta vaglia . . . [Fu] Eolo Rè de venti singolarmente da un basso sanese rappresentato. . . . Era questi [Bellerofonte] il non mai a bastanza lodato Signor Michele Grasseschi contralto del Serenissimo Prencipe Matthias di Toscana . . . Archimene figliola regia, rappresentata dalla Signora Anna Renzi Romana idea verace della Musica, e singolar stupor delle Scene, che nel corso della Favola, mentre hor sfogò hor finse, hor scoprì, ed hor pianse le sue amorose passioni, ed incontri si rese all'ordinario donna de gl'animi e degl'affeti, conseguì alla fine il suo amato Bellerofonte in isposo. (*Descrittione*, pp. 12–19)

21. NICCOLÒ ENEA BARTOLINI, *Venere gelosa* (Surian, 28 January 1643)

Quest'Opera fatta per cantare . . . non teme il concorso di quelle che solamente si recitano. . . . Se la poesia non è copiosa di sentenze ed'arguzie non può chiamarsi, però fredda nè senza spirito; hò sostenuto lo stile, e con la diversità de metri, e con la proprietà delle parole, mi son ingegnato d'irritare la bizzaria di chi doveva accompagnarla con le note. . . . Per voi ho speso ancor io molti mesi indarno per dilettarvi (preface, n.p.)

22. *Apparati scenici per lo Teatro Novissimo* (Vecellio e Leni, 24 January 1644, Giacomo Torelli), Descrittione del Signor Conte Maiolino Bisaccioni

a. Venetia sempre, & in ogni occasione meravigliosa, & che non si stanca giamai di mostrar le sue grandezze, anco nel virtuoso diletto ha ritrovato il mirabile, havendo introdotto alcuni anni sono il rappresentare in musica attioni grandi con apparati, e machine tali, che avanzano ogni credenza, & quello che posson con qualche difficoltà nelle Regie Sale gli errarij più abondanti (e rare volte ancora) qui si vede con privata commodità facilmente esseguirsi non in una sola, ma in tre orchestre ad un tratto; e gareggiando questa con quella di maggiori squisitezze, chiamano tutti dalle più remote parti d'Italia i spettatori. Io non prendo a scrivere quello che si è fatto nella Venere Gelosa, perche la stimi la più riguardevole delle Teatrali di quest'anno, e di questa Città; ne perche la mia elettione sia per togliere i pregi alle altre; ma perche di questa io mi sono prima compiaciuto, e n'ho riserbata la memoria più viva. . . . Ma ne meno di questa voglio scriver tutte le parti, parendomi bastante il portar le cose più importanti del Drama, quanto che basta a mostrare quali siano stati le [*sic*] vestiti Scenici, ò diciamo apparati. (p. 6)

b. Al natale di questa Scena dovea tutto il Teatro, non che il Palco, o gl'edifitij sollevarsi, e ben sollevossi, poichè al muovere di quei gran telari allo sparire del cielo, & al veder tutte le cose di quella gran machina rivolgere, e sconvolgersi, non restò alcuno de' spettatori fermo, s'alzò, si rivolse, e non sapeva, che si vedesse, ò aspettasse se non una gran novità, ma ben presto l'occhio restò pago, poiche rappresentò la Scena tratta in vago & dilettevole Giardino Reale, egli era di gran lunga diverso da quanti mai se ne sono rappresentati, e su le scene, e su le stampe. (p. 39)

c. Questi Apparati sono stati così maravigliosi, & esquisitamente rappresentati, che hanno persuaso il genio di chi hà operato à lasciarle vedere anco quest'anno 1643 [1644]. Et in vero hà havuto molto giuditio, poiche se n'è ricevuta sodisfattione indicibile, in modo, che sono stati da molti tenuti per novi, e da altri per migliorati, e ciò per l'aggiunta di altre bellissime scene quì connesse, e per essere riuscito il Drama bello à maraviglia; onde si è veduto in effetto, che il repetere le cose belle anco due volte è lodabile. (*Descrittione*, p. 42)

23. Scipione Herrico, *Deidamia* (Leni e Vecellio, 5 January 1644)

a. Questa Gran Città, si come è nel sito, tal sempre si è dimostrata, & dimostra, e nelle publiche, e nelle private attioni ammirabile, e rara. Stupisce in questi tempi il forastiero, vedendo gli adorni Teatri, ne' quali si rappresentano in Musica tante Opere Drammatiche, così ingegnosamente composte, e di varie, e meravigliose apparenze ripiene. Onde si porge occasione à tanti belli ingegni di essercitarsi con lor molta lode, ò nella Poesia, ò nella Musica, ò nella fabrica delle machine, ò in altre simili honorate, ed à ciò appartenenti fatiche.

Hor io venendo in questo Nobile Asilo d'ogni virtù, ammirando così belle gare sono stato pur anco eccitato dal fervore Poetico, e quella istessa ragione, che mi persuadeva à non voler concorrere con tanti huomini dotti; mi stimolava con un soave desiderio d'imitarli. Finalmente à questo mio interno affetto, aggiungendosi le continue inchieste de gli amici mi son posto all'arringo à compiacenza di essi, i quali han guidato il mio stile, che da tal sorte di poetare suole essere affatto lontano.

b. Hò composta per recitarsi nel Teatro Novissimo la presente Opera, la quale per maggior commodità de gli Spettatori, dovendo uscire alle Stampe, hò voluto, che comparisse alla luce del Mondo adornata del nome di V. S. Illustrissima, la quale si degnerà riceverla tanto in mio nome, come in tributo della mia devota servitù: quanto in nome di coloro, che nella inventione, e ne' concetti meco n'hebbero parte. (preface, pp. 5–6)

24. Maiolino Bisaccioni, *Ercole in Lidia* (Vecellio e Leni, 1645)

a. Ordij questa favola, e la disposi in scene, mà perche già molti anni la Musa havea preso da me congedo, & io manomessala, come poco valevole, massime in questi tempi di finezza, ò di supercilio, che non degna, se non cose strane. Pregai una penna florida, e sublime ad intesser le mie fila di parole, rime, e concetti di lei degni. Vi si applicò ben cortese come suole, ma poscia occupata in materie sode, non passò più oltre del prim'Atto.

b. Io che nell'otio del letto (se però l'otio, & i dolori della podagra si accoppiano) haveva bisogno di solievo, mi diedi per ischerzo à tesser di mio filo . . . l'ordito [di questo dramma], e tanto m'inoltrai, che mi sono trovato al fine, quando meno lo credei. (preface, pp. 5–6)

25. Pietro Paolo Bissari, *Torilda* (Valvasense, 1648)

a. Tra le più osservate curiosità de' moderni Drammi, habbiamo la varietà delle Scene, che tratte in giro, ò condotte per canaletti di legno con Machina ch'ad un subito le ricambia, vanno per ogni parte aprendo nuovi prospetti. (p. 4)

b. Ne sarà fuor di quell' uso, che 'l Dramma con musica si rappresenti, sapendosi, che Frinico fù per ciò eletto Capitano, che faceva cantare le sue Tragedie *cum melis, & melopeis*, ch'eran tuoni dicevoli alla battaglia. (p. 5)

c. A gli scherzi, e balli, che s'intessono alle moderne rappresentanze s'innovano quell'antiche *emmeleia* che rendevan men noiose le lor Tragedie. . . . Di questi adornate le nuove Scene, non si diran manchevoli de gli usati chori, già, che i Chori per lo più ne Balli si dimostravano; e le Danze cuì sarà co'l suono aggiunto il canto, non saran dissimili da quella Iporchematica, di che scrive Atheneo, che con canti, e suoni si distingueva. (p. 7)

d. Non son manchevoli quest'Opre di quei precetti di quantità in rappresentar per lo più gli avenimenti di un solo giorno nello statuito termine di quattr' hore.

e. . . . in queste [opere] tutte, anziche interrotti, sembrino ravvivati gli antichi instituti. (preface, p. 8)

26. BISSARI, *Bradamante* (Valvasense, 1650)

L'haver goduto la Città di Venetia in pochi anni circa cinquanta Opere Regie, delle quali à fatica ne han veduto qualcheduna poche Città, ò nelle Nozze, ò in altra solennità de' lor Prencipi; hà insterilito chi compone, e nauseato chi ascolta; riuscendo difficile il trovar cose non vedute, o il farle così ben comparire, che con pompa, & apparenza maggiore non siano per avanti comparse. (preface, p. 7)

27. GIOVANNI BATTISTA FUSCONI [PIETRO MICHIELE AND FRANCESCO LOREDANO], *Amore innamorato* (Surian, 1642)

a. Questa Favola hà tutte le buone regole insegnate da' Maestri; che termina co 'l giro d'un giorno, ò poco più; ch'è un'attione sola; che non hà accidente, che sia incompatibile; e che non travia punto dal costume;

b. Mà stimo poca prudenza il prendersi briga per difendere una cosa trascurata anche dagli stessi Autori. Tanto più, ch'essendo al presente il secolo composto d'opinioni, e d'interessi non crede ad altre regole, che à quelle del capriccio, e della passione. (p. 7)

c. Questo dovrebbe sodisffare ad alcuni, che non s'appagano, che di miracoli, e che sprez-zarebbero l'armonie del Cielo, se l'ascoltassero più d'una volta. (preface, p. 8)

28. FUSCONI [MICHIELE], *Argiope* (Pinelli, 1649)
[Dedication to Anna Renzi, 29 December 1645]

a. Per servire a V.S. misi dapprima la mano a quest'opera, & a suo contemplatione l'hò finalmente perfetionata; onde a lei debbo ancora per ogni riguardo inviarla, come a colei ch'è destinata a felicitar gli errori della mia Penna con la divinità del suo canto, che trasporta le Sirene sù i Teatri, anzi porta in Terra l'armonia delle sfere. Doverei quì in applauso all'eminenza de' vostri meriti, che vi predica una Musa novella al nostro secolo, sciogliere canti di Cigno: ma dove parla un Mondo epilogato in questa augustissima Città, stupenda acclamatrice della vostra virtù: sarebbe temerario il suono della voce di chi non vanta altro pregio, che d'unico ammiratore d'un Merito sovrahumano. Vi dedico adunque quest'opera non per obligarvi a protegerla, bastandole per potente diffesa l'essere beatificata dal vostro canto: ma per viva espressione de gli oblighi immortali ch'io professo alla vostra ineffabile gentilezza, della quale perpetuo Idolatra vi prego dal Cielo nella eternità della vostra gloria eterno corso di felicissima fortuna. (dedication, p. 3)

b. L'Orditura di questa Favola venne a preghiere d'Amici più tosto precipitata, che tessuta in quatordici sere dalla penna di quel famosissimo Cigno dell'Adria, che mantiene al nostro secolo in Vita la Poesia Italiana: poiche essendo egli allhora di partenza, & in aspettatione della discretione de' venti, che gli aprissero la strada per un lungo viaggio maritimo non potè applicarvisi, che a momenti rubati al sonno. (p. 5)

c. Spero . . . che la diversità pur troppo apparente dello stile verrà resa uniforme dalla musica impareggiabile (ancorche diversa) delli Signori Gio. Rovetta, & Alessandro Leardini Prencipi de Musici Moderni. (preface, p. 6)

d. Gli accidenti, che mutano l'essere alle cose in un istante, havendo privato della seconda gloria il nostro Dramma, la quale sarebbe stata la musica del Sig. Rovetta, unita a quella del Sig.

Leardini, ti lasceranno godere dell'armonia d'un solo Orfeo, mentre io te ne havea apparecchiata quella di due. (postscript, p. 96)

29. FRANCESCO SBARRA, *Alessandro vincitor di se stesso* (Batti, 20 January 1651)
"Lettera dell'autore al signor Michel'Angelo Torcigliani" (Lucca, 29 December 1650)

a. Il padre Cesti, miracolo della Musica, con altri Virtuosi rappresentò nel passato Autunno un gentilissimo Dramma nella Città nostra [*Giasone*]; io se bene all'hora relegato in letto da una lunga, e pericolosa indispositione, a dispetto del male, che voleva trà l'altre miserie, che seco adduce, privarmi ancora della vista di questa virtuosa Attione, mi portai a vederla: il gusto ch'io ne retrassi fù riconosciuto da me per l'unico mio rimedio. . . .

b. Per sodisfare all'istanze di questi Virtuosi, da' quali riconosceva la ricuperata salute, intrapresi, & ultimai un Dramma, in quei pochi giorni, che d'otio mi concesse la mia convalescenza, tempo maggiore, e più opportuno non venendomi permesso dalla necessità, che tenevano di rappresentarlo prontamente in Venetia. I parti, che sono concepiti in stato simile di non intera sanità, sono sempre imperfetti: ma questi è più d'ogni altro,

c. non havendo havuto ben minimo tempo di rivederlo, necessitato dall'angustia del Tempo a lasciarlo metter sotto le note nella stessa forma, che alla giornata l'andava abbozzando. S'aggiunge, che per esser riuscito troppo lungo per la Musica, è convenuto à i medesimi d'accorciarlo, sì che è impossibile, che qualche storpiatura non apparisca, & in questa maniera mi avvisano, che sono necessitati à stamparlo.

d. In questa stretta, ch'è la maggiore, che possa incontrarsi, trattandosi della reputatione, ch'è l'anima d'un galanthuomo, ricorro al favore di V. S., supplicandola à farmi gratia di rivedere, & emendare à suo modo quest'Opera, prima che si stampi. . . . Vi ritroverà molti errori di lingua, assai languidezze, e durezze di versi, nel giocoso infinità d'Idiotismi nostri, che altrove non quadrano, oltre à molti sconcerti causati dall'accorciamento dell'Opera. (author's letter, pp. 4–5)

e. Sò che l'Ariette cantate da Alessandro, & Aristotile, si stimeranno contro il decoro di Personaggi si grandi; ma sò ancora, ch'è improprio il recitarsi in Musica, non imitandosi in questa maniera il discorso naturale, e togliendosi l'anima al componimento Drammatico, che non deve esser altro, che un'imitatione dell'attioni humane, e pur questo difetto non solo è tolerato dal Secolo corrente; ma ricevuto con applauso; questa specie di Poesia hoggi non hà altro fine che il dilettare, onde conviene accommodarsi all'uso de i Tempi;

f. se lo stile recitativo non venisse intermezzato con simili scherzi, porterebbe più fastidio, che diletto. (preface)

30. SBARRA, *L'amor della patria superiore ad ogn'altro* (Pezzana, 1668)

Per ben conoscere il soprafino talento, e fertilissimo ingegno del Sig. Francesco Sbarra, basta dar un'Occhiata all'Opere sue; frà le quali soggetto, che mira co 'l più vivo dell'Anima, il maggior bene della Serenissima Republica; come suddito fedelissimo, hà scielto quella Intitolata L'AMOR DELLA PATRIA. . . . Perche pare, che s'aggiusti alla misura del Grado, nel quale si trovano i publici interessi; già tanto proditoriamente versati dall'Immanità Ottomana; Hà stimato proprio, ch'io (come già feci dell'Erudita Tirannide dell'Interesse dello stesso Autore) per mezzo delle mie Stampe, debba Publicar anco la presente, accresciuta dal medesimo Signor Sbarra; acciòche quanto 'l ferventissimo zelo è sviscerato applicato al Publico sollievo, altretanto possano Tutti egualmente comprendere, con i dovuti riflessi, quali siano le proprie incombenze; e l'obligo de ciascuno di concorrer efficacemente con l'Affetto, e con gl'effetti al respiro, e Prosperità dell'Amata Patria.

Raccogliendo quel Generoso eccitamento, che da quest'Opera viene proposto, del più memorabile Essempio d'un intiera Republica, con Attioni così gloriose, che sono ben degne d'esser scolpite à Caratteri d'oro Adamantini, negl'animi veramente Amanti della riverita, Adorabile Patria, per conservar il pretiosissimo Tesoro dell'Inestimabile Gemma della sicura libertà; Unico Oggetto, che move all'espressione di questi devotissimi ossequij; con infiammato desiderio, che nei Cuori de tutti venga Universalmente impresso, sostenuto, e coll'opre comprobato, ch'attualmente sia L'AMOR DELLA PATRIA SUPERIORE AD OGN'ALTRO. (printer's preface, pp. 3–4)

31. GIOVANNI FAUSTINI, *Egisto* (Miloco, 1643)

a. Per non lasciar perire la Doriclea ho formato con frettolosa penna l'Egisto, quale getto nelle braccie della fortuna: s'egli non sarà meritevole de' tuoi applausi scusa la qualità del suo essere, perchè nato in pochi giorni si può chiamare più tosto sconciatura, che parto dell'intelletto. L'ho fabricato con la bilancia in mano, & aggiustato alla debolezza di chi lo deve far comparire sopra la Scena. I Teatri vogliono apparati per destare la meraviglia, & il diletto, e tal volta i belletti, gl'ori, e le porpore ingannano gl'occhi, e fanno parere belli li oggetti defformi. Se tù sei Critico non detestare la pazzia del mio Egisto, come imitatione d'un'attione da te veduta altre volte calcare le Scene, trasportata dal Comico nel Dramatico Musicale, perchè le preghiere autorevoli di personaggio grande mi hanno violentato a inserirla nell'opera, per sodisfare al Genio di chi l'hà da rappresentare.

b. L'Episodio d'Amore . . . ti confesso d'haverlo tolto d'Ausonio, con quella licenza, ch'usarono i Pocti Latini di togliere l'inventioni da' Greci per vestire le loro favole, & i loro Epici Componimenti. (preface, pp. 3–4)

32. FAUSTINI, *Doriclea* (Miloco, 1645)

Non posso più raffrenare, Eccellentissimo Signor mio, gl'empiti generosi di Doriclea: intollerante di rimanere sepolta nell'angustezze della Casa paterna, si parte dalle mosse per giungere alle mete d'una gloria immortale. Semplice, ella è giovane, e guidata dalla cieca scorta del suo ardimento non pavenca gl'Alcidi, che la sfidano, e non mira l'insidie, apprestatele per impedirle il camino, da due potenti nemiche, l'emulatione interessata, e l'Ignoranza pretendente. . . . Tocca à V. S. . . . per l'affetto, che porta à questa Amazone, quale hà tratto, si può dire, i primi vagiti nelle sue braccia, ad assicurarle il sentiero, & à diffendere la sua riputatione contro la sfacciata ambitione di certi rozzi versificatori, che poveri d'inventioni, ò per dir meglio, dissipatori dell'altrui, trattano l'arti della maledicenza, tentando di deturpare le Compositioni de gl'ingegni migliori de' loro, non sapendo queste Piche la difficoltà dell'inventare, perche non hanno giamai inventato, e ch'egli è, come mi disse lei una volta, un filosofare. (dedication)

33. FAUSTINI, *Oristeo*, Favola Ottava (Pinelli, 1651)

a. Io non son di quelli . . . che scrivono per dilettare il proprio capriccio; Affatico la penna, le confesso la mia ambitione, per tentare, s'ella potesse inalzarmi sopra l'ordinario, & il commune de gl'ingegni stupidi, e plebei. Questa honorata pazzia, che cominciò quasi ad assalirmi uscito da' vincoli delle fascie, non cessando mai dalle sue instigationi, mi necessita alle assidue fabriche di varie tessiture.

b. Composi però, senza l'impulso dell'ambito fine l'Oristeo, e la Rosinda, gettato poco tempo nella loro creatione, per sgravarmi dalle obligationi, che inavertito mi havevano racchiuso trà le angustezze d'un Teatro dove, se non altro, l'occhio avezzato alla vastezza di Scene Reali s'inviliva, nella vicinanza dell'apparenze. È vero, che non dissimile dall'Orchestra sudetta, nella quale comparsero Ersilla, & Euripo, e dove di poi dovevano farsi vedere questi gemelli, è il Palco da me eretto, per decapitare l'otio della institutione del mio viver libero, ma è anco verissimo che da loro, come da Cadaveri, non pretendo di trarre voci d'applauso, riserbando à tempi più lieti, & à Teatri più maestosi l'Eupatra, l'Alciade, & il Meraspe, Heroi usciti d'Embrioni, e quasi perfettionati. (dedication)

34. FAUSTINI, *Rosinda*, Favola Nona (Pinelli, 1651)

Mi dichiarai nell'antecedente Oristeo, che questi duo Drami furono da me composti per disobligatione di debito, non per avidità d'applauso. (preface)

35. FAUSTINI, *Eritrea*, Drama Undecima Postumo (Giuliani, 1652)

a. Mentre una finta morte d'Eritrea lusingherà a V.S. Illustriss. dolcemente l'orecchio, la pur troppo vera del Sig. Giovanni Faustini le commoverà dolorosamente l'anima. Morì pochi giorni sono questo celebre Litterato, & doppò la tessitura di undici Opere, hà lasciato sotto il Torchio quella della sua cara Eritrea. Questa povera Regina tutta abattuta per gl'incontri sinistri, per la stravaganza delli accidenti, compare alla fine alla luce, obligata d'ubbidire à quel genitore, che la promise nella Calisto. Non hanno mancato intoppi da trattenerla nel viaggio, oltre la perdita di quello, che generata, doveva assisterle ancora. Hà pur anco smarrita in dietro la compagnia del virtuoso Bonifatio, che nel principio del camino fermò col passo la vita. (p. 5)

b. La Scena degli Elefanti, ch'in molte parti dell'opera osserverà V.S. Illustriss. chiamata; e che fu inventione del Poeta, si lascia da parte, non convenendo al decoro di Regina vestir un'habito, che destinato per lei habbia prima servito ad'altri. (dedication by Giacomo Batti, bookseller, p. 6)

[*second ed.*] (Batti, 1661)

c. Ecco, che ad onta del tempo (e pur ha per gloria di strugerlo) di nuovo si fà vedere alla luce l'Eritrea. La virtù di chi la compose servì di scudo per riparo ai colpi dell'oblivione. Puote ben il tempo trionfar della vita dell'Auttore: ma in vano s'affaticò d'ecclissar il nome d'un che tuttavia risorge al mondo. Mà perchè vi sono state aggionte, et levate mille cose sì è stato proprio il ristamparla prima nella forma stessa, che fù già con molto splendore rappresentata in questa città, & nella guisa apunto, che dall'Auttore fù fabricata; poi seguente havrai nel medesimo libretto quella, che al presente si recita; essendosene così compiaciuto, chi n'era padrone per incontrare nelle sodissfationi de suoi amorevolissimi padroni a quali si tiene molto obligato, onde così non rimarà deffraudato il merito di chi la compose, & rimarano consolati quelli che al presente la fanno rappresentare. (dedication)

36. FAUSTINI, *Eupatra*, Favola Duodecima (Ginammi, 1655)

a. Non ha strale la morte, che offender possa la vita di coloro, che vivono per merito di virtù, & muoiono solo per necessità di natura. Uno di questi è il Sig. Giovanni Faustini di gloriosa ricordanza, che piansimo già morto, anzi ammiramo rapito dalle mani della morte, & aplaudemmo sposato con l'immortalità. Il livore medesimo non hà veleno per attossicar questa gloria, nè caligini per offuscar questo splendore, mentre tuttavia escono alla luce del mondo novi parti di quel nobilissimo ingegno, tra quale è l'Eupatra, che non può dirsi Orfana, mentre il Padre nella memoria de posteri è vivente, e Vostra Signoria Illustrissima nella protetione di lui è più, che mai vigoroso. (printer's dedication)

b. Ecco finalmente l'Eupatra già anni quattro promessa. Duodecima fatica drammatica del Sig. Gio. Faustini di felice memoria. Se le sue opere hanno in questa Città, e nell'Italia tutta, dove frequentemente vengono rappresentate ottenuti gl'applausi universali, non si deve temere, che anco questa Principessa non habbia a conseguire i dovutili allori. Sarà ammirabile per l'inventione, e per la tessitura:

c. molti desiderarebbero di vederla comparire in Teatro più grande, mà di ciò compiacendosene chi la fa rappresentare non devono prendersene altro pensiero. Il Teatro è ristretto frà l'angustezze de' muri, nè oltre essi può estendersi, tuttavolta con l'artificio s'è procurato d'ingannar l'occhio, che in simili apparenze deve anco godere d'essere ingannato.

d. L'Autore quasi presago di sua intempestiva morte lasciò di suo pugno ne' fogli alcune notarelle, onde andavano poste certe canzonette, che sono poi state fatte da virtuosissimo soggetto. A gl'Idioti paiono oscure quelle favole, che sole si svelano nell'ultime Scene, ma gl'intendenti, e studiosi l'amirano, poiche in simili compositioni devono tenersi sospesi anco gl'ingegni più curiosi, che così ha sempre professato l'Autore, non solo nelle dodeci opere fin'hora stampate, mà in altre ancora, che si riserbano gl'anni venturi,

e. havendo egli sempre applicato tutto l'animo all'inventione, da che, per la continua, &

incessante applicatione, ne derivò l'origine di sua infermità, che troppo acerbamente in età di trentadue [sic] anni gli levò la vita. (printer's preface, pp. 7–8)

f. Per aggradirti eccoti stampate l'aggiunte all'Eupatra fatte da virtuosissimi soggetti lequali però sempre furono abborite dal genio dell'autore. Nondimeno si sono andate disponendo in maniera, che niente levano al sussiego dell'opera: il cui stile erudito e sollevato non può biasimarsi, che da chi vive povero di talenti necessarij in simili compositioni; poiche scrivendosi per dilettare una Città imparegiabile, e che propriamente deve nominarsi Città de Heroi, devesi anco scrivere (dà chi sà però farlo) sollevato e con le forme dovute, e proprie à personaggi, che s'introducono, & agl'ingegni nobili, & eruditi, ch'ascoltano, e leggono. (printer's postscript)

37. FAUSTINI–NICOLÒ MINATO, *Elena* (Giuliani, 26 December 1659)
a. Il Soggetto di questo drama uscì dal Felicissimo ingegno del già Sign. Giovanni Faustini di famosa memoria: e della cui Virtù stupirono i Teatri non solo di questa Città, ma quelli ancora de' più remoti Paesi. Molte penne sublimi son state richieste, doppo la di lui Morte, a vestirlo col manto della Poesia, e con varie ragioni ciascuno ha ricusato. Io non hò saputo rifutar quest'honore. . . .

b. Prego il Cielo, che la Pace delle sue Ceneri non resti turbata da chi delle mie imperfettioni prenda ardimento di farne risentire alla di lui Virtù qualche tocco. Mi dichiaro però, che, ciò, che v'è di male è mio, e tutto ciò, che vi risplende di buono è suo. Tu Lettor Cortese ammira il Soggetto, compatisci le Parole. (Minato's preface)

38. FAUSTINI, *Alciade*, Drama Decimoquarto (Nicolini & Curti, 1667)
a. Il Signor Giovanni Faustini nell'età sua più giovenile per diletto proprio applicò l'ingegno alle compositioni Dramatiche musicali, nelle quali riuscì ammirabile nell'inventione in particolare: Onde nel corso di soli anni nove (essendo stato troppo prematuramente rapito dalla morte l'anno 1651, nel trigesimo secondo dell'età sua) si viddero rappresentare ne i Theatri di questa Città con gli applausi maggiori La Virtù de'Strali d'Amore, L'Egisto, L'Ormindo, il Titone, la Doriclea, L'Ersilla, L'Euripo, L'Oristeo, La Rosinda, La Calisto, L'Eritrea, & doppo la di lui morte ancora L'Eupatra, poi l'Elena rapita da Teseo, vestita col manto di Poesia da sublime virtuoso, tutte poste in musica, ò dalla virtù singolare del Signor Francesco Cavalli dignissimo Organista della Serenissima Republica, ò dal Signor Don Pietro Andrea Zianni hora Maestro di Capella della Maestà dell'Imperatrice, incontrarono non solo nel genio, & nella sodisfattione di questa Città tanto delicata nell'udire simili rappresentationi, mà di molte altre principali dell'Italia, nelle quali, più, e più volte sono state rappresentate con ogni pienezza d'applauso; anzi che con l'Inventioni multiplici, & varie d'esse quasi come di cose obliate si sono addobbate, & arrichite altre compositioni. Restano ancora tre fatiche di questo virtuoso: La Medea placata, L'Alciade, & il Meraspe, overo il Tiranno humiliato d'Amore: L'Anno presente compariranno nel Nobilissimo Theatro Grimano prima l'Alciade, & poi il Meraspe, promessi dall'Auttore nelle sue stampe l'anno 1651, che passò ad altra vita.

b. L'inventioni saranno nuove, curiose, & dilettevoli, havendo procurato d'allontanarsi da introdurvi in esse femine in habito virile datesi à credere per huomeni, & altre cose ancora, più, & più volte vedute, & rappresentate; Onde si può credere, che anco queste siano per incontrare nella sodisfattione della Città. Nell'Alciade si sono aggiunte alcune cose, composte da virtuoso soggetto per favorire, & à richiesta di chi fà rappresentare il DRAMA. La compositione della Musica d'Esso è del Signor Zianni, che conforme al suo solito hà fatto cose mirabili. (printer's preface)

39. FAUSTINI, *Il tiranno humiliato d'Amore overo il Meraspe*, Soggetto Decimoquarto (Bruni/Bati, 12 December 1667)
Il presente Drama fù lasciato imperfetto dal già Signor Giovanni Faustini, mentre nè compose solamente due Atti, ma scarsi d'ariette, & la maggior parte in stile recitativo, come s'acco-

stumava in quel tempo onde per ridurlo all'uso corrente è stato necessario che vi s'affatichi più d'una penna; senza alterar punto il Soggetto, & il scenario Lasciato dall'Auttore in tutta perfettione, come anco il Prologo. Nel verso però vi sarà qualche cosa framischiata dell'auttore stesso, che per dar forza al titolo dell'opera è stato neccessario inserirla. (printer's preface, p. 3)

40. GIACOMO CASTOREO, *Pericle effeminato* (Batti, 7 January 1653)
a. Se vi ritroverai qualche cosa che tiene del Historico, sappi che il resto è mera Inventione, onde perderai la fatica, se anderai a ventilar Plutarco, e Tucidide per conoscer se mi son allontanato dal vero; Perche non intendo di riferirti un historia, ma di rappresentarti una favola, che non ha d'historico, che il nome. È ben vero che l'Attione principale di essa, è tratta da Plutarco, che scrive gli Amori di Pericle ed'Aspasia per le quali s'acquistò il nome effeminato: ma però nel inserirli nel Drama, hò seguito il proprio Capriccio.
b. Se non hò osservato ne il decoro nei personaggi, ne il verisimile negli accidenti, non mi riprendere, perche seguo l'abuso, introdotto da molti, e praticato da tutti. Quelle metafore, che hanno titolo di giocoso, lontane però in qualche parte dalla modestia morale; ascoltele come ti piace; ma sappi, che la mia Intentione non è mai stata d'inserirvi l'oscenità; anzi d'indurti a compianger meco la depravata corutella del Secolo, nel quale la facoltà poetica, che altre volte fù stromento d'intimorir i tiranni con la Civiltà de Costumi, non trovi mezo per dilettarti che con la sfacciatagine de moti inhonesti. (preface, pp. 8–9)

41. CASTOREO, *La guerriera spartana* (Batti, 6 January 1654)
Vi fu . . . chi accusava [la guerriera] di furto per haverli osservato al lembo d'una Veste certo ornamento, che par tessuto ad'un'istesso telaro con quello d'un'altro: Mà di questo non se ne parli; perche potrò io bene difenderla quando occorresse. (preface)

42. NICOLÒ MINATO, *Antioco* (Giuliani, 21 January 1658)
Il Xerse, e l'Artemisia, fiachi delineamenti della mia penna, furono da tè compatiti fra le pompe sublimi del Felicissimo Teatro à SS. Gio: e Paolo: hora mi tocco pregarti à compatire questa mia Nuova debolezza, destinata al Teatro à S. Cassano. Sò che ti moverà sensi di curiosità la mutatione: rendila però sodisfatta col sapere, che con amatissimo Amico, che hà sortito, fin l'Anno trascorso, di far risplendere le sue meravigliose Virtù in quel Teatro, io non hò voluto tentar concorrenza, sì perche sarei rimasto perdente, come perche il mio costume regolato dalla rettitudine non usa di insidiare la Fortuna de gl'Amici. (preface)

43. MINATO, *La caduta di Elio Seiano* (Heredi Leni, 3 February 1667)
E se trovi chi s'esprima, che non gli vadano à senso, osserva, e vedrai esser persone di basso grado che non arrivano à concepire elevati sentimenti d'Anima Eroica. Rammentati, che le Rappresentationi di questi Drami furono dagl'Antichi inventate per insegnar la perfettion de' costumi onde l'Attioni, che vi si figurano, devono formarsi all'Idea di quelle che doverebbe essere, se non di quello che è. (preface)

44. AURELIO AURELI, *La costanza di Rosmonda*, Favola Quinta (Valvasense, 15 January 1659)
a. Per non fastidirti con la lunghezza del Drama, hò levato nell'ultime prove tutto quello, che ho stimato superfluo; ma perche il primo Atto era già passato sotto il torchio della Stampa, ti prego a scusarmi, & à supplire con la velocità dello sguardo, dove non è potuto giunger à tempo la tardità della penna a segnarti con i punti quei versi che non si cantano.
b. Nella scena XIV, dell'Atto Primo dove dice Clitennestra sopra una Loggia, s'è pensato di farla comparire in scena per esponerla à gli occhi di tutti, & in particolare à quelli, che saranno ne i palchi. (postscript, p. 91)

45. AURELI, *Antigona delusa da Alceste*, Favola Settima (Batti, 15 January 1660)

a. Quanto sia facile ad ingannarsi l'opinione del Volgo, questa volta lo vedrai da gli effetti; mentre essendosi per la Città di Venetia diseminata una voce, che quest'anno non s'havrebbe recitato nel Teatro à SS. Gio: e Paolo, questo hà dato motivo à chi assiste al dominio, e protettione del medesimo Teatro di farti vedere nel breve corso di questo Carnevale, che non solo si recita, mà di più à comparir sù la Scena doi Drami. (p. 7)

b. . . . per la strettezza del tempo mi è convenuto aggiustare il Drama sopra le Scene (trattane sol una) sopra i medesimi Balli, e sù parte delle machine inventate dall'Illustrissimo Sig. Zaguri. (preface, p. 9)

46. AURELI, *Le fatiche d'Ercole per Deianira*, Favola Decima (Nicolini, 1662)

a. Sò d'essermi espresso più fiate, ch'io scrivo per mero capriccio, e per obbedire à chi me lo comanda, e non per ambitione d'immortalarmi con quell'opere, che per essere tutte composte in Musica non hanno altro fondamento, che l'aria. . . .

b. Sono hoggidì le persone della Città di Venetia divenute così svogliate nè i gusti de i Drami, che non sanno più, che desiderar di vedere, ne l'intelletto di chi compone sà più, che inventare per acquistarsi gl'applausi de' spettatori, ò per incontrare la sodisfattione della maggior parte (che di tutti è impossibile).

c. Se tal ora non m'è riuscito il poter colpire nel segno, sappi, ch'anco non sempre hò havuto per potervi applicare quella opportunità di tempo, che si ricerca in simili compositioni. Che ciò sia vero lo vedrai dà gl'effetti, mentre spero, che in queste mie fatiche destinate per Ercole conoscerai la differenza, che v'è dallo scrivere in fretta, al componere con la mente quieta, e à bell'agio. Confesso d'essermi in queste affaticato più, che negl'altri miei Drami per incontrar il tuo genio. (preface, pp. 5–6)

47. AURELI, *Gli amori d'Apollo e di Leucotoe*, Favola Undecima (Nicolini, 8 January 1663)

Mi dichiaro che sono così capricciosi i geni del nostro secolo, & è sì difficile da contentarsi il Popolo di Venetia, satio hormai reso dalla rappresentatione di tanti Drami, ch'io non stimarei spropositi il fare degli spropositi, quando fossi sicuro, che questi dovessero dilettar gl'ascoltanti, e gradire a chi spende. (preface)

48. AURELI, *Perseo*, Favola Decimaterza (Nicolini, 1665)

Sò, ch'il gusto del Popolo di Venetia è arrivato à tal segno, che non sà più che bramar di vedere, nè i Compositori sanno più che inventar per sodisfar al capriccio bizarro di questa Città. (preface)

49. AURELI, *Eliogabalo*, Opera Decimaquarta (Nicolini, 10 January 1667 [1668])

Torno ad infastidirti con la mia debolezza: E quando credevo arrecarti men noia con un'altro Eliogabalo parto di sollevato ingegno già estinto, ornato di varie gemme di Veneta penna erudita, aggiustato da mè in qualche parte all'uso del genio corrente, & in fine nobilitato dalla Musica singolare del Signor Francesco Cavalli, m'è convenuto impensatamente per vigoroso commando di chi devo obbedire terminar frettolosamente questo mio Eliogabalo parto legitimo della mia penna in tutto diverso di costumi, e d'attioni dall'altro, qual già due anni principiai à componere con diligente studio di formar un Drama adeguato al tuo genio. (preface)

50. AURELI, *Claudio Cesare*, Opera Decimasesta (Nicolini, 27 December 1672)

a. Ti presento il mio Claudio ricco più di canzoni, e d'ariette, che d'accidenti. Basti il dire, che sia Drama per Musica. Che si può fare? s'oggi dì i capricci di Venetia così la vogliono, io procuro d'incontrar il lor gusto (preface).

b. Doppo stampata, e provata l'Opera sovra la Scena s'hà stimato bene l'abbreviarla in varie parti superflue; Onde sei pregato a trascorrer benignamente con l'occhio alquanti versi, e qualche

Scena, che per maggior brevità si tralasciano, non havendo potuto apportarli per esser la stampa già fatta. Qui sotto leggerai anco trè ariette mutate, il tutto fatto à solo fine di cantar solo quello, che si vede, che possa maggiormente dilettar gl'Uditori.

c. Compatisci la difficoltà ch'oggidì provano li compositori nel poter sodisfare non solo à tanti capricci bizarri di questa Città; mà anco a gl'humori stravaganti de' Signori Musici recitanti. (postscript)

51. Aureli, *Antigona delusa d'Alceste*, Drama Rinovato (Curti/Nicolini, 18 January 1669 [1670])
Se qui dentro vi conoscerai repplicata alle tue orecchie la vaghezza di qualche sua arietta [del Ziani] da te forse altre volte udita o in Venetia o alla grandezza di quella Corte Cesarea . . . considera che il tutto s'è fatto a solo fine di maggiormente compiacerti. (preface)

52. Francesco Piccioli, *L'incostanza trionfante overo il Theseo* (Giuliani/Batti, 16 January 1658)
L'autore [hà] con tutto lo studio evitato d'innestar in questo Drama quegl'intrecci, che sono stati, e sono communi à quasi tutte simili Compositioni. Non vi vedrai perciò, ne Lettere, ne Ritratti, ne Monili, ne Prencipi, ne Prencipesse in Habiti mentiti, ne Parti supposti da' Nutrici, ne altre pretese inventioni tali, che se bene si producono per nuove, e diverse, sono però sempre le stesse, nè possono certo più dilettare. Vi troverai bensì un'ordine continuato di simulationi, cabale, ed artificij, che caminano con puro passo Naturale, ò Politico, e che come spero non ti spiaceranno. (printer's second preface)

53. Giovanni Maria Milcetti, *Hipsicratea*, secondo musical drama (Batti, primo dell'anno 1660)
a. Quest'Opera è stata composta nella Badia delle Carceri; e di la transmessa foglio per foglio a Murano; secondo ricevea l'essere, e disponevasi nelle sue scene. Chi sà la distanza de' luoghi, non si darà maraviglia, se la vedrà con qualche varietà di versi, e parole tra lo stamparsi, e il rappresentarsi, poiche in effetto avanti si sia veduta compita, & organizzata di Poesia era di già animata di Musica, e di già cantava le sinfonie. (preface, p. 7)
b. Già, che la lontananza non mi dà d'essere così pronto per sovenire ai bisogni di questo mio Drama; mi contento, che V.S. v'inserisca le canzonette che mi descrive. Ben la prego di segnarle in Margine con una stellata * overo con un segno ,, si come s'è usato in altre. E dico questo, perche si come non mi piace vestire il mio con gl'ornamenti de gl'altri; così godo in estremo, che sia distinto. (postscript)

54. Anon., *Achille in Sciro* (Curti, 29 January 1664)
Se [questo Drama] non camina con le regole severe d'Aristotile, siegue la piacevole usanza del secolo, essendo questa una sorte di compositione nuova, ch'à differenza dell'antiche, hà più per fine il dilettevole, che l'utile. (printer's preface)

55. Giovanni Filippo Apolloni, *Argia* (Nicolini, 13 January 1669)
Sentirai alcune ariette udite in altra occasione; ma perche sia noto, che furon prese da questo Drama vi si hanno lasciate si per essere di pochissimo numero, come anco di singolare esquisitezza. (printer's preface)

Appendix II: Treatises, Critical and Historical Accounts

◆ ◆ ◆

1. ANON., *Il corago o vero alcune osservazioni per metter bene in scena le composizioni drammatiche* (MS I-Mbe y.F.11), ed. Paolo Fabbri and Angelo Pompilio (Florence, 1983)

a. Primo perché è privo della perfetta imitazione delli affetti e del commun ragionare, perché se bene un'aria allegra significa l'affetto allegro, tuttavia non esprime nel particulare ciascun verso e parola nel modo che si dovrebbe. (p. 60)

b. Per cominciare da personaggi o interloquitori che la rappresentazione armonica pare che più convenevolmente abbracci, sembrano molto a proposito per le azioni profane le deità antiche come Apollo, Teti, Nettuno et altri stimati numi, come anche i semidei et eroi vetusti, massime tra i quali si possono annoverare i fiumi, laghi, massime i più celebri appresso le muse come Peneo, il Tebro, il Trasimeno e sopra tutti quei personaggi che stimiamo essere stati perfetti musici, come Orfeo, Anfione e simili. La ragione di tutto questo si è perché vedendo troppo bene ciascuno auditore che almeno nelle parti più conosciute della terra non si parla in musica ma pianamente dalli uomini ordinarii, più si conforma con il concetto che si ha dei personaggi sopra umani il parlar in musica che con il concetto e manifesta notizia delli uomini dozzinali, perché essendo il ragionare armonico più alto, più maestrevole, più dolce e nobile dell'ordinario parlare, si attribuisce per un certo connaturale sentimento ai personaggi che hanno più del sublime e divino. . . .

c. Se noi prendiamo per interlocutori le persone vicine ai nostri tempi e di costumi più manifestamente simili ai nostri, troppo apertamente ci si appresenta subito improbabile et inverisimile quel modo di parlar cantando. (p. 63)

d. Nelle [azioni] ridicole sono a proposito le persone più sciocche e che abbino notabile modo di ragionare con inflessioni plebee e che sono da noi conosciute, perché l'imitazione dei loro modi quanto più si accosta cantando al parlare di quelli, tanto più riesce giocondo et ammirabile. (p. 64)

e. Sopra tutto per esser buon recitante cantando bisognerebbe esser anche buono recitante parlando, onde aviamo veduto che alcuni che hanno avuto particolar grazia in recitare hanno fatto meraviglie quando insieme hanno saputo cantare. Intorno a che alcuni muovono questione se si deva eleggere un musico non cattivo che sia perfetto recitante o pure un musico eccellente ma di poco o nessun talento di recitare, nel che si è toccato con mano che sì come ad alcuni pochi molto intendenti di musica sono più piaciuti l'eccellenti cantori quantunque freddi nel recitamento, così al co[mu]ne del teatro sodisfazione maggiore hanno dato i perfetti istrioni con mediocre voce e perizia musicale. Pertanto dovendo il musico distribuire a proposito le parti e servirsi di tutti a perfezione, procurerà per quanto si mostrerà possibile di imitar li eccellenti cantori ma [mettendo quelli] esangui et in età nel recitare in parti che non siano molto attuosi e che abbino molti ornamenti a torno come in nuvole et altre machine per aria dove non si richiede tanto moto né espressione di atteggiamenti istrionici. (pp. 91–92)

2. GIULIO STROZZI, *Le glorie della signora Anna Renzi romana* (Venice: Surian, 1644)

a. L'azzione con la quale si dà l'anima, lo spirito, e l'essere alle cose, deve esser governata dal movimento del corpo, dal gesto, dal volto, e dalla voce, hora innalzandola, hora abbassandola, sdegnandosi, & tornando subito a pacificarsi: una volta parlando in fretta, un'altra adagio, movendo il corpo hor a questa, hor a quella parte, raccogliendo le braccia, e distendendole, ridendo, e piangendo, hor con poca, hora con molta agitatione di mani: la nostra Signora Anna è dotata d'una espressione sì viva, che paiono le risposte, e i discorsi non appresi dalla memoria, ma nati all'hora. In somma ella si trasforma tutta nella persona che rappresenta, e sembra hora una Talia piena di comica allegrezza, hora una Melpomone ricca di Tragica Maestà. . . . Padroneggia la Scena, intende quel che proferisce, e lo proferisce si chiaramente, che non hanno l'orecchie, che desiderare. (p. 6)

b. Hà una lingua sciolta, una pronuntia suave, non affettata, non presta, una voce piena, sonora, non aspra, non roca, ne che ti offenda con la soverchia sottigliezza: il che nasce dal temperamento del petto, e della gola, per la qual buona voce si ricerca molto caldi, che allarghi le vie, e tanto humido, che le intenerisca, e mollifichi. (p. 9)

c. Per questo ella hà il passaggio felice, e 'l trillo gagliardo, doppio, e rinforzato, ed è intervenuto à lei, che ben venti sei volte, con reggier tutto il peso d'un opera, l'hà replicata quasi una sera doppo l'altra, senza perder pur un caratto della sua teatrale, e perfettissima voce. (pp. 9–10)

d. Io hò considerato, oltre la fisonomia, che in lei non mentisce esser vero ancor quello, che per formar un ingegno sublime si ricerca, cioè grande intelletto, molta imaginativa, e bella memoria, come se non fussero queste tre cose contrarie, e non havessero nell'istesso sogetto alcuna naturale oppositione. Dono tutto della cortese natura, che sà, ma radevolte, unir questi tre habiti, quasi in republica, senza la maggioranza dell'uno, o dell'altro. La Signora Anna di temperamento malinconico per adustione hà nel discorso poche parole, mà quelle accorte, sensate, e degne per i suo' bei detti del premio della Lode. (p. 10)

e. Cosi ella và tacitamente osservando le azzioni altrui, e quando poi hà da rapresentarle, aiutata dal sangue, del quale ella è copiosissima, e dalla bile, che se le accende (senza la quale non possono gli huomini intraprender cose grandi) mostra lo spirito, e valor suo appreso con lo studio delle osservationi fatte: Onde ella hà havuto i Cieli molto propitij per renderla d'un ingegno sì riguardevole, e singolare. (pp. 10–11)

3. GIOVAN DOMENICO OTTONELLI, *Della cristiana moderatione del theatro* (Florence: Bonardi, 1652)
Libro IV, detto l'Ammonizione ai Recitanti, Nota terza: "Delle comedie cantate a nostro tempo, e di quante sorti, e di che qualità si rappresentino" (quoted in Ferdinando Taviani, *La commedia dell'arte e la società barocca: La fascinazione del teatro* [Rome, 1969], pp. 509–13)

a. Le seconde comedie cantate sono quelle che rappresentano tal volta alcuni gentiluomini, o cittadini virtuosi, o accademici eruditi, secondo la incidenza di qualche buona ragione. (p. 511)

b. La terza sorte delle comedie cantate . . . sono propriamente le mercenarie e dramatiche rappresentazioni musicali, cioè le fatte da que' mercenarii musici che sono comedianti di professione, e che raccolti in una compagnia sono diretti, e governati da un di loro, come principale d'autorità, e capo degli altri. (p. 512)

c. Si sforzano di radunar tanti virtuosi compagni, che la sola compagnia, composta di mercenarii comici professori, basti a condurre l'impresa, senza la necessità di chiamar per aiutanti altri cantori o sonatori: e sortiscono qualche volta l'intento, e qualche volta no. E quando nol sortiscono, non s'abbandonano; ma sen vanno con la compagnia, almeno cominciata, ad una principal città; . . . [e] fanno pratica per sapere, se prima non sanno, che cantore e sonatore sia nella città, o secolare, o ecclesiastico, o religioso, che possa essere invitato con premio, overo pregato con affetto, et anche tal volta quasi sforzato col mezzo d'intercessori grandi, ad accettar una, o più parti di musico aiutante in publico teatro, per compir il numero sufficiente a far udir, veder, e gustar il drama, o la comedia musicale al popolo uditore, e spettatore. (p. 512)

4. LEONE ALLACCI, *Drammaturgia di Leone Allacci divisa in sette indici* (Rome: Mascardi, 1666)
Avviene per tanto che doppo lette, [le opere dramatiche] si reiettano, e non se ne fa più conto di loro, così per le sciocchezze, che d'ordinario in molte si scorgono, onde vengono a perdersi gli esemplari, & oscurarsi non solo le memorie di chi, con suo grande scomodo, e curioso studio si

procurò qualche nome, ma delle patrie, e delle famiglie: come per essere al parere di qualcheduna in non poca parte tolte dalle antiche, e non variarsi l'una dall'altra nella inventione, e nel soggetto, e non intervenendo ritrovi novi, sono perciò venute a tanta noia, che come si sente nell'argumento, che in presa di Città, o sacco si sono smarriti bambini, o fanciulli, fanno conto di haverlo gia lette, e volentieri s'astengono di vederle, conoscendo chiaramente come diceva il Burchiello esser rappezzi di panni vecchi, stiracchiate, e rubacchiate di quà e là, per non haver via ne verso, ne capo, ne coda. (preface)

5. CRISTOFORO IVANOVICH, *Poesie* (Venice: Catani, 1675)
Letter to Giovanni Maria Pagliardi, 26 June 1673, transcribed in *Quellentexte zur Konzeption der europäischen Oper im 17. Jahrhundert*, ed. Heinz Becker (Kassel, 1981), 63–64

a. Hanno scelto per il venturo Carnevale il mio Lismaco i Sig. Conduttori del Teatro de' SS Gio. e Paolo. . . . Riceverà dunque ella in copia il Drama sudetto, qual prego sia letto per gentilezza, e riletto per grazia; a finche osservato con attenzione si renda più famigliare alle sue erudite note, essendo mira universale di far cosa da riuscire; giache il benefizio del tempo somministra i rimedij giovevoli. . . . Osserverà Ella, che l'Invenzione hà per fondamento una Storia famosa, che forma azioni Eroiche con un'amoroso patetico. Lo stile hò procurato facile, ed espressivo, l'ariette con qualche spirito, ma naturale. Mi spiacerebbe la sua lontananza, se la sua esperimentata Intelligenza non mi promettesse quel frutto, che maturarebbe una personale comunicazione; mentre saprà distinguer i sensi, comprender gli affetti, ed esprimere la loro forza. Hò frammesso qualche numero d'ariette da me stimato proprio al bisogno, compartito alle parti, che spero avranno occasione i Musici di farsi onore. Hò adoperata varietà di metri; a finche campeggiano nella loro bizzarria gli andamenti della sua musica, e se vi sarà cosa, che non le piaccia, si contenti darmi avviso per potervi rimediare. Nelle parti amorose vi sono sparsi alcuni lamenti, a' quali sarà dirizzata principalmente la curiosità, ed io gli hò maneggiati con qualche forma nuova, che potrà dilettare.

b. Se poi ritrovasse qualche affetto nel recitativo, che si possa ridurre in una cavata, non tralasci di farlo, che vien gradito qualche risalto improviso. Intorno poi al numero delle ariette, da farsi con le Sinfonie, si rimette alla sua discrezione con mira alla brevità tanto; quì, desiderata. In somma il Genio di questa Città inclina, che l'Eroico sia grave, ma vivace, il patetico non soverchiamente languido, ed il giocoso tutto brio; ma facile. Condoni V. S. la libertà di queste mie riflessioni dettatemi dal zelo del ben comune. Suppongo, che riceverà la lista de' musici, per adattare all'abilità delle loro voci la musica, in ciò consistendo la maggior importanza. Con l'onore delle sue umanissime attendo pure i suoi liberi sensi intorno al Drama per ricavare motivi di qualche perfezione.

6. IVANOVICH, "Le memorie teatrali di Venezia," in *Minerva al tavolino* (Venice: Pezzana, 1681)
a. Dedication: Mostra l'Autore d'avere scritte le Memorie Teatrali di Venezia, col fondamento delle Glorie Grimane, i di cui Teatri sono ammirati dal Mondo tutto. ([p. 363])

b. Hò maggiore [ragione] di reverire V.V. E.E. per i veri Apolli, se con la magnificenza de 'l oro Teatri, con la generosa profusione dell'oro fanno sentire i più elevati metri e le più isquisite voci. ([p. 363])

c. Con i lumi delle vostre Glorie hò formato la chiarezza all'opera; poiche il fregio maggiore nasce dal genio Eroico di V.V. E.E. e de' vostri gran progenitori, per opera de' quali si rinovò a' tempi nostri in questa inclita Città, la sontuosità di più Teatri, punto non inferiore à quella, che in Roma ostentarono i Marcelli, ed i Pompei. ([p. 364])

d. Capitolo I: Non vi fù mai alcuna Republica nel Mondo, che meglio superasse tutte le altre Republiche, che quella di Roma; nè alcun'altra, che meglio imitasse questa, che la Republica di Venezia. (p. 369)

e. [I trattenimenti Carnovaleschi di Venezia] sono oggetti di sopraffina Politica, da' quali dipende la felicità del governo, l'abbondanza, ed i giuochi, mediante i quali usati à misura del l'onesto, s'acquista il Prencipe l'amore de' Popoli, che mai meglio si scordano del giogo, che satollati ò trattenuti ne' piaceri.

La Plebe quando non hà che da rodere, rode la Fama del Prencipe, e quando non hà trattenimenti, può coll'ozio facilmente degenerare ne' disegni di pessime consequenze. (pp. 370–71)

f. Principiano le prove dell'Opere in Musica prima nelle Case de' Cavalieri Protettori, ò interessati de' Teatri, e poi sulle Scene, con curiosità delle voci novelle, che poi si godono con genio in tempo di publica Comparsa. (p. 377)

g. Primi sono i Teatri di Musica à principio con una pompa, e splendore incredibile, punto non inferiore à quanto si pratica in diversi luoghi dalla magnificenza de' Principi con questo solo divario, che dove questi lo fanno godere con generosità, in Venezia è fatto negozio, e non può correre con quel decoro, che corre nell'occasioni, in cui da' medemi Principi si celebrano spesso le Nascite, e gli sposalizij à maggior ostentamento della propria Grandezza. (pp. 377–78)

h. Capitolo IV: . . . Ora i Teatri sono capaci di poco numero di persone, in riguardo agli Antichi; di più, che in vece di scalinate, sono fabricati più ordini di Palchetti, la maggior parte à comodo de' Nobili; mentre le Dame vogliono stare smascherate in quelli, e godere tutta la libertà. Nel campo di mezzo s'affittano di sera in sera scagni, senza distinzione di persone, poiche l'uso delle Maschere leva la necessità del rispetto, che s'usava a' Senatori, e alle Matrone di Roma, che comparivano con maestà, volendo anco in questo Venezia, come nata libera, conservar à tutti la libertà. (pp. 387–88)

i. Se v'era figurato il precipizio di Fetonte, si facea piombar dal Carro qualche misero condannato frà gli applausi Popolari. Lo stesso si facea, introducendosi Muzio Scevola, che abbruciasse la mano, e altre simili rappresentazioni volendo assuefare quel Popolo alle stragi, e agli orrori.

j. Oggi, però è introdotto il Teatro con la Musica, per sollievo dell'animo, e per una virtuosa ricreazione, vedendosi comparire Machine spiritose, suggerite dal Drama, che allettano molto fra le Pompe di Scene ed abiti, ch'appagano al sommo la curiosità universale. (p. 388)

k. Capitolo V: . . . L'anno 1636. nacque generoso desiderio in alcuni miei amici, e compagni in Padova, di ordinar un Torneo; onde io per nobilitarlo maggiormente, presi per mano la Favola di Cadmo, e ne composi l'Introduzione, che fù poi posta in Musica nella forma, che comparve stampata in publica vista. Si fece à questo oggetto serrar un luogo spazioso contiguo à Pra della Valle, e con machine a Cavallo; come si vede in questi disegni, si perfezzionò un pomposo spettacolo. Fù numeroso il concorso di Nobiltà Veneta, di Cavalieri di Terraferma, e di Scolari dello Studio; mentre seguì la comparsa il mese d'Ottobre, destinato per ordinario al villeggiare. Sia stata la fortuna de' Cavalieri, che lo composero, o pure la bontà di chi intervenne, riuscì d'universal'applauso. . . . Di qui venne, che l'anno addietro con la protezione di più Nobili, s'unirono diversi Virtuosi professori della Musica, mediante i quali comparve l'anno 1637 nel Teatro di S. Cassiano l'Andromeda di Benedetto Ferrari Poeta, Musico, e Suonatore eccellente della Tiorba. (pp. 390–91)

l. E quello, ch'è più considerabile, la diversità de' prezzi alla Porta facilita maggiormente i concorsi. Poiche i Nobili, e Mercanti col comodo dell'entrate, e de' negotij, anno il modo di soddisfarsi continuamente, e il Popolo ancora col prezzo assai minorato di prima, come si dirà à suo tempo. (p. 392)

m. [Il Teatro della Musica è] avanzata a' segni incredibili della soddisfazione universale, che si compra à vil prezzo, già introdotto come si dirà à suo tempo da un privato fine di putrido interesse à pregiudizio della Virtù, che già caminava, e sù i Teatri de' Comici, e della Musica col suo decoro. (p. 394)

n. Sono erretti in questa Città quattro principalissimi Teatri, uno situato sù le Fondamenta nuove detto de' Santi Gio: e Paolo, per esser ivi vicino di Giovanni Grimani, che per esser prima fabricato di Tavole, e non tutto sopra il suo terreno, lo trasportò con prestezza incredibile in poca distanza sopra il suo fondo . . . facendolo erger tutto di pietra. (p. 396, quoting Martinioni)

o. Capitolo IX: Quanti Teatri siano stati, e sono al presente in Venezia, ed il tempo della loro comparsa. (p. 397)

p. Il primo fu aperto à San Cassiano in Corte Michela, dietro al Campanile. . . . Durò qualche anno; ma fabricatosene nella detta Contrada un'altro, ch'è quello, che al presente si trova degli Eredi di Carlo Andrea Tron, restò desolato il primo, ch'appena oggi convertito in alcuni compartimenti d'affittanze conserva qualche vestigio in ombra. Il presente dunque ha servito da recitar prima Comedie, e poi l'anno 1637. da rappresentar l'Andromeda, che fu il primo Drama, che si sentisse in Musica a Venezia. . . . L'anno 1629 provò gravissimo incendio; fù però rimesso con prestezza. (p. 398)

q. Si recitò in quello [Teatro Novissimo] in Musica sino l'anno 1646, restando poi affatto distrutto, e il suo luogo era dove al presente è introdotta la Cavallerizza dietro a' Mendicanti verso le Fondamenta nuove. (p. 399)

r. L'undecimo à San Gio: Grisostomo eretto con mirabil prestezza l'anno 1678 da Gio: Carlo, e Abate Vincenzo fratelli Grimani d'Antonio, Nipoti, & eredi di Giovanni sudetto, mostrando in questo modo d'aver ereditata non meno la magnificenza che il genio virtuoso, per cui rendono maggiormente cospicua la Nobiltà, e di stirpe, e d'animo. (p. 401)

s. Capitolo XII: . . . Molti Magistrati, che rappresentano la maestà del Dominio, vi anno la competente ingerenza. In ordine a che ogni anno sono tenuti i Principali del Teatro, a far istanza qualche giorno prima delle Recite al Magistrato de' Proveditori di Comune, accioche ordini al suo Architetto di portarsi all'osservazione dello stato d'essi Teatri; se le mura sono sussistenti, e se i Palchetti sono lontani d'ogni pericolo . . . e v'è di mezzo tempo opportuno in caso di bisogno d'applicarvi il dovuto rimedio. . . . Secondariamente non si può principiar la Recita, ne esporre in pubblico il cartello solito, se prima non si ottiene la licenza da' Capi dell'Eccelso Consiglio de' X, quale ottenuta la prima volta disobliga il Teatro d'ogni altra nuova licenza tutto quel Carnovale. Da questo supremo Tribunale per lo più si prescrive l'ora in cui debba terminar l'opera per il comodo universale. . . . Per ultimo lo Stampatore, che ottiene licenza da' Superiori di dar l'Opera alle stampe, come si pratica con altri libri; prima di vender i libretti stampati, è tenuto, a presentarsi a' Proveditori sudetti di Comune, per ricever la limitazione del prezzo a' medemi, e giusto la medema farne l'esito a beneficio di chi si dira a suo tempo. (pp. 405-7)

t. Capitolo XIII: La spesa, ch'è tenuto à fare il teatro. (p. 407)

u. Ne' principij de' Teatri non caminava il rigore de' prezzi; poiche avea i suoi riguardi la discrezione, e l'onestà, e venivano più gradite, e compatite le fatiche de' Virtuosi; dove al presente il genio è fatto così incontentabile, ch'è di necessità il perder in luogo di avanzare; e per lo più sopra tutti gli utili, che si cavano, si rimette considerabilmente per pagamenti eccedenti de' Musici. Dal principio bastavano due voci isquisite, poco numero d'arie per dilettare, poche mutazioni di Scena per appagare la curiosità; ora più si osserva una voce, che non corrisponda, che molte delle migliori c'abbia l'Europa. Si vorebbe, ch'ogni Scena del Drama caminasse con la mutazione, e che l'invenzioni delle Machine si andassero a ritrovare fuori del Mondo.

v. Queste sono le cause per le quali cresce ogni anno più la spesa; mà non cresce di già; anzi si diminuisce il pagamento alla porta, che pone a rischio d'impossibilitar la continuazione, se non si dà regola migliore alle cose correnti. (p. 408)

w. Capitolo XIV: . . . La . . . riuscita [dell'opera], o buona, o cattiva, dipende da mille accidenti per lo più originati da' giuochi stravaganti d'una ridicola fortuna, che ordinariamente suole sposarsi col giudicio del Volgo. (p. 410)

x. Capitolo XV: . . . L'utile della porta, ch'è fondamento principale dell'interesse, in vece di crescere si và diminuendo con evidente pregiudizio, e pericolo di tralasciarsi la continuazione di questo nobilissimo trattenimento. Il poco prezzo lieva il modo alla spesa considerabile delle pompe, introduce più facilmente il Volgo ignorante, e tumultuario, e fà perder il decoro à quella Virtù, che comparisce non meno per diletto, che per profitto. L'anno primo, che comparì in

Venezia il Drama in Musica fù del 1637. Si limitò come onesta contribuzione il pagamento di lire quattro per bolletino, che serve di passaporta nel Teatro. Durò l'uso della medesma inalterabile, non ostante qual si sia fortuna sinistra incontrassero le recite fino l'anno 1674, e durerebbe ancora, se Francesco Santurini quell'anno col comodo del Teatro di San Moise preso ad affitto vantaggiosamente con le Scene, e Materiali, che servirono l'anno innanzi ad una generosità Accademica, e con una mediocre compagnia de' Cantanti non violava l'integrità dell'uso sudetto, con un quarto di ducato alla Porta. Questa novità vantaggiosa piacque all'universale; ond'egli allettato dal profitto, venendogli contrastata la continuazione del Teatro di S. Moise sudetto, pensò, e gli sortì di fabricar il Teatro di Sant'Angelo, col beneficio del regalo di Palchetti, ed aprirlo col prezzo medemo alla Porta l'anno 1677. . . . Gli esempij di novità s'abbracciano volentieri quando ridondano in beneficio. Un calo eccedente la metà allettò il concorso col pregiudicio de' Teatri soliti a ricever le lire quattro sudette, facendo, che il famoso Teatro di San Giovanni, e Paolo, si riducesse doppo quaranta anni di così decorosa contribuzione al sudetto quarto l'anno 1679, e coll'esempio di lui l'anno 1680. quelli di San Salvatore, e di San Cassiano,

    y. non rimanendo altro al prezzo primiero, che il Novissimo di S. Gio. Grisostomo; dove si vede impiegata tutta la magnificenza maggiore da' sudetti fratelli Grimani. (pp. 411–12)

    z. Capitolo XVI: . . . Dal principio, che comparve il Drama in Musica sui Teatri di Venezia, era contento l'Autore di quella Gloria, che gli sortiva dall'Applauso.

    aa. Col progresso di tempo il numero de' Teatri, non trovando così facilmente l'incontro; perche in quei principij pochi erano i compositori; cominciò a dar qualche regalo per allettar maggiormente i genij Poetici alle fatiche del Drama,

    bb. che non era aggravato da tanti riguardi, che si praticano al presente. Ogni assunto serviva, ogni intreccio era gradito, ogni frase era ammirata; come si vede in ogni genere di cose, quando compariscono di nuovo. Oggidì s'ascrive a gran miracolo, se la incontrano le più bizzarre, e peregrine invenzioni, disposizioni, & elocuzioni; tanto sono svogliati, e fatti incontentabili gli animi delle delicie più soavi della Virtù. A questa causa fu introdotto l'uso, che tuttavia si pratica di lasciar all'Autore del Drama per premio delle sue fatiche tutto quello si cava dalla vendita de' libretti stampati a sue spese, e dalla Dedicatoria, che si fa a sua libera disposizione, e quest'utile dipende dalla riuscita del Drama, (pp. 413–14)

    cc. Capitolo XVIII: . . . Il Teatro è stato prima, e sarebbe ancora di gran bene, se si conservasse il decoro della sua prima origine, se l'abuso non avesse luogo, e se i genii si temprassero di miglior sentimento. (p. 422)

    dd. Capitolo XIX: Nacque l'introduzione de' Drami in Musica, come s'è detto, l'anno 1637 sotto il Principato di Francesco Erizzo, e in tempo, che la Republica godea una tranquilissima pace. E' dover dunque un trattenimento si virtuoso, e dilettevole, introdotto a' giorni nostri di registrare con esattezza di tutte le notizie più degne; acciochè la memoria non termini col suono degli stromenti, e delle voci, come già fece quella delle Tragedie, e d'altre Rappresentazioni Teatrali di Roma, di cui non fù chi con diligenza pari alla presente informasse la Posterità, che ne vive affatto all'oscuro, e che non resti sepolta fra l'ombre allo smorzar de' lumi, che l'accompagnano. Una memoria si degna, che obliga a renderla cospicua, e segnalata, gl'ingegni più elevati con le invenzioni più curiose, e nobili, che uscissero giammai alla vista degli uomini merita d'esser depositata all'immortalità; onde in ogni tempo apparisca il merito della Virtù ad esempio, ed eccitamento di chi n'avrà genio d'esercitarla à sua maggior gloria. A queste Memorie Teatrali di Venezia siegue per tanto un Catalogo generale, in cui dall'anno 1637 . . . fino a quest'anno 1681 si farà distinta, e puntuale menzione . . . l'anno . . . il Teatro . . . il titolo del Drama . . . il nome dell'Autore, e . . . quello del Compositore di Musica. (pp. 423–24)

    ee. La prima [tavola] sarà di tutti i titoli de' Drami, e gioverà il sapergli a chi compone, per ischivargli, o pure per diversificare gli assunti sovra le azioni del Protagonista, com'è praticato Ercole con più titoli, Alessandro, e Pompeo. La seconda sarà di tutti i nomi degli Autori, che gli anno composti. La terza di tutti i nomi de' Compositori di Musica. . . . Gioveranno parimenti queste Tavole a molti, che averanno spirito, e talento per intraprender con la fatica virtuosa le carriere d'un Aringo si lodevolmente battuto dalle prime, e più rinomate Penne della Republica Letteraria. (p. 424)

ff. Capitolo Ultimo: . . . Dalla lettura de' Drami citati dalle presenti Memorie nel Catalogo, risulterà appresso i Posteri la lode degli Autori, meglio, che non è risultata nel tempo delle Recite per più cause. (p. 425)

gg. Varie sono le cause, e stravaganti gli accidenti, che accompagnano il Drama sulla Scena, ogni uno de' quali è bastante a dare, e negare l'applauso all'Autore. Di già si sono veduti alcuni Drami di tutto merito contrariati dalla Fortuna con molto stupore di chi ne professò la cognizione, o perche fosse ordinaria la scelta de' Cantanti, o debolezza di Musica, o mancanza di machine, o imperfezione di Scene, o povertà d'abiti, circostanze tutte fuori della colpa dell'Autore, e nul-ladimeno ogn'una pregiudiziale alla riuscita; dove all'incontrario alcuni Drami ripieni di difetti mostruosissimi, e per disposizione, e per elocuzione incompatibili, sono stati favoriti dal con-corso, o per una voce di nuovo sentita, o per una Musica di metro bizzarra, o per una machina di stravagante invenzione; in somma parendo, che la fatalità per lo più concorresse a favorire i meno meritevoli. Quindi avverrà, che dalla lettura de' Drami citati nel Catalogo delle presenti Memorie, potranno sperare quei Virtuosi, ch'anno affaticato nobilmente l'ingegno, dal giudizio dispassionato de' Posteri la dovuta lode; meglio, che da quello di chi al presente glielo nega per natural'inclinazione, che s'ha d'invidiar la fama d'Uomini insigni, mentre vivono, e di lodarli mentre muoiono.

hh. Considerazioni diverse intorno a' teatri, a' drami, ed agli abusi correnti: . . . Si fanno furti non solo degli Accidenti più ingegnosi; ma anche dell'ariette, e di versi interi, cosi, che talvolta si adoperano pretesti d'amicizie, artifizii di apparenti confidenze, ne v'è più strada sicura di potersi fidare. (pp. 428–29)

ii. Con una libertà indiscreta si comincia a far Notomia della medema [il libretto], e col capriccio di pochi, che pretendono di formar giudizio universale, si lacera, si smove, e si scom-pone il modello, s'urta l'Invenzione, si difforma la Disposizione, e peggiora l'Elocuzione, in tal guisa, che viene ad esporsi in publico un parto difforme, com'era la statua in Atene. Passando poi alla considerazione della riuscita, e qual si può sperare da un componimento disordinato da tante alterazioni? Non v'è scrupolo se s'incorra negli Anacronismi. . . . Non v'è difetto, se la Storia, o la Favola si diversifichi. . . .

jj. Si stima picciol'errore, che con lo stile medesimo si dica l'Eroico, ed il ridicolo; che il patetico, ch'è l'anima del Drama, si ristringa, che l'ariette occupino il luogo del recitativo ne-cessario. (p. 430)

7. GIOVANNI MARIA CRESCIMBENI, *La bellezza della volgar poesia* (Rome: Buagni, 1700)

Giacinto Andrea Cicognini intorno alla metà di quel secolo . . . introdusse i Drammi col suo Giasone, il quale per vero dire è il primo, e il più perfetto Dramma, che si trovi; e con esso portò l'esterminio dell'Istrionica, e per conseguenza della vera, e buona Comica, e délla Tragica stessa; imperciocchè per maggiormente lusingare colla novità lo svogliato gusto degli spettatori, nau-seanti ugualmente la viltà delle cose Comiche, e la gravità delle Tragiche, l'inventor de' Drammi unì l'una, e l'altra in essi, mettendo pratica con mostruosità non più udita tra Re, ed Eroi, ed altri illustri Personaggi, e Buffoni, e Servi, e vilissimi uomini. Questo guazzabuglio di personaggi fu cagione del total guastamento delle regole Poetiche, le quali andarano di tal maniera in disuso, che nè meno si riguardò più alla locuzione; la quale, costretta a servire alla musica, perdè la sua purità, e si riempiè d'idiotismi. Fu tralasciato il maneggio regolato delle figure, che nobilitano l'orazione, che si restrinse per lo più dentro i termini del parlar proprio, e famigliare, il quale è più adattato per la musica; e finalmente il legame di quei piccoli metri, appellati volgarmente Ariette, che a larga mano si spargevano per le scene, e la straboccevole improprietà di fare altrui parlar cantando, tolsero affatto da i componimenti la forza degli affetti, e l'artifizio di muovergli negli ascoltanti. (pp. 106–7)

Appendix III: Correspondence and Documents

• • •

A. Venice, Archivio di Stato: Scuola grande di San Marco

1. FRANCESCO CAVALLI TO MARCO FAUSTINI, 23 JULY 1654 (*b.* 188: 14), facsimile in Jane Glover, "The Teatro Sant'Apollinare and the Development of Seventeenth-Century Venetian Opera" (Ph.D. diss., Oxford University, 1975)

Benche V.S. Ecc^{ma} negha l'affetto c'hò sempre portato à lei, al suo Teatro, riverenzia insieme à gli Ill^{mi} interressati; Le fò sapere, come io ultimamente mi abboccai coll'Illmo Duodo; e frà le cose concertate assieme per frase nella scrittura fermo questi.

Che non si parlasse di far suonare quel 3° stromento, bastando solo la mia esibitione in Voce.

Che fatta la prima Recita mi fosse datto scudi d'Argento 100.

Che ogni 4 Recite mi fossero datto Ducati 50 fino all'interà sodisfattione delli Ducati 400.

Queste cose mi furno cortessissimamente promesse da detto S^{re} mà non attese poi nella scrittura ch'in vece di fornire (come l'appuntato) li scudi 100 la prima sera gli hà posti doppo la 3ª sera. Li Ducati 50 in cambio delle 4 gli hà posti doppo le sei; onde io vedendo che non mi si manteneva in scritto, quel trato ch'in Voce mi s'era promesso, regolai detta scrittura, e si come esso Illmo Duodo sua l'havea mandata à me; Io la rimandai à esso S^{re} Covretta in questa forma, a ciò fosse sotto scritta, et ultimate queste righe, in cominciato sia questa quadragess^{ma}. Veggo però dalle longhezze di questo neg° et della dilationi nel concludere, la poca stima che si fà della mia persona, che perciò un Mese fà mi licentiai (con una mia) dall'Illmo Duodo, mà per portar mi la anco più àllungo non vuolare accettarla onde pervenirne à un fine, scrivo questa à lei che servirà per tutta la Compag^a e per informatione che se per tutto Dimani, che sara li 24 del Corrente non mi haveranno rissolto con la sotto scrittione alla scritt^a inviata, io mi dichiaro libero del trattato fin hora havuto insieme.

V.S. Ecc^{ma} non havrà occasione di dolersi di me, mentre stà à loro S^{ri} l'havermi; dichiarandomi pronto à servirli, mentre mi sij sotto scritta la scrittura, che non è stravagante, ma è confirm a del concerto pred^{to}: ne è variata in altro (nella forma del pagamento) che di due sere più, overo, dell'esborso delli 100 scudi et di una sera di meno, di questo delli Ducati 50 cosa che non sò credere che vi sij Cagioni di non mi contentare con una sodisf^{ne} di si poco momento. Serva però come ho detto questa per avviso, che s'io non riceverò da questa sotto scrittione per tutto mercoredi come sopra, m'intenderò fuori d'ogni obligatione con loro Sⁱ. E le b. la mano.

2. CAVALLI CONTRACT WITH FAUSTINI, 24 JULY 1658 (*b.* 194: 266–67), quoted in *Quellentexte zur Konzeption der europäischen Oper im 17. Jahrhundert*, ed. Heinz Becker (Kassel, 1981), p. 72

Sig.^r Cavalli debba per tre Anni prossimi poner in musica ogn'Anno, un Opera da Rappresentarsi nel Teatro di S. Cassiano, et ciò con li patti e' conditioni infra scritte.

P° . . . facendo à tutte sue spese far tutte le Copie et Originali che seranno necessarij.

2°. Che d.° Sig.^r Cavalli sia tenuto et obbligato assister personalm.te a' tutte le prove che seranno necessarie come anco mutar parte, alterar, sminuir et aggionger quello fosse necessario nella musica et servitio dell'Opera secondo l'occorenze et emergenze che succedono in simili Occasioni.

3°. Non possa . . . nel corso di d.^{ti} 3 Anni poner in musica altra opere che s'havesero a recittare in questa Città cosi in Theatri Publici con pagamento come privati . . . senza il quale detti

Ill.^{mi} et Compagni non sarebbero devenuti alla stipulatione della presente scrittura. Non resti però prohibito ad esso Sig.^r Cavalli il poner in musica in d.° tempo Opere che fossero per recitarsi fuori della Città.

4°. Sij tenuto d.° Sig.^r Cavalli sonar nell'Opera il P.° istromento ogni sera che si recita. . . . Et all'incontro per recognitione delle soprad.^{te} obligationi, detti Ill.^{mi} et Compagno s'obbligano d'esborsar ogni Anno al d.° Sig.^r Fran.^{co} Cavalli D.^{ti} Quatro Cento correnti da £6 ij 4 per ducato . . . fatta la P.ª Recita gli sijno contati D.^{ti} 150 et per il restante, ogni 5 Recite, D.^{ti} 50 sino all'intero pagamento, dovendo però li detti D.^{ti} 400 esserli pagati senza alcuna contraditione à tutti li modi ò siano poche ò molte le recite che si faranno dell'oppera.

3. CAVALLI TO FAUSTINI, 8 AUGUST 1662 (*b.* 188: 380), facsimile in Wolfgang Ost-hoff, "Cavalli," *La musica* 1 (Turin, 1966): 829.

a. Alle sue instanze . . . a quelle (a nome suo) fattemi dall'Ecc.^{mo} Minato non ho potuto resistere, ond^e hò condisceso à compiacerla e servirla, col porre in musica l'opera si come ho sempre fatto, sebene havevo stabilito di non prendere più questo impaccio;

b. ma à questa affettuosa risolut^{ne} mi s'interpone un intoppo, posto però da V. S. e non da mè; perche ella vorrebbe due opere, et io per il poco tempo, non posso prometterglile, havendo anco altri miei interessi proprij, che mi tengono occupato. . . . S'assicuri, che se il tempo me lo permetesse [non] risparmiarei fattica anco d'avvantaggio [di acconten]tarla in tutto.

4. CAVALLI, CONTRACT WITH FAUSTINI, 29 JUNE 1667 (*b.* 194: 50), quoted in Bruno Brunelli, "L'impresario in angustie," *Rivista italiana del dramma* 3 (1941): 334–35

Il Sig. Fran^{co} Cavalli s'obbliga di poner in musica con tutta diligenza, et applicatione un'opera all'Ecc.° Sig. Marco Faustini, che nel presente Anno deve rappresentarsi nel Teatro di S. Gio. e Paolo, dovendo assister alle prove et occorrendo anco aggiunger, alterare, et levare quelle cose, che fossero necessarie, et occorressero conforme alla sodisfatione d'esso Sig. Faustini, al quale doverano restare l'originali. All'incontro esso Sig. Cavalli . . . conseguirà dal d.° Sig. Faustini ducatti quattrocento cinquanta, ciascuno di lire sei soldi quattro per ducato, quali gli saranno . . . pagati dal d.° Sig. Faustini le prime quattro recite.

5. PIETRO ANDREA ZIANI TO FAUSTINI, 25 JULY 1665 (*b.* 188: 82–83)

a. Mi pare che l'opera sia un poco secca particolarm.^{te} solliloquij assai lunghi, come sterile di Canzonette. Vedrà che ho cavato anco qualche arietta di più del suo aviso per rallegrarla più che sia possibile ma dubito (se non la guarnisse di Arie) vogli buttar inseriora; lei sa l'uso hod-ierno, e li solliloquii così lunghi vengono abborriti da tutti sì che io l'aviso per tempo acciò si risolvi per il meglio. Io ho troppo in urto prima l'opera del Beregano che ha molto grido sì per esser nuova e desiderata, come perchè è in gran stima; e la Doriclea (e ben belliss.^{ma}) mà è opera vecchia e già sentita altre volte per la poesia, e veramente non mi pare che possa star a petto del Tito. . . .

b. Quanto poi al regallo che dice di farmi di 200 ducati per la mia fatica col movermi in Consideratione quello hebbi l'ultima volta per l'Amore Guerriero etc. . . . per haver fatto un Annibale in sei giorni, col espormi à cimenti così pericolosi, ho saputo far guadagnare a V. S. tanto che non solo ha pagate tutte le sue spese in un Anno, che egli sovrastava tanta Rovina ma ha saputo molto bene regalare tutti li musici, ed a me causa principale di tanto beneficio, non solo mi si è dato regallo, ma mi si levò 70 ducati del mio solito salario, e se bene non fu lei la cagione di farmi operare, ma altri, tutto ciò lei hebbe il guadagno, ed io la lode come il Corvo ed altri il formaggio.

c. . . . Se lei paga un musico 150 e 100 doble l'uno, perche à un Maestro di nomina che è la prima careta di far comparire un opera, non se gli dovrà dare almeno ò l'equivalente ò poco meno?

6. ANTONIO CAVAGNA TO FAUSTINI, 17 OCTOBER 1665 (*b.* 188: 212)

Io resto molto confuso et perplesso nel sentire la compagnia che tiene così diversa da quello c'hammi di prima insinuato, non havendo Donne di credito et pochi homini, questo mi passa l'anima; in quanto alla mia parte havevo già pensato et trovato il loco in due parti dove si potea aggiongier senza alteratione una arietta . . . per altro poi io intendo di cantar sopra li instrumenti della orchestra accordati al giusto tono di Roma, e non più come ho fatto nella Statira, nel Teseo et altri, e questo per esser di maggior vantaggio alla mia voce, e lo dico io hora acciò niuno si lamenti di ciò.

7. CAVAGNA TO FAUSTINI, 2 NOVEMBER 1665 (*b.* 188: 46^v)

In quanto all'arietta di dolce foco io non trovo bene di riccantarla per esser cosa molto affettata et mendicata onde potra farlli fare una musica nova. L'aria io non la tengo ne meno.

8. SEBASTIANO CIONI TO FAUSTINI, 6 NOVEMBER 1665 (*b.* 188: 129–30)

La Signora Anna stuona. . . . Non la vogliono più sentire. . . . Signor Cavagnino resterà molto scandalizzato quando si vedrà a petto una Donna tale.

9. PIETRO DOLFIN TO FAUSTINI, 12 NOVEMBER 1665 (*b.* 194: 115)

Mi piacque [l'opera] per ogni rispetto (con la consideratione però d'esser à Verona) così la Sig.^{ra} Anna rapresentante la parte di Romilda mi spiaque ad un [tal] segno, che mi riescì insoportabile, nè solo à me, ma à tutti chi erano con me, et à tutta l'assistenza dandogli ogni volta ch'usciva si può dire la subiata per il riso, che facevano ne' suoi trilli, et nelle sue cadenze. E' tanto odiosa, che lei sola è bastante di precipitar un'opera e tanto sgraziata che l'altra di Mantova, et Orsetta paiono angioli.

10. ZIANI TO FAUSTINI, 28 NOVEMBER 1665 (*b.* 188: 354)

Non hò più inteso che il S. Giuseppino, fratello del S.D. Giulio Cesare, faccia il Contralto come lei mi significa per il restante della parte d'Euristo che doverà esso recitare. Ne hò parlato perciò col sud: S.D. Giulio e m'ha appunto risposto che ciò gli pare impossibile, mentre lui ha sempre cantato il sop.°; che ben è anco vero che tal Volta cantò il contralto, che potrebbe essere che di nuovo gli fosse venuto questo pensiero di cantarlo, onde non partirò dal suo ordine, e gli scriverò que poco che avanza in contralto. Devo dirle che la parte del Nocchiero e di Lerilda nella prima scena del 3.° Atto non è stata da V.S. assignata per chi la dovrà recitare, che perciò io per non perder tempo ho messa la parte del Nocchiero in Basso per D. Giacinto, che mi pare proprio (tanto più che ha pochis.^{ma} parte) e quella di Lerilda l'ho posta per un soprano che vedo ne ha d'abondanza. Resta solo che anco V. S. mi avisi (se pure sarà in tempo) la parte nel 3.° Atto per la Vecchia Clipea, che non la vedo notata nella destinatione delle altre parti che io penso in tanto (per non perder tempo) di porla per il Sig.^{r} Antonio da Murano che fa la parte di Idiotea che osservo non comparisce in Scena un tempo fà. . . . V.S. osserverà ne la scena 12 del 2.° Atto la Cantata in forma di lamento d'Alciade, *Più per me non vi è contenti*, che è la mia favorita per il S. Cavagnino, che stimo portera il Vanto di tutto il resto, pur che sia cantata adasio e le Viole discrete, e qui piace tanto à S.M. che ne ho fatto copia e aggionte parole per non perderla.

11. ZIANI TO FAUSTINI, 9 MAY 1666 (*b.* 188: 279)

a. Può rengraziar il Cavalier Beregano quella Virtuosa da Roma che ha sostenuta la sua opera che del resto il Tito era ito. Per il verso non se può aggiungere, ma per l'intrecchi è stato pochissimo stimato e il Pompeo molto più per la Grandezza e Pompa nella scena che qui viene predicata per singolarissima e anche più di San Gio e Paolo.

b. Prego Dio gli dia buona fortuna, e si come io prego Dio di accomodar ben bene i fatti miei per non più faticare in simili materie, così loderò sempre il Signor Cavalli à rinunziar le armi al Tempio mentre non altro che l'età, e le comodità le rendono di poca sodisfatione. Lui è gran Virtuoso e sarà anco maggiore quando che non havendo lui dibisogno di faticare volontariamente si ritirerà.

12. ZIANI TO FAUSTINI, 12 JUNE 1666 (b. 188: 268)

Quando io veda V. S. sola a recitare in Venezia, dirò sarà la prima volta, ma non lo credo. Se fosse direi (V. S. mi scusi) che in Venezia tutti li matti fossero divenuti savii. Si racordi che anco lei haveva fatto voto di non più impegnarsi etc. Il teatro di S. Salvatore fu fatto in un tempo che lei doveva esser sola per ogni rispetto e questo sempre farà contraposto al Grimano. È troppo un bel gioiello, se Marco Mozzoni havesse hauto buona direzione, e compagnia fedele etc. Non haveria totalmente perso, se bene sono informato che il suo male non è tanto quanto vien fatto.

13. GASPARO ORIGO TO FAUSTINI, 2 OCTOBER 1666 (b. 188: 292)

Mi ha detto che ottima resolutione farebbero a far recitare in loco di questa l'Argia o l'Alessandro, e che quando si risolvessero di far recitar l'Argia la Sig.ʳᵃ Giulia s'obligarebbe, che l'Apolloni autor dell'Opera gl'aggiungerebbe e leverebbe tutte le scene che volessero . . . solo gli dico che mutandosi Opera, leverebbe ogni dubbio della parte, tanto più che la Sig.ᵃ Giulia molto è inclina havendo l'essempio di ciò che fece la Rosilena.

14. FAUSTINI TO GASPARE ORIGO, [?] OCTOBER 1666 (b. 188: 294–95)

Tutte due l'opere sono del Sig. Gio: Faustini di felice memoria mio fratello, che morì 1651 in età giovenile di anni 30. [sic] et che ha stampato et fato recitare 14 opere [tutte composte in musica dal Signor Cavalli et dal Signor Ziani] & che fù amirabile nell' inventione [et dalle quali tutti questi Sig.ⁱ che sin hora hanno in questa città fato opere hanno rubbato l'inventioni bellissime di esse] et che vengono quasi ogn'anno recitate nelle principali Theatri musicali d'Italia; onde consideri V.S. Ill.ᵐᵃ se Io sono per tralasciare di far rappresentare queste, che sono da lui state lasciate per predilette et promesse nelle sue stampe per far rappresentare l'Argia et Ales.° opere già fate et viste in Venetia; . . . la prima d'Alciade fù stata lasciata . . . in tutto perfettione; la seconda intitolata il Tiranno humiliato d'Amore meno perfetto. Sarea indecenza toccare in alcuna parte il belliss.ᵐᵒ soggetto; ho fato fare l'atto primo dall'Ill.ᵐᵒ Beregano, et più non havendo lui potuto continuare il 2.° es 3.° [no date] a soggetto [valorosi.] valoroso, che molto bene hà inserito [nel genio] della [. . . ?] onde l'opera sarà amirabile per ogni rispetto. Sono stato troppo prolisso con questa parte, ma si scuserà, perchè son troppo interessato nel [fare rappresentare] l'opere d'un mio fratello, inalzate al magior segno da tutti che le ha sentite, et per orazione delle quali ho pigliato il Teatro.

15. CORESI TO FAUSTINI, 3 NOVEMBER 1666, (b. 194: 14), quoted in Brunelli, "Angustie," pp. 333–34

Circa al prologo che V.S. mi manda sono quattro parole e ben corte, però la prego con tutto l'affetto dell'Anima a non me lo far fare, perchè non havendo io mai fatto prologo non voglio ne ancora cominciare, e questa parte è una parte che ogn'uno la puol fare.

16. CAVAGNA TO FAUSTINI, 14 [NOVEMBER] 1666 (b. 188: 37)

Due cose sole mi spaventano, l'una, di dover cantar con la Maschera da Moro, cosa non più usata da me, et non mai compresa che doppo haver letto il terzo atto; l'altra dover cantar in mezo di due angioli, la Sig.ʳᵃ Antonia et la Sig.ʳᵃ Giulia; la canzonetta che mi manda per agionta mi scusi chi l'à fatta, è per un contralto et non per Soprano, et molto diferente dalla maniera del Sig.ʳ Ziani, onde mi contentarò cantare il duetto et che la Sig.ʳᵃ Giulia canti la sua canzone sola.

17. CORESI TO FAUSTINI, 13 JUNE 1667 (*b.* 188: 164)
a. Mi pare che nel principio ci sia di gran dicerie, come sarebbe nella scena quarta dell'atto secondo, dove dice (Piange Olinda), la quale è una diceria che non puol mai far bel sentire, che, come sà, a Venezia bisogna sfuggirle.

b. Nella scena seconda dell'atto terzo vi è una canzona, la quale comincia (Ride il core), la quale non val niente essendo già stata vista dai primi virtuosi di Roma, però o V.S. la faccia mutar lei o vero la farò mutar io, non havendo io altra fine se non che mia moglie quest'anno si faccia honore, però bisogna che lei si contenti che la parte si accomodi dove è bisogno, che così resterà V. S. ben servita e noi sodisfatti. . . .

c. Mi favorisca presentar l'inclusa al Sig. Francesco Cavalli, al quale io dico dove arriva mia moglie acciò egli possa ben favorirla.

18. GIUSEPPE DONATI TO FAUSTINI, 23 JULY 1667 (*b.* 188: 174)
Dal Sig. Coresi mi vien dato per parte sua una lettera come anco la parte di Mer^pe dove la trovo sattisfattione, ma per esser un poco troppo alta bisogna accomodarla però in qualche loco si che per non far torto al compositione di essa; senza [il suo] consenso non la moverò ma per esser cosa di poco momento credo sia per contentarsi non ne havendo di bisogno solo che nelle cadenze avezo in certi luochi che stà ferma nel alta dove senza muovere il Basso continuo si puol accomodare che non perdi la sua solita armonia, si che senza suo avviso non moverò nulla acciò conoscha ch'io non pretendo di mettere le mani ove non mi tocca.

19. CORESI TO FAUSTINI, 13 AUGUST 1667 (*b.* 188: 169), quoted in Brunelli, "Angustie," p. 337
Ho ricevuta la parte di Caristo, quale rimando a V.S. in dietro perchè non è parte da mandare a dun pari mio . . . e se l'anno passato pigliai detta parte fu perchè lei non me ne dede altro che una scena, ma adesso che l'ho vista tutta, hò scoperto la poca stima che lei fa di me . . . però, V.S. mostri questa parte a Venezia, che vedrà che è una parte da darla al minimo straccion che sia tra i musici.

20. CORESI TO FAUSTINI, 27 AUGUST 1667 (*b.* 188: 166), quoted in Brunelli, "Angustie," p. 338
Io sempre gli ho detto che non mi curo di recitare come non hò parte da farmi honore, e per esser le parti da farsi honore non basta l'haver quantità di versi, che se fussero mille versi tutte botte e resposte, queste non si chiamon parte bone, già che lei ò non lo conosce ò non lo vol conoscere; non vi essendo in quella parte nè anche una riga di canzona.

21. CORESI TO FAUSTINI, 10 SEPTEMBER 1667 (*b.* 188: 167)
Nel terzo atto non ci ha altro che seconda e terza scena, onde mi pare impossibile che non ce ne sia d'altra, però avverta non haverne lasciata qualche scena, perchè ella finisce con quel duo che dice: "vincerai-vincerò" e poi quella canzonetta che è chiusa dell'opera.

22. FAUSTINI TO GRIMANI BROTHERS, 15 DECEMBER 1667 (*b.* 188: 199–200)
[che] i detti Ill^mi Grimani . . . habbino facoltà libera di far recitare in esso [SS. Giovanni e Paolo] l'opera del Meraspe di già principiata, e proseguirla per tutte quelle recite che stimeranno più proprie senza ingerenza alcuna di esso S. Faustini, dovendo tutto l'utile che se ne ricaverà così di bolettini come de Scagni, cedere solo a loro benefitio. E' di più anco possano fare rappresentare d'altra opera dell'Eliogabalo composta dal Sr Aurelio Aurelli o altra, che fosse di loro sodisfattione.

B. Hannover, Staatsarchiv: Aktes-Korrespondenzen italienischer Kardinäle und anderer Personen, besonders Italiener an Herzog Johann Friedrich

1. FRANCESCO MASSI, 13 DECEMBER 1669 (Cal. Br. 22, vol. 4, no. 627, f. 152)

Devo dar parte a V.S. di haver visitato il povero Sig Aurelio nostro quale, dopo la sua malatia che lo condusse all'estremo, è rimasto come un cadavere, affatto distrutto. Iddio ha voluto preservarlo per il bene di quelle sue povere creature, casa povera di fortune, et hora affatto caduta in miseria. Stimerei atto degno della Pietà di V.S. il farli qualche pietosa rimostratione per sostenerli.

2. PIETRO DOLFIN, 26 DECEMBER 1669 (vol. 2, no. 625, f. 405)

Come là ben nota impareggiabile generosità di V.A.S. m'hà impedito pubblicamente dedicar la mia Ermengarda alla sua autorevol protettione cosi l'humilissima riverenza mia mi hà prohibito appoggiarla ad alcun' altra persona mentre non ha chi può guidarmi nel mondo, che l'A.V. Sua. Se nelle stampe però non ho fatto spiccar il suo nome resta ben impresso nel mio core divoto, col quale non ho mancato di presentargliela com'hora pur faccio, . . . [solazione]. Riceveti adunque il Drama per l'A.V. e per la Sig^ra sua, qual è certo riuscito con grande applauso non per la debbolezza della compositione poetica, mà per la dolcissima musica del Sig^r Sartorio, comendata al più alto segno da tutti, e per la [presenza?] della mia nova cantatrice, che non da loco a S. Gio e Paolo.

3. MASSI, 20 AUGUST 1670 (vol. 4, no. 627, f. 196)

Questa nobilissima sfera [di donne] riceve mirabile adornamento dalla Bellissima Giovinetta Cantatrice che esso Sig Pietro [Dolfin] tiene presso di se; la quale fatta eccellente dal continuato studio e dalla sonorissima voce è però l'idolo amato dello stesso Sig. Pietro, che ne vive a meraviglia geloso; a questa, già pose l'occhio addosso quel caro concupissibile lupatto del nostro Sig. Nicola; ma il Sig. Pietro, che è formica, non lo vuole d'intorno. Accortosi di ciò il Sig. Nicola, per far dispetto al Sig. Pietro nello stesso tempo che questo componeva il Dramma per San Zuanne, e Polo, si è messo lui a rintracciare l'occasione di intrudersi in quel Theatro, et ha fatto tanto, che si ha fatto dar parola di esser insomma lui il melodrammatico per quest'anno. Il Sig Pietro che già haveva composto il Dramma non si è cavato, ha ceduto questa Bizzarria al Sig. Nicola; quale, presso li Sig. Grimani ha fatto tanto, che sia restato con uffici impegnato il Sig. Pietro a dar, tra gl'altri famosissimi Virtuosi, e virtuose, anco la sua dolcissima, onde il Sig. Nicola, vive hora a bocca dolce di dover pure con questo artificio pascer nel teatro la vista, e d'insinuarsi se le potesse venir fatta. Ma altro e tanto accorto l'altro, che già vede la furberia amorosa, si è premunito coll'animo deliberato, di non lasciar il suo bene, nè meno per un momento; onde se V.A.S. sarà a Venetia per questo Carnevale, potrà godere di trovarsi spettatore di due drammi ad un tempo, l'uno in musica, e l'altro in prosa, l'uno coll'attione delli giuochi Pantomimi alla muta, e l'altro con le note, e con le voci. Così di Barzelletta in Barzelletta haverà doppio godimento, in vedere nell'una rappresentari i finti, e nell'altra, i veri amori.

4. DOLFIN, 19 DECEMBER 1670 [1671] (vol. 2, no. 625, ff. 409-10)

Mancandomi di quà l'occasioni tutte di dimostrare all'A.V.S. l'Illma mia oservanza, prendo questa picciola congiuntura di trasmettere alla sua gran bontà le due opere, che sin hora si van rappresentando l'anno corrente. Dalle medesme intenderà la loro essenza, quale pare a me poco buona sebben questa da S. Luca riesce bene et la altra ha dato un crolo che se la copia d'esquisiti Cantanti non la sostentasse si sarebbe sin hora chiuso il Teatro, ne all'A.V.S. scrivo le distinte informationi dell'una e dell'altra parte, per non portargli soverchio il disturbo, già tutto havendo significato al Sig. Antonio Sartorio suo Mastro di Cappella. Replicherò solo ciò ch'à lui scrissi. Quanto alli due virtuosi di Costà, che Vicentino si fa gran honore, mà che il povero Mutio ha una parte così contraria alla sua attitudine (facendo quella d'Ercole) che non può far spiccare la sua virtù. Viene però somamente lodato il suo Canto, et nella ventura opera certo vien detto ch'egli spiccherà grandemente. La putta di mia casa fa il dio caduto, ottima riuscita se ben anch'essa ha una parte per lei non propria.

5. MASSI, 26 DECEMBER 1670 (vol. 4, no. 627, f. 224)

Nel Teatro di S. Zuanipolo è cascata la prima opera cioè è restata senza concorso; et ivi hanno rimessa insieme la Dori, quella bell'opera tanto applaudita, dove Giulia Romana faceva sentire meraviglie, quale riproduce nello stesso teatro con più zucchari, e con più Netare che non fece nelle prime scene.

6. MASSI, 6 FEBRUARY 1671 (vol. 4, no. 627, f. 227)

L'opera del Sig. Nicola [*Heraclio*] è cosi bella, che non satia mai. Tale è il concetto che se ne forma, che il Sig. Nicola si è Deificato in quel Teatro, dove, se lui non dirà, niente sarà fatto per l'avvenire, e se lui inventerà nuovi mondi di esquisitezze, concorreranno tutti per ammirarlo; non trovandosi veramente sogetto che lo pareggi nell'Inventione, nella magnificenza, e nella Piramide del suo Ingegno.

7. DOLFIN, 15 APRIL 1672 (vol. 2, no. 625, f. 420)

Et se ciò credessi, o almeno sperassi, vorrei stimolar alla recita d'opere in S. Salvatore molti che hanno intentione di formar nova Compagnia quando potessero havere il Sig. Antonio Suo Maestro di Cappella. Non solo per la di lui ben esperimentata virtù, ma perch'egli tiene il potere d'accordo de' Principi di Baviera e del Formenti, quali si dichiarano, che se il detto facesse la musica sarebbero infa[llibilmente?] del partito suo. . . . Anche Giulia si potrebbe havere, non fermata da Grimani, anzi come licentiata havendo scritto per Tonina, Ciecolino, e di già in parola col Sig Vend[rami]no. Lucretia sua humilissima serva in tal caso sarebbe pur del partito.

8. MASSI, 9 DECEMBER 1672 (vol. 4, no. 627, f. 271)

Si vanno preparando li Teatri delle opere, conforme al solito . . . è venuta la solita sirena del Tevere Sig. Giulia per far languire il Teatro Grimano colle sue dolcissime tenerezze; si è detto che sia per venir Ciecolino, ma non si vede ancora comparire.

9. MASSI, 16 DECEMBER 1672 (vol. 4, no. 627, f. 273^v)

Già si è aperto il Teatro di S. Luca, dove già due volte si è recitata l'opera intitolata l'Orfeo, dramma dell' Aurelij, e musica del valoroso Sig. Sartorio, Maestro di Cappella di V.A. S. Li Drammatici principali sono li virtuosi di V.A.S. molto applauditi, e particolarmente il baritono, lodato anco dalla Piramide [Beregan], se bene è il mecennate di San Zuanepolo, assai lo loda, e vi è la cantatrice romana detta Tonina [Antonia Coresi]: di voce meravigliosa esquisita, furba, et attrattiva per esser Romana, mà di maniera non arriva all'altra detta la Dori [Giulia Masotti], stimata però valorosa; et il Sig. Nicola [Beregan], se bene è Giuliano, mutarebbe volontieri casaccha, perche questa Tonina è più buona robba, et ha più amabil volto, e più belle sembianze; più brillo, e più succho, et anco più flessibile; dice però esserne padrone, e gode in se stesso; l'opera è ben galante, più Pastorale, che cosa Heroica. Ha grandissimo concorso, perche è la prima, che sodisfa nel bel principio. Hor là, concorrono tutti i soli[ti], et in pomposa mostra riempino i Palchi.

10. DOLFIN, 23 DECEMBER 1672 (vol. 2, no. 625, ff. 436^v–37^v)

Sappi adunque come mirabile riesce sin hora la musica del Sig^r. Ant. [Sartorio]. Li musici di V.A. l'uno piaciuto in estremo da moltissimi: più del Torto Fusai, et è il Baritono. L'altro pur piaciuto, et da mè stimato il meglio di ogni altro soprano per la maniera seben debbolissima di voce anco minorata doppo l'arrivo in Venetia. L'opera intitolata l'Orfeo dell'Aureli (che da mè sarà il primo ordinario all'A.V. trasmessa) pessima, gl'altri musici ascoltabili, Tonina Divina, così che la Pia peggiorata anco nella crudezza della voce dall'anno passato in quà non fa figura alcuna. Scene, et Abbiti pur ordinarii, et priva di ogn'altra curiosità, che dell'accennate. Ma che dirà l'A.V. quando sentirà un altra curiosa novella a publica gloria del suo sire. Antonio Sartorio, Sappi che doppo esser stata composta in musica la 2ª opera dal valoroso acreditatissimo Cavalli, per non piacer la medesima alle prove, per esser quella mancante di briose ariette l'ha tolta al med^{mo} Cavalli e data dà riffare al Sartorio, quale doppo haver fatto passare col mio consiglio complimentoso ufficialmente col detto l'hà doppo gl'avisi delle sue benigne grazie presa, et hoggi darà principio à comporla con tanto suo honore, et utile ancora, quanto l'A.V. potra argomentare. . . . Lucretia poi che per le grazie dalla sua generosità ricevute può ardire di porsi anch'ella in questo numero, non reciterà quest'anno per quanto si crede sin hora, mentre ricercata (come dal A.V.S. in altra mia significai) dà gl'Ecc Vend[rami]no & Molino per la 2da opera havendogliel'io concessa con la riserva di voler ceder per la parte destinatogli questa osservata da me per inferiore à quelle dà le sostenute benche debbolmente: negl'anni passati, io non hò voluto, che reciti, onde in suo loco ho fermato la putta protetta dall'Ecc. Sig^r Leonardo Loredano, quale per quello che s'è pubblicato doppo esser stata sentita da gl'interessati, e da altri, non si può sentire; onde dà una parte temendo, chè col pomo guasto rovini gl'altri buoni, dall'altra temendo di disgustar il Prottettore non sa, che fare gl'interessati medesimi, et io quest'anno godo fuori d'ogn'altro impiccio, che di quello che potesse apportarmi qualche torto che venisse [inperito à sen di V.A. quale non posso sin hora prevedere, ne credo possa succedere. Al S. Giovanni e Paolo pur son confusi per la ondata conseguita di quest'anno, non havendo d'esquisito che Giulia.

11. DOLFIN, 30 DECEMBER 1672 (vol. 2, no. 625, f. 439)
a. Io non glie l'hò voluta concedere, dicendogli che se l'havev negata à quegli di S. Luca per la parte non di mia sodisfatione non era di dovere, ch'io la concedessi à loro, come si suol dir per stroppa buco per imparar la parte in due giorni è stata adunque fortunata a non esser con quei straccioni.

b. È capitato il Sig. Ant. Rivani detto Ciecolino, che volontariamente è venuto à recitare nella 2da opera credo partito dalla Maestà dell'Imperatrice con molta sodisfattione della medesima al solito della sua impertinenza.

c. À S. Gio. Paolo hà dato cativo augurio a buoni successi che potessero li Sig. Grimani sperare la morte del povero Gio. Ant. Borretti maestro della musica di detta opera, ben conosciuto dall' A.V. et che sicuramente dalla sua bontà compatito, spirò ieri doppo quindici giorni di male perche la sua opera andasse in Scena, onde se la medesima [*Domitiano*] formava l'esequie alla sua morte non poteva che riuscir funesta. Riceverà l'A.V. li due libretti, che con la presente gli trasmetto, come farò pure degli altri due dell'opere seconde con le distinte notitie d'ogni successo, et a buon conto. Le giuro, che s'imortala il Sig. Ant. [Sartorio] per la benignità di V.A. quest'Anno, mentre il marito della Sigra Tonina mi hà questa mattina detto esser meravigliosa la parte del primo atto data alla med^{ma} della seconda opera [*Massenzio*] e può dir di restar solo in materia di compor opere hor ch'è morto il povero Borretti certo in tal facenda esquisito.

12. MASSI, 30 DECEMBER 1672 (vol. 4, no. 627, f. 266^v)
Il Teatro Grimano non riesce con applauso per altro rispetto che Sig. Giulia, e per le scene, lo vince quello di San Luca, ne l'uno ne l'altro molto a proposito, perche mancano le due colonette dell'anno passato; la Sig^{ra} Lucretia, et il castratino Lassi. Anco a San Moise si fa opera in musica, e non si fa pagare alle porte, ma dispensano bollettini; chi ha palco proprio, non paga manco all'entrare, et è accomodato di quattro bollettini per goder nel suo palco quattro amici cosi gratis; e quelli che non hanno il palco pagano li bollettini, et il palco se lo vogliono.

13. NICOLÀ BEREGAN, 30 DECEMBER 1672 (vol. 1, no. 624, ff. 172–73)
Hieri sera li 30 Xre fù dato principio all'Opera di S. Gio. e Paolo intitolata il Domitiano del Noris la quale veramente è posta superbamente in scena con bellissime rappresentanze ma cosi

povera di cantanti che fa compassione e fuori della Signora Giulia non hanno soggetti che la cantino, à talé stato sono ridotte l'opere di Venetia. è vero che quelli di S Lucca non ostante un'opera stracciata dell'Aureli intitolata l'Orfeo per havere huomeni migliori trionferanno à confusione de S. Gio. Polisti. . . . La Lucretia del nostro S. Pietro Dolfino ricercata ultimamente dalli Sig Grimani non hà prudente[mente] voluto recitare, sapendo, che con una compagnia di tal [carico?] poco poteano riuscire le cose.

14. MASSI, 8 JANUARY 1673 (vol. 4, no. 627, f. 520^v)

È riuscita molto piacevole l'opera di San Moise, e vi è stata assai gente, massime per il vantaggio che non si paga alle Porte; e per questo sarà quest'anno il più frequentato di tutti gli altri Theatri.

15. MASSI, 13 JANUARY 1673 (vol. 4, no. 627, f. 493)

Qua non corrono novità. San Moise ha grandissimo concorso, e ne penuriano gl'altri theatri. È arrivato qua Cecolino, ma tardi per recitare. Ho inteso che è stato da V.A.S. Procurerò di vederlo.

16. DOLFIN, 20 JANUARY 1672 [1673] (vol. 2, no. 625, ff. 440^v–41)

a. Questa sera farà l'ultima recita della prima opera al S. Luca, et mercordi si darà principio alla 2da che mirabile riuscirà per la musica del Sig. Sartorio composta in così breve tempo. Li musici suoi continuano poi con l'universale applauso, et il Gratianini estraordinario piace così che nella 2ª opera fà la prima parte mentre prende il titolo dal suo nome Ciecolino poi che per quant'egli afferma (et si va scorgendo veridici i suoi detti) non è partito con disgratia, ma di sotisfatione di Sua Maestà, stà così bene in voce, che estraordinariamen^{te} darà nel genio. La Putta dell'Ecc. Sig. Leonardo Loredano, ch'à forza di Broglio, non havendo io voluto, che reciti Lucretia, è stata presa per la 3ª parte, riesce insoportabile.

b. Anco à S. Moisè si fa un opera, senz'altra spesa che quella del Palco, mà è tanto poco di buono, che più d'una volta non torna il conto di vederla, e pur questa hà l'applauso, et è sempre ripieno il Teatro.

17. MASSI, 27 JANUARY 1672 [1673] (vol. 2, no. 625, f. 442)

Dopo l'andata in scena dell'opera di S. Gio. e Paolo ha certo accumulato concetto l'Orfeo di S. Luca, così ch'a tutta la Città è riuscita dispiacevole la fermata di quello per far la seconda quale ancoche riesca bene son sicuro che bisognarà tornar a fare per un paio di volte per sodisfar l'utile. L'Orfeo mentre sebben l'opera era Aureliana, haveva però qualche buona scena et la musica haveva modo di spiccare tra tante belle ariette. Dimani sera si darà principio alla nuova [*Massenzio*], et io non manco di trasmetterla all'A.V., pregandola compatirmi se non le mando questa ne l'altre legata per haver havuto anco gran fattica a poter far acquisto alle tre di questa notte dell'acclusa come la prima che sia uscita dalla mano dello stampatore. Io non posso dargli relatione alcuna di questo per non haver mai voluto veder, nemmeno una prova, et per la compositione, l'A.V.S. havrà sotto l'occhio la medesima da farne più prudente giuditio. Per quel poco ch'ho letto ho trovato che nel voler adornar il Drama ha il Poeta piantata una selva di Eruditioni così folta, ch'ha oscurata la compositione, et perdendosi il gusto ha nella povertà degl'accidenti durato fattica ad uscirne il bene. Tant'è non mi formalizzo su l'opinione mia, ma venerdi prossimo gliene portarò le più certe notitie dall'esito delle recite.

18. DOLFIN, 3 FEBRUARY 1673 (vol. 2, no. 625, f. 444)

Servirà la presente per semplice informatione dell'opera di S. Luca et de servitori di V.A.S. La medesima adunque riesce mirabile, per due capi. L'uno per la musica bella bellissima et meravigliosa, per esser stata composta in tredici giorni in loco del altra dello stesso Maestro, et meglio ancora della prima. Onde in parola d'honore e con la mia solita ingenuità le giuro che ha obbligatione il Sartorio all'A.S. della vita stessa havendolo con il suo benigno bene placito reso nella fama imortale, et unico, non havendo certo chi l'uguagli, per detto universale. L'altro capo è l'esquisitezza de musici, tra quali il suo Sire Gratianino spicca meravigliosamente bene cosi che mi ha fatto risvegliar la vena per haverlo una volta in una mia opera . . . che in cinque giorni ho fatto un atto della medesima.

19. MASSI, 24 FEBRUARY 1673 (vol. 4, no. 627, f. 435ᵛ)

A quest'hora ho dato l'ordine diretto al Sig. Daniel, che siino pagati li due Palchi di V.A.S. a San Samuele, et a San Zuanepolo; e sta bene l'esser pontuali a pagarli, perche non resti un minimo attacco, o pretesto da metterci in continguenza di qual che lite. Che mano in mano farò che siino pagati anchor quelli di San Moise, e di San Cassano, et io conservo le ricevute dell'ordini delli sudetti pagamenti.

20. MASSI, [. . .] 1673 (vol. 2, no. 625, ff. 456–57)

Questa volta si, ch'io spero d'haver resa ben servita L.A.V. Ill.ᵐᵃ et nell'ordine et nel merito nell'acquisto fattogli fare del più bel palco, non solo, che sia nel Teatro di S. Salvatore, mà che sia in Venetia, e per dir il vero, con quelli cautioni più aggiustate, che mai si possa praticare. . . . Non col palco dunque ma una stanza haverà su la scena essendomi riuscito l'intento di preventare anco l'altro da V.A.S. nel contiguo all'acquistato, et sicome non più di cento scudi d'Argento volevo dargli del palco sudetto acquistato cosi col'ottenimento in concambio dell'altro vicino mi sono (mediante l'autorità dall'A.V. benignamente inpartitami) presa la risolutione di promettergli cinquanta doble, e venti se di quel sporcheccio da S. Cassiano ha dato cent'e cinquanta d.ᵗⁱ questo ne dovrebbe valere più d'altre tante. Se la Serⁿⁱˢˢ. adunque verrà à goder col Carnovale Venturo havrà sicuro addatato alla sua grandezza. Perche però sarebbe troppo osservabile, e mal inteso, il lasciar palco cosi cospicuo senze esser foderato di polite tavole, con tutte le sue ablutie, e pertinentie, io glielo farò aquisitare. . . . L'affitanza, che tiene A.V. per il palco di S. Cassiano non hà nessuna imaginabile sicurezza, così, che se quest'anno, ò l'altro tempo si facesse opera, andarebbe il medmo disfatto, senza restitutione del donativo.

21. MASSI, 10 FEBRUARY 1673 (vol. 4, no. 627, f. 487)

Qua il carnevale è passato bene, e San Luca ha portato il vanto delli Theatri. Li Sig. Grimani hanno descapitato L. 3000: e per compimento di questo infortunio, in sul meglio, è stata sbarrata una archibugiata ad un Musico recitante di quel Theatro, et è restato mortalmente colpito in Gondola, mentre esso era nella medema con quattro, o cinque altri Musici. Li virtuosi modesti di V.A.S. si sono portati valorosamente, e sono vittoriosi. In questi pochi giorni che restano del Carnevale, col la severità, e bellezza del tempo si vedono Mascare a diluvio, et è la Piazza piena di Paradisi. Il Sig. Nicola vanta di essersi provisto di una Dea caduta apposta dal terzo giro per lui. Mi sono informato, et ho saputo, che è una pettegola petaiizza piena di mal francese.

22. MASSI, 20 OCTOBER 1673 (vol. 4, no. 627, ff. 423–24ᵛ)

a. Quà si comincia a lavorare nelli Teatri per l'ammanimento delle opere. Ho veduto questa matina aperto il Teatro Grimano. E arrivata quà una Cantatrice romana famosa nominata Orsola. E bella e questo basti a persuadersi che la faccia subito il concorso delli più famosi Grifoni Cantalordini. E poi soavissima, e condisce si bene la conversatione, che fà crescere appetito sopra appetito; si vede che fa egregiamente il Mestiere di Cantatrice Zitellotta romana; Parla, canta, racconta, moteggia, fà vezzi colla bochetta, cava quella anco fuori il linguino mostrando con esso di rinfrescarsi il labro afaticato da tanta armonia che esce da quella bella boccha. E furba come un Diavolo; piena di sucho, tutta brio, presta come una Dondola; ha bella taglia, belissima fronte, occhi neri, sempre ridenti; Già dissi della boccha: bel seno, bellissima mano, e ignuda deve essere a meraviglia gentile. Il Sig. Marchese Rangoni, con tutto che ha una cantatrice famosa tutta sua, in Casa sua, che è l'anima sua; Con tutto ciò, è caduto tra i lacci della bella Romana; la frequenta giorno, e notte; la serve, la assiste, e non può simular che l'ama. Quel che si sia del cuore del suo più domestico caro pene, V.A.S. può considerarlo, basta a dire che son femine; la Donzella Rangoni si diede a i pianti amari per ammollire al represo il cuore del Marchese; lui, e tenerissimo, fù visto a consolarla con protestar di esser suo in ogni modo, non ostante le Cortesie che sentiva di fare alla Romana; levi l'amaro della Donzella; ma ritornata nella solita Gelosia,

b. haveva risoluto di non cantar mai più, quando pur stimolata da gl'amici del marchese in piena conversatione prese a cantar un lamento, giusto giusto tagliato al suo dosso, bellissima poesia e musica perfettissima. Hor chi non vede quella scena non sà, che cosa e trasformarsi per il canto. Ella movea se stessa, e per la natura del lamento, pregava, ammolliva, chiamava il suo usurpatore bene; dolcemente lo persuadeva, lo guardava, e vibrava svisceratezze da gl'occhi; piangea con lacrime di fede; protestava che il cuore era l'altare, ove mai sempre ardea, fuoco d'immenso affetto; che lui era il Rè della gran regione de suoi pensieri, che perciò non l'abandonasse; seguitava con atti disperati con tutto furore, e tanto, che parea propriamente una furia arrabbiata; ma nominando in un passo la sua rivale, volse gl'occhi al cielo et esclamando *ahahahh!* che sia maledetta. Tornò poi col cuore a segno, e del caso suo accagionando più l'ira de fati, che l'incostanza del suo caro finisce il lamento ch'ella tramortì.

c. Racconto a V.A.S. questo per una cosa insigne, perche non crederò di sentir mai cosi più bene, e più di Cuore rappresentata al vivo; cosa di stupore, ritene ognuno. Il Marchese ammutì, e se ben stava col labro suo ridente come suol per natura, mostrava nondimeno d'haver il suo cuor confuso, perche veramente il Cimento era stato grande, et insigne. Si alzò su la Romanina, furba che il tutto haveva benissimo inteso, e con un sforzo strapazzativo cantò un arietta in sprezzo della gelosia, una arietta ridiculosa, ma bene assai gentile, e la Donzella Rangoni arrabbiava; oh che gusto, oh chi potesse veder quei cuori! Queste cosinee si godono a Venetia Sereniss. Princ. e senza teatri ancora ogni cosa è Teatro; per che, dove si tratta di dolcezze, di piaceri, e de godimenti, Venetia ha rivi di Manna, Canali di miele, e Canal Grande pieno di Elixir vite. Il buono è che di quella dolcissima conversatione adesso l'istoria incomincia. Io pagherei la mia Arzetta, che è l'unica gioia ch'io ho, che V.A.S. potesse esserci presente. Vi è di male, che non vogliono quelle due cantar più insieme. Si aspeta la Sig.ra Lucretia Dolfina, e questa compirà il numero delle tre gratie.

23. MASSI, 6 JUNE 1674 (vol. 4, no. 627, f. 568)
Il Sig. Pietro Dolfino sta nella diligenza delli Palchi del Theatro di San Salvador, et godo di vederlo fuori de gl'impegni della sua opera, con la quale si procurava mille incomodi, e mille impegni, col frutto delle ordinarie censure, e di irreparabili passioni. Io non consigliarei mai niuno amico a mettersi a far Drammi a Venetia.

24. BEREGAN, 20 SEPTEMBER 1675 (vol. 1, no. 624, f. 180)
Es parsa fama, che il S. Gratianino se ne venga prima del Carnevale in Italia—il che essendo vero, prendo ardire come emissario dell'A.V.S. tanto per mio nome, quanto per nome del S. Marchese Guido Rangoni di riverentemente supplicare la bontà di V.A.S. a restar servita d'impegnar il medesimo Sig. Gratianini che capitando à Venetia, e prima d'impegnarsi con alcun delli Teatri per la recita, faccia capo con mè, poiche dovendosi nel Teatro di S. Lucca recitar quest'anno un mio Drama sperarei di farlo spiccar maggiormente quando avessi questa parte.

25. BEREGAN, 17 NOVEMBER 1675 (vol. 1, no. 624, f. 181)
Suppilcai sino il passato Sett.bre con miei Eumilissi.mi caratteri la bontà di V.A.S. perche restasse servita di Commandare al S. Gratianini Cantante e Musico di V.A.S. che capitando in Venetia per questo prossimo Carnevale impiegasse la sua virtù nel recitare à S. Lucca un mio Drama intitolato l'Ottaviano Cesare Augusto, il quale con tutta pompa viene fatto recitare dal S.r Marchese Rangoni.

C. *Venice, Biblioteca nazionale marciana: Avvisi*

1. 21 NOVEMBER 1682 (I-Vnm, It. VI 459 [12103])

Nel mentre si vanno seguitando le comedie nel Teatro di San Samuele seguita a divertirsi il Serenissimo di Mantova, questa sera resta destinata di far la prova gente all'opera in musica in quello di San Cassano per essere in scena nella ventura, havendo già pronto tutte le cose necessarie per tale effetto.

2. 5 DECEMBER 1682 (I-Vnn, It. VI 459 [12103])

Nel mentre discorendosi, che il Serenissimo di Mantova dovesse per suoi particolari affari dara una scorza a suoi stati, havendo quei del Teatro di San Cassan ottenuta licenza di poter andare in scena con quella di Santi Gio e Paolo, ha differito la sua andata e hieri sera si diede principio alla prima opera, intitolata Temistocle in bando e questa sera l'altra intitolata Ottone il grando, andandosi per tanto da tutti gl'altri Teatri in musica mettendosi all'ordine il necessario per poter anch'essi essere in scena, essendo arrivate tutte le cantatrici, e musici.

3. 30 JANUARY 1683 (I-Vnm, It. IV 460 [12104])

Nel Teatro di S. Luca metteranno fuori una nuova opera publicando la fama che sarà più bella che la prima, e lo stesso pure si farà nel Teatro Griman Grisostomo . . . la quale ha più concorso che mai non ostante il pagamento delle 4 lire per ciascheduna persona.

4. 6 FEBRUARY 1683 (I-Vnm, It. VI 460 [12104])

Essendosi nel Teatro di San Cassiano cominciata la recita del nuovo Dramma intitolata L'innocenza risorta et in quello di S. Angelo Cornelio Silla che sono riuscite assai più grate delli primi, e dimane sera si principierà l'altra opera nel Teatro Vend. a S. Luca, ma in quello de Grimani à S. Giovanni Grisostomo non sarà rinnovata mentre continua ad esser la prima de comune sodisfatione pensandosi solo d'aggiungere alcune canzonette.

5. 11 DECEMBER 1682 (I-Vnm, It. VI 460 [12104])

Lunedi comparerà qua il Duca di Mantova con numerosa comitiva e si porta a godere la recita dell'opera nel Teatro di San Luca che fù principiata sin sabato della passata contro il parere dei musici, che non volevano acconsentirci, dicendo che tutti non erano pienamente instrutti per bene rappresentare le loro parti, e non ostante questo dubio riuscì d'universale sodisfattione, ma nelle sere seguenti non vi è stato quel concorso, che si sperava, e ciò a causa delle frequenti pioggie e malignità de tempi. Si crede, che in breve principieranno l'altre ne teatri di SS. Giovanni e Paolo, il San Giovanni Grisostomo, & altre.

Bibliography

◆　　◆　　◆

Abert, Anna Amalie. *Claudio Monteverdi und das musikalische Drama.* Lippstadt, 1954.

Ademollo, Alessandro. *I primi fasti della musica italiana a Parigi (1645–1662).* Milan, 1884.

———. *I teatri di Roma nel secolo decimosettimo.* Rome, 1888.

Allacci, Leone. *Drammaturgia di Leone Allacci accresciuta e continuata fino all'anno MDCCLV.* Venice: Giambattista Pasquali, 1755.

Antonicek, Theodor. "Die Damira-Opern der beiden Ziani." *Analecta musicologica* 14 (1974): 176–207.

Applausi poetici alle glorie della Signora Leonora Baroni. Rome: Costazuti, 1639, 1641.

Arnold, Denis. "Performing Practice." In *The New Monteverdi Companion,* edited by Denis Arnold and Nigel Fortune, 319–33. London, 1985.

Balsano, Maria Antonella, and James Haar. "L'Ariosto in Musica." In *L'Ariosto: La musica, i musicisti,* edited by Maria Antonella Balsano, 47–88. Florence, 1981.

Battagia, Michele. *Delle accademie veneziane.* Venice, 1826.

Beare, W. *The Roman Stage: A Short History of Latin Drama in the Time of the Republic.* London, 1964.

Becker, Heinz, ed. *Quellentexte zur Konzeption der europäischen Oper im 17. Jahrhundert.* Kassel, 1981.

Bellina, Anna Laura. *L'ingegnosa congiunzione: Melos e immagine nella "favola" per musica.* Florence, 1984.

Bellina, Anna Laura, and Thomas Walker. "Il melodramma: Poesia e musica nell'esperienza teatrale." In *Storia della cultura veneta dalla controriforma alla fine della repubblica: Il seicento* 4.1: 409–32. Vicenza, 1983.

Belloni, Antonio. *Storia letteraria d'Italia: Il seicento.* Milan, 1943.

Benedetti, Silvano. "Il teatro musicale a Venezia nel '600: Aspetti organizzativi." *Studi veneziani* 8 (1984): 185–220.

Bertelli, Pietro. *Diversarum nationum habitus centum et quatuor.* Padua, 1589.

Bianconi, Lorenzo. "Caletti." *Dizionario biografico degli italiani,* 16: 686–96. Rome, 1973.

———. "Scena, musica e pubblico nell'opera del seicento." In *Illusione e pratica teatrale: Proposte per una lettura dello spazio scenico dagli intermedi fiorentini all'opera comica veneziana,* 15–24. Exhib. cat. Venice, 1975.

———. "L'Ercole in Rialto." In *Venezia e il melodramma nel seicento,* edited by Maria Teresa Muraro, 259–72. Florence, 1976.

———. "Funktionen des Operntheaters in Neapel bis 1700 und die Rolle Alessandro Scarlattis." In *Colloquium Alessandro Scarlatti: Würzburg 1975,* edited by Wolfgang Osthoff and J. Ruile-Dronke, 13–116. Tutzing, 1979.

———. "Cesti." In *Dizionario biografico degli italiani,* 24: 281–98. Rome, 1980.

———. *Il seicento.* Storia della musica a cura della società italiana di musicologia 4. Turin, 1982. Translated as *Music in the Seventeenth Century.* Cambridge, 1987.

———. "Il cinquecento e il seicento." In *Teatro, musica, tradizione dei classici,* 319–63. Letteratura italiana 6. Turin, 1986.

———. Preface to Giulio Strozzi and Francesco Sacrati, *La finta pazza,* ed. Lorenzo Bianconi and Thomas Walker. Drammaturgia musicale veneta 1. Milan, in press.

Bianconi, Lorenzo, and Thomas Walker. "Dalla 'Finta pazza' alla 'Veremonda': Storie di Febi-armonici." *Rivista italiana di musicologia* 10 (1975): 379–454.

———. "Production, Consumption, and Political Function of Seventeenth-Century Opera." *Early Music History* 4 (1984): 209–96.

Bjurström, Per. *Giacomo Torelli and Baroque Stage Design*. Stockholm, 1961.

———. *Feast and Theater in Queen Christina's Rome*. Stockholm, 1966.

———. "Unveröffentlichtes von Nicodemus Tessin d. J.: Reisenotizen über Barock-Theater in Venedig und Piazzola." *Kleine Schriften der Gesellschaft für Theatergeschichte* 21 (1966): 14–41.

Bonini, Severo. *Discorsi e regole sopra la musica*. 1640. Edited by Leila Galleni Luisi. Cremona, 1975.

[Bonlini, Carlo.] *Le glorie della poesia e della musica contenute nell'esatta notitia de teatri della città di Venezia*. Venice: Bonarigo, 1730. Reprint. Bologna: Forni, 1979.

Bontempi, Angelo. *Historia musica*. Perugia: Costantini, 1695.

Boretti, Giovanni Antonio. *Ercole in Tebe*. Facsimile. Edited by Howard Mayer Brown. Italian Opera, 1640–1770 6. New York: Garland, 1982.

Borsetta, Maria Paola. "Teatro dell'arte e teatro d'opera nella prima metà del seicento." Tesi di laurea, Bologna University, 1986.

Bouwsma, William J. *Venice and the Defense of Republican Liberty: Renaissance Values in the Age of the Counter Reformation*. Berkeley and Los Angeles, 1968.

Brizi, Bruno. "Teoria e prassi melodrammatica di G. F. Busenello e 'L'incoronazione di Poppea.'" In *Venezia e il melodramma nel seicento*, edited by Maria Teresa Muraro, 51–74. Florence, 1976.

Brockpähler, Renate. *Handbuch zur Geschichte der Barockoper in Deutschland*. Emsdetten, 1964.

Brown, Howard M. *Sixteenth-Century Instrumentation: The Music for the Florentine Intermedi*. Musicological Studies and Documents 30. [Rome], 1973.

Brunelli, Bruno. "L'impresario in angustie." *Rivista italiana del dramma* 3 (1941): 311–41.

Burke, Peter. *The Historical Anthropology of Early Modern Italy*. Cambridge, 1987.

Burt, Nathaniel. "Opera in Arcadia." *Musical Quarterly* 41 (1955): 145–70.

Caffi, Francesco. *Storia della musica sacra nella già cappella ducale di S. Marco in Venezia (dal 1318 al 1797)*. 2 vols. Venice, 1853. Rev. ed. Edited by Elvidio Surian. Venice, 1987.

———. "Storia della musica teatrale in Venezia." 4 vols. MS. I-Vnm It. Cl. IV. Cod. 747–49 (10462–65).

Camerini, Paolo. *Piazzola*. Milan, 1925.

Cametti, Alberto. *Il teatro di Tordinona poi di Apollo*. Tivoli, 1938.

Carile, Antonio, and Giorgio Fedalto. *Le origini di Venezia*. Bologna, 1978.

Castronovo, Valerio. "Maiolino Bisaccioni." *Dizionario biografico degli italiani*, 10: 639–43. Rome, 1968.

Cavalli, Francesco. *Gli amori d'Apollo e di Dafne*. Facsimile. Edited by Howard Mayer Brown. Italian Opera, 1640–1770 1. New York: Garland, 1978.

———. *L'Oristeo*. Facsimile. Edited by Howard Mayer Brown and Eric Weimer. Italian Opera, 1640–1770 62. New York: Garland, 1982.

———. *Scipione affricano*. Facsimile. Edited by Howard Mayer Brown. Italian Opera, 1640–1770 5. New York: Garland, 1978.

Cecchetti, Bartolomeo. "Carte relative ai teatri di S. Cassiano e dei SS. Giovanni e Paolo." *Archivio veneto* 17 (1887): 246.

Cessi, Roberto. *Storia della repubblica di Venezia*. Milan and Messina, 1968.

Cesti, Antonio. *L'Argia*. Facsimile. Edited by Howard Mayer Brown. Italian Opera, 1640–1770 3. New York: Garland, 1978.

———. *La Dori*. Facsimile. Edited by Howard Mayer Brown and Eric Weimer. Italian Opera, 1640–1770 63. New York: Garland, 1982.

———. *Orontea*. Edited by William C. Holmes. Wellesley Edition 11. Wellesley, Mass. 1973.

Chiarelli, Alessandra. " 'L'incoronazione di Poppea' o 'Il Nerone': Problemi di filologia testuale." *Rivista italiana di musicologia* 9 (1974): 117–51.

Cicogna, Emmanuele A. *Saggio di bibliografia veneziana*. Venice, 1847.

Clinkscale, Martha. "Pier Francesco Cavalli's *Xerse*." Ph.D. diss., University of Minnesota, 1970.

Clubb, Louise G. *Italian Plays (1500–1700) in the Folger Library*. Florence, 1968.

———. "The Making of the Pastoral Play: Italian Experiments between 1573 and 1590." In *Petrarch to Pirandello: Studies in Italian Literature in Honor of Beatrice Corrigan*, edited by Julius A. Molinaro, 45–72. Toronto, 1973.

Corrigan, Beatrice. "All Happy Endings: Libretti of the Late Seicento." *Forum italicum* 7 (1973): 250–67.

Cozzi, Gaetano. *Paolo Sarpi tra Venezia e l'Europa*. Turin, 1979.

Crescimbeni, Giovanni Maria. *La bellezza della volgar poesia*. Rome: Buagni, 1700.

Croce, Benedetto. "Appunti sui costumi e letteratura spagnuola in Italia." In *Nuovi saggi sulla letteratura italiana del seicento*, 235–39. Bari, 1949.

Curtis, Alan. "*La Poppea impasticciata*, or Who Wrote the Music to *L'incoronazione* [1643]?" *Journal of the American Musicological Society* 42 (1989): 22–54.

Dahlhaus, Carl. "Drammaturgia dell'opera italiana." In *Storia dell'opera italiana*, edited by Lorenzo Bianconi and Giorgio Pestelli, 6: 79–162. Turin, 1988.

Damerini, Gino. "Cronache del Teatro Vendramin." *Il dramma*. 36–37, no. 291 (1960): 101–15; no. 294 (1961): 49–58; no. 296 (1961): 41–52; no. 302 (1961): 55–68.

———. "Il trapianto dello spettacolo teatrale veneziano del seicento nella civiltà barocca europea." In *Barocco europeo e barocco veneziano*, edited by Vittore Branca, 223–39. Florence, 1962.

Da Mosto, Andrea. "Il teatro a Venezia nel secolo XVII." *Rivista politica e letteraria* 8 (1899): 144–64.

———. "Uomini e cose del '600 veneziano (da un epistolario inedito)," *Rivista di Venezia* 12, no. 3 (1933): 117–22.

Dean, Winton. Review of *Erismena, The Musical Times* 108 (1967): 636.

Degrada, Francesco. "Gian Francesco Busenello e il libretto della 'Incoronazione di Poppea.' " In *Congresso internazionale sul tema "Claudio Monteverdi e il suo tempo,"* edited by Raffaello Monterosso, 81–102. Verona, 1969.

Della Corte, Andrea, ed. *Drammi per musica dal Rinuccini allo Zeno*. 2 vols. Turin, 1958.

De' Paoli, Domenico. *Claudio Monteverdi*. Milan, 1979.

Di Benedetto, Renato. "Poetiche e polemiche." In *Storia dell'opera italiana*, edited by Lorenzo Bianconi and Giorgio Pestelli, 6: 3–76. Turin, 1988.

Discorsi academici de' Signori Incogniti havuti in Venetia nell'academia dell'Illustrissimo Signor G. F. Loredano. Venice: Sarzina, 1635.

Doni, Giovanni Battista. *De' trattati di musica*. Florence: A. F. Gori, 1763. Vol. 2, part 2: *Trattato della musica scenica* (1640).

Durante, Sergio. "Il cantante: Aspetti e problemi della professione." In *Storia dell'opera italiana*, edited by Lorenzo Bianconi and Giorgio Pestelli, 4: 350–415. Turin, 1987.

———. "Vizi privati e virtù pubbliche del polemista teatrale da Muratori a Marcello." In *Benedetto Marcello: La sua opera e il suo tempo*, edited by Claudio Madricardo and Franco Rossi, 415–24. Florence, 1988.

Echi poetici all'armonia musicale della signora Isabella Trevisani Romana. Bologna: Ferroni, 1648.

Einstein, Alfred. *The Italian Madrigal*. 3 vols. Princeton, 1949.

Elwert, W. Theodore. *Italienische Metrik*. Munich, 1968. Translated as *Versificazione italiana dalle origini ai giorni nostri*. Florence, 1983.

Evelyn, John. *The Memoires of John Evelyn*. 2 vols. Edited by W. Bray. London, 1819.

Fabbri, Paolo. *Monteverdi*. Turin, 1985.

———. "Alle origini di un 'topos' operistico: La scena di follia." In *L'opera fra Venezia e Parigi*. Papers read at a conference held at the Fondazione Giorgio Cini, September 1985. In press.

———. "Istituti metrici e formali." In *Storia dell'opera italiana*, edited by Lorenzo Bianconi and Giorgio Pestelli, 6: 165–233. Turin, 1988.

———. *Il secolo cantante: Per una storia del libretto d'opera nel seicento*. Bologna, 1990.

Fabbri, Paolo, and Angelo Pompilio, eds. *Il Corago o vero alcune osservazioni per metter bene in scena le composizioni drammatiche*. Florence, 1983.

Falavolti, Laura, ed. *Commedie dei comici dell'arte*. Turin, 1982.

Feldman, Martha. "Venice and the Madrigal in the Mid-Sixteenth Century." 2 vols. Ph.D. diss., University of Pennsylvania, 1987.

Fenlon, Iain. "The Mantuan 'Orfeo.' " In *Claudio Monteverdi: Orfeo*, edited by John Whenham, 1–19. Cambridge, 1986.

Fortune, Nigel. "Monteverdi and the 'Seconda Prattica.' " In *The New Monteverdi Companion*, edited by Denis Arnold and Nigel Fortune, 183–97. London, 1985.

Franco, Giacomo. *Habiti delle donne venetiane*. Venice, 1610.

Freeman, Robert S. *Opera without Drama: Currents of Change in Italian Opera, 1675 to 1725*. Ann Arbor, 1981.

Gallico, Claudio. "Discorso di G. B. Doni sul recitare in scena." *Rivista italiana di musicologia* 3 (1968): 286–302.

———. *Monteverdi*. Turin, 1979.

Galvani, Livio Niso [Giuseppe Salvioli]. *I teatri musicali di Venezia nel secolo XVII, 1637–1700*. Milan, 1879.

Giazotto, Remo. *La musica a Genova nella vita pubblica e privata dal XIII al XVIII secolo*. Genoa, 1951.

———. "La guerra dei palchi: Documenti per servire alla storia del teatro musicale a Venezia come istituto sociale e iniziative privata nei secoli XVII e XVIII." *Nuova rivista musicale italiana* 1 (1967): 245–86, 465–508; 3 (1969): 906–33.

———. "Nel CCC anno della morte di Antonio Cesti. Ventidue lettere ritrovate nell'Archivio di Stato di Venezia." *Nuova rivista musicale italiana* 3 (1969): 496–512.

Gilbert, Felix. "Venice in the Crisis of the League of Cambrai." In *Renaissance Venice*, edited by J. R. Hale, 274–92. London, 1973.

———. *The Pope, His Banker, and Venice*. Cambridge, Mass., 1980.

Gilmore, Margaret. "Monteverdi and Dramatic Music in Venice, 1595–1637." MS.

Glixon, Beth. "The Letter-Writing Scene." Paper delivered at the annual meeting of the American Musicological Society, Philadelphia, 1984.

———. Review of Drammaturgia musicale veneta, vols. 4, 6, 12, 18, 24, 26. *Current Musicology* 39 (1985): 74–84.

———. "Recitative in Seventeenth-Century Venetian Opera: Its Dramatic Function and Musical Language." Ph.D. diss., Rutgers University, 1985.

Glixon, Beth, and Jonathan Glixon. "Marco Faustini and Venetian Opera Production in the 1650s: Recent Archival Discoveries." Paper delivered at a meeting of the South-Central Chapter of the American Musicological Society, Lexington, Kentucky, 1990.

Le glorie degli Incogniti o vero Gli huomini illustri dell'Accademia de' Signori Incogniti di Venetia. Venice: Valvasense, 1647.

Le glorie della musica celebrate dalla sorella poesia, rappresentandosi in Bologna la Delia e l'Ulisse nel teatro de gl'Illustriss. Guastavillani. Bologna: Ferroni, 1640.

Le glorie dell'armi venete celebrate nell'accademia de' Signori Imperfetti per la vittoria ottenuta contro l'armi ottomane. Venice: Pinelli, 1651.

Le glorie della Signora Anna Renzi romana. Venice: Surian, 1644.

Glover, Jane. "The Teatro Sant'Apollinare and the Development of Seventeenth-Century Venetian Opera." Ph.D. diss., Oxford University, 1975.

——. "The Peak Period of Venetian Public Opera: The 1650s." *Proceedings of the Royal Musical Association* 102 (1975–76): 67–82.

——. *Cavalli.* London, 1978.

——. "The Venetian Operas." In *The New Monteverdi Companion,* edited by Denis Arnold and Nigel Fortune, 288–315. London, 1985.

Goldschmidt, Hugo. "Cavalli als dramatischer Komponist." *Monatshefte für Musikgeschichte* 25 (1893): 45–48, 53–58, 61–111.

——. *Studien zur Geschichte der italienischen Oper im 17. Jahrhundert.* Leipzig, 1901–4. Reprint. Hildesheim: Olms, 1967.

Groppo, Antonio. *Catalogo di tutti i drammi per musica recitati ne' teatri di Venezia dall'anno 1637 in cui ebbero principio le pubbliche rappresentazioni de' medesimi, fin all'anno presente 1745.* Venice: Groppo, 1745. Reprint. Bologna: Forni, 1979.

Grout, Donald J. "The Chorus in Early Opera." In *Festschrift Friedrich Blume,* edited by Anna Amalie Abert and Wilhelm Pfannkuch, 151–61. Basel, 1963.

Grubb, James S. "When Myths Lose Power: Four Decades of Venetian Historiography." *Journal of Modern History* 58 (1986): 43–94.

Guarino, Raimondo. *La tragedia e le macchine: "Andromède" di Corneille e Torelli.* Rome, 1982.

Hanning, Barbara Russano. "Apologia pro Ottavio Rinuccini." *Journal of the American Musicological Society* 26 (1973): 240–62.

——. "Glorious Apollo: Poetic and Political Themes in the First Opera." *Renaissance Quarterly* 32 (1979): 485–513.

——. *Of Poetry and Music's Power.* Ann Arbor, 1980.

Herrick, Marvin. *The Fusion of Horatian and Aristotelian Literary Criticism, 1531–1555.* Urbana, Ill., 1946.

Hill, John W. "Le relazioni di Antonio Cesti con la corte e i teatri di Firenze." *Rivista italiana di musicologia* 11 (1976): 27–47.

Hjelmborg, Bjørn. "Aspects of the Aria in the Early Operas of Francesco Cavalli." In *Natalicia musicologica Knud Jeppesen septuagenario collegis oblata,* edited by Bjørn Hjelmborg and Søren Sørensen, 173–98. Copenhagen, 1962.

Holmes, William C. "Comedy–Opera–Comic Opera." *Analecta musicologica* 5 (1968): 92–103.

——. " 'Orontea': A Study of Change and Development in the Libretto and the Music of Mid-Seventeenth Century Italian Opera." Ph.D. diss., Columbia University, 1968.

——. "Giacinto Andrea Cicognini's and Antonio Cesti's *Orontea* (1649)." In *New Looks at Italian Opera: Essays in Honor of Donald J. Grout,* edited by William W. Austin, 108–32. Ithaca, N.Y., 1968.

Ivaldi, Armando Fabio. "Gli Adorno e l'hostaria-teatro del Falcone di Genova (1600–1680)." *Rivista italiana di musicologia* 15 (1981): 87–152.

Ivanovich, Cristoforo. *Minerva al tavolino.* Venice: Pezzana, 1681. 2d ed., 1688.

Jander, Owen. "The Prologues and Intermezzos of Alessandro Stradella." *Analecta musicologica* 7 (1969): 87–111.

Jeffery, Peter. "The Autograph Manuscripts of Francesco Cavalli." Ph.D. diss., Princeton University, 1980.

Kapp, Volker. "Liebeswahn und Staatsräson in der Oper L'Incoronazione di Poppea. Zur Verarbeitung von Seneca und Tacitus durch Monteverdis Text-Dichter Giovanni Francesco Busenello." In *Italia viva: Studien zur Sprache und Literatur Italiens.* Festschrift für Hans Ludwig Scheel, edited by Willi Hirdt and Reinhard Klesczewski, 213–24. Tübingen, 1983.

Kerman, Joseph. *Opera as Drama*. New York, 1956. Rev. ed. Berkeley and Los Angeles, 1988.

Kretzschmar, Hermann. "Die venetianische Oper und die Werke Cavallis und Cestis." *Viertel-jahrschrift für Musikwissenschaft* 8 (1892): 1–76.

———. "Beiträge zur Geschichte der venetianischen Oper." *Jahrbuch der Musikbibliothek Peters* 14 (1907): 71–81.

———. "Weitere Beiträge zur Geschichte der venetianischen Oper." *Jahrbuch der Musikbibliothek Peters* 17 (1910): 61–71.

———. "Schlussbeitrag zur Geschichte der venetianischen Oper." *Jahrbuch der Musikbibliothek Peters* 18 (1911): 49–61.

Kuzmick Hansell, Katherine. "Il ballo teatrale e l'opera italiana." In *Storia dell'opera italiana*, edited by Lorenzo Bianconi and Giorgio Pestelli, 5: 177–306. Turin, 1988.

Labalme, Patricia H. "Personality and Politics in Venice: Pietro Aretino." In *Titian, His World and His Legacy*, edited by David Rosand, 119–32. New York, 1982.

Lavin, Irving. *Bernini and the Unity of the Visual Arts*. New York, 1980.

Leclerc, Hélène. *Venise et l'avènement de l'opéra public à l'âge baroque*. Paris, 1987.

Legrenzi, Giovanni. *Totila*. Facsimile. Edited by Howard Mayer Brown. Italian Opera, 1640–1770 9. New York: Garland, 1978.

Leich, Karl. *Girolamo Frigimelica Robertis Libretti (1694–1708): Ein Beitrag insbesondere zur Geschichte des Opernlibrettos in Venedig*. Schriften zur Musik 26. Munich, 1972.

Leopold, Silke. " 'Quelle bazzicature poetiche, appellate ariette': Dichtungsformen in der frühen italienischen Oper (1600–1640)." *Hamburger Jahrbuch für Musikwissenschaft* 3 (1978): 101–41.

———. "Madrigali sulle egloghe sdrucciole di Iacopo Sannazaro." *Rivista italiana di musicologia* 14 (1979): 75–127.

———. *Claudio Monteverdi und seine Zeit*. Laaber, 1982.

Lindgren, Lowell, and Carl B. Schmidt. "A Collection of 137 Broadsides concerning Theatre in Late Seventeenth-Century Italy: An Annotated Catalogue." *Harvard Library Bulletin* 28 (1980): 185–233.

Livingston, Arthur. "Una scappatella di Polo Vendramin e un sonetto di Gian Francesco Busenello." *Fanfulla della domenica*, 24 September 1911.

———. *La vita veneziana nelle opere di Gian Francesco Busenello*. Venice, 1913.

Loredano, Giovanni Francesco. *Bizzarrie academiche*. Venice: Sarzina, 1638.

———. *Bizzarrie academiche del Loredano*. Parte seconda. Bologna: G. Longhi, 1676.

Lorenz, Alfred. *Alessandro Scarlattis Jugendoper*. Augsburg, 1927.

Lucio, Francesco, and Aurelio Aureli. *Il Medoro*. Facsimile. Edited by Giovanni Morelli and Thomas Walker. Drammaturgia musicale veneta 4. Milan: Ricordi, 1984.

Magini, Alessandro. "Indagini stilistiche intorno *L'incoronazione di Poppea*." Tesi di laurea, Bologna University, 1983–84.

———. "Le monodie di Benedetto Ferrari e *L'incoronazione di Poppea*: Un rilevamento stilistico comparativo." *Rivista italiana di musicologia* 21 (1987): 266–99.

Malipiero, Federico. *La peripezia d'Ulisse overo la casta Penelope*. Venice: Surian, 1640.

———. *L'imperatrice ambiziosa*. Venice: Surian, 1642.

Mancini, Franco, Maria Teresa Muraro, and Elena Povoledo, eds. *Illusione e pratica teatrale: Proposte per una lettura dello spazio scenico dagli intermedi fiorentini all'opera veneziana*. Exhib. cat. Venice, 1975.

Mangini, Nicola. *I teatri di Venezia*. Milan, 1974.

Matteini, Nevio. *Il "Rimino," una delle prime "gazette" d'Italia: Saggio storico sui primordi della stampa*. Bologna, 1967.

Maylander, Michele. *Storia delle accademie d'Italia*. 5 vols. Bologna, 1926–30.

Medin, Antonio. *La storia della repubblica di Venezia nella poesia*. Milan, 1904.

Ménestrier, Claude-François. *Des Representations en musique anciennes et modernes*. Paris, 1681.

Molinari, Cesare. *Le nozze degli dei: Un saggio sul grande spettacolo italiano nel seicento.* Rome, 1968.

———. *La commedia dell'arte.* Milan, 1985.

Molmenti, Pompeo. "Venezia alla metà del secolo XVII descritta da due contemporanei." In *Curiosità di storia veneziana,* 281–456. Bologna, 1920.

———. *La storia di Venezia nella vita privata dalle origini alla caduta della repubblica.* 7th ed. 3 vols. Bergamo, 1927–29.

Monson, Craig. "*Giulio Cesare in Egitto* from Sartorio (1677) to Handel (1724)." *Music and Letters* 66 (1985): 313–37.

———. "A Seventeenth-Century Opera Cycle: The Rise and Fall of Aelius Sejanus." MS.

Monteverdi, Claudio. *Tutte le opere di Claudio Monteverdi.* 17 vols. Edited by Gian Francesco Malipiero. Asolo, 1926–42.

———. *L'incoronazione di Poppea.* Venice manuscript. Facsimile. Edited by Giacomo Benvenuti. Milan: Bocca, 1938.

———. *L'incoronazione di Poppea.* Venice manuscript. Facsimile. Edited by Sergio Martinotti. Bologna: Forni [1969].

———. *L'incoronazione di Poppea.* Edited by Alan Curtis. London, 1989.

———. *Orfeo.* 1609 ed. Facsimile. Edited by Adolf Sandberger. Augsburg, 1927.

———. *Orfeo.* 1615 ed. Facsimile. Edited by Denis Stevens. Westmead, Farnsborough, Hants, England: Gregg, 1972.

———. *Claudio Monteverdi: Lettere, dediche, e prefazioni.* Edited by Domenico de' Paoli. Rome, 1973.

———. *The Letters of Claudio Monteverdi.* Edited by Denis Stevens. Cambridge, 1980.

Morelli, Giovanni. *Scompiglio e lamento (simmetrie dell'incostanza e incostanza delle simmetrie): "L'Egisto" di Faustini e Cavalli.* Gran Teatro La Fenice, Opere-Concerti-Balletti, 1981–82. Venice, 1982.

———. "Povero Bajazetto: Osservazioni su alcuni aspetti dell'abbattimento tematico della 'paura del turco' nell'opera veneziana del sei-settecento." In *Venezia e i Turchi,* 280–93. Milan, 1985.

———. "La scena di follia nella 'Lucia di Lammermoor': Sintomi, fra mitologia della paura e mitologia della libertà." In *La drammaturgia musicale,* edited by Lorenzo Bianconi, 411–32. Bologna, 1986.

———. "Il filo di Poppea: Il soggetto antico-romano nell'opera veneziana del seicento, osservazioni." In *Venezia e la Roma del Papa,* 245–74. Milan, 1987.

Morelli, Giovanni, and Thomas Walker. "Tre controversie intorno al San Cassiano." In *Venezia e il melodrama nel seicento,* edited by Maria Teresa Muraro, 97–120. Florence, 1976.

———. "Migliori plettri." In Aurelio Aureli and Francesco Lucio, *Orfeo,* ed. Giovanni Morelli and Thomas Walker, IX–LVII, CXXXI–LXIV. Drammaturgia Musicale Veneta 4. Milan, 1986.

Mueller, Reinhard. "Basso ostinato und die 'imitatione del parlare' in Monteverdis 'Incoronazione di Poppea.'" *Archiv für Musikwissenschaft* 40 (1983): 1–23.

Muir, Edward. *Civic Ritual in Renaissance Venice.* Princeton, 1981.

Muraro, Maria Teresa. "La festa a Venezia e le sue manifestazioni rappresentative: Le compagnie della Calza e le *momarie.*" In *Storia della cultura veneta dal primo quattrocento al concilio di Trento,* 3.3: 315–42. Vicenza, 1983.

Murata, Margaret. "The Recitative Soliloquy." *Journal of the American Musicological Society* 32 (1978): 45–73.

———. *Operas for the Papal Court, 1631–1668.* Ann Arbor, 1981.

———. "Classical Tragedy in the History of Early Opera in Rome." *Early Music History* 4 (1984): 101–34.

———. "Why the First Opera Given in Paris Wasn't Roman." In *L'opera tra Venezia e Parigi.* Papers read at a conference held at the Fondazione Giorgio Cini, September 1985. In press.

————. "Singing about Singing, or The Power of Music, Sixty Years After." In *In cantu et in sermone: For Nino Pirrotta on His 80th Birthday*, edited by Fabrizio della Seta and Franco Piperno, 363–82. Florence, 1989.

Nolhac, Pier de, and Angelo Solerti. *Il viaggio in Italia di Enrico III re di Francia e le feste a Venezia, Ferrara, Mantova e Torino*. Turin, 1890.

Noske, Frits. *The Signifier and the Signified: Studies in the Operas of Mozart and Verdi*. The Hague, 1977.

Odorisio, Ginevra Conti. *Donna e società nel seicento*. Rome, 1979.

L'orologio del piacere che mostra l'ore del dilettevole soggiorno havuto della serenissima d'Ernest Augusto Vescovo d'Osnabruc, duca di Branswich, Lunebergo, etc. Piazzola, 1685.

Osthoff, Wolfgang. "Die venezianische und neapolitanische Fassung von Monteverdis 'Incoronazione di Poppea.' " *Acta musicologica* 26 (1954): 88–113.

————. "Trombe sordine." *Archiv für Musikwissenschaft* 13 (1956): 77–95.

————. "Zu den Quellen von Monteverdis *Ritorno di Ulisse in patria*." *Studien zur Musikwissenschaft* 23 (1956): 67–78.

————. "Neue Beobachtungen zu Quellen und Geschichte von Monteverdis 'Incoronazione di Poppea.' " *Die Musikforschung* 11 (1958): 129–38.

————. "Zur Bologneser Aufführung von Monteverdis 'Ritorno di Ulisse' im Jahre 1640." In *Mitteilungen der Kommission für Musikforschung*, 155–60. Vienna, 1958.

————. "Antonio Cestis 'Alessandro vincitor di se stesso.' " *Studien zur Musikwissenschaft* 24 (1960): 13–43.

————. "Maske und Musik: Die Gestaltwerdung der Oper in Venedig." *Castrum peregrini* 65 (1964): 10–49. Translated as "Maschera e musica." *Nuova rivista musicale italiana* 1 (1967): 16–44.

————. "Cavalli." In *La musica*, 1: 825–34. Turin, 1966.

————. "Händels 'Largo' als Musik des goldenen Zeitalters." *Archiv für Musikwissenschaft* 30 (1973): 177–81.

————. "Filiberto Laurenzis Musik zu 'La finta savia' im Zusammenhang der frühvenezianischen Oper." In *Venezia e il melodramma nel seicento*, edited by Maria Teresa Muraro, 173–97. Florence, 1976.

————. "La musica della pazzia nella 'Finta pazza' di Francesco Sacrati." In *L'opera fra Venezia e Parigi*. Papers read at a conference held at the Fondazione Giorgio Cini, September 1985. In press.

————. "Musica e versificazione: Funzioni del verso poetico nell'opera Italiana." In *La drammaturgia musicale*, edited by Lorenzo Bianconi, 126–32. Bologna, 1986.

Palisca, Claude. "The Alterati of Florence: Pioneers in the Theory of Dramatic Music." In *New Looks at Italian Opera: Essays in Honor of Donald J. Grout*, edited by William W. Austin, 9–38. Ithaca, N.Y., 1968.

————. *Humanism in Italian Renaissance Musical Thought*. New Haven, 1985.

Pallucchini, Rodolfo, and Paola Rossi. *Tintoretto: Le opere sacre e profane*. Milan, 1982.

Papadopoli-Aldobrandini, Nicolò. *Le monete di Venezia descritte ed illustrate*. 4 vols. 1893–1919.

Pavanello, Giuseppe. "S. Marco nella leggenda e nella storia." *Rivista della città di Venezia* 7 (1928): 293–324.

Pavoni, Giuseppe. *Diario . . . delle feste nelle solennissime nozze delli serenissimi sposi il sig. duca Ferdinando Medici e la sig. donna Christina di Lorena*. Bologna: Rossi, 1589.

Petrobelli, Pierluigi. " 'L'Ermiona' di Pio Enea degli Obizzi ed i primi spettacoli d'opera veneziani." *Quaderni della Rassegna musicale* 3 (1965): 125–41.

————. "Francesco Manelli: Documenti e osservazioni." *Chigiana* 24 (1967): 43–66.

Pirrotta, Nino. "Tre capitoli su Cesti." In *La scuola romana: G. Carissimi–A. Cesti–M. Marazzoli*, 27–79. Siena: Accademia musicale Chigiana, 1953.

————. "*Commedia dell'Arte* and Opera." *Musical Quarterly* 41 (1955): 169–89. Reprinted in *Music and Culture in Italy from the Middle Ages to the Baroque* (henceforth *Essays*), 343–60. Cambridge, Mass., 1984. Translated as "Commedia dell'arte e l'opera" in *Scelte poetiche di musicisti* (henceforth *Scelte*), 147–72. Venice, 1987.

————. "Falsirena e la più antica delle cavatine." *Collectanea historiae musicae* 2 (1957): 355–66. Reprinted in *Scelte*, 255–64. Translated as "Falsirena and the Earliest Cavatina." *Essays*, 335–42.

————. "Ferrari." *Enciclopedia dello spettacolo*, 5: cols. 187–88. Rome, 1958.

————. "Il caval zoppo e il vetturino: Cronache di Parnaso 1642." *Collectanea historiae musicae* 4 (1966): 215–26. Reprinted in *Scelte*, 265–76. Translated as "The Lame Horse and the Coachman: News of the Operatic Parnassus in 1642." *Essays*, 325–34.

————. "Early Opera and Aria." In *New Looks at Italian Opera: Essays in Honor of Donald J. Grout*, edited by William W. Austin, 39–107. Ithaca, N.Y., 1968. Reprinted in *Music and Theatre from Poliziano to Monteverdi*, by Nino Pirrotta and Elena Povoledo, ch. 6. Cambridge, 1982.

————. "Scelte poetiche di Monteverdi." *Nuova rivista musicale italiana* 2 (1968): 10–42, 226–54. Reprinted in *Scelte*, 81–146. Translated as "Monteverdi's Poetic Choices." *Essays*, 271–316.

————. "Early Venetian Libretti at Los Angeles." In *Essays in Musicology in Honor of Dragan Plamenac*, edited by Gustave Reese and Robert Snow, 233–43. Pittsburgh, 1969. Reprinted in *Essays*, 317–24. Translated as "Antichi libretti d'opera veneziani a Los Angeles." *Scelte*, 243–54.

————. "Teatro, scene e musica nelle opere di Monteverdi." In *Congresso internazionale sul tema "Claudio Monteverdi e il suo tempo*," edited by Raffaello Monterosso, 45–67. Verona, 1969. Reprinted in *Scelte*, 219–42. Translated as "Theater, Sets, and Music in Monteverdi's Operas." *Essays*, 254–70.

————. "Monteverdi e i problemi dell'opera." In *Studi sul teatro veneto fra rinascimento ed età barocca*, edited by Maria Teresa Muraro, 321–43. Florence, 1971. Reprinted in *Scelte*, 197–218. Translated as "Monteverdi and the Problems of Opera." *Essays*, 235–53.

————. *Music and Culture in Italy from the Middle Ages to the Baroque*. Cambridge, Mass., 1984.

————. *Scelte poetiche di musicisti*. Venice, 1987.

Pirrotta, Nino, and Elena Povoledo, *Li due Orfei*. Turin, 1969. 2d ed. 1975. Translated as *Music and Theatre from Poliziano to Monteverdi*. Cambridge, 1982.

Porter, William. "Peri's and Corsi's 'Dafne': Some New Discoveries and Observations." *Journal of the American Musicological Society* 18 (1965): 170–96.

Povoledo, Elena. "Lo Schioppi viniziano pittor di Teatro." *Prospettive* 16 (1958): 45–50.

————. "Una rappresentazione accademica a Venezia nel 1634." In *Studi sul teatro veneto fra Rinascimento ed età barocca*, edited by Maria Teresa Muraro, 119–69. Florence, 1971.

————. "Scène et mise en scène à Venise: De la décadence des compagnies de la Calza jusqu'à la représentation de L'*Andromeda* au Théâtre de San Cassian (1637)." In *Renaissance, Maniérisme, Baroque: Actes du XIᵉ Stage International de Tours*, 87–99. Paris, 1972.

Powers, Harold S. "Il Serse trasformato." *Musical Quarterly* 47 (1961): 481–92; 48 (1962): 73–92.

————. "L'Erismena travestita." In *Studies in Music History: Essays for Oliver Strunk*, edited by Harold S. Powers, 259–324. Princeton, 1968.

————. "Il *Mutio* tramutato, Part I: Sources and Libretto." In *Venezia e il melodramma nel seicento*, edited by Maria Teresa Muraro, 227–58. Florence, 1976.

————. " 'La solita forma' and 'The Uses of Convention.' " *Acta musicologica* 59 (1987): 65–90.

Prota-Giurleo, Ulisse. *Francesco Cirillo e l'introduzione del melodramma a Napoli*. Grumo Nevano, 1952.

Prunières, Henry. *L'Opéra en France avant Lulli*. Paris, 1913.

————. *Cavalli et l'opéra vénitien au XVIIᵉ siècle*. Paris, 1931.

Pullan, Brian. *Aspetti e cause della decadenza economica veneziana nel secolo XVII.* Venice and Rome, 1961.

———, ed. *Crisis and Change in the Venetian Economy in the 16th and 17th Centuries.* London, 1968.

Puppi, Lionello. "Ignoto Deo." *Arte veneta* 23 (1969): 169–80.

———. "Il teatro fiorentino degli Immobili e la rappresentazione nel 1658 dell' 'Ipermestra' del Tacca." In *Studi sul teatro veneto fra Rinascimento ed età barocca*, edited by Maria Teresa Muraro, 171–92. Florence, 1971.

Quirini, Leonardo. *I vezzi d'Erato.* Venice: Hertz, 1653.

Ramous, Mario. *La metrica.* Milan, 1984.

Rapp, R. T. *Industry and Economic Decline in Seventeenth-Century Venice.* Cambridge, Mass., 1976.

Reiner, Stuart. " 'Vi sono molt'altre mezz'arie. . . .' " In *Studies in Music History: Essays for Oliver Strunk*, edited by Harold S. Powers, 241–58. Princeton, 1968.

———. "La vag'angioletta (and others)." *Analecta musicologica* 14 (1974): 26–88.

Ricci, Corrado. *I teatri di Bologna.* Bologna, 1888.

Ridolfi, Carlo. *Le maraviglie dell'arte.* [Venice, 1648.] Edited by Detlev Freiherrn von Hadeln. Berlin, 1914–24.

Robinson, Michael F. "Provenzale." In *The New Grove Dictionary of Music and Musicians*, 15: 316–17. London, 1980.

Romanin, Samuele. *Storia documentata di Venezia.* 10 vols. Venice, 1853–61.

Rosand, David. " 'Venetia Figurata': The Iconography of a Myth." In *Interpretazioni veneziane: Studi di storia dell'arte in onore di Michelangelo Muraro*, edited by David Rosand, 177–96. Venice, 1984.

———. "Venezia e gli dei." In *"Renovatio urbis": Venezia nell'età di Andrea Gritti (1523–1538)*, edited by Manfredo Tafuri, 201–15. Rome, 1984.

Rosand, Ellen. "Aria in the Early Operas of Francesco Cavalli." Ph.D. diss., New York University, 1971.

———. " 'Ormindo travestito' in 'Erismena.' " *Journal of the American Musicological Society* 28 (1975): 268–91.

———. "Aria as Drama in the Early Operas of Francesco Cavalli." In *Venezia e il melodramma nel seicento*, edited by Maria Teresa Muraro, 75–96. Florence, 1976.

———. "Comic Contrast and Dramatic Continuity: Observations on the Form and Function of Aria in the Operas of Francesco Cavalli." *Music Review* 37 (1976): 92–105.

———. "Music in the Myth of Venice." *Renaissance Quarterly* 30 (1977): 511–37.

———. "Barbara Strozzi, *virtuosissima cantatrice*: The Composer's Voice." *Journal of the American Musicological Society* 31 (1978): 241–81.

———. "The Descending Tetrachord: An Emblem of Lament." *Musical Quarterly* 55 (1979): 346–59.

———. "Boretti." In *The New Grove Dictionary of Music and Musicians*, 3: 48. London, 1980.

———. "In Defense of the Venetian Libretto." *Studi musicali* 9 (1980): 271–85.

———. "*L'Orfeo*: The Metamorphosis of a Musical Myth." *Israel Studies in Musicology* 2 (1980): 101–20.

———. "Minato." In *The New Grove Dictionary of Music and Musicians*, 12: 332. London, 1980.

———. "L'Ovidio trasformato." In Aurelio Aureli and Antonio Sartorio, *Orfeo*, ed. Ellen Rosand, IX–LVII. Drammaturgia musicale veneta 6. Milan, 1983.

———. "Orlando in Seicento Venice: The Road Not Taken." In *Opera seria as a Social Phenomenon*, edited by Michael Collins and Elise Kirk, 87–104. Austin, 1984.

———. "Seneca and the Interpretation of *L'incoronazione di Poppea*." *Journal of the American Musicological Society* 38 (1985): 34–71.

———. "Iro and the Interpretation of *Il ritorno d'Ulisse in patria*." *Journal of Musicology* 7 (1989): 141–64.

———. "Monteverdi's Mimetic Art: *L'incoronazione di Poppea*." *Cambridge Opera Journal* 1 (1989): 113–37.

———. "The Opera Scenario, 1638–1655: A Preliminary Survey." In *In cantu et in sermone: For Nino Pirrotta on His 80th Birthday*, edited by Fabrizio della Seta and Franco Piperno, 335–46. Florence, 1989.

———. "Operatic Madness: A Challenge to Convention." In *Music and Text: Critical Inquiries*, edited by Steven Paul Scher. Cambridge, in press.

Rosselli, John. *The Opera Industry in Italy from Cimarosa to Verdi: The Role of the Impresario*. Cambridge, 1984.

———. "The Castrati as a Professional Group and a Social Phenomenon, 1550–1850." *Acta musicologica* 60 (1988): 143–79.

———. "From Princely Service to the Open Market: Singers of Italian Opera and Their Patrons." *Cambridge Opera Journal* 1 (1989): 1–32.

Rossi, L. "Michelangelo Buonarroti il Giovane." *Dizionario biografico degli italiani*, 15: 178–81. Rome, 1972.

Rutschman, Edward Raymond. "The Minato-Cavalli Operas: The Search for Structure in Libretto and Solo Scene." Ph.D. diss., University of Washington, 1979.

———. "Minato and the Venetian Opera Libretto." *Current Musicology* 27 (1982): 84–91.

Sacrati, Francesco, and Giulio Strozzi. *La finta pazza* Facsimile. Edited by Lorenzo Bianconi and Thomas Walker. Drammaturgia musicale veneta 1. Milan: Ricordi, in press.

Saint-Disdier, Alexandre-Toussaint de Limojon, Sier de. *La Ville et la République de Venise*. Paris: Barbin, 1680.

Salerno, Henry F., trans. *Scenarios of the Commedia dell'Arte: Flaminio Scala's Il teatro delle favole rappresentative*. New York, 1967.

Sansovino, Francesco. *Venetia città nobilissima et singolare . . . con aggiunta di tutte le cose notabili . . . da D. Giustiniano Martinioni*. Venice: Curti, 1663.

Sartori, Claudio. "La prima diva della lirica italiana: Anna Renzi." *Nuova rivista musicale italiana* 2 (1968): 430–52.

———. "Un fantomatico compositore per un'opera che forse non era un'opera." *Nuova rivista musicale italiana* 5 (1971): 788–98.

———. "Ancora della 'Finta pazza' di Strozzi e Sacrati." *Nuova rivista musicale italiana* 11 (1977): 335–38.

———. "Primo tentativo di catalogo unico dei libretti italiani a stampa fino all'anno 1800." MS. Ufficio Ricerca Fondi Musicali, Milan.

Sartorio, Antonio. *Adelaide*. Facsimile. Edited by Howard Mayer Brown. Italian Opera, 1640–1770 8. New York: Garland, 1978.

Sartorio, Antonio, and Aurelio Aureli. *L'Orfeo* Facsimile. Edited by Ellen Rosand. Drammaturgia musicale veneta 6. Milan: Ricordi, 1983.

"Satire, et altre raccolte per l'Academia de gl'Unisoni in casa di Giulio Strozzi." MS. I-Vnm It. Cl. X Cod. 115 (7193).

Saunders, Harris Sheridan, Jr. "The Repertoire of a Venetian Opera House (1678–1714): The Teatro Grimani di San Giovanni Grisostomo." Ph.D. diss., Harvard University, 1985.

———. "The Teatro Grimani di San Giovanni Grisostomo: The Interaction of Family Interests and Opera in Venice." Paper delivered at the annual meeting of the American Musicological Society, New Orleans, 1987.

Scala, Flaminio. *Il teatro delle favole rappresentative*. [Venice: Pulciani, 1611.] 2 vols. Edited by Ferruccio Marotti. Milan, 1976.

Schmidt, Carl. "The Operas of Antonio Cesti." Ph.D. diss., Harvard University, 1973.

———. "Antonio Cesti's *La Dori*: A Study of Sources, Performance Traditions, and Musical Style." *Rivista italiana di musicologia* 10 (1975): 455–98.

————. " 'La Dori' di Antonio Cesti: Sussidi bibliografici." *Rivista italiana di musicologia* 11 (1976): 197–229.

————. "An Episode in the History of Venetian Opera: The *Tito* Commission (1665–66)." *Journal of the American Musicological Society* 31 (1978): 442–66.

Schwager, Myron. "Public Opera and the Trials of the Teatro San Moisè." *Early Music* 14 (1986): 387–94.

Selfridge-Field, Eleanor. *Pallade veneta: Writings on Music in Venetian Society, 1650–1750.* Venice, 1985.

Sella, Domenico. *Commerci e industrie a Venezia nel secolo XVII.* Venice and Rome, 1961.

Skippon, Sir Philip. *Journey through the Low Countries, Germany, Italy, and France.* London, 1682. Reprint. 1752.

Solerti, Angelo. "Le rappresentazioni musicali di Venezia dal 1571 al 1605." *Rivista musicale italiana* 9 (1902): 503–58.

————. *Gli albori del melodramma.* 3 vols. Milan, Palermo, and Naples, 1904.

Spingarn, Joel E. *A History of Literary Criticism in the Renaissance.* 2d ed. New York, 1908.

Spini, Giorgio. *Ricerca dei libertini: La teoria dell'impostura delle religioni nel seicento italiano.* Rome, 1950. 2d ed. Florence, 1983.

Stassi, Maria Gabriella. "Le novelle di Maiolino Bisaccioni tra 'favola' e 'istoria.' " In *L'arte dell'interpretare: Studi critici offerti a Giovanni Getto,* 291–316. Cuneo, 1984.

Sternfeld, Frederick W. "The Birth of Opera: Ovid, Poliziano, and the 'Lieto Fine.' " *Analecta musicologica* 19 (1979): 30–51.

Strozzi, Giulio. *La Venetia edificata, poema eroico di Giulio Strozzi, con gli argomenti del Sig. Francesco Cortesi.* Venice: Pinelli, 1624.

Sweykowska, Anna. "Le due poetiche venete e le ultime opere di Claudio Monteverdi." *Quadrivium* 18 (1977): 149–57.

Tarr, Edward, and Thomas Walker. " 'Bellici carmi, festivo fragor': Die Verwendung der Trompete in der italienischen Oper des 17. Jahrhunderts." *Hamburger Jahrbuch für Musikwissenschaft* 3 (1978): 143–203.

Taviani, Ferdinando. *La commedia dell'arte e la società barocca. La fascinazione del teatro.* Rome, 1969.

Taviani, Ferdinando, and Mirella Schino. *Il segreto della commedia dell'arte: La memoria delle compagnie italiane del XVI, XVII, e XVIII secolo.* Florence, 1982. 2d ed. 1986.

Termini, Olga. "The Transformation of Madrigalisms in Venetian Operas of the Later Seventeenth Century." *Music Review* 39 (1973): 4–21.

Tessari, Roberto. *La commedia dell'arte nel seicento.* Florence, 1969.

Testi, Fulvio. *Lettere.* Edited by M. L. Doglio. Bari, 1967.

Tieri, Guglielmina Verardo. "Il Teatro Novissimo: Storia di 'mutationi, macchine, e musiche.' " *Nuova rivista musicale italiana* 10 (1976): 555–95.

Tilmouth, Michael. "Music on the Travels of an English Merchant: Robert Bargrave (1628–61)." *Music and Letters* 53 (1972): 143–59.

————. "Grossi." In *The New Grove Dictionary of Music and Musicians,* 7: 743–44. London, 1980.

Timms, Colin. "Bontempi." In *The New Grove Dictionary of Music and Musicians,* 3: 37–38. London, 1980.

————. "The Cavata at the Time of Vivaldi." In *Nuovi studi vivaldiani,* edited by Antonio Fanna and Giovanni Morelli, 451–77. Florence, 1988.

Tolnay, Charles de. "Tintoretto's Salotto Dorato Cycle in the Doge's Palace." In *Scritti di storia dell'arte in onore di Mario Salmi,* 3: 117–31. Rome, 1961–63.

Tomlinson, Gary. "Madrigal, Monody, and Monteverdi's *via naturale alla immitatione.*" *Journal of the American Musicological Society* 34 (1981): 60–108.

————. "Music and the Claims of Text." *Critical Inquiry* 8 (1982): 565–89.

————. "Twice Bitten, Thrice Shy: Monteverdi's 'finta' *Finta pazza.*" *Journal of the American Musicological Society* 36 (1983): 303–11.

——. *Monteverdi and the End of the Renaissance*. Berkeley and Los Angeles, 1987.

——, ed. *Italian Secular Song, 1606–1636*, 7 vols. New York, 1986.

Tramontin, Silvio. "San Marco." In *Culto dei santi a Venezia*, 41–73. Venice, 1965.

Vassalli, Antonio. "Il Tasso in musica e la trasmissione dei testi." In *Tasso: La musica, i musicisti*, edited by Maria Antonella Balsano and Thomas Walker, 59–90. Florence, 1988.

Vaumorière, Pierre d'Ortigue de. *Lettres sur toutes sortes de sujets*. Paris: J. Guignard, 1690. 2d ed. Paris, 1696. 5th ed. Brussels, 1709.

Vayne, Paul. *Le Pain et le cirque: Sociologie historique d'un pluralisme politique*. Paris, 1976.

Vecellio, Cesare. *Degli abiti antichi e moderni*. Venice, 1589.

Veglia prima de' Signori academici Unisoni havuta in Venetia in casa del Signor Giulio Strozzi. Venice: Sarzina, 1638.

Velimirović, Miloš. "Cristoforo Ivanovich from Budva, the First Historian of the Venetian Opera." *ZVUK* [Yugoslav Music Review] 77–78 (1967): 135–45.

Viale Ferrero, Mercedes. "Repliche a Torino di alcuni melodrammi veneziani e loro caratteristiche." In *Venezia e il melodramma nel seicento*, edited by Maria Teresa Muraro, 145–72. Florence, 1976.

——. "Luogo teatrale e spazio scenico." In *Storia dell'opera italiana*, edited by Lorenzo Bianconi and Giorgio Pestelli, 5: 1–122. Turin, 1988.

Vigilante, M. "Giacinto Andrea Cicognini." In *Dizionario biografico degli italiani*, 25: 428–31. Rome, 1981.

Von Fischer, Kurt. "Eine wenig beachtete Quelle zu Busenellos 'L'incoronazione di Poppea.'" In *Congresso internazionale sul tema "Claudio Monteverdi e il suo tempo,"* edited by Raffaello Monterosso, 75–80. Verona, 1969.

Walker, Thomas. "Gli errori di *Minerva al tavolino*: Osservazioni sulla cronologia delle prime opere veneziane." In *Venezia e il melodramma nel seicento*, edited by Maria Teresa Muraro, 7–20. Florence, 1976.

——. "Acciaiuoli." In *The New Grove Dictionary of Music and Musicians*, 1: 33–34. London, 1980.

——. "Anna Renzi." In *The New Grove Dictionary of Music and Musicians*, 15: 745–46. London, 1980.

——. "Cavalli." In *The New Grove Dictionary of Music and Musicians*, 4: 24–34. London, 1980.

Weaver, Robert Lamar. "Sixteenth-Century Instrumentation." *Musical Quarterly* 47 (1961): 363–78.

——. "The Orchestra in Early Italian Opera." *Journal of the American Musicological Society* 17 (1964): 83–89.

Weaver, Robert Lamar, and Norma Wright Weaver. *A Chronology of Music in the Florentine Theater, 1590–1750*. Detroit, 1978.

Weinberg, Bernard. *A History of Literary Criticism in the Italian Renaissance*. 2 vols. Chicago, 1961.

Weiss, Piero. "Pier Jacopo Martello on Opera [1715]: An Annotated Translation." *Musical Quarterly* 66 (1980): 378–403.

——. "Neoclassical Criticism and Opera." *Studies in the History of Music* 2 (1987): 1–30.

Wellesz, Egon. "Cavalli und der Stil der Venetianischen Oper, 1640–1660." *Studien zur Musikwissenschaft* 1 (1913): 1–103.

Whenham, John. *Duet and Dialogue in the Age of Monteverdi*. 2 vols. Ann Arbor, 1982.

——, ed. *Claudio Monteverdi: Orfeo*. Cambridge, 1986.

Wiel, Taddeo. *I codici musicali contariniani del secolo XVII nella R. Biblioteca di San Marco in Venezia*. Venice, 1888. Reprint. Bologna: Forni, 1969.

——. *I teatri musicali veneziani nel settecento: Catalogo delle opere in musica rappresentate nel secolo XVIII in Venezia (1701–1800)*. Venice, 1897.

——. "Francesco Cavalli (1602–1676) e la sua musica scenica." *Nuovo archivio veneto*, n.s., 28 (1914): 106–50. Partial translation, "Francesco Cavalli (1602–1676)," *Musical Antiquary* 4 (1912–13): 1–19. Reprint, 1968.

Wolff, Helmut Christian. *Die venezianische Oper in der zweiten Hälfte des 17. Jahrhunderts*. Berlin, 1937. Reprint. Bologna: Forni: 1975.

———. "L'influsso di Monteverdi sull'opera veneziana." *Rivista italiana di musicologia* 2 (1967): 382–86.

———. "Italian Opera from the Later Monteverdi to Scarlatti." In *The New Oxford History of Music*, 5: 1–72. Oxford, 1975.

———. "Manierismus in den venezianischen Opernlibretti des 17. Jahrhunderts." In *Venezia e il melodramma nel seicento*, edited by Maria Teresa Muraro, 319–26. Florence, 1976.

Wolters, Wolfgang. *Der Bilderschmuck des Dogenpalastes: Untersuchungen zur Selbstdarstellung der Republik Venedig im 16. Jahrhundert*. Wiesbaden, 1983.

Worsthorne, Simon Towneley. *Seventeenth-Century Venetian Opera*. Oxford, 1954. Rev. ed., 1968.

Yates, Frances A. *Astraea: The Imperial Theme in the Sixteenth Century*. Boston, 1975.

Zorzi, Lodovico. *Il teatro e la città: Saggi sulla scena italiana*. Turin, 1977.

Zorzi, Lodovico, Maria Teresa Muraro, Gianfranco Prato, and Elvi Zorzi, eds. *I teatri pubblici di Venezia (secoli XVII–XVIII)*. Exhib. cat. Venice, 1971.

Musical Examples

◆　　◆　　◆

Example 1.　Claudio Monteverdi, *Il ritorno d'Ulisse in patria* (1640), 1.9, Ulisse: "Ò fortunato Ulisse" (A-Wn 18763: 40ᵛ–41ᵛ)

continued

continued

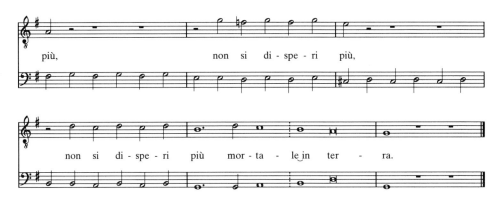

più,   non si di-spe-ri più,

non si di-spe-ri più mor-ta-le_in ter - ra.

Example 2.   Claudio Monteverdi, *Il ritorno d'Ulisse in patria* (1640), 3.8, Ericlea:
"Ericlea che vuoi far" (A-Wn 18763: 120^r–123^r)

Ericlea:

E - ri-cle - a,   E - ri-cle - a,   che vuoi far,   Vuoi ta-cer, ò par-

-lar?   Se par - li tu con - so - li,   Ob - be - di - sci se ta - ci.

Sei te - nu - ta_a ser - vir, Ob - bli - ga - ta_àd a - mar,   Vuoi ta-

-cer,   vuoi ta - cer, vuoi ta-cer, ò par - lar?   Mà   ce - da al-l'ob-be-dien - za

continued

continued

Ericlea:

Me - di - car chi lan-gui - sce, me - di - car chi lan - gui - sce, __

__ o che di - let-to. Mà che in-giu - rie e di-spet-to Sco-prir l'al-trui pen - sier. Bel - la

co - sa tal - vol - ta è un bel ta - cer, Bel - la co - sa tal - vol - ta è un bel ta -

-cer, Bel - la co - sa tal - vol - ta è un bel ta - cer. È fe-ri-tà cru -

-de - le Il po - ter con pa-ro - le Con-so-lar chi si duo-le, e non lo far, e non lo far,

Ma del pen-tir-si al - fin As-sai lun-ge è il ta - cer più che'l par - lar, as-sai lun-ge è il ta -

-cer più che'l par - lar, as - sai lun-ge è il ta - cer più che'l par - lar.

Rit. ut sopra

continued

Example 3.   Francesco Sacrati, *La finta pazza* (1641), 3.3, Eunuco: "Io non son buono" (I-Isola bella, private collection: [94^r])

continued

Example 4.   Francesco Cavalli, *Didone* (1641), 3.6, Enea: "Acate, Ilioneo" (I-Vnm, It. IV, 355 [=9879]: 113ᵛ–116ᵛ)

continued

Il ciel, il ciel ful - mi - na - tor de pet - ti re - i Chia - ma dal co - - re i pen - ti - men - ti mie - i. Ac - ce - le - riam l'an - da - ta, e ta - ci - tur - ni La - sciam di Li - bia i mi - nac - cia - ti li - di, Ci pro - met - ton le stel - le al - ti sus - si - di, Sù via dal por - to u - -sciam che - ti e not - tur - ni, Si ch'il ru - mor non giun - ga al - la ma - gio - ne Del - l'in - fe - li - ce mia dol - ce Di - -do - ne. _____ Fie - ris - si - mo con - tra - sto, a - spro con - flit - to; A - mor

continued

m'in-du-ce ai pianti a vi - va for - za, Ho-nor tro-va le la - gri-me e le

sfor-za A' sof-fo-car - si in me-zo il co - re af - flit - to. Son pian-ta com-bat-

-tu - ta da due ven - ti, E ven-gon da due in-fer-ni i miei tor -

-men - ti. ____ Ma la pie-tà di pa - dre,

e ver-so ai di - vi Re - li - gi-on hor chia-ma al-la par-ti - ta, ___

Ma Di-don il mio cor, ahi __ la mia vi - ta Co-m'ab-ban-do - no

in la - gri-mo - si ri - vi? In fiam-me già la-

continued

-sciai la pa-tria an-ti - ca,   La-scio in ac - que di pian - ti ho - - ra l'a-mi - - ca.

3[♯] 4   3

Dor - mi ca - ra,   dor - mi ca - ra Di - do - ne, _____

♯

il ciel cor - te - se Non ti fac - cia so - gnar l'an - da - ta

♯   [♯]

[♭]   ♭

mi - a, Il cor - po in na - - ve, e   l'al - ma à   te s'in -

[♯]

-vi - a, _____ Non fian mai spen - te ____ le mie ___ vo - glie ac - ce -

-se,   I - te sot - to al guan-cial del mio te - so - ro, O miei so -

♯

-spi - ri, o miei so - spi - ri,   e di te ch'io _____   mi

continued

-drai lun - ge mie ve - le,   Bel - la   Di - don,   bel - la   Di - don,

non mi   chia - mar,   non mi   chia - mar___   cru - de - le.

Example 5.   Francesco Cavalli, *Ormindo* (1644), I.8, Erisbe: "Fortunato mio cor"
(I-Vnm, It. IV, 368 [=9892]: 48ᵛ–49ᵛ)

Erisbe:

For - tu - na - to, for - tu - na - to, for - tu - na - to mio

cor,   for - tu - na - to, for - tu - na - to   mio   cor,

continued

Example 6a.   Francesco Cavalli, *Ormindo* (1644), 1.5, Melide: "Frena il cordoglio, frena" (I-Vnm, It. IV, 368 [=9892]: 28^v–29^r)

continued

Example 6b.   Francesco Cavalli, *Ormindo* (1644), 1.5, Erice: "Rasserena la fronte"
(I-Vnm, It. IV, 368 [=9892]: 29ʳ)

Example 7.   Francesco Cavalli, *Ormindo* (1644), 1.7, Erisbe: "Se nel sen di giova-
netti" (I-Vnm, It. IV, 368 [=9892]: 34ʳ–35ᵛ)

continued

continued

Fa - me - li-ca, e di - giu - na Di dol - cez - ze ve - ra - ci, Con so -
-spi - ri_in - te - rot - ti Pas - so le tris - te not - ti, Sa - tia di
fred - di, e di scia - pi - ti ba - ci. Pas - co sol di de -
-sio l'a - vi - de bra - me, E à men - sa Re - al mo - ro di fa - me.

[*Se nel sen,* + Rit.]

Example 8.   Francesco Cavalli, *Ormindo* (1644), 1.5, Sicle: "Chi, chi mi toglie al
          die" (I-Vnm, It. IV, 368 [=9892]: 29ʳ–30ʳ)

Sicle:

Am - mu - ti - te, ta - ce - te, Con sì va - ni con - for - ti Con - so - lar - mi cre - de - te?

Am - mu - ti - te, ta - ce - te. Chi, chi, chi mi to - glie_al

continued

di - e,   Car - ne - fi - ce pie - to - so Del-le scia - gu - re mi -

-e,   Chi,   chi,   chi mi to-glie, chi mi to - glie al di - e

Ritornello

An-go-scie a - spre e a-

-cer - be,   Se tan-to fie-re sie - te,   Per-che,   per-che non m'uc-ci - de - te?   Del-

-la sua vi-ta pri-va non vi-va più la mi-se-ra,   non vi - va. __   Chi,   chi,

chi mi to-glie al di - e,   Car - ne - fi-ce pie - to - so Del-le scia - gu-re mi -

-e,   Chi,   chi,   chi mi to-glie, chi mi to - glie al di - e.

Example 9.   Francesco Cavalli, *Ormindo* (1644), 2.5, Melide: "Volevo amar an-ch'io" (I-Vnm, It. IV, 368 [=9892]: 84^r–85^v)

continued

Example 10.   Francesco Cavalli, *Ormindo* (1644), 3.12, Erisbe and Ormindo: "Ah, questo è l'himeneo" (I-Vnm, It. IV, 368 [=9892]: 166^v–172^v)

continued

continued

continued

continued

continued

Example 11.   Francesco Cavalli, *Giasone* (1649), 1.14, Medea: "Dell'antro magico"
(I-Vnm, It. IV, 363 [=9887]: 58ᵛ–62ᵛ)

continued

continued

gle - be Gran mo - nar - ca del - l'om - bre in - ten - to a scol - ta - mi,

E se i dar - di d'A - mor già mai ti pun - se - ro, A - dem - pi ò Rè de i sot - te - ra - nei

po - po - li L'a - mo - ro - so de - sio, che'l cor mi sti - mo - la,   E

tut - to, tut - to A - ver - no,   e tut - to, tut - to A - ver - no al - la bell' op - ra u -

-ni - sca - si.   I mo - stri for - mi - da - bi - li, Del bel vel - lo di

Fris - so, Sen - ti - nel - le fe - ro - ci in - fa - ti - ca - bi - li,   Per po - ten - za d'a -

-bis - so Si ren - do - no a Gia - son   og - gi do - ma - bi - li.

continued

Dall' ar - sa Di - te (Quan-te por-ta-te Ser-pi al-la fron-te) Fu - rie ve-

-ni - te, E di Plu-to gl'im-pe - ri a me sve-la - te. Già que-sta ver - ga io

sco - to Già per - co-to Il suol col piè: Or - ri - di De - mo - ni,

Spi - ri - ti D'E - re-bo, Vo - la - te a me. Co-si, co-si in dar-no vi

chia - mo? Quai stre - pi - ti, Quai si - bi - li, Non la-scian pe - ne-trar nel cie - co

ba - ra-tro Le mie vo - ci ter - ri - bi-li? Dal - la sab - bia

Di Co - ci - to Tut - ta rab - bia Quà v'in - vi - to,

continued

Al mio so - glio, Qua, qua ___ vi vo - glio.

A che si tar - da più?   Nu - mi Tar-ta - re - i sù, sù, sù, sù!

[Coro di spiriti, Volano spirito]
Medea:

Si, si, si, Vin - ce - rà Il mio re, Si, si, si, Vin - ce -

-rà, vin - ce - rà il mio re, Al suo pro De - i - tà Di la

giù Pu - gne - rà, pu - gne - rà, pu - gne - rà, Si, si, si, vin - ce -

-rà, vin - ce - rà, si, si, si, vin - ce - rà, vin - ce - rà.

Example 12.   Francesco Cavalli, *Giasone* (1649), 3.10, Delfa: "È follia" (I-Vnm, It. IV, 363 [=9887]: 144ᵛ–145ʳ)

Example 13.   Francesco Cavalli, *Giasone* (1649), 3.1, Oreste and Delfa: "Nel bo-schetto" and "L'ombra à me" (I-Vnm, It. IV, 363 [=9887]: 116ᵛ–117ʳ)

[Oreste, 2ⁿᵈ strophe]

Example 14.   Francesco Cavalli, *Giasone* (1649), 3.2, Medea and Giasone: "Dormi, dormi" (I-Vnm, It. IV, 363 [=9887]: 120^r–122^r)

continued

Giasone:

Dor - mi,   dor - mi,   dor - mi ch'io dor - mo,   ò bel - la, _

E men-tre i sen - si miei con-se-gno al son - no,   Og - gi per te Gia - son van-tar _

si _ puo - le, D'ha-ver l'al - ma trà l'om - bre, tra l'om - bre e in

brac - cio il so - le.   Dor - mi,

continued

Example 15.   Antonio Cesti, *Alessandro vincitor di se stesso* (1651), 1.5, Alessandro: "Tua virtù" (I-Rvat Chigi Q.V. 61: 37ᵛ)

Example 16.   Antonio Cesti, *Alessandro vincitor di se stesso* (1651), 1.6, Alessandro:
"Tua bellezza è celeste" (I–Rvat Chigi Q.V. 61: 44[r])

Example 17.   Francesco Sacrati, *La finta pazza* (1641), 1.3, Achille: "Ombra di timore" (I-Isola bella, private collection: [16^{r–v}])

Example 18.   Francesco Cavalli, *Didone* (1641), 3.10, Jarba: "O benefico Dio" (I-Vnm, It. IV, 355 [=9879]: 129^v–130^v)

continued

Example 19. Francesco Cavalli, *Didone* (1641), 2.2, Jarba: "Rivolgo altrove il piede" (I-Vnm, It. IV, 355 [=9879]: 54[r–v])

continued

Example 20.   Francesco Cavalli, *La virtù de' strali d'Amore* (1642), 1.9, Erino: "Stolto chi fa d'un crine" (I-Vnm, It. IV, 373 [=9897]: 24^{r-v})

continued

Ritornello [à 5, only two parts given in manuscript]

Example 21.   Francesco Cavalli, *Egisto* (1643), 2.8, Dema: "Piacque a me sempre più" (A–Wn 16452: 61ᵛ–62ᵛ)

Dema:

Piac-que a me sem-pre ____ più La va-ga ____ gio-ven-tù d'o - gni al-tra e - ta - de; Sem-pre quel - la bel - ta - de Mi por-se più con - ten - to, Che non ha - vea ru - vi - do pe-lo al men - to Chi ha pro-va - to il mio a-

continued

continued

Example 22.   Francesco Cavalli, *Erismena* (1655), 1.12, Erismena: "Comincia à respirar" (I-Vnm, It. IV, 417 [=9941]: 25^r–26^r)

continued

Example 23.   Antonio Cesti, *Argia* (1669), 1.2, Feraspe: "Aurette vezzose" (I-Vnm, It. IV, 391 [=9915]: 8^{r-v})

continued

Example 24.   Giovanni Antonio Boretti, *Eliogabalo* (1668), 1.19, Flavia: "Cieca dea la tua possanza" (I-Vnm, It. IV, 412 [=9937]: 31^v–32^r)

continued

Example 25. Pietro Andrea Ziani, *Le fortune di Rodope e Damira* (1657), 2.7, Lerino: "Voglio un giorno innamorarmi" (I-Vnm, It. IV, 450 [= 9974]: 57^v–58^r)

continued

da _ voi non _ vò.   So ch'a-man-do tra - di-te,   e scal-tre o-gn'ho -

-ra, Voi la fa - te sù gl'oc-chi, voi la fa - te su - gl'oc-chi à   chi _

_ v'a   do   ra,   Voi la   fa - te sù gl'oc-chi, voi la

fa - te su-gl'oc-chi à _   chi   v'a - do   ra.

[Ritornello]

Example 26.   Pietro Andrea Ziani, *Le fortune di Rodope e Damira* (1657), 1.8,
Rodope: "Luci belle, se bramate" (I-Vnm, It. IV, 450 [=9974]: 22^(r-v))

continued

Example 27.   Francesco Cavalli, *Ormindo* (1644), 1.3, Nerillo: "O sagace chi sà"
(I–Vnm, It. IV, 368 [=9892]: 17^r–20^v)

continued

-gir _____ co-me il suo peg-gio La don-ne - sca bel - tà.

Bel - tà   men-ti-ta, e va - na   Che per far lac-ci à co - ri Và ru-ban-do i ca-

-pel - li A te-schi in-fra-ci-di-ti en-tro gl'a-vel - li: _____   Ma   che par-lo de'

5   6#

mor-ti, Se con vez - zi la-sci - vi Pe-la spie-ta-ta-men-te   in-si-no i vi-vi?

[*O sagace, Rit. da capo*]

continued

Example 28.   Francesco Cavalli, *La virtù de' strali d'Amore* (1642), 3.9, Mercurio:
"Donne s'amar volete" (I-Vnm, It. IV, 373 [=9897]: 90^(r–v))

Example 29.   Francesco Cavalli, *Doriclea* (1645), 3.4, Melloe: "Voglio provar anch'io, che cosa è amor" (I-Vnm, It. IV, 356 [=9880]: 85^{r-v})

Example 30.   Francesco Cavalli, *Xerse* (1654), 2.8, Eumene: "La bellezza è un don fugace" (I-Vnm, It. IV, 374 [=9898]: 90ᵛ–91ʳ)

continued

2^(da) stroffa ut sopra si replica con il Ritornello

Example 31.   Francesco Cavalli, *Doriclea* (1645), 1.5, Eurinda: "Udite amanti, udite" (I-Vnm, It. IV, 356 [=9880]: 22^v–24^v)

continued

cor _____ più

lie - to, più lie - to _____ cor, non si tro - va del

mio   più lie - to, più lie - to ____ cor _____

_____ più lie - to, più lie - to _____ cor.

Ritornello

6

continued

continued

schie - re d'A - mor   Si può tro - var ___ del mio   più lie - to, più

lie - to ___ cor, ___ più

lie - to, ___ più ___ lie - to ___ cor,   si può tro - var ___ del

6♯

mio   più   lie - to,   più   lie - to ___ cor, ___

___ più   lie - to, ___ più ___ lie - to ___ cor?

[Rit., 2ⁿᵈ strophe, Rit.]

Example 32.   Francesco Cavalli, *Xerse* (1654), 2.13, Amastre: "Morirò: volete più"
(I-Vnm, It. IV, 374 [=9898]: 101ᵛ–102ʳ)

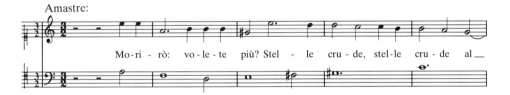

Amastre:

Mo - ri - rò: vo - le - te   più? Stel - le   cru - de, stel - le   cru - de   al

continued

Si replica da capo

Example 33.   Francesco Cavalli, *Xerse* (1654), 2.15, Romilda: "Amante non è"
(I-Vnm, It. IV, 374 [=9898]: 108ᵛ–109ʳ)

continued

[2nd strophe]

Example 34.   Francesco Lucio, *Medoro* (1658), 2.14, Miralba: "Non dovevi innamorarti" (I-Vnm, It. IV, 436 [=9960]: 58[r]–59[r])

continued

Example 35.   Antonio Sartorio, *Orfeo* (1673), 1.13, Orfeo: "Cerco pace e mi fà guerra" (I-Vnm, It. IV, 443 [=9967]: 23ᵛ–24ʳ)

continued

Example 36.   Francesco Cavalli, *Xerse* (1654), 2.1, Amastre: "Speranze fermate"
(I-Vnm, It. IV, 374 [=9898]: 68^{r-v})

continued

Example 37.   Antonio Sartorio, *Seleuco* (1666), 1.7, Seleuco: "Tardanza noiosa"
(I-Vnm, It. IV, 454 [=9978]: [14ᵛ–15ᵛ])

continued

Example 38.   Francesco Cavalli, *Erismena* (1655), 3.12, Aldimira: "Ch'io parta? non posso" (I-Vnm, It. IV, 417 [=9941]: 99ᵛ–100ʳ)

continued

Example 39.   Pietro Andrea Ziani, *Le fortune di Rodope e Damira* (1657), 3.8,
Rodope: "Rendetemi il mio ben stelle fatali" (I-MOe Mus. F 1301: 138ᵛ–141ᵛ)

continued

continued

continued

continued

Example 40.   Francesco Cavalli, *Mutio Scevola* (1665), 1.13, Elisa: "Fermo scoglio è la mia fede" (I-Vnm, It. IV, 364 [=9888]: 34ʳ)

continued

Example 41.   Francesco Lucio, *Medoro* (1658), 3.11, Angelica: "La mia mente è un vasto Egeo" (I-Vnm, It. IV, 436 [=9960]: 85^r–86^r)

continued

continued

Example 42.   Francesco Cavalli, *Xerse* (1654), I.I, Xerse: "Ombra mai fù"
(I-Vnm, It. IV, 374 [=9898]: 1^r–3^v)

continued

continued

[Rit., 2nd strophe, refrain: *Ombra mai fù*]

Example 43.   Francesco Lucio, *Medoro* (1658), 1.8, Medoro: "O luce serena"
(I-Vnm, It. IV, 436 [= 9960]: 20ʳ–21ʳ)

continued

continued

O luce serena da Capo

Example 44.   Francesco Cavalli, *Erismena* (1655), 2.7, Aldimira: "Vaghe stelle"
(I-Vnm, It. IV, 417 [=9941]: 48^v–51^v)

continued

continued

continued

continued

Example 45.   Antonio Cesti, *Argia* (1669), 2.5, Alceo: "Io pensavo innamorarmi"
(I–Vnm, It. IV, 391 [= 9915]: 67^{r-v})

continued

Example 46.   Giovanni Antonio Boretti, *Ercole in Tebe* (1671), 1.13, Clitarco: "Fier tiranno" (I-Vnm, It. IV, 316 [=9940]: 23ᵛ)

continued

continued

Example 47.   Antonio Sartorio, *Orfeo* (1673), 1.4, Erinda: "S'io potessi ritornar"
(I-Vnm, It. IV, 443 [= 9967]: 10^{r-v})

continued

continued

Example 48.   Antonio Sartorio, *Orfeo* (1673), I.17, Euridice: "Non sò dir" (I-Vnm, It. IV, 443 [=9967]: 29ᵛ–30ʳ)

continued

Example 49.   Antonio Cesti, *Argia* (1669), 1.5, Atamante: "Nascer grande"
(I-Vnm, It. IV, 391 [=9915]: 15ᵛ–16ʳ)

[Rit. à 5]

Example 50.   Antonio Sartorio, *Adelaide* (1672), I.11, Annone: "Le grane di Tiro"
(I-Vnm, It. IV, 380 [= 9904]: 29^{r-v})

Example 51.   Antonio Sartorio, *Orfeo* (1673), 1.5, Autonoe: "Ruscelletti" and
"Qual spirto dannato" (I-Vnm, It. IV, 443 [=9967]: 10ᵛ–12ʳ)

continued

continued

continued

Example 52.   Francesco Cavalli, *Giasone* (1649), 2.11 (= libretto 2.12), Alinda: "Quanti soldati" (I-Vnm, It. IV, 343 [=9887]: 101^r–102^r)

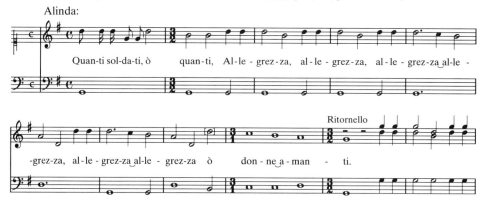

continued

Example 53.   Francesco Cavalli, *Giasone* (1649), 2.11 (=libretto 2.12), Besso and
Alinda: "Non più guerra" (I-Vnm, It. IV, 343 [=9887]: 105^r–106^v)

continued

continued

continued

6

continued

Example 54.   Francesco Sacrati, *La finta pazza* (1641), 1.3, Deidamia: "Suona d'intorno la fiera tromba" (I-Isola bella, private collection: [17ʳ])

Example 55.   Francesco Cavalli, *Doriclea* (1645), 1.12 (=libretto 1.11), Venere and Coro: "Amori all'armi, all'armi" (I-Vnm, It. IV, 356 [=9880]: 32^r–36^r)

continued

continued

continued

continued

continued

continued

Example 56.   Pietro Andrea Ziani, *Le fortune di Rodope e Damira* (1657), 2.15,
Rodope: "Vendetta mio core" (I-MOe, F 1301: 111ʳ–112ʳ)

continued

continued

Example 57.   Antonio Sartorio, *Adelaide* (1672), 1.1, Adelaide: "Vitrici schiere"
(I-Vnm, It. IV, 380 [=9904]: 1ʳ–3ʳ)

continued

continued

continued

Example 58.   Giovanni Legrenzi, *Totila* (1677), 2.6, Totila: "Crudo mostro e gelosia" (I-Vnm, It. IV, 460 [=9984]: 73^v–74^r)

continued

Di Ce-ra-ste ha il crin in - vol - to, Na - ta già di Sti - gio in se - no,

L'ar - mi a - sper - se ha di _ ve - le - no, l'ar - mi a-

-sper - se ha di ve - le - no, E al mio cor, _____

e al mio cor dà pe - na ri - a, dà pe - na, dà

pe - na ri - a. Cru - do mo - stro, cru - do

mo - stro è ge - lo - si - a, cru - do mo - stro è ge - lo - si - a.

Ritornello [à 5, bass only in manuscript]

Example 59.   Francesco Cavalli, *Giasone* (1649), 2.11 (=libretto 2.12), Alinda and Besso: "Ma quanto più" (I-Vnm, It. IV, 343 [=9887]: 104^v–105^r)

Example 60.   Antonio Sartorio, *Seleuco* (1666), 2.4, Antioco: "Aria non trovo"
(I-Vnm, It. IV, 454 [=9978]: 36^v–39^r)

continued

Antioco: Silo:

Non più, non più trop-po m'an-no — ia.   O - di que - sta, si - gno - re:

Ritornello

43

Musico:

Ar - do_ohi - mè   ne so di che,   Son fe - ri - to e non so

co — me,   Son pia - ga - to e non so_il dì. Ne men que-sta mi pia - ce.

Ritornello

6   6   6   6

continued

continued

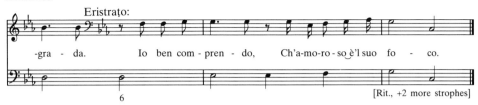

Example 61.   Francesco Cavalli, *La virtù de' strali d'Amore* (1642), 3.15, Meonte and
Eumete: "O mia vita" (I-Vnm, It. IV, 373 [=9897]: 112^v–116^r)

continued

continued

continued

continued

-diam ch'A-mor   c'in - vi - ta   à i   bac - ci, à i   bac - ci,

-diam ch'A-mor   c'in - vi - ta   al

à i   bac - ci, à i   bac - ci, al   let - to, al

let - to, al   let - to, à i   bac - ci, à i   bac - ci, al   let - to, al

let - to,   al   let - to,   al   let -   to. _____

let - to,   al   let - to, al   let -   to.

Example 62a.   Antonio Cesti, *Argia* (1669), 3.17, Argia and Lucimoro: "Si, si, si"
(I–Vnm, It. IV, 391 [=9915]: 142^{r-v})

Example 62b.   Pietro Andrea Ziani, *Annibale in Capua* (1661), 3.20, Emilia and
Floro: "Sin che l'alma in petto havrò" (I-Vnm, It. IV, 387 [=9911]: 86[r])

Example 62c.   Giovanni Antonio Boretti, *Eliogabalo* (1668), 3.21, Flavia and
Eliogabalo: "Al ferir, al gioir" (I-Vnm, It. IV, 412 [=9937]: 102[r])

continued

Example 62d.   Antonio Sartorio, *Orfeo* (1673), 3.16, Autonoe and Aristeo: "Mia vita, mio ardore" (I-Vnm, It. IV, 443 [=9967]: 85[r–v])

continued

Example 63.   Claudio Monteverdi, *L'incoronazione di Poppea* (1643), 2.12, Poppea:
"Amor, recorro a te" (I-Vnm, It. IV, 439 [= 9963]: 75^v–76^r)

Example 64.   Francesco Cavalli, *Giasone* (1649), 2.1, Isifile: "Alinda è troppo vana"
(I-Vnm, It. IV, 343 [=9887]: 65^{r-v})

Example 65.   Antonio Cesti, *Orontea* (Innsbruck: 1656), 2.4, Alidoro: "Ma lasso, e
qual affanno" (I-Rsc: 111^{v})

continued

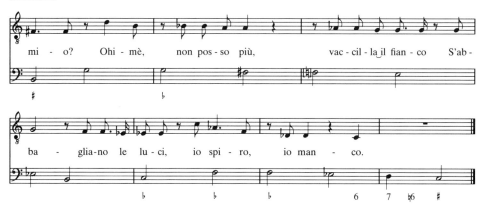

Example 66.   Giovanni Antonio Boretti, *Ercole in Tebe* (1671), 2.20, Megera: "Se nel vincer di Alcide" (I-Vnm, It. IV, 316 [=9940]: 76^r–77^v)

continued

continued

son - no _____ i miei, i miei tor - -men - ti, _____ Se - pel - li - sci nel son - no i miei tor - men - ti,

continued

Example 67.   Francesco Cavalli, *Didone* (1641), 1.7, Ecuba: "Tremulo spirito"
(I-Vnm, It. IV, 355 [=9879]: 32ʳ)

continued

Example 68.   Francesco Cavalli, *Calisto* (1651), 1.13, Satirino and Linfea: "Io son d'origine" (I–Vnm, It. IV, 353 [=9877]: 39ᵛ–40ᵛ)

continued

continued

Example 69. Pietro Andrea Ziani, *Annibale in Capua* (1661), 1.19, Alcea: "O voi de l'Erebo" (I-Vnm, It. IV, 387 [=9911]: 25ᵛ–26ʳ)

continued

Example 70.   Francesco Sacrati, *La finta pazza* (1641), 2.9, end, 2.10, excerpts, Deidamia: "Guerrieri, all'armi, all'armi" (I-Isola bella, private collection: [69ʳ–73ʳ])

continued

continued

continued

continued

continued

Ch'ei fà dal cie - lo in ter - ra Mi ri - e - sce so -

-ven-te il gran to - nan - te Un son-nac - chio - so a - man - te. _ [Diomede, then Uno del Coro]

(h)
Deidamia:

Deh, dim-mi, dim-mi il ve - ro, Se lo di - ce - sti mai, Che fis - sa pe - co - rag - gi - ne ti as-

-sa - le? Di che ti me-ra-vi - gli? Cut - tret-to-la, Frin-guel-lo, O - cha, Frus-so-ne, Bar-bag-

-gian - ni, Ba - bus - so; Non sò per qua-le in - flus - so, Ne' miei se - gre - ti a -

-mo-ri, Ur-to o-gn'ho-ra in sog - get - ti Più sto-li-di e peg - gio - ri. Non si può più par-la - re,

O-gn'un, à quel che sen - to, Hog - gi mi vuol glos-sa - re, Mi vuol far il co-men - to,

4   3

continued

A stri-de quie - te, dun - que, Ad in - ten - der-si à cen - ni, Al - la

mu - ta, al-la mu - ta, Pron-ta man, oc-chio pre-sto, Quel che di-ria la lin - gua, quel che di-ria la

(i)
Deidamia:

lin - gua e-spri - ma il ge - sto.   [Eunuco, Diomede,   Ohi - mè que-
                                        then Uno del Coro]

-st'on - da, ohi-mè, È l'ul - ti - ma per me; Dun - que pie - ta-de in voi non hà più

luo - go?   Non ve - de - te ch'af-fo - go,   af - fo - go,   af - fo - go.

(j)   #6
Eunuco: Deidamia:

E non ti ba - gni un pe - lo. __   Ah, so ben i - o Qual di rac-

-chiu-so pian-to al me - sto co - re   Fa la - go il mio do - lo - re.

4   #

continued

(k)

Example 71a.   Francesco Cavalli, *Egisto* (1643), 3.5, Egisto: "Celesti fulmini"
(A-Wn 16452: 90^r–95^r)

continued

continued

continued

continued

continued

continued

-de te at-te-rar - mi Ò pal - li - de fan - ta - sme,   O por-ten-to - si mo - stri?

Non m'ar-re-cò ter-ro - re Fan-ta-sma, e mo-stro rio di voi mag-gio - re.   Tan - ta-lo,

pren - di,   pren-di il   fug-gi - ti - vo po - mo,   To - gli,   to - gli del-l'ac-qua a-

va - ra, Be - vi, be - vi,   che fa - i?   Ah, ah,   per-che la spu - ti?   As-sag-

-giar-la anch' io vò,   se'l ciel   m'a-iut - ti. ____   Hai tù rag-gio - ne,

el - la è ben trop - pa a - ma - ra.   Oh   di Da - nao ho - mi

ci - de E mal-na - te fi - glio-le Clo - ri,   Clo - ri   non è con vo - i?   In-se-

continued

-gna - te - la, in - se-gna - te - la à mè,   Di - te,   di - te,   dov' è.

Ree d'u-na stes - sa   col - pa Me la ce - la-te in va - no,   La tro - ve - rò   ben

i - o,   La   vò   tan - to sfer-zar con que-ste   ser - pi, Sin che de - sti pie -

-tà del suo mar -ti - re Nel-le   fu - rie so - rel - le Di lei com - pa - - gne fel - - le.

Ec - co, ec - co la scel -le - - ra - ta, Che dal con - ca - vo   vo-stro Fat - ti - co - so stru-

-men-to In cui s'e - ra ce - la - ta, u-sci - ta fug - ge,   Fug-gi pur, fug-gi pu - re,   Ch'io

se-gui-rò le tue fu-ga-ci pian - te   Sin nel-le go-le del ma-stin la-tran - te.

Example 71b.   Francesco Cavalli, *Egisto* (1643), 3.9, excerpts, Egisto: "Rendetemi Euridice" (A–Wn 16452: 102ᵛ–104ʳ)

continued

continued

Quan-to mi fa . . .   *Ride*   mi fa-te ri - de - re.   Ohi-me, ohi-me, fug-gia-mo, fug-

-gia - mo, ohi-me.   E - gli vie - ne di là,   Nò, nò,   fer - ma - te il piè,

Sie - te, sie - te pur scio - chi,   *Riso* ah, ah, ah, ah, ah.

Example 72.   Claudio Monteverdi, *Il ritorno d'Ulisse in patria* (1640), 3.1, excerpts,
Iro: "O dolor" (A-Wn 18763: 103^v–107^r)

Iro:

l'ho di - strut-ta,   l'ho di - strut-ta,   l'ho di - strut-ta,   l'ho di - strut-ta,   l'ho di - strut-ta,

l'ho di-strut-ta, l'ho di-strut-ta,   l'ho di-strut-ta, l'ho di-strut-ta,   l'ho di-strut-ta, l'ho di-strut-ta,

l'ho vin - ta,   l'ho vin - ta [etc.]

continued

continued

Example 73.   Francesco Cavalli, *Giasone* (1649), 2.14, Isifile: "Indietro ria canaglia"
(I-Vnm, It. IV, 343 [=9887]: 116ʳ)

Example 74.   Pietro Andrea Ziani, *Le fortune di Rodope e Damira* (1657), 2.10,
Damira: "Tra nozze si liete" (I-Vnm, It. IV, 450 [=9974]: 69ʳ–73ʳ)

continued

ti, si suo - ni, si   can   -   ti, Al -

-le - gri e fe - stan - ti, Ò   spo - se go - de - te, ò spo - si __ go - de - te, __

[♮5]

__ al - le - gri e fe - stan - ti   ò   spo - si go - de - te, ò   spo - si __ go -

-de - te. _____

Rodope:

Go - dia - mo, si, go - dia - mo,   go - dia - mo, si, go - dia - mo,   go - dia - mo, si,

Creonte:

Go - dia - mo, si, go - dia - mo,   go - dia - mo, si,   go -

continued

Example 75a.   Domenico Freschi, *Helena rapita da Paride* (1677), 2.23 (libretto = 2.24), Euristene: "Su le rive d'Acheronte" (I-Vnm, It. IV, 357 [= 9881]: 61$^\mathrm{r}$)

continued

Example 75b.   Domenico Freschi, *Helena rapita da Paride* 2.23 (libretto = 2.24),
Euristene: "Se non fuggi amante insano" (I-Vnm, It. IV, 357 [=9881]: 62ʳ)

Example 76a.   Giovanni Legrenzi, *Totila* (1677), 3.15, Publicola: "Sù, stringetevi"
(I-Vnm, It. IV, 460 [=9984]: 59ᵛ)

continued

Bac - cia - te - vi,   bac - cia - te - vi   Se ba - ciar voi non sa -

-pe - te   Co - me si ba - cia   o - ra dà mè ap-pren-de - te.

Example 76b.   Giovanni Legrenzi, *Totila* 3.15, Publicola: "Bel Narciso" (I-Vnm, It. IV, 460 [=9984]: 59ᵛ)

(b)

Publicola:

Bel Nar - ci - so   Lun - gi dal   fon - te,   Co - me so - lo qui

Desbo:

ti   veg - gi - o.   In no-vo la-be - rin-to o - ra son i - o.

Publicola:

Per far   spec - chio à   la tua   fron - te   Cer - chi   for - se no -

Desbo: Publicola:

-vel - lo un ri - o?   E quan-do mai?   Que - ste   chio-me con   au - rei

[♮]

continued

gi - ri   À più nin - fe la - gna il cor,   Con tue guan - cie ___
let - te de fio - ri   Ai nu - di_a - mo - ri   E be vez - zo - sa for -
-man - do   và.   Chi non le bac - cia pia - cer non ___ ha, pia -
-cer non ___ hà,   chi non le bac - cia pia - cer non ___ hà.

Desbo:

In - ten - do_il re - sto_a - fè,   Ad - dio,   que - sta paz - zi - a non fa   per

Publicola:

me.   Co - sì ri - tro - so?   Sin che spun - ta l'a - stro di Ve - ne - re

Me - co qui sie - di_in grem - bo,   me - co qui sie - di_in grem - bo à l'er - be   te - ne - re.

continued

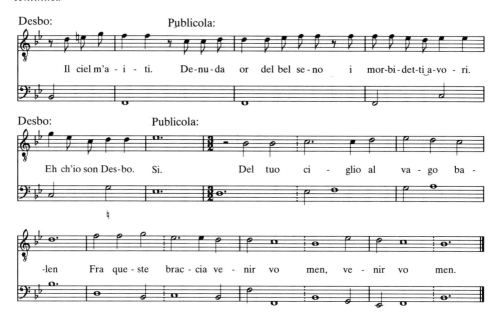

Example 77.   Francesco Cavalli, *Le nozze di Teti e di Peleo* (1639), 3.6, Teti: "Pure orecchi sentiste" (I-Vnm, It. IV, 365 [=9889]: 88ᵛ–90ᵛ)

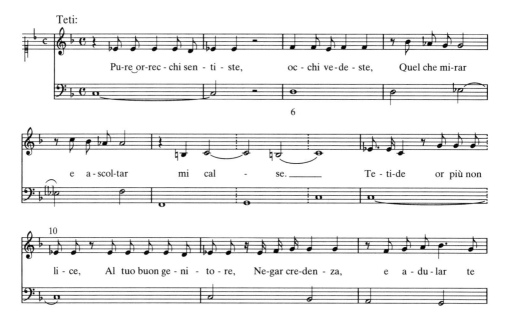

continued

continued

continued

continued

Example 78.   Francesco Cavalli, *Gli amori d'Apollo e di Dafne* (1640), 3.3, Apollo:
"Ohimè, che miro" (I-Vnm, It. IV, 404 [=9928]: 85ʳ–88ᵛ)

continued

continued

continued

continued

continued

continued

Example 79.   Francesco Sacrati, *La finta pazza* (1641), 2.6, Deidamia: "Ardisci, animo ardisci" (I-Isola bella, private collection: [57^v–58^r])

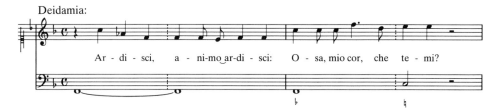

continued

continued

Example 80.   Francesco Cavalli, *Doriclea* (1645), 3.1, Doriclea: "Se ben mai non mi vide" (I-Vnm, It. IV, 356 [=9880]: 76^r–81^r)

continued

continued

continued

mio con - sor - te ò ven - ti, _____ Que -

- ste, que - ste que - ste vo - ci,

que - ste vo - ci do - len - ti: __

continued

Ah ple-be de-gli De - i, Su-per-bis - si-mi A-stre - i, In ve-ce di por-

6

-tar-le à lui se-cre-te A l'ae-re le get-ta-te, e di-sper-de - te? Nel-le con-ca-ve

7   6

rup - pi Eo - lo vi ser - ri, V'an-no-din sem-pre ad' a-man-ti-ni fer - ri. ___

6

Ohi-mè Ti-gra-ne, ohi-mè, del'l'em-pio As-si - ro Pri - gion io vi ri - mi - ro,

continued

Do-ve lo scu-do,   do-ve lo scu-do e l'ha-sta, Chi mi da l'ar - mi ò là,   Ri - tor-ni in li-ber

tà Il mio ca - ro si-gno - re,   La-scia-lo, la-scia-lo tra-di-to - re.

Che va - neg - gio in - fe - li - ce?   e quai mi

det - ta Fu - ne-sti au - gu - ri il duol?   la spe - me si - a   De

7   6   #

l'e - gro spir - to   mio   me - di - ca   pi - a. _____

[5♮]

continued

Example 81.   Francesco Cavalli, *Giasone* (1649), 3.21, Isifile: "Infelice ch'ascolto"
(I-Vnm, It. IV, 343 [=9887]: 159^v–162^v)

continued

continued

-tu - ra   O - bli-ga à gl'a-li - men-ti an - co le   fie - re,   Fà   che   ma - no pie-to - sa   Gli

so-mi - ni-stri al-men   vit - to men-di - co,   E non sof-frir   ch'i   tuoi scet-tra - ti   fi - gli

Per la   fa - me lan-guen - ti   Spi-rin   l'al-me   in-no - cen - ti.

Re - gi - na,   E - ge - o,   a-

-mi - ci,   Sup - pli - ca - te   per   me   que - sto,   que - sto cru-

-de - le, _____   Che   nel   fe -

-rir   mi   la - sci   Que - ste   mam - mel - le   da   suoi   col - pi   in-

continued

-tat - te, _____ Ac - ciò nu -

-tri sca al - men i fi - gli mie - i Dal mor - to sen ma -

-ter - no un fred - do lat - te. _____

Pre - ga - te - lo pie - to - si Che que-

-gl'an - gel' in - fan - ti As - si - sti - no à i mar - ti - ri Del-la ma - dre tra-

-di - ta, E ch'ad' o - gni fe - ri - ta Ch'im-pri-me - rà nel mio pu - di - co pet - to

Be - vi-no quel-li il san-gue mio stil - lan - te, Ac - ciò ch'ei tra-pas - san - do Nel-le lor pu - re

continued

continued

mio,   e   pa - dre,   pa - dre vo - stro. ___   Fi - gli   v'at -

-ten - do,   v'at-ten-do e mo - ro,   E   te Gia - son,   Gia - son   ben ch'ho-mi -

Giasone:

-ci - da,   a - do - ro. ___   Non ho più cor in   pet-to   [etc.]

Example 82.   Table of tetrachord basses in laments of Francesco Cavalli

(a)
Inverted: *Hipermestra* (1658) 3.11

(b)
Chromatic: *Egisto* (1643) 2.6

(c)
Arpeggiated: *Eliogabalo* (1667) 1.16

(d)
Embellished and extended: *Ormindo* (1644) 3.11

(e)
Embellished, then inverted: *Statira* (1655) 3.4

continued

(f)
Implied: *Artemisia* (1656) 2.12

Af-fli - ge-te-mi   do - len- - - ti,

(g)
Ritornello only: *Artemisia* 3.19

Di - spe - ra - te pu - pil - le,_____ hor si pian - ge - te

Example 83.   Francesco Cavalli, *Ciro* (1654), 3.16 (=libretto 3.15), Ciro:
"Negatemi respiri" (I-Vnm, It. IV, 354 [=9878]: 102^v–104^r)

Ciro:

Ne - ga - te mi re - spi - - ri au-

- re, au - re vi - ta - li, Si   ch'io non vi - va ___ più, si

ch'io non vi - va ___ più,   non vi - va, non vi - va,   si   ch'io non

continued

continued

mi re - spi - ri, au - re, au - re vi -

-ta - li. _____

Pom-pe a - dul - te - re, e voi, e voi ben - de re -

-a - li, I - te, i - te lun - gi da me, i - te, i - te lun - gi da

me, i - te, i - te i - te, lun - gi da me: _____

Cal - cai già po - co un

tro - no Hor Ci - ro, Ci - ro più, più non

continued

Example 84.   Antonio Cesti, *Argia* (1669), 3.18 (= libretto 3.17), Selino: "Dissera-tevi abissi" (I-Vnm, It. IV, 391 [= 9915]: 138^{r-v})

continued

Example 85.   Carlo Grossi, *Romilda* (1659), 3.15, Altemira: "Ahi vista, ahi, conoscenza" (I-Vnm, It. IV, 379 [=9903]: 110ᵛ–111ᵛ)

continued

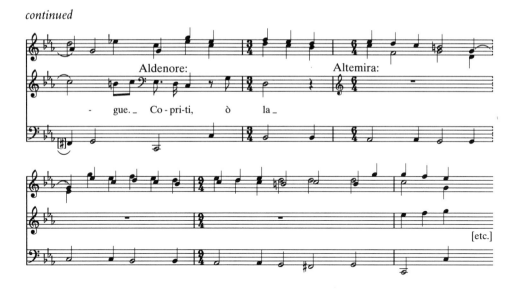

Example 86.   Carlo Grossi, *Artaxerse* (1669), 3.11, Ormonda: "Lacrimate Eurimene" (I-Vnm, It. IV, 394 [=9918]: 79^v–80^r)

continued

continued

Example 87.   Pietro Andrea Ziani, *Le fortune di Rodope e Damira* (1657), 3.4,
Nigrane: "Rodope, dove sei" (I-Vnm, It. IV, 450 [=9974]: 84^{v}–86^{r})

continued

continued

Example 88.   Antonio Cesti, *Tito* (1666), 3.8, Polemone: "Berenice, ove sei"
(I-Vnm, It. IV, 459 [= 9983]: 123ᵛ–126ᵛ)

continued

continued

continued

-v'è,   do - v'è,   di - te do - v'è.

Example 89.   Giovanni Battista Rovettino, *Gli amori d'Apollo e di Leucotoe* (1663), 3.11, Leucotoe: "Pria giusto Re, che genitor pietoso" (I-Vnm, It. IV, 386 [=9910]: 84ᵛ–85ᵛ)

Leucotoe:

Pria giu-sto Re,   che ge-ni-tor pie-to-so,   Bar-ba-ro   di-spie-ta-to, Mo-stro dis-hu-ma-

-na - to,   Ne giu-sto Re, ne ge - ni - tor   mi se - i: Qual leg - ge,   qual

leg - ge v'è, che ne-ghi Pie-ta-de ai fi-gli,   e le dif-fe-se, le dif-fe-se ai re - i?

Nel - le Cau-ca-see ta-ne,   Dal-le ti - gri più   cru-de Lat - te di fe-ri-ta-de em - pio suc-

-chia-sti,   Nò,   non mi ge-ne-ra-sti,   Che se pa-dre mi fos-si,   che se pa-dre mi

continued

continued

mi - e   vi las-so he-re - di.   Ca - ri al-

-ber - ghi   ca - ri ca - ri,   ne mai Fe - bo vi nie - ghi

i lu - mi-no   si, lu - mi - no-si ra - i, ____ Stian di

Giu - no per voi chiu - se le por - te,   Ad-dio reg - gia,   ad-dio

cor - te,   ad-dio reg - gia,   ad-dio cor-te.

Example 90.   Giovanni Antonio Boretti, *Eliogabalo* (1668), 2.11, Domitiano: "O del ciel perfide stelle" (I-Vnm, It. IV, 412 [= 9937]: 57^r–58^v)

continued

Mai non vie-ne per me stil-la di pie-tà   Deh, _____

_ tor - na - te-mi un dì la _____ li - ber - tà, _

deh,   deh tor - na - te-mi un dì la _____

li - ber - tà,   la li - ber - tà, _____   tor -

6   5   4
4   3   2

continued

Example 91.   Francesco Cavalli, *Scipione affricano* (1664), 2.9 (=libretto 2.8), Sofonisba: "Di misera Regina" (I-Vnm, It. IV, 371 [=9895]: 70^v–71^v)

continued

fa - to di-ven - ti,   mu - ta con - vien ch'io vi - va,   Che sup-pri - ma i la -

-men - ti,   Che le per - di - te mie   si - mu - li, e ce - li,   Che'l ce - ne-re in-fe -

-li - ce Del e-stin - to mio Re pa - ce non pre - ghi,   E'l tri-bu - to del pian-to an -

- co gli ne - ghi, __   Chi tan-to me-co ò stel-le A in-cru-de-lir v'ha mos-so?

Son in - fe - li - ce, e so-spi - rar non __ pos - so,

son in - fe - li - ce, e so-spi - rar non __ pos - so.

Deh pie - to - se Ver-di her - bet - te, Ru - gia-do - se, Mor - bi -

continued

-det - te, S'io non pos - so   dir   ohi - mè,   La - gri - ma - te   voi   per

6   6♯   [♯]

[♯]

me,   s'io non pos - so   dir   ohi - mè,   La - gri - ma - te   voi   per   me.

♯

Index

◆ ◆ ◆

NOTE: Page numbers in italics refer to musical examples.